SUPERCOMPUTER SYSTEMS TECHNOLOGY

STATE OF THE ART REPORT

SUPERCOMPUTER SYSTEMS TECHNOLOGY

EDITOR: F SUMNER

SERIES 10
NUMBER 6

THE STATE OF THE ART REPORTS - 1982 SERIES

1 Network Architectures

2 Programming Technology

3 Business Graphics

4 Computer Operations

5 Integrated Office Systems

6 Supercomputer Systems Technology

7 Database - The Second Generation

8 Technology Management

Published by Pergamon Infotech Limited,
Maidenhead, Berkshire, England.

Printed by A Wheaton & Company Limited,
Exeter, Devonshire, England.

UDC 681.3
Dewey 658.505
ISBN 008 028569 4

CONTENTS

BIBLIOGRAPHY AND ANALYSIS REFERENCES

INDEX

INTRODUCTION

BY KENNETH BAKER MP, MINISTER FOR INFORMATION TECHNOLOGY

As you will know, 1982 is Information Technology Year - a year in which industry and government are working together to promote the use of IT devices and the development of IT products. Although our efforts and aspirations are concentrated firmly on 1982, we are conscious that the real success of the enterprise will not be known for many years. Only with hindsight will we know if the fundamental attitudes of the rising generation have been influenced significantly.

We are looking to the future, which is why I particularly welcome a publication such as this. The starting point here is with the relative advantages and disadvantages of the CRAY and Control Data's Cyber 205, but we must also consider Japan's aspirations to build a machine that can handle 100 billion instructions per second, and how such awesome power might be used.

Before we anticipate the future it might be salutory to consider the past. Some 35 years ago a university professor with excellent credentials predicted that just a few computers would be sufficient to solve all the world's needs - and he was talking about computers with about as much power as a Sinclair ZX81! His mistake was in thinking that computers would merely replace machines used for calculations in scientific laboratories - his vision did not include the wider markets implied by data, as opposed to number, processing. More understandably, he did not foresee that computers would drop in price in real terms by a factor of several thousand. We can only be smug about his shortcomings if we feel confident that we know what we will be doing with the £1000 supercomputer in our pockets in 2010!

The computer industry has obviously seen remarkable advances in the past 30 years - the big question is whether such rapid advance will continue, or whether the technology curve is flattening out. Will current research to extend semiconductor technology yield dramatic or only marginal results? Will biotechnology or other new technologies cause a new leap forward? Or will the computer industry follow the example of the aircraft industry and enter a period where economy and refinement are more important than speed and range?

The Japanese Fifth Generation conference brought many of these questions into focus. While Japan's market penetration with their current computers is relatively modest, the new programme with its emphasis on very large scale integration, new architectures, and Expert Systems may open up new markets with vast commercial potential. A distinguished body has been set up by the Department of Industry to review progress in this field and make recommendations.

Although most of the major advances so far have been in computer hardware, much of the research effort now must concentrate on software refinements. With current machines it has been sufficient to break down the complexity of programming by partitioning it into modules which can then be subdivided, but this approach is becoming increasingly difficult because many of the new applications just cannot be defined in a rigorous logical form. One of the avenues of software development is designed to meet this problem head on. Much research has been devoted to how to specify the job in a more precise and rigorous way, including how to validate the specification. Other approaches involve advances in compilers, operating systems, and other support tools.

It is far from certain, however, that such developments can cope with the next level of complexity which affects a wide range of applications - the sort of office application, for example, where 'human experience' is a significant factor. Two new techniques are emerging in this area - one is concerned with logic languages which use more rigorous but easy to apply logic terms, and the other with using knowledge engineering techniques to permit a degree of flexibility by a trial and error approach. Many countries are concentrating on these fields, and in the UK we are considering drawing together the skills of scientists in industry, the universities, and government in a way which would be unparalleled in thirty years of computer development in universities and government laboratories.

The government's commitment to Information Technology necessarily carries with it a commitment to investigate areas such as these and, if we cannot foresee the end result, then that only increases the excitement of the chase, for supercomputer technology is still a relatively unexplored and very exciting area indeed.

EDITOR'S FOREWORD

At the time of the publication of the last State of the Art Report on supercomputers, very few such machines had been delivered to users and most of these could be fairly classified as organisations with specialised computing needs. During the last three years, over 30 CRAY systems have been delivered into a wide variety of environments and the machine is being used as a general 'FORTRAN work horse' as well as for specialised calculations. The basis of this expansion of usage is the provision of suitable compilers and packages. The CDC supercomputer, the CYBER 205, is also firmly established with several computers on customer sites. However, there appears to have been little development in array processors and the competition for the NASA aerodynamic computer appears to have been won by a vector machine rather than an array processor. Since 1979, the performance in MFLOPS of large IBM and IBM-like systems has increased considerably and the range of performance available to the customer is more or less continuous. The next step forward in supercomputer power, the CRAY-II, is now clearly defined and the details of its performance and construction are available.

In 1979 'supercomputer' meant 'super' in terms of the number of MFLOPS: nowadays systems are being discussed which merit the 'super' in terms of facilities offered to the user, or in their capacity for highly specialised data processing. Examples of these are the Japanese Fifth Generation concept and dedicated image processing systems.

The papers in this State of the Art Report address all the above points, together with the advances in technology and an updated view of future developments. Some of the papers are concerned with the successful efforts that have been made to widen the range of applications for supercomputers and the place of supercomputers within an organisation's computer centre.

F Sumner: Editor

F SUMNER's first contact with computers was in 1962, programming the Ferranti Mark 1 to solve quantum chemistry problems. He worked at Manchester University on the Mark 1 Mercury on pattern recognition and was one of the designers of the Atlas and the MU5. He became Professor of Computer Science at Manchester in November 1967 and in November 1980 was appointed to the newly created Barclays chair of Microprocessor Applications in Industry.

PUBLISHER'S NOTE

This Report is divided into three parts:

1 ANALYSIS.

2 INVITED PAPERS.

3 BIBLIOGRAPHY.

The Analysis

1 Serves as an introduction to the major technical advances in supercomputer systems technology.

2 Provides a balanced analysis of the state of the art in supercomputer systems technology.

The Analysis is constructed by the editor of the Report in the form of a discussion among the chief authorities in this field. The quotations from these authorities are selected by the editor to present a balanced and comprehensive view of the latest developments in supercomputer systems technology: design and applications. To enable readers to follow up points of interest, the sources of all quotations are given in the Bibliography which follows the Invited Papers.

The following editorial conventions are used throughout the Analysis:

1 Material in Courier italic (this typeface) is written by the editor.

2 Material in Courier roman (this typeface) *is contributed by the person or publication whose name precedes it. The contributor's name is set in* **Diplomat;** *a number in the range* 100-199 *in brackets following the name refers to the original source, as specified in the Bibliography. Numbers within the text from* 200 *onwards follow the same convention. A name without a reference refers to an Invited Paper published in this Report.*

3 The quotations in the Analysis are arranged at the discretion of the editor to bring out key issues. Three or four dots within a single quotation indicate that a portion of the original text has been removed by the editor to improve clarity.

The Invited Papers in this State of the Art Report examine various aspects of supercomputer systems technology. If a paper cites references they are given at the end of that paper, numbered in the range 001-099.

The Bibliography is a specially selected compilation of the most important published material on the subject of supercomputer systems technology. Each key item of the literature is reviewed and annotated to assist in selecting the required information.

ANALYSIS

1: Introduction

A brief description of the development of high performance computers is given in order to highlight the relationship between advances in technology and architecture. Parallelism/concurrency and store organisation are also discussed and component technology is examined. Silicon technology is the dominant component technology, but there has been considerable research into the use of Josephson junction devices and other technologies, and these are assessed. Memory technology is considered, with particular reference to magnetic bubble memories and new directions in magnetic recording.

INTRODUCTION

The adjective 'super' has been applied to computers since the arrival of the first electronic system and possibly even before that! In the late Forties all electronic computers were supercomputers as compared with the mechanical and electromechanical devices, which were all that were previously available.

As computers have developed over the last 35 years or so, super has been reserved for the 'best' computer available, STRETCH, ATLAS, and the CDC 6600 being three successive holders of the title in the Sixties. Of the present commercially available systems, supercomputer is generally applied to the various CRAY systems and the CDC CYBER 205 family.

Looking at this list gives a very clear indication as to what has been regarded as 'best'. For the last 35 years supercomputers have been those that could perform the most operations per second. The units by which this performance has been measured have steadily changed from Kinstr/sec (thousands of instructions per second) to million instr/sec, then as supercomputers tended to be purely for scientific applications into MFLOPS (millions of floating-point operations per second) and now for the purposes of NASA we have reached GFLOPS.

In the days when Grosch's Law was valid, this concept of 'best' was acceptable. Nowadays 'best' probably means most cost effective for any particular application, so that under the right circumstances almost all existing computers could qualify for the title 'best'. Against this background super has become restricted to the computers capable of performing the most floating-point operations per second.

This definition of super is far too restrictive. There are many areas of computer applications other than scientific computation where vast amounts of computing are required and super should be an acceptable description for the best computers designed for these applications. Two obvious areas are pattern recognition or picture processing and knowledge-based systems (expert systems). Array processors seem to be ideally suited to the first area and the major thrust of the Japanese Fifth Generation project is to produce supercomputers for the second area.

The above paragraph indicates a change that has occurred during the last 10 years. Until the early Seventies supercomputers were general-purpose computers. Today there are still very powerful general-purpose computers that are certainly the 'best' for the applications on which they are used, but the term super has become restricted to computers that are particularly good at certain types of floating-point calculations. The additional speed has been achieved by making the architecture of the computer fit the structure of this class of problems with the result that as well as being very good at solving the right kind of problem the same computer can be relatively very bad at solving other problems.

Before discussing the architectural features of these problem-specific supercomputers a brief description will be given of the development of high-performance computers to show the relationship between the advances in technology and the advances in architecture.

DEVELOPMENT OF PERFORMANCE

The performance of a computer is attributable to two major factors, firstly by the speed of the technology and secondly by the architecture. The speed of the technology may be characterised by the time taken to perform the basic logical operations and the time taken to read and write data from and to the storage medium (or media). The architecture is the way in which the different parts, arithmetic units, stores, fast registers etc are organised and manipulated by the instruction set.

Hockney and Jesshope **(200)** *give a great deal of credit to the computer architect for the vast increase in performance over the last 30 years.*

HOCKNEY and JESSHOPE (200): We may compare the clock period, as a measure of the speed of the technology, with the number of useful arithmetic operations performed per second on an actual problem as a measure of performance. Wilkes quotes an execution time of $18n$ msec for evaluating a series of n terms ($2n$ arithmetic operations) on the EDSAC1 which had a clock period of 2 μsec. This is an average rate of 100 arithmetic operations per second, which we may compare with a performance of 130 million arithmetic operations per second on the CRAY-1 for matrix multiplication. Since the CRAY-1 has a clock period of 12.5 nsec, we have an improvement in total performance of 10^6 over the period of about three decades, of which only about a factor of 160 can be attributed to improvements in technology.

While accepting the overall factor of 10^6 for the increase in performance most computer designers would take a rather different point of view of the division of the credit between technology and architecture. For example Lincoln **(201)** *is in no doubt as to what is the driving force.*

LINCOLN (201): The beginning point for a supercomputer development is the acquisition of the fastest, densest technology available in a given generation (about six to ten years) of circuitry. The clock cycle of a fast computer is then determined by the speed of the basic gate and the time delay of all the interconnections between circuits....

The electronic element which is the keystone of performance in the CYBER 205 is a newly developed, high-powered, large scale integration (LSI) circuit. This device provides 168 emitter-coupled logic (ECL) gates which have an average switching time of 600-800 psec. It resulted from a research effort begun by Control Data's Advanced Design Laboratory in 1972 in conjunction with several key semiconductor vendors.

Similar views are held by Ibbett **(202)** *who argues that the increased reliability and reduced heat dissipation of components has permitted computer architects to consider more complex structures, which would previously have been unworkable.*

IBBETT (202): Technological improvements include increases in the speed of logic circuits and storage devices, as well as increases in reliability. Thus the use of transistors in ATLAS, for example, not only allowed individual circuits to operate faster than those in MERCURY, but also allowed the use of parallel adders, which involved many more logic circuits but which produced results very much more quickly than the simple serial adders used in earlier machines. Corresponding changes can be seen today as the scale of integration of integrated circuits continues to increase, allowing ever more complex logical operations to be carried out within one silicon chip, and hence allowing greater complexity to be introduced into systems while keeping the chip speed and overall system reliability more or less constant.

It is more realistic to use the gate delay as a basis for comparison rather than the clock period as it is necessary to define how many operations occur within a clock period for this to be a valid comparison. Taking as the basis for our comparison, two extremes of technology, as typified by the Ferranti Mark 1 (the world's first available electronic computer), which was installed in 1951, and the technology used in today's supercomputers, the two gate delays are 100 nsec and 500 psec, ie a factor of 200 which is not very different from the 160 technology factor derived by Hockney and Jesshope. However, the technology factor that vitally influences performance is the access time to the memory for instructions and operands. In this case the two extremes are 400 μsec and 40 nsec, giving a ratio of 10 000. A factor of about 50 within this is due to the parallel transfer of data. However, the serial transfers in early computers were necessary because of the technological difficulty of implementing parallel transfers, not because they were thought to be better - after all mechanical calculators had been parallel transfers for years. If a copy of the Ferranti Mark 1 were made using today's technology without any concurrency techniques it would operate at 120 nsec/instr compared with the 1.2 msec of the actual machine.

These arguments suggest a factor of 10 000 as a consequence of improvements in technology and a factor of 100 as a consequence of advances in architecture.

The role of the computer architect is defined by Ibbett **(202)** *as capitalising on the benefits offered by the technology.*

IBBETT (202): Making more effective use of existing technology is the chief concern of computer architecture, and almost all of the techniques used can be classified under the headings of either storage hierarchies or concurrency. Storage devices range from being small and fast (but expensive) to being large and cheap (but slow); in a storage hierarchy several types, sizes, and speed of storage device are combined together, using both hardware and software mechanisms, with the aim of presenting the user with the illusion that he has a fast, large (and cheap) store at his disposal.

Storage hierarchies can be extended to include high-speed buffers, which permit a factor of four on the access time for instructions and operands, for example in the CYBER 205 as stated by Lincoln **(201)**.

LINCOLN (201): The CYBER 205 possesses a memory hierarchy which was necessitated by the range of cost, performance, power, and density characteristics of available technology, and the need for speed on one hand and large capacity on the other. The most crucial memory, in terms of dictating the clock rate of the CPU, is the register file ... This issue rate was targeted at one instruction per clock cycle, thus imposing high demands on the register file technology.... The chip nearest to possessing these qualities was a 4-bit wide by 16-bit deep chip with separate read and write address registers; this chip could read one operand and write one operand in about 8-10 nsec.

Most of the factor of 100 is, however, due to the utilisation of concurrency or parallelism.

PARALLELISM/CONCURRENCY

Some of the concurrency in early high-performance systems was real and some was only apparent. An excellent discussion of this categorisation is given by Lorin (203) *for architectures up to about 1972.*

One way of categorising the different degrees of parallelism is into invisible parallelism and visible parallelism. The user of the computer is obviously unaware of the former and this category includes parallel data transfers, parallel arithmetic, and input/output/computing parallelism of multiprogrammed systems.

Parallelism in arithmetic can be taken to considerable lengths, for example a simple 48-bit multiplier could take 48 add times. In the CDC 7600 it takes five add times.

The principal forms of visible parallelism are summarised by Hockney and Jesshope.

HOCKNEY and JESSHOPE (200):

1 *Pipelining:* the application of assembly-line techniques to improve the performance of an arithmetic or control unit.

2 *Functional:* providing several independent units for performing different functions, such as logic, addition, or multiplication, and allowing these to operate simultaneously on different data.

3 *Array:* providing an array of identical Processing Elements (PEs) under common control, all performing the same operation simultaneously but on different data stored in their private memories, ie lockstep operation.

4 *Multiprocessing:* the provision of several processors, each obeying its own instructions, and usually communicating via a common memory.

Visible parallelism can be ignored by the user but can be utilised to yield greatly increased performance. For example, the multiple functional units of the CDC 7600 with careful programming (in machine code) can yield performance improvements of several 100% depending upon the problem and the skill and determination of the programmer.

Requiring or encouraging users to do this type of programming runs contrary to all the developments of high-level computing languages. The visible parallelism is therefore often hidden from the user by the compiler. The optimising FORTRAN compiler of the 7600 makes an excellent job of utilising the functional parallelism and the vectorising compilers of the CRAY and the CYBER 205 attempt to make use of the extensive pipelining available in these computers. Unfortunately efficient use of these systems requires intervention by the programmer although one or two days work on a program can have a dramatic effect. The efficient use of visible parallelism will be discussed in more detail later.

STORE ORGANISATION

Getting instructions and operands from the main store fast enough to keep the high-performance CPU busy has always been difficult and as the degree of parallelism has increased so has the degree of difficulty.

Instruction buffers, fast registers, cache memories, interleaved memories, and very wide memories have all been used. The successful solution of memory management is vital to the efficient use of vector and array processors and will be discussed in detail in a later section of this analysis.

COMPONENT TECHNOLOGY

The rate of change in silicon technology can be judged from the fact that graphs of cost per gate or gates per chip are always drawn on logarithmic scales. The following two graphs show a) complexity and b) cost reduction in silicon integrated circuits and are from a paper given in 1979 by D H Roberts the Director of Research for GEC **(203)**. *A variation of the second graph (b), which plots transistors per chip, has become generally known as Moore's First Law.*

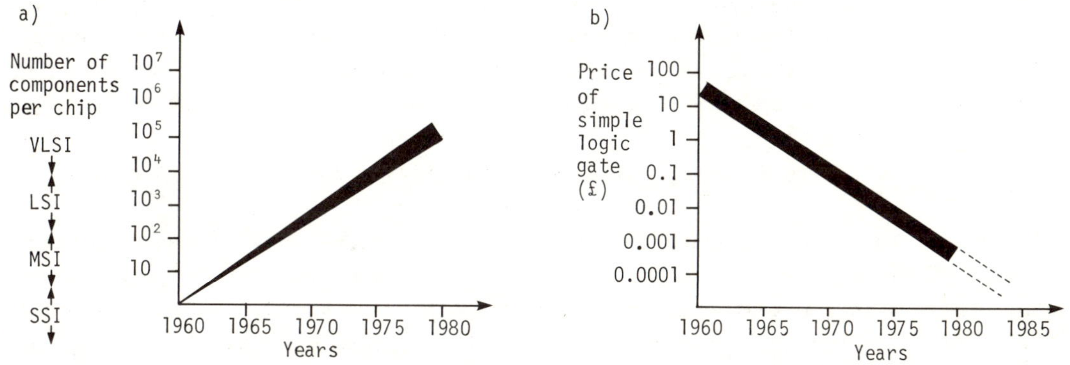

While silicon technology is the dominant component technology there has been extensive research mainly by IBM into the use of Josephson Junction devices. There is an excellent description of this work in the March 1980 issue of the IBM Journal of Research and Development. *A selection of quotations from the introductory paper by Anacker gives a clear indication of the potential for these devices and the problems that will have to be overcome. For example, as the operation is based on superconductivity they must be operated at very low temperature, about four degrees above absolute zero. The coolant therefore has to be liquid helium. This was one of the main obstacles to the development of Cryotrons in the Fifties. The potential for Josephson technology is very exciting.*

ANACKER (204): Josephson computer technology provides excellent potential for ultra-high-performance computer mainframes complete with processors and memory hierarchies. Ultra-high performance may be defined in this context as ranging from 500 to 5000 psec in processor cycle time with commensurately fast-access cache and main memories to support such ultra-high-performance processors. This range of processor cycle times, combined with current computer architecture, could provide mainframes with 10- to 100-fold higher computing rates than that of an IBM 3033 mainframe system.

It is illustrative to assess the implications of ultra-high performance as defined above by postulating a hypothetical mainframe, without regard to technology, comprising a 1-nsec uniprocessor backed by a 2-nsec cache and a 10-nsec main memory. If constructed in IBM 3033 system architecture, it is estimated that this mainframe would provide about 250 million instr/sec of computing power and it would comprise about 300 000 processor circuits, 256K bytes of cache and at least 64 Mbytes of main memory capacities, the latter increased about eight- to ten-fold over current main memory capacities in an attempt to bridge the access gap between the contemplated ultra-high-performance mainframe and conventional I/O and auxiliary storage systems.

Anacker gives three attractions of Josephson devices; obviously the first is extremely fast switching, less than 10 psec.

ANACKER (204): The first characteristic is clearly a prerequisite for fast logic speed and cache memory access. It poses, however, problems which will be common to all technologies attempting to reach into the ultra-high-performance range as defined. These problems arise since electrical signal pulses with rise times of less than 10 psec render all strip lines of more than about 2-mm length on-chip and throughout a package electrically long. It is therefore advisable to terminate these lines properly and it is mandatory to match discontinuities along their lengths, eg fan-out tabs, beam leads, solder bonds, and pluggable connectors, to the line impedance. This avoids signal reflections and distortion, and thus reduces effective signal delay and disturbance. Such signals, with frequency spectra up to 35 GHz, will also substantially couple into adjacent and crossing lines unless proper precautions are taken, as anyone familiar with microwave technology will appreciate. How one might solve these problems in room-temperature semiconductor technologies is not clear to date, yet it appears that solutions are at hand in Josephson technology.

The second attraction is extremely low power dissipation, less than 500 nW per circuit.

ANACKER (204): The second characteristic, low-power dissipation, offers advantages since it allows the transfer of heat directly from chips into the liquid coolant bath. This is in contrast with the need for voluminous heat sinks necessary in current high-performance semiconductor technology to prevent thermal runaway. Circuit miniaturisation will not alleviate this problem in semiconductor technology, since the density of circuits is likely to go up faster than the power per circuit decreases, thus causing the chip power density to remain high, especially if higher switching speed is demanded. Cooling in liquid nitrogen will not alleviate this problem either because chips would be superheated by several hundred degrees at the onset of film boiling once the 'critical power density' was exceeded. Since the power dissipation of Josephson logic and cache memory chips, for current experimental circuits, is more than three orders of magnitude smaller, they will not suffer from this problem.

The third attraction is operation at very low temperatures.

ANACKER (204): The third characteristic, low-operating temperature, not commonly recognised as a benefit, can provide very desirable features for ultra-high-performance computers, since the low temperature allows the use of superconducting strip lines and ground planes with zero electrical resistance. The strip lines can therefore transmit electrical signals unattenuated and with minimum distortion (when properly terminated) even when they are arranged close to the ground plane, made thin and narrow, and are closely spaced. Close proximity to a ground plane yields low characteristic impedance and all but eliminates cross-talk between parallel and crossing lines. Thin lines provide a low aspect ratio of height to width which is beneficial for microcircuit fabrication and lithographic patterning. Narrow and closely spaced lines provide high wiring-channel density and thus are favourable for system wiring. It is estimated that one x- and one y-wiring plane will suffice on-chip and throughout the package for total interchip connections in Josephson mainframes.

Low temperature can provide still more benefits. The thermal energy (kT) is about 100 times smaller at 4K than at 360 to 380K where semiconductor circuits are operated. This leads to smaller thermally-induced electrical noise, and helps to maintain good signal-to-noise ratio even when signal bandwidth is increased and signal energy is reduced. The low energy (kT) also affects the rates of thermally activated physical and chemical processes such as diffusion, corrosion, and electromigration. These processes are temperature dependent and are at a virtual standstill at 4K. A potential exists therefore for ultra-high reliability and longevity of components in Josephson technology.

Low power dissipation also permits resistive termination of all strip lines on-chip and throughout the package. In fact, the power dissipation of 500 nW per circuit previously cited includes the power dissipated in the line termination resistors, and it is planned to terminate all signal lines in Josephson processors and to do it on-chip. Direct heat transfer from chip to bath is not impeded by this measure.

Furthermore, low power dissipation avoids an increasingly difficult problem observed in high-performance semiconductor technologies as they are miniaturised.

Other potentially fast technologies are based on III-V ion implantation techniques. These are so called as they use elements from groups III and V of the periodic table: the most widely used combination at the moment is gallium arsenide. These films have a higher electron mobility than silicon and are therefore potentially faster: like silicon they work at normal temperatures. A paper by Eden et al **(205)** *gives an indication of the possibilities of gallium arsenide technology. Power dissipations for a 64 gate array are sufficiently low to make VLSI circuits achievable.*

The amount of research going on in these new technologies and in the expansion of silicon-based technology can be judged from the number of papers published in journals such as the IEE Journal of Solid States Circuits; *the April 1982 issue of this journal is devoted to VLSI and would provide an excellent starting point for anyone wishing to carry out more detailed reading on this subject.*

From the point of view of designing and building computers, speed is only one of the parameters in the argument. Of equal importance is the problem of cooling. Seymour Cray has been quoted as saying that the major problems in the design of the CRAY-1 were associated with plumbing.

At the moment, higher speeds are obtainable using ECL technology rather than NMOS or CMOS, but only at the cost of greater power dissipation per gate. The 168 gate array of the CYBER 205 represented a high level of integration for ECL technology at the time it was developed (1972 onwards). Even this level of integration presents problems.

LINCOLN (201): Power requirements of even this level of integration make extraordinary demands on creative packaging and cooling of the parts, individually and collectively.

In fact Lincoln appears to have similar opinions to those attributed to Seymour Cray.

LINCOLN (201): The circuit family chosen for the CYBER 205 possessed many pleasant attributes for design engineers but exhibited one challenging characteristic: high power dissipation. The average power per chip was about 5W. To maintain a desirable junction temperature of 55°C at this dissipation level demanded some creativity from the packaging and cooling engineers. The solution finally obtained was to bring a liquid coolant (Freon) into contact with each and every chip. Air cooling was discarded early as an alternative since each printed circuit board was designed to hold 150 arrays and thus would be emitting 750W in less than a square foot of chassis area. Other conductive techniques, using metal heat transfer paths, also yielded thermal resistances too high to manage. The reason for this is that any liquid coolant system cannot create exposed surfaces cooler than a nominal dew point in today's standard machine room. If this were not so, then a very low temperature medium could be used as a cooling agent, overcoming deficiencies in the thermal pathing.

Other major aspects of circuit technology after speed and cooling are circuits per chip, availability and price. All these lead Kinniment to the conclusion that silicon-based technology is by far the most important for the next 10 years and possibly longer.

KINNIMENT: Undoubtedly one of the most significant influences on computer design over the next 10 years will be developments in ... silicon technology, which is now the only fabrication technology capable of VLSI in a cost-effective form. The implications of the probable reductions in system cost, and size, as well as the improvements in performance are such that in my opinion silicon VLSI will be the natural implementation medium for most computer systems, and its characteristics will be one of the main influences on the architecture of the machines themselves.

Kinniment indicates the probable increases in the levels of integration based on reducing the lateral dimensions of the components and the thickness of the materials.

KINNIMENT: Since there are fields in both vertical and lateral directions, and because etching processes will only succeed in producing fine lines if the material thickness is reduced, the vertical dimensions of the transistor must be reduced in step with the lateral dimensions. A 'scaled' device may thus be produced which performs in the same qualitative way that the original transistor performed. Present standard technology produced line widths of 5μ in 1980 with corresponding gate delays of 5-10 nsec. By using techniques now available and likely to be in production by 1990, line widths as low as 0.25μ are possible, and the potential of this is a 400-fold increase in the level of integration.

Kinniment gives two definitions of VLSI as opposed to LSI. These are less than 2μ line widths and 'the point at which the problem of complexity overwhelms all other problems'. Figures 1 and 2 from Kinniment's paper make these definitions very clear.

One effect of scaling the dimensions on a chip is to magnify the relative effects of interconnection both on and off the chip.

KINNIMENT: The results are to magnify the relative effects of interconnections both from the point of view of supplying power to the chip, since the series resistance of the metal will present problems not previously encountered, and from the point of view of system performance, since although the individual gates have improved in performance the interconnect has become worse both in absolute and relative terms.... within VLSI computation is relatively cheap and communication relatively expensive. The interconnections even within a chip are costly in terms of silicon area and costly in terms of performance, so that if it is possible to avoid moving data long distances either on or off a chip it pays to do so.

Date	(a) Chip size	(b) Minimum line width	$(a/b)^2 \div 50$ Transistors/chip
1960	1mm × 1mm	30μ	18
1970	2.5mm × 2.5mm	10μ	1250
1980	6mm × 6mm	3μ	80 000
1990	10mm × 10mm	0.5μ	8 000 000
	1M gates/chip by 1990?		

Figure 1: Trends in integration

In the early days of computer design it was possible to make developments using the same technology as would be used for the final product. Furthermore, this development could be done within any small research group in either industry or university. The advent of integrated circuit technology made it more diffucult to design and build computers in such groups. One very exciting development of silicon technology is the 'silicon foundry' which permits all designers to have access to circuit production facilities, and this magnifies tremendously the design effort available for the development of new applications of VLSI.

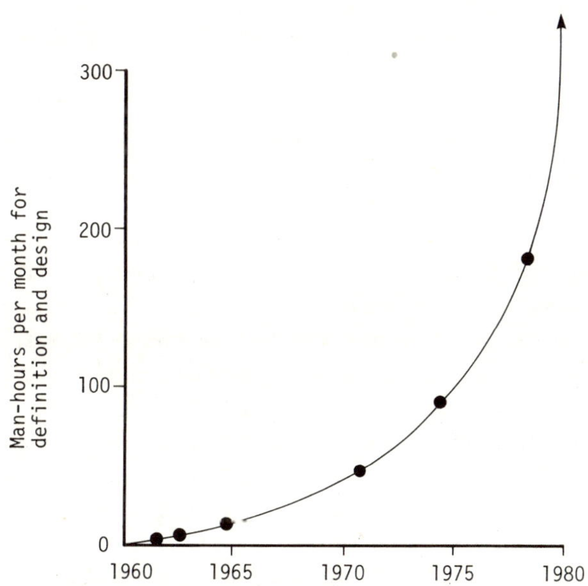

The man-hours per month required for ic product definition, design, and layout grow exponentially

Moore's 2nd law 5-10 transistors/day

(Barron's corollary: 1m transistors, 30 men = 10 years)

Figure 2: VLSI design effort

KINNIMENT: The design of systems on the chip has, up to now, been the prerogative of relatively few people in semiconductor houses or large computer manufacturers such as IBM. The reasons for this are the very high capital costs of the fabrication equipment required and the reluctance of companies to share the details of their processes with competitors. This scene has recently undergone a dramatic change, partly aided by the emergence of relatively standard processes, partly by excess silicon capacity in the industry, but mainly by the need to tap design expertise wherever it exists.

This trend is best exemplified by the MultiProject Chip activity initiated at Caltech by Carver Mead and brought to maturity by Lynn Conway at Xerox PARC in 1979. The emergence of Electron Beam Lithography has allowed several chip designs to be easily incorporated on the same mask, and hence manufactured on the same wafer. The costs of a mask set and the processing of a batch of wafers can thus be shared between the designs, reducing the cost per design to levels comparable to other implementation methods even on a one-off basis.

Other impressive aspects of MPC79 were the turn-around time of 29 days from design cut-off to packaged chips, and the inclusion of a LISP microprocessor design 6mm × 7.5mm which functioned correctly first time. This was essentially a US university exercise but has since been repeated in other countries including the UK in 1981. It is obvious that if this kind of design is economic from the system designer's point of view as well as the semiconductor house, then there will be an explosion of activity bringing together fabrication capacity with design expertise, and indeed this can already be seen to be happening with the formation of 'silicon brokerage' companies whose function is to act as the catalyst and to provide the bridge between design and implementation.

While there are a number of possible and established limits to the reduction in dimensions of MOS devices, Kinniment sees a factor of at least 10 in dimension and 100 in packing density before 1990.

He does not see the same improvement in bipolar technology and believes that MOS will catch up during the next 10 years.

KINNIMENT: The main reason for this is that one of the important determinants of the speed of a bipolar transistor is the base transit time, and this is dependent on the base width of the transistor. Bipolar transistors are made in a different way from MOS devices, the base width being defined by the vertical difference between two diffusions rather than a surface dimension produced by photolithography. As a result it has been possible to produce transistors with base widths of less than 1μ for some years and ECL gates can currently be produced with propagation delays of 0.5 nsec or less. There is very little room for reduction in vertical dimensions of the transistor before quantum limits are reached, and also little room for reductions in gate output voltage swings which are already dangerously close to the curvature of the Vbe characteristic with voltage changes of 0.45V in ECL.

The only remaining possibility is a scaling of surface dimensions which would reduce collector currents at a similar rate to the corresponding capacitances. Gate speed thus remains fairly constant, and power per chip also remains constant in a 'stuffed' technology ... MOS is likely to catch up with the best bipolar technology over the next 10 years without the same penalty in process complexity.

Within MOS technology there is considerable potential for CMOS.

KINNIMENT: The great advantage of CMOS is that while conductor current densities will increase in the same way as NMOS, leading to the eventual dominance of power supply problems and interconnection performance limitations, the power requirements of a CMOS circuit start from a much lower base, typically 20 times less than the equivalent static NMOS device. It has much more mileage as a VLSI process, and also has the possibility of somewhat faster circuits. The greater silicon area required by CMOS is less of a difficulty in an environment where the circuit area is mainly occupied by interconnections in any case, and the need for many interconnection layers is likely to increase the process complexity required for NMOS.

As is clearly evident from Figure 2, of man-hours per month, efficient design is essential if full use is to be made of VLSI technology. The problems are not dissimilar to those in creating large software systems and the ultimate hope is to produce a 'silicon compiler'.

KINNIMENT: Many of the ideas already used to create large software systems may also be helpful in the design of VLSI hardware. In dealing with a complex problem, splitting the design up into a number of simple modules, each communicating with the others in a defined and predictable way, prevents the spread of design problems and allows the design of each part to proceed relatively independently. In addition to the existing software problems of complexity VLSI introduces a whole series of further difficulties:

- Each module must fit into a two-dimensional space
- Communication between non-adjacent modules is difficult
- Timing problems exist as well as those of sequencing
- The fabrication process is subject to faults as well as the possibility of designer error
- Turn-around time from design to chip is long, therefore testing difficulties are encountered.

These are problems which will have to be overcome before the idea of a 'silicon compiler' analgous to compilers of high-level languages can become a reality, and a specification can be compiled directly into a chip layout.

The problems of design can be reduced by the use of uncommitted logic arrays.

KINNIMENT: It is in this area of the market-place that uncommitted logic arrays are now making a significant impact, sales being expected to more than triple from \$60 million per year in 1981 to \$200 million by 1984. The cost per circuit (and the performance) of an Uncommitted Logic Array (ULA) function implementation is likely to lie somewhere between full custom design and the same function implemented in standard off-the-shelf integrated circuits.

The advantage in speed and ease of design comes from the fact that the chip is designed with an array of prediffused components allowing a range of standard gates or functions to be produced simply by interconnecting the components in a predefined way. This allows:

- The designer to think in terms of familiar objects such as gates or MSI components
- Easy conversion of design automation software intended for PCBs
- The majority of masking stages to be done on a large scale before final commitment of the circuit to a particular design.

All of these factors make for a quick and easy design process though not necessarily an efficient one, again a turn-around time of three months from system specification to prototype chip in a commercial environment is typical. Computer manufacturers from IBM to Sinclair by way of DEC have all recently taken advantage of gate array technology.

Gate array technology has advanced considerably from the 168 gates referred to by Lincoln above.

KINNIMENT: Both bipolar and CMOS gate array designs are now available commercially with capabilities of up to 1000 gates in bipolar and 5000 gates in CMOS. While bipolar arrays can offer sub-nsec gate delays, the power dissipation per chip required to achieve this performance is such that further increases in speed or density will be difficult.

No such limitation exists for CMOS arrays and in consequence they will dominate the market in the near future.

MEMORY TECHNOLOGY

Cache memories, Random Access Memories (RAMs) and Read-Only Memories (ROMs) utilise the same technology as the logic components with the added advantage that the regularity of a memory array makes the design process much easier and permits more efficient use of the chip area. In his IFIP 80 paper, Terajima **(206)** *predicts that a 4-Mbyte memory chip will be possible by 1990 at the latest and that ultimately 100 Mbits on a 5-inch wafer will be achievable using 1μ channel lengths and defect-tolerant designs.*

In all computer systems to date, there has been a demand for far more memory than can be supplied at the very fast level. This will continue to be the case and developments in backing store technology are of vital importance. The use of storage technology depends on cost per bit and access time. Figure 3 from Hoagland's paper illustrates this including RAM as well as backing store.

Over the past few years there has been considerable publicity for Charge-Coupled Devices (CCDs) and Magnetic Bubble Memories (MBMs) with many authorities arguing that such technologies will replace high-speed drums and possibly other forms of magnetic surface recording. Hoagland believes that CCDs will not have a sufficient advantage over RAMs.

HOAGLAND: CCD obtains a cost advantage over RAM by storing information in packets of charge rather than by means of bistable circuitry in a serial-parallel type organisation. The technological similarity, while a great asset, may in fact retard the wide acceptance of CCDs for storage because, compared to RAMs, the obtainable cost reduction may not be enough to offset the associated great decrease in access time, except in very specific applications.

Hoagland discusses the subject of magnetic bubble memories.

HOAGLAND: The MBM also uses a shift-register type organisation. Magnetic bubbles are small cylindrical magnetic domains formed in certain thin magnetic films when an external magnetic bias field is applied normal to the plane of the film. These 'bubble' domains are magnetised in the reverse sense to that of the film itself.

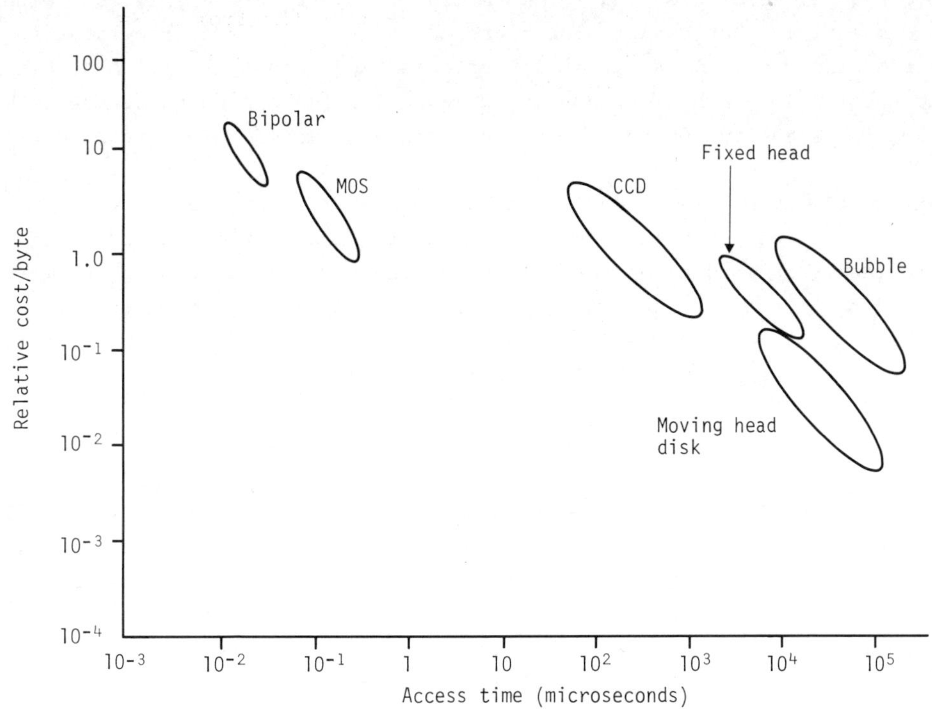

Figure 3: Performance levels and costs for storage technologies

Information is coded in terms of the presence or absence of bubbles. MBM is non-volatile and non-mechanical. 1-Mbit chips are now being offered (2 to 3-μ bubbles). The factor curtailing the wider use of bubbles is cost, with the interface circuitry and power being significant factors. It is not clear that their cost will ever get lower than the rapidly moving semiconductor technology, much less disk.

Hoagland concludes that from the standpoint of cost per bit neither CCDs nor MBMs are a threat to moving head disks as auxiliary storage.

MBMs are being used where their particular characteristics match those of the problem being solved, for example, in database management systems (DBMSs).

During the last 25 years there has been a factor of 10^4 in disk storage density. Density increases should continue at the same rate during the Eighties. Higher storage densities have been achieved through head-to-surface spacing, head materials, disk coatings, and track densities.

HOAGLAND: Progress in reducing the head-to-surface spacing has been the key factor in increasing the linear density of disk storage. A boundary layer of air is used to provide an air bearing, which in turn determines the spacing. Progress in air-bearing technology has reduced head-to-disk spacing from 900 μinches to 10 μinches.

Read/write head materials have been improved from laminated mu-metal, to ferrite, to batch fabricated thin film. The thin film approach offers higher frequency capability and much better control for the fabrication of narrow track widths. Fabrication technology has reduced the gap length a factor of 40, from 1000 to 25 μinches. Improved spin-coating processes have reduced particulate iron oxide coating thickness by a factor of 150, from 1200 to 20 μinches. To date, advances in disk media have been made by going to thinner and smoother particulate coatings to improve spatial resolution and reduce medium demagnetisation effects. With newer head materials that can provide higher write fields, higher coercive force media (which also reduce demagnetisation effects) and thin sputtered or chemically deposited metal films with high saturation magnetisation are being pursued. With these films it is easily possible to produce medium layers of less than 10 μinches.

Track density of moving-head magnetic disks is determined by the accuracy and tolerance of the head-positioning mechanism and the transverse resolution of the read-write head: as long as an adequate signal:noise ratio is available, track width is reduced. Over the same time period track density has increased from 20 to almost 1100 track/inch. Placing servo information with the data and better head-disk assembly packaging will lead to further advances.

Hoagland anticipates progress in several new directions in magnetic recording.

HOAGLAND: New directions in magnetic recording include higher coercive force film media, array (multi-element) heads, and vertical recording. Vertical recording utilises a medium than can be magnetised normal to the plane of the medium. At high densities demagnetisation considerations favour this mode for the writing of narrow stable transitions. This approach calls for a departure from current media but could lead to a significant further gain in linear density.

At the end of his paper Hoagland makes a point about mature technologies and new technologies. His remarks apply not only to magnetic surface recording but also to silicon technology as compared with other VLSI techniques, as argued by Kinniment.

HOAGLAND: It is frequently said that there are mature technologies and new technologies, with the inference that the rate of progress will be much greater in a new alternative. This can be misleading. For any technology to succeed it must offer something superior to a current technology at the time of its actual introduction. Existing technologies are moving targets. Thus one cannot begin at a rudimentary state with a new approach, but must develop the technology at least far enough to gain initial market acceptance. While no technology can be economically improved indefinitely, technological potential is not so much a function of newness as it is of intrinsic physical and engineering limits.

2: Architecture

Classifications of computer systems are examined and the high performance yields of different approaches are discussed. Pipelined vector processors are assessed with reference to CYBER 205, CRAY 1, CRAY X-MP, and CRAY 2. SIMD processors are examined, including the NASF, the DAP, and the Goodyear Aerospace Massively Parallel Processor (MPP). MIMD processors are also considered. The advantage of including distributed computing alongside supercomputers is emphasised and one example of a network of microcomputers is described. Finally, store management is examined with reference to memory problems in pipelined vector processors and high performance SISD systems. In addition, new architectures are assessed.

CLASSIFICATION OF SYSTEMS

Computer architecture has been defined in a number of ways. Two alternatives will suffice to illustrate this.

IBBETT (202): Computer architecture has been defined in a number of ways by different authors. Amdahl, Blaauw, and Brooks, for example, the designers of the IBM System 360 architecture, used the term to 'describe the attributes of a system as seen by the programmer, ie the conceptual structure and functional behaviour, as distinct from the organisation of the dataflow and controls, the logical design, and the physical implementation'. Stone, on the other hand, states that 'the study of computer architecture is the study of the organisation and interconnection of components of computer systems'.

The design of computer systems has often been referred to as an art rather than a science. This worry with respect to the scientific integrity of the subject has possibly been the motive behind several attempts at classification or computer taxonomies. Probably the most famous is attributable to Flynn **(207)** *who classified computers according to instruction and datastreams. A good summary of Flynn's taxonomy is given by Hockney and Jesshope.*

HOCKNEY and JESSHOPE (200):

1 SISD: single instruction stream/single datastream. This is the conventional serial von Neumann computer in which there is one stream of instructions (and therefore, in practice, only one instruction processing unit) and each arithmetic instruction initiates one arithmetic operation, leading to a single datastream of logically related arguments and results. It is irrevelant whether pipelining is used to speed up the processing of instructions or the arithmetic. It is what we have previously called a serial scalar computer. Examples are: CDC 6600 (unpipelined); CDC 7600 (pipelined arithmetic); AMDAHL 470V/6 (pipelined instruction processing).

2 SIMD: single instruction stream/multiple datastream. This is a computer that retains a single stream of instructions but has vector instructions that initiate many operations. Each element of the vector is regarded as a member of a separate datastream hence, excepting the degenerate case of vectors of length one, there are multiple datastreams. This classification therefore includes all machines with vector instructions. Again it is irrelevant whether the capability of vector processing is realised by pipelining or by building arrays of processors. Examples are: CRAY-1 (pipelined vector computer); ILLIAC IV (processor array); ICL DAP (processor array); OMEN-64 (processor array).

3 MISD: multiple instruction stream/single datastream. This class seems to be void because it implies that several instructions are operating on a data item simultaneously. However Flynn **(207)** states that it includes specialised streaming organisations using multiple instruction streams on a single sequence of data. However no examples are given.

4 MIMD: multiple instruction stream/multiple datastream. Multiple instruction streams imply the existence of several instruction processing units and therefore necessarily several datastreams. This class therefore includes all forms of multiprocessor configurations, from linked mainframe computers to large arrays of microprocessors.

The above classification clearly covers early computers (SISD), lock step array processors such as ILLIAC IV or DAP (SIMD), and multiprocessor systems such as Cm (MIMD). However, it fails to classify the most important of today's supercomputers: the CRAY and the CYBER 205. These do scalar operations as SISD and vector operations as SIMD with the distinction that the single instruction is applied successively to a vector of operands rather than in parallel to an array of operands, as in other SIMD architectures. The significant features of these two machines are the extensive pipeline and the ability to operate at high speed on vector and scalar operands. It is therefore becoming accepted to put them in a classification of their own pipelined vector processors.*

A second taxonomy by Shaw **(208)** *identifies six different types of computer. One corresponds to SISD, four are subclassifications of SIMD, and the final one covers logic in memory systems and associative processors.*

Hockney and Jesshope **(200)** *have developed a precise algebraic notation to describe computer designs which is probably best illustrated by the definitions they give for several well-known computers.*

HOCKNEY and JESSHOPE (200):

$$C(Z80 + \text{memory}) = C(Z80)_8 - M_{64K*8}\ ;C(Z80) = I_8^{250}[B_{8\ 8} - M_{18*8}]$$

$$C(\text{INTEL } 8086) = I_8[B_{16\ 16} - M_{13*8}]_{16} - M_{1M*16}$$

$$C(\text{EDSAC1}) = I[B_1 - M];\ M = M_{512*35}$$

$$C(\text{IBM } 7090) = I[F_{36} - M]$$

$$C(\text{CDC } 6600) = I[10E - 32M - 10\overline{P}]_r\ ;10E = \{4F_{60}, 6B\}$$

$$C(\text{CDC } 7600) = I[9Ep - M - 16\overline{P}]_r\ ;9Ep = \{3Fp, 6B\};M = 32M1 - 8M2$$

$$C(\text{IBM } 360/195) = Ip^{54}[2C - 32M1^{160}(1KB) - 16M2^{800}];$$

$$2C = \{C1, C2\};C1 = I[3Fp - M];C2 = I[B - M]$$

$$C(\text{CRAY-1}) = Iv^{12}[12Ep^{12} - 16M^{50}]_r\ ;12Ep = \{3Fp_{64}, 9B\}$$

$$C(\text{CYBER } 205) = Iv^{20}[4\overline{F}p_{64} - 512M^{80}_{16K*32}]$$

$$C(\text{TIASC}(2\text{IPU, } 4 \text{ pipe})) = 2Ipv[2\overline{F}p] - 8M - 8\overline{P}$$

$$C(\text{ILLIAC IV}(4 \text{ quadrant})) = C1[4C2^{80}[64\overline{P}]_1^{1} - {}^{nn}];\ P = F_{64}^{600} - M_{2K*64}^{400}$$

$$C(\text{PEPE}) = C1[31[288\{\overline{3E - M}\}]_1^{0} - {}^{nn}];\ C1 = C(\text{CDC } 7600)$$

$$C(\text{BSP}) = Ip[16\overline{F} \times 17\overline{M}]_1$$

$$C(64 \times 64 \text{ ICL DAP}) = C[64^2\overline{P}]_1^{1} - {}^{nn}\ ;P = B_1 - M_{4K*1}$$

$$C(\text{STARAN}) = I[32[256\overline{B}_1 \times O_{256*256}]_1] - M$$

$$C(\text{OMEN-64}) = I_{16}[64\overline{B}_1 - O_{64*16} - E_{16}]_1$$

$$C(\text{HYPERCUBE}) = I[2^4\overline{C}];\ C = C(2*\text{INTEL } 8080)$$

Anderson and Jenson **(209)** present a naming scheme for different systems of interconnecting computers.

The pursuit of classifications or taxonomies seems a rather pointless activity. The language of Hockney and Jesshope for precise pictorial description has considerably more merit, but it is difficult to see how any of these activities will lead to advances in computer designs.

For the remainder of this analysis the three approaches to high-performance computers will be taken as:

1 Pipelined vector processors: computers in which the operation of each instruction is divided into many (the number varies considerably) stages so that many instructions, or the same instruction on many data items, can be in the process of being obeyed at the same time.

2 SIMD: an array of processors working in step from a common instruction stream but with each having its own datastream.

3 MIMD: an array of some (again the number varies considerably) processors and memories each obeying their own instruction streams on their own data but collaborating to solve a single unified problem; all processors share most, often all, of primary memory.

HOW DO THE DIFFERENT APPROACHES YIELD HIGH PERFORMANCE?

Going back to the Ferranti Mark 1 computer in 1951, which had a single address format, the instruction was obeyed in four beats:

- Accessing the store for the instruction
- Decoding and calculating the operand address
- Accessing the store for the operand
- Performing the arithmetic.

The same structure continued in the MERCURY and into the initial design of the ATLAS, the increased speeds of the machines coming from faster components, parallel arithmetic, and engineered floating-point. During the design of the ATLAS, it was realised (after about 20 years of building computers!) that these four stages were, for most instructions, independent of each other and, of equal importance, independent of the effects of the previous three instructions. Therefore, in theory, if the four stages were of equal length the timing of a sequence of instructions would be

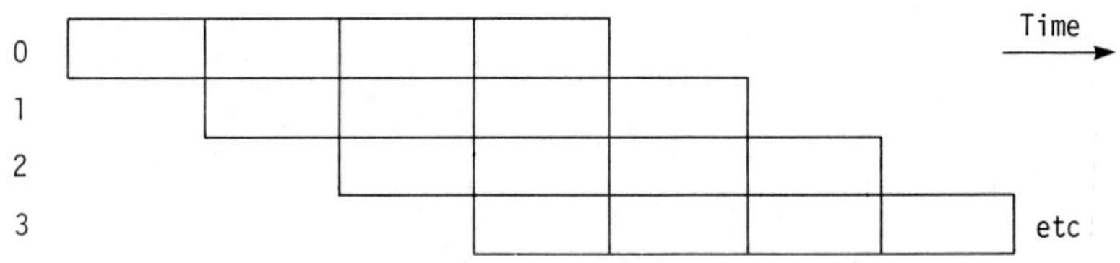

Obviously, each instruction takes the same time as it would without overlapping (as the technique was then called) but the average rate of completing the instruction is four times greater.

In practice the stages of instructions are not equal in length nor are instructions always completely independent of the three preceding instructions. The most obvious example is of a conditional branch order which can completely destroy the overlapping of instructions. An indication of these difficulties is that the effective overlap of the ATLAS over a complete program was approximately 2 rather than the theoretical maximum of 4.

The concept of pipelining developed quite rapidly from these beginnings. In synchronous computers, the instructions were divided into equal stages which greatly simplified the overlapping. Modifications of the ATLAS concept are obviously necessary for 0, 2, and 3 address systems.

Up to the CDC 6600, the MU5, and large IBM computers of the same period, this type of division was the limit of pipelining although the concept of multiple arithmetic units was introduced to permit long arithmetic operations to be overlapped with each other in the same way as other parts of the instruction. Each arithmetic operation was, however, an indivisable object. Incidentally, it should be noted that the implementation of multiple arithmetic units requires a 2 or 3 address format.

The CDC 7600 divided the operation of some of the slower arithmetic units into stages so that the concept of pipelining could be extended into the arithmetic. For example, the floating-point add takes four stages and the floating-point multiply takes five. The longer the pipeline, ie the greater the number of subdivisions, from starting the instruction to completing it, the more difficult it is to keep the pipeline full and thus achieve maximum performance. These difficulties arise for the same reasons as on the ATLAS and on the 7600; the effect is that the pipeline on average is only 25% full.

The processing of vectors of data is the obvious way of keeping the pipeline full. It is the same as obeying a long sequence to, say, add orders with the necessity of only accessing the operands from the memory. Vector pipelines are thus a natural solution to the problem created by the introduction of overlapping or pipelining to increase the speed of SISD computers.

The potential of high performance of SIMD and MIMD is obvious: the more processors working on the same problem the faster the overall computation. However, it is clearly obvious that there can be considerable degradation of performance if it is not possible to map the problem efficiently onto the structure of the computer. Both of these classes of computer attempt to achieve maximum flexibility by the methods of interconnection of the processors and memories. This is a very active area of research, mostly on theoretical solutions for non-existent machines, and, rather than consider such general solutions, the way in which specific high-performance computers have tackled the problems will be covered in the next subsection, where the designs of several high-performance systems are looked at in more detail.

CYBER 205

For most computer systems it is difficult to find publications describing their important features. For the 205 there is a paper on the 203 by Kascic **(210)**, *CYBER 203 and 203E being early names for the system now marketed as the CYBER 205. Hockney and Jesshope* **(200)** *and Ibbett* **(202)** *have produced excellent descriptions of the system by studying the hardware reference manuals published by CDC.*

The STAR-100 had many problems that have been modified by the 205.

IBBETT (202): The STAR-100 was criticised on a number of grounds by users who wished to apply it to more general computing problems than those for which it was designed. The grounds for criticism were mainly the long vector start-up time and poor performance on scalar arithmetic, both of which were inevitable consequences of the design. These problems are largely overcome in the CYBER 205 by the use of a very much faster (80 nsec access time) semiconductor memory and by the inclusion of a high-performance scalar unit. The overall performance of the CYBER 205 is further enhanced by its implementation in specially developed ECL LSI ULA technology, allowing a reduction of the clock period from the 40 nsec used in the STAR-100 to 20 nsec.

Figure 4 shows the units and their interconnections.

In pipeline computers one of the degrading effects is memory clashes, where the memory is busy when an item of data is requested. In the ATLAS the concept of multiple banks was introduced, each bank being independent so that requests to different banks could take place at the same time. This concept was greatly extended in the 6600 and 7600 where 32 separate banks were used.

Another problem in high-performance computers is getting the operands to the arithmetic unit at a sufficient rate. In the 205 scalar operands are stored in a bank of 256 fast registers and each can be both read and written to within one clock cycle of 20 nsec. Vector operands, on the other hand, are streamed directly from store and are not kept in fast registers. This is one of the significant differences from the CRAY-1.

IBBETT: Internally the memory is organised such that within each unit of one million words there are 16 interleaved 32-bit stacks allowing eight sequentially addressed 64-bit words (512 bits) to be accessed in parallel. Each stack is divided into eight independent banks, each holding 16K words. A new bank read access can be initiated in every clock period, provided it is to a bank which is not already

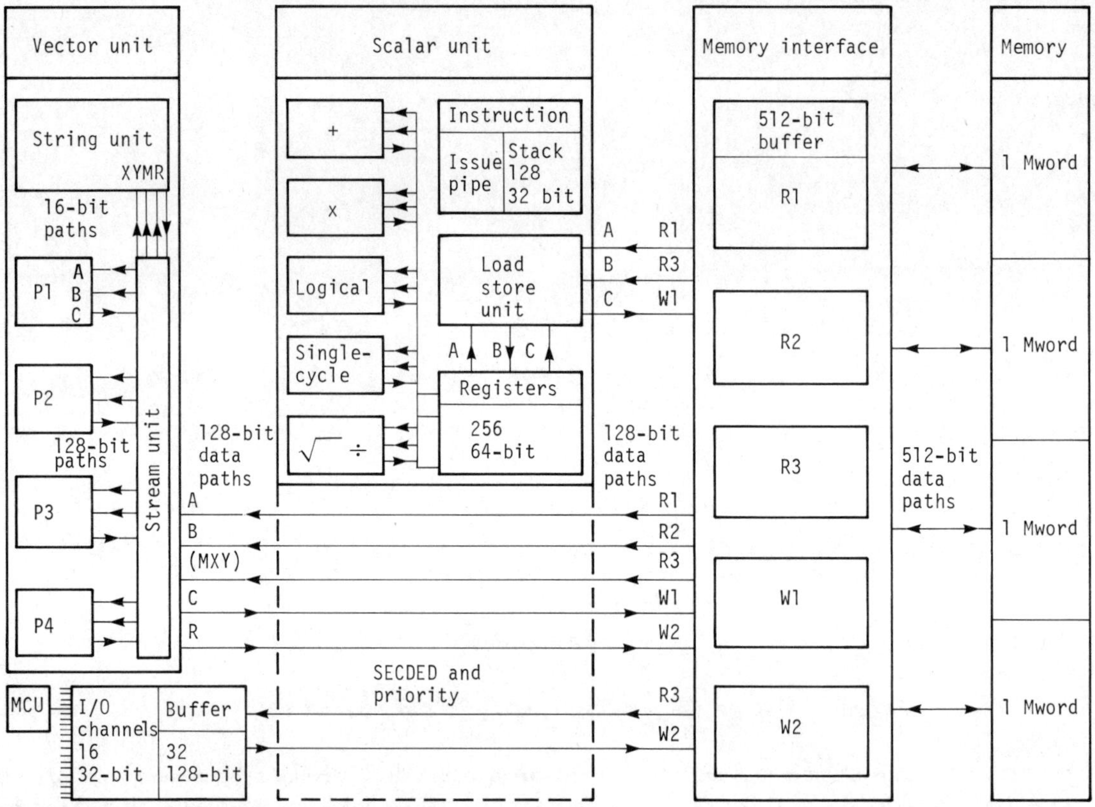

Figure 4: Architectural block diagram showing the principal units and data paths of the CDC CYBER 205 (reproduced from **(211)***)*

busy, and the banks can share a single stack data path since this path is only required during the last clock period of the four clock period bank cycle.

An important difference between the 205 and the CRAY-1 is that the 205 uses virtual addressing.

High-speed scalar arithmetic is very important in vector processors as all calculations have a proportion of scalar arithmetic and an imbalance between the scalar and vector units can adversely affect a computer's performance. This was the case with the STAR-100. As well as getting operands it is vital that the correct instructions are available in the processing unit. Most high-performance computers, for example IBM 195 and the CDC 7600, have instruction buffers to trap loops and store new instructions after branch orders, together with an early call system to ensure that the instructions are in the CPU when required.

IBBETT (202): The design of the CYBER 205 scalar processor is largely derived from that of the CDC 7600. The instruction stack is filled from central memory (under control of the branch/prefetch unit) two superwords ahead of the instruction currently being executed, and can contain up to eight associatively addressed superwords. Instructions are taken from the stack by the instruction issue unit, which decodes each instruction in turn and sends it to the appropriate functional unit for execution. Vector and string instructions are sent to the vector processor while scalar instructions are sent to one of five arithmetic subunits within the scalar floating-point unit. The add/subtract, multiply, logical and single cycle units are all pipelined and can accept a new pair of input operands at every clock cycle.

The scalar operations read from and write to the bank of 256 fast registers. The speed of the scalar operations is similar to that of the 7600.

HOCKNEY and JESSHOPE (200):

Functional unit	Unit time (nsec)	Unit time (clock periods)
Load/store	300	15
Addition/subtraction	100	5
Multiplication	100	5
Logical	60	3
Single cycle	20	1
Division, square root, conversion		
• for 64 bits	1080	54
• for 32 bits	600	30

All these times are 'shortstop times'.

IBBETT (202): Shortstopping is a technique which allows a result required as a source operand by a succeeding instruction to be returned directly to the input of an arithmetic unit. This is the scalar equivalent of chaining in the CRAY-1, and although similar in some respects to data forwarding in the IBM System 360 Model 91, it is different in that a shortstopped result in the CYBER 205 is sent as an input operand to an arithmetic unit at the same time as being written into the register file. In the Model 91 a result is not written into a register at all if it is forwarded.

A vector pipeline of the 205 is illustrated in Figure 5. A system can have two or four pipes.

The individual arithmetic units are themselves pipelined and the pipelines are fed with operands by a streaming unit.

HOCKNEY and JESSHOPE (200): Operations on vectors of numbers or strings of characters are performed in the vector section which comprises either one, two or four *floating-point pipelines* and a *string unit* that are fed with streams of data by a *stream unit*. Unlike the CRAY-1 there are no vector registers, and all vector operations are main memory to main memory operations, necessitating data to travel a round trip of about 50ft, compared to less than 6ft on the CRAY-1. This difference partly explains the much longer vector start-up time on the CYBER 205. A vector may comprise up to 65 635 consecutively addressed elements. If the required data is not consecutively stored the required elements can be selected by a *control vector* of bits, one bit for each word of the vector. The operation is then only performed for elements for which the corresponding control bit is one. However all elements of the consecutively stored vector must be read from memory even though only a small fraction may be operated upon. Alternatively if the control vector is sparse in ones, the specified elements of a long vector may be selected by a *compress* operation and restored consecutively. Subsequent operations may then be performed with better efficiency on the new compressed vector. In addition efficient scatter/gather instructions are implemented by microcode in the stream unit. These reference memory either randomly according to an index list, or periodically (ie at equal intervals).

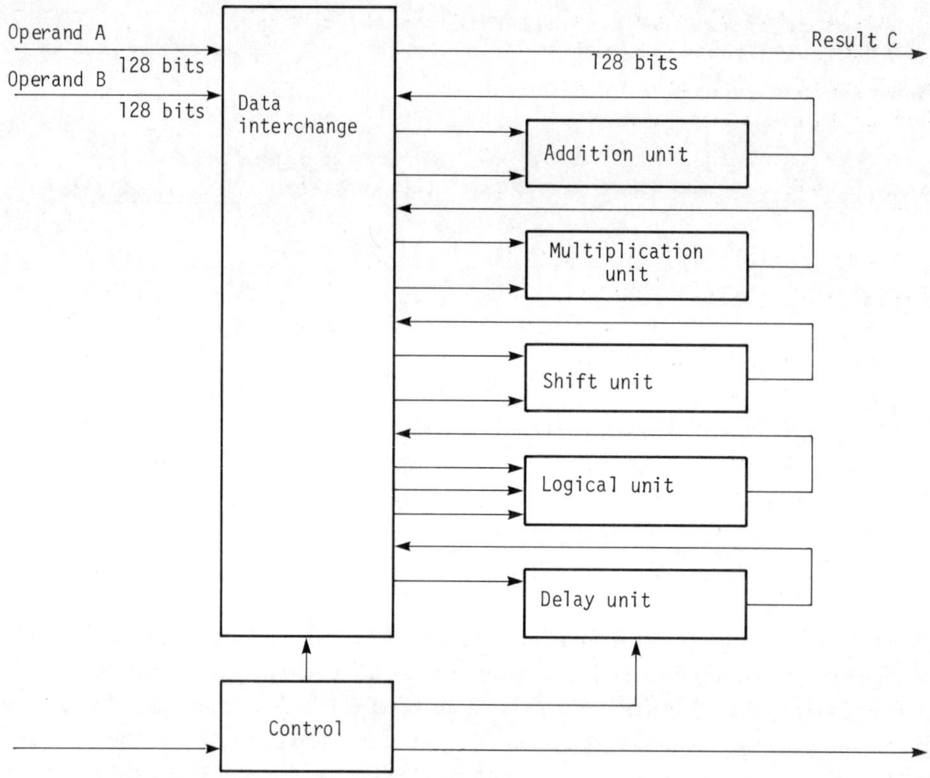

Figure 5: CYBER 205 vector pipeline (from (211))

The difficulty with streaming operands from memory occurs when accessing columns on a matrix that has been stored in row order.

IBBETT: One of the criticisms levelled at the CYBER 205 is that, as in the STAR-100, vectors may only be accessed on the basis of a unit increment between successive elements, so that matrices stored by row, for example, cannot easily be accessed by column. However, the high memory bandwidth of the CYBER 205 is only obtainable because many adjacent elements can be read out in parallel in each memory cycle, and to allow different accessing patterns in standard vector orders would severely degrade performance. Provision of increments different from unity would also require changes to the instruction format, and alternative general mechanisms for the reordering of operands are provided instead. These mechanisms are invoked in indexed list operations which allow for the gathering or scattering of periodic or random data within a data structure.

During execution of a scatter operation (Transmit List -> Indexed C), for example, two source vectors (A and B) are normally read from memory and a result vector (C) is written to memory. Source vector A is a list of indices referring to positions in the result vector, while source vector B is the sequential list of 32-bit or 64-bit operands to be written. During each cycle of operation, the index taken from vector A is shifted appropriately and added to the result vector origin to form a memory address. This address is then sent to memory, accompanied by appropriate write control bits and by the corresponding operand taken from vector B. The index list may be formed either by geometrical considerations or by data-dependent considerations. Sparse vectors with a population density of the order of 0.1%, for example, can be dealt with more efficiently by this mechanism than by the alternative Boolean control vector technique which is also available in the CYBER-205 and which is suitable for population densities in the range 1-10%.

In a gather operation (Transmit indexed list -> C), source vector A is again a list of indices, but these indices refer to positions in source vector B rather than the result vector. Addresses formed by adding each index from vector A in turn to the origin of vector B are used to access operands from vector B, and these operands are then written to sequential result vector locations.

The potential speed of the 205 is greater than that of the CRAY-1.

IBBETT: In the typical two-pipeline CYBER 205 system, two 64-bit operands can be transferred into the floating-point pipeline on each of its two input highways, and two 64-bit results transferred out, in one 20 nsec clock period. This corresponds to an execution rate for 64-bit floating-point numbers of 100 MFLOPS, or 200 MFLOPS for 32-bit numbers. For linked triadic operations, or during the execution of the scalar product operation, this rate is doubled to 200 MFLOPS for 64-bit numbers or 400 MFLOPS for 32-bit numbers. The memory bandwidth required to support this execution rate is six 64-bit words per 20 nsec interval, or 300 Mwords/sec. Since the data highway between each one million words of central memory and the memory interface is 512 bits wide, and since a read or write transfer can occur every 20 nsec, memory bandwidth is actually 400 Mwords/sec. A one million word memory configuration can therefore support a two-pipeline system without difficulty. For the four-pipeline system at least two million words of central memory are required, with each one million words being connected to the memory interface via its own data highway. In this case the maximum execution rate is 800 MFLOPS for 32-bit linked triadic or scalar product operations.

Where accessing patterns involving non-unary increments are required, performance is reduced because the vector arithmetic instruction must be preceded by a gather instruction or succeeded by a scatter instruction. These instructions themselves run at less than the full arithmetic rate and have been measured to proceed at an average rate of 40 million operations/sec. This performance is an average of many operations running at a rate of 50 million/sec with occasional periods of 12.5 million/sec.

The CYBER 205 has a much shorter vector start-up time than the STAR-100 but it is still longer than that of the CRAY-1. The effect of this is illustrated by the speeds in MFLOPS for different vector lengths for the two computers (see Figure 6).

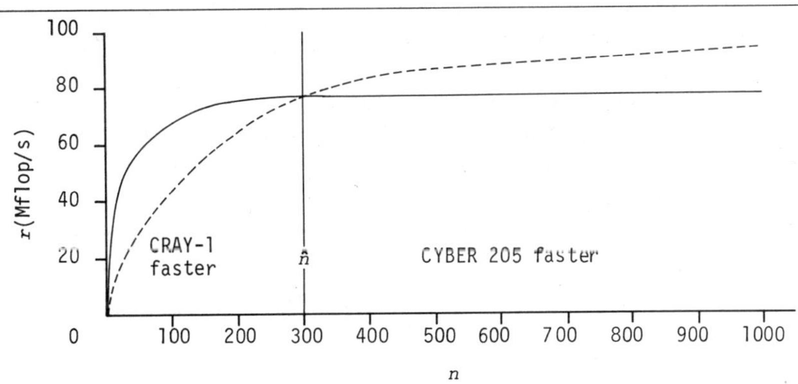

Figure 6: Comparison of CRAY-1 and CYBER 205 speeds (from (200)*)*

CRAY-1

The CRAY-1 is a logical extension of the 6600 and 7600. A simplistic definition is that it was in fact just the same with the addition of vector operations using banks of 64 element vector registers instead of scalar registers in the three address operations of the 6600 or 7600.

The features of the CRAY-1 are well summarised in Figure 7 **(212)**.

Computation section

- Scalar and vector processing modes
- 12.5 nsec clock period operation
- 64-bit word size
- Integer and floating-point arithmetic
- 12 fully segmented functional units
- Eight 24-bit address (A) registers
- 64 24-bit intermediate address (B) registers
- Eight 64-bit scalar (S) registers
- 64 64-bit intermediate scalar (T) registers
- Eight 64-element vector (V) registers (64 bits per element)
- Vector length and vector mask registers
- One 64-bit real-time clock (RT) register
- Four instruction buffers of 64 16-bit parcels each
- 128 basic instructions
- Prioritised interrupt control.

Memory section

- 1 048 576 64-bit words (plus eight check bits per word)
- 16 independent banks of 64 536 words each
- Four clock period bank cycle time
- One word per clock period transfer rate for B, T, and V registers
- One word per two clock periods transfer rate to instruction buffers (up to 16 instructions per clock period).

I/O section

- 24 I/O channels organised into four 6-channel groups
- Each channel group contains either six input or six output channels
- Each channel group served by memory every four clock periods
- Channel priority within each channel group
- 16 data bits, three control bits per channel, and four parity bits
- Maximum channel rate of one 64-bit word every 100 nsec
- Maximum datastream rate of 550 000 64-bit words/sec
- Channel error detection.

Figure 7: CRAY-1 CPU characteristics summary

The interrelationship of the various parts is clearly shown in Figure 8.

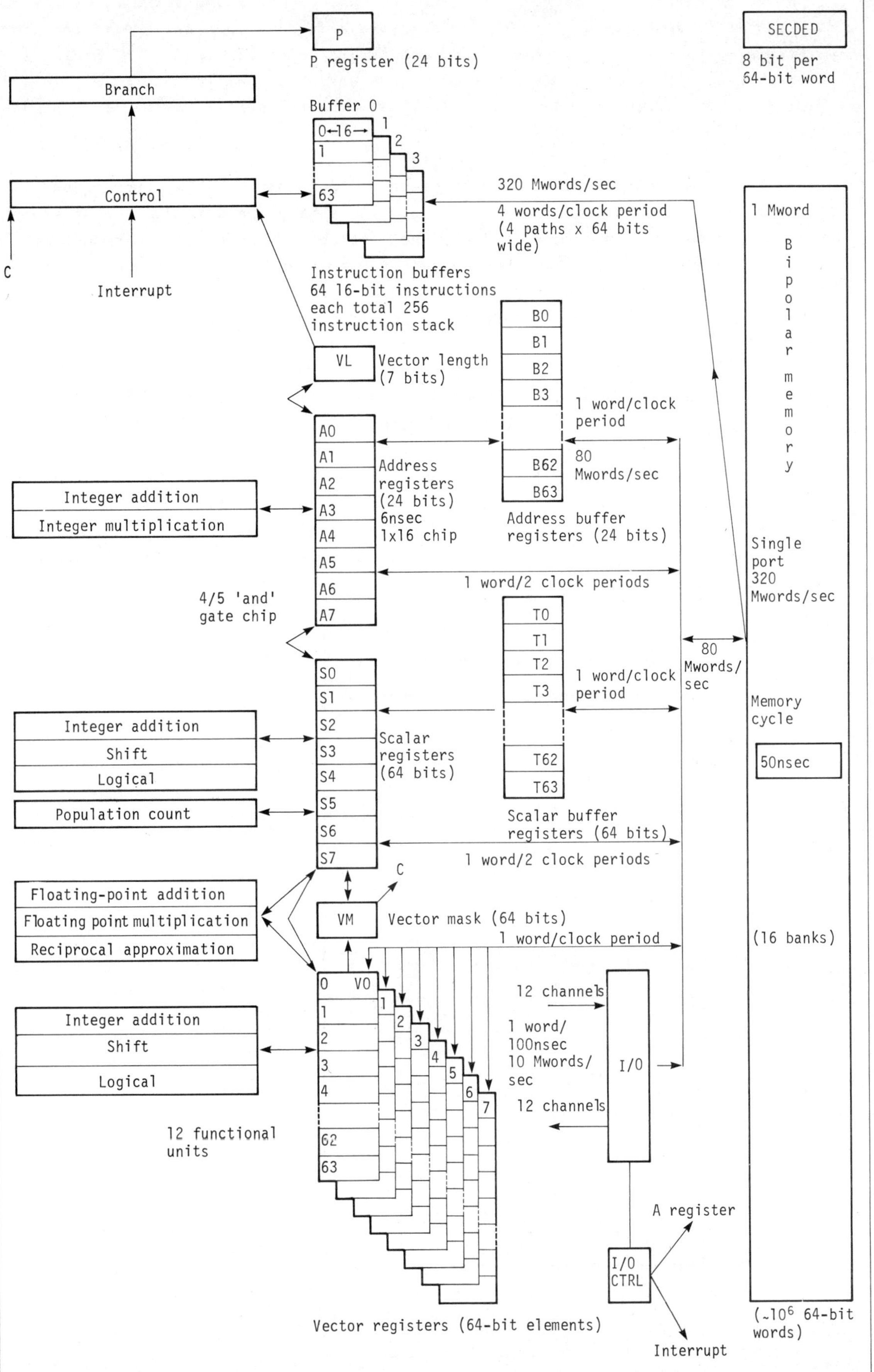

Figure 8: Interrelationship of parts in CRAY-1 (reproduced from **(200)***)*

The significant differences between the CYBER 205 and the CRAY-1 are the clock times of 20 nsec and 12.5 nsec respectively (but what happens in one clock period?); the store access times of 80 nsec and 50 nsec; and most important of all the use of banks of registers to store vectors in the CRAY-1. The extensive use of registers is also exemplified in the design of the instruction buffer in the CRAY-1, which is very much bigger than the buffer in the CYBER 205.

IBBETT (202): The need for instruction prefetching and loop catching techniques arises from the impracticability of having a large high-speed random access store close to the central processor, and all the instruction buffering techniques with which we have dealt so far have been aimed at circumventing this problem. With the advent of MSI and LSI storage technologies, however, different hardware organisations have been made possible. An example of this can be seen in the instruction buffering mechanism used in the CRAY-1.

The overall structure and instruction set of the CRAY-1 are largely derived from the CDC 6600 and 7600, with instructions being executed by a set of parallel functional units. The processor obtains all its instructions directly from a set of instruction buffers, however, and does not send a stream of instruction requests to the main store. These buffers are organised as shown in Figure 9. Each of the four buffers holds 64 consecutive 16-bit instruction parcels, and if an instruction request cannot be satisfied from within these buffers, a full 64-parcel block of instructions is transferred from main store into one of them.

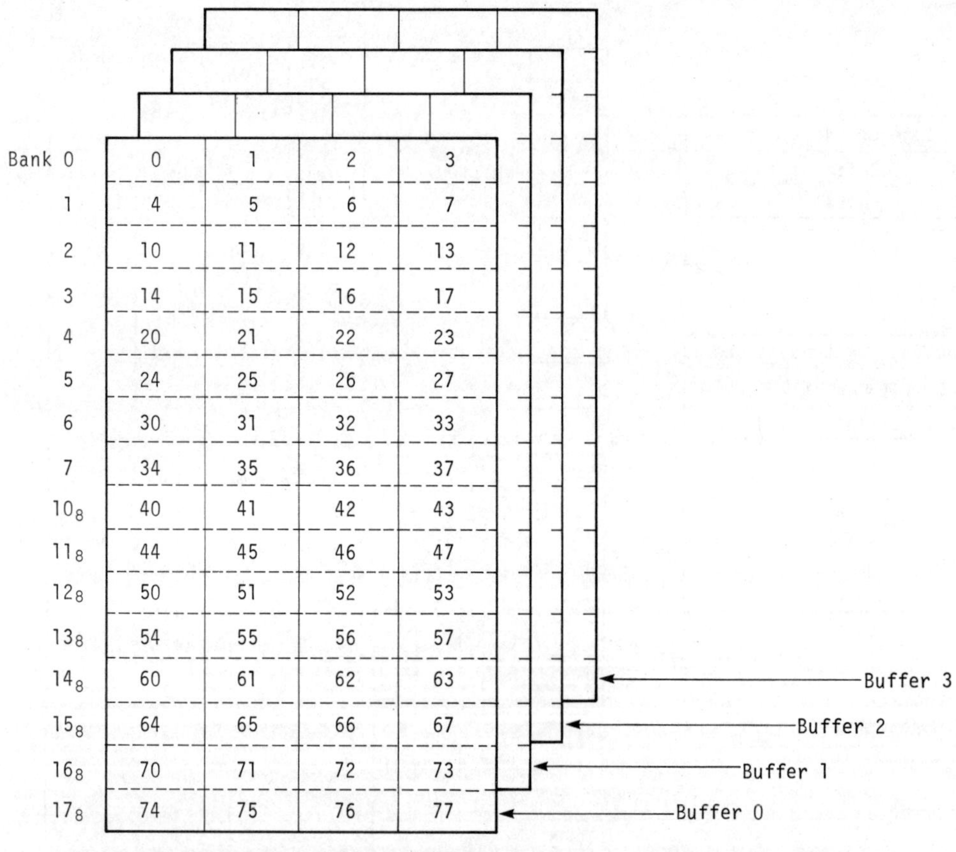

Figure 9: CRAY-1 instruction buffers (reproduced from (202))

CRAY X-MP

The first CRAY-1 was delivered to Los Alamos in 1976. Since then over 50 systems have been delivered throughout the world making it easily the most widely used of all the supercomputers. In April 1982, Cray Research announced a new series, the CRAY X-MP (see Figure 10), with four systems scheduled for delivery in 1983.

The technology of the new system shows clearly that at the present level of circuit development very high speeds cannot be achieved by using high levels of integration.

CRAY RESEARCH (213): Throughout the CRAY X-MP CPUs, 16-gate array integrated circuits are used. These circuits which are faster and denser than the circuitry used in the CRAY-1, contribute to a clock cycle time of 9.5 nsec and a memory bank cycle time of 38 nsec.

This is to be compared with the clock period of the CRAY-1 which is 12.5 nsec.

The X-MP is a dual processor with two identical processors sharing a common memory which has either 2M or 4M 64-bit words.

The recognition of the need for a high bandwidth between the CPU and the memory is shown by the fact that the 4M word memory is organised in 32 banks and that there are four parallel memory ports to each of the two processors. The X-MP has eight times the memory bandwidth of the CRAY-1.

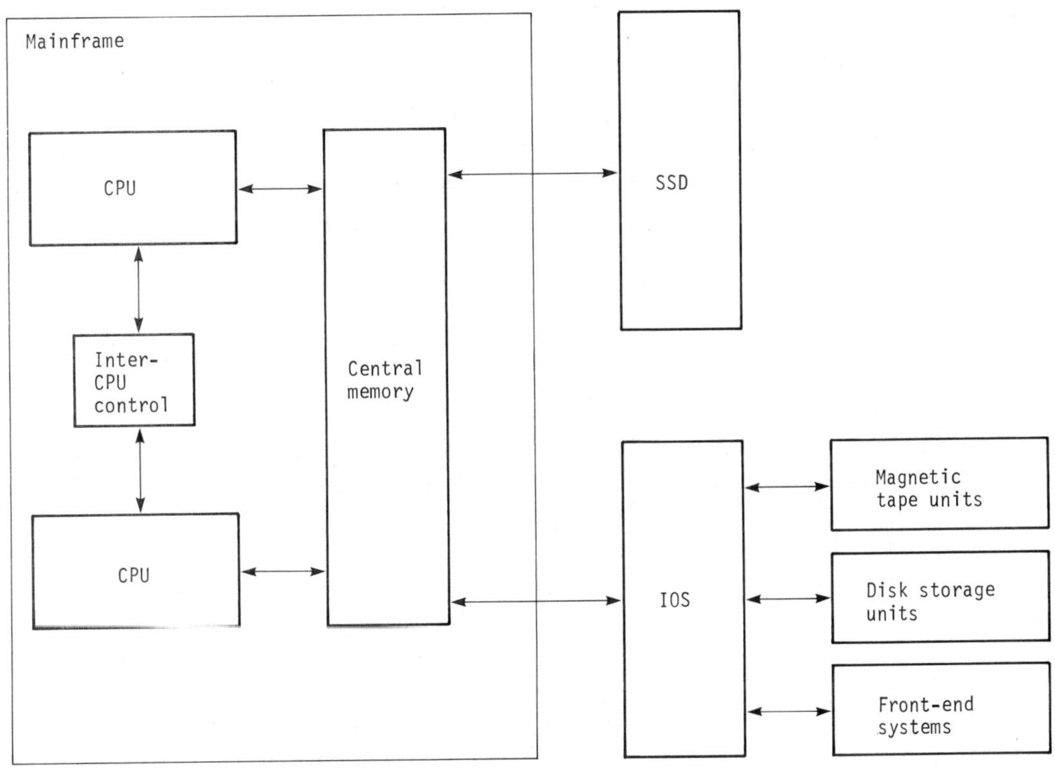

Figure 10: CRAY X-MP overall system organisation (reproduced from **(213)***)*

The value of an effective instruction buffer is also re-enforced by the doubling of the size of the instruction buffer in each processor as compared with that of the CRAY-1 to four buffers each holding 128 16-bit instruction parcels.

A summary of the X-MP architecture is shown in Figure 11. The potential performance is quite impressive.

CRAY RESEARCH (213): The X-MP is capable of an overall instruction issue rate of over 200 million instr/sec. Computation rates of over 400 million 64-bit floating-point operations (MFLOPS) are possible and combined arithmetic/logical operations can exceed 1000 million operations per second (MOPS).

Using conventional disk files as backing store would lead to severe bottlenecks with this speed of computing. This problem has been avoided by the provision of the Solid-state Storage Device (SSD) which can have a capacity of up to 256 Mbytes arranged in 64 banks connected by a high-speed channel of 1250 Mbyte/sec into the X-MP memory.

CRAY RESEARCH (213): Complementing the CRAY X-MP architecture, the SSD connects to the mainframe through a specially designed high-speed channel capable of maximum burst transfer rates of 1250 Mbyte/sec (10 Gbyte/sec) (see Figure 12). Performance improvement factors over disks of 50 to 100 are possible for short random or long sequential transfers, respectively.

CRAY-2

The next computer system from Cray Research is a continuation of the approach of the X-MP. The CRAY-2 is expected to be six to twelve times as fast as the CRAY-1 and the first customer deliveries are expected in 1985.

The clock period will be 4 nsec and the system will consist of four identical processors sharing a 4M word memory which will have a cycle time of 12.5 nsec.

High-density packaging of components is obviously essential if speeds of this level are to be achieved and the size of the total system is expected to be only one tenth of that of the CRAY-1 (26 inches high by 36 inches long).

CRAY RESEARCH (214): Modules for the CRAY-2 are packaged closely in three dimensions, as compared with two dimensions on the CRAY-1. Each CRAY-2 module consists of eight layers. This design substantially reduces the lengths of connecting wires, thus taking advantage of the fact that shorter wires result in greater potential speed. The longest wire in the CRAY-2 will be 16 inches compared to 4 feet in the CRAY-1.

Cooling is obviously going to be a major problem also with the high-packing density. It is in this area that the biggest technological advance has probably been made.

CRAY RESEARCH (214): Cray applied liquid immersion technology in the design of the CRAY-2 to solve a basic problem in computer design, that of cooling. By immersing the computer in a bath of clear inert liquid, the cooling problems inherent in large computer systems are substantially reduced. The resultant cooling system is extremely efficient and enables higher density packaging of components.

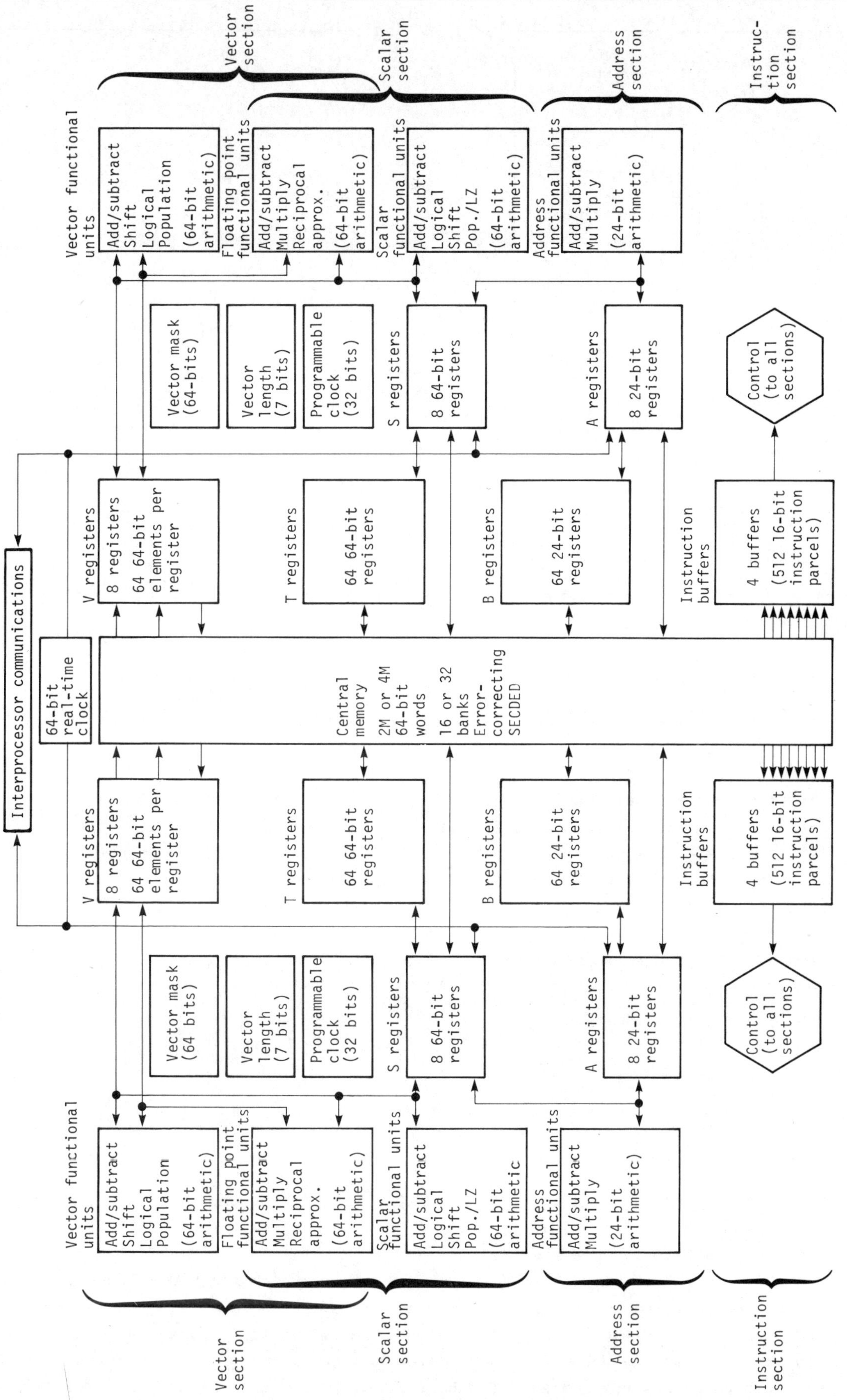

Figure 11: Summary of X-MP architecture (reproduced from **(213)***)*

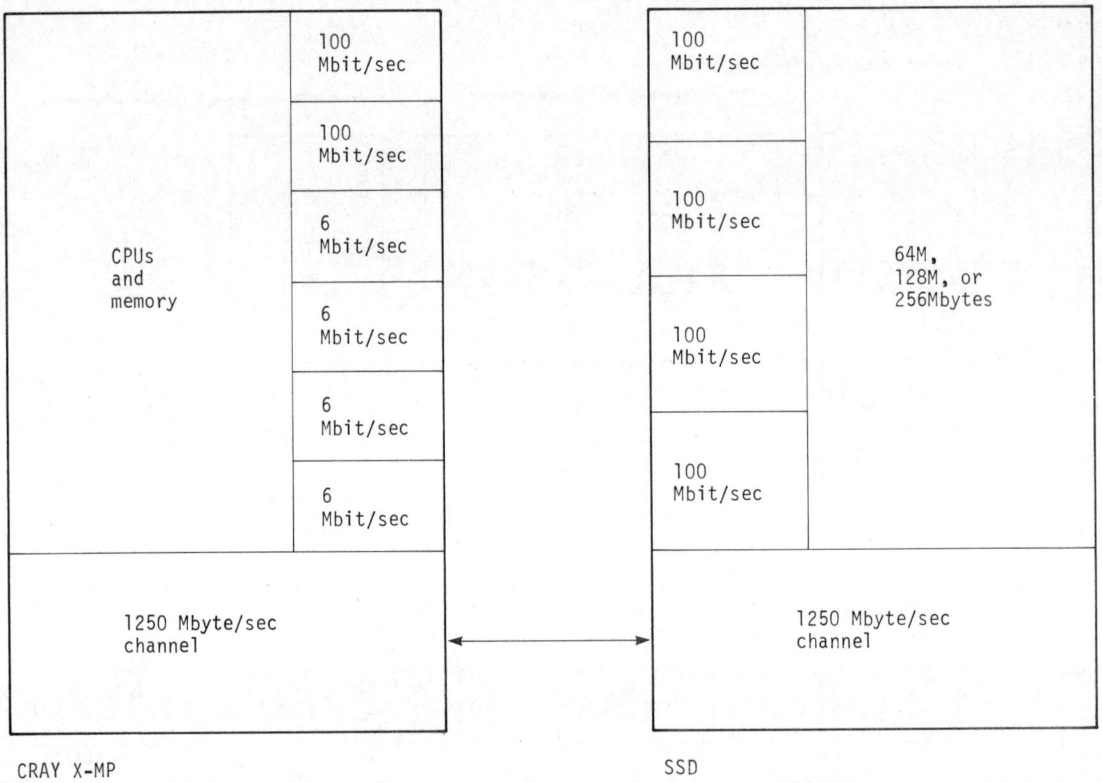

Figure 12: Provision of SSD in the CRAY X-MP (reproduced from (213))

The coolant is a pure fluorocarbon liquid which has been used for years in many industrial applications.

CRAY RESEARCH (214): An interesting sidelight to the liquid immersion technology is that it has an unusual functional value. The fluorocarbon liquid is normally quite clear and the consistency of salad oil. However, engineers have observed on the prototype module that when the circuits are on, the liquid becomes somewhat turbulent due to heat generation. The turbulence has been described as 'quite beautiful to watch', and it also indicates where hot spots are located in the computer. For these two reasons, the company may enclose the CRAY-2 in a clear frame.

Perhaps computer design has now become an 'art form' that can be appreciated visually.

<u>NASF</u>

MAI TIN (215): A project was initiated at NASA (National Aeronautics and Space Administration, USA) in 1977 to develop a special-purpose Numerical Aerodynamic Simulation Facility (NASF) to enhance the nation's aerodynamic design capability in the Eighties. In 1977, two contractors, Control Data Corporation and Burroughs Corporation, carried out preliminary studies for the facility. The goal was a 1 GFLOP machine to solve the three-dimensional hydrodynamic differential equation with about 100 mesh points along each direction, in about 10 minutes elapsed time. Each mesh point was associated with about 30 to 40 floating-point variables. This facility was to be operational in the 1982-1983 timeframe.

This is to be compared with the maximum quoted speed of the CRAY X-MP of 400 MFLOPS. Clearly speeds of over 1 GFLOP are only possible for problems that have a very high degree of parallelism which can be efficiently mapped onto the architecture of the computer.

The CDC proposal was a development of the design of the CYBER 200 series. A good description is given by Stevens **(216)** *from whose paper Figure 13 is taken (see over). Each of the five pipelined vector units at the right-hand side of Figure 13 has a structure as shown in Figure 14 (see over).*

The clock period is 8 nsec, which gives a basic performance of 500 MFLOPS. However, as each result may be formed from up to three floating-point operations the maximum processing rate is 1.5 GFLOPS for 64-bit operands and 3 GFLOPS for 32-bit operands. It is expected that 32-bit arithmetical precision will be adequate for large parts of the calculation.

The major problem in the design is getting operands to the pipelines fast enough to sustain these rates. The memory is arranged in a hierarchy of three levels: 8M words of very fast ECL memory, 32M words of MOS memory, and 128M words of CCD memory. There is extensive hardware for memory mapping between the 32M word and the 8M word memories in an attempt to ensure that the right operands are transferred into the fast memory irrespective of the direction of sweeping through the three-dimensional array of data.

The practicability of designs of this complexity, which are also rather problem specific, has to be seriously questioned.

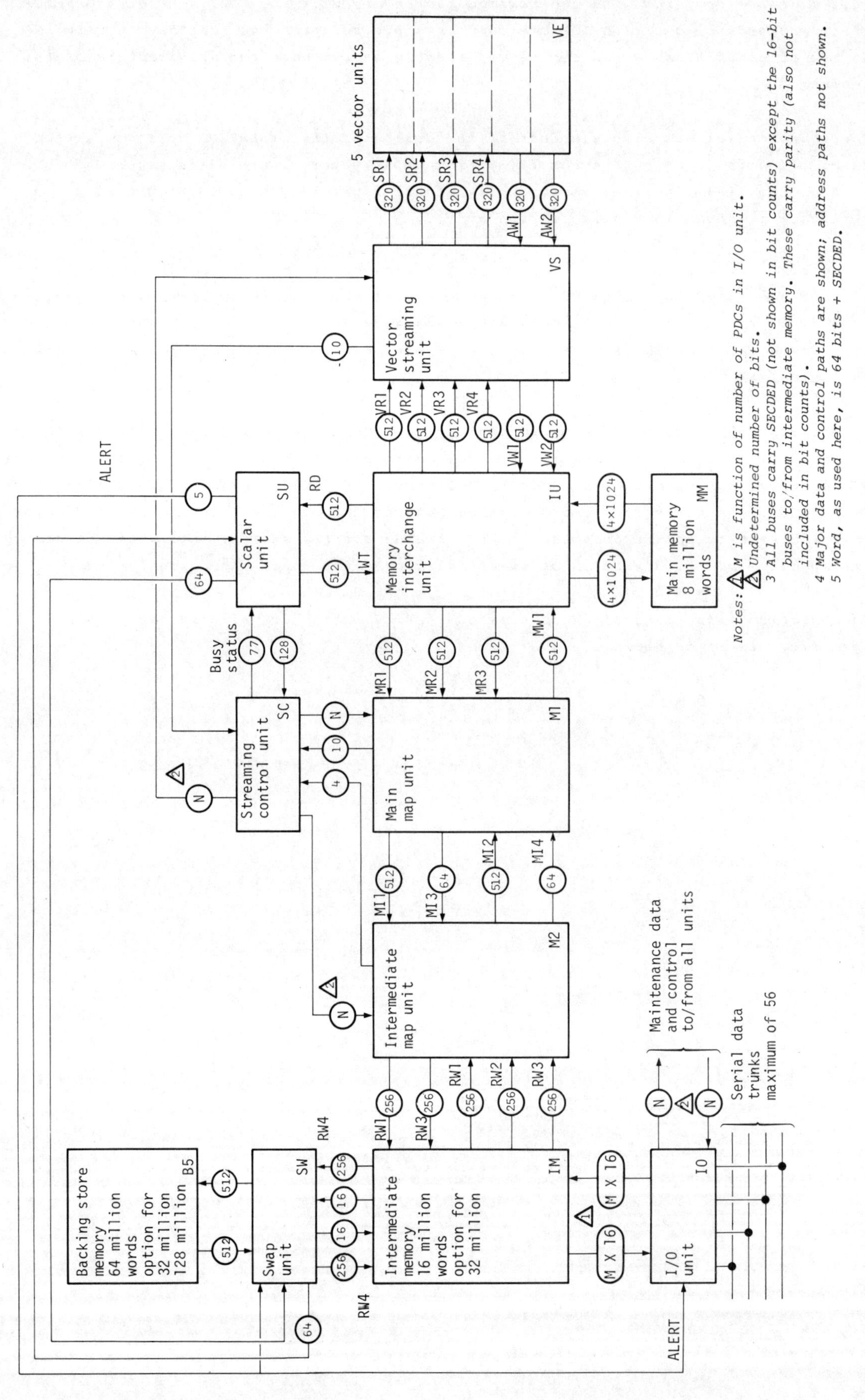

Figure 13: CDC FMP configuration

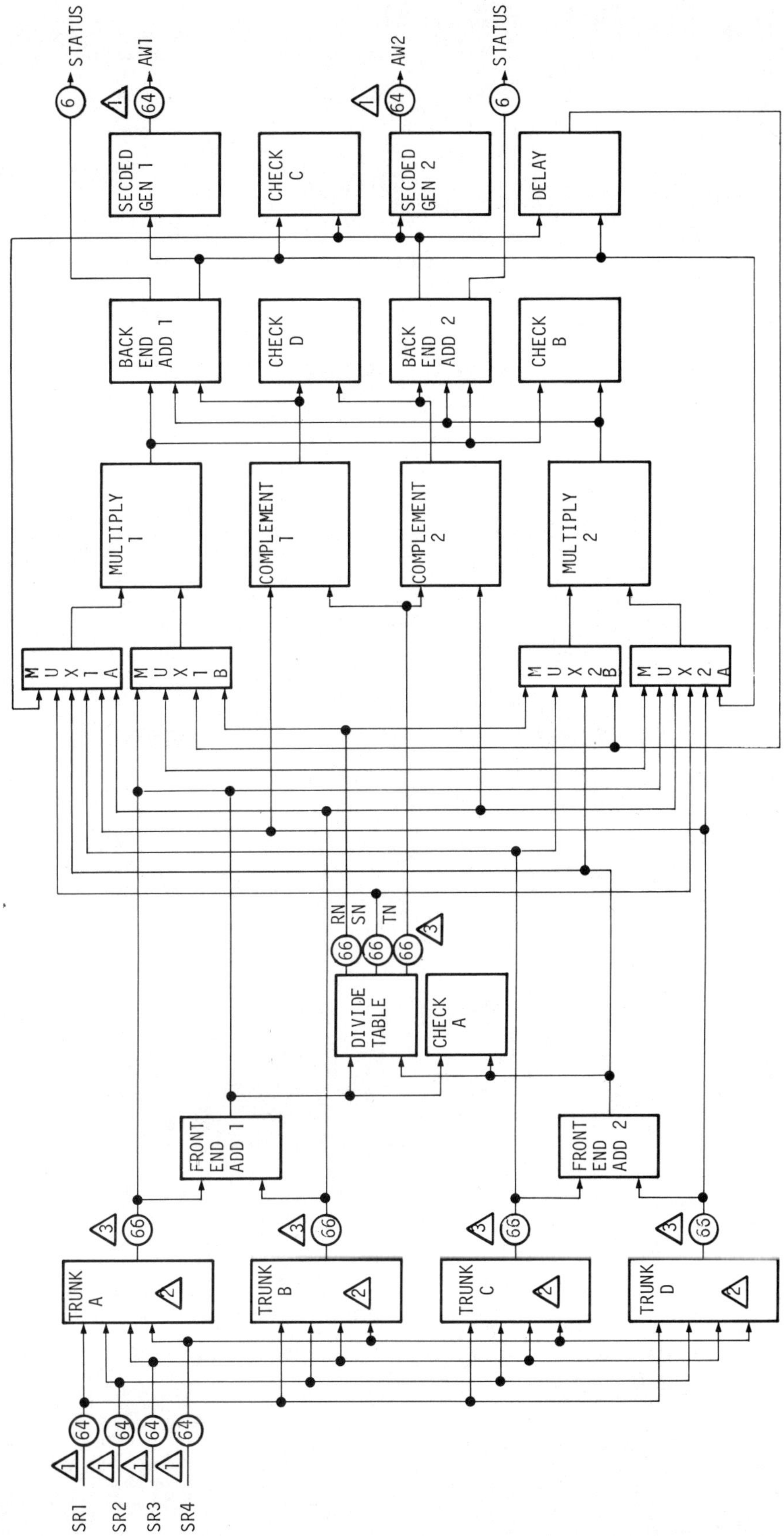

Notes:

1 These buses carry SECDED (not shown in bit widths)

2 Includes SECDED correct network

3 Duplicate sign bits

4 All inputs/outputs are from/to vector streaming unit

Figure 14: One CDC vector pipeline

SIMD PROCESSORS

During the last three years there has been virtually no development in supercomputers of this classification as compared with the advances made in pipeline vector designs. In fact one of the machines described by Hockney and Jesshope in Supercomputers **(212)**, *the Burroughs BSP, has now been withdrawn. Of the two NASF designs selected by NASA for further investigation the CDC system appears to be the one with the greater chance of success. The Burroughs design is included in this analysis as it has several interesting features.*

NASF

Burroughs produced a solution to the NASA problem based on an array of 512 processors (see Figure 15). There is little information available beyond the NASA reports **(114)** *and the paper by Stevens* **(216)**.

The two major problems are memory management and the control of the array of 512 processors.

Each processor has 16K 48-bit words giving a total of 8M words at the fastest level. The next level is 34M words of MOS memory, and the final level is 256M words of CCD memory (this is very like the three memories in the CDC approach). The memory mapping between the MOS memory and the 512 local memories is done by a complex switching network. The MOS memory is in 521 banks (521 being the first prime number greater than 512).

HOCKNEY and JESSHOPE (200): The NASF design has an array of 512 floating-point processors and like the BSP has a prime number of memory banks, 521, which is the next prime number larger than 512. In order to make use of this configuration of memory and processors to provide conflict-free access, a full connection network must be used. The BSP used two crossbar switches; however, the cost of crossbar switches to connect 512 processors to 521 memory banks would be astronomical. Thus Burroughs have been forced to consider the alternative of multistage networks. This has been one of the major design constraints in the Burroughs NASF. The final design uses a pair of omega networks called upper and lower. Because there are 521 memory banks and because the omega network must be configured in powers of two, each connection network comprises a 1024 × 1024 switch. Thus each processor is connected to two ports on each network. The first 512 memory banks are connected to the network ports using their bit-reversed address, with the remaining memory banks distributed randomly among the unused ports.

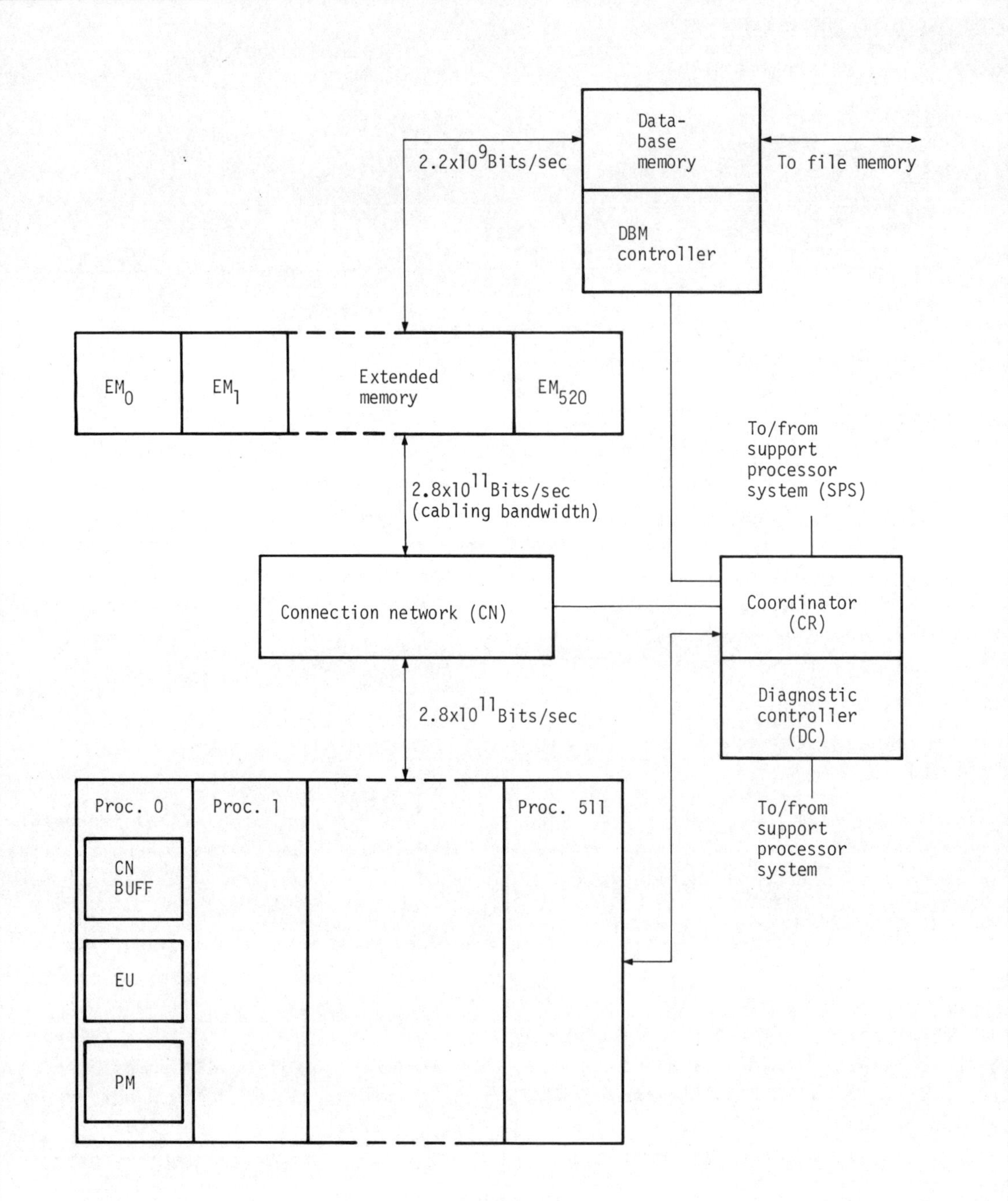

Figure 15: Burroughs organisation of FMP

The omega network can be self-seeking. For example, packets of addressed data can be placed at one node and then forwarded to their destination. This requires queues at intersections in the network, with data forwarding strategies. The access priorities of the upper network are opposite to those of the lower and if access cannot be completed on one, the other will automatically be tried. The cycle time of the network is 120 nsec, which is three times longer than the 40 nsec cycle of each processor.

The 512 processors do not work off a common instruction stream. Each processor has its own program so that the design could be classified as MIMD. However, the code is generally the same and the 512 processors are periodically resynchronised by the control unit.

Simulations of the design suggest a performance in line with the requirements of NASA.

DAP

A production model of a 64 × 64 element DAP connected to an ICL 2980 has now been in operation at Queen Mary College, London for a few years. It is currently being modified to increase the memory per processing element from 4K bits to 16K bits as the smaller memory was found to be rather restrictive.

The most significant development in this area has been the announcement by ICL of a single user workstation comprising a 32 × 32 DAP array connected to a PERQ computer. For problems amenable to the DAP architecture this should give a personal workstation with the power of a CDC 7600.

The Goodyear Aerospace MPP

HOCKNEY and JESSHOPE (200): The Goodyear Aerospace Massively Parallel Processor (MPP) is being designed in response to another NASA project. The requirement is a computer to process LANDSAT-D satellite images, preferably in real-time. This satellite has a data bandwidth of $>10^6$ picture elements (pixels) per second and depending on the processing required each pixel needs 100 to 10 000 operations. Thus the requirement is for a processing rate in excess of 1000 MOPS.

Because pixel information is generally held in short integers (eg 8-bit precision), the obvious choice of architecture is a DAP-like structure, to process data in parallel by the bit slice. Goodyear Aerospace did in fact choose this approach, but went for a larger array (128 × 128) with a slightly more complex 1-bit processor.

The overall architecture of the MPP is shown in Figure 16.

The MPP should perform eight times faster than the DAP and be capable of a speed of 2 GOPS when doing 8-bit integer arithmetic.

MIMD PROCESSORS

The paper by Jones and Schwarz **(218)** *contains a nice statement which encapsulates the activities in the area of MIMD architectures.*

JONES and SCHWARZ (218): Surprisingly few different multiprocessor designs have actually been built. Not much information is available on their actual use - a contrast to the abundance of descriptions of possible architectures. In addition, the bulk of extant multiprocessors are what we might call *timid* multiprocessors, both as to the number of processors involved (two is the prevalent number) and because they execute uniprocessor software that has been patched and mutated to function on multiple processors. Few multiprocessor operating systems have actually been implemented. In most cases the adapted uniprocessor operating systems provide acceptable performance when executed on a small number of processors, perhaps two or three. But because of the gross grain of synchronisation used, most such systems would have unacceptable performance if executed on 10 or more processors.

In MIMD systems the hardware interest is in the processor/memory interconnections rather than in the design of the individual processors which are treated more as components and are generally off-the-shelf minis or micros. The success or failure of

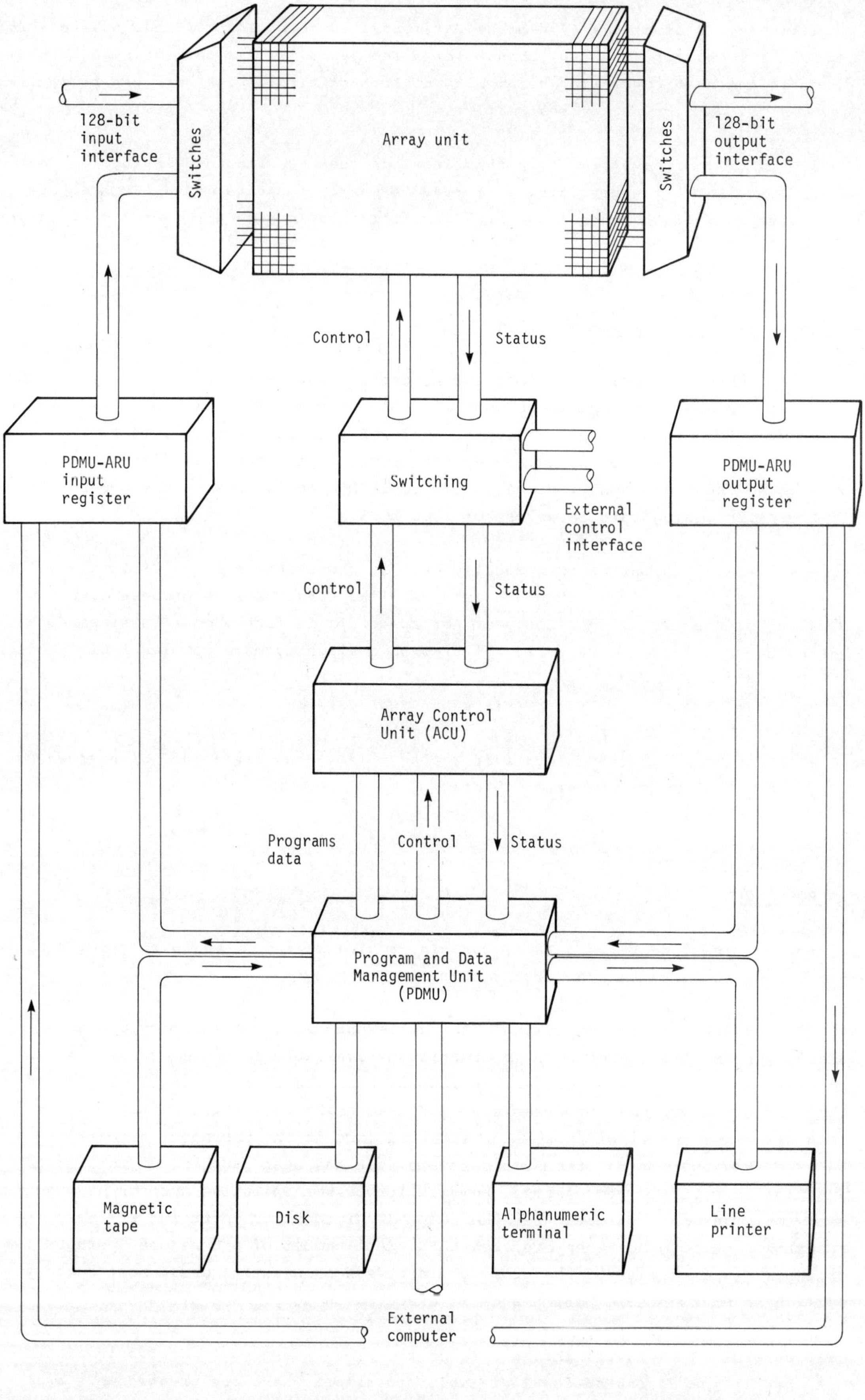

Figure 16: Overall architecture of the MMP (reproduced from **(200)***)*

MIMD systems is very dependent on the effectiveness of the operating system and the high-level languages available to the user.

The importance of the operating system in MIMD architectures is clearly indicated in the paper by Jones and Schwarz by the way in which they identify the three systems that they discuss by using the names of both the hardware system and the operating system.

C.mmp

The first system that they describe was the result of the initial work at Carnegie-Mellon University using PDP-11 processors.

JONES and SCHWARZ (218): C.mmp is composed of slightly modified DEC PDP-11/40 processors augmented with a writable control store. Up to 16 of these processors may be connected to up to 16 shared memory modules through a 16 × 16 *cross-point switch*, thus providing a maximum physical address space of 32 Mbytes (see Figure 17). The current configuration consists of 11 processors and 2.5 Mbytes of shared memory. An interprocessor bus connects the processors and allows any one to interrupt any other.

All processors are capable of accessing all of memory with equal cost, although the PDP-11's 16-bit architecture limits the amount of memory directly addressable at any given time to 64 Kbytes. This immediate address space consists of eight pages of 8K bytes, and software operations specify which eight pages of physical memory are immediately addressable out of a possibly larger set of accessible pages. The time required to access shared memory is approximately 1 μsec, assuming no contention at the referenced memory module. To reduce memory contention, a per-processor cache was planned, but not implemented. Without the cache approximately three processors can simultaneously reference the same memory module without experiencing degradation due to contention. In addition to shared memory each processor has 8K bytes of private local memory, which is used by the operating system for per-processor data structures and a few frequently executed routines such as context-swap and low-level synchronisation.

Cm*

The second system is a natural development of the first using LSI-11 processors.

JONES and SCHWARZ (218): Anticipating the era of the 'computer on a chip', the Cm* multiprocessor is composed of 50 *computer modules*, each consisting of a DEC LSI-11, a standard LSI-11 bus, memory, and devices. All primary memory in the system is accessible to each processor. In contrast to C.mmp, where processors and memories are connected with a *centralised* cross-point switch, Cm* contains a *distributed switch*. Each computer module includes a local switch, the *Slocal*, which routes processor memory references to memory outside the module via the *map bus* and accepts references from distant sources to its local memory. Up to 14 computer modules may be connected to a map bus so that they share the use of a single *Kmap*, a processor responsible for mapping addresses and routing data between Slocals.

Together, the computer modules, Kmap and map bus comprise a *cluster*, as shown in Figure 18. The current configuration contains five clusters connected by *intercluster buses* between the Kmaps. A Cm* configuration can have an arbitrary number of clusters.

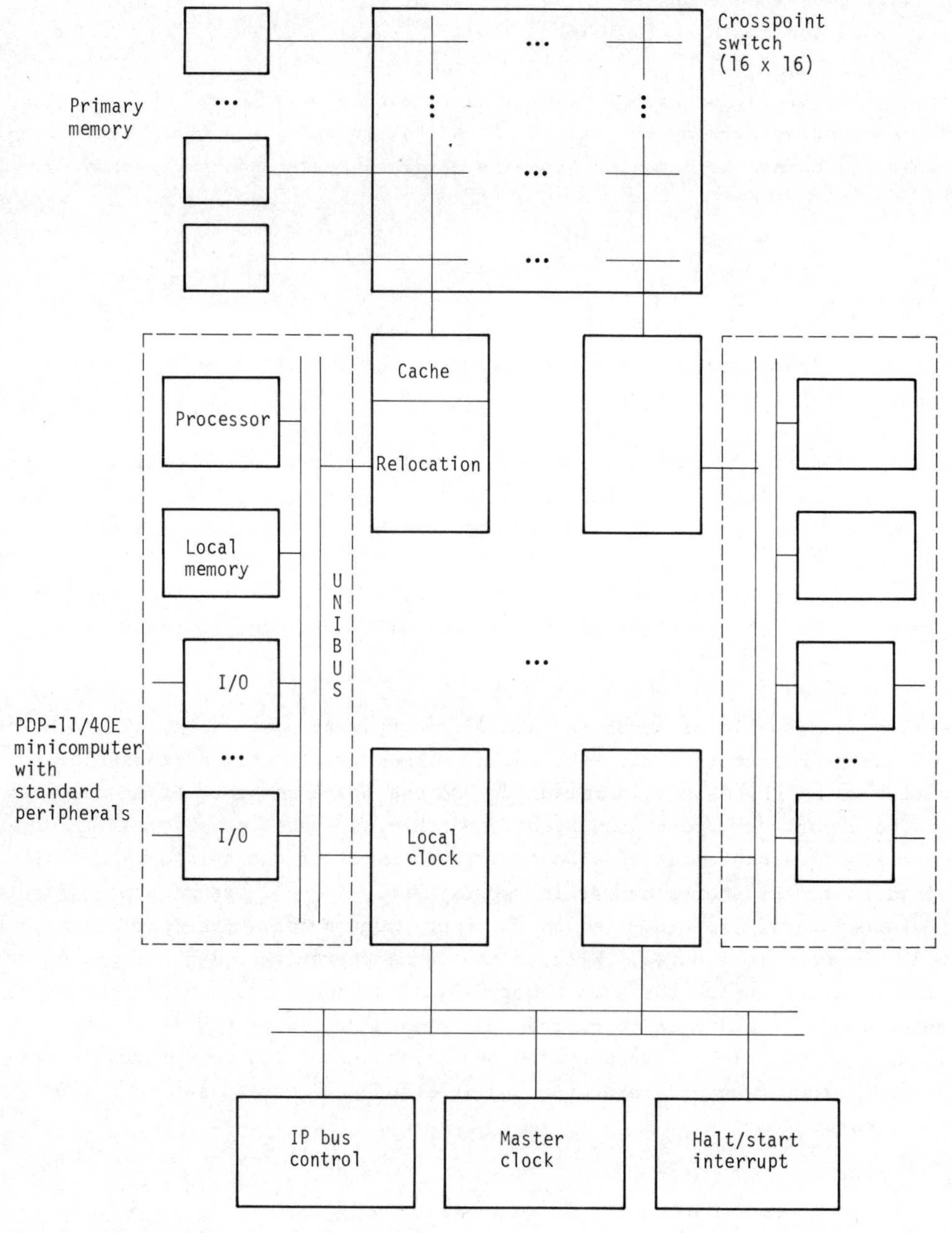

Figure 17: The structure of C.mmp. (reproduced from **(218)***)*

Collectively, the Kmaps and the Slocals form the distributed memory switch. They mediate each non-local reference, thus sustaining the appearance of a single, large, *uniformly addressed* memory. However, memory reference costs are not uniform; approximate interreference times for local, intracluster, and intercluster references are 3, 9, and 26 μsec, respectively.

Pluribus

The third system is a contemporary of C.mmp using Lockheed SUE processors and buses.

JONES and SCHWARZ (218): The prototype PLURIBUS is employed as an Interface Message Processor (IMP) for the ARPANET; it consists of 13 processors on seven processor buses with 8K bytes of private memory per processor, two common memory buses of

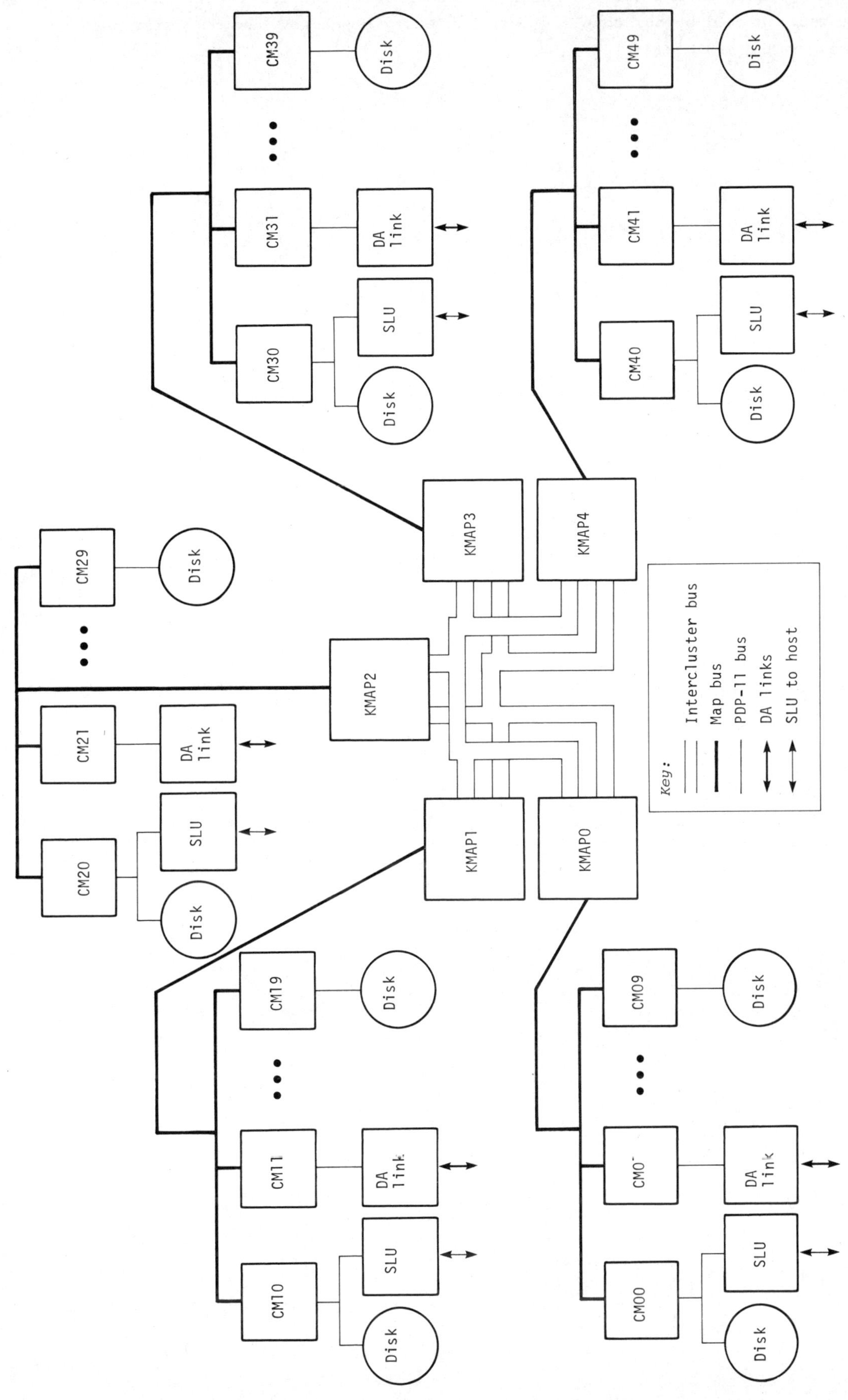

Figure 18: A five-cluster CM configuration (reproduced from* **(218)***)*

32K bytes each, and two I/O buses. These modules are completely and symmetrically interconnected by bus couplers, so that every processor bus can reference every memory and I/O bus.

DISTRIBUTED COMPUTING

The term distributed computing has been used so widely over the past few years that it is difficult to arrive at a generally accepted definition of the term.

A reasonable definition is a collection of individual computers connected together by a local or wide area network so that as well as operating independently they can share resources and can also collaborate in varying degrees for the solution of suitable problems.

Distributed computing is therefore very much about networks where the nodes are computers and the links between them are any of the numerous interconnection systems (local, national, and international) that are being developed.

The argument for including distributed computing alongside supercomputers is that many companies have gone from large central computers to distributed networks of smaller computers rather than increase the size of the single system. Also, regarding the company's computing as a single entity, the power of the distributed system both in operations per second and storage capacity is easily in the same league as the commonly accepted supercomputers.

The potential range of the term distributed computing can be seen by reference to the paper by Crook. He defines three elements of the system:

- *Processing*
- *Control*
- *Database.*

Processing can extend over a range from separate specialised computers to multiple computers, often physically apart. Control can vary from fully centralised to completely decentralised cooperating nodes. The database can be centralised, decentralised with central control, duplicated, or physically distributed.

CROOK: We do have a spectrum of distribution. In terms of processing the use of multiple processors and multiple computers are the key interests. In the control area it is the multiple nodes cooperating on subtasks through to fully cooperating capability that is the interesting and relevant point. The database becomes interesting with distributed files using a single central directory. The ultimate node is a fully partitioned database with no master file or directory.

The resulting distributed system, therefore, is not a fixed systems concept, but involves a spectrum of options and capabilities involving control, processing, and database.

The attractions of the use of a distributed system can be summarised as below.

CROOK:

- Reliability
- Availability
- Modular growth (cost/flexibility)
- Resource sharing
- Adaptability
- Graceful degradation
- Flexible growth path.

Before discussing distributed computing as just defined it is of interest to look at the degree of distribution present in systems not normally regarded as falling within this classification.

All large mainframes have computing power outside the main central processor, for example the peripheral processors of the CDC 6600 and 7600 and the channels of IBM systems. Computers such as the CRAY-1 and the CYBER 205 are always operated with front-end processors to look after communication with the outside world and the management of the file store.

Most installations with supercomputers link them either to other supercomputers or more generally to a variety of smaller computers, using very high-capacity channels (several millions of bit/sec). This permits the sharing of items such as mass stores, laser printers, etc and links to the numerous local and remote terminals that need to have access to the system. These are the same motives as some of those listed above for less exotic systems.

The new system to be installed at the University of Manchester Computing Centre will use a CDC loosely-coupled network to connect together a CYBER 205, two CDC 7600s, a mass storage system, a large CYBER system used for interactive computing, and a front-end processor to manage the mass store and to provide access to the system for several hundred terminals and about 50 remote job entry stations scattered among some 30 universities.

Probably the most exotic 'distributed system' is the OCTOPUS network at the Lawrence Livermore National Laboratory as described in the paper by Rodrigue, Giroux, and Pratt **(219)** *(Figure 19).*

Since the publication of this paper the lab has installed or ordered a further three CRAY systems proving that all distributed systems have the attractive facility of modular growth.

Returning to the more generally accepted concept of distributed computing, Crook introduces his paper as follows:

CROOK: This paper ... will concentrate on the newly evolving systems design using multiple microcomputers linked together over a local area network. It is believed this approach will be the most relevant one over the next 10 years.

TECHNOLOGICAL DEVELOPMENTS

The rapid advances in technology will increase the attractions of distributed computing.

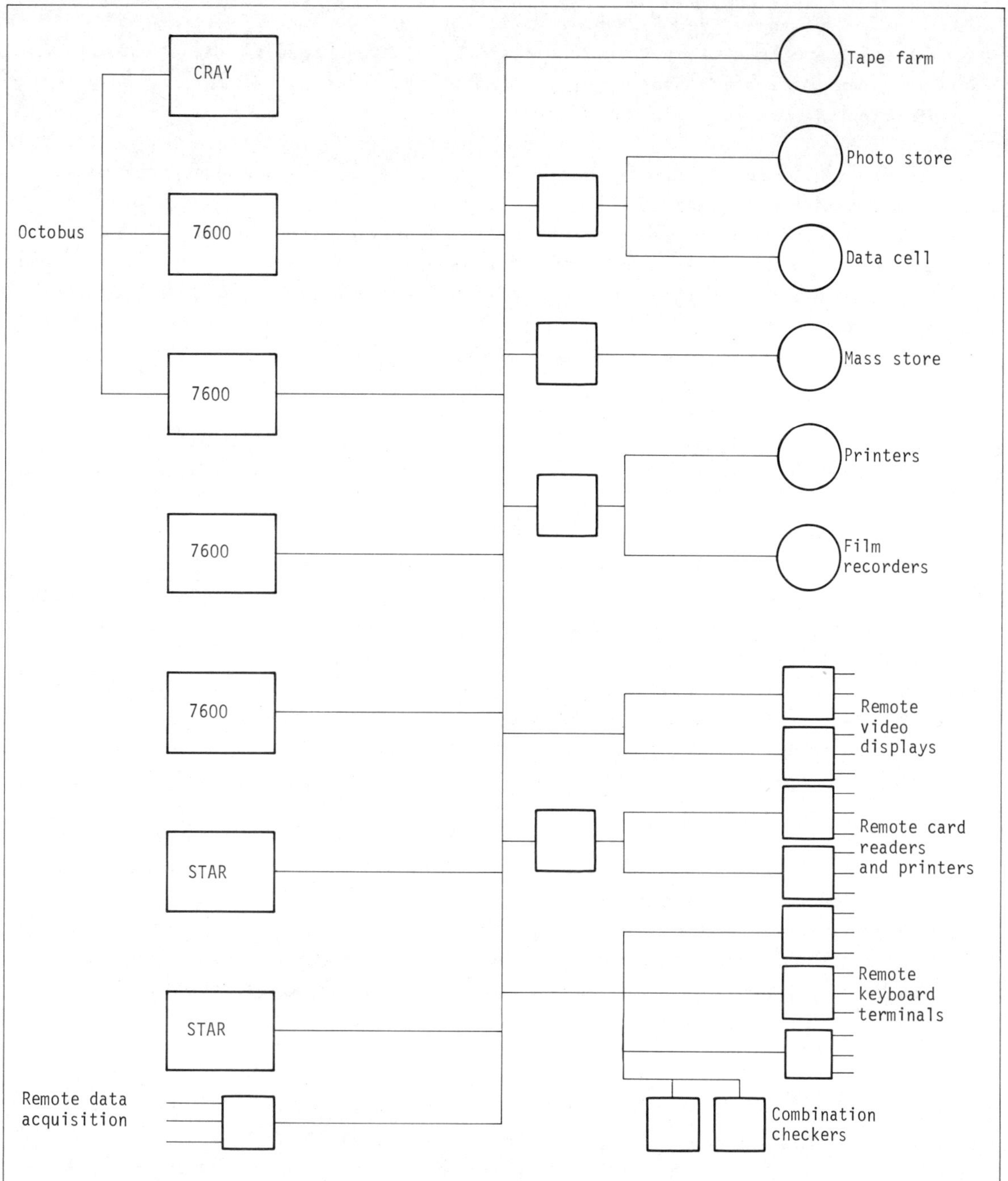

Figure 19: Octopus network (reproduced from **(219)***)*

CROOK: The whole area of communications/information technology is expanding and presenting systems designers with the need to address both local and wide-area communications. Consequently, isolated stand-alone computer systems are unlikely to be very acceptable to the user. The ability to communicate with other systems over short or long distances or to access databases, etc will be critical. This very fact will enhance the need for a distributed systems style of thinking.

Other relevant developments are those involving memory technology. Mass storage devices are becoming both cheaper and available in volume. Current Winchester disk and related technology looks like it will provide capacities of 1 Gbyte. Also optical memory technology will further enhance the cost/performance developments. The use of mass consumer software and such developments as 'expert systems' promises a revolution in the software industry. This is not yet perceived though some evidence is already beginning to appear.

In summary, we can see several fundamental forcing functions at play in the general market-place and technology. These are going to have a massive impact on all computer and information systems developments. The question of their relevance to distributed systems needs rapid evaluation.

Local, powerful, and distributed processing nodes (personal computer workstations) are the most obvious trend. Each node will also have a low cost and a plentiful front-end storage system. Mass back-end storage systems, again involving low-cost technology, will be accessed by many users as a common database. Multiple systems will be feasible due to the excellent price structure. The rapid developments in communications technology will facilitate high-capacity local-area (1km) interconnects between nodes; access to a world-wide network will also be required by the user and the implementation will be feasible.

There are two major questions to be answered in any distributed system. Should the nodes be the same type of computer? If the same should they use the same software system?

CROOK: Various models of distributed systems involving local networks specify the ideal of a range of dissimilar processors all being able to communicate and perform tasks together. The practical attainment of such systems is very hard to identify. The advent of the low-cost personal computer has elevated this issue to one of immediate practical concern. It must be intuitively evident that a homogeneous mix of nodes greatly facilitates the cooperation of such nodes in a system, but even this coherent mix of nodes still presents non-trivial problems, involving a mix of languages and operating systems....

A mix of homogeneous machine nodes does facilitate the construction of practical distributed network systems capable of undertaking meaningful commercial tasks. Again, evidence has accumulated which supports the concept of local autonomy. Here the user simply wants the best of both worlds: the ability to operate in isolation and to select the optimum language, operating system or applications program for the issue at hand while at the same time accessing other nodes in the system and also utilising system resources and capabilities as transparently as possible.

The role of the physical network in distributed computing is nicely defined by Crook.

CROOK: A significant issue is that concerning the degree to which the user perceives the network and the distribution of its resources. The individual user ideally must see no network or systems software.

MICROCOMPUTER NETWORKS

There are now many networks of microcomputers, one example being the Zynar/Nestar system.

CROOK: When discussing distributed computing, the use of personal workstations places considerable emphasis on local autonomy. This reflects the actual way in which such computers are going to be used. The great appeal of the personal computer is exactly that! The computer is personal. Therefore many of these new distributed systems place great emphasis on local autonomy and responsiveness. Essentially the user perceives his/her own workstation with its dedicated processing power available exclusively. Local autonomous facilities are available such as printer, other I/O devices and local bulk storage....

The network makes available a wide range of attached special 'servers' or resources. These span the following:

1 Multiple file servers with a comprehensive range of software for multiuser use.

2 Print servers covering the ability to handle multiple networks, languages, operating systems, printer types, etc.

3 Network gateways to both wide-area networks and other networks/computers, eg:

- File transfer server via dialled-up lines via the PTT
- Dial-in remote station server
- Viewdata server
- Telex server
- 3780 server.

Consequently the user node has access to a very 'rich' set of capabilities previously not considered practical with small personal computers. The system therefore provides for three types of system components: the computing nodes, special servers, and a communications substrate.

It should be stressed that this type of network is not intended to work on a total system task over a set of fully cooperating nodes.

CROOK: Many of the tasks required by a user of the system are stand-alone but with access to system capabilities such as mass storage, communications, etc. This is in contrast to many supposed distributed systems involving the execution of a total systems task over a complete set of fully cooperating nodes.

Crook identifies three advantages of a network of microcomputers availability, modular growth, and resource sharing.

CROOK: Availability is another key issue - the ability to move from one workstation to another and still perform the assigned task, together with the wide distribution of system assets, enhances the availability of the system as experienced by the user.

Modular growth, in terms of cost and flexibility, is a key feature. Above a specified minimum entry level, increases in capability can usually be achieved with a specific number of user nodes. The ability to increase in small increments provides for total efficiency. The alternatives of a large central processor resource always tend to imply under-utilised overheads. The purchaser does not wish to buy a system and then find out that the system is already operating at close to maximum capacity.

Resource sharing is another key feature. Expensive and high-grade professional server attachments can be added to a network. The costs are shared among the total user community.

The theoretical potential of networks of personal computers to work efficiently when collaborating on a single task has led to quite a large amount of research.

CROOK: Recent ideas have reflected upon the issue of developing programs which exploit spare computational capacity in a network during periods of low activity (eg at night). These programs represent one of the most difficult forms for distributed computing implementation. Given a local network involving many distributed nodes, then it is possible to conceive of an approach involving a program which can enter spare computational capacity existing at a node and use it. During quiescent periods the program can expand and use the network's full distributed capacity. During busy periods the program would retreat and 'lie low' in a small set of unused nodes. In essence, the program would start on one machine, then it would locate 'spare' machine capacity at a node. It would then enter that spare node and seize its processing power. Operating under a concept of segmentation and replication, the program could expand and contract according to network usage.

One of the attractions of low-cost hardware is that you do not feel guilty if it is not being used. Trying to use spare capacity in a network for low priority background computing must have some detrimental effect on the normal use of the network and seems to run contrary to the general trend of using cheaper hardware to keep the computational organisation, especially the operating system software, as simple as possible.

This leads to an apparent need for a modification of the definition of distributed computing given at the beginning of this subsection. Should the phrase 'and can also collaborate for the solution of a single problem' be deleted? If the collaboration is doing sections of the same program in parallel on different processors with all the problems of synchronisation then surely it should be deleted. However, very profitable collaboration can occur when different processors are doing distinct tasks using the same database and communicating via this database. This type of collaboration is easily managed and can lead to very efficient use of the total system.

STORE MANAGEMENT

INTRODUCTION

The point was made in Section 1 that the realisation of the potential speed of very high-performance computers depends on getting the instructions and operands to the control unit and arithmetic units fast enough to permit them to compute at the high rates of which they are capable. References to the problem and parts of the solution were made in the sections dealing with the particular architectures.

Most of the discussion in this subsection will relate to memory problems in pipelined vector processors and high-performance SISD systems. In SIMD and MIMD the processors are of lower power and generally each has its own memory so that memory transfer rates are of less importance. In these systems the problem is processor/memory interconnection to permit access to data in the store of some other processors. In the DAP access is to the north, south, east, and west neighbours; in the ILLIAC IV the step lengths are 1 and 8. Numerous other interconnection topologies have been studied.

In the introduction to his paper Ibbett makes the following observations:

IBBETT: The design of a vector processing system involves a variety of considerations relating to main storage. Since vector processing is generally used as a means of obtaining high performance on scientific processing, the rate at which operands can be transferred between main storage and the floating-point execution unit is of prime importance. This is a 'real store' problem; in systems which use virtual addressing there are also 'virtual store' problems associated with the address translation mechanism. Also important is the nature of the hardware/software interface of the system (defined by the instruction set and the addressing structure) since this determines the amount of support which the hardware can provide for software running on the system. In seeking to obtain higher levels of machine performance, these facets of design must all be taken into account, and an analysis of existing systems gives considerable insight into the problems involved.

Fundamentally, data (instructions or operands) can either be held in very fast registers, which have to be periodically reloaded from the main store causing delays, or alternatively they can be streamed from the main store, which must have a bandwidth sufficient for the streaming to provide data at the required rate. There will, of course, be a delay while the streaming is initiated.

DATASTREAMING

The CRAY-1 follows the CDC 6600 and 7600 designs in using fast registers and leaving the loading and unloading of these to the software.

IBBETT: The problem of executing floating-point operations at a rate in excess of one per clock is overcome in the CRAY-1 processor by the use of vector orders, which cause streams of up to 64 data elements to be processed as a result of one instruction issue. Vectors are contained in a set of eight V registers, each capable of holding 64 elements (each of 64 bits), and a typical vector instruction causes sets of operands to be taken from two V registers and the results to be returned to a third.

The loading of the registers, especially the vector registers, relies for its speed on the basic speed of the memory and the interleaving of consecutive addresses across independent memory banks.

IBBETT: Block copy operations ... normally proceed at a rate of one per clock period. The semiconductor memory has a cycle time of 50 nsec (four clock periods), and for contiguous addresses ... must be at least 4-way interleaved to allow this rate to be achieved. In practice the memory in a CRAY-1 is 8-way or 16-way interleaved and contains 0.5M, 1M, 2M, or 4M words according to the configuration. When non-contiguous addresses are used, however, store clashes can occur and the maximum rate cannot be maintained. When a vector is accessed from store into a V register a starting address and increment are supplied by the program. This allows for complete flexibility in accessing arrays by row, by column, or by diagonal, but can lead to store clashing if, for example, an increment of 16 is used in a 16-way interleaved store.

Delays can occur in the CRAY-1 if two vector register loads occur in consecutive instructions

memory → V1
memory → V2

IBBETT: The second instruction cannot issue until all the elements of V1 have been accessed from memory. There is thus an effective start-up delay in this sequence equal to the time required to load V1. The separation of store accessing and arithmetic operations within the instruction set of the CRAY-1 (made possible by the presence of the various processor registers) allows these activities to be overlapped to a large extent, but the start-up delay can nevertheless occur quite frequently and can reduce overall performance.

This has been solved on the CRAY X-MP by the provision of multiple memory ports.

IBBETT: The CRAY X-MP mainframe contains the equivalent of two CRAY-1 processors, re-engineered to allow a clock period of 9.5 nsec, and to allow both processors to occupy roughly the same physical space as a single CRAY-1 processor. These two processors share a common central memory, into which each has four independent access ports. The memory itself consists of 2M or 4M 64-bit words interleaved 32 or 64 ways according to the configuration. With this arrangement two vectors can be accessed in parallel from memory by either of the processors, provided there are no store clashes at the individual memory banks. If the two vectors reside in exactly the same set of memory banks, for example, then the accesses will become synchronised such that elements of one of the vectors are accessed one memory cycle behind the other. This gives an effective start-up time of one memory access time for one of the vectors and a start-up time one memory cycle longer than this for the other vector, a considerable improvement over the CRAY-1 where the effective start-up time for this sequence could be of the order of 64 memory access times.

While the Cray approach permits very high performance the attainment of this performance depends upon properly managing the reloading of the 64 element V registers. This is left entirely to the software. The best results can only be obtained by a good knowledge of the data structures of the problem. However, very good results can be obtained by using the CRAY vectorising FORTRAN compiler in a straightforward manner. Other machines deal with vectors in a different way.

IBBETT: Although the accessing mechanisms in the CRAY machines offer complete flexibility in the handling of vectors which are actually sub-arrays, the entire management of all forms of data structure is left to the software. Vectors with more than 64 elements, for example, must be broken up into sets of 64 elements or less and processed separately. This problem does not arise in the CYBER 205 unless vectors of more than 64K elements are used, and here each vector is essentially identified by a descriptor (containing an origin address and a length) held in the register file and accessed from there when required by an instruction. The use of descriptors to identify vectors can have a number of other benefits from a software point of view, as has been shown in the MU5 computer and its commercial derivatives at the top of the ICL 2900 Series.

The CYBER 205 is a three-address computer. The vector operations have two input streams, one output stream, and a control vector stream.

IBBETT: These streams are specified by the origin addresses, field lengths, and off-sets or indices selected from locations in a register file by the instruction before it leaves the scalar processor, and sent to the vector control unit when the instruction is issued. During the setting up of a vector instruction within the vector processor, off-set values are added to the corresponding origin addresses and subtracted from the field lengths before being sent to the stream addressing unit. For each datastream the stream addressing unit generates sequential store addresses (normally to 512-bit words) by incrementing the original address until the field length, which is decremented correspondingly, reaches zero.

The addressing unit is sufficiently intelligent to avoid memory bank conflicts.

IBBETT: The generation of addresses for each input and output stream is treated as an independent operation within the stream addressing unit. This allows each operation to be stopped and started independently, and allows the stream addressing unit to avoid bank busy conflicts in central memory. Since the banks have an 80 nsec cycle time, a request to any one bank causes a four clock period busy condition, and a subsequent request to the same bank is not allowed to proceed until a further three clock periods have elapsed. In addition the priority of requests must be taken into account; within the vector processor input operand requests have highest priority, vector write requests have second priority, string write requests third, and control vector read requests fourth. A request of low priority must therefore be checked against higher priority requests to the same bank up to three clock periods ahead and up to three clock periods behind the clock period in which it will itself access central memory.

The processing of non-contiguously stored vectors results in a decrease in the rate of flow of data. Scatter and gather functions are provided to alleviate the problem by reordering operands.

IBBETT: One of the criticisms levelled at the CYBER 205 is that, as in the STAR-100, vectors may only be accessed on the basis of a unit increment between successive elements, so that matrices stored by row, for example, cannot be easily accessed by column. However, the high memory bandwidth of the CYBER 205 is only obtainable because many adjacent elements can be read out in parallel in each memory cycle, and to allow different accessing patterns in standard vector orders would severely degrade performance. Provision of increments different from unity would also require changes to the instruction format, and alternative general mechanisms for the reordering of operands are provided instead. These mechanisms are invoked in indexed list operations, which allow for the gathering or scattering of periodic or random data within a data structure.

Virtual addressing introduced in the early Sixties has now become very widely used. It has many advantages but if improperly used can lead to considerable degradation. This appears to be particularly true in vector processors and problems with virtual store management were severe in the STAR-100.

In the original paging system on the ATLAS there were 32 pages each of 512 words with a total storage size of 16K and there were 32 fast associative registers for very high-speed translation of virtual addresses into real addresses. Slow table look-up to locate virtual addresses only occurred when the page containing the required address was on the drum backing store. As memory sizes have increased the number of pages in real store has also increased particularly if the page size has not increased. With a large number of pages it is not possible to provide full cover of the memory with associative registers and in modern computers the number of associative registers is considerably smaller than the number of pages in real store, the associative registers are therefore current page registers containing the most recently used virtual pages. In many systems the remainder of the page address table is held in central memory and when a particular address is not found in one of the associative registers this page table is searched automatically. This is, however, quite slow and the operating system does its best to avoid it.

In the STAR-100 with 1M words of store, two-page sizes were allowed 512 and 64K.

LINCOLN (220): The space permitted for the implementation of the virtual memory mapping scheme permitted a maximum of 16 entries to be held in associative registers. Any entry in the associative registers could be matched to a request in essentially zero time, relative to the time cost of the actual memory access. A one million word CDC STAR-100 can contain up to 2000 entries to map the entire physical memory into virtual pages. The table can contain a good deal more entries as the same physical memory page can be specified in more than one page table entry. The time required to search the entire table is 1000 machine cycles or 40 μsec. The time required to perform a vector add operation of an entire small page of data is 256 machine cycles or 10 μsec. Page-table searching can thus increase the apparent vector overhead by a substantial amount. In practice, the depth of a particular table search has been about 100 entries, with the page then being referenced by more than one vector operation, thus reducing the search costs imposed by the use of virtual memory.

Before a search of the virtual page table is initiated, the associative registers must be stored into memory so that they can be used for the search operation. At the conclusion of the search, these registers must be loaded again, before continuing the operation in progress. This process can take almost 6 μsec thus ensuring that the minimum table search will require almost as much time to match a single page as it does to process the data in the page (10 μsec) with a vector arithmetic instruction.

Using too few pages can also have disastrous effects.

LINCOLN (220): From the previous discussion it should be apparent that when one wants to maximise the high performance execution of vector operations on STAR, data should be aggregated into large pages of 65 536 words. In this mode the entire physical memory of one million words can be mapped by only 16 entries in the virtual table, one for each large page.

A side effect of the use of large pages was not discovered until after the CDC STAR-100 machines had been in production operation at customers' sites for a while. The phenomena called stalling arose as a variety of jobs were run concurrently on the machines, combining both large and small page tasks in memory at one time. Some preproduction jobs were run in large page mode, in the interactive environment, to debug various computational and I/O aspects of the program. In this mode the operating system might permit a maximum of four or five large pages to be resident for a given job at any time. The effect of this, in some cases, was to bring that job execution to a complete standstill. The reasons, after brief analysis, were all too clear. A simple vector add operation needs two input datastreams, one output datastream, and perhaps a control vector stream, plus the instruction stream containing the vector operation itself. If each of the streams were to be stored in a different large page, then the nominal number of pages needed for a job would be five. More pages can in fact be needed, however, as the need to have a look-ahead output page requires the presence of an additional page. Further, if the data from one of the input streams bridges two large pages, under some circumstances at least an additional input page must be in memory at the same time as all of the other pages. If the operating system limitation is five pages, we are treated to the spectacle of the monitor evicting the very page we need to run the vector operation in order to bring in another page, also needed for the vector instruction. Each time the instruction tries to restart it finds a page missing, creates an access interrupt, and causes the operating system to evict a vital page, bring in one that it has just evicted, and then begin the cycle all over again. It became necessary for the hardware to set a stall bit in the user's invisible package to tell the operating system that this condition has arisen, since the software detection of the condition in all cases was almost impossible.

This concept of stalling should not be confused with the notorious phenomena of thrashing which has been the bane of virtual memory machines for years. In the latter case, the machine is being used inefficiently as a great deal of overhead is invoked for a small quanta of work accomplished, in order to swap pages to and from memory. In the stalling case, no work is accomplished at all, and no basic changes in program structure (except for the physical reallocation of the affected data) can improve the situation.

Vector operations cannot be interrupted and this can lead to problems in virtual store management.

IBBETT: Since different programs running on the CYBER 205 require differing numbers of pages, a mechanism is required to prevent the hardware searching invalid page or space table entries. An 'end-of-table' marker is used for this purpose. If this marker is found in a page table register when there is a page fault, an interrupt is generated immediately and the space table is not searched. If the end-of-table marker is in the space table, however, then it will only be read and an interrupt generated after all valid entries in the space table have been examined. Such interrupts can, of course, occur during the execution of a vector order because the vector lengths associated with these orders are such that it is inevitable that the operand fetches will eventually cross a page boundary into a page for which no page or space table entry has been set up. While it might be possible to ignore some types of interrupt for the duration of one of these orders, a page fault must be dealt with immediately since the order itself cannot continue until the appropriate action has been taken. This requires a clean shut-down of the order, the preservation of essential state information, and the transfer of control to the interrupt code. The use of a long arithmetic pipeline in the CYBER 205 and the presence of significant amounts of buffering in the stream units means that in order to achieve the full vector rate, while still responding to these page fault interrupts, a one-page look-ahead is required on the output stream to ensure that operands progressing through the processor can be returned to store before shut-down. Once the interrupt has been processed, the state information is restored and the order restarted from where it left off.

In the CYBER 205 the second level of storage is on disks, which is very slow compared with the fast memory; therefore, paging faults must be avoided if at all possible.

STORAGE HIERARCHIES

The classical storage pyramid is given in Figure 20.

The complete memory hierarchy contains many different speeds and size of memory from fast registers to mass stores (the latter are now replacing tapes to a great extent in high-performance systems). Figure 21 indicates the relation of the different levels.

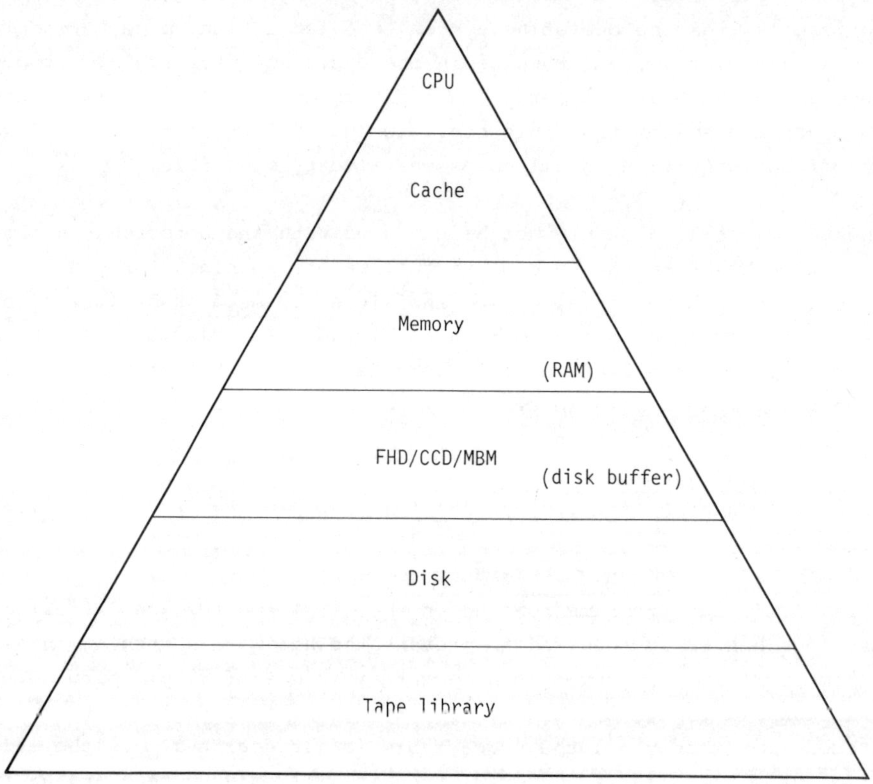

Figure 20: The classical storage pyramid

Pohn and Smay give a very detailed description of cache memories, their structure and efficiency.

POHN and SMAY (221): The concept of an nsec/μsec hierarchy (a cache) was proposed more than a decade ago. Its early implementation was unfeasible because of the lack of suitable technology. In fact, as early as 1962 Bloom, Cohen, and Porter proposed a technique known as a look-aside memory to improve the logic-to-memory speed ratio by the use of an associative memory. Lee had tried to simulate the concept of implementing a look-aside memory and had found that by adding an associative memory of about 256 words with a 100-nsec cycle time, an effective cycle time of about 250-400 nsec could be obtained in a memory system whose main memory cycle time was 1 μsec. This concept of an nsec/μsec hierarchy was also implemented in embryonic form in other computers like the Ferranti ATLAS and ETL-Mk-6.

Device and common technology	Access plus transfer time	Speed reduction	Memory size bits	Cents/bit* (system level)
Register (semiconductor flip-flops)	2-20 nsec	1	10^3-10^4	20-100
Cache (semiconductor RAM)	20-200 nsec	10	10^4-10^5	1-10
Main memory (semiconductor memory, ferrite core)	200-2000 nsec	100	10^6-10^8	0.1-0.5
Backing memory (fixed-head disk and drum, magnetic bubble)	1-10 msec	10^5-10^6	10^7-10^9	0.05-0.2
Secondary memory (moving-head disks)	20-100 msec	10^6-10^7	10^9-10^{11}	0.01-.0005
Mass memory (automated tape handlers, optical disks, microfilm handlers, strip handlers)	10-100 sec	10^8-10^9	10^{11}-10^{12}	2-8 10^{-5}

* The cost of memory cells diminishes typically 20% or 30% per year, so the values given are representative of the 1979-80 timeframe.

Figure 21: Spectrum of storage device technologies

With the availability of semiconductor monolithic memories, an nsec/μsec hierarchy (cache system) was implemented in 1968 for the first time in the IBM 360 Model 85, a large-scale computer. In such a system a fast and small memory, called a buffer or cache, is interposed between the central processor and the main memory, where it serves as the user-transparent bridge between speeds. It is transparent in the sense that it is not directly addressable by the user. However, by providing the processor with all the current information it requires, the cache gives the illusion of having a large main memory operating at the speed of the processor. Hence, the processor tends to operate with a memory of near cache speed but with a cost near that of the main system.

A paged virtual memory system combines a random-access main memory with an auxiliary store, such as a disk, in a manner logically similar to that used in the cache system. Such a system tends to achieve the speed of main memory at the cost of auxiliary memory, whereas a cache memory system tends to achieve the high speed of the cache memory at the lower cost of the main memory. Thus, for any virtual memory system, one level is characterised by its serving as a buffer to the next level. However, the terms 'cache virtual memory system' or 'buffered virtual memory system' are most typically applied only to systems which have a very small high-speed memory between the processor and the main memory.

A cache or buffer tends to provide a required or localised subset of information to the processor at a faster speed and a lower price than a single fast, large memory and can provide the illusion of a larger main memory operating at the speed of the cache. As long as present memory speed-price conditions persist, such 'buffering' will be a cost-effective solution for matching speed between the processor and memory system.

A cache memory is generally part of a multilevel hierarchy invisible to the user. Pohn and Smay give an illustration of a three-level system in Figure 22.

POHN and SMAY (221): The directories hold a map of blocks from the next higher level memory which are currently held in a particular level of memory. The directory associated with the cache needs to be in hardware for speed reasons, ie the presence of desired information in the cache must be quickly determined. The directory which maps the secondary store to the main memory can be implemented in software if desired, because typically the secondary disks or drums have access times of a few msec. The general scenario is to look for a word in the cache; if it is not found in the cache, the main memory is examined. If the word is still not found, it is obtained from the secondary memory and brought into the lower two levels.

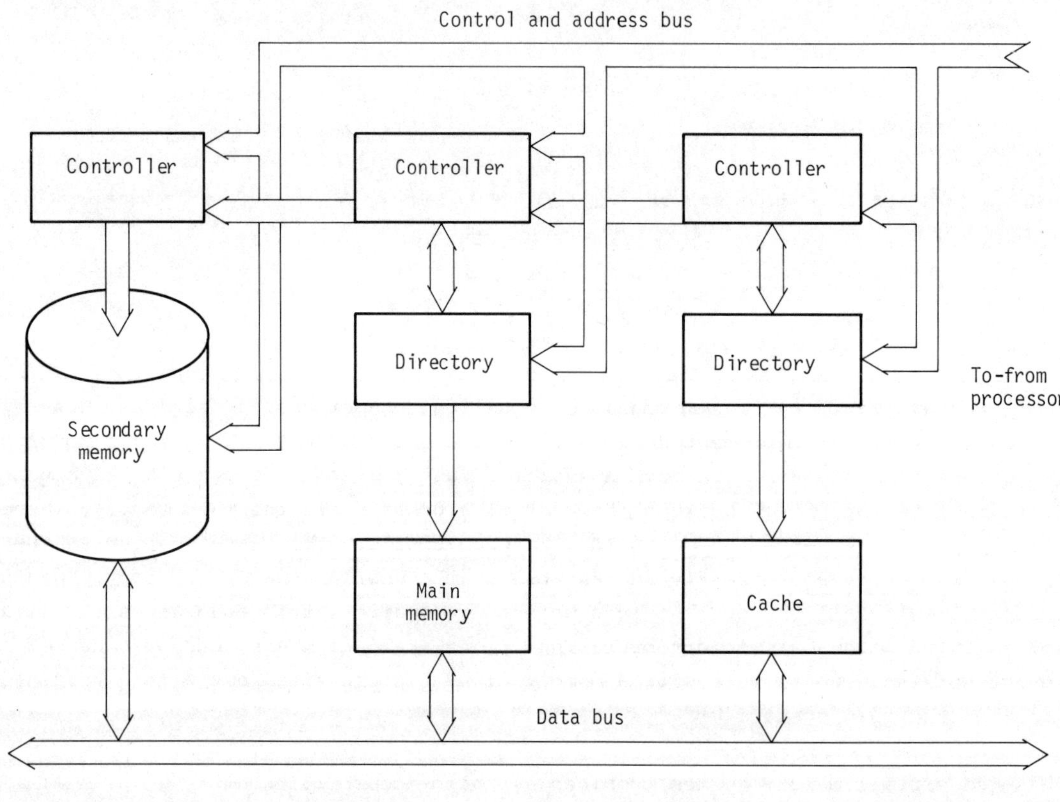

Figure 22: A three-level system

Numerous designs are discussed, together with an analysis of replacement algorithms and efficiencies, of cache memories.

POHN and SMAY (221): A variety of swapping algorithms can be used to manage the movement of words or blocks into and out of a buffer. The behaviour of four of these algorithms will be briefly examined for a small memory system.

1 *Write through:* whenever a word is written into the buffer, an updated copy is written into the backing store as well. CPU operation begins as soon as possible if overlap is used.

2 *Simple swap:* when a desired word is not found in the buffer, the old word is first written from the buffer into the backing store and then the new word is brought in. Operation begins as soon as the new word is available, if overlap is used.

3 *Flagged swap:* a flag is maintained for each word to indicate that a word in the buffer block has been altered after it was brought into the buffer. When a new word is needed, the old buffer word is swapped out only if it has been altered. If not, the new word is brought in directly from the backing store.

4 *Flagged, registered swap:* In order to speed access, a buffer word to be replaced is first loaded into a register; the new word is immediately brought into the buffer from the backing store, and subsequently the registered word is written into the backing store. Again, CPU operation is started as soon as possible.

It is assumed that the buffer memory operation is overlapped with the completion of backing or main store. In the graphic results that follow, it is implicitly assumed that a single job is involved.

Figure 23 illustrates the effect of various replacement algorithms on the effective cycle time for memory systems as the hit ratio is varied with fixed proportions of reads. The effective cycle time is defined as the average time to read or write the memory, assuming requests are always present. In a real processor this may not be the case, because some instructions may be longer than the main memory cycle time. The results indicated in Figure 23 clearly demonstrate the superiority of the flagged algorithms for the systems employing single main modules or multiple modules operating in unison. The write-through algorithm is very sensitive to the fraction of words written.

INSTRUCTION BUFFERS

For instructions most computers rely on streaming the ones required from memory. Branch orders disrupt this flow and cause delays in computing. Many different types of instruction buffer have been developed to attempt to solve the various problems. Descriptions of significant designs are contained in Ibbett's book **(202)**. *Two designs will be mentioned here as they typify alternative approaches to the problem.*

The CDC 7600 instruction stack is relatively simple.

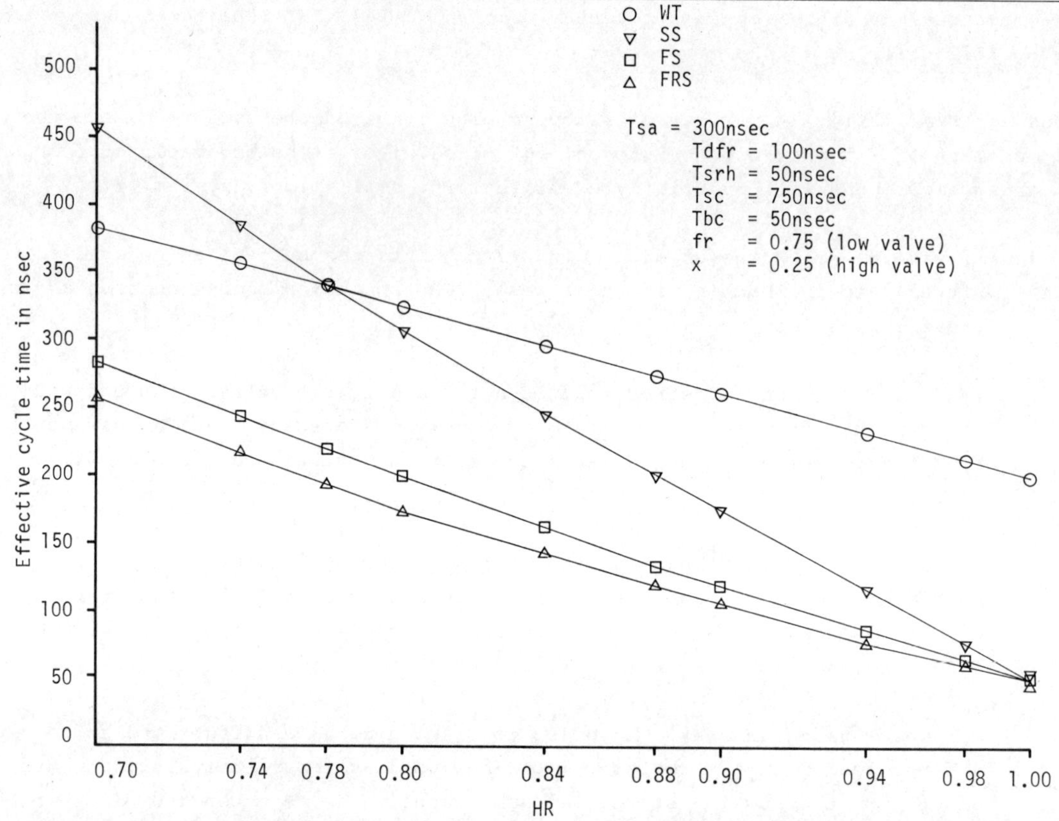

Figure 23: Effect of replacement algorithms on the performance of 50nsec buffer systems

IBBETT (202): The 7600 instruction word stack is made up of 12 60-bit registers, compared with the eight used in the 6600, and each register also has its own 18-bit associative address register in an instruction address stack (Figure 24).

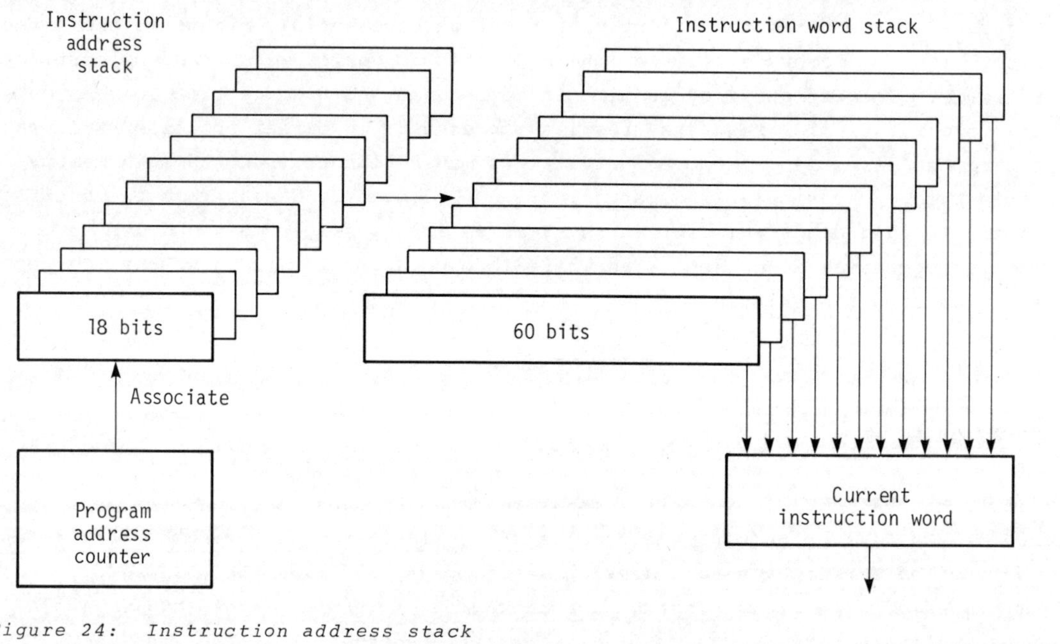

Figure 24: Instruction address stack

The instruction stack is filled two words ahead of the instruction currently being executed, thus giving a greater degree of prefetching than was possible in the 6600, and hence overcoming the storage access delay for sequential instructions. Furthermore, instructions are obeyed from a current instruction word register, rather than from the bottom stack register, and a complete 60-bit word is transferred from the instruction stack into this register whenever the word address changes in the program address counter. This transfer can be made from any of the 12 registers in the instruction word stack, allowing a considerable degree of flexibility in prefetching and loop catching. Whenever a new word is required in the current instruction word register the address in the program address counter is compared with the entries in the instruction address stack, and if a coincidence occurs for any of these entries, the content of the corresponding register in the instruction word stack is transferred into the current instruction word register.

When obeying sequential code the required word will normally be in one of the bottom two registers. When a branch instruction is executed and the branch taken, the required word may already be in one of the top 10 registers, obviating the need for a store access, and giving improved performance. If the required word is not in the stack, the first two words at the target address are immediately requested from store and instruction execution continues when the first of these is received. Whenever an instruction word is received from store all the entries in the instruction word stack and the instruction address stack are simultaneously moved up one position, with the new address and instruction word being entered at the bottom of the stack and the oldest entry being lost. Entries in the stack are only invalidated by the execution of a subroutine call or exchange jump, and not by normal branch instructions, so that a program may branch back and forth between short sequences of non-contiguous code held in the stack.

The size of instruction buffer needed on very high-performance computers can be seen from the details given above for the CRAY-1 and for the CRAY X-MP.

An alternative approach to dealing with branch orders was developed on the MU5 computer at the University of Manchester.

IBBETT (202): The system used in the MU5 Instruction Buffer Unit (IBU) involves an eight-line associatively addressed 'jump trace' store which attempts to predict the outcome of an impending control transfer. Whenever a new instruction address is generated by the IBU it is presented to the associative 'jump-from' address store before being sent to the local store via the Store Access Control unit (SAC). If an equivalence is found, this address is replaced by the corresponding 'jump-to' address, so that prefetching of the new sequence takes place instead. When the control transfer instruction which gave equivalence in the trace is [*obeyed*], it is accompanied by a bit indicating that the instructions following it are 'out of sequence'. This bit is used to determine the action after execution of the control transfer. If the following instructions have been correctly predicted, execution of instructions continues uninterrupted. If the instructions are not out of sequence, but should have been, a request is made to SAC for the instructions at the 'jump-to' address, and at the same time a line in the jump trace is loaded with the 'jump-from' and 'jump-to' addresses. Thus when the 'jump-from' address reoccurs within the IBU, the instructions at the 'jump-to' address are automatically prefetched.

Simulation studies of this system indicated that about 75% of control transfers could be trapped using an eight-line store, and that, as before, increasing the number of lines in the store did not significantly improve the performance. The apparent drop in performance as compared with the first system considered occurs because the prediction mechanism sometimes predicts a transfer which does not occur. No attempt is made to correct the jump trace when a predicted branch does not occur, however, since the drop in performance is more than offset by the fact that the prediction mechanism allows useful overlapping of instructions to continue when the prediction is correct.

Instruction buffering and coping with branch orders is one of the outstanding difficulties in the design of high-performance pipeline computers.

NEW ARCHITECTURES

The writing of correct programs for complex applications is extremely difficult and there has been extensive research into development methods in an attempt to minimise the problem. Any system of hardware and software that significantly reduced these difficulties could merit the prefix 'super' in terms of the saving of time taken to develop a correct program. The advocates of functional and applicative languages seem to have no doubts that their approach is the correct one.

DARLINGTON and REEVE (241): It has become increasingly evident that the conventional approach to programming using high-level languages such as ALGOL or PASCAL is inadequate to cope with the size or complexity of the applications now being tackled. Critics of these languages trace their shortcomings to their connection with the von Neumann model of computation and highlight their non-mathematical behaviour, in particular the lack of referential transparency.

In contrast, the applicative or functional languages (eg HOPE or KRC) are based on firmer mathematical foundations. This, it is claimed, makes programming and program understanding a much simpler activity, a point that is made forcibly by Backus in his ACM Turing Award Lecture.

The languages, however, cannot operate efficiently on conventional computers.

DARLINGTON and REEVE (241): Despite the numerous advantages of applicative languages their poor performance on conventional machines has meant that they have not gained widespread acceptance. This poor performance may be attributed to their natural mode of evaluation being far removed from the von Neumann model. In an attempt to alleviate this problem alternative computer architectures are being sought. The applicative languages are natural candidates for parallel evaluation since by definition they are free from side effects and thereby permit the independent evaluation of sub-expressions.

One of the reduction type architectures that have been proposed recently is called ALICE.

REEVE (242): ALICE (Applicative Language Idealised Computing Engine) is a general-purpose multiprocessor parallel computer system being developed at Imperial College by John Darlington and Mike Reeve. ALICE is based on an extended graph reduction model of computation and may be viewed as a parallel production system.

To ensure that continuing research at the implementation level does not affect the applications programming level, an implementation-independent Assembly code has been developed to provide a stable base for software projects. Known as the ALICE Compiler Target Language (ALICE CTL), it is intended to be the code produced by compilers or written by programmers wishing to exploit ALICE facilities not accessible through any of the available high-level languages. It is designed so that only a simple translator is required to convert it to the form specific to any particular implementation.

At present an ALICE simulator (written in PASCAL) permits the execution of programs written in the ALICE CTL.

An interesting feature of many of the papers in this area is the use of 'von Neumann architectures' as a term of approbation. The new approaches may in fact be valid but they have a long way to go and the arrogance with which the ideas are advanced is only matched by the degree to which they have failed to convince the world of practical computing of the validity of the methods. Other advocates of new approaches to computer design (for example dataflow architectures) have had the courage to design and (start) to build systems embodying their ideas, which will permit realistic evaluations to be made of their approach as compared with using the new technologies in more conventional ways.

DATAFLOW

GURD: In the recent search for improvements in computing speed, system reliability, software manageability, and cost effectiveness there have been several attempts to establish a viable alternative computer architecture to replace the traditional 'von Neumann' organisation on which our present computing practices are based. Dataflow is one possible alternative which shows promise of allowing very high-speed computing by efficient exploitation of vast software parallelism in a highly parallel system of processing hardware. The name 'dataflow' is derived from the graphical model of computation which is used to describe how programs are executed. In this model, data is active and flows asynchronously through the two-dimensional program, activating each instruction when all required input data has arrived. This is in direct contrast to the 'von Neumann' model in which data passively resides in store while instructions are executed one-at-a-time according to a defined sequence controlled by a 'program counter'.

Dataflow is an attempt to exploit the parallelism of the problem. In his paper Gurd starts by postulating definitions of parallelism that are an advance on those of Flynn referred to at the beginning of this analysis. Gurd considers Flynn's classification to be too simple.

GURD: Nowadays this classification is considered too simple, although no generally accepted taxonomy is emerging. The difficulty is that the hardware parallelism may be implemented at a different level of 'granularity' to the obvious software parallelism; eg in an instruction pipeline, where small parts of the execution of successive instructions are processed concurrently in an overlapped fashion, regardless of program parallelism. It would be helpful if a level-independent taxonomy existed, but in its absence we have found it useful to compare dataflow machines with conventionally-based parallel systems by distinguishing between 'regular' and 'irregular' parallelism.

Regular parallelism is that exploited in pipeline vector processors and in SIMD systems.

GURD: Regular parallelism exists wherever the same task is to be performed many times over, usually on disjoint data. With connected data it may be necessary to exploit regular parallelism via a pipeline, as in the instruction pipeline cited above. Otherwise, eg for the first, or SIMD, kind of software parallelism, a lock step parallel array of hardware, as in the DAP or ILLIAC IV, can be used. In either case, the actions being performed concurrently are highly regular, and the performance of systems depends on the executing programs providing enough work with the required form of regularity.

Most of the parallel computers so far constructed exploit regular parallelism of one form or another and, in practice, it has proved extraordinarily difficult to arrange for programs to continually provide sufficient parallelism of the required regular nature. Consequently, the applications run at variable speed, the regular parts executing rapidly while other parts necessarily go more slowly. In many cases the slow segments dominate overall performance and reduce the total speed-up of programs to a fraction of the theoretical maximum.

Irregular parallelism is tackled to some extent in MIMD systems but this area of parallelism has not been efficiently exploited.

GURD: Few parallel computers exist to exploit irregular parallelism on a large scale, and it is in this area that most of the interesting experiments in computer architecture are now being conducted. The best known examples use parallelism at the 'process' level in languages such as CONCURRENT PASCAL, MODULA, DISTRIBUTED PROCESSES and COMMUNICATING SEQUENTIAL PROCESSES, implemented on shared-memory or message-passing multiprocessors. Dataflow systems attempt to exploit irregular parallelism at a lower level, approximating to the conventional machine code 'instruction' level.

Regular parallelism can be expressed by vector notations. An effective notation for instruction level irregular parallelism is required. Gurd develops a graphical notation using as an example a representation of the code for the evaluation of the following sequence of expressions:

G = A*B
H = C*D
I = E*F
K = G*H*I

Gurd represents the sequence by a data dependence or dataflow graph:

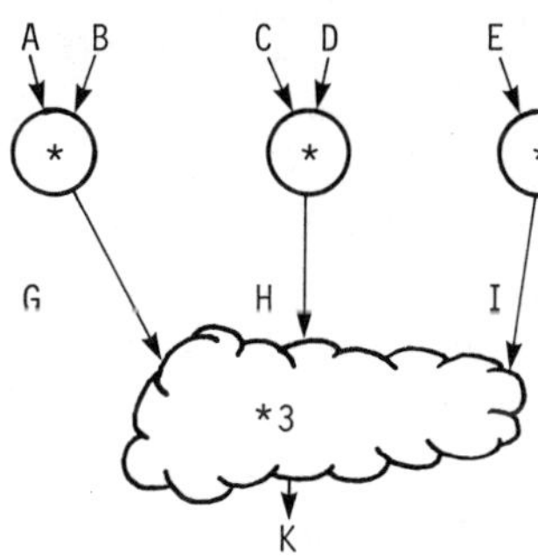

A machine-level program graph for the above sequence is:

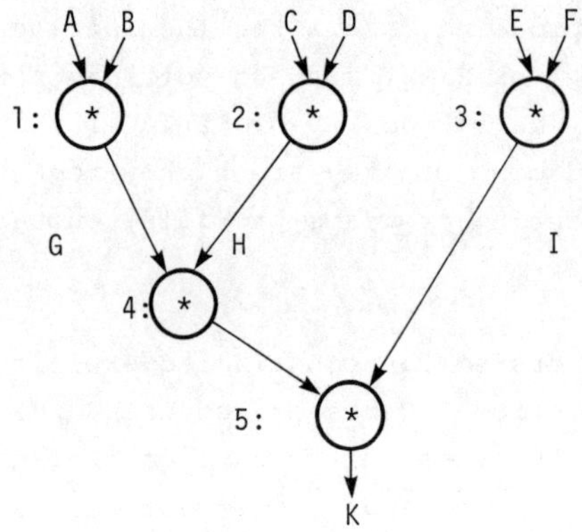

GURD: Remember that the idea of this notation is to allow all potentially concurrent instructions to execute simultaneously. In the original sequential program we would expect the multiplications to be performed in the order {1}, {2}, {3}, {4}, {5}, producing the answer in five multiplication times. On the graph we can see that either of the parallel execution orderings {1, 2, 3} ,{4} ,{5} or {1, 2} {3, 4} {5} will produce the answer in three multiplication times (given at least three and two multipliers, respectively). The problem for the parallel execution model is to cause one of these parallel execution orderings to occur: how can this be achieved?

This is followed by an impassioned plea on behalf of research workers in this area.

GURD: The above points have been laboured because together they form a compelling reason for abandoning program counters in instruction-level parallel computers. Dataflow researchers often feel persecuted because conventional computer scientists think they are studying obscure architectures for the sake of doing something different. In the context of the development of parallel computing, they are actually studying an *improvement* over conventional techniques. The key to this improvement is to notice that a data dependence graph shows how *instructions are dependent on data*. It makes no sense to execute an instruction before the data it requires is all available: conversely, once an instruction has finished executing, all other instructions that are waiting for its output data to be produced can safely be activated. The simplest way to execute a graph program is to send the data from instruction to instruction according to the data dependence arcs, and to allow each instruction to execute when and only when it has all the required input data available. In this way the graph program becomes *data driven*.

The execution of graph programs is best illustrated by introducing the concept of 'tokens'.

GURD: We can illustrate data-driven execution of graph programs by introducing data carriers (usually called *tokens*, after PetriNet terminology) onto the data dependence graph. Each token carries one data value and is constrained to move (at any speed it can) from tail to head of one dependence arc. Tokens wait at the head of dependence arcs until all other arcs (if any) pointing to the subsequent instruction have tokens at their heads and then the subsequent instruction is executed, taking an arbitrary amount of time before producing (a) result token(s) at its output arc(s). The tokens causing the execution are no longer required and they can be safely removed from the input arcs.

Figure 1 of Gurd's paper (see page 253) shows the flow of tokens, represented by black dots, through the graph as the program is executed. The name 'dataflow' thus becomes obvoius.

Conditional assignments are an important part of any problem representation and it is, therefore, essential that the dataflow notation can implement such assignments.

GURD: We can implement a FORTRAN conditional assignment such as:

```
C = A
IF (B.EQ.D)  C = F
```

as the following graph:

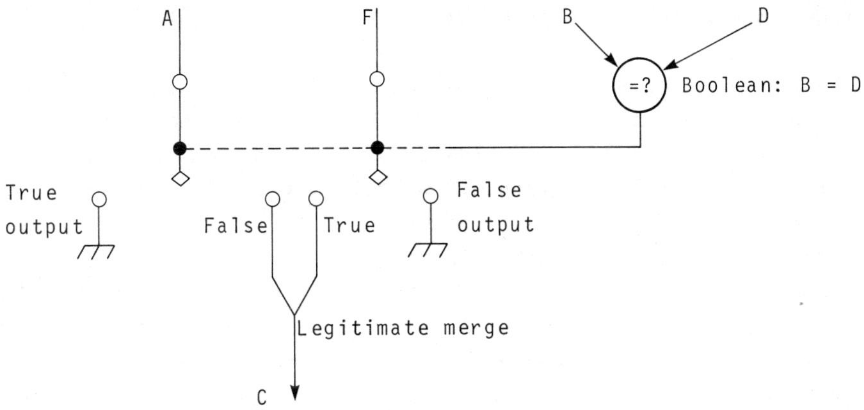

where  indicates that any token on this arc is destroyed, and the =? instruction generates a Boolean value indicating whether its data inputs are equal.

Dataflow graphs can be generated from conventional programming languages such as FORTRAN. More suitable languages are the single assignment languages (SALs) and the suitability of the dataflow approach to functional or applicative languages has recently received considerable attention.

GURD: Functional languages are based on the mathematics of functional algebra and have no concepts of storage state and assignment. In fact, they are sometimes called Zero Assignment Languages (ZALs). One interesting point that has recently emerged is that if assignment is restricted to occur only once for each variable in a program, the effect is the same as if there were no assignment at all, and 'assignment' statements were treated as *definitions* of variables. In this way SALs and functional languages are identical, and it is not surprising that absence of GOTOs and side-effects are common to them both. However, functional algebra allows higher level programming than most SALs permit by means of higher order functions and more comprehensive data structuring facilities. Consequently there is not a direct equivalence of the two. Nevertheless, they have enough in common to make it highly probable that functional languages will be amenable to efficient implementation on dataflow systems. Research is in progress to demonstrate operational compilers in this area.

Any hardware to implement dataflow will have to perform at least three major tasks.

GURD:

1 The program graph must be stored somewhere.

2 Data tokens that flow through the graph and match together with appropriate partners must be implemented.

3 Suitable data processing facilities must be provided.

The approach in the UK that has attracted most attention and which is well on the way to achieving a working system is that of Gurd and Watson at the University of Manchester.

GURD: In the basic ring-structured system the three dataflow tasks, namely matching tokens together, relating matched tokens onto the program graph, and performing the data processing, are implemented in three separate hardware modules. The individual actions in each of these modules are dependent only on the current input data, so that successive actions may be overlapped by connecting the modules in a pipeline. One additional pipeline module is provided to queue excess jobs when highly parallel programs are running. Hence the overall structure of the ring-structured processor is a four-stage pipeline as shown in Figure 6 [*see page 264*].

The fundamental unit of information in the switch is a token package, representing a notational tagged token on an arc of the graph. The token has a data value and tag, and the arc is represented by the address in the program graph store of the instruction at its head (the 'destination'). This token is the smallest data package, and so the queue module is inserted at this point. Queued tokens are presented one-at-a-time to the matching unit, which is responsible for grouping together tokens that have the same tag and are heading for the same destination. In the Manchester system tokens may only be grouped in ones and twos. Unmatched tokens, ie those that arrive at the matching unit before their partner (if they have one), are kept in the unmatched token store attached to the matching unit. After matching has successfully occurred, matched token pairs are sent to the program graph store. The tag and destination fields for the pair are of necessity identical. The program graph is stored as an array of instructions, each one representing a node and its associated output arcs. The incoming destination is used to address the next instruction, which defines an opcode to perform at this point and up to two destinations to which the result should be sent. The now complete executable package is sent to the processing unit, which executes the required opcode on the input data, and sends the results back into the communication switch.

The critical task is token matching. Unmatched tokens have to be stored; the ideal form for this store would be an associative memory, although the implementers have been constrained to use slower hash table techniques. The average match time is 300 nsec with the technology used, which limits the execution rate to 3.3 million instr/sec.

Other implementations of dataflow architectures have been produced or are being planned. One system was built at Texas Instruments in 1978 using four 9900 microprocessors. A more advanced system is being developed by Dennis at MIT which is one of the major centres for dataflow research. A VLSI dynamic tagged dataflow processor is also being constructed at MIT under the direction of Arvind. This is briefly described in the paper by Gurd.

GURD: A second research group at MIT, under the leadership of Arvind, is constructing a VLSI-based dynamic-tagged dataflow processor. An outline system design is shown [*see page 265*]. The structure is quite complex but in essence it is similar to the ring-structured system. The two main differences are *firstly* that data structure accesses are handled differently from ordinary data token activities and *secondly* that there is a two-tiered communication system.

Data structure operations are treated separately so that they can be performed quickly and so that the related tokens do not fill up the unmatched token store. The two-tiered communication structure relieves the general communication switch of a lot of traffic as long as programs exhibit strong locality (ie local processing activity is likely to remain in the same area of the graph and hence the same processor, rather than communicating randomly with all other processors). In fact, locality also benefits the size of unmatched token store, and current plans at MIT are to implement a 64-word store only, as opposed to the 16K-word store being used at Manchester.

One of the most significant paragraphs in Gurd's paper is the last.

GURD: Little has yet been published about the performance of dataflow systems in practical applications, but the existence of so much operational hardware should lead to a great expansion of assessment work and subsequent results in the near future.

When the assessment does take place then a realistic evaluation of these alternative architectures can be made. It is interesting that the Japanese Fifth Generation and Intelligent Knowledge Based Systems (KBSs) seem to base their hardware hopes on these as yet unproven architectures.

3: Software

Operating systems for supercomputers of the vector pipeline class are discussed, with particular reference to the CRAY 1, CYBER 205 and MIMD systems. In distributed computing, the individual nodes each have their own operating system and they communicate through the network and the software supporting network. The International Standards Organisation has proposed a network protocol of seven layers: the ISO Open Systems Interconnection Reference Model is described briefly. FORTRAN and PASCAL compilers are considered in detail and package software is also briefly examined.

Supercomputers of the vector pipeline class are essentially batch processors - preferably, from the point of view of efficiency, of large or very large jobs. The operating systems are therefore comparatively straightforward.

The CRAY-1 Operating System (COS) is a multiprogramming batch system capable of supporting 63 active user programs at one time. The basic flow of a job is described below.

CRAY (222):

1 A user submits a job to the front-end computer via a normal batch stream or local/ remote terminal/RJE station. The job deck is recognised by software running on this front-end machine as a job destined to run on the CRAY-1 system.

2 Front-end station software (which has been specifically written for the particular front-end machine) sends the job to the CRAY-1 where it is put into an input queue by the CRAY-1 operating system.

3 COS examines the parameters on the JOB card to determine what resources are requested and when they can be met (ie the class of job, priority, etc).

4 When the job is selected for execution, the job control statements are read, interpreted, and executed.

5 Any data files required by the job can be accessed if they are permanent files on the CRAY disks or staged from the front-end machine if they are resident on disk or magnetic tape on the front-end. Any files created by the executing job can similarly be saved on the CRAY disks or staged to the front-end.

6 When the job completes the output file from the job, a job log is then sent back to the front-end machine.

7 The front-end station software receives the job and takes the appropriate action as specified by the user (ie print locally or remotely).

8 If, for any reason, the job aborts or a system error occurs, COS will take appropriate action which may include the rerunning of a job, or reacquiring a file from the front-end.

Within the main store each program area is defined by an item of data and limit pair. Addresses in each program run from 0 to the assigned limit.

COS has the normal batch system facilities, job control language, file management, job scheduling, and accounting.

The contribution of the operating system to system efficiency is in ensuring that a job is available in fast memory ready for execution when the current job ends or is halted. Otherwise there would be a considerable loss of computing time if a new job had to be rolled in off the disk system.

The operating system for the CYBER 205, CYBER 200-OS, is logically more complex than that of the CRAY - it supports batch and interactive computing. However, these and all input/output have to go over the loosely coupled network to and from the front-end processor.

CDC (223): CYBER 200-OS permits concurrent and parallel operations of many computational and I/O activities. The user interfaces with the system via the front-end computer. Information is passed between the front-end computer and the Model 205 computational facility using the CDC loosely coupled network. Any required data conversion of binary and coded information is handled by the access devices within the network prior to transmission between computer systems.

Since a distributive concept was the major guideline in the hardware design of the CYBER 200 computer, a distributed system and processing approach is also the most logical choice in the software design to achieve economic functioning within the total CYBER 200 data processing complex. Thus, a major attribute of the software system is its high modularity and task-oriented structure, based on an efficient file concept.

The major characteristics of CYBER 200-OS are given below.

CYBER (223):

- File-oriented system with security and back-up facilities based on high performance random access mass storage
- Support of virtual memory addressing
- I/O may be performed implicitly or explicitly
- Implementation of a multitasking concept
- Extensive accounting and resource utilisation information
- Job and file recovery
- User and system checkpoint/restart.

The CYBER 205 has a very large virtual memory together with the advantages of a segmented virtual address system.

CDC (223): CYBER 200-OS considers every program to be executable only in virtual memory, which means that every page in virtual memory has a corresponding space on the disk storage system. Executable code exists first as a file on mass storage. This file, called a program file, is built by the loader and contains a map at the beginning of the file called the minus page. This map corresponds to the virtual page addresses and relates them to corresponding logical disk addresses.

The program file exists as read only, and the integrity of the program file is never violated.... The code and the data of the program need not be in contiguous physical memory locations.

During program execution the program can either open existing file space or create new file space and assign the type of access it desires to that file. It can assign a read-only type access to the file in which case the programmer would be notified if any attempt were to be made to write into that file. It can assign a read/write access to the file in which case the data is swapped into memory and back to the file.... The user never needs to issue any input or output commands with this virtual memory scheme. The only thing the user needs to do is reference data. The operating system intervenes to bring the referenced data into main memory if it is not already there. This type of I/O is called implicit I/O. In other words, when implicit I/O is being used the user never issues a read or write command, allowing greatly simplified program structures to be developed. Using implicit I/O, however, the job's execution is interrupted until the appropriate page has been transferred from mass storage to central memory. For most jobs this is acceptable, especially in multiprogramming mode, because another job can have access to the central processor while the interrupted program is waiting until the implicit I/O is completed.

The dangers with this approach are obvious. Insufficient fast store for any job could cause 'thrashing' to some degree and with the relatively very slow speed of the disk backing store the performance degradation could be enormous.

For very large programs or in other circumstances where demand paging could be an embarrassment the operating system provides the user with two methods of helping the operating system to efficiently manage the virtual memory.

CDC (223): The first is the ADVISE request by which the user informs the system, in advance, of the next pages of data which are required, and the system, in parallel with the job execution, streams the data from mass storage to central memory. Then when the job references the data, it is available in central memory and no program interruption takes place. The second is an alternative method of performing I/O, called explicit I/O. This is the type of I/O that all programmers are accustomed to, that is, the programmer explicitly uses read and write statements to acquire or store his data. With explicit I/O, a program may be reading, writing, and executing simultaneously. This can be important for the effective utilisation of the machine in the previously mentioned environments.

In an SIMD system, such as the DAP, the operating system is that of the host computer. This is VME/B for the 2900/DAP and UNIX for the proposed PERQ/DAP.

In MIMD systems the performance can be severely degraded if the software does not efficiently manage the links between the multiple memories, which constitute the common memory of the system, or fails to make use of the local memories of the individual processors. Jones and Schwarz conclude that there is little difference, at least in appearances, from the operating systems for conventional multiprogrammed uniprocessors.

JONES and SCHWARZ (218): Perhaps the first issue to raise in a discussion of multiprocessor software is the question of how it differs from uniprocessor software. In particular, how does software written to execute on multiple processors differ from that written to execute in the more familiar multiprogramming (uniprocessor) environment? Differences may stem from two sources:

- Architectural attributes unique to the multiprocessor
- A new programming style peculiar to parallel applications.

The attribute that all multiprocessors share is *replicated components*, especially multiple general-purpose processors. This is precisely the attribute simulated by multiprogramming operating systems; its users visualise multiple 'virtual processors'. For example, a UNIX user routinely requests the concurrent execution of multiple programs with the output of one program 'piped' as input to the next program. Each process can be thought of as executing on a virtual processor. Consequently there are few differences between multiprogrammed systems with and without multiple processors.

Non-homogeneous multiprocessors present difficulties as the non-homogeneity must be hidden from the user. Even if the components have the same architecture, problems arise if they are of different performance. C.mmp had this problem of asymmetry as it contained two different PDP-11 models. It is significant that the problem was solved by making all the processors the same rather than by tackling the software difficulties.

JONES and SCHWARZ (218): Viewed from the programmer's perspective, multiprocessor architectures do not introduce unique new problems not shared by other architectures. Replicated components, particularly those that are non-homogeneous or asymmetric, increase the amount of management that must be provided by either the operating system or the application - or both.... Management of multiple components, whether physical or virtual, is required in any computer system; the problem is exacerbated in any architecture in which components proliferate. We believe that those architectures with fewer management problems will eventually dominate.

Problems may also arise due to a different style of programming when using an MIMD system.

JONES and SCHWARZ (218): There is a second potential source of differences between multiprocessor and uniprocessor software, a programming style peculiar to parallel applications. One commonly believed myth is that parallel systems of programs are intrinsically different, that they require specialised control structures or data accessing facilities. In general, our experience has not shown this to be true.... Parallel programming does not give rise to the need for substantially new and different paradigms or methodologies. The art of programming is evolving.... some of the newer methods and methodologies that have evolved to cope with the rising complexity of software are non-sequential. Hence they are well suited for implementation on a multiprocessor.

Jones and Schwarz provide firm evidence that parallel software is not more difficult to implement than serial software. However, the behaviour of the running system is much more complex.

JONES and SCHWARZ (218): Although parallel solutions may not be more complex to implement, understanding the *behaviour* of the running system is indeed more complex. Non-determinacy is natural in distributed systems; yet it complicates any attempt to obtain a precise snapshot of the system state. Any programming style that makes it necessary to be able to capture such snapshots of the state will yield programs that are exceedingly difficult to debug and maintain. Though the occasion does arise when a snapshot is needed, it is rare.

In multiprogramming systems the operating system implements virtual memory and paging to remove the need for store management from the user. However, ignoring the existence of two levels of store can lead to severe degradation through threshing. In MIMD systems the operating system can also hide the distributed nature of the common memory (using the Kmap in Cm). Data items can be regarded as being anywhere in the common memory. However, ignoring the advantages of proper use of memory can lead to degradation similar to that caused by ignoring paging.*

JONES and SCHWARZ (218): Consider the synchronous parallel method of solving partial differential equations. This PDE solution method dedicates a processor to each of p processes, and each process iterates on a fixed subset $(m*n/p)$ of the $m \times n$ array of components. The important attributes are that newly computed values are written directly back into the shared global array without synchronisation, and that processes do not synchronise their iterations.

Figure 25 shows speed-up under several conditions. If all code and global variables are shared, and if references to the stack and local variables require Kmap assistance (ie are mapped), adding processors beyond four does not contribute to speed-up of the computation because both contention and memory reference cost contribute to inadequate utilisation of the system. If only the globals are shared, even though Kmap assistance is still required for every access, about six processors can be usefully employed.

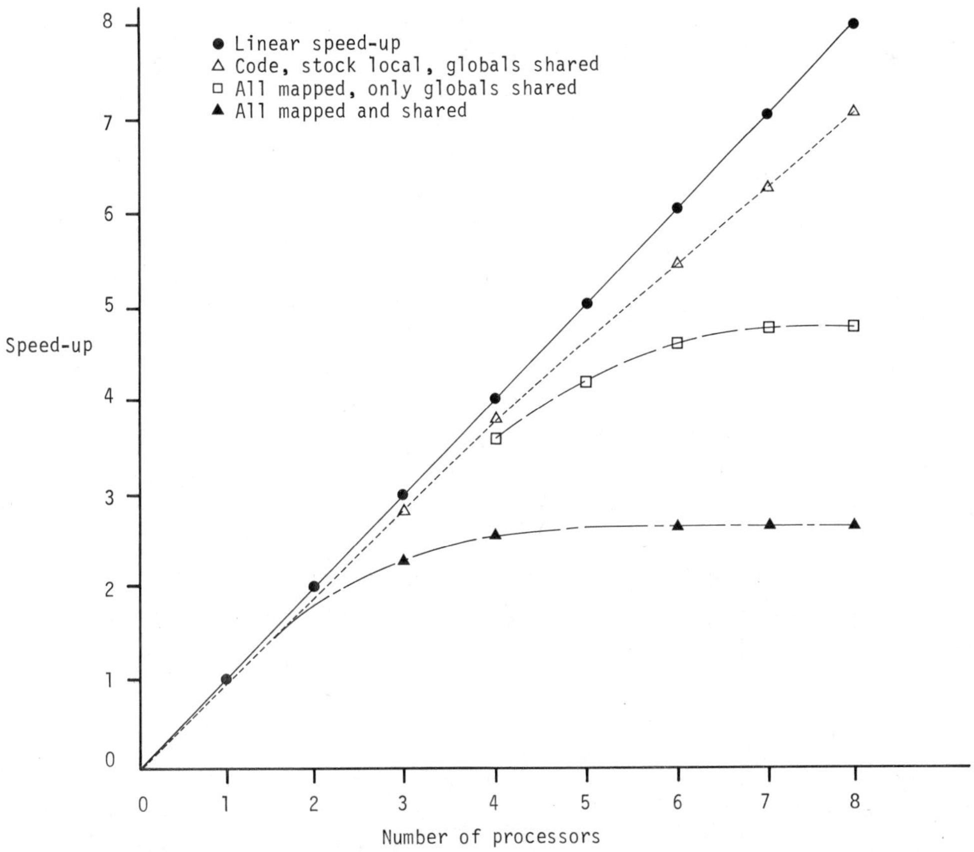

Figure 25: Speed-up of partial differential equation solver

Clearly, if contention for memory containing code is eliminated, two additional processors contribute fruitfully to the computation.

Finally, when code, stack, and local variables are all not only local but also unmapped, with only access to the global variables requiring Kmap assistance, each new processor up through the eighth contributes to the PDE solution (no more than eight processors were available when this experiment was performed), and the result is close to linear speed-up. The rather obvious conclusion is that performance degradation is substantial if program reference patterns are not considered in making resource allocation decisions.

In an MIMD system with several programs sharing data, for example a matrix stored in the common memory which is being used to perform an iterative numerical algorithm, there can be very severe synchronisation problems in accessing the memory. Jones and Schwarz describe the various synchronisation mechanisms used in C.mmp/HYDRA. These obviously increase the complexity of the operating system but they can be very successful in solving the problems.

JONES and SCHWARZ (218): Measurements on locking within the HYDRA operating system show that if *data* is locked instead of critical *code* sections, synchronisation can be negligible. In measurements involving 14 processors, idleness due to locking consumed less than 1% of the processors.

In distributed computing the individual nodes each have their own operating system and they communicate through the network and the software supporting the network. The International Standards Organisation (ISO) has proposed a network protocol of seven levels.

COLE (224): The ISO reference model is biased towards protocols based on X.25, and because of this, protocol hierarchies based on other mechanisms (such as those used on the ARPA network) do not fit the proposed model very well. This does not mean that one way is correct, merely that there is more than one way of designing a protocol hierarchy. The ISO model has seven levels as shown in Figure 26:

1 Physical circuit level.
2 Link level.
3 Network level.
4 Transport level.
5 Session level.
6 Presentation level.
7 Application level.

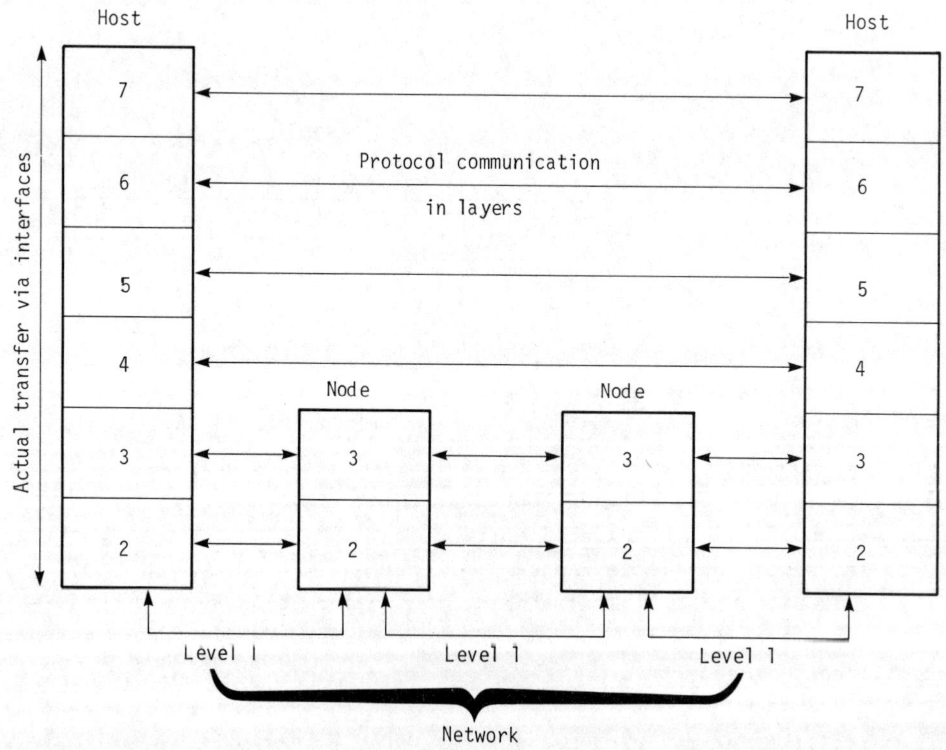

Figure 26: The seven protocol layers of ISO

The first three levels are the same as the three levels of the X.25 access protocol.

COLE (224): In the X.25 parlance a host is called a DTE (Data Terminating Equipment) and a node is called a DCE (Data Communications Equipment).

The physical circuit

COLE (224): This level provides the physical communication by specifying the electrical signals, voltages, plus shape, and pin assignment that the DTE needs to connect physically to the DCE.

The link level

COLE (224): The purpose of level 2 is to control the physical link between the two ends of the level 1 circuit to provide a reliable transfer of information for level 3 between the DTE and DCE. X.25 level 2 uses a link control protocol based on the ISO HDLC (Higher Data Link Control) protocol. The advantages of using an existing protocol are greater than those to be gained from designing a new one. For instance, a new protocol would have to be adopted by a large number of people wishing to communicate; adoption of the protocol would then require a lot of effort. Other link protocols have been designed: IBM uses one called SDLC (Synchronous Data Link Control) which is not dissimilar to HDLC and DEC have their own as well.

The network level

COLE (224): The function of level 2 is to carry a level 3 packet across a link. The function of level 3 is to carry a piece of information from one host (DTE) to another via intermediate network nodes. The transfer of the level 3 information will involve a number of level 2 links. The X.25 specification only covers the link between the DTE and DCE, but we will assume a similar protocol is used between each node of the network as well. Each level 3 packet contains a certain amount of level 3 protocol information in a header, then possibly some user data (from level 4). The major differences between levels 2 and 3 are the use of addresses and logical channel numbers. Most hosts will be connected to the network by one level 2 link. This link then has to be used to enable the host to communicate with several other hosts by multiplexing logical channels onto the one physical link. Level 3 is used to achieve this multiple connection via a single link. Using level 3 a host establishes a logical channel to another host by making a connection request using the full address of the remote host. When the connection is established it becomes a logical channel with a unique number, the logical channel number. Using the logical channel concept, packets for several calls may pass across the same level 2 link as they are all identified by a unique channel number. At the DCE the channel number is used to decide which route the packet will take. The logical channel is in fact a virtual circuit.

The remaining four levels are explained below.

The transport level

COLE (224): This level separates the host from the network, level 3, by providing interprocess communication rather than host-to-host connection. A transport level connection may exist over several networks, each of which will have its own level 3 and may be different in some respects. The transport level is responsible for the safe transfer of a message, or datastream, from one application process to another; as processes run on hosts this level is only implemented on the hosts. Level 4 provides addressing to a user application (rather than a host as in level 3), sequencing (so that the data arrives in the same order it was sent), multiplexing of connections, and some error and flow control.

The session level

COLE (224): This level is responsible for the management of resources used by the network applications, such as the operating system, the use of buffers, and the interprocess communication interface between the applications process and the transport level process. Addressing mapping between network addresses and the actual processes is the concern of this level.

The presentation level

COLE (224): The application or user process will not want the full generality of a network but a specific service such as a file transfer, or on-line access via a terminal, etc. This level is concerned with mapping the user's requirements into network actions. As this is the area of mapping the user's view of the network into the actual facilities, it is the level at which such features as device independence, address to service mapping, and virtual terminals are implemented. Many specific functions are implemented at this level for specific functions such as file transfer, message service, interactive use, etc.

The application level

COLE (224): This level contains the processes within the host computer that are capable of using a network, or the human user at a terminal. It may be a language with network facilities, or a standard set of commands for terminal usage over the network. As all work in a computer is achieved by an active process, it is convenient to think of the process as the beginning and end of the network connection, especially for addressing purposes. However, all processes must work for someone, so it is reasonable to think of a human user beyond the application process.

Networks are a very active area of research and a good source of detailed information is the State of the Art Report Networks (225).

One of the most important areas in MIMD systems is the management of the database which can be shared or distributed (226).

COMPILERS AND PACKAGES

COMPILERS

Most supercomputers can generally only be efficiently used if the problem can be mapped onto the hardware. On the other hand, most users wish to write in standard high-level languages, in particular in FORTRAN. This is not only because they know these languages but so that they can move their programs to other computers. Furthermore, many packages are written in standard high-level languages and it is highly desirable that these can be used without conversion. These conflicting requirements have led to the development of compilers that will accept programs in, for example, standard FORTRAN but will produce object code that will be efficient on the particular hardware. Early examples of this were the FORTRAN compilers of the CDC 6600 and 7600, which optimised the use of the fast registers and the multiple arithmetic units. The CRAY-1 and CYBER 205 both have vectorising compilers which attempt to detect parallelism and use the vector instructions.

CRAY (222): CFT analyses the innermost DO loops of the FORTRAN programs it compiles to determine whether vector processing methods can be applied to improve overall program efficiency. If so, the execution sequence of the code it produces contains vector instructions to drive the high-speed vector and floating-point functional units and the eight-vector registers in their integrated processing of the specified operation. This feature of CFT is automatically activated through compiler analysis of statements contained in certain DO loops in the program without special notation on the part of the programmer. Thus, no special provisions are required that would encumber the programmer or affect the transportability of the programs produced or used.

Not all DO loops are vectorisable. The programmer can enhance the performance of his programs by avoiding certain constructs.

CRAY (222): To be vectorisable, a DO loop must manipulate or perform calculations on the contents of one or more arrays. Additionally, a vectorisable DO loop may contain the following types of constructs:

- Calls to CRAY-1 FORTRAN intrinsic functions
- Arithmetic, relational, and logical operators in expressions
- Non-unit incrementing or decrementing of subscripts (so every third element of an array could be addressed, either explicitly or implicitly as part of a multi-dimensional array reference)
- Subscripts containing simple expressions
- Scalar variables (ie no subscript) holding an intermediate result which is set in the loop to an expression manipulating arrays.

Loops containing a GOTO, IF, CALL, or any I/O statement are not vectorisable. Any procedure named in an EXTERNAL statement also inhibits vectorisation of an inner DO loop referencing it. However, a user-supplied vector external function can be supplied, which will allow vectorisation to take place.

CDC have a similar FORTRAN compiler.

CDC (223): The source language for CYBER 200 FORTRAN is ANSI (ASA document X3.9-1966) with extensions. The extensions provide vector language syntax and direct access to all central processor instructions which make efficient machine utilisation possible without the necessity for Assembly language programming. The FORTRAN compiler, object time library, and generated object programs are location independent.

The CYBER 200 FORTRAN compiler provides code optimisation, loop collapsing into vector instructions, and effective utilisation of the large CYBER 200 register file. Programmers can write in traditional FORTRAN allowing the compiler to optimise and collapse loops; or, they may utilise the extensions which permit direct access to the hardware capabilities of vector and string manipulation. Efficient code development is aided by a symbolic cross reference and a symbolic debugging package.

The FORTRAN compiler for the BSP was more ambitious than those of the CRAY and CYBER 205.

HOCKNEY and JESSHOPE (200): Although the BSP compiler contains many parallel constructs, it also contains a vectorising capability. This combination gives the dual advantage of being able to run existing sequential codes using the vectorising capability and/or rewriting code explicitly in parallel constructs.

The BSP vectoriser is described in detail by Austin **(227)**.

HOCKNEY and JESSHOPE (200): The BSP vectoriser is considerably more sophisticated than the CFT compiler. It analyses more than one level of nested loops and can perform certain order transformations on statements and DO loops. In addition to this, the compiler will vectorise loops containing first-order linear recurrences and also certain loops containing IF statements. The following examples of the vectorising capability of the BSP FORTRAN compiler are taken from Austin **(227)**. The vectorisation transformation is expressed in terms of BSP parallel constructs.

```
C     LOOP CONTAINING AN IF STATEMENT

        DO 2 I = 1, N-1
           IF (M.GT.3) A(I) = A(I+1) + C(I)
2     CONTINUE

C     IF LOOP VECTORISED

        WHERE (M.GT.3) A(1:N-1) = A(2:N) + C(1:N-1)

C     MULTISTATEMENT CONDITIONAL

        DO 3 I = 1, N
           IF (A(I).LT.B(I)) GOTO 31
              C(I) = E(I) + 2
              A(I) = 0
           GOTO 3
```

```
31          C(I) = F(I)
3     CONTINUE

C     MULTISTATEMENT LOOP VECTORISED

        LOGICAL L(N)
        L = A(1:N).GE.B(1:N)
        WHERE (L) DO
           C(1:N) = E(1:N) +2
           A(1:N) = 0
           OTHERWISE
              C(1:N) = F(1:N)
           ENDWHERE

C     MULTISTATEMENT LOOP WITH NON-VECTORISABLE RECURRENCE

        DO 4 I = 2, 100
           A(I) = B(I) + 1
           C(I) = D(I-1) + E(I)
           D(I) = C(I) + A(I)
4          F(I) = D(I) + 2

C     PARTIAL VECTORISATION

        A(2:100) = B(2:100) + 1
        DO I = 2, 100
           C(I) = D(I-1) + E(I)
           D(I) = C(I) + A(I)
        END DO
        F(2:100) = D(2:100) + 2

C     LOOP REQUIRING STATEMENT REORDERING

        DO 5 I = 1, N
           A(I) = B(I) + C(I)
           C(I) = B(I-1)
5          B(I) = 2*A(I+1)

C     VECTORISED WITH TEMPORARY AND REORDERING

        REAL TEMP(N)
        TEMP(1:N) = A(2:N+1)
        A(1:N) = B(1:N) + C(1:N)
        B(1:N) = 2*TEMP(1:N)
        C(1:N) = B(0:N-1)

C     LOOP REQUIRING REORDERING

        DO 6 I = 1, N
        DO 6 J = 1,N
        DO 6 K = 1, L
           A(I,J+1,K) = B(I,J-1,K)
6          B(I,J,K) = A(I,J,K)
```

```
C     VECTORISATION WITH REORDERING

          DO 7 J = 1, N
             A(1:M, J+1, 1:L) = B(1:M, J-1, 1:L)
7            B(1:M, J, 1:L) = A(1:M, J, 1:L)
```

In this last example a recurrence in J has been isolated and the innermost and outermost loops in M and L have been vectorised. Notice that although the BSP hardware can handle first-order linear recurrence, the recurrence vectorisation process will only be invoked if no other vectorisation can be performed on a given set of DO loops. This is because the parallel evaluation of a first-order linear recurrence is not 100% efficient.

Comparing these examples with the CRAY-1 CFT compiler demonstrates that Burroughs has advanced the state of the art in this field of automatic vectorisation. This is apparent from the final three examples, where for the CFT compiler, the transformations would have had to be made by hand.

Another useful feature of the BSP compiler is the analysis of the vectorisation process, which is produced as a compiler diagnostic report. This provides a learning tool for the programmer who is inexperienced in parallel structures and programming techniques.

Vectorising compilers accept code that will run on other computers. As soon as special functions are added, the FORTRAN program becomes non-portable. However, special constructs that match the architecture can greatly increase the performance.

The DAP has a form of FORTRAN which reflects the 64 × 64 array structure.

HOCKNEY and JESSHOPE (200): Arrays are declared in DAP FORTRAN in the usual way, using the DIMENSION or TYPE statement; however, vectors are declared with their first dimension elided and matrices with the first two dimensions elided. These are the constrained dimensions, which take on the DAP size of N elements for a vector and $N \times N$ for a matrix. Sets of these objects may also be declared by using other dimensions.

```
DIMENSION V( ), VSET(,4)
REAL      M(,), MSET(,,4)
```

The examples above therefore define a single vector V and vector set VSET of four vectors, followed by a matrix M and matrix set MSET of four matrices. The unconstrained dimensions are for sequential access only and map onto the DAP store. These dimensions are treated exactly as in standard FORTRAN.

Because expressions in DAP FORTRAN can be matrix or vector valued, the function subprogram definition has been extended to include matrix and vector valued functions, as well as the more usual scalar valued function. The type of the function is declared in the function statement. Thus

```
REAL MATRIX FUNCTION MATMULT
```

declares a function MATMULT which returns a real matrix valued result.

In addition to the extension of a user-defined function, the standard or built-in

FORTRAN functions have been made polymorphic. They return a value of the same type as their argument, with matrix and vector types being evaluated in parallel. Other built-in functions introduced into DAP FORTRAN include data manipulation functions, shift functions, selection functions, and reduction functions. The reduction functions operate over either or both of the constrained dimensions, using arithmetic, relational or logical operators. Some examples are given below.

ALL	.AND. over rows and columns
ANY	.OR. over rows and columns
ANDROWS	.AND. over rows
ORCOLS	.OR. over columns
SUM	+ over rows and columns
MAXP	⩾ over rows and columns (gives logical position only)

Nearly all programming on supercomputers is in FORTRAN. As this type of machine begins to be installed in general as well as specialised user communities, interest in other languages is increasing. One obvious example is PASCAL and Cray Research are collaborating with the University of Manchester in the production of a compiler (Wilson et al).

WILSON *et al*: PASCAL compilers are commonly based on one of the three compilers originally implemented at Zurich, each for a different level of language provision. These compilers are single pass, with a recursive-descent recognition directly producing code for an interpretive or real machine. This reflects the simple LL(1) nature of the syntax and semantics of the language. However, a high degree of code optimisation necessitates knowledge of the complete program being compiled, which in turn implies a multipass compilation technique.

In order to achieve high execution rates, efficient use must be made of the fast registers of the CRAY.

WILSON *et al*: With high memory-to-register and register-to-register transfer rates, a PASCAL program on the CRAY-1 is expected to achieve high execution speeds. However, the ratio of memory-to-register to register-to-register transfer speeds is 1:11. Therefore, it is important to minimise the number of store/loads in a procedure by devising a suitable register allocation scheme and by interleaving instructions so as to minimise 'hold' conditions arising from store accesses. This interleaving carried out by the compiler is called 'scheduling'.

With reference to the scalar capabilities of the CRAY-1, there are 64 intermediate B/T registers each. Hence, there is a possibility of utilising these registers as cache memory. Surprisingly, it will be shown that this number is more than the average number of variables declared in a procedure and comparable to the total number of variables declared in a program. Consequently, use of B/T registers to hold variable values is a major factor in reducing the number of store/loads required in a program.

With reference to the vector capabilities, there are eight vector registers, each of which has sixty-four 64-bit elements. While these are obviously utilised for vector processing, it is conceivable to utilise them as an 8 * 64 scalar cache memory. A closer investigation suggests that the benefits thus gained, compared to store/loads, may not be significant, especially when the selection of a particular vector register is difficult and an A register load is required. Also, a store/load may not result in a significant delay if data transfer overlaps with concurrent processing. This is a scheduling problem.

In computers with small memory size there generally has to be a tradeoff between runtime efficiency and compiler size/speed. Runtime efficiency generally induces complexity, which in turn increases compiler size and representation data size. In contrast, the 8 Mbyte typical memory size of the CRAY-1, enables an optimising multipass PASCAL compiler to be feasible. In general, this should assist in runtime efficiency of PASCAL programs on the CRAY-1.

The compiler must also make efficient use of the independent functional units.

WILSON *et al*: In addition to the parallelism implied in vector operations and autonomous store accesses, the CRAY-1 has independent pipelined functional units that may carry out several arithmetic and logical operations concurrently. The pipelining also permits each unit individually to accept functional requests at 12.5 nsec clock intervals even if the functional operation occupies several clocks. To take advantage of this, the compiler must further interleave the instructions by choosing registers and scheduling appropriately.

The problems of branch orders have been discussed earlier. This is of particular importance in PASCAL.

WILSON *et al*: The high proportion of control transfers inherent in PASCAL programs suggests careful examination of the instruction buffering mechanism on the hardware. This is significant in size, the 256 instruction units being approximately five times that on a CDC 7600. It also has a minimal structure consisting of four separately loaded buffers, but has no intelligence regarding choice of release, look-ahead filling, or heuristics and each buffer must be treated as a contiguous unit. Clearly, loops which fit totally into these buffers and cover no more than four disjoint address spaces, will benefit from a lack of hold conditions arising from instruction store fetches. However, any deviation from these rules incurs the penalty of apparently increased time to process a control transfer from a minimum of 2 clocks in the case of no-transfer conditional to a worst-case buffer 'thrashing' of 25 clocks.

The development of structured programming means that an efficient procedure-calling system must be implemented.

WILSON *et al*: With the provision of the procedural abstraction facility in PASCAL and a wide acceptance of structured programming principles, a large usage of procedures is expected in PASCAL programs to be run on the CRAY-1, and this will be demonstrated later. Hence, it is important to have an efficient procedure-calling sequence....

In the CRAY-1 PASCAL compiler (CP) the substitution of suitable procedures is neither performed by a preprocessor nor by the code generator. Instead, it is performed at the internal representation level, where there is a knowledge of the properties of the procedure concerned and the cache register allocation scheme has already been applied.

PASCAL permits better use to be made of the particular register types.

WILSON *et al*: PASCAL is a strongly typed language. This enables compile time selection of a suitable type of register for an operand, since conversion, subrange information, etc is known at compile time. Consider the following declarations as an example:

```
var I : 1..10; (*index variable*)
        B : boolean
```

A 24-bit A register is more suitable than a 64-bit S register, given the bounds of variable I; whereas, an S register is more suitable for variable b, since logical operations on the CRAY-1 are performed in these registers. This contrasts with the lack of such information in FORTRAN.

Wilson et al also discuss the provision of vector facilities.

WILSON *et al*: Vector facilities can be provided by language extension as in CFD on the ILLIAC IV, by provision of subroutines which may be called by the user as in the STAR FORTRAN on the CDC STAR-100 and CFT on the CRAY-1 or by use of an entirely new language which reflects the vector parallelism as does the ACTUS language of Perrot. These approaches have obvious benefits in guaranteeing the maximum extraction of vector parallelism at a minimum compilation cost. However, they do put a varying degree of burden on the user and remove all possibility of porting the application to or from other (possibly scalar) processors. PASCAL enthusiasts would see this latter point as particularly important, in a context where a CRAY-1 is necessarily part of a multimachine configuration. Thus CRAY-1 CFT and CRAY PASCAL have been aimed at automatic vectorisation of standard scalar written programs.

They also discuss the problems of vectorisation and present an interesting analysis of loops in a PASCAL program. Surprisingly few are found to be vectorisable.

WILSON *et al*: In an attempt to isolate the nature of loops and those features which were preventing vectorisation, the static analysis presented earlier was extended. The static analyser program was modified to detect the occurrence of constructs within FOR loops which were known to enforce scalar operation. Where no such difficulty was detected, a data dependency analysis of the statements within the loop was undertaken. This was capable of determining whether the loop was a vector one or could be manipulated to be so. The results in Figure 27 for a program known to be highly numerical in content show relatively few vectorisable loops (16 out of 191). Of course, it is possible that the knowledge in CP of the form of side effects in each user procedure would permit the elimination of a procedure call as a definitive block to vectorisation.

The necessity for scalar optimisations determines the point at which vector operations are detected by the compiler.

WILSON *et al*: The detection of vector operations during compilation may be achieved at one of several points. The source text may be preprocessed into a vector form, as may be achieved in the Parafrase system described by Kuck *et al*. Alternatively, vectorisation may be achieved within the compiler by operating on the internal representation of the program, either before or after scalar optimisations. In the case of CP, scalar optimisations require the modifiable tree-structure representation to be changed to a directed graph form. In contrast, vectorisation may involve changing the structure of the program by loop splitting, for example. Thus in CP, vector operations are detected prior to scalar optimisations and a modified form of the triples is produced.

It is hoped that this PASCAL compiler will manage scalar operations more efficiently than CRAY FORTRAN, and will be equally capable of detecting and implementing vectorisation.

Summary of vector failures

Inner loop found	18	10.98
Procedure/function found	63	38.41
Nested if found	4	2.44
Index expression failed	2	1.22
GOTO/label found	5	3.05
Case statement found	2	1.22
LHS is constant	61	37.20
Const inc expression expected	8	4.88
Non-index use of control variable	1	0.61

Total failures = 164

Data dependence analysis of 27 loops led to:

3	Scalar ,	15.79
16	Vector ,	84.21

Figure 27: Vectorisation static analysis

PACKAGES

There has been a relatively slow build-up in the availability of package software which will run on machines such as the CRAY-1 and CYBER 205. As the number of installations has increased and as the user community has become more general, the demand for packages has increased. Many packages are written in FORTRAN so that it is relatively easy to get these running. However, the production of packages which make use of the vector features of the computers is considerably more difficult. This is a very important aspect and many packages, such as the NAG library which are very widely used, have been properly converted. It is unlikely that the non-availability of suitable packages will inhibit the use of vector-pipelined supercomputers.

For processors such as the DAP the user community is still very small and the availability of packages is severely limited.

4: Performance

A formal definition of performance for different computer architectures is discussed and a procedure for evaluating the products on the market is described. The problems encountered by a university or general scientific computing centre when considering the purchase of a pipelined vector processor are examined. Techniques for efficient parallel computing are assessed. A single problem may have several solutions, each suited to computation on different architectures. In considering parallel solutions, the space of the solution can be characterised by three dimensions. The size exhibited by the solution in these dimensions indicates the type of parallel computer best suited to the solution.

The best attempt to arrive at a formal definition of performance for different computer architectures has been made by Hockney **(228)** *and Hockney and Jesshope* **(200).**

A good starting point is the illustration in Figure 28 of three different ways of performing the addition of two floating-point vectors x_1 *and* y_1 *assuming that each addition can be divided into four equal length suboperations.*

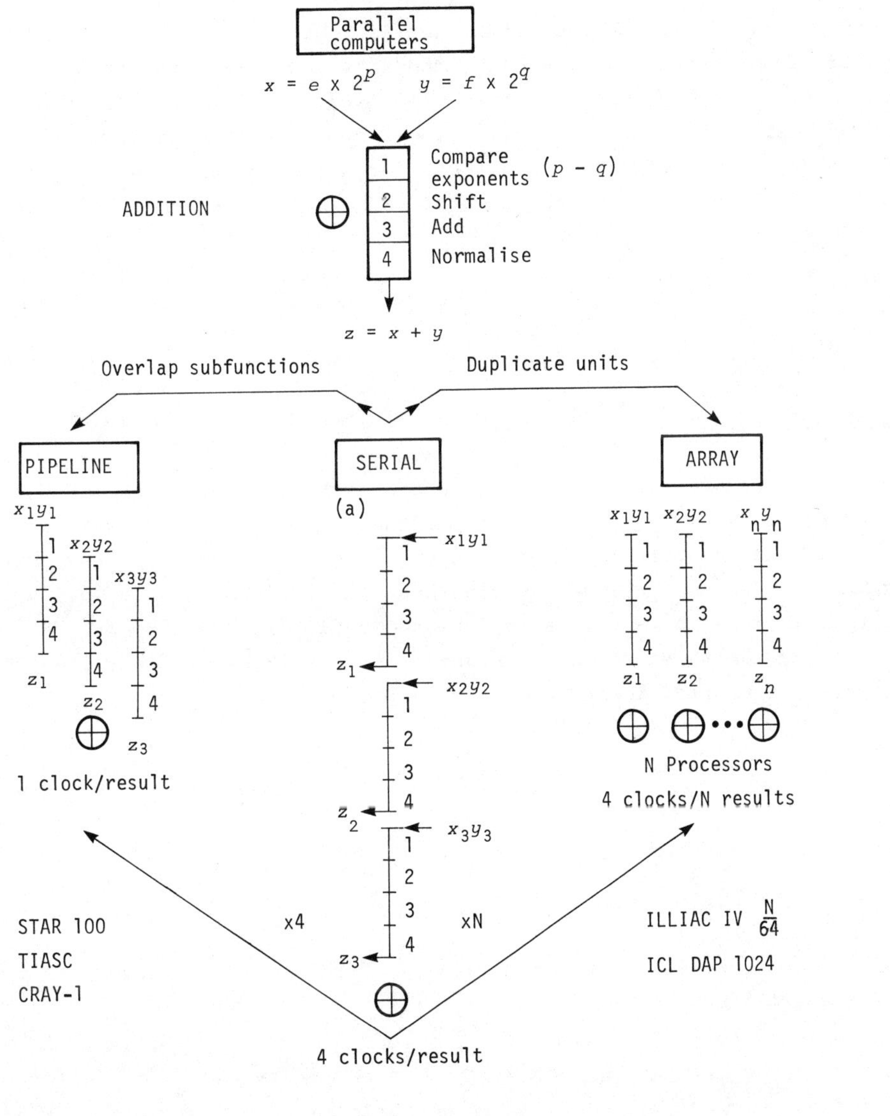

Figure 28: Three different ways of performing floating-point vector additions

Serial computers

HOCKNEY and JESSHOPE (200): If ℓ is the number of suboperations (in this case, $\ell=4$) and τ is the time required to complete each (usually the clock period) then the time to perform an operation on a vector of length n is

$$t_{\text{serial}} = \ell\tau n,$$

and the maximum rate of producing results is

$$r_{\infty\text{serial}} = (\ell\tau)^{-1}.$$

Pipelined computers

HOCKNEY and JESSHOPE (200): The time to perform the operation on a vector of length n is therefore

$$t_{\text{pipe}} = [s + \ell + (n-1)]\tau,$$

where $s\tau$ is a fixed start-up time that is required to set up the pipeline for the vectors in question, ie to compute the first and last addresses for each vector and other overheads. It also includes the fixed time for numbers to be transferred between memory and the arithmetic pipeline. ℓ is the number of stages or segments in the pipeline and therefore differs for different arithmetic operations. When full, and therefore operating smoothly, a pipeline delivers one result every clock period τ, hence

$$r_{\infty\text{pipe}} = \tau^{-1}.$$

Array processors

HOCKNEY and JESSHOPE (200): If there are N such processors and $N < n$, the first N argument pairs (x_1, y_1) can be sent to the PEs and the first N results found simultaneously in a time of one parallel operation on all elements of the array, say $t_{\|}$/(4τ in our example). The next N elements can then be loaded and also computed in parallel in a further $t_{\|}$ time units. This is repeated until all the elements are computed. The timing diagram is shown on the right of Figure 28 and we conclude that the time to compute a vector of length n on such a processor array is

$$t_{\text{array}} = t_{\|} \lceil n/N \rceil$$

and

$$r_{\infty\text{array}} = N/t_{\|},$$

where $\lceil x \rceil$ - the ceiling function of x - is the smallest integer that is either equal to or greater than x.

Hockney and Jesshope use the performance of a computer doing a single arithmetic operation on a vector of length n, as the criterion for comparison of architectures.

HOCKNEY and JESSHOPE (200): The performance of the computer during a single arithmetic operation on a vector of length n. This will be fitted as closely as possible to the following generic formula for the time of the operation, t, as a function of the vector length:

$$t = r_{\infty}^{-1}(n + n_{1/2}).$$

The two parameters $n_{1/2}$ and r_{∞} completely describe the hardware performance of the idealised generic computer and give a first-order description of any real computer. These characteristic parameters are called:

1 *The half-performance length* $n_{1/2}$: the vector length required to achieve half the maximum performance.

2 *The maximum or asymptotic performance* r_{∞}: the maximum rate of computation in units of equivalent scalar operations performed per second. For the generic computer this occurs asymptotically for vectors of infinite length, hence the subscript. The common unit for floating-point execution is MFLOPS.

Expressions for $n_{1/2}$ and r_{∞} for serial, pipeline, and array processors are given by Hockney and Jesshope.

HOCKNEY and JESSHOPE (200): The half-performance length ($n_{1/2}$), on the other hand, is a measure of the amount of parallelism in the computer architecture. We shall see that it varies from $n_{1/2} = 0$ for serial computers with no parallel operation to $n_{1/2} = \infty$ for an infinite array of processors.

For serial computers

$$n_{1/2} = 0 \quad \text{and} \quad r_{\infty} = (\ell\tau)^{-1}.$$

For pipelines

$$n_{1/2} = s + \ell - 1 \quad \text{and} \quad r_{\infty} = \tau^{-1}.$$

And for array processors (with N processors in the array)

$$n_{1/2} = \infty \quad \text{and} \quad r_{\infty}/n_{1/2} = t_{\parallel}^{-1} \quad \text{for } n \leq N.$$

$$n_{1/2} = N/2 \quad \text{and} \quad r_{\infty} = N/t_{\parallel} \quad \text{for } n > N.$$

Computer architectures can be quantitatively compared by using these two parameters.

HOCKNEY and JESSHOPE (200): The two parameters $n_{1/2}$ and r_{∞} provide us with a quantitative means of comparing the parallelism and maximum performance of *all* computers. It is most instructive to examine the relative position of different computers on the ($n_{1/2}$, r_{∞}) plane. Such a diagram, which may be regarded as separating the computers into a spectrum, is shown in Figure 29. The vertical axis (r_{∞}) is the maximum performance in MFLOPS of the computer and the horizontal axis ($n_{1/2}$) is the amount of parallelism in the architecture. A computer is then represented by a dot in the diagram, except that in most cases a computer may be used in different modes with different levels of parallelism. We thus find that one computer is often represented by a solid line connecting the points representing its different modes of operation. We also show by directional broken lines computer designs that are evolutionary developments of each other. Since we use a logarithmic scale, we arbitrarily plot serial designs ($n_{1/2} = 0$) on the line $n_{1/2} = 1$. This is quite

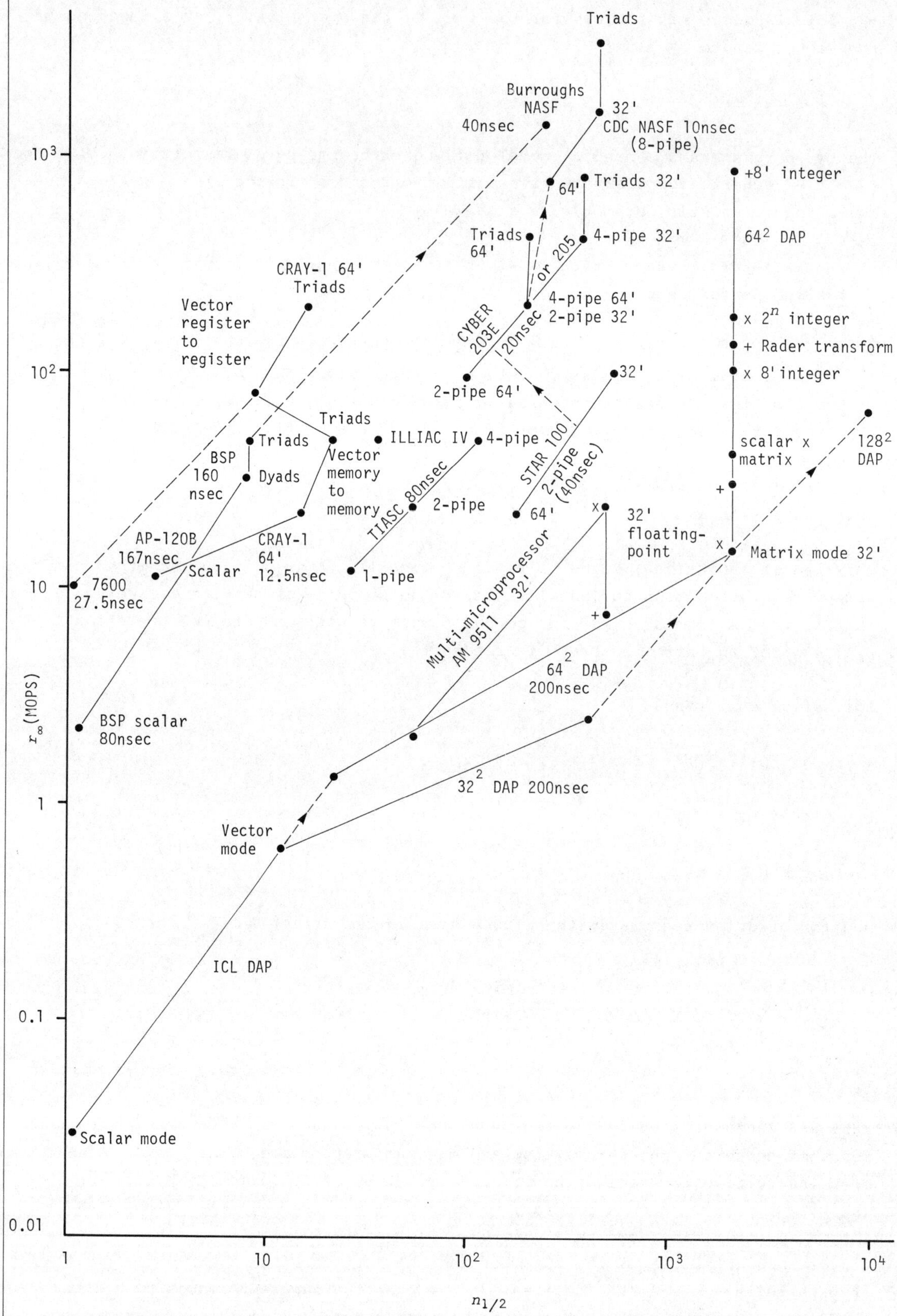

Note:

Diagonal lines at roughly 45° correspond to development by increased replication. Operations are floating-point except where stated. A prime denotes the number of bits in the representation of a number.

Figure 29: The two-dimensional spectrum of computers plotted on the $(n_{1/2}, r_\infty)$ plane

reasonable because serial computers, when programmed to process a vector, do display a small non-zero value of $n_{1/2}$.

The preceding formal approach is very useful in categorising architectures and physical implementations of these architectures. However, if an establishment is planning to buy a new computer how does it evaluate the performance of the possible choices? The standard procedure is for the organisation to produce a 'benchmark', which is a set of carefully chosen programs that can be taken to be representative of the present or preferably the expected workload. Running the benchmark on different computer systems provides a basis for comparison relative to each other and relative to a base line that is generally the performance of the organisation's present computer.

When the pattern of work is not expected to change significantly and when the architectures being compared are similar to each other and to the existing system then this technique is quite accurate and it is relatively easy to decide whether or not the change to the new system will be cost effective. There are two major difficulties with supercomputers. Firstly, the organisation buying one probably wants to push its applications into new areas which were not previously possible. Secondly, the design of supercomputers is such that the delivered power is very dependent upon the workload. In these circumstances, the benchmark has to be carefully chosen to prevent silly comparisons. An extreme case that occurred recently was of a FORTRAN program written for an IBM system, which used double length floating-point numbers, ie 64 bits rather than 32 bits. This was originally run on a CRAY-1 with the request for double length included, ie using 128 bits rather than 64. Double length arithmetic is relatively very slow on the CRAY so the result of this comparison was rather misleading.

PIPELINED VECTOR PROCESSORS FOR GENERAL SCIENTIFIC COMPUTING

The early customers for these systems have been places such as the Lawrence Livermore Laboratory, Los Alamos, and weather forecasting centres. They all have very large programs which they wish to transfer to the new system and will happily use the new system on a small number of programs. Of course, if it turns out to be of more general applicability this is a bonus. In such a situation it is possible to make a fairly accurate assessment of the expected performance both for transferring the work directly and after careful optimisation to fit the particular architecture.

When a university or general scientific computer centre considers the purchase of a pipelined vector processor the problems of assessment and comparison are much more difficult.

Consider a batch of FORTRAN programs running on a CDC 7600 and a CRAY-1. The maximum performance of a 7600 is one result per clock period or approximately 40 MFLOPS and that of the CRAY-1 is 160 MFLOPS. The operating speed of a 7600 with an average (whatever this means) workload is about 10 MIPS and Hockney quotes a rate of about 3 MFLOPS for a particular FORTRAN program. This program cannot be vectorised and for it the CRAY-1 runs at 5 MFLOPS, ie a factor of about 1.7. If all the programs to be run had similar characteristics to this one then the correct choice could well be to buy a second or even a third conventional high-performance computer such as a 7600 or a big IBM or AMDAHL system. With a batch of FORTRAN programs representative of the workload of the University of Manchester the ratio of performance between a CRAY-1 and a 7600 was about 2.7. The improvement over the lower limit given by Hockney is obviously due to the vectorising capability of the CRAY compiler and the existence of a significant number of DO *loops which can be vectorised. Some 22 of the larger programs were optimised by hand; the average optimisation changed about 25 lines per program and took approximately one man-day. After this optimisation the ratio of performance was about 6.*

The difference between 2.7 and 6 is obviously very significant and shows that any generalised use of a pipelined vector processor without some attempt at optimising the code reduces the power of the pipelined vector processor to something little different from that which could be supplied for the same expenditure by one or more high-performance conventional computers.

The figures for the CYBER 205 with the same collection of jobs are very similar, being about 2 for the unoptimised and 7 for the optimised set of programs. This fits with the slower scale of speed of the 205 and the longer vector start-up time; the CYBER 205 has a larger value of $n_{1/2}$. *For the CYBER 205 the ratio to the 7600 varies tremendously for the different jobs in the benchmarks: the lowest factor, after optimisation, is about 3 and the highest 33.*

The effort in optimisation to get the increased performance on either the CRAY-1 or CYBER 205 is negligible and shows very clearly that a pipelined vector processor can be used efficiently in a general scientific computing environment where the users wish to use standard languages, particularly FORTRAN and standard packages. They do not wish to spend a long time on optimising their numerical methods or in reprogramming in languages containing parallel constructs which could not then be ported to other systems.

Some users did rewrite their programs completely, still using FORTRAN, and some also changed the numerical method that they were using. These users frequently obtained a factor greater than 10 over a 7600 and in one case a factor of over 30 was achieved.

These latter figures support the arguments given above that computers which obtain their high performance from a highly structured design must have the problems adjusted to fit this structure if they are to be used to their full effect.

TECHNIQUES FOR EFFICIENT PARALLEL COMPUTING

The point is made by Jones and Schwarz that a single problem may have several solutions each suited to computation on different architectures.

JONES and SCHWARZ (218): A problem may have a number of distinct and different solutions, each of which may or may not be well suited to implementation on a particular architecture. The alternative solutions to a problem are often limited less by attributes of the problem than by the creativity of the problem solver. Historically, problem solvers start with a particular architecture in mind and attempt to find a solution that exploits it. Because of this procedure new architectures can stimulate new solutions.

In considering parallel solutions the space of the solution can be characterised by three dimensions:

- *The computation unit*
- *Communication patterns*
- *Patterns of reference to data.*

The size exhibited by the solution in these dimensions indicates the type of parallel computer best suited to the solution.

The computation unit

JONES and SCHWARZ (218): The unit of computation, potentially performed in parallel with others, may be as small as one stage of a multiply operation or as large as an arbitrarily long sequence of instructions. This *granularity* of the computation unit determines whether the parallelism exhibited by a solution is well matched to a pipeline architecture, a multiprocessor, or a network. Whatever the grain size, book-keeping is necessary to keep track of the relative progress of the individual computation units. If the grain size must be small, as for a vector or pipelined architecture, performance constraints require that this book-keeping be minimal, and it is usually performed in hardware. In contrast, when the computation unit is a software *process*, ... its maintenance is non-trivial and is usually performed in software.

The computation units that collectively make up a solution are either *homogeneous*, ie functionally identical, or they are *heterogeneous*. This attribute affects whether a solution and an architecture are well matched. For example, only a solution involving homogeneous computation units is suitable for implementation on an SIMD stream architecture such as ILLIAC IV.

In contrast, a multiprocessor is constructed of a collection of processors, each capable of independent and sequential execution of a program. Consequently, the process is a natural choice for the computation unit. Multiprocessors are thus ideally suited for solutions with large-grain, possibly heterogeneous, computation units. Of course, homogeneous computation units can also be supported conveniently and efficiently and may share a single copy of code.

Communication patterns

JONES and SCHWARZ (218): Concurrently executing computation units which together accomplish one task need to communicate both data and control information. Both the *frequency* with which units communicate and the *amount* of information that must be communicated bear on the type of architecture that is well matched to a particular solution.

Patterns of reference to data

JONES and SCHWARZ (218): Both the *regularity* of references to a data structure and their relative *locality* influence how well matched an architecture is to a solution. For example, a typical signal-processing solution accesses data vector elements in an order determined by a simple function, so that the index of the next accessed element is easily calculable; given one index, the next index can be computed with a single arithmetic operation. Vector and systolic architectures are designed to reflect the reference patterns of limited, but important, classes of problem solutions....

Even when reference patterns have no discernible regularity, they may exhibit locality. An implementation may exploit locality so that each computation unit primarily accesses local data, generating very few, if any, references to more distant data. Network architectures are well matched to solutions that exhibit locality. In a multiprocessor, locality may or may not be exploitable.

Techniques suitable for serial computation are often not suitable for parallel architectures.

One of the basic rules for doing parallel computation is to question the validity of algorithms used in serial computation.

PARKINSON: The greatest hurdle that a new programmer has to overcome is to learn to consider applications rather than algorithms. The last 30 years of application development have been concerned with exploiting the essentially serial nature of computer processing and finding methods which maximise the benefits to be gained by choosing a correct ordering. The advent of parallel computing means that many of the basic assumptions behind the algorithms are incorrect and that alternative ways of solving tasks are more efficient. The challenge for the application programmer is to discover the inherent parallelism in a task - a parallelism which has often been obscured by serial computer programming methodology.

Parallelism often exists in a problem but is not apparent at first sight. Parkinson illustrates this by studying the iterative solution of sets of linear equations.

PARKINSON:

$$x_{i,j} = \alpha\left[x_{i-1,j} + x_{i+1,j} + x_{i,j+1} + x_{i,j-1}\right] + B_{ij}$$

These equations are often solved by iterative methods where $x^n_{i,j}$ is the nth approximation to $x_{i,j}$.

The Jacobi method is obviously parallel.

PARKINSON: The Jacobi scheme computes the n+1 iteration from the nth iteration using the formula:

$$x^{n+1}_{ij} = \alpha\left[x^n_{i-1,j} + x^n_{i+1,j} + x^n_{i,j} + x^n_{i,j-1}\right] + B_{ij} \quad \text{all } i \text{ and } j$$

If we assume that we have an estimate for $x^n_{i,j}$ for all i and j then it is evident that we can compute all the x^{n+1}_{ij} quantities in any order as the values are not dependent on each other; hence the Jacobi iteration scheme is easily implemented on a parallel computer and can readily use as many processors as there are unknowns (N*M). Typical large problems may have 10^4 unknowns (or even 10^6 unknowns for the three-dimensional analogue) and it is easy to see that Jacobi-type algorithms will map well onto highly parallel DAP-like systems.

The Jacobi method is not attractive on serial computers and a well-known scheme is the Gauss-Seidel algorithm.

PARKINSON:

$$x^{n+1}_{i,j} = \alpha(x^{n+1}_{i-1,j} + x^{n+1}_{i,j-1} + x^n_{i,j+1} + x^n_{i+1,j}) + B_{ij}$$

This scheme has no obvious parallelism and is just one example of an algorithm developed to maximise the benefits of serial computation. The uneducated programmer will dismiss this algorithm as unsuitable for parallel computation as 'obviously we cannot compute x^{n+1}_{ij} until $x^{n+1}_{i-1,j}$ and $x^{n+1}_{i,j-1}$ are known and so only one value may be computed at a time'.

More careful examination reveals that this is false.

PARKINSON: Suppose we have an estimate for $x^{n}_{i,j}$ for all i,j then the iteration scheme only allows us to compute a new value for $x^{n+1}_{1,1}$ as indeed our beginner would deduce. Once $x^{n+1}_{1,1}$ is known then we have all the information needed to compute $x^{n+1}_{1,2}$ and $x^{n+1}_{2,1}$ so two points may be computed in parallel. Once these two points have been computed it is possible to compute $x^{n+1}_{1,3}$; $x^{n+1}_{2,2}$; $x^{n+1}_{3,1}$ simultaneously. In general it turns out that one can compute simultaneously all values $x^{n+1}_{i,j}$; $i+j = k$ if $x^{n+1}_{i,j}$ for $i + j = k-1$ are known. The 'one degree' of parallelism has immediately turned into up to N degrees of parallelism, ie a point at a time has turned into a diagonal at a time.

Further examination reveals even more parallelism.

PARKINSON: It is of the essence of the algorithm that many iterations are going to be done and therefore it is *not* essential to wait until one iteration is completed before the next is started. If we carefully examine the known data when we are about to compute:

$$x^{n+1}_{1,3} ; x^{n+1}_{2,2} ; x^{n+1}_{3,1}$$

we have computed:

$$x^{n+1}_{1,2} ; {}^{n+1}_{2,1}$$

which are the two values needed to compute $x^{n+2}_{1,1}$! We therefore may start the next iteration. Further study shows that when the diagonal $x^{n+1}_{i,j}$ $\{i+j = K\}$ is being computed then we can:

Compute the diagonal $K - 2$ for iteration $n + 2$
Compute the diagonal $K - 4$ for iteration $n + 3$
Compute the diagonal $K - 6$ for iteration $n + 4$

The end result of this investigation is that by overlapping iterations we can compute every other diagonal simultaneously and hence update half the equations. This simple study has taken us from one degree of parallelism to N degrees of parallelism to $N^2/2$ degrees of parallelism without altering the fundamental mathematical processes.

There are two major lessons to be learnt in using parallel systems.

PARKINSON:

1 Be careful not to make hasty judgements about algorithms because they appear serial in nature.

2 Be careful not to put artificial unnecessary constraint on subproblems.

This second point is most important; if the programmer insisted on trying to replicate the subproblem of computing x^{n+1} given x^{n} then the maximum degree of parallelism is N. The task is not just to repeat the subproblem a large number of times, it is to solve the equations and artificially constraining the real task can lose the parallelism.

Another way of expressing this lesson is to realise that although loops in serial programs are indicative of potential parallelism it is often the case that the innermost loop is not the best one to exploit and a reordering of the loops is often beneficial.

The potential gain from reordering the loops may be considered for the three loops of matrix multiplication.

$$c_{ij} = \sum_K A_{ik} B_{kj}$$

which in FORTRAN is:

```
      DO      1  1 = 1,N
      DO      1  J = 1,N
      DO      1  K = 1,N
   1  C(1,J)       = C(1,J)  +  A(1,K) * B(K,J)
```

The papers in Volume 1 of the State of the Art Report Supercomputers **(212)** *consider the problem in detail. The same material is covered in* **(200)** *and it is from this latter source that the quotation is taken.*

The first reordering of the loops is the middle product method which yields a parallelism of n and is ideally suited to pipelined vector processors.

HOCKNEY and JESSHOPE (200): The middle-product method is obtained by interchanging the order of the DO loops in the code. If we bring the loop over rows, *I*, to the innermost position, we have code that computes the inner product over all elements of a column of C in parallel:

```
            DO 1 J = 1, N
            DO 1 K = 1, N

            DO 1 I = 1, N
   1  C(I,J) = C(I,J) + A(I,K)*B(K,J)
```

Every term in the loop over *I* can be evaluated in parallel, so that the loop can be replaced by a vector expression. In an obvious notation, the code can be written:

```
            DO 1 J = 1, N
            DO 1 K = 1, N

   1  C( ,J) = C( ,J) + A( ,K)*B(K,J)
```

where C(,J) and A(,K) are vectors composed of the *J*th and *K*th columns of C and A. The addition, +, is a parallel addition of *n* elements, and the multiplication, *, is the multiplication of the scalar *B(K,J)* by the vector A(,*K*). The parallelism of the middle-product code is therefore *n*, compared with 1 for the original inner-product method.

If written carefully in Assembly language this method yields one of the highest attainable computation rates on the CRAY-1.

HOCKNEY and JESSHOPE (200): The middle-product method, when programmed in Assembler, is found to be the best code on the CRAY-1 computer. Supervector performance of 138 MFLOPS is observed. This implies that, on average, almost two arithmetic operations are being performed per clock period (one operation per clock is equivalent to 80 MFLOPS). This is possible because the multiplication and addition operations can be chained to act as a single pipelined composite operation delivering one element of the result vector C(,*J*) per clock period.

For array processors the better reordering is the outer product method which yields a parallelism of n^2.

HOCKNEY and JESSHOPE (200): The outer-product method is obtained by moving the loop over K in the code to the outside, as follows:

```
          DO 1 K = 1, N

          DO 1 I = 1, N
          DO 1 J = 1, N
1   C(I,J) = C(I,J) + A(I,K)*B(K,J)
```

The code can be replaced by a single array-like statement in which one term of the inner product is evaluated in parallel for all n^2 elements of C.... C stands for the whole array and we may write:

```
          DO 1 K = 1, N
1      C = C + A( ,K)*B(K, )
```

where the multiplication operation is an element-by-element multiplication of an $n \times n$ matrix made by duplicating the Kth column of A, and an $n \times n$ matrix made by duplication of the Kth row of B. The addition operation is an element-by-element addition of $n \times n$ elements. This is expressed in DAP FORTRAN by:

```
          DO 1 K = 1, N
1   C = C + MATC(A( ,K))*MATR(B(K, ))
```

where the function subprogram MATC(X) forms a matrix all of whose columns are the vector X. MATR(X) similarly forms a matrix all of whose rows are the vector X. Two functions are required because otherwise the coercion of a vector into a matrix is ambiguous.

The outer product is clearly highly suitable for a processor array that has the same dimensions as the matrices (eg multiplying 64 × 64 matrices on a 64 × 64 ICL DAP). In this case the parallelism of the hardware is exactly matched to the parallelism of the algorithm. Because the parallelism has been increased from n to n^2, compared with the middle-product method, the outer-product method is also likely to be superior on pipelined computers with a large value of $n_{1/2}$.

An interesting problem for array processors is when the dimensions of the matrices are small compared with the dimensions of the array.

PARKINSON: If the matrices which arise in a particular application are very small compared with the DAP eg 4 × 4 then the application programmer is encouraged to examine the loop within which these multiplications occur and look for ways to perform many multiplications simultaneously.

The problem of multiplying two 16 × 16 matrices on a 64 × 64 DAP has been studied by Jesshope and Craigie **(229)** *and summarised in Hockney and Jesshope.*

HOCKNEY and JESSHOPE (200): Jesshope and Craigie note that there are n^3 multiplications in the product of two $n \times n$ matrices (n^2 inner products, each with n multiplications) and that all these products can be evaluated simultaneously with a parallelism of n^3. The summation of the n terms of all the n^2 inner products can be achieved in $\log_2 n$

steps, also with parallelism n^3, using the cascade sum method. The equivalent FORTRAN code is:

```
      DO 1 I = 1, N
      DO 1 J = 1, N
      DO 1 K = 1, N

1     C(I,J,K) = A(I,J,K)*B(I,J,K)

      DO 2 L = 1, LOG2N
         K1 = 2**(L-1)
      DO 2 K = 1, N - K1
      DO 2 J = 1, N
      DO 2 I = 1, N

2   C(I,J,K) = C(I,J,K) + C(I,J,K+K1)
```

In the above, the first loop performs all the n^3 multiplications and the second loop evaluates the cascade sum.

For the case of 16 × 16 matrices on a 64 × 64 ICL DAP, we have $n = 16$ and $n^3 = 4096$, hence the parallelism of the algorithm exactly matches the parallelism of the hardware.

The above analysis of matrix multiplication techniques yields good parallel algorithms which are also good serial algorithms. Sometimes a good parallel algorithm is not a good serial algorithm. Parkinson considers the LU decomposition algorithm used in the solution of sets of equations $Ax = b$.

PARKINSON: Briefly A is decomposed into the product of two matrices $A = LU$ where L is a lower triangular matrix with unit entries along the main diagonal and U is an upper triangular matrix. Then to complete the solution of $Ax=b$ the following steps are performed:

y is evaluated from $L\underset{\sim}{y} = \underset{\sim}{b}$

x is evaluated from $U\underset{\sim}{x} = \underset{\sim}{y}$

.... If different right-hand sides are needed with the same matrix A then the LU decomposition need only be performed once and each new set of equations requires only $O(n^2)$ operations for its full solution. The result is so powerful and widely known that it appears natural to ask, 'How does one perform LU decomposition in a parallel computer and how does one solve triangular systems on a parallel computer?'. These are the wrong questions - the correct questions are: 'How does one solve sets of equations on a parallel computer?', and 'How does one solve multiple sets of similar equations on a parallel computer?'.

In particular, Parkinson considers the case where the number of equations is equal to or less than the dimensions of the DAP memory.

PARKINSON: The LU decomposition algorithm steps through the rows of the original matrix sequentially and subtracts a multiple of that row (the pivot row) from all rows so far unused. To implement this on a parallel computer with N rows and N columns requires fewer and fewer processors to be active at each step. The Gauss-Jordan algorithm substracts multiples of the pivot row from all other rows and so exercises more processors in each step. As a result after N steps (each with one parallel add, multiplication, and division) the LU algorithm produces the decomposed form LU but the Gauss-Jordan algorithm has produced the full solution. Hence the Gauss-Jordan algorithm is faster than the LU algorithm for the solution of a single set of equations.

There is no known parallel algorithm for solving a triangular system of N equations in N unknowns (using N^2 processors) in less than N steps (one multiplication and addition per step) and hence the solution of the equations $LU\tilde{x} = b$ takes twice the time than the solution of the equations $A\tilde{x} = \tilde{b}$ (by Gauss-Jordan) hence the LU factorisation is inappropriate. The situation is even stranger - not only is the LU factorisation not appropriate for a parallel environment but, if the problem 'solve, using N^2 processors, the set of N equations $LU\ \tilde{x} = \tilde{b}$ for a set of different right-hand sides, was posed, then a good strategy would be to compute $A = LU$ and then solve $A\tilde{x} = \tilde{b}$, which is the very inverse of serial computing practice.

When MIMD systems are considered, solutions for which the computation units are large are more suitable. Jones and Schwarz consider several techniques for deriving parallel solutions suitable for MIMD systems.

JONES and SCHWARZ (218): The first technique for devising parallel solutions involves noting when a problem exhibits inherently independent subparts, since each can be realised as an independent process having little or no communication with other processes. For example, a timesharing service can be implemented so that each user's work is performed by one or more parallel processes. Similarly, in a real-time control system, each different device in a factory can be monitored and controlled by a different process. In either case processors might even be dedicated to subsets of the processes.

For problems in which computation is performed on localised portions of the input data, a parallel solution can be constructed by *partitioning* the data and replicating processes, such that each computes using one partition of data. An example application for which this is a fruitful technique is reduction of an image by averaging the values of a contiguous set of pixels from the original image to obtain the value of one pixel in the reduced image....

Another alternative approach is *pipelining*, which is applicable if the computation can be divided into parts so that the output of one or several collected parts is the input for another part. Because each computation part is realised as a separate process, communication costs may be high unless communication is achieved by address transmission....

Note that the processes that result from pipelining are heterogeneous, while those resulting from partitioning are homogeneous....

Yet another technique that has been demonstrably useful is that of *relaxation*....

Processes depend on data produced by other processes, but iterations need not be synchronised; one process can use data produced by others in either earlier or later iterations. The objective of applying this technique is to reduce synchronisation, not to subdivide either data or computation in order to increase parallelism.

One more technique that deserves mention is the one flippantly called the *Chinese army* technique. Taking advantage of parallel processing, one creates a large number of processes, each performing precisely the same function, such as a search. When one of the processes achieves the collective goal, it notifies the others to cease this iteration and to reinitialise themselves for further iterations, if any. Note that no assumptions are made about localised, or even limited, accessing of the data by an individual process.

A frequently made statement about MIMD systems is that overheads prohibit the attainment of linear speed-up. Jones and Schwarz describe some recent work on Cm on the asynchronous parallel PDE solution.*

JONES and SCHWARZ (218): Theoretical speed-up is linear. Each point on the curve (see Figure 30) shows the speed-up of the PDE computation when some number of processes executed, each on a dedicated processor. When 18 processes were used, the computation

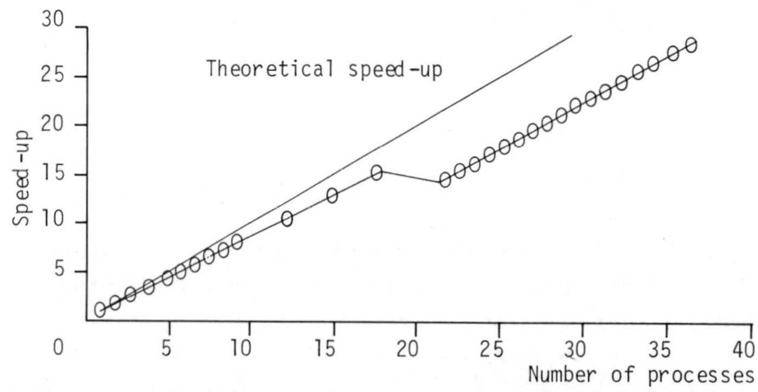

Figure 30: Speed-up of the asynchronous parallel PDE solution

was performed 15 times faster than with one process. With 37 processes, speed-up is 28. Note that as the number of processes increases from 25 to 37, the curve is rising in a roughly linear fashion. We believe that the 'hitch' in the curve between 18 and 22 processes derives from a combination of the Cm* architecture and the way the data was distributed.

In terms of performance MIMD systems do not appear to be very attractive. However, if reliability is a highly desired feature of the system then MIMD may be the best approach. VLSI technology may also increase the attractiveness of MIMD systems.

In SIMD systems such as a DAP, where the processors are single-bit computers, all the arithmetic is done by software. This can be very attractive as, for any particular problem or part of a problem, it is unlikely that the fixed length of hardware arithmetic will be optimum.

In earlier discussions of pipelined processors the disruptive effect of branch orders was found to be very severe. In these machines great effort has been put into the design of instruction fetching and buffering systems to attempt to minimise the problem. In fact it is this problem that makes the manipulation of long vectors attractive as the proportion of branch orders per arithmetic operation is much lower than with scalar operations.

Parkinson makes a very interesting point with regard to the DAP and problems with a high proportion of decisions or branches.

PARKINSON: The DAP is primarily a 'decision engine' and is therefore well suited to applications which require many data-dependent decisions. The realisation of this fact has been one of the most stimulating facets of our experience with the DAP. Initially it was felt that an ideal DAP problem would be one in which all processors would be kept fully occupied (ie problems such as matrix addition) and that performance degradation would take place if decisions required processors to be disabled. Comparison with other computers, however, shows that the relative performance improvement shown by DAP is greatest for problems with many data-dependent decisions. As decisions are implemented by 'switching-off' processors this leads to an apparently paradoxical result:

- Relative to classical serial machines the performance of the DAP rises as one switches off processors!

The paradox is resolved by realising that the measurement is relative and that what is really happening is that the performance of the serial machine is degraded by decisions and that degradation is greater than the degradation experienced by the DAP.

It is difficult to arrive at a precise value for the performance of the DAP. The machine at Queen Mary College London has now been in use for about two years and from looking at the applications for which there are results it would appear that the performance is within a factor of two, up or down, of a CRAY-1. This is very good considering the price of the DAP but it is, of course, for problems well suited to the architecture.

DISTRIBUTED COMPUTING

The attractions of homogeneous networks have already been covered in Section 2 and in Crook's paper. Non-homogeneous networks of large systems represent a good basic structure for specialised architectures for use by users with special problems. All users attached to such a system by either local or wide area networks can use any of the systems which could include conventional computers, pipelined vector processors, a DAP or similar array processor, a database system, an image processor, and any other specialised system that is developed. All will share the same mass storage facilities and other specialised high-cost I/O equipment. For very large centres, with large numbers of users from different disciplines, such a collection of interconnected different systems would appear to be an excellent solution capable of giving the best performance for any class of problem.

5: Applications

Current supercomputer applications in such diversified areas as the petroleum industry and the film industry are discussed. Special-purpose processing is assessed, with particular reference to image processors. Management of the knowledge database is a fundamental part of the Japanese Fifth Generation computer system proposals and of all intelligent knowledge-based systems. Database machines are examined in detail. Expert systems and PROLOG are also considered, together with the Japanese Fifth Generation proposals. Finally, possible future developments are discussed.

The only widely used supercomputers are pipelined vector processors and at the moment only the CRAY-1 has a large user base although some CYBER 205 machines have been installed and several more will be in use within the next year. We have argued that a pipelined vector processor could be used in a general scientific computing environment as well as on specialised applications. The application area of these computers is therefore virtually unlimited; a good indication of the range of uses may be obtained from the list of titles of the papers contained in an SERC report of work done in the last two years on the CRAY-1 at the Daresbury laboratory.

SERC (230):

1 *Time-dependent Hartree-Fock analysis of heavy ion collisions* J M Irvine (University of Manchester).

2 *Atomic calculations on the Daresbury CRAY-1* K T Taylor (SERC Daresbury Laboratory).

3 *Applications of the CRAY-1 for quantum chemistry calculations* V R Saunders and M F Guest (SERC Daresbury Laboratory).

4 *Studies of biological macromolecules made possible by the CRAY-1 computer* W C A Pulford and D C Phillips (University of Oxford).

5 *The electronic properties of solids* J B Pendry (Imperial College).

6 *Use of the CRAY for computer simulation calculations on one-dimensional magnetic systems* J M Loveluck (Rutherford and Appleton Laboratories).

7 *The CRAY-1S system in lattice simulation studies* C R A Catlow, A N Cormack, and J R Walker (University College).

8 *Simulation studies of water around biomolecules* P Barnes, J L Finney, B J Gellatly, J M Goodfellow, J E Quinn, and H F J Savage (Birkbeck College).

9 *Simulation of the interface between an ionic crystal and water* N Anastasiou, D Fincham, and K Singer (Royal Holloway College).

10 *Use of the CRAY-1 in plasma physics* T J M Boyd and G A Gardner (University College of North Wales Bangor).

11 *Use of the CRAY computer for research in astronomy* M J Seaton (University College).

12 *Simulation of particle problems in astrophysics* R A James (University of Manchester).

13 *NERC use of the CRAY-1 computer: an overview* D P Edwards (NERC Swindon).

14 *Tidal modelling carried out by IOS Bidston* N S Heaps (IOS Bidston).

15 *Climatic modelling at the University of Exeter* D R Davies (University of Exeter).

16 *Numerical modelling of the atmosphere at the University of Reading* B J Hoskins (University of Reading).

A few specific application areas will be quoted to illustrate the diversity of areas where the use of a supercomputer has proved to be a sensible choice.

The European Centre for Medium Range Weather Forecasting (ECMWF) and the National Centre for Atmospheric Research (NCAR) use a CRAY-1 to simulate atmospheric conditions using world-wide data in numerical weather models. The use of supercomputers in this area is proving to be very valuable - even more powerful systems are required. An interesting result in ship routing using the ECMWF computer has recently been reported.

CRAY (231): The shipping industry is one of many that benefits greatly from accurate weather forecasts. Shippers face the age-old problem of transporting cargo quickly and safely. Encountering poor weather conditions may slow a ship's progress or damage the ship and its cargo considerably.

The Royal Netherlands Meteorological Institute (KNMI) has provided weather routing information for transatlantic voyages since 1959. To date, the organisation has weather routed over 8000 crossings, evaluating surface weather patterns subjectively derived from the best available weather data.

More recently, accurate forecasts obtained from the ECMWF using its CRAY-1 system have provided substantial benefits in determining optimum routes for ships faced with adverse weather conditions.

As an example, let us consider the crossings of two large container ships that took place last February [*1980*]. Experience shows that the crossing normally takes about seven days for these vessels. However, the ships must avoid beam waves of greater than six metres in order to prevent damage due to excessive rolling.

Each ship set out following its great circle route, the shortest distance between two points on the earth's surface. By early 19 February, it became clear from the ECMWF forecast that if no evasive action were taken, both vessels would pass through a dangerous wavefield by the 21st. In order to avoid damage, the westbound vessel was advised to deviate to pass north of the high waves, adding about 110 nautical miles (nm) to the trip. The eastbound vessel was told to deviate to the south, with an extra mileage of 135 nm. Taking these modified routes, both vessels successfully avoided the high-beam waves.

Evaluations of the crossing were completed afterwards to compare actual wave conditions along alternative routes. The least-time routes were constructed for each ship, and the differences in travel time between the least-time route and the actual route taken by each ship was also computed. Evaluation showed that in spite of the extra mileage of the actual route, the westbound ship saved 10 hours and the eastbound ship eight hours compared with the great circle route. Furthermore, the westbound ship could have saved two more hours by modifying its route slightly a day earlier than advised. However, the eastbound ship followed a path corresponding closely to the least-time route.

In the Petroleum Industry reservoir simulation is extremely important and can lead to increased productivity.

CRAY (214): For any given reservoir, many different methods of extraction are possible. The petroleum engineer has the difficult job of determining which method will maximise recovery over time, and a mathematical model run on a large-scale computer is usually the tool of choice. A reservoir model solves the set of equations that describe the physical processes taking place in the reservoir in terms of background assumptions and operating constraints. By studying the effect of the various recovery methods, a petroleum engineer can estimate approximate total recovery.

The first step for the engineer in modelling a reservoir is to establish a basic description of the reservoir. The reservoir simulation enables an engineer to 'experiment' on a field by trying out alternative methods of recovery. The goal of simulation is to determine output quantities and costs for each of a variety of recovery methods. By analysing the alternatives, the most attractive development methods for a field can be identified before any actual production work is undertaken....

ARCO Oil and Gas Company was faced with a decision about the method of development to use for a Prudhoe Bay field on the north slope of Alaska. Analysis of the field on the CRAY-1 resulted in a decision that is expected to produce about 7% more oil. On a field estimated at over 20 billion barrels, 7% is extremely significant, both in terms of product and additional profit - enough to pay for the CRAY-1 a number of times over.

Computers are now used extensively in animation both for scientific applications and in the entertainments industry. The film industry has now moved into the use of supercomputers for animation.

CRAY (231): Digital Productions recently installed a CRAY-1 S/1000 at its offices in Los Angeles, California. The company will use its CRAY-1/S to synthesise realistic-appearing motion pictures of objects described mathematically. The digital synthesis of these pictures is so computationally demanding that supercomputer power was deemed mandatory.

Digital Productions plans to develop software and hardware to service the motion picture and scientific communities.... Digital Productions foresees a strong future in high-quality three-dimensional computer graphics. It expects to be able to display gases, fluids, and solids, depicting density and composition accurately.

Interactive two- and three-dimensional computer graphics is extremely important in many areas, (for example circuit design) and is seen as one of the major uses of the proposed PERQ/DAP workstation.

In a large scientific laboratory computers for numerical simulation are vital, for example at the Lawrence Livermore Laboratory.

RODRIGUE, GIROUX, and PRATT (219): At large scientific laboratories the computer has emerged, in the past two decades, as one of the most heavily used scientific tools. Detailed numerical simulations of physical processes substitute for actual experiments and predict the effects of known or extrapolated characteristics of matter and energy. Using simulations has several advantages:

1 Computer simulations are far cheaper than experiments.

2 Computer versatility means that a wider range of problems can be analysed.

3 The computer gives an understanding of physical problems that cannot be obtained from experiments alone.

Increased use of computer simulation has not, of course, eliminated the need for laboratory experiments. Rather, numerical models must be constantly improved to agree with experimental results.

The strong interaction among experiment, theory, and computation is shown in Figure 31. Typically, a prototype experiment is performed and the numerical models are refined until the computations are accurate. The interaction can, however, be more complicated: theoretical science develops mathematical models that computational science solves numerically; the numerical results may then suggest new theories. Experimental science provides data for computational science, and computational science can model processes that are hard to approach in the laboratory - particle fusion is an example of such a process.

Numerical modelling for large problems is almost always limited by the computing power available.

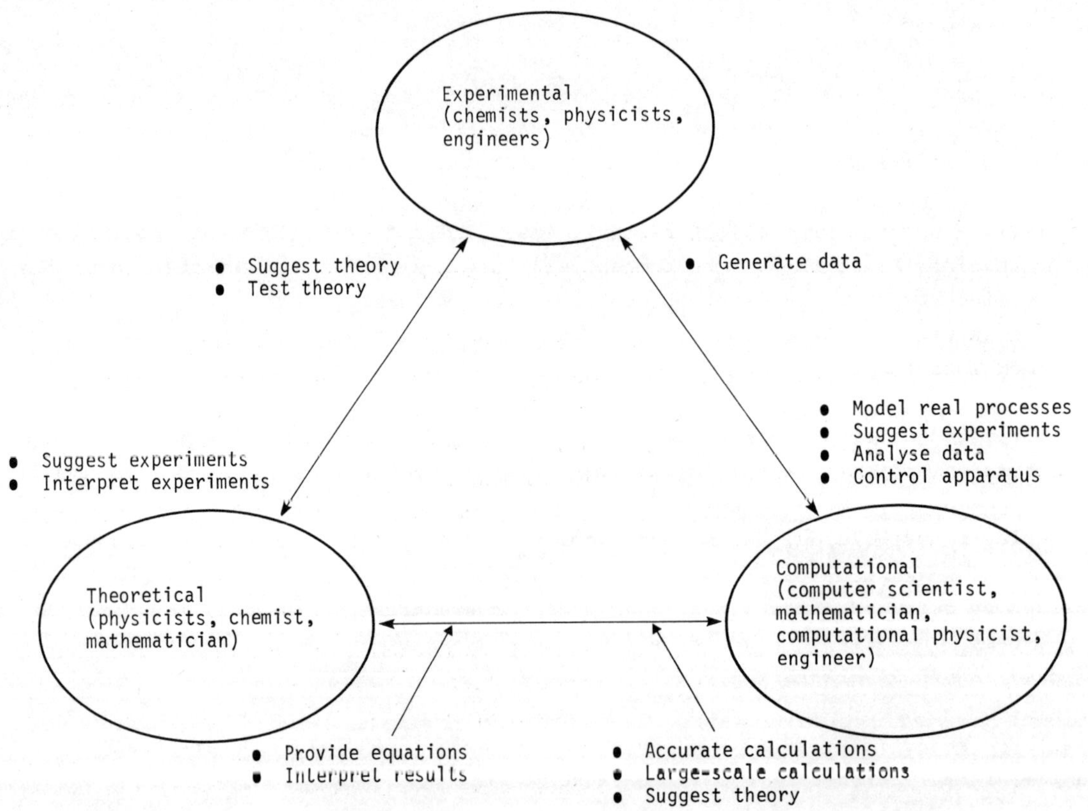

Figure 31: Schematic representation of the interaction among experiment, theory, and computation

RODRIGUE, GIROUX, and PRATT (219): Scientific computation at LLNL deals mainly with formulating and solving problems associated with the dynamics of large mechanical systems that are composed of particles (for example, electrons or photons) or assemblies of particles (for example, plasmas and chemical compounds). The particles in a system are too numerous to be counted, yet they do not form a continuum. Thus, the basic problem in scientific computation: how is a physical system represented in a computer whose arithmetic power and storage capacity are both finite? To solve this problem, one must make one of two assumptions:

1 The particles describing the physical system form a continuum and can be treated as a fluid.

2 The particles describing the physical system are finite in number.

With the fluid method, integral or differential equations are derived by applying the laws of Newtonian mechanics. Problems arise when we try to solve these integro-differential equations in the computer. With the finite particle method, mathematical models describing particle interactions are formulated; solution of these models yields the dynamics of the finite particle system. Here, computational problems arise in the techniques used to compute particle behaviour.

In either case, the complexity of the mathematical models is limited, at least in part, by the ability of the computer to solve them. Other factors to consider include accuracy of the solutions, computer hardware demands, and computational time.

That computing power will continue to be a limiting factor for the numerical modelling of fluid flow is clearly the case in the field of computational aerodynamics.

MAI TIN (215): Computational Aerodynamics provides a rapid and inexpensive means for simulating aerodynamic flows through the numerical solution of approximating sets of the fluid dynamics equations (Navier Stokes equations) using fast computers. This discipline emerged in the Fifties when electronic digital computers first became available to researchers, and now has become an important design tool, although it is not yet possible to design a complete aircraft from computer results.

There are both technical and economic reasons for accelerating progress in this field. The costs associated with wind tunnel experiments are increasing rapidly with time, as labour and energy costs escalate. More important still, the actual amount of experimentation required with each new generation of vehicle is increasing almost exponentially. On the other hand, the cost of computational power is decreasing with time, and the numerical methods for solving the hydrodynamic equations are continuously improving.

Figure 32 from **(238)** shows the evolution and current capacities of this discipline. The Stage I approximations to the governing equations neglect all viscous terms, as well as the inviscid non-linear terms. Such flow simulations can only complement experimental results in a minor role. The present (1977) or Stage II approximations neglect the viscous terms in the Navier Stokes equations, and therefore only problems in which viscous effects are not dominant can be adequately modelled with these equations. Nevertheless, this capability has provided engineers with a new and valuable tool, and in some cases results can be obtained which are impossible to derive from experimental facilities.

	Stage	Approximation	Computer class for practical 3-D engineering computations
I Past	Inviscid linearised (Sixties)	Viscous and non-linear terms neglected	IBM 360 CDC 6600
II Present	Inviscid non-linear (1977)	Viscous terms neglected	CDC 7600 STAR-100 CRAY-1 ILLIAC IV
III Next step	Reynolds time-averaged Navier Stokes (early Eighties)	No terms neglected turbulent momentum and heat transport terms modelled	At least 40 times current computers
IV Far future	Full time- dependent Navier Stokes (c 1990)	Subgrid scale turbulence modelled	At least 100 times requirement for Stage III

Figure 32: Stages of approximation to three-dimensional numerical aerodynamic simulations (from **(238)***)*

In the Stage III approximations, no terms are neglected in the full Reynolds-averaged Navier Stokes equations, although certain terms involving turbulent behaviour are modelled. Comparatively long computing times are still required. While the two-dimensional simulations take less than an hour on a CDC 7600 computer, routine computations of three-dimensional flows are not practical since about 100 times as much computation is necessary. With the improved turbulence models expected in the near future, however, this could become feasible with a computer only 40 times faster than current supercomputers.

The final stage solves the complete time-dependent Navier Stokes equations of viscous fluid motion. All turbulent eddies of signfiicant size would be computed, but small-scale turbulent motion would still be modelled, in order to retain a practical mesh size. This stage would only be reached if computational facilities are developed to meet the requirements of Stage III....

Much faster machines with considerably larger memories would be required to solve three-dimensional flows in a short enough time to be practical for routine engineering use. This time is found, from experience, to be about 10 minutes and the corresponding speed of the machine would therefore be at least 1 billion FLOPS.... This is the minimum speed, and assumes that future numerical methods are at least four times as efficient as they were in 1976. This indicates that the special processor for solving fluid dynamics problems must be at least 40 times as powerful as the current supercomputers.

These arguments led to the NASF designs of CDC and Burroughs.

Image analysis is a major application for array processors as well as for pipelined computers. Davies discusses the image analysis associated with a bolt location problem.

DAVIES: Thus the total number of machine operations for the complete bolt location problem would be close to $100 \times 256^2 \times 50 \simeq 300$ million. This implies that the recognition process would take of the order of three minutes on machines such as a PDP-11.

Clearly, this situation is unrealistic for real-time applications, and some form of hardware parallelism is required. One approach is to employ a parallel processor of the DAP or CLIP4 variety, which will handle whole image operations in one machine cycle. The other approach is to make use of the fact that many different image processing operations are being implemented in sequence on a given image, so that a type of pipelined processor would operate efficiently. The parallel processor implementation would be able to handle the bolt problem in about 2 msec, while an optimised video-rate pipelined processor would carry it out in about 100 msec.

The Goodyear Aerospace MPP project is an outcome of the need to process in real-time the LANDSAT-D satellite images. The data bandwidth is more than 10^6 pixels per second which leads to a processing rate of greater than 1000 MOPS. Most of the operations are on 8-bit integers which is why a DAP-like structure has been chosen.

SPECIAL-PURPOSE PROCESSING

IMAGE PROCESSORS

Picture processing, image processing, or pictorial information systems are all names used to describe essentially the same subject area. The interest in this area is now very great. A recent SERC Report (232) *refers to the strong support for Pattern Recognition and Image Processing (PRIP) in other countries.*

SERC (232): It is typified by the Pattern Information Processing Systems (PIPS) project in Japan. This 10-year project which commenced in 1971 with a budget of about £10 million per year encompassed the development of the theory, algorithms, software, and special hardware including VLSI devices. It focused on a number of case studies which eventually led to the development of commercial systems for character recognition, speech processing, image processing and recognition, and others. The chairman of SRC was very impressed with this project during his visit to Japan and asked the information engineering committee to consider whether PRIP deserved special attention over and above the normal responsive mode of SERC support. Efforts on a similar scale, albeit less publicised, are evident in a number of European countries and the US.

PRIP also plays a prominent role in the current long-term Japanese research programme - the Fifth Generation computer development project - especially in the areas of man/machine interface, intelligent robots, office automation, and medical care.

The same report stresses the importance of visual data and the many applications for PRIP techniques.

SERC (232): Visual data constitutes practically all the estimated 10^9 bits of information received by human sensory receptors every second. The list of applications where it would be desirable to aid or replace human perceptual processing of images by machine processing already spans every walk of life. Furthermore, all the time new imaging sensors are devised, and data not originally derived from images is increasingly presented in that form, thus expanding the scenic world beyond that naturally perceivable by man. There is no doubt that machine image processing activities should and will grow in the future.

The report lists some of the possible applications:

- *Remote sensing*
- *Astronomy*
- *Bubble chamber photograph processing*
- *Industrial inspection*
- *Robotics*
- *Medicine*
- *Material science*
- *Military applications*
- *Life sciences*
- *Man/machine interface*
- *Document processing.*

Davies indicates the expansion of the subject and identifies five separate areas.

DAVIES: After more than two decades of development, the field of Image Processing (IP) is still expanding rapidly and now has a large range of industrial, commercial, medical, forensic, space, remote sensing, military, and scientific applications. At the same time, the techniques of IP have crystallised into a number of rather separate areas of study including, in particular, image enhancement and restoration, image coding, image analysis for recognition, image reconstruction, and image database management.

Danielsson and Levialdi identify three areas which they then define.

DANIELSSON and LEVIALDI (233): Broadly speaking, IP can be broken down into three categories:

- Image database management
- Image coding
- Image analysis for pattern recognition.

Image database processing is, of course, dominated by storing, updating, and retrieval problems but could also involve magnification/demagnification, rotation, and other operations related to display functions. Image coding aims towards data compression and therefore could be an important and integrated part of an image database system.

Image analysis differs from the other two activities in the sense that it irreversibly reduces the image data to a set of features (first step) and eventually to a member of a small output set (second step). In some applications, the output set has only two members, eg GO/NOGO.

Davies has a wider definition of image database management and also has two areas not included by Danielsson and Levialdi, namely image reconstruction and image enhancement and restoration.

DAVIES: Image database management is a special discipline in which satellite and aerial images are normalised in orientation and size, and corrected for geometric and projective distortions; their borders, intensities, and colours are matched to help constitute a database which is then available (at least in principle) for a variety of geographic, cartographic, military, national, and other needs.

Image reconstruction is a highly sophisticated technique which aims to reconstruct detailed images of the interiors of objects from sets of projections, using, for example, transmitted X-ray beams. The method has recently become important, under the name 'computed tomography', for providing remarkable brain and body scan pictures....

Image enhancement and restoration aim respectively to make images more easily interpretable by eye and to restore blurred images (degraded by atmospheric disturbances, motion smearing, etc) to a form as close to their original as practicable. Thus these types of IP are concerned with obtaining improved versions of images, and specifically transforming one image into another. This contrasts with image analysis, where images are transformed into data sets whose outputs may include coordinates of objects, size and shape information, and so on.

Both papers concentrate on image analysis and have similar definitions. Danielsson and Levialdi adopt a simple two level computational model for image analysis.

DANIELSSON and LEVIALDI (233): The computational model we adopt is shown in Figure 33. It is partitioned into two distinct levels. The lower level performs operations like noise suppression, edge and line detection, and masking, all of which could be called filtering in the most general sense. Besides this function, the computer structure at this lower level must also be able to input image data and to convey output feature data to the higher level. These features are, for instance, grey-scale histograms, object counts, area and perimeter counts, or coordinates for detected keypoints. The features are evaluated by the higher level, resulting in a final output and/or a new-task command fed back to the lower level.

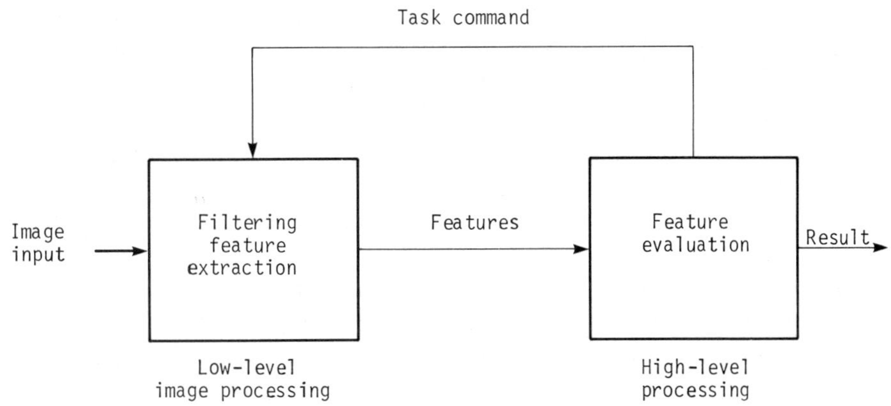

Figure 33: The computational model

Thus, implicit in the model is the fact that the higher level is in control of the lower level, including the image input. Furthermore, each command from the higher level defines an *image processing task*, which in most cases is allowed to proceed data-independently until finished. A low-level task can be very simple, eg delivering a histogram, or it can be complex, involving a sequence of sophisticated linear and non-linear filters, masking and other combinations among multiple images, iterative logical operations, grey-scale transforms, etc.

DAVIES: The complete IP and recognition system can be refined considerably by a feedback loop wherein the recogniser is able to pass instructions on specific tasks to be performed back to the image processor. For the purpose of the present discussion, a pattern recogniser may be considered as a device which accepts abstract input data and classifies it into one of a number of categories, according to the data set it was trained on.

The basic low-level operations are neighbourhood operations and global transfers.

DANIELSSON and LEVIALDI (233): Low-level operations can be categorised as follows:

- Image input and (for human interaction) image output
- Point-wise operations between two or more images
- Neighbourhood operations
- Global transforms
- Feature output.

Image input operations need no further comment for the moment. Point-wise operations are of the type ADD, SUB, AND, XOR, MAX, etc with two different images as operands. Actually, point-wise operations can be considered a special case of neighbourhood operations, with a neighbourhood size of 1 × 1 pixel, provided we allow enough space in each pixel for data from both of the original images. Neighbourhood operations are applied uniformly over the image plane and compute an output pixel as a function of a neighbourhood of input pixels. These operations encompass not only convolutions (linear filters with moderate-size kernels) and a variety of non-linear filters (median, zonal, direction sensitive, etc), but also logical transforms on binary images of the expand/shrink type (very often iterated). The number of published algorithms utilising neighbourhood operations is steadily growing. By global transforms, we mean Fourier, Cosine, Hadamard, and the like. For image analysis, this type of transform has proved to be of limited value.

Davies agrees that global transforms are not suitable for IP applications.

DAVIES: Perhaps the most basic function of IP is to generate one image from another. Clearly, the simplest way to do this is by a pixel by pixel copying operation. Convolution is an immediate generalisation of copying, which permits the output image to be closely related to the input image, while retaining a high degree of latitude in the form of the output picture. It is certainly not completely general in that (a) it is a linear operation and (b) its action is spatially invariant. While the latter property is normally useful in IP, restriction to linear processes may not be so relevant. On the contrary, linear processing precludes decision making and is therefore inappropriate for some image analysis and recognition tasks. Nonetheless, the simplicity of linear operations, coupled with the fact that theoretical analysis of their properties is mathematically tractable, results in their wide application in IP.

It is well known that the effects of convolution operations can be computed in the spatial frequency domain if their Fourier transforms are first obtained. In two-dimensional IP applications an initial conversion of an image to the spatial frequency domain is followed by multiplicative application of the transformed convolving functions, which is then followed by conversion back to the image domain. This means that three operations have been substituted for the original (single) direct operation, implying an increase in computational complexity. Indeed, it will be clear that this 'global transform' approach results in making every new image pixel depend on every pixel of the original image, rather than (as is the case for a great number of IP tasks) depending on a limited number of pixels in the neighbourhood of the output pixel. (This comment is also valid for the other well known global transform methods, including Cosine, Hadamard, Harhunen-Loeve, etc).... Thus there is likely to be a considerable processing overhead associated with the global transform approach.

This, coupled with the fact that linear operators are not decision oriented, leads to global transform methods being, on the whole, unsuitable for image analysis applications - especially those where real-time processing is vital. The areas where global transform methods do come into their own is in image preprocessing, image enhancement, and (particularly) image restoration.

Before discussing specialised hardware for neighbourhood operations it is useful to look at the descriptions of some of the basic operations given by Davies.

NOISE SUPPRESSION

DAVIES: Often, processing by global transform methods is unnecessary and indeed too computationally expensive for the task in hand. All that may be needed is the application of a simple neighbourhood operator which replaces the centre pixel of

```
1 1 1
1 0 1
1 1 1
```

by 1, and the centre pixel of

```
0 0 0
0 1 0
0 0 0
```

by 0, throughout the image.

Impulse noise of these two types (often termed 'salt and pepper' noise) can thus be eliminated conveniently by a simple recognition and decision process applied to every part of a digital image. There are numerous variants on such noise removal processes: one modifies the centre pixel to the value expressed by all but one (rather than all) of the surrounding pixels; another (which is a generalisation to cover the case of grey-scale images) prevents the centre pixel being greater than the maximum of the surrounding values, or less than the minimum. A very commonly used variant is the median filter which essentially orders the values within the 3×3 window and returns the median value, this being better than the mean value in that it has a less deleterious effect on image detail. In fact, the median filter tends to produce a more pleasing effect than normal averaging and also copes well with impulse noise. All these filters can be applied several times to give greater smoothing effect, though it will often be more effective to apply a larger (5×5) implementation of the same general process (eg for the median filter one finds the median value of 25 instead of 9 pixel values).

Low-pass spatial frequency filtering by global transform methods can be mimicked by neighbourhood operators using local expand-then-shrink and shrink-then-expand operations (for binary images) or local max-then-min and min-then-max operations (for grey-scale images).... While such operators are non-linear, linearised versions can be constructed by employing averaging convolutions, of the following form:

```
1 1 1       1 2 1
1 1 1   or  2 4 2   etc.
1 1 1       1 2 1
```

However, it is usual for the total weight to be normalised to unity, so that the average brightness of the image is unaffected by noise-filtering operations.

It should be noted that noise-removal operations can easily be taken too far, since there is a danger that edges and, particularly, texture will be smoothed out, thereby ruining later processing capabilities.

EDGE ENHANCEMENT

DAVIES: Broadly, edge enhancement means improving the appearance of images that have become degraded by some possibly unknown blurring operation. This can be achieved in the spatial frequency domain by suitable high-frequency emphasis filtering. However, a simpler approach is often permissible using the technique of 'sharp/unsharp' masking. Here the new image is formed by subtracting a deliberately blurred version of the received image from a multiple of the received image and renormalising, in an attempt to cancel the blur. The effect may be achieved by sharp/unsharp masking, using the following averaging convolution as the deliberate blurring function:

$$\frac{1}{16}\begin{pmatrix} 1 & 2 & 1 \\ 2 & 4 & 2 \\ 1 & 2 & 1 \end{pmatrix}$$

This crude method of emphasising high frequencies tends to produce such problems as 'ringing' (which takes the form of thin dark or light bands surrounding objects). However, applied carefully, it is efficient, effective, and useful.

Any technique of edge enhancement must, in principle, involve high-frequency emphasis filtering, and will therefore tend to emphasise noise: for this reason careful optimisation is called for.

Although Davies considers global transforms to be less suitable for IP he believes that a dichotomy exists which will have to be resolved before IP architecture can be optimised.

DAVIES: In this respect it is relevant to highlight an interesting dichotomy that exists in current IP methodology - that of traditional applied mathematical methods versus simple logical and integer operations on images. The former are typified by linear processing using Fourier transform techniques, curve-fitting by least squares calculations, shape description by moments, and so on. The latter are typified by shrink and expand operations, median filters, etc: they broadly consist of the 3 × 3 neighbourhood operations discussed throughout this paper. As noted ... the dichotomy sometimes holds implications about decision making and recognition processes. More often, however, it merely represents an alternative strategy for performing IP operations that has grown up largely by chance. Although it was implied that global transform methods are likely to be less efficient for image analysis applications, it is by no means obvious that traditional mathematical methods, which normally require inherently slow floating-point computations, will always be less efficient overall than processing requiring simple logical and integer operations. Until the dichotomy is fully understood the problem of optimising IP architectures will not finally be solved.

Danielsson and Levialdi also believe that IP architectures are still not well defined.

DANIELSSON and LEVIALDI (233): However there is as yet no consensus on computer architecture for general-purpose pictorial systems - not even for the somewhat restricted purpose of low-level image analysis. Also, there is a striking difference between the feverish experiments in parallelism in research environments and the fairly conservative approach taken by the commercial manufacturers. The reason is probably that the applications of image analysis so far have been restricted to a few areas such as particle measurements and pixel-wise operations on satellite images. When a more varied field of application matures (biomedical imagery, robot vision, automatic inspection, etc), new architectures will establish themselves more firmly

A very powerful SIMD system is STARAN which was under continuous development and refinement by Goodyear Aerospace from 1972. Those aspects of STARAN-E which make it particularly suitable for image processing are described by Potter **(234)** *(see Figures 34 and 35).*

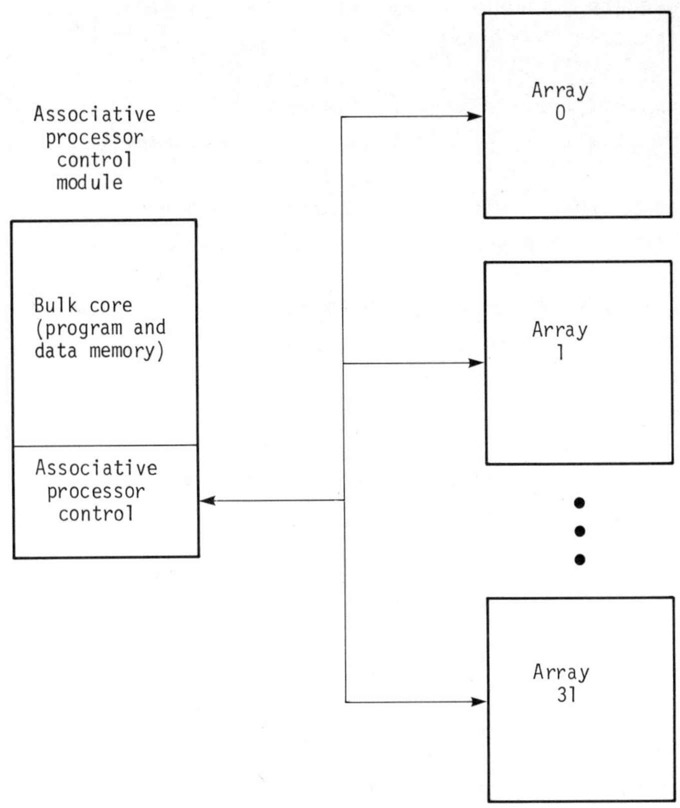

Figure 34: Basic STARAN architecture (reproduced from (234)*)*

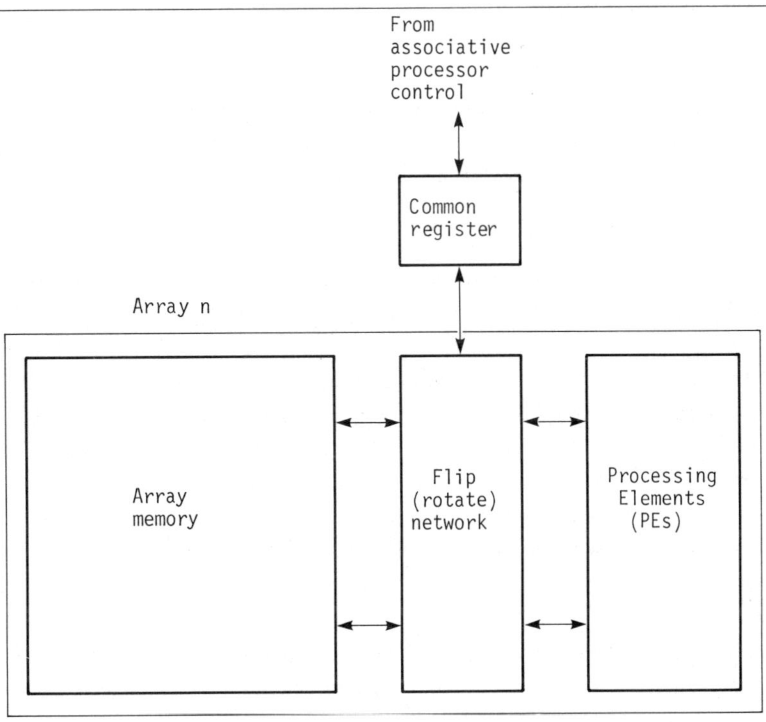

Figure 35: Flip network (reproduced from (234)*)*

There are 256 processing elements in each array, which gives a maximum processing capability of 356 million instr/sec.

Neighbourhood operations require pixel neighbours in the two-dimensional plane to be readily accessible. The flip network makes such operations very efficient.

POTTER (234): This network performs as a specialised shift register and provides great flexibility in accessing pixels which are spatially related.

In particular, the flip network can accomplish power of two rotates within power of two sized fields with no time penalty. This is, a 1-bit rotate in 128 2-bit fields; 1- and 2-bit rotates in 64 4-bit fields; 1-, 2-, and 4-bit rotates in 32 8-bit fields; on up to 1-, 2-, 4-, 8-, 16-, 32-, 64- and 128-bit rotates in one 256-bit field. This means that interword operations at these intervals can be performed in parallel at the same rate as intraword operations. Moreover, all interword operations can be performed with only a slight penalty.

STARAN is also good at parallel decision making and has the high-volume I/O facilities required for IP.

POTTER (234): The multiple datastream parallelism of the STARAN allows it to perform a 'serial' algorithm on up to 8192 data elements simultaneously. This is important in IP where large volumes of data are processed. Images are inherently two dimensional, but the large array size of the STARAN-E readily allows an entire 512 × 512 8 bit/pixel image to be stored in one array with essentially its two-dimensional topography intact. The array addressing structure and the array flip network provides easy access to every pixel and its neighbours in a simple efficient manner. The mask (M) register operation in an array enables complex decision processes to be made on any subset of pixels in an array. All of the above aspects of the STARAN's architecture would not be valuable if it could not be efficiently used. The three I/O paths into every array provide the capability to broadcast parameters and constants efficiently as well as loading and unloading image data in an expeditious manner. Thus it is apparent that many of the architectural features of STARAN are ideally united for IP and pattern recognition.

Goodyear Aerospace are currently implementing the MPP which owes much of its design to STARAN and also the ICL DAP. The MPP is to be used for processing satellite photographs.

DANIELSSON and LEVIALDI (233): The massively parallel processor is currently under design at Goodyear. It contains a minimum of 128 × 128 = 16 384 processors. For I/O MPP relies on two specially designed buffer memories called staging memories registers, with room for 2.5 Mbytes. In these, a scanning-fashion input datastream is converted to bit-planes of 16 384 bits each that can be shifted into the array at 160 Mbytes/sec. Thus, the staging memories can be identified with the two-stage interfaces of CLIP IV. But unlike CLIP IV, MPP has no special hardware for feature extraction.

The processing units are of the type shown in Figure 36. To each unit is allocated a 1K bit (provisions are made for more) high-speed RAM that contains the image data.

The processor is bit-serial, not unlike the one in CLIP IV, but is more oriented towards arithmetical operations. Only the four nearest neighbours are interconnected. The variable-length shift register greatly enhances multiplication. Estimated speeds for pixel-wise operations are exemplified by 6553 MOPS for 8-bit integer addition and 216 MOPS for 32-bit floating-point multiplication. The very high throughput rates

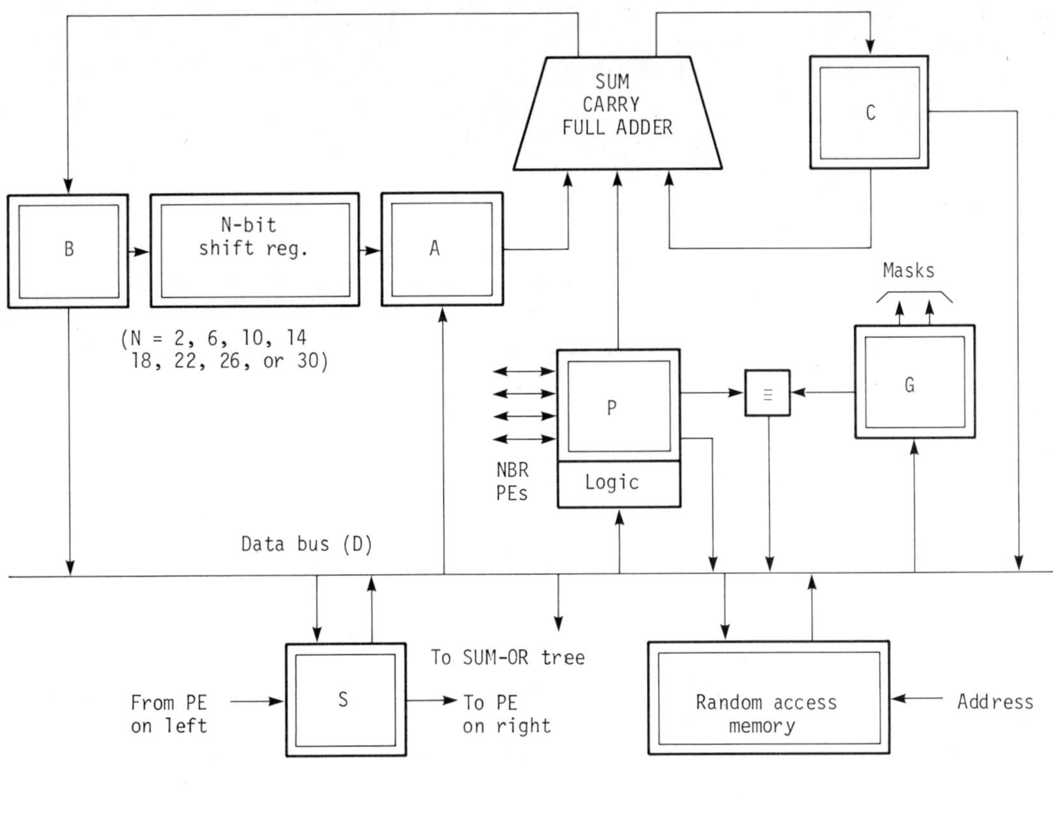

Figure 36: MPP processing units

result not only from the high degree of image parallelism (16 384) but also from the very short instruction cycle (100 nsec) that is anticipated. During this 100 nsec period, both data read/write and the operation itself must be carried out.

One of the early processors designed for neighbourhood operations in IP was the Perkin Elmer GLOPR which was a hexagonal grid so that each pixel has six equidistant neighbours. An enhanced commercial version of GLOPR was Diff3.

DANIELSSON and LEVIALDI (233): GLOPR operates on binary images only and utilises a hexagonal grid, therefore having six equidistant neighbours for each pixel. Image data is shifted into place, as shown in Figure 37, so that the parallel neighbourhood logic can get immediate and address-free access to all seven of the bits in the neighbourhood. This way of accessing a window is typical for all neighbourhood parallel designs.

GLOPR allows processing of up to 128 × 128 binary pixels and has proved to be successful in automatic recognition of white blood cells. The operation performed by the processor is based on the so-called Golay surrounds. In a binary hexagonal neighbourhood, only 14 different surrounding patterns of 1s and 0s exist if patterns identical after rotations are considered to be equivalent. In GLOPR, the programmer may specify the output to be 1 (or 0) for an arbitrary subset of the 14 surrounds.

Diff3, the commercial and enhanced version of GLOPR, contains four 1-bit 64 × 64 image registers, and for each operation an arbitrary Boolean function of any two registers can be used as input to the Golay processor. A typical utilisation of this point-wise operation is masking image A with image B. Thus, one could claim that there is a pipeline depth of $k_o = 2$. Diff3 also has image parallelism of degree $k_i = 8$, since

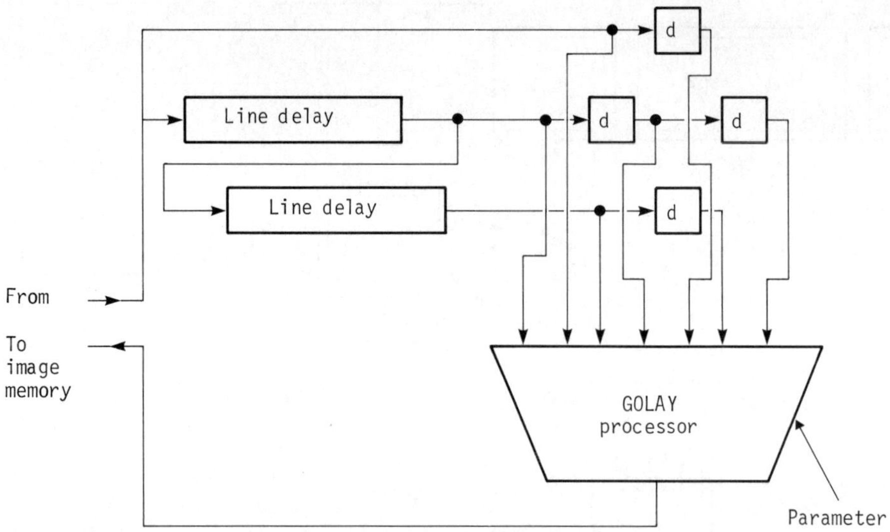

Figure 37: Placement of image data

eight output pixels are produced simultaneously with eight different processors. This can be accomplished by splitting each of the shift registers in GLOPR into eight shorter ones, as shown in Figure 38. The total parallelism of Diff3 is consequently $2 \times 8 \times 7 \times 11 = 112$. With a clock frequency of 5MHz, one instruction cycle takes $64 \times 64 / 8 \times 5 = 102.4$ μsec.

Diff3 is most effective for binary images. A grey-scale image can be processed only indirectly, by multilevel thresholding at the image input. Linear filters (convolutions) are virtually impossible to perform.

Pipelined vector processors of the CRAY-1 type have been discussed in great detail. Pipeline processors of a different type have been used in IP. One system with extensive pipelining is the Cytocomputer (Figure 39) which contains no less than 88 processor stages of one type and 25 of a second type.

DANIELSSON and LEVIALDI (233): The so-called two-dimensional stages are 3 × 3 neighbourhood, parallel processors performing operations on 8-bit pixels. They are similar to the logical processor of Picap I in the sense that the first step is to compare each pixel with an individual constant. In the Cytocomputer, this constant can be biased with the centre pixel value. After this transformation of the incoming 9 × 8 bits to a 9-bit Boolean vector, this vector is passed to a 512 × 8-bit programmable RAM for table look-up. Thus, any neighbourhood logic function may be implemented. Depending on the RAM output, either this output or the original centre pixel value is used for further processing (of Picap I). Finally, the two-dimensional processor passes this value to a second 256 × 8 RAM to deliver a final output from the stage. Obviously, each two-dimensional stage is a powerful device. Since each pixel represents 8 bits, it is possible to carry up to eight binary images along with the pipeline.

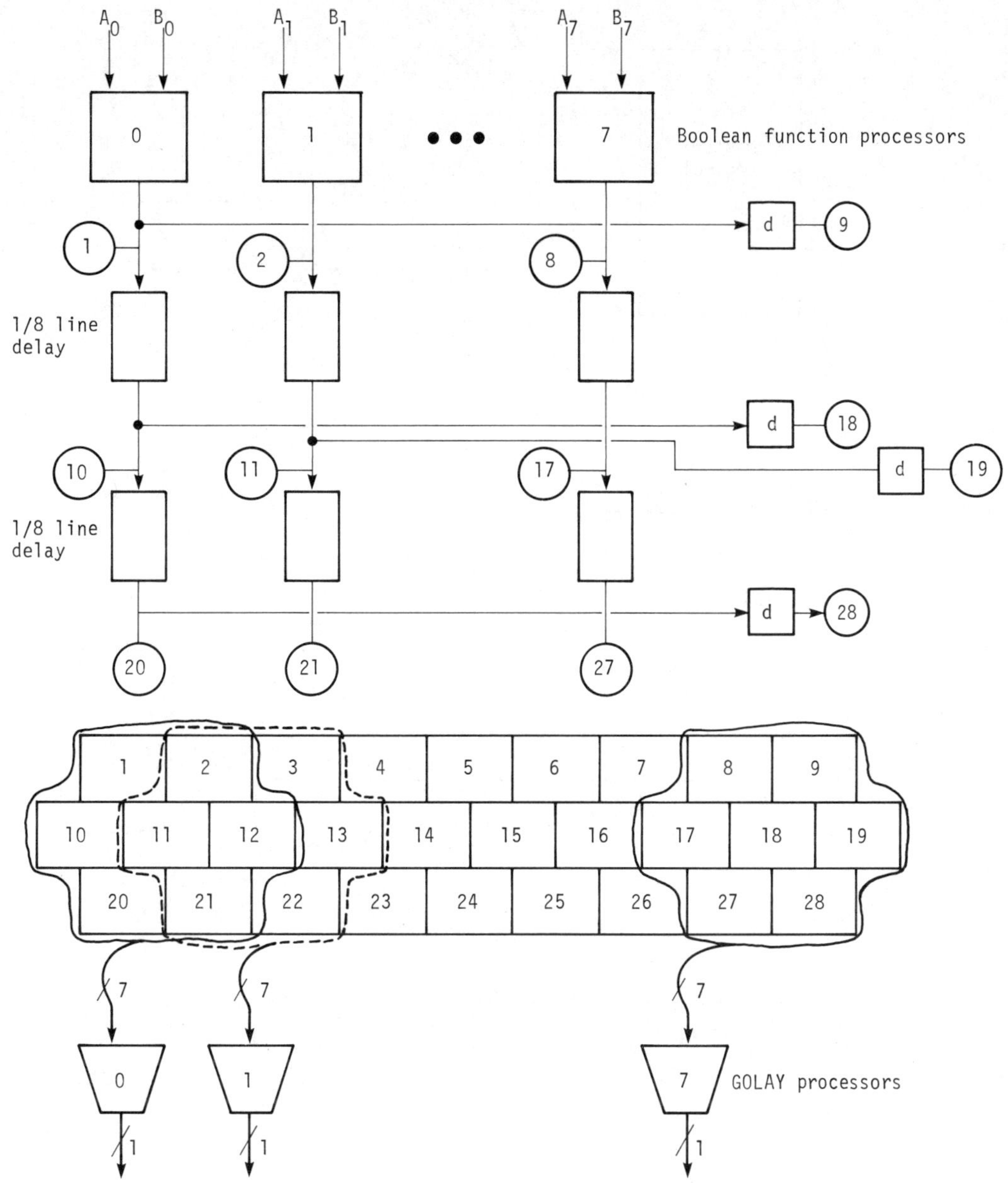

Figure 38: Splitting the shift registers

The so-called three-dimensional stages are more arithmetical in nature. From a 3 × 3 neighbourhood, each 8-bit pixel is incremented with an individual constant and also (at the programmer's will) with the centre pixel value. Next, the maximum values of these are retrieved. Finally, the output from the three-dimensional state is obtained by a table look-up in a 256 × 8 RAM.

The three-dimensional stages are not convolution processors. Rather, they perform operations that are motivated by the set algebra developed by Matheron and Serra. Sternberg has carried these ideas further (as have Serra and others) by considering grey-scale pictures as surfaces of a three-dimensional volume. Two fundamental transforms on binary images are expansion and shrinking (also called dilation and erosion). Their generalisation for grey-scale images are MAX (neighbourhood) and MIN (neighbourhood); these are the basic operations of the three-dimensional processors in the Cytocomputer.

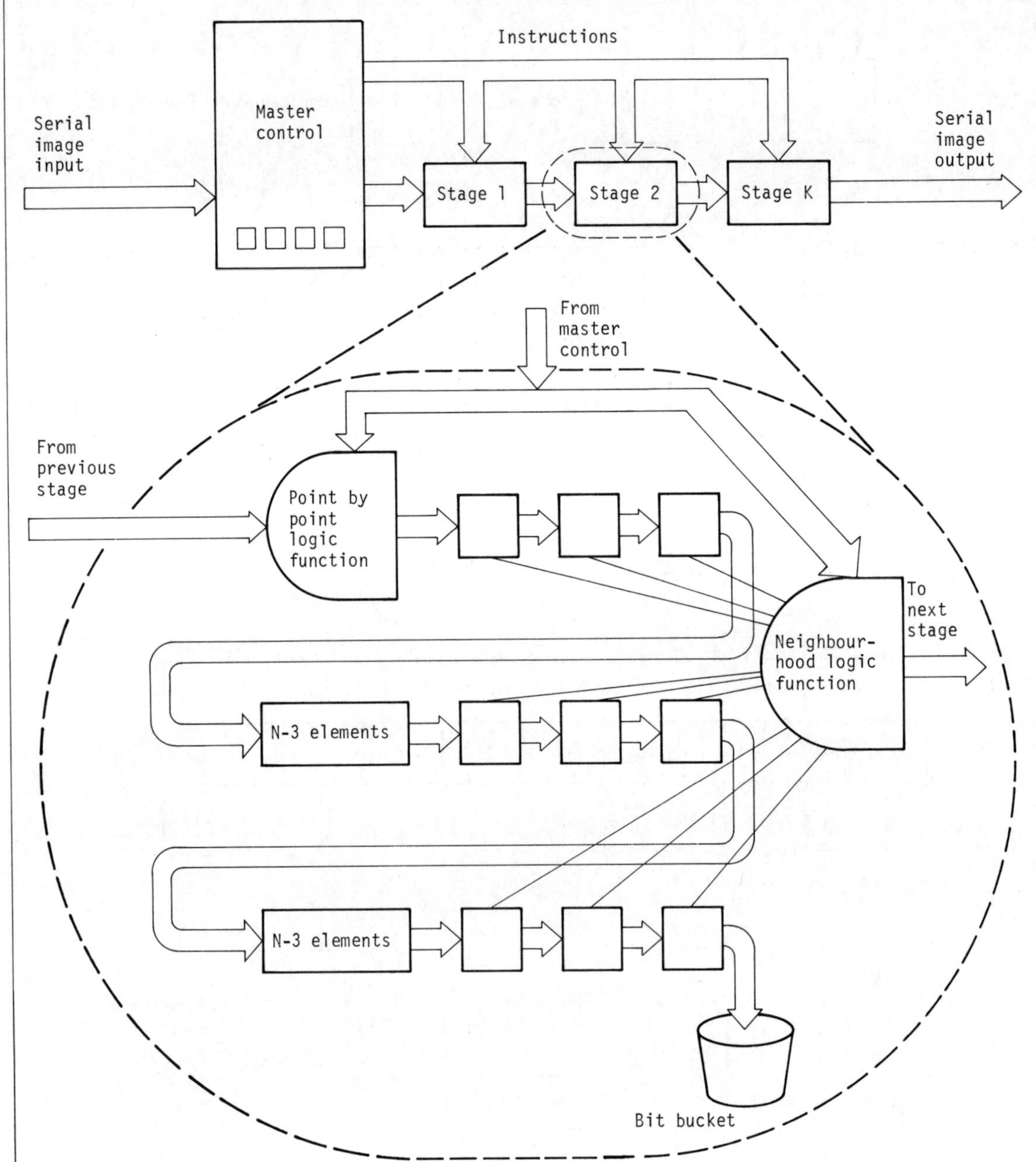

Figure 39: The Cytocomputer

The Cytocomputer needs an elaborate program set-up for each task. All the RAMs of the active stages have to be loaded, an operation said to require in the order of 1 msec per stage. The bandwidth of the pipeline is 1.6 Mbyte/sec. This means that a 256 × 256 image is processed with a multiple of operations in 40 msec.

The Cytocomputer is only efficient when the problem is large, in which case the total parallelism is 6336.

The first image parallel processor was proposed by Unger who suggested a tightly connected array of simple binary processors where the transformation of each point depended on its own state and the states of its four nearest neighbours.

One of the first attempts to implement such a structure was ILLIAC III which was a 32 × 32 array. Though never operational, it was a big influence on later designs. One design, the MPP, has already been referred to; another family of designs have been developed over the past few years at University College London. The latest in the series is CLIP IV which is an array of 96 × 96 identical processors each having the structure shown in Figure 40. The operation of CLIP IV is summarised in the paper by Danielsson and Levialdi.

DANIELSSON and LEVIALDI (233): In the centre is an array of 96 × 96 processors, which is surrounded by a data-shuffling system that interfaces the array to scanning I/O devices. A selected 96 × 96 × 6-bit window of the TV frame is first stored in six long shift registers, one for each bit-plane. One such bit-plane is then converted back to a 96 × 96 square format that can be shifted over the edge into the two-dimensional array. The necessity for extra I/O hardware is not unique for CLIP IV but rather is typical for image-parallel processors. But CLIP IV also has a unique feature-extraction output in the form of a summing pyramid tree connected to one of the edges. A complete bit-count is obtained by shifting out one bit-plane.

The processor array itself consists of bit-serial processors of the type shown in Figure 41. A common instruction/control bit-vector is broadcast to all processors, which run in perfect synchronism. The local memory of a processor consists of 32 1-bit registers, two general 1-bit registers (A and B), and a carry register (C). All processors are connected to their eight nearest neighbours. Either the neighbourhood logic or the B-output can be used as the second operand to the Boolean processor. Any possible two-input function can be generated. Furthermore, the other gates enable the CLIP processor to perform the full-adder function.

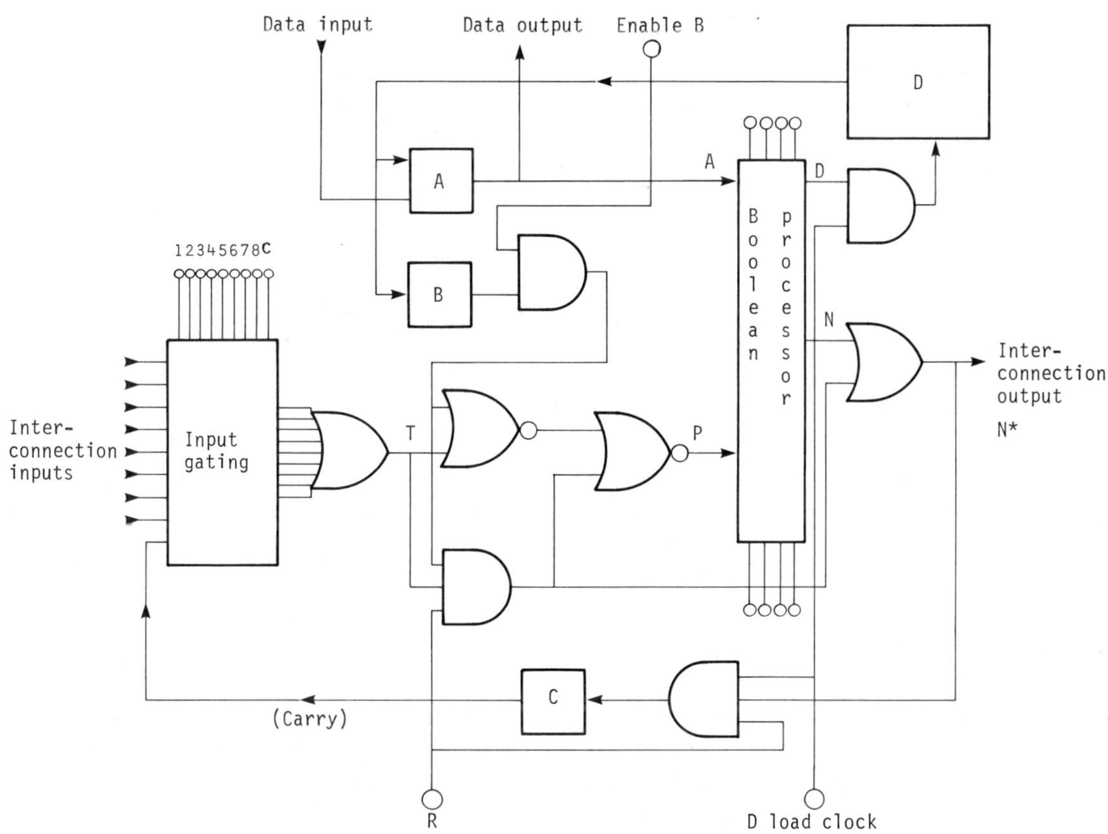

Figure 40: The CLIP IV logic and memory structure

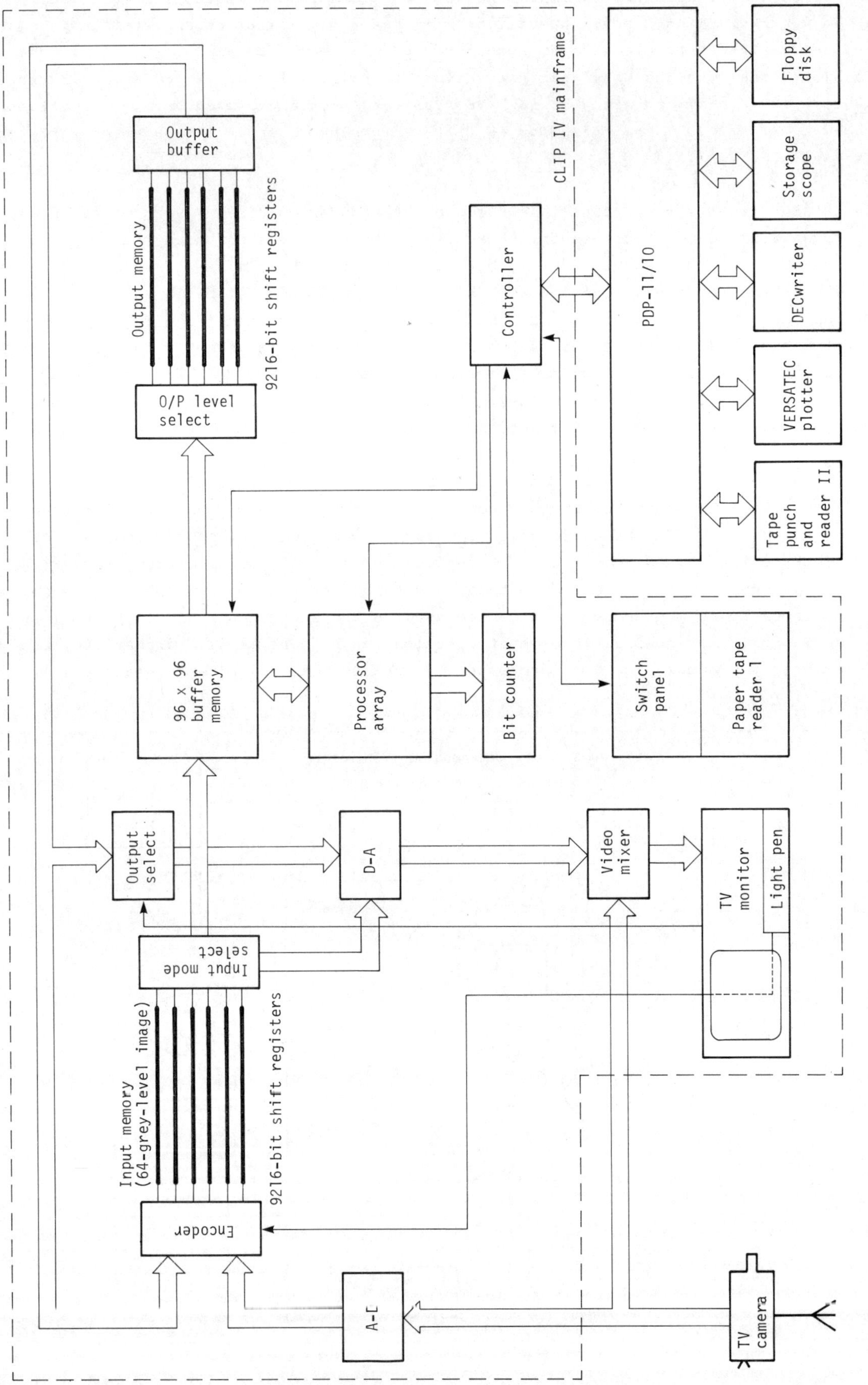

Figure 41: CLIP IV image-parallel machine

The processor is seen to be extremely simple, and the power of the system relies simply upon the fact that there are no fewer than 9216 copies of them. For binary 3 × 3 logic operations, CLIP IV is indeed very fast, and operations of the shrink/expand type are performed in only one instruction cycle. A more complicated thinning algorithm iterated six times takes about 1 msec.

Another classification of IP is bus oriented.

DANIELSSON and LEVIALDI (233): Some IP systems possess architectures that are more or less dominated by a bus structure that enables flexible communication between memory on the one hand and input, output, and processors on the other. All these systems contain several processors - sometimes different ones for different types of operations, sometimes identical processors for a multitude of operation types. In any case, these processors fetch data from a fairly large image memory and proceed sequentially over the image plane. This does not mean that we do not find parallelism in these systems. On the contrary, all four types of parallelism can be found in different versions and combinations.

The number of new IP systems has been growing almost explosively in recent years, especially in the academic environment.

Two systems will be described briefly: TOSPICS and Picap II. For TOSPICS, an overall block diagram (Figure 42) and a more detailed block diagram of the parallel pattern processor (Figure 43) are given in the paper by Mori et al.

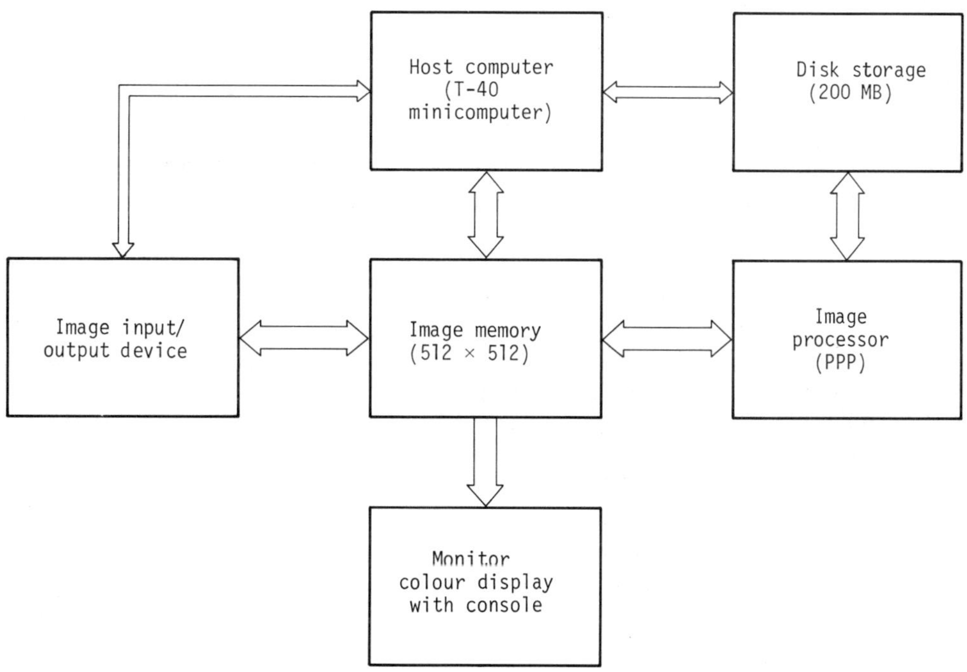

Figure 42: TOSPICS block diagram (reproduced from **(236)***)*

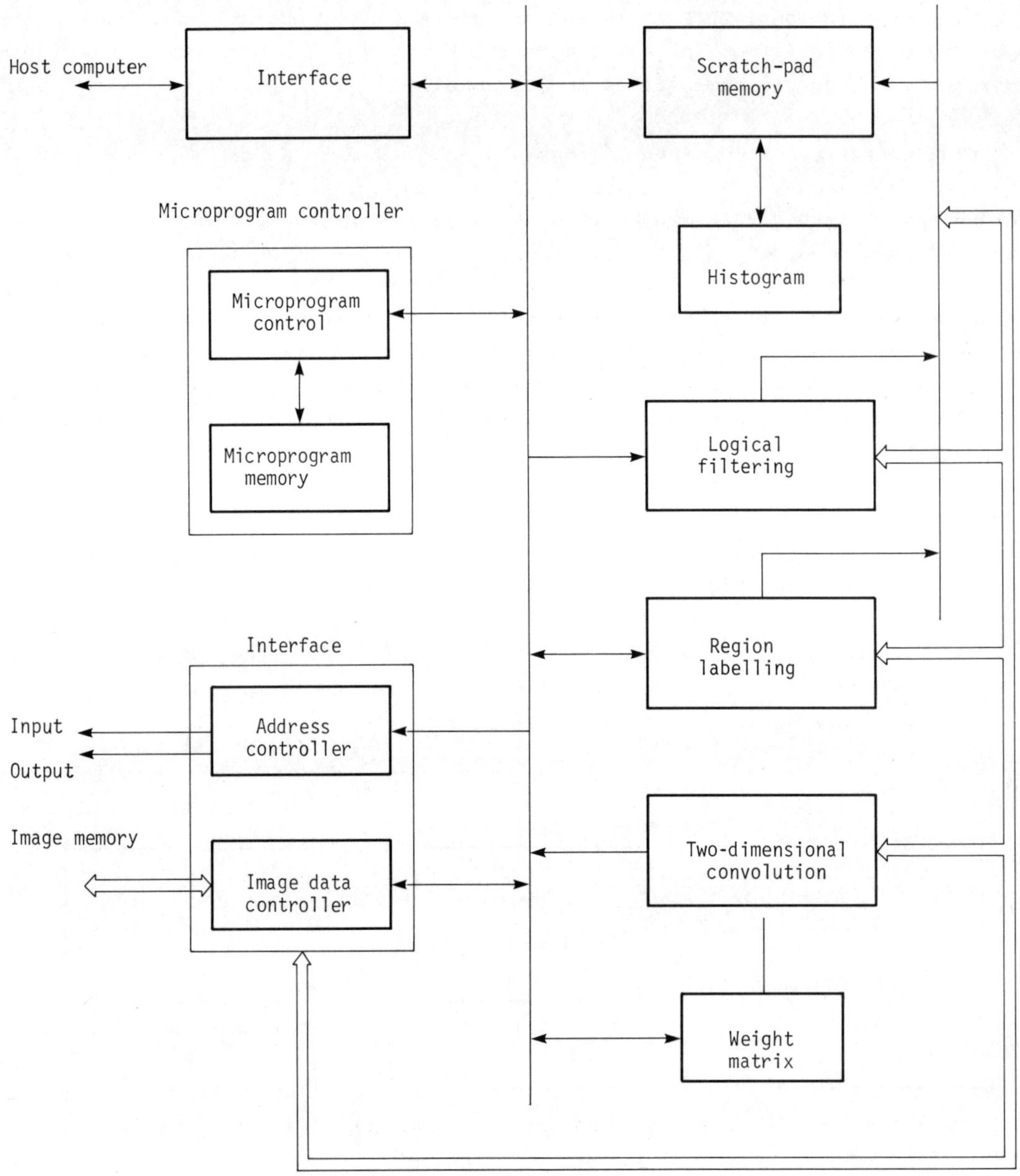

Figure 43: Local parallel pattern processor block diagram (reproduced from (236)*)*

MORI *et al* **(236)**: The Parallel Pattern Processor (PPP) includes seven special-purpose modules for two-dimensional convolution, point mapping, linear coordinate transformation, logical filtering, histogram generation, region labelling, and pixel operations. These functions can be combined for more global and complex functions such as texture analysis, shape identification, region separation, and so on. By using dynamically rewritable microprogram architecture, powerful and flexible programs of image processing were designed and demonstrated in the interactive IP system TOSPICS.

The host computer in TOSPICS is a minicomputer TOSBAC-40C with 64K bytes of memory. The image memory, the TOSPICS pivot, consists of four layers of 512 × 512 pixels, 8 bit per pixel, and four planes of 512 × 512 binary graphic memory. The two-dimensional convolution module includes a buffer memory of a shift register and a weighting matrix memory. The shift register storing the image data of n lines enables a parallel accessing of $n \times n$ image data for the local parallel calculations. The

512-byte scratch-pad memory is needed for table look-up operations in logical filtering, point mapping, and region labelling. It is also used as 256 registers of 16 bit length in histogram generation.

The image memory is connected to the high-speed bus in the PPP, which has a transfer rate of 4 Mbyte/sec. The interface to the image memory has two address controllers which independently calculate the input and output memory addresses and transfer image data simultaneously to or from any image memory layer or graphic plane. Those address controllers are used for the linear coordinate transformation of image data. They are capable of calculating next memory addresses automatically and checking the boundary of image data.

The microprograms and execution commands are transferred through the interface from the host computer with a set of parameters to execute those programs and commands. The processed image data is usually transferred to an image output device, but data can also be stored in the disk memory for the higher level processing, such as image understanding.

Picap II has been developed at Linköping University (Figure 44). Its principal feature is a very high-speed bus with a basic cycle time of 100 nsec. Another interesting feature is that the multiple processors can, in fact, operate as an MIMD architecture.

DANIELSSON and LEVIALDI (233): The basic bus cycle time is 100 nsec and this timeslot can be grabbed by any of the active units (called processors) that are connected to the bus. The data width of the bus is 32 bits in both directions (to and from the memory); hence, a gross data rate of 40 Mbyte/sec is possible. Contention problems are automatically resolved for each memory access on a fixed priority basis, but because of the high total bandwidth of the bus, the activity of one processor is normally completely transparent to another. The physical extension of the bus is on the order of one metre.

The memory (4 Mbytes) is divided into 16 modules that are activated independently of each other. However, all images are distributed over the modules by normal address interleaving, so that the whole memory constitutes one single linear address space.

The processors are activated by the host computer, which delivers parameters (and sometimes also microcode) over a control bus. After completion of an instruction, a processor signals back to the host and (in some cases) delivers feature data. The processors in Figure 44 are simply drawn as blank boxes, but normally they are all different and are specialised for different functions (compare TOSPICS). But unlike TOSPICS, each processor has its own microcontrol and address generator. Thus, Picap II is capable of multiple-instruction multiple-datastream processing, orchestrated by the host computer. The bus allows 15 processors to be connected. Among those operational in mid-1981 are a video input processor, a display processor, an interface to a high-capacity, high-speed disk memory, and a filter processor.

The need for very high-performance special-purpose processors for IP has already been established. The needs, however, will continue to expand and it is probably true to say that architectures for IP will be one of the most important activities over the next 10 years. An indication of the possible processing and memory requirements is given in a paper by Nudd **(237)** *(see Figure 45).*

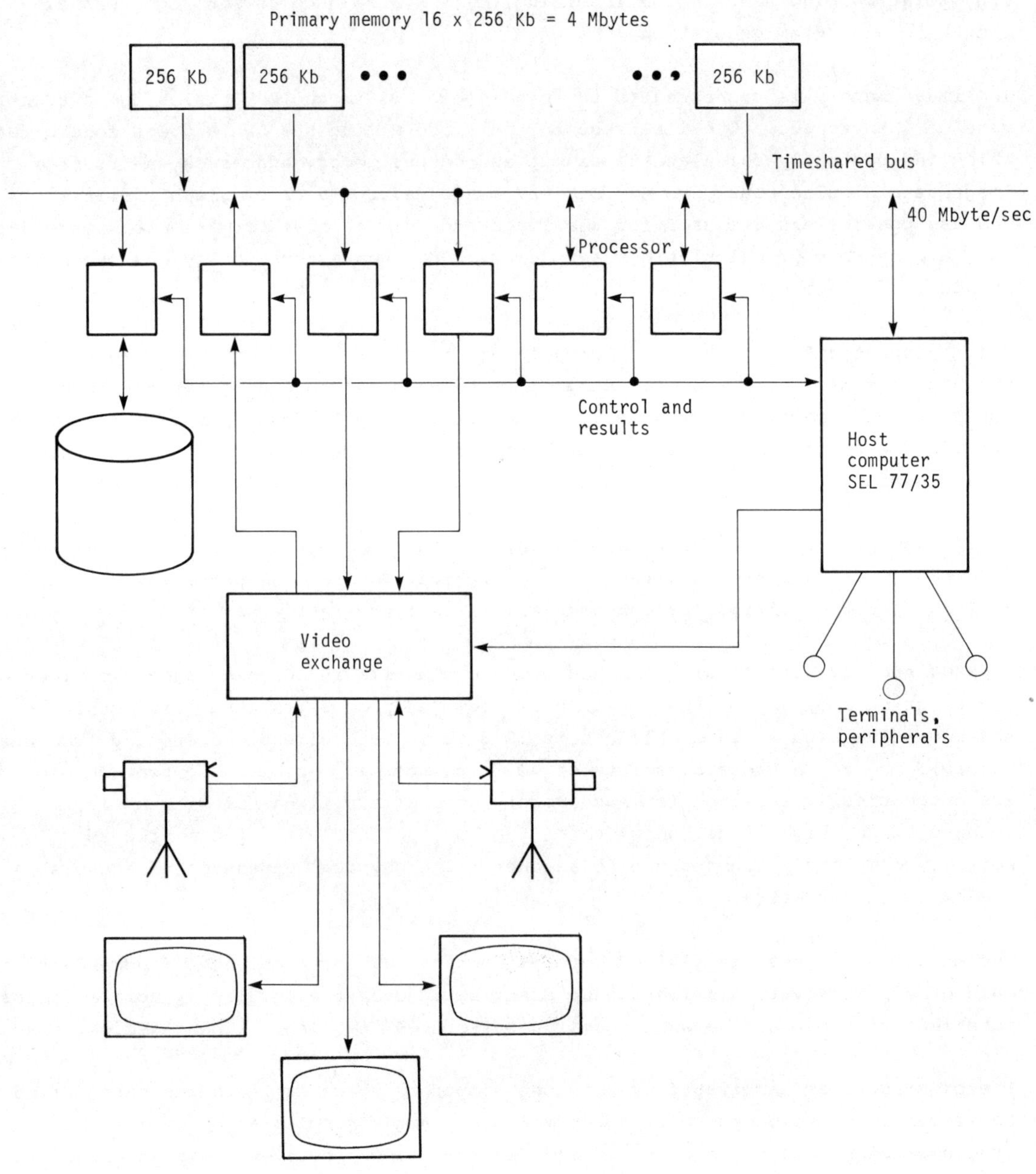

Figure 44: Linkoping's Picap II

The developing area of computed tomography will require considerable computing power and possible new architectures as the problem is the processing of three-dimensional digital images. The basic element is now a voxel, short for volume element, which is the three-dimensional equivalent of a pixel. In two-dimensional operations three tessellations are possible, whereas in three-dimensional only the cube yields close-packed tessellation. A single voxel will have either six face neighbours, 18 face and edge neighbours, or 26 face, edge, and vertex neighbours. The problems of data representation and the complexity of computing are obviously great.

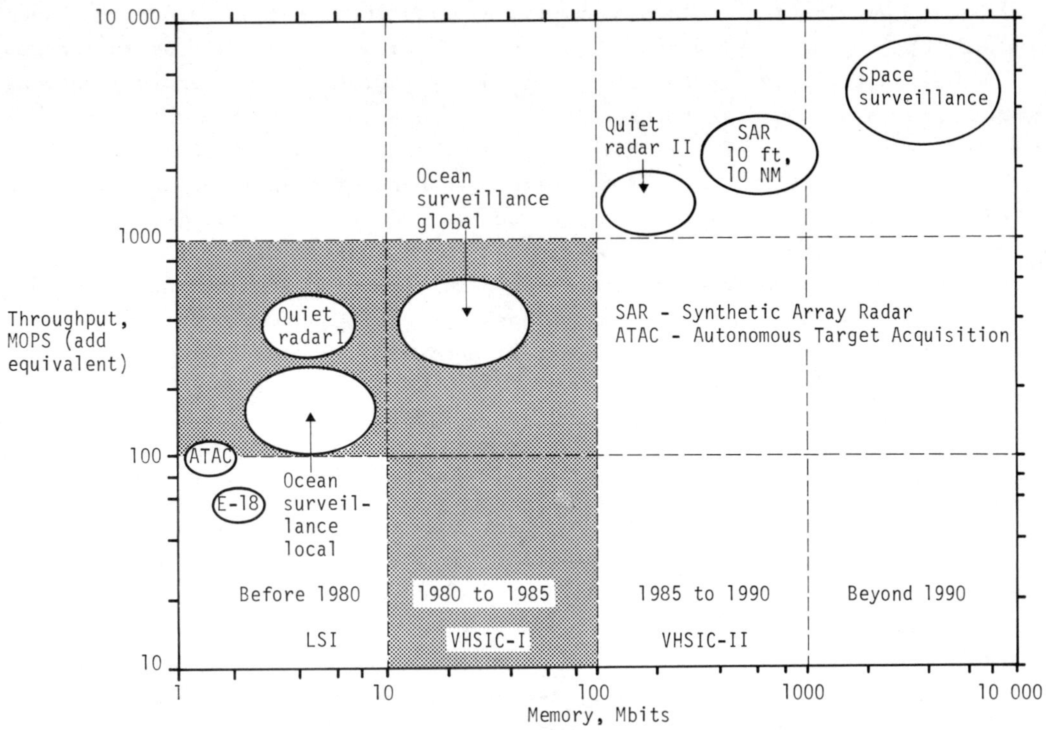

Figure 45: Estimation of processing and memory requirements for potential military systems

DATABASE MACHINES

The management of databases has become increasingly important during recent years and it will be seen in a later section that management of the knowledge database is a fundamental part of the Japanese Fifth Generation proposals and of all intelligent knowledge-based systems.

In many commercial organisations the management of the database has become one of the most time-consuming activities.

MARYANSKI (238): The introduction of generalised database management systems in the late Sixties resulted in a substantial increase in the capabilities of business data processing installations. Unfortunately, this increase in data processing capability has stimulated a corresponding increment in the demand for services. As a result many installations have reached the point of resource saturation. The obvious, yet increasingly unappealing, recourse to saturation is a mainframe upgrade. A recently devised alternative to such an upgrade is the offloading of database management functions from an existing mainframe to a directly attached minicomputer. This alternative configuration is known as a back-end database management system (DBMS).

The movement of computing from numeric manipulation to data manipulation is recognised by Su et al **(239)**, *who also point out the unsuitability of the von Neumann architecture to this type of activity.*

SU *et al* **(239)**: The primary application for digital computers is shifting from numeric to non-numeric applications. In non-numeric applications, the user retrieves and manipulates data by specifying the attributes and values of the data he is interested in, ie addressing data by contents, rather than by addressing the memory locations where the interested data is stored. The basic operations required are SEARCH, RETRIEVE, UPDATE, INSERT, DELETE, MOVE-DATA, etc, rather than ADD, SUBTRACT, SHIFT, etc. The mismatch of the von Neumann design to non-numeric applications is the main cause of the complexity and inefficiencies of the present systems. The large and growing market for database systems warrants a re-evaluation of the relationship between technology and database applications. If technology can be matched more closely to database applications, then perhaps advanced functionality, ease-of-use, and data independence can be achieved cost effectively.

Most database management operations can be done in parallel and the conventional sequential machine is not appropriate.

SU *et al* **(239)**: In all considerations however, the most serious drawback is the lack of appropriateness of the sequential machine for the parallel process of data manipulation. One can liken this to the analogy of viewing a three-dimensional cube on a two-dimensional surface. Some forms are still recognisable: However, many others are skewed and hence do not appear 'normal'. So it is with processors. The software problems become necessarily more complex, simply because the representation is not appropriate. By providing a more appropriate environment, perhaps the 'skewedness' of present problems can be reduced.

While new architectures are desirable it is interesting to note the view expressed by Maryanski in 1980 when discussing back-end DBMSs, which will be covered in more detail later in this section.

MARYANSKI (238): Since the development of the first prototype back-end DBMS by Canaday *et al* at Bell Laboratories many commercial and research groups have evaluated and prototyped similar systems. However, according to the definitions presented here, the author is unaware of any back-end DBMS available in the market-place.

The arguments for implementing the functions in hardware are very strongly made by Su et al *both in terms of performance and increasing sophistication.*

SU *et al* **(239)**: There seem to be two major performance bottlenecks in the present systems: the staging bottleneck and the communication bottleneck. In conventional systems, data is not stored at the place where it is processed. To 'stage' data into main memory for processing is very time consuming, and often ties up the important resources of a computing system, such as communication channels. Database applications will continue to demand larger and more complicated databases, requiring more time to stage and process the data files. In order to support very large databases (greater than 10^{10} bytes), or databases requiring both fast update and/or complex query, it is necessary to exploit specialised hardware to eliminate unnecessary data staging and to carry out database management functions efficiently. Data communication over long distances is expensive and limited in speed. This forces many database systems to physically distribute data to locations where usage is highest. Data redundancy is often purposefully introduced in distributed systems to avoid excess amounts of data transfer and to improve performance and reliability. However, many additional problems on data updating, recovery, integrity, and security in distributed systems are introduced by the above techniques. Special-purpose hardware tailored toward managing distributed database management and supporting data communication would be very useful....

DBMS users are continuously demanding more sophisticated DBMS capabilities. Capabilities such as automatic database restructuring and system tuning, automatic data distribution and redistribution, back-up and recovery, integrity and security controls, etc are generally handled by software in the traditional systems. Tremendous overhead is generated in implementing these capabilities. Because systems are currently pushing software complexity barriers, performance improvements in this area are not likely without dedicating hardware to unburden saturated systems.

Similar arguments are advanced by Berra who also lists the desirable elements of a DBMS.

BERRA: One field that has received increased attention *vis-à-vis* movement of software functions to hardware is the database management field. Owing to size and complexity, managing databases becomes increasingly difficult. Over the past few years, increasing effort has been expended in the study of new types of hardware called database machines which are designed solely for the purpose of managing data. This research has been driven by the decreasing cost of hardware *and* by the need for performance improvements due to increased database size and complexity and a maturing database theory.

The desirable attributes of a database management environment include the following:

- Large capacity storage which is both modular and low in cost per bit
- Ease of mapping between the conceptual schemata and the internal schema
- Variable length data formats
- Fast retrieval and update of data
- Content search operations such as 'equal to', 'greater than or equal to', 'less than or equal to' etc
- Context search such as and, or and not
- Complete instruction sets which are conceived with database management functions in mind.

Specialised database machines make extensive use of parallel techniques and can be placed clearly in the supercomputer class as defined by the number of operations per second. They are an excellent example of specialised architectures, designed to fit the structure of the problem, that achieve high performance as a result of the accuracy of this matching.

Current work on database machines is divided by Berra into six categories and this classification will be used in presenting the ideas of Berra and other workers. The first classification has already been referred to, namely back-end database systems. Maryanski introduces the concept of a back-end system by first considering the operation of application programs on a database in a single machine environment, which he identifies as having six major components (see Figure 46).

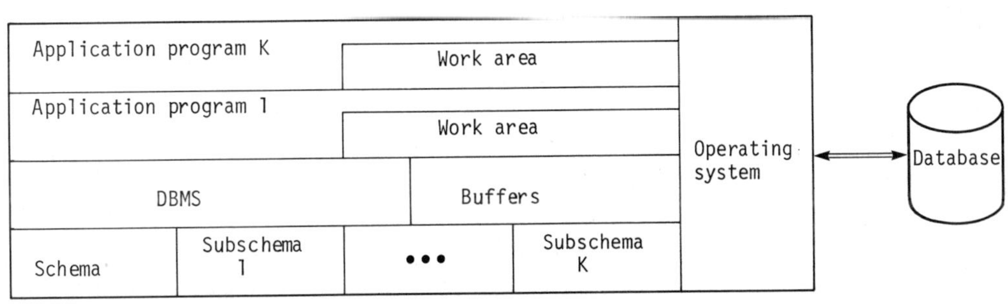

Figure 46: Single-machine DBMS

MARYANSKI (238):

1 The database software (DBMS).

2 The application programs.

3 The operating system and its buffers.

4 The schema, which is a logical description of the entire database.

5 The subschemata, which describe the portion of the database available to the individual application programs and provide a mechanism for validating the program's access rights to the data.

6 The work areas, which are shared by the application programs and the DBMS.

He then lists the sequence of operations for a retrieval operation.

Origination and validation

MARYANSKI (238):

1 The application program issues a request to the DBMS indicating the operation required and the data to be operated upon.

2 The request is validated against the subschema to ensure that the application program has the right to issue the request.

Data access

MARYANSKI (238):

3 The DBMS checks its buffers to determine if the request can be satisfied with currently available data. If this is the case, step 8 is executed next.

4 The DBMS requests that the operating system perform a transfer between the secondary storage device containing the requested data and the system buffers.

5 The operating system initiates the transfer between secondary storage and primary memory.

6 The data is transferred from secondary storage into the system buffers. This may require that a portion of the existing contents of the buffer space be written onto secondary storage in order to provide sufficient space for the new data without loss of previous information.

7 The operating system notifies the DBMS that the transfer is complete.

8 The DBMS places the data and status information in the work area of the application program that issued the request.

Completion

MARYANSKI (238):

9 The application program may access the data and status information in the work area in the course of its execution.

The communication system must provide the facilities for the transmission of commands, data, and status information between the host and back-end machines. The control of the physical links, proper utilisation of line protocols, transmission error detection and correction, processor and task synchronisation, and management of message buffers are among the responsibilities of the communication system. Since a back-end DBMS is a special case of a computer network, the communication facility need not contain all the features of a full-scale network communication system. For example, a routing mechanism is unnecessary in a two-machine back-end DBMS.

The interprocessor link should be of at least channel speed if intermachine communication is not to become a bottleneck. Simulation studies have indicated that intermachine links with speeds of 1 Mbaud or greater will produce only minimal communication delays. Configurations with the host and back-end processors sharing common memory have been proposed for situations in which quick response is necessary.

Figure 47 shows several (k) database tasks in the back-end system.

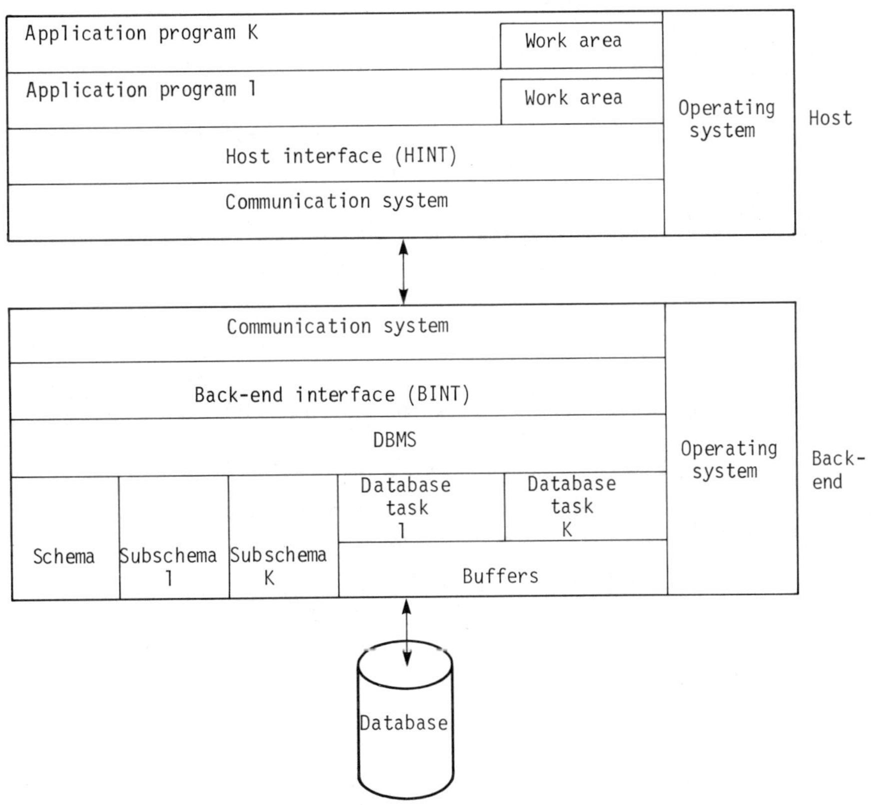

Figure 47: Software organisation of back-end DBMS

MARYANSKI (238): If a back-end is to operate efficiently, the DBMS module must be multiprogrammed. Therefore several tasks capable of presenting database requests to the DBMS must reside on the back-end machine. The database requests presented to the DBMS by the database tasks are those that have originated in the application program and are transmitted through the interface routines and the communication system to the database tasks. The database task acts as a surrogate on the back-end machine for an application program on the host. When the database request is complete, the database task returns the resulting data and status information to the back-end interface, which initiates the transmission of the result to the host machine.

The function of the back-end processor is obviously to reduce the load on the front-end, or host, so that it is not swamped by the database activities.

SU *et al* **(239):** The key concept of back-ends is to offload the database management functions from the host computer to dedicated processor(s) in order to:

1 Release the host from tedious and time-consuming operations involved in database manipulation, maintenance and control.

2 Increase system performance through functional specialisation of and through parallel processing among the host and the back-end(s).

The primary impetus for the back-end approach is, of course, to reduce the cost of managing data. The back-end approach can be viewed as a cost-effective alternative to upgrading the host or to achieve the level of functionality and performance that no conventional system can provide.

The separation into front- and back-end has several advantages including those associated with modularity. Systems can have multiple hosts or multiple back-ends as shown in Figures 48 and 49.

SU *et al* **(239):** The isolation of the DBMS, the mass storage devices, and the database from the host can bring a number of additional advantages.

1 Several hosts, possibly dissimilar, can share on-line data in the configuration shown in Figure 48. A single back-end may handle the processing of the database and present data in forms suitable to the dissimilar hosts.

2 Databases and the DBMS itself can be transported from an old mainframe to a new one with relatively little conversion effort. Similarly, changes to the databases, the mass storage devices, and the DBMS (eg adopting a standard DBMS) can be made without entailing changes to the host.

3 Storage devices including special-purpose cellular-logic devices or bubble devices can be made available through back-ends to mainframes that do not otherwise support these devices because of I/O or operating system constraints.

4 Multiple numbers of back-ends (see Figure 49) can be used to process large databases which can be stored either in a distributed manner across secondary memory devices to facilitate parallel processing or in a manner such that one database can be processed by one back-end.

5 The enforcement of database integrity and security can be separated from that of operating system integrity and security; thus the failure of one will not endanger the other.

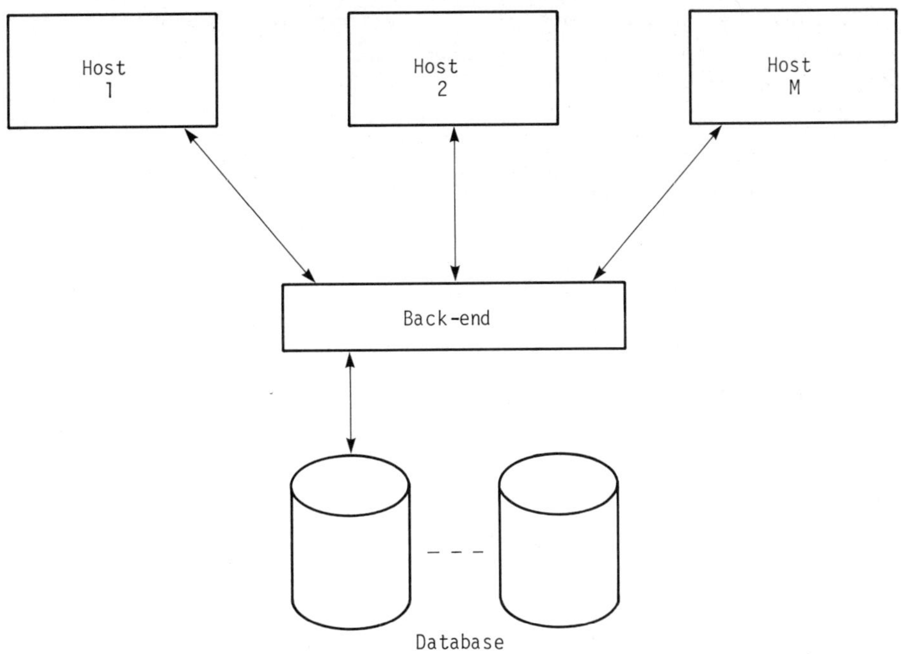

Figure 48: Multiple host configuration

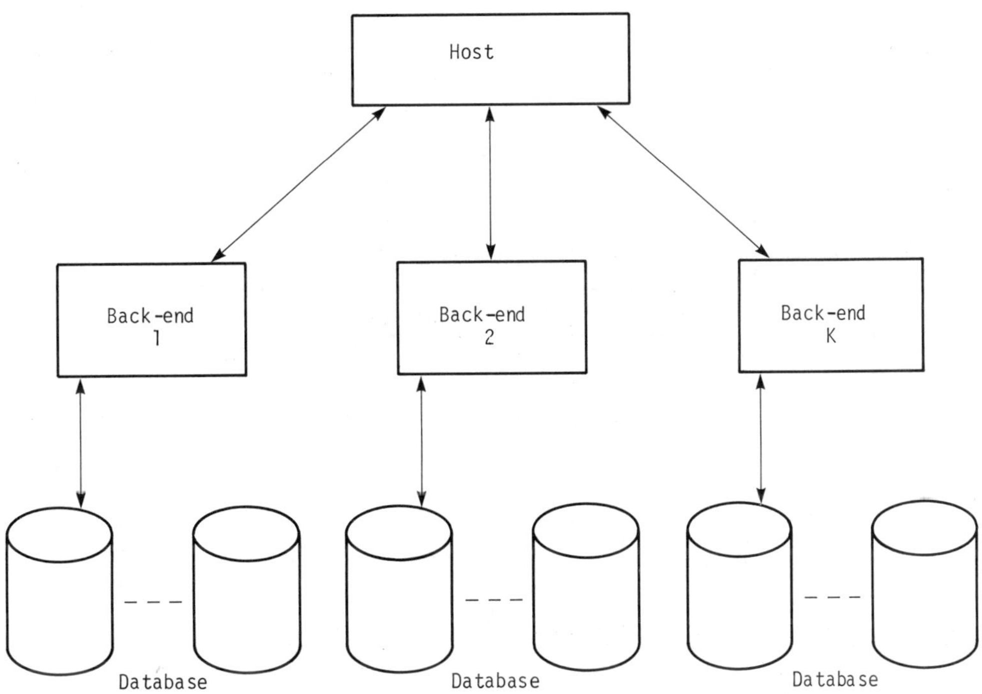

Figure 49: Multiple back-end configuration

The realisation of these attributes can be clearly seen in the Britton-Lee IDM 500 which is illustrated in Berra's paper.

Berra's second class of systems uses associative memories. These are potentially very fast, but as is usually the case they are also expensive. The method of operation is to load a register with the pattern to be searched for and a second register with a mask so that comparisons are only made over the selected fields. The whole of the associative memory is then searched in parallel, each line of the memory is logically 'anded' *with the mask and the output compared with the pattern being looked for. Any matches are then indicated. Berra gives a very clear description of the operation.*

BERRA: Shown in Figure 50 is a telephone example, albeit somewhat trivial, in which data has been loaded into the associative array. In this search the object is to obtain the records (tuples) of those persons who live on an avenue (AVE) and have a 4 as the first digit of their telephone number. The values AVE and 4 are loaded into the comparand register in the proper places; the mask register is set such that only the fields of interest are searched and then an exact match search is executed. The results appear in the response store. In this example an and operation is performed between the responders to the AVE argument and the 4 argument. Thus, the records of Pamela Drew and Alvin Zwing are responders.

The size of the associative memory is obviously limited by cost so that a system of streaming the data through the associative memory is required with a fast parallel search of each set of data as it passes through the associative memory. STARAN which has been described in an earlier section is a good example of the associative memory approach. The benefits and drawbacks of this approach are well summarised by Su et al.

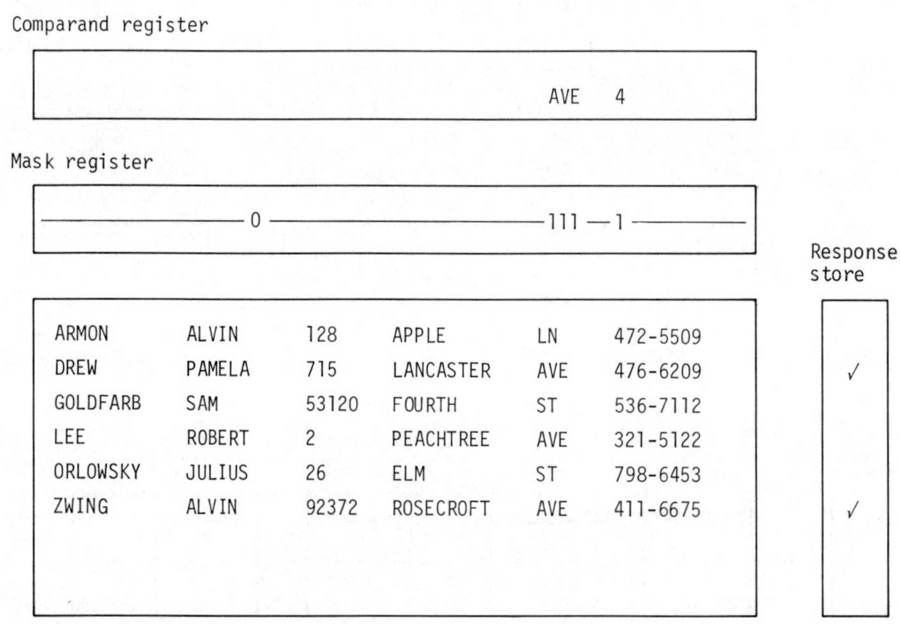

Figure 50: Associative memory telephone example

SU *et al* (239): The principal benefit of this approach is improved performance. The use of high-speed associative memory reduces the effective access time of the mass memory where databases are stored. However, due to the high cost of building this type of memory and processor, the size of associative memory is rather small. In a database management environment, considerable amounts of data will have to be paged in and out of the associative memory to take advantage of its capability. Although data can be searched in high speed once the data is in the memory, to stage data into the memory can become a bottleneck of this type of system. For certain types of application such as table look-up and directory processing, the use of high-speed associative memory will result in an order of magnitude improvement in performance at relatively low incremental cost. Where there is little locality of references, however, the potential cost benefit will not be realised.

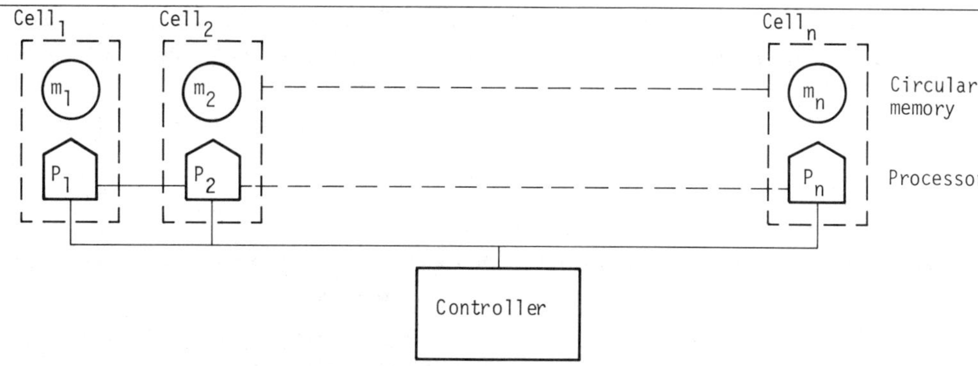

Figure 51: Cellular-logic configuration (reproduced from (239)*)*

The third class is cellular logic devices. Such a device can be the back-end of a front-end/back-end system. The principal feature of these devices is that there is a processor with each cell of memory, where a cell can be a track on a disk, a CCD loop, or a magnetic bubble loop, ie any memory device which acts logically like a delay line. The organisation of such a device is shown in Figure 51.

The principal feature is the exhaustive search of the database which is achieved with a high degree of parallelism.

SU *et al* (239): The data stored on the rotating devices such as disks, drums, CCDs, or magnetic bubble memories are systematically and exhaustively searched by the processing elements, one for each physical or electronic track of the rotating memory. Thus, data is processed on the same device where it is stored. Irrelevant data can be filtered out by the secondary storage devices and only the relevant data is brought into the main memory for further processing.... Furthermore, since the entire database is exhaustively searched in each circulation of the memory, data can either be searched associatively by contents (ie by specifying what data is to be searched rather than where the data can be found) or by contexts (ie by specifying the neighbourhood where relevant data can be found). The content and context search techniques in the cellular-logic devices offer uniformity and fast response time for search and update operations without the need to build and maintain special supportive structures such as indexes, hash tables, pointers, etc used in the conventional systems.

Several systems have been designed based on the cellular approach. One of these, RAP, which was started at the University of Toronto, is described by Berra. The similarity of the structure to the general diagram above is very clear. The merits of this approach are clearly summarised by Su et al.

SU *et al* **(239)**: The distinguishing features of the cellular-logic approach are as follows:

1 Increased processing capabilities in secondary storage devices to reduce the need for data staging in the main memory.

2 Search time is independent of the database size.

3 Elimination of the need for building, updating, and protecting auxiliary structures.

4 The use of identical cells to increase reliability and flexibility in adding or reducing the number of cells and to reduce the cost of production.

5 The potential for extremely high speeds as cell sizes decrease and memory density and speed increase (ie increase in the ratio of processing power to memory).

This approach can clearly benefit from the ease of application of units which is possible in VLSI.

Multiple processor database machines are Berra's fourth class. He describes a specialised MIMD architecture designed to support relational DBMSs. As can be seen from Figure 52 this class is another instance of a front-end/back-end system.

One of the basic techniques used today to increase performance and reliability is to implement, in hardware, a function which would, more traditionally, have been performed by software on a general-purpose computer. This is the characteristic of systems in Berra's fifth class.

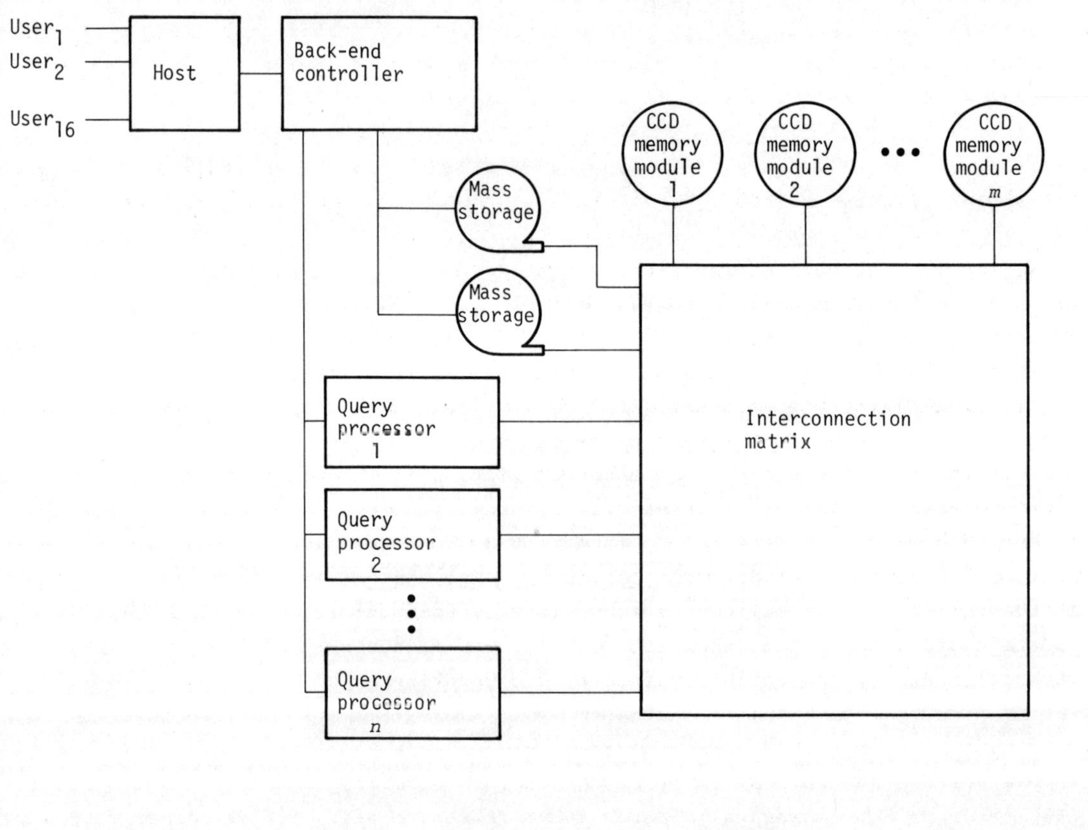

Figure 52: Direct system architecture

BERRA: The basic philosophy behind the development of a Special Purpose Function Architecture (SPFA) is to transfer a clearly defined function that is currently performed in software, to hardware. Several factors motivate the decision to make this transfer, including the decreasing cost of hardware, the ability to perform the function in a much shorter period of time, the clearness of the definition of the function, and the compatability with the current DBMS. In the latter case there is likely to be a considerable investment in the current DBMS that must not be discarded. It is therefore desirable to increase the performance of one or more clearly defined functions without adversely affecting the current system. The development of an SPFA is a possible solution to this problem.

The motives for this approach are put very strongly by Hsiao.

HSIAO (240): The database machine is made of specialised computer hardware which supports basic database management functions found in most contemporary software DBMS. The main motives for developing such machines are to enhance the reliability and performance of the system beyond that which can be obtained from a software-based system.

Database management software grows in complexity and size. This growth is prompted by the increase in user database management requirements and the recent change of data processing mode from an off-line, batched, single-user environment to an on-line, concurrent and multi-user environment. Large and complex software systems tend to be failure-prone. Furthermore, practical verification methods for software systems are still not in sight. On the other hand, methods for verifying hardware functionality, design, and production have long been available. Advanced technology has also overcome some of the problems of the logic complexity and capacity requirements, making the construction of relatively large and complex machines viable. By incorporating basic database management functions into hardware, not only can we provide more reliable basic functions, but we can also improve the software reliability since the software requirements will be less complex and the system software will be smaller in size.

Conventional computer systems were not designed for database management. These von Neumann-type computers are good for the preparation and execution of programs for numerical computations and for simple data processing. Database management activity, on the other hand, is concerned with the storage, retrieval, and management of large databases and requires quick search and good update operation for concurrent access. For example, it is well known that the execution of any IMS data management call on an IBM 370 computer takes several hundred CPU instructions for preparations of an eventual I/O. Thus, a typical conventional computer spends much of the time interpreting data management calls instead of executing them. Consequently, the response time for a call is degraded. By relegating the database management functions to specialised hardware (ie the database machine), the response time can be improved. Furthermore, the von Neumann type computer can concentrate on its traditional role of program preparation and execution with the CPU cycles released. Both the general-purpose conventional computers and special-purpose database machines can then yield high performance.

With the advances in silicon technology and the advances in design techniques (also the use of uncommitted logic arrays), this approach of building hardware to perform a clearly identifiable task is certain to become more and more widely used.

Berra illustrates his final class, information and storage retrieval systems, by a brief description of the High Speed Text Search (HSTS) machine.

BERRA: For several years research has been conducted that is aimed at the development of machines concerned with information storage and retrieval. The initial research was directed primarily towards the document retrieval problem, which is more closely aligned with database management. However, in the more recent work the emphasis has been on the processing of full text.

A full text machine that has recently been delivered is the HSTS machine (see Figure 53). This machine uses finite state automation in order to identify words, word stems, continuous word phrases, word proximity, etc along with fixed and variable length 'don't care' facilities.

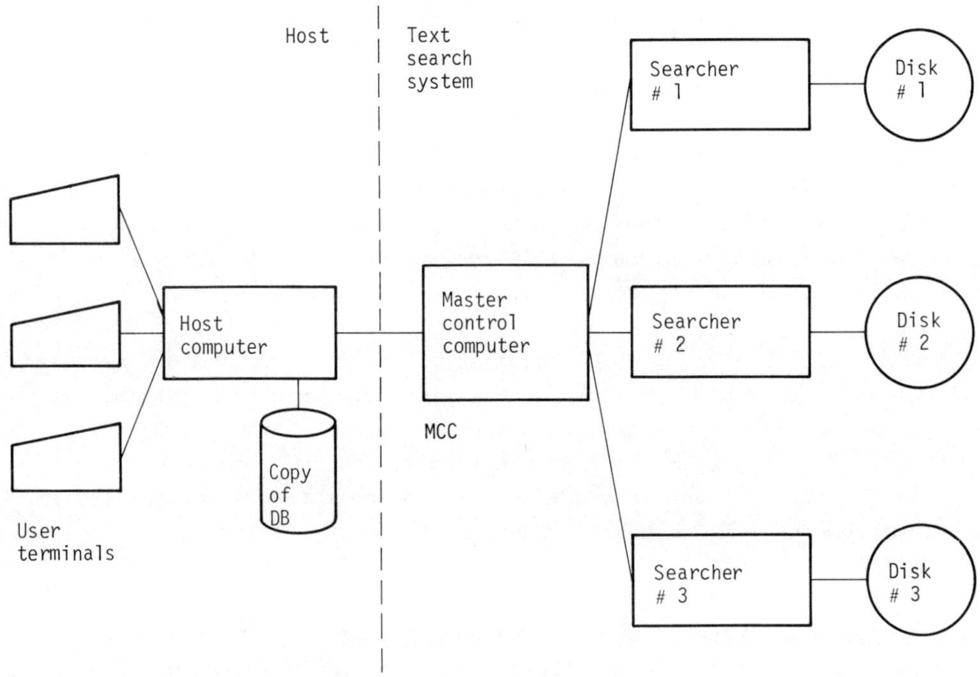

Figure 53: High Speed Text Search (HSTS) configuration

This system again shows the use of parallelism, which can be seen to be the common attribute of the various database architectures referred to above. DBMSs will therefore advance rapidly as a result of the developments in VLSI and the various storage technologies.

SU *et al* **(239)**: What impact do hardware technologies and database machines have on the database management area? The answer is: they are all making data processing less expensive and more accessible (to both large and small users). The low-cost, computational, logic, and control capabilities have already made microprocessors ubiquitous. Bubbles and CCDs offer modular storage coupled with data storing, arranging, and managing capabilities. Their impact will be twofold:

1 They will extend database management capabilities to smaller data collections for smaller users in smaller machines.

2 They will be useful in large database systems as nodes in a network, as servers, and as components amenable to parallel operations.

Advances in database machine technology will be required to solve many DBMS problems so that the promise of the database gospel can be delivered to users. Progress toward producing these machines will depend heavily on the improvements in price/performance of basic memory and processor technologies. A better understanding of the partitioning of the total problem will also aid special device development. The trend will be toward defining integrated database machines. Thus, workers in this area will find it necessary to have a good understanding of database application and software issues, as well as hardware architecture and technology issues.

The advances in DBM technology will not only have great impact on the implementation of DBMS software but also have profound effect on the designs of DBMS architectures, data models, and data languages. Database machines can make it very cost effective to support high-level data models and data languages, which are necessary for improving user/programmer productivity and to support multischema DBMS architectures, which are necessary for achieving data independence. The existing database machines have demonstrated their capabilities to make data mapping between schemata a simpler task and to support the existing data models with considerable improvement in cost/performance. Furthermore, database machines are particularly suitable for supporting high-level, non-procedural, and set-oriented data languages. Thus, we should establish a standard DBMS architecture or a data model based on user benefits and assume with confidence that the performance gap will gradually close up. High-level, non-procedural and set-oriented operations that score high in both user productivity and technology considerations should be incorporated in a standard data language.

EXPERT SYSTEMS

The study of Artificial Intelligence (AI) has been an active part of the computing scene since the development of the first electronic computers. The publicity side of the subject has never suffered from false modesty. Claims were being made 20 years ago for the understanding of continuous speech, automatic translation, and the understanding of natural language. While considerable achievements have been made, they have rarely, if ever, matched the preresearch publicity that has been used to generate funding for many of the projects. This has resulted in considerable distrust of the claims and also in a reduction of funding; in the UK, the publication of the Lighthill report caused a significant reduction in the funding of AI projects

In recent years, progress has been steady and the published ambitions less extravagant - that is until the appearance of the proposals for the Japanese Fifth Generation.

One highly successful area has been the development of expert systems which have also captured the imagination of workers outside the academic community, including many branches of industry.

Following a recent meeting organised by the British Computer Society specialist group on expert systems a report is to be published which is intended to provide a tutorial introduction to expert systems techniques, to discuss the technical context in which they will be further developed over the next decade, and to identify implications for effective commercial and industrial exploitation. The report is expected to be published towards the end of 1982. A summary of conclusions has been published by the authors.

d'AGAPEYEFF (243):

1 Expert systems combine pattern matching and heuristic search techniques from research in AI to provide a *very different but entirely general style of programming*. A program written in this style is a set of pattern-cum-action statements (rules) directly representing human knowledge of the application.

2 Rule-based programming confers advantages in *the scope of potential applications*, in *the ease with which application experts can specify the program*, and in the ability of such systems to *explain their behaviour on demand*.

3 The knowledge rules are amenable to consistency checking. They are machine independent and are not confined to execution on von Neumann architectures. However, a practical difficulty is the discontinuity with programming practice for currently popular procedural languages (eg COBOL and FORTRAN).

4 Existing software products in the UK have shown that modest expert systems can

be implemented on inexpensive microcomputers. It is likely that this will shortly lead to domestic and industrial equipment which explains their operation, to a consumer market in machines offering 'intelligent' advice, and to a demand for information systems that can be understood and refined by end users.

5 In the long run, expert systems will have a substantial impact upon the competitiveness of both users and suppliers of computers, upon the wealth of nations, and the quality of life in technological societies.

An expert system can be regarded as consisting of two parts:

- *A knowledge base*
- *An inference machine.*

BRATKO: The knowledge base contains facts, relations between facts, and possibly methods for solving problems in the domain of application. The inference machine implements algorithms which solve problems and answer user queries by either simply retrieving facts from the knowledge base, or by inferring new facts from the facts that are explicitly stored in the knowledge base. Inferring new facts involves the use of general relations, or principles, which can also be stored in the knowledge base.

A major problem is the organisation of the knowledge base. Several techniques have been investigated but the rule-based approach has become the accepted method. It is the method used in most of the well known expert systems.

BRATKO: In general, rules are of the form 'if-then', but they can have different interpretations. Examples are:

'If precondition P then conclusion C.'

'If situation S then action A.'

'If conditions C1 and C2 hold then condition C does not hold.'

A more concise notation is often used, for example:

P ---> C

The meaning of this depends on interpretation, eg 'if precondition P then conclusion C'.

The desirable features of if-then *rules are listed by Bratko.*

BRATKO:

- *Modularity:* each rule defines a small, relatively independent piece of knowledge
- *Incrementability:* new rules can be added to the knowledge base relatively independently of other rules
- *Modifiability:* old rules can be changed relatively independently of other rules
- Support system's *transparency*.

One example of the if-then *rules illustrated by Bratko is taken from the MYCIN system for medical consultation.*

BRATKO:

> If 1 the infection is primary-bacteremia, and
> 2 the site of the culture is one of the sterile sites, and
> 3 the suspected portal of entry of the organism is the gastrointestinal tract,
> then there is suggestive evidence (0.7) that the identity of the organism is bacteroides.

An if-then rule from the MYCIN system for medical consultation (the parameter 0.7 says to what degree the rule can be trusted).

Rule systems are closely related to pattern-directed systems for the architecture of software systems. A very clear comparison with the conventional approach is given by Bratko (see Figure 54).

In the pattern-directed approach, modules communicate with the data environment rather than with other modules. The structure is obviously sympathetic to parallel computation using the MIMD type of architecture.

In view of the popularity of the principles of structured programming the following quote from Bratko is very interesting.

BRATKO: From the viewpoint of the principles of structured program design, the structure (b) seems almost shocking. However, it also has certain advantages. One major advantage is that the design of the system does not require all the connections between modules to be carefully planned and defined in advance. Consequently, each module can be designed and implemented relatively autonomously, and is less dependent on other modules than in conventional systems. This renders a high degree of modularity. The level of modularity is manifested, for example, in that the removal of some module from the system is often not fatal. After the removal, the system would typically still be able to solve problems; only the way of solving problems might change. The same is true for the addition of new modules and for modifications of the existing modules. If similar modifications are arrived at in systems with conventional organisation, at least the calls to other modules have to be properly modified.

This high degree of modularity is specially desirable in systems with complex knowledge bases because it is difficult to predict in advance all the interactions between individual pieces of knowledge in the base. The pattern-directed architecture offers a natural solution to this: each piece of knowledge, represented by an if-then rule, can be regarded as a pattern-directed module.

The basic life-cycle of such a pattern-directed system is defined by Bratko as consisting of three steps.

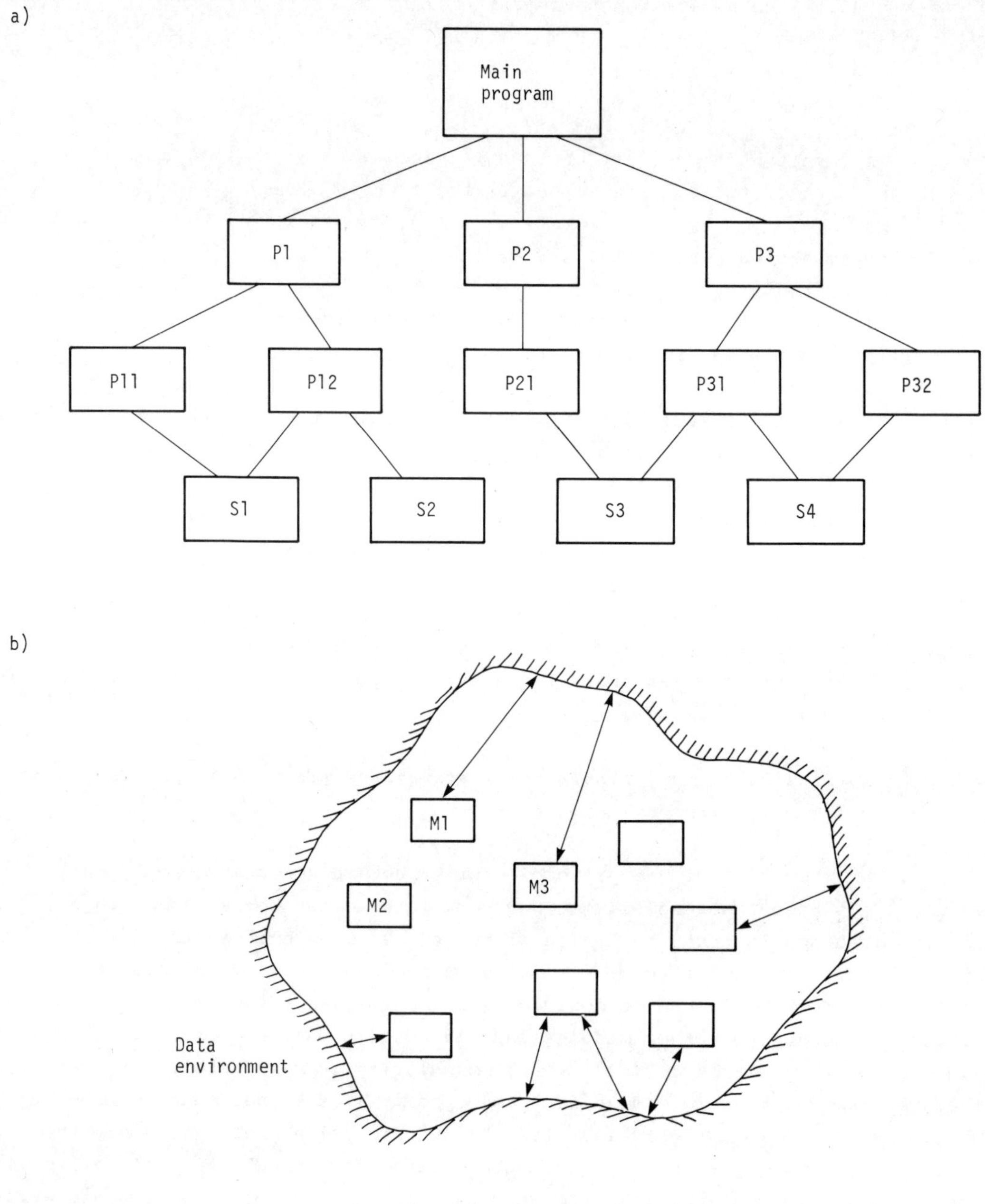

Figure 54a: Example of conventional system organisation
Figure 54b: Example of pattern-directed system
Figure 54: Comparison of conventional and pattern-directed architecture

BRATKO:

1 *Pattern-matching:* find in the database all the occurrences of the condition patterns of the program modules. This results in a conflict set.

2 *Conflict resolution:* choose one of the modules in the conflict set.

3 *Execution:* trigger the execution of the module that was chosen in step 2.

Today's 'expert systems' are highly specialised and the aim of research must be to produce general Intelligent Knowledge-Based Systems (IKBSs).

IKBSs are the central component of the Japanese Fifth Generation proposals. These proposals look into the future, covering the next five to 10 years. They do, however, contain references to two developments that are currently in progress:

- *Dataflow architectures which have been discussed above*
- *The language PROLOG, which is particularly suited to the solving of problems that involve objects and relations between objects.*

PROLOG

The syntax of PROLOG is based on the syntax of first order predicate calculus restricted to Horn clauses only. PROLOG is a non-procedural language. The execution of the program can be regarded as the evaluation of relations. Programming in PROLOG is very different from programming in algorithmic or procedural languages. Detailed descriptions of PROLOG can be obtained from Periera et al **(244)** *and Clockson and Mellish* **(245)**.

Bratko provides a good introduction to PROLOG with several examples, one of which will be summarised in this analysis.

Consider the representation of a small family tree and the provision of the ability to answer questions on the relationships contained in the tree.

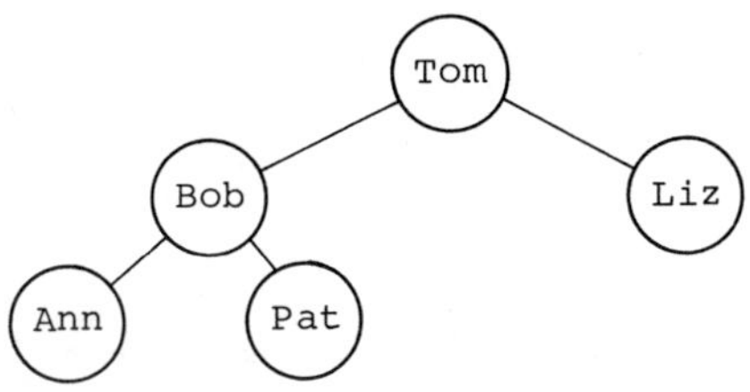

BRATKO: A small database shown above defines the parent relation. In PROLOG this relation can be defined by the following piece of program:

```
parent(tom,bob).
parent(tom,liz).
parent(bob,ann).
parent(bob,pat).
```

The successor relation can be derived from the parent relation. The general rule defining the successor relation can be stated in PROLOG by two statements:

```
succ(X,Y) :- parent(Y,X).
succ(X,Y) :- parent(Y,Z), succ(X,Z).
```

The first statement above says: 'For all X and Y, X is a successor of Y if Y is a parent of X.'

The second statement recursively defines indirect successors and can be read: 'For all X and Y, X is a successor of Y if there exists a Z such that Y is a parent of Z and X is a successor of Z.'

Now the PROLOG system can be asked: Who are the children of Bob? This question to PROLOG is:

```
?- parent(bob,X).
```

PROLOG's answer is:

```
X = ann;
X = pat
```

We can also ask: Who are the predecessors of Pat? That is: we are looking for all the people whose successor is Pat.

```
?- succ(pat,Y).
```

Answer:

```
Y = bob;
Y = tom
```

We can also ask for all the pairs successor-predecessor:

```
?- succ(S,P).
```

PROLOG will answer with all instances of the variables P and S so that they satisfy the successor relationship:

```
P = tom, S = bob;
P = tom, S = liz;
P = tom, S = ann;
etc.
```

The areas for which PROLOG is and is not suitable are summarised by Bratko.

BRATKO: PROLOG is an efficient tool for non-numerical problems which involve objects and relations. It is, on the other hand, in its present form completely unsuitable for more traditional, numeric-type computations.

It is rather obvious that PROLOG is extremely well suited for the development of expert systems. It facilitates experimenting with alternative ways of representing and using knowledge in the system....

PROLOG can be naturally used as a query language for relational databases; [*it can also be used*] as a specification language for information system design.

THE JAPANESE FIFTH GENERATION

The proposals presented for Fifth Generation Computer Systems (FGCSs) must have received more publicity than any previous forward look in computer design and applications There was an international conference in Tokyo in October 1981 with 86 overseas guests. A report in the January 1982 edition of Datamation *clearly illustrates the effect on the people attending the conference. Edward Feigenbaum of Stanford University was very enthusiastic.*

DATAMATION (246): 'The Fifth Generation system project aims to build the artificial intelligence machine that we have all been waiting for. If successful, the project will have a revolutionary impact on the computing world. I believe it is the right concept at the right time on the right schedule.'

A more down to earth opinion was expressed by McCormick of the University of Illinois.

DATAMATION (246): No supercomputer project in the past - whether it be the Univac LARC or the IBM STRETCH or the ILLIAC - came near its stated goal or achieved commercial success. The FGCS project is a supercomputer development project and is an attempt by the Japanese to get up to speed in knowledge engineering.

The chairman of the Fifth Generation project is Professor Moto-Oka so that the paper by Moto-Oka and Tanaka may safely be regarded as definitive. In the introduction to their paper they indicate the application areas where computers have not yet been successful.

MOTO-OKA and TANAKA: However, there are still some application fields in which computers have not been able to demonstrate their power satisfactorily; these are pattern recognition, natural language translation, summarising capabilities of sentences, learning capability of past experiences, global decision making through various kinds of information, and so on.

We are also facing a serious problem, namely the 'software crisis'. This arises because of the gap between the logic level required by applications and the one offered by high-level languages. As the application field expands more, the gap becomes broader and broader. This means that computers should support a higher logic level which is at the same time friendly and familiar for humans. We call such computer systems Fifth Generation Computer Systems (FGCSs). In other words, the FGCSs are Knowledge Information Processing Systems (KIPSs); they have knowledge bases and are able to infer from the knowledge and solve problems as humans do. Only when computers gain such capability, can they be truly useful and tide us over the software crisis. To realise such high-level computers, various kinds of technology are required such as knowledge representation, inference operation, knowledge acquisition, very efficient parallel execution mechanism, VLSI technology and so on. These technologies are not completed yet, but we think that the time is now ripe to start a project to develop Fifth Generation computers which are based on artificial intelligence.

If the use of computers is to expand into these areas the following problems will have to be solved.

MOTO-OKA and TANAKA:

1 To realise such basic functions as inference, association, and learning as the nucleus functions of the Fifth Generation computers, which are going to be implemented by hardware.

2 To equip perfectly various kinds of basic software for artificial intelligence, thus mastering the basic functions.

3 To realise friendly man/machine interfaces which are natural for human beings, through utilising the research results of pattern recognition technology and artificial intelligence.

4 To realise some excellent developing support systems to resolve the so-called software crisis and to make the productivity of software high.

Figures 55 and 56 are taken from Moto-Oka and Tanaka's paper and give the basic configuration of the FGCS. The main concept of FGCS is knowledge information processing and the functions of FGCS can be divided into three.

MOTO-OKA and TANAKA:

1. *Problem-solving and inference function* means that it is necessary to establish a high-level architecture based on the computation models of a functional or predicate calculus type, which are higher in the logic level than the conventional von Neumann architecture.

2. *Knowledge-base management function* aims at the realisation of large-scale databases which are needed to make up the many application systems of knowledge information processing, and at the perfect provision of high-speed inference and retrieval processing capability.

3. *Intelligent interface function:* the objective is to offer some friendly means which facilitate natural information processing for humans through dialogue with computers using voice, images, or natural languages.

PROLOG and dataflow appear to have important roles in the research and development programs.

MOTO-OKA and TANAKA: A language which includes the language PROLOG will be used as the interface between software and hardware. The knowledge-base management function is an innovative database management function which is enhanced by the processing function of semantic information. The relational datamodel is selected as the

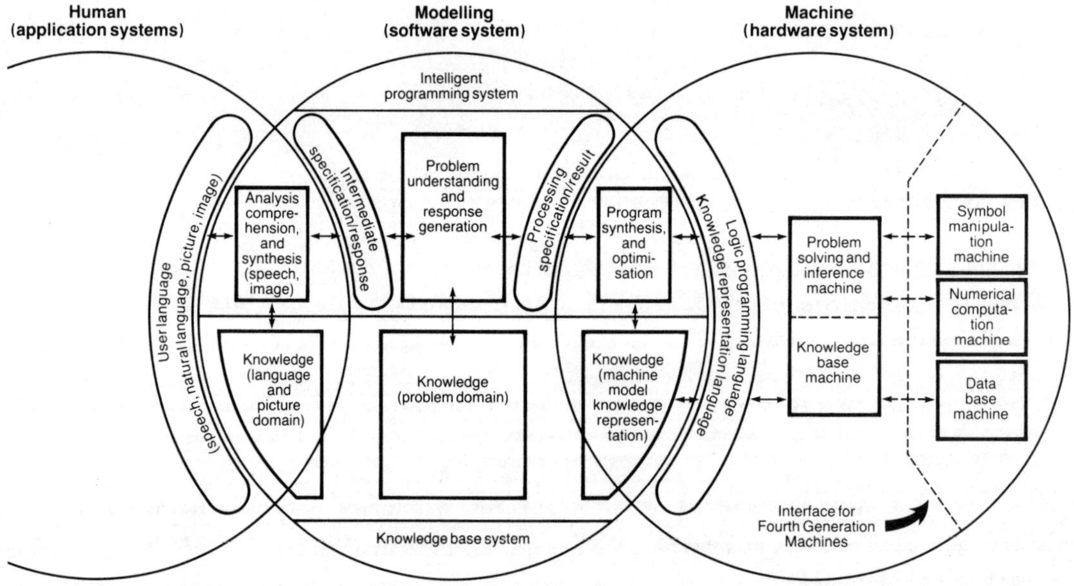

Figure 55: Conceptual diagram of the Fifth Generation Computer Systems

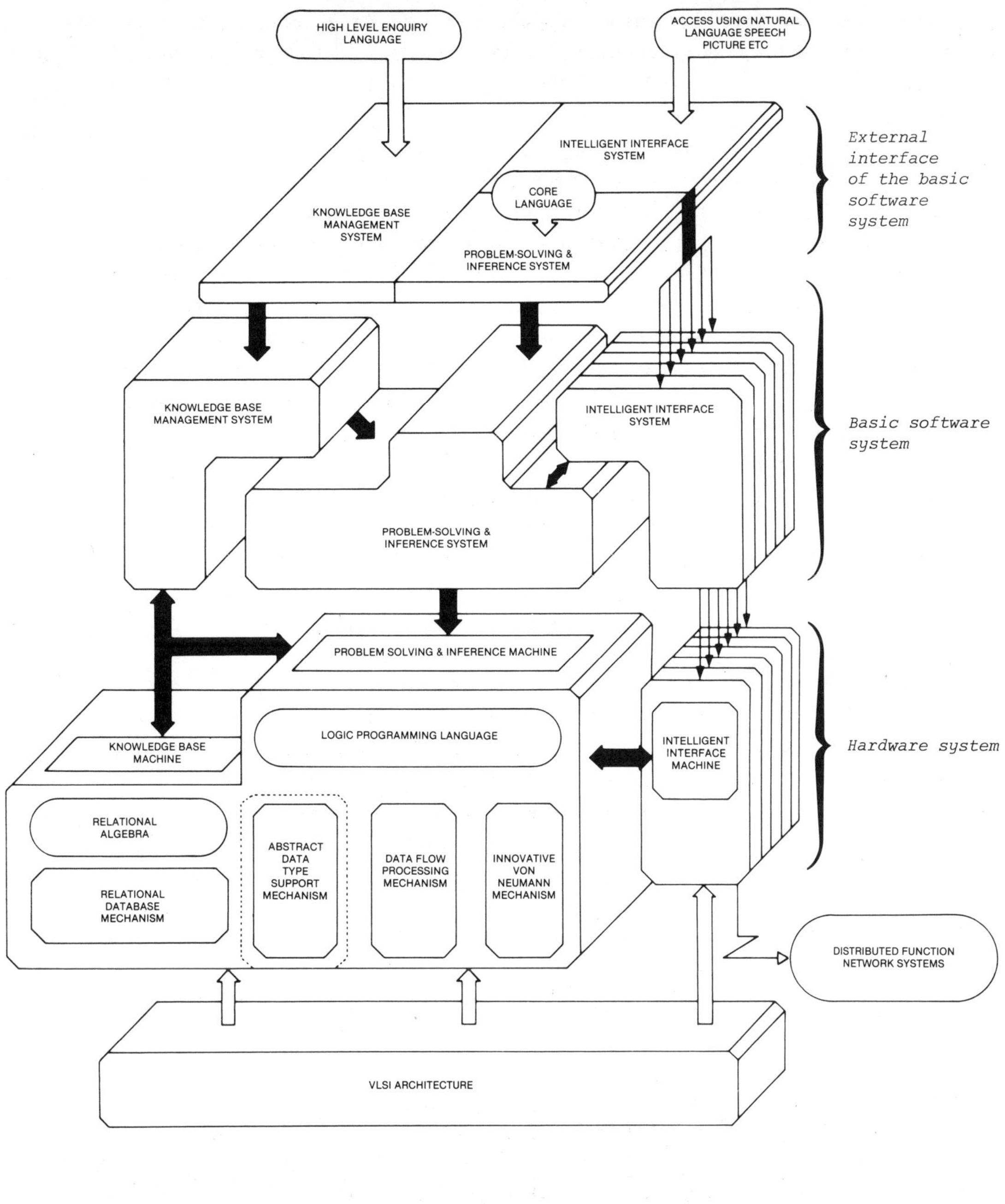

Figure 56: Basic configuration image of the Fifth Generation Computer Systems

basic data model, which matches PROLOG very well. The software of knowledge-base management will be implemented over the hardware function which processes the relational algebra in parallel.

We think that the dataflow architecture will fit the basic hardware mechanism of the inference machine very well. The dataflow architecture can not only pull out as many parallelisms contained in the program as possible, but also matches very well to functional languages which can be good interfaces to the inference processing.

We regard the relational database machine as the basic mechanism of the knowledge-base machine. The relational operations will be supported by the high level of parallel and pipeline processing mechanisms based on the concept of dataflow and stream processing. On the mechanism which implements relational operation, some expansion and improvement will be done to support the knowledge operations. At the final stage of development, the basic processing mechanism of the knowledge base will be extracted from the fused mechanism of the inference function and the knowledge-base management function rather than be based on the relational database machine.

The plans for the intelligent interface, particularly in the area of speech I/O, appear very extravagant.

MOTO-OKA and TANAKA: At the intelligent interface function, we can provide functions to enable human interaction with the computer very naturally through natural language, voice, figures, and images. As natural language processing gives the basis of translation, the foreign languages (such as English) as well as Japanese can be set as the object languages. The final target is a system which can handle more than 10 000 basic words, with the exception of professional words, with less than 2000 grammatical rules, and can also analyse syntactically 99% of input sentences correctly.

The target of voice processing is a system which can handle multispeaker and continuous spoken Japanese with a vocabulary of more than 50 000 words and whose word-recognition rate is more than 95% at a rate three times faster than the real-time speech.

Regarding figure and image processing, we are going to develop a system whioh stores hundreds of thousands of pieces of figure and image information together with their structure information and which can be used for the knowledge information processing system.

Massive advances in VLSI technology and improvements in computer performance will be needed for the program to be possible. Figures given in the Datamation *report suggest expert systems capable of 100 000 times as many inferences per second as compared with existing systems, a personal dataflow machine with a speed of 10 million instr/sec, and a huge dataflow system made up of 1000 to 10 000 processors with a store of from 1 to 10 Gbytes.*

Some applications for FGCS are given by Moto-Oka and Tanaka.

MOTO-OKA and TANAKA: The basic applications systems, which we imagine will be the basic and common systems for a wide variety of applications in the 1990s, are the machine translation system and the many kinds of consultation system. The machine translation system is expected to have the capability of translating several languages and being able to handle hundreds of thousands of words with 90% precision; the rest of the translation is human aided. This system will be developed as a total system used by computers at each stage between the text editing and the final printing of translated results. The total translation cost is expected to be less than 30% of the cost of human translators.

Examples of consultation systems are found in medical diagnosis, natural language understanding, computer-aided design of machines, computer users' consultation, computer system diagnosis, and so on. Each system will be made of more than 5000 objects and more than 10 000 inference rules and use more than 5000 words. It is expected to have semi-automatic knowledge acquisition capability with the system interface of natural language and speech.

A wider picture is given by some proposals for systems to demonstrate the validity of IKBS.

Pre-GP health advisor	-	*domestic use, low cost; with voice I/O*
Workshop guide	-	*semi-professional, eg for car maintenance; voice I/O, animated synthetic graphics*
Teacher's auxiliary	-	*testing, textbook replacement for domestic use, eg for maths, languages, music; voice I/O, graphics*
Citizen's helper	-	*for consultation eg on planning regulations; voice I/O*
Tactical decision aid	-	*eg defence command and control, business, economics, public service*
Hardware/software	-	*detailing, validating; graphics*
Design mate		
Technical translator		
Fourth-generation robot	-	*sensing, planning*
Office manager/personal assistant	-	*scheduling, prompting, circulating, filing*
Report subeditor	-	*checking, amplifying; graphics*
'Masterminder'	-	*leisure question and answer, trial of skill*
Brief writer	-	*summarising, updating; voice I/O, graphics*
Home servant	-	*monitoring, switching*
Factory/plant manager	-	*process control; voice I/O, graphics*
Movie maker	-	*cartoons from text, cues*
Personnel aide	-	*detecting potential problems, career development needs.*

The response in the UK to the Japanese proposals has been a significant increase in awareness of IKBS and the need to be able to compete in the areas of hardware, software and peripheral devices. The paper by Malik reviews the response to date and it is hoped that tangible improvements in research activities will follow within the next year.

FUTURE PREDICTIONS

Information technology may be regarded as consisting of three components:

- Computing
- Storage
- Communications.

In the next few years the greatest impact from the user's point of view will probably come from communications.

The extensive introduction of local area networks and open networks all with wide bandwidths will mean that every user could access any local or remote computer. The advances in VLSI and other integrated circuit technology will have a big impact on the nature of the user terminal. Many terminals are still 'dumb' but there is a rapid move towards intelligent terminals using 8- or 16-bit microcomputers. Single user workstations such as the APOLLO and the PERQ are also becoming more widely used. As 'terminals' or 'workstations' increase in power the need for most users to go beyond their own personal system for computing power will rapidly diminish. A major contributory factor in this will be the increase in the size of local fast memories, which will permit them to accommodate most package software. There will still be the need to access remote databases and other specialised facilities. The situation will be generally similar to that described by Crook.

With the increase in power of workstations, the type of central computer will also change. Very powerful computers or special-purpose processors will still be needed, indeed the requirement for this type of computing will continue to increase. However, the role for today's large mainframes will diminish.

For high-performance computers there appears to be little competition over the next few years for pipelined vector processors. Of the other types discussed, SIMD computers will be widely used, sometimes in scientific computing, eg DAP, or in special applications such as IP. IP and pattern recognition of all types will be vital in the improvement of the man/machine interface, which is of paramount importance to the future development of computing. MIMD processors will probably find a home in database machines where the different tasks can best be tackled by different architectures. This is clearly what is planned in the Japanese Fifth Generation project where several distinct activities for the hardware are identified. There does not, however, appear to be much evidence that MIMD systems consisting of several identical computers will have an exciting future.

The future for totally new architectures (like dataflow) is bound up with the development of languages (like PROLOG) that are required for new areas of application (like IKBS), which will run more efficiently on the new architectures than they do on the conventional ones of today.

The development of software to permit problems to be expressed clearly is obviously of the greatest importance. A representation of parallel constructs for vector processors and array processors and the expression of relationships for the newer languages are essential for the efficient use of high-performance systems and the development of IKBS.

Looking into the future is always difficult but it seems certain that in the next few years developments in hardware and software will continue at least at the rate of previous years and that, as in the past, the inhibiting factor to the adoption of advances in technology will be the inertia of investment in existing methods.

INVITED PAPERS

SOME ARCHITECTURES FOR DATABASE MANAGEMENT

P B Berra

Syracuse University
Syracuse
NY

P B BERRA is Professor of Industrial Engineering and Operations Research at Syracuse University, New York. In addition to Syracuse, he has taught at the University of Michigan Dearborn Campus, Boston University, and Purdue University, and has also worked in industry with IBM, Bendix, and Hughes Aircraft. He has been active in a number of special interest groups and technical committees on database management, with a special interest in computer architecture for data management. He has published over 30 technical papers and has given numerous technical presentations. He is currently a Senior Editor for the IEEE Computer Society Press.

SOME ARCHITECTURES FOR DATABASE MANAGEMENT

Current developments in database machines are divided into six groups and these are discussed in detail. They are: the front-end/back-end system; the associative memory/processor group; cellular logic devices; multiple processor systems; special-purpose function architectures, and information storage and retrieval systems. Finally, future trends in technology are assessed and the revolutionary and evolutionary approaches to database machines are compared.

INTRODUCTION

The cost of hardware components that make up modern day digital computers continues to drop at a rapid rate. Along with this cost reduction there exists a simultaneous increase in the number of components that one can place on an integrated circuit chip. This leads to what seems to be an ever decreasing cost of hardware combined with a continued increase in functional capability. When these improvements are coupled with the ever increasing costs of software, primarily caused by increased personnel costs, it becomes imperative to consider moving functions that are primarily executed in software, to hardware.

One field that has received increased attention *vis-à-vis* movement of software functions to hardware is the database management field. Owing to size and complexity, managing databases becomes increasingly difficult. Over the past few years, increasing effort has been expended in the study of new types of hardware called database machines which are designed solely for the purpose of managing data. This research has been driven by the decreasing cost of hardware *and* by the need for performance improvements due to increased database size and complexity and a maturing database theory.

The desirable attributes of a database management environment include the following:

- Large capacity storage which is both modular and low in cost per bit
- Ease of mapping between the conceptual schemata and the internal schema
- Variable length data formats
- Fast retrieval and update of data
- Content search operations such as 'equal to', 'greater than or equal to', 'less than or equal to', etc
- Context search such as and, or and not
- Complete instruction sets which are conceived with database management functions in mind.

The current work in database machines can be divided into six somewhat overlapping groups. The first group is the front-end/back-end system. In this group the database functions are moved to a sequential computer back-end. The second is the associative memory/processor group. This involves hardware associative memories or processors being utilised to perform a variety of functions such as content search in parallel and parallel arithmetic operations. An example of this type of device is the Staran associative array processor (001).

The third class of database machines is cellular logic devices. The main attribute of these devices is that some of the intelligence of the central processing unit is moved closer to secondary memory, usually composed of disks, but often charge-coupled devices or magnetic bubble memory. Examples of this type of system include the Context-Addressed Segment Sequential Memory (CASSM) system (002) and the Relational Associative Processor (RAP) system (003).

The fourth class of systems can be called multiple processor systems in that they are composed of several distinct processors, each of which performs a separate function. Examples of this type of system include the Ohio State Database Computer (004), the Infoplex system (005), the Direct system (006) and the Relational Associative Computer System (RELACS) (007).

The database machines of the fifth class are Special Purpose Function Architectures (SPFAs). This class concentrates on a clearly defined function and develops an architecture that is concerned only with that function. Examples of SPFAs include the content-addressed file store (008), the search processor (009), merge processors (010), inverted file processors (011), directory processors (012) and dictionary and partial directory processors (013).

The sixth class involves machines that are concerned with information storage and retrieval problems. The most interesting of these systems are concerned with the processing of full text. Examples of these systems include the Associative File Processor (AFP) (014) and the High Speed Text Search (HSTS) system (015,016).

In this paper examples of the six approaches are discussed. The paper concludes with some comments on future directions in the database machines field.

THE FRONT-END/BACK-END SYSTEM

Figure 1 shows a front-end/back-end organisation. The basic reason for the existence of this organisation is to allow the host computer to perform the data processing functions that it was designed to perform while off-loading most database management functions to the back-end. An example of a front-end/back-end organisation is the Britton Lee IDM 500 (017) as shown in Figure 2. As indicated in the figure the IDM 500 serves as the interface between the front-end host device and the database. The database commands are passed from the front-end to the IDM 500 for execution with subsequent results being returned. For a review of back-end systems the reader is referred to Maryanski (018).

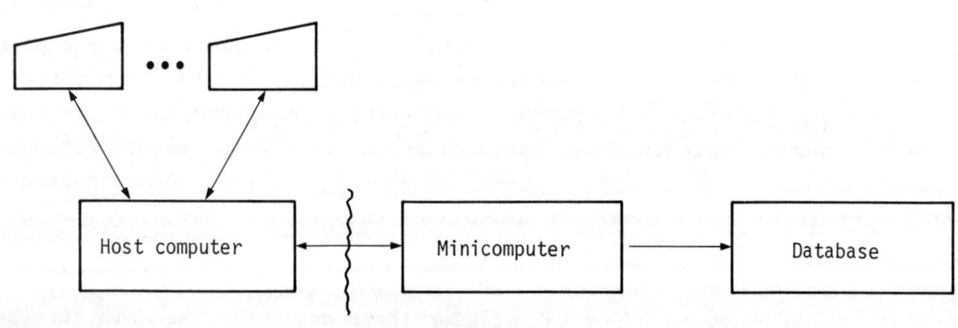

Figure 1: Front-end/back-end organisation

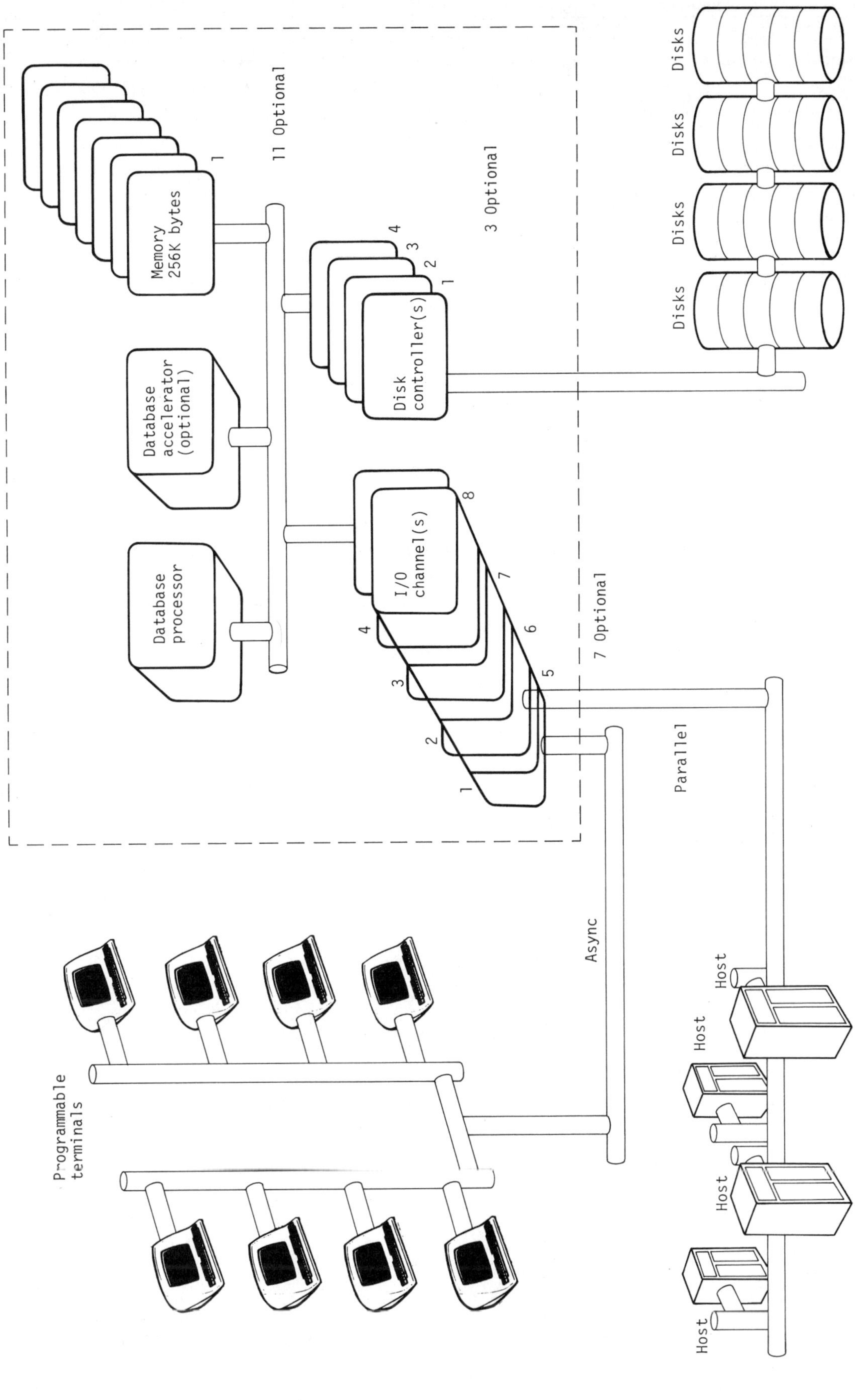

Figure 2: The Britton-Lee Intelligent Database Machine

ASSOCIATIVE MEMORIES AND PROCESSORS

Figure 3 shows a general block diagram of an associative array processor. The shaded areas are of most interest here. The data to be searched is loaded into the associative array from the auxiliary memory. The search argument is loaded into the comparand register and a mask is set so that only the data of interest will be searched. A search command such as 'equal to comparand' is executed and the resulting hits are indicated in the response store. The system then gives these hits to the user or performs further processing if required.

Shown in Figure 4 is a telephone example, albeit somewhat trivial, in which data has been loaded into the associative array. In this search the object is to obtain the records (tuples) of those persons who live on an avenue (AVE) and have a 4 as the first digit of their telephone number. The values AVE and 4 are loaded into the comparand register in the proper places; the mask register is set such that only the fields of interest are searched and then an exact match search is executed. The results appear in the response store. In this example an and operation is performed between the responders to the AVE argument and the 4 argument. Thus, the records of Pamela Drew and Alvin Zwing are responders.

The main attributes of associative memories/processors *vis-à-vis* database machines are content addressing and parallelism. That is, the device accesses data by content rather than by hardware storage address and does so in parallel. Conceptually, one can view associative memories/processors as having large word lengths (256 to 9K bits) with perhaps 1024 words, with each word having a simple processing element. These devices access data by content and execute search instructions such as 'exact match', 'next higher', 'next lower', 'less than', 'greater than', 'between limits' etc, and

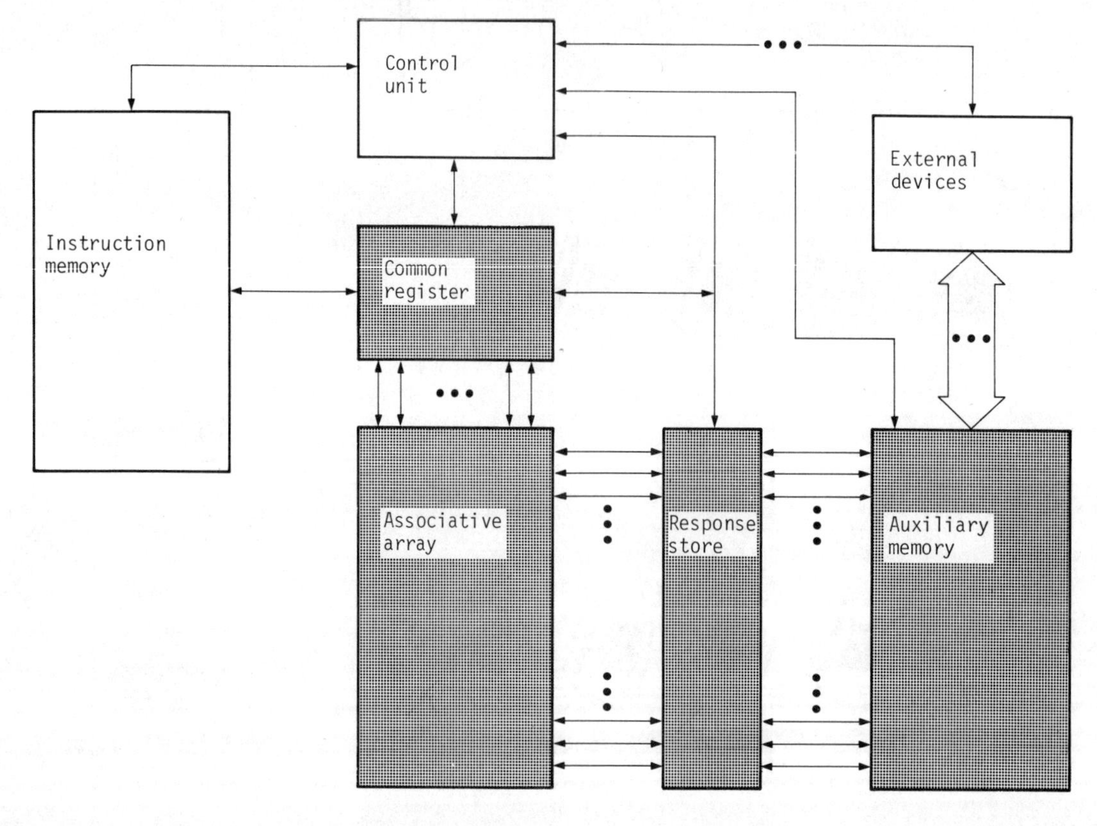

Figure 3: Block diagram of associative array architecture

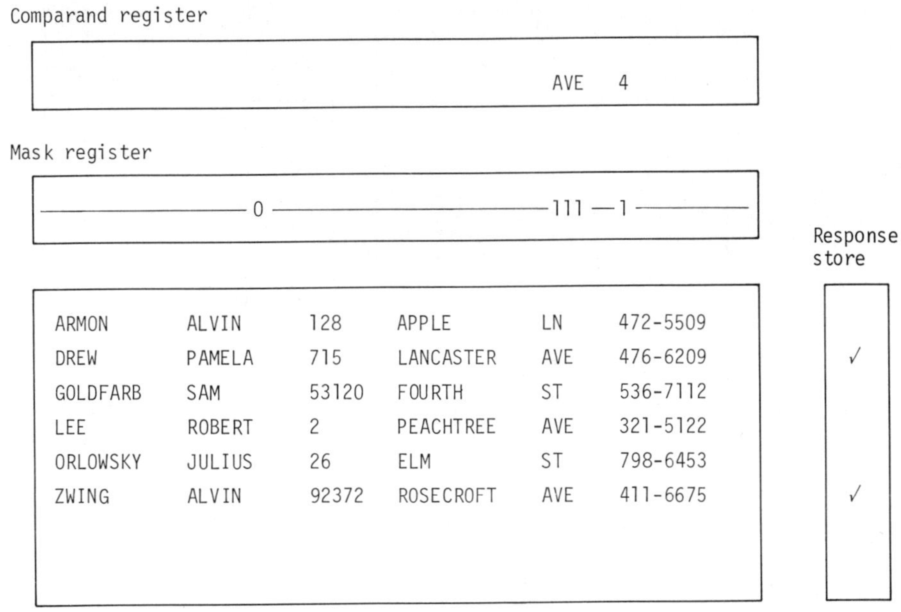

Figure 4: Associative memory telephone example

perform Boolean operations. Associative processors possess the same capabilities as associative memories but have the added capability of parallel arithmetic operations.

In order to keep an associative array processor supplied with data one must utilise a configuration such as that shown in Figure 5. In this configuration the array size is 256 bits by 1024 words and there are 100 standard disks. The fast buffer memory has two ports with data being staged out of it into the associative array and into another part of it from the disks. With this configuration the speed of the array is balanced with the input/output speed. That is, the time to process data in the array is approximately equal to the time to load the array. More details regarding this configuration can be found in (001). Other work that has been performed in the associative memories/processors area includes references (019,020).

CELLULAR LOGIC

Shown in Figure 6 is a general block diagram of a front-end/back-end architecture in which the back-end has been modified to form a database machine. In this type of machine some of the capability of the standard sequential computer CPU is replicated and distributed closer to the secondary memory. In the configuration shown each cell has a processing element that interacts with its memory, although in some configurations there may be intercell communications. In executing a search the controller broadcasts to each cell an instruction (ie 'exact match') previously received from the front-end. The instruction is executed simultaneously in each cell and each processing element accesses its memory by content. In this way, parallelism and content addressing are implemented in this type of device. There have been several projects in which this

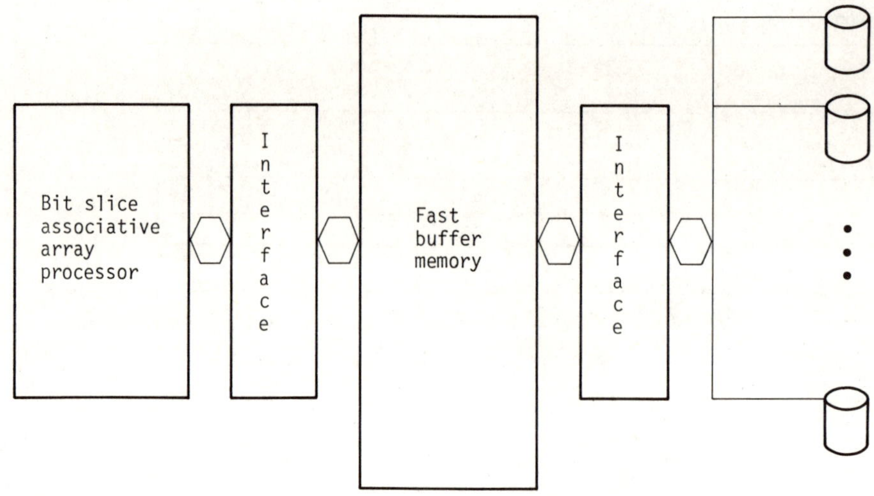

Figure 5: Associative array processor/buffer memory/disk

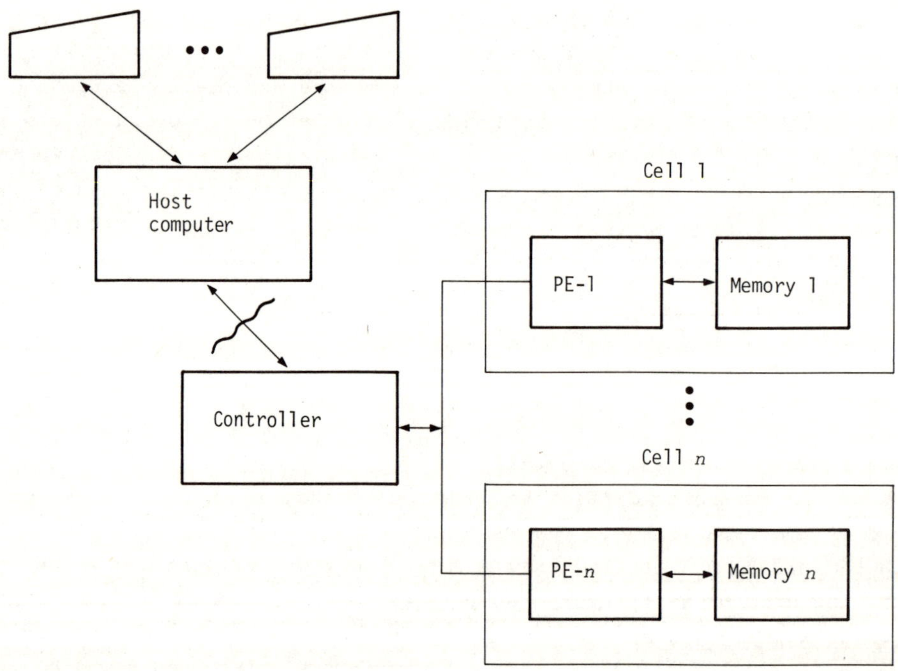

Figure 6: Cellular logic

concept has been used to develop a database machine. Some of these projects are discussed in (021).

The Relational Associative Processor (RAP) can be used as an example for making remarks about these systems. Figure 7 shows a general block diagram of the RAP architecture. The statistical arithmetic unit is responsible for certain operations performed over all cells. These operations include 'count', 'sum', 'maximum', 'minimum', and 'average' and generally compiling intermediate results. The controller is responsible for overall coordination of the cell processors, error checking, serial parallel conversion, data transfers to and from the host computer as well as a variety of other control operations.

Figure 8 provides a more detailed block diagram of a RAP cell. The data is read from the memory into the buffer, processed and read back to memory if required. The information search and manipulation unit is responsible for such operations as intercell communication, decoding commands sent by the controller and evaluation of search criteria. The arithmetic logic unit performs arithmetic and set function operations.

MULTIPLE PROCESSOR SYSTEMS

As was pointed out earlier, there are several multiple processor database machine projects underway. As an example of one of these projects we will consider the Direct system (006).

The Direct system is a multiple instruction stream, multiple data stream architecture which supports relational database management systems. As indicated in Figure 9 its

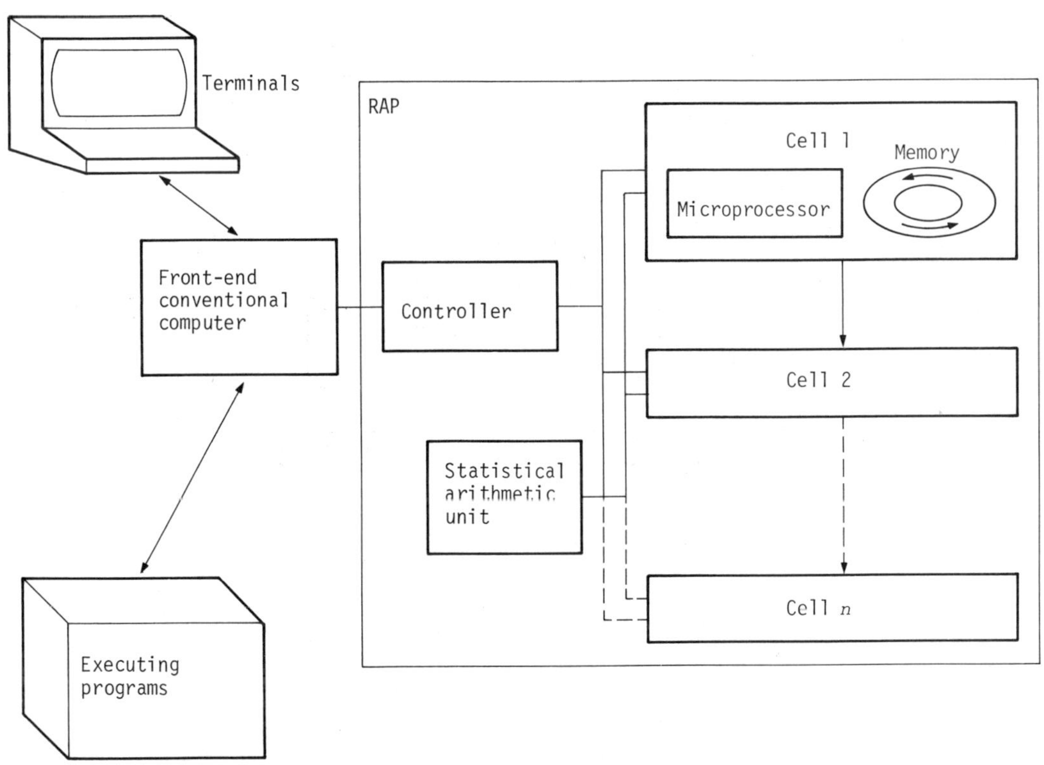

Figure 7: Overview of Relational Associative Processor (RAP) architecture

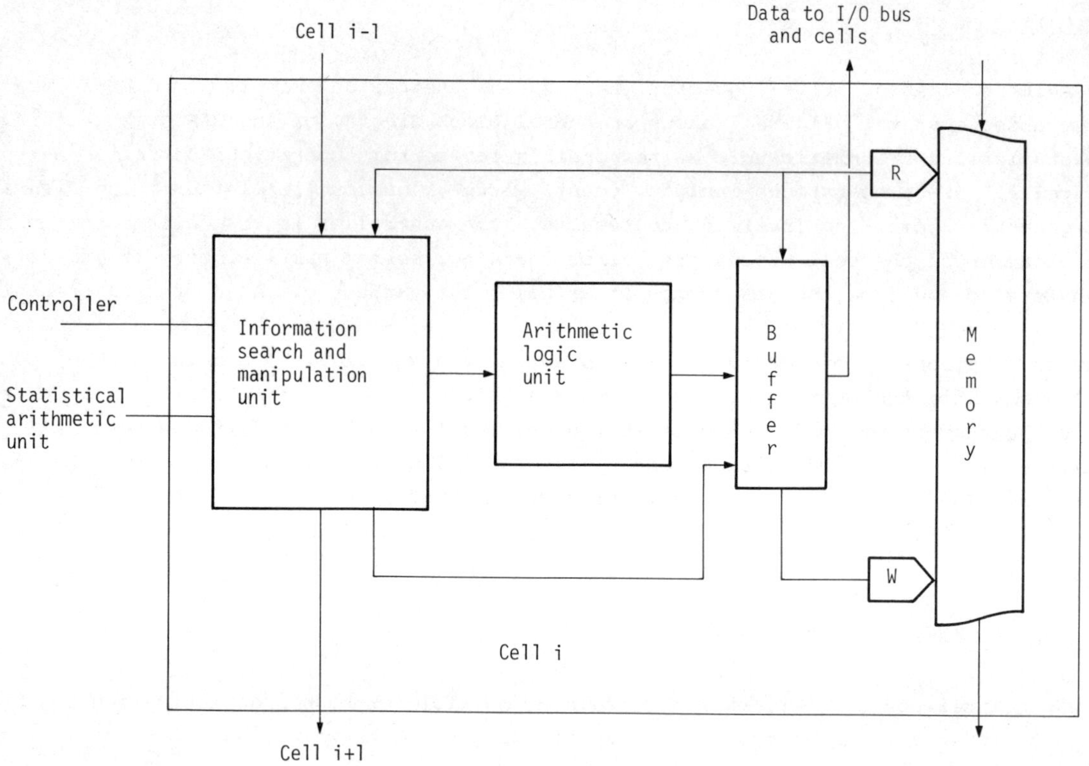

Figure 8: The RAP cell structure

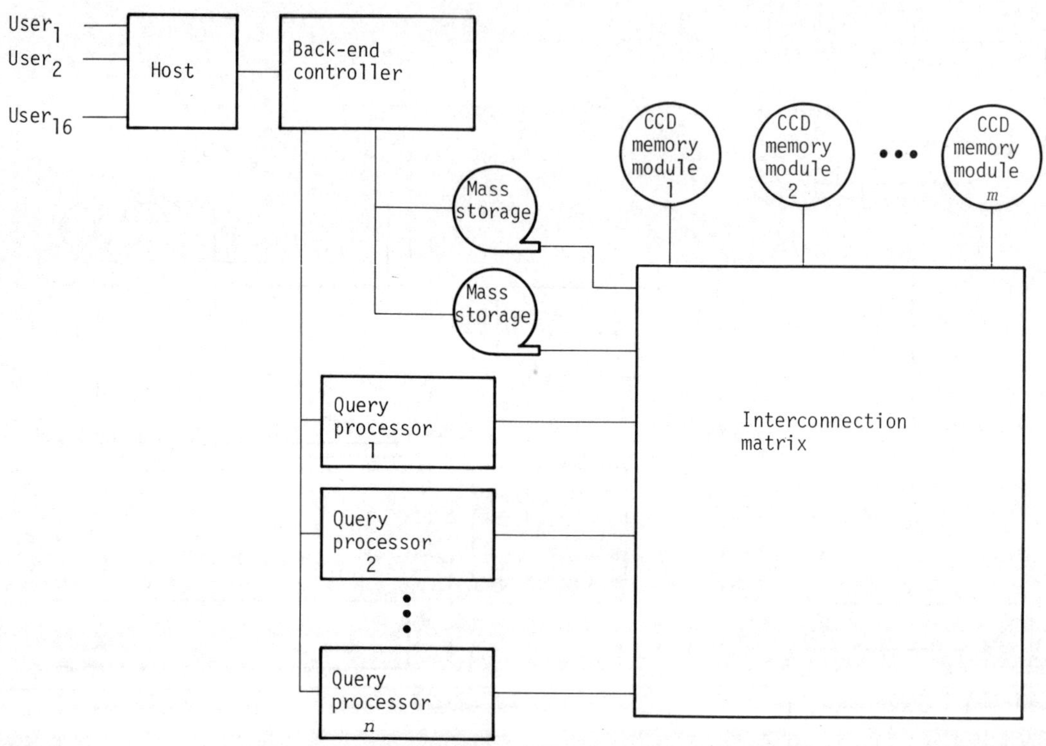

Figure 9: Direct system architecture

initial configuration consists of a number of query processors, a number of memory modules, an interconnection matrix that connects query processors to memory modules, one or two disk storage devices, a back-end controller and a host processor. The system can support both intraquery and interquery processing. That is, a number of processors may be processing the same query simultaneously while a number of other processors may be processing one or more other queries.

Direct is compatible with the Ingres (022) relational database management system. The user interacts with Ingres through the front-end processor in order to formulate a query that is sent to the back-end controller for execution. The back-end controller determines the number of query processors that will be assigned to each query, ensures that the query is executed properly, and finally returns results to the host processor.

In addition to those multiple processor systems previously mentioned, a number of other designs are in various stages of development. The systems include the Univac system (023), and the Dialog system (024).

SPECIAL PURPOSE FUNCTION ARCHITECTURES

The basic philosophy behind the development of a Special Purpose Function Architecture (SPFA) is to transfer a clearly defined function that is currently performed in software, to hardware. Several factors motivate the decision to make this transfer, including the decreasing cost of hardware, the ability to perform the function in a much shorter period of time, the clearness of the definition of the function and compatability with the current database management system. In the latter case there is likely to be a considerable investment in the current database management system that must not be discarded. It is therefore desirable to increase the performance of one or more clearly defined functions without adversely affecting the current system. The development of a SPFA is a possible solution to this problem.

As an example of one of these systems, consider the Dictionary Directory Processor (DDP) (013). Figure 10 gives a general block diagram of this system. The system is designed to perform the following six functions:

1 To determine if attribute or relation names exist in the database and, if so, to provide their shortened (coded) names.

2 To determine if attributes have synonyms and, if so, provide the synonym names.

3 To determine which attributes are part of which relations.

4 To determine whether logical relationships in a user's query can be constructed (ie to determine if a join can be performed).

5 To provide descriptor data for attributes in a query.

6 To provide primary key values and location information for the relations that are referenced.

Figure 11 shows an expanded block diagram of the associative memories and arrays of Figure 10. Several interconnections are apparent in the figure. Associative Memory 1 (AM1) holds the attribute names and is connected with AM2 which holds the attribute

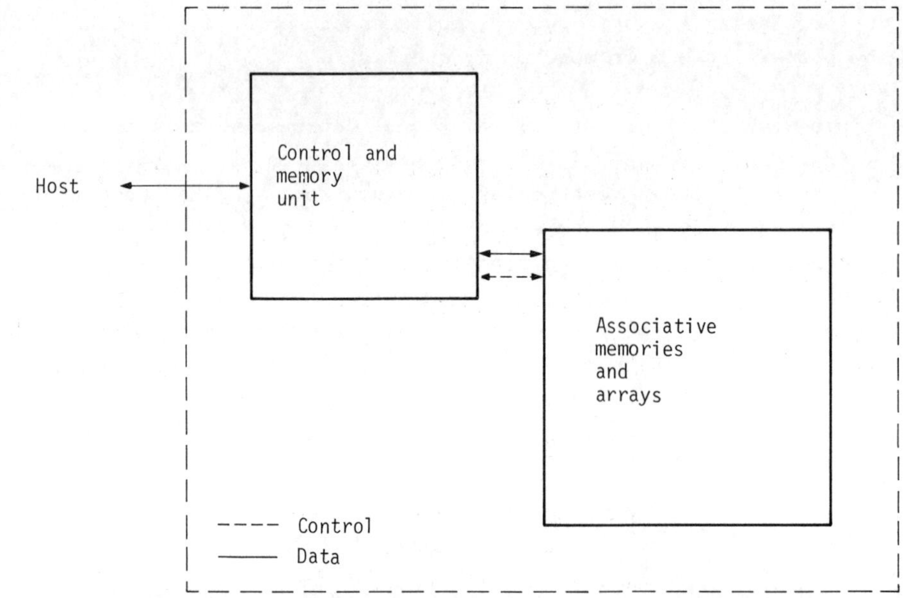

Figure 10: An overview of the Dictionary Directory Processor (DDP)

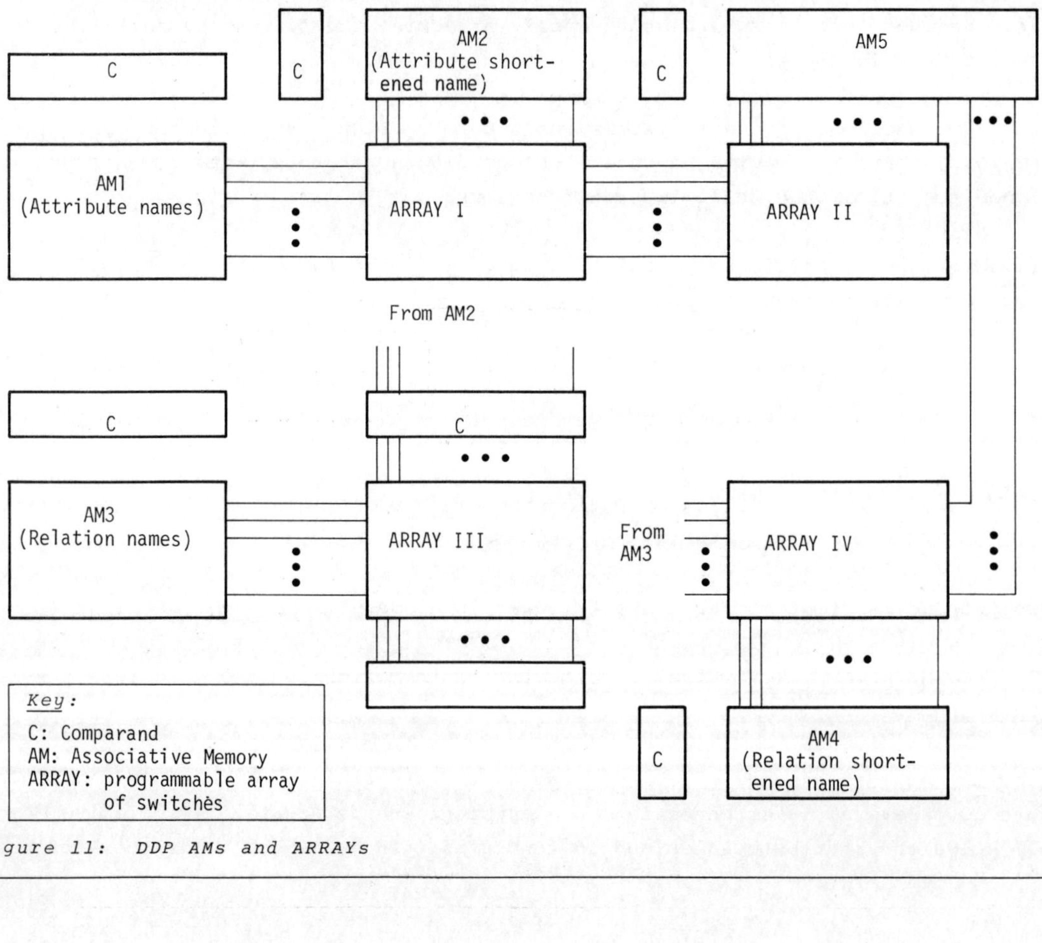

Figure 11: DDP AMs and ARRAYs

shortened names. The connecting device is ARRAY 1 which contains a mechanism for determining if synonyms appear in the databases. AM3, which contains the relation names, is connected to AM4 which contains the relation shortened names. These two AMs are connected via ARRAY IV which provides primary key and location information. ARRAY III contains a bit map that is utilised to determine which attributes belong to which relations. Finally ARRAY II contains descriptor data concerning attributes and other data such as access privileges, security levels etc.

Some additional works regarding SPFAs is concerned with the feasibility of developing a Database Machine Architecture Development facility (DMAD) (025). This work concerns the use of an emulation facility to select a candidate function to be moved to hardware, the creation of an SPFA that will perform the function, the testing and evaluation of the SPFA, and finally, the substitution of the SPFA into the working environment.

INFORMATION STORAGE AND RETRIEVAL SYSTEMS

For several years research has been conducted that is aimed at the development of machines that are concerned with information storage and retrieval (011,026). The initial research was directed primarily toward the document retrieval problem which is more closely aligned with database management. However, in the more recent work the emphasis has been on the processing of full text.

A full text machine that has recently been delivered is the High Speed Text Search (HSTS) machine (016) (see Figure 12). This machine uses finite state automation in order to identify words, word stems, continuous word phrases, word proximity etc. along with fixed and variable length 'don't care' facilities.

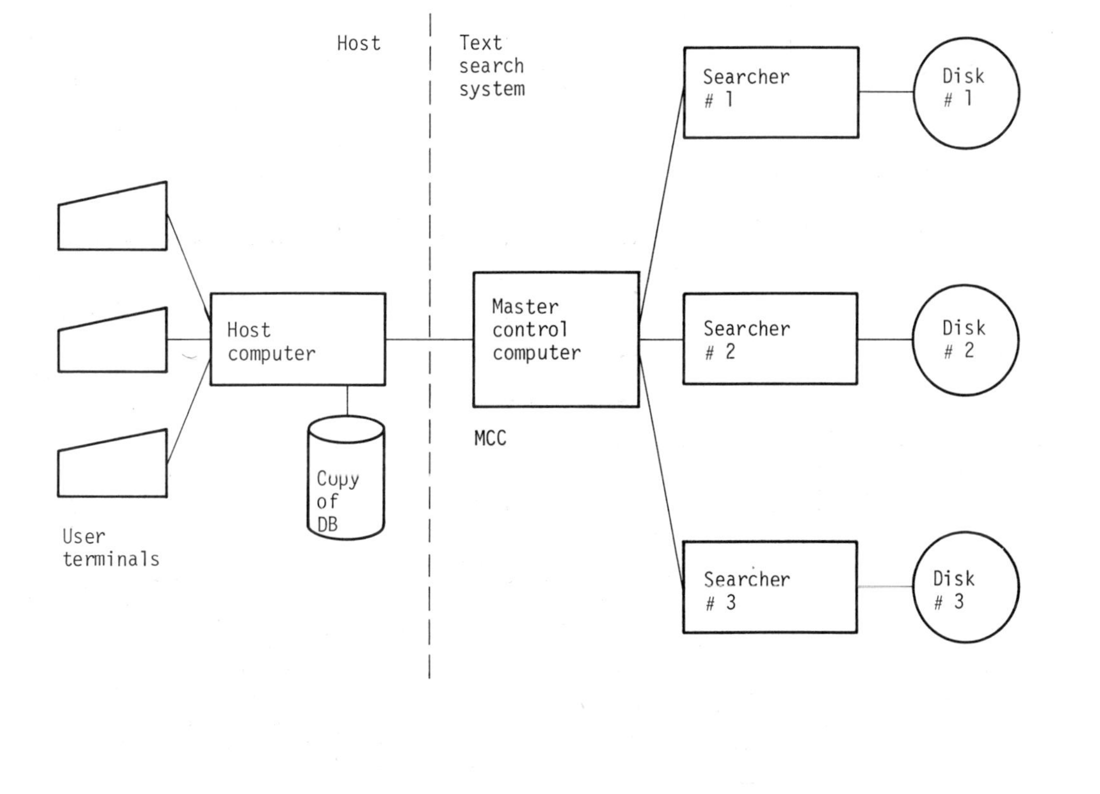

Figure 12: High Speed Text Search (HSTS) configuration

CONCLUSIONS AND FUTURE DIRECTIONS

In the next 10 years there will continue to be phenomenal improvements in technology. As we move to VLSI, these improvements will continue to take the form of decreased size and increased function with a simultaneous decrease in cost, so much so that by the end of the 10 years we can expect to hold in our hand a computer that has the power of the large mainframes that are in operation today. As this trend continues, advances in technology will have significant effects on all phases of computing and changes will take place in areas of our lives that most people never thought possible.

These trends in technology will have profound effects on how we deal with data through database management systems. There is no doubt that database machines will become a reality; the question concerns how we get there from here. There are two fairly distinct approaches that one can identify on each end of the spectrum of possible approaches; the revolutionary approach and the evolutionary approach. The revolutionary approach concerns using a database machine straight away. There are at least two types of group that will take the revolutionary approach to database machines. The first group includes those organisations who do not have much of an investment in current database management software and data. This group will in a sense leap-frog current sequential database management systems and go directly to database machines. Obviously, this route is riddled with problems, but nevertheless some organisations will take it. The second identifiable group that will take the revolutionary route includes organisations that are heavily involved in database management today and whose requirements have exceeded the capabilities of current systems. This group will have to discard much of their current investment in favour of trying to attain order of magnitude increases in performance and increases in function.

However, by far the largest group of database management system users will take the evolutionary approach. These are the organisations that have tremendous investments in software and data but who are able to 'get along' with current systems. Initially, these users will see increases in performance and/or throughput as technological and architectural advances take place. Most of the impact will come from special purpose function architectures such as search processors, merge processors, data dictionary/directory processors etc. That is, there will be a 'bottom-up' approach in which enhancements will be made to existing systems at the hardware/firmware level without the user really knowing about it. All the user will see is the resulting increase in performance and/or throughput. As this evolution continues there will invariably be increases in functional capability which the user will soon recognise. Then the user will want to take advantage of these increases. This represents the next major step in the evolutionary approach. The trend will continue until many organisations have developed the use of database machines.

Obviously all of the above prognostications could be incorrect. One thing, however, is sure, the database machine field will develop and those persons involved with it will live through some very exciting times.

REFERENCES

001 BERRA P B and OLIVER E
Associative array processor utilisation in database management
Computer vol 12 no 3 pp 53-61 (March 1979)

002 SU S Y W, NGUYEN L H, EMAM A and LIPOVSKI G J
The architectural features and implementation techniques of the multicell CASSM
IEEE Transactions on Computers vol C-28 no 6 pp 430-446 (June 1979)

003 SCHUSTER S A, NGUYGEN H B, OZKARAHAN E A and SMITH K C
RAP2 - an associative processor for databases and its implications
IEEE Transactions on Computers vol C-28 no 6 pp 446-458 (June 1979)

004 BANERJEE J, HSIAO D K and KANNAN K
DBC - a database computer for very large databases
IEEE Transactions on Computers vol C-28 no 6 pp 414-430 (June 1979)

005 MADNICK S E
The Infoplex database computer: concepts and directions
IEEE COMPCON Spring 79 Digest of Papers pp 168-176 (Feb 1979)

006 DEWITT D J
Direct - a multiprocessor organisation for supporting relational database management systems
IEEE Transactions on Computers vol C-28 no 6 pp 395-406 (June 1979)

007 OLIVER E
RELACS, an associative computer architecture to support a relational data model
PhD dissertation Syracuse University (June 1979)

008 MALLER V A J
The Content-Addressed File Store (CAFS) system
ICL Technical Journal (Nov 1979)

009 LEILICH H O, STIEGE G and ZEIDLER H C
A search processor for database management systems
Proc Fourth Intl Conf on *Very large databases* pp 280-287 (Sep 1978)

010 HOLLAAR L A
A design for a list merging network
IEEE Transactions on Computers vol C-28 no 6 pp 406-414 (June 1979)

011 HOLLAAR L A
Text retrieval computers
Computer vol 12 no 3 pp 40-50 (Mar 1979)

012 SINGHANIA A K
A multiple associative memories system for pipelining a directory to a very large database
PhD dissertation Syracuse University (May 1977)

013 CAPRARO G T
A database management modelling technique and special function hardware architecture
PhD dissertation Syracuse University (Mar 1978)

014 BIRD R M, TU J C and WORTHY R M
Associative parallel processors for searching very large textual databases
Proc Third Workshop on Computer Architecture for Non-numeric Processing pp 8-16 (May 1977)

015 ROBERTS D C
A specialised computer architecture for text retrieval
Proc Fourth Workshop on Computer Architecture for Non-numeric Processing pp 51-59 (Aug 1978)

016 MOORE G
HSTS, High Speed Text Search system
Operating Systems Inc Woodland Hills CA (*circa* May 1980)

017 IDM 500 Literature
Britton-Lee Inc Albright Way Los Gatos CA

018 MARYANSKI F J
Back-end database systems
ACM Computing Surveys vol 12 no 1 pp 3-25 (Mar 1980)

019 DEFIORE C and BERRA P B
A quantitative analysis of utilisation of associative memories in database management
IEEE Transactions on Computers vol C-23 no 2 pp 121-123 (Feb 1974)

020 MOULDER R
An implementation of a data management system on an associative processor
AFIPS Conf Proc vol 42 pp 171-176 (June 1973)

021 SU S Y W
Cellular-logic devices: concepts and applications
Computer vol 12 no 3 pp 11-25 (Mar 1979)

022 STONEBRAKER M *et al*
The design and implementation of Ingres
ACM Transactions on Database Systems vol 1 pp 189-222 (Sep 1976)

023 FREEMAN H A *et al*
Database computer research
Sperry Univac Final Report Contract no N00014-78-C-0487 (Nov 1979)

024 WAH B W and YAO S B
Dialog, a distributed processor organisation for database machine
NCC 80 AFIPS Press vol 49 (May 1980)

025 LIUZZI R A
A study of a database machine architecture development facility and its feasibility for developing special purpose function architectures
Unpublished doctoral dissertation Syracuse University (Apr 1980)

026 STELLHORN W H
An inverted file processor for information retrieval
IEEE Transactions on Computers vol C-26 pp 1258-1267 (Dec 1977)

EXPERT SYSTEMS AND PROLOG

I Bratko

J Stefan Institute
and
E Kardelj University
Ljubljana
Yugoslavia

I BRATKO received his PhD in computer science in 1978 from the University of Ljubljana. He is a reader in computer science in the Electrical Engineering Faculty, E Kardelj University, and a research fellow at the J Stefan Institute, Yugoslavia, where he leads a research group for artificial intelligence. His research interests include artificial intelligence, applications of artificial intelligence methods, heuristic methods for problem solving, expert systems, combinatorial optimisation problems and computer chess. From 1977 to 1981 he visited the Machine Intelligence Research Unit at the University of Edinburgh several times, conducting research in knowledge-based systems and computer chess. Dr Bratko is the author of many papers on artificial intelligence.

EXPERT SYSTEMS AND PROLOG

The basic features of rule-based systems, pattern-directed architecture, and PROLOG are discussed, and their uses in the design and implementation of Expert Systems are assessed. The rule-based representation of knowledge is examined with particular reference to 'if-then' rules. Rule systems are closely related to a relatively new architecture of software systems called pattern-directed systems and these are discussed in detail. PROLOG, a non-procedural programming language, is well suited to solving problems involving objects and relations between objects and examples are given in order to illustrate the nature of PROLOG programming. Finally, some implementations and applications of PROLOG are given.

INTRODUCTION

Expert systems can usually be viewed as composed of two modules, as shown in Figure 1: a *knowledge base* and an *inference machine*. This structure nicely reflects the two main tasks of knowledge engineering which are:

1 Representing and storing large amounts of problem-domain knowledge in the computer.

2 Actively using the problem-domain knowledge for solving problems and answering user queries.

The knowledge base contains facts, relations between facts, and possible methods for solving problems in the domain of application. The inference machine implements algorithms which solve problems and answer user queries by either simply retrieving facts from the knowledge base, or by inferring new facts from the facts that are explicitly stored in the knowledge base. Inferring new facts involves the use of general relations, or principles, which can also be stored in the knowledge base.

A number of tools and techniques have been developed in the field of artificial intelligence for the design and implementation of expert systems which have the same structure as shown in Figure 1, and which use knowledge-representations that satisfy certain criteria as explained later in this paper. These tools and techniques include rule-based systems, the architecture of pattern-directed systems, and programming languages for artificial intelligence. Among recently developed languages PROLOG is perhaps the most important and revolutionary innovation. This paper outlines basic ideas and features of rule-based systems, pattern-directed architecture, and PROLOG, and demonstrates their use in the design and implementation of expert systems.

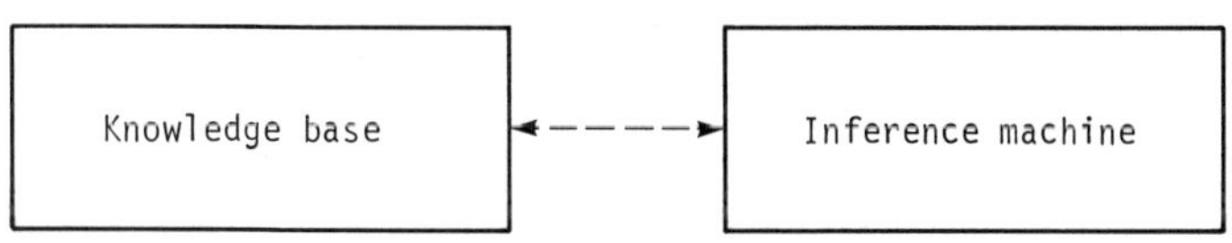

Figure 1: Structure of expert systems

RULE-BASED REPRESENTATION OF KNOWLEDGE

One major problem of artificial intelligence is concerned with the question of what form the knowledge should be organised into so that it can be efficiently used by the inference machine. In addition to this requirement, the technology of expert systems also requires that the representation of knowledge be:

- Transparent to the user
- Easy to increment by the (human) expert for the domain of application
- Easy to modify by the expert.

Several schemes have been proposed and used in knowledge-based systems, such as semantic networks (001), frames (002), and advice tables (003). Another schema, the rule-based representation, has however become overwhelmingly popular. Most well-known examples of expert systems, such as MYCIN (004) and PROSPECTOR (005) make use of rule-based representations.

In general, rules are of the form 'if-then', but they can have different interpretations. Examples are:

'If precondition P then conclusion C.'

'If situation S then action A.'

'If conditions C1 and C2 hold then condition C does not hold.'

A more concise notation is often used, for example:

```
P ---> C
```

The meaning of this depends on interpretation, eg 'if precondition P then conclusion C'.

If-then rules usually turn out to be a natural form of expressing knowledge, and have the following additional desirable features:

- *Modularity*: each rule defines a small, relatively independent piece of knowledge
- *Incrementability*: new rules can be added to the knowledge-base relatively independently of other rules
- *Modifiability*: old rules can be changed relatively independently of other rules
- Support system's *transparency*.

This last property is one of the most important and distinguishing demands of knowledge engineering. By transparency of the system we mean the system's ability to explain in terms which are understandable to the user its decisions and solutions. If-then rules facilitate answering two basic types of user's questions: '*How?*' and '*Why?*'. This is illustrated by the following example. Let a small knowledge-base consist of the rules:

```
b ---> a          (Meaning: if b then a)
c ---> b
d ---> b
e ---> d
f ---> d
```

This system of rules can be represented by the graph in Figure 2.

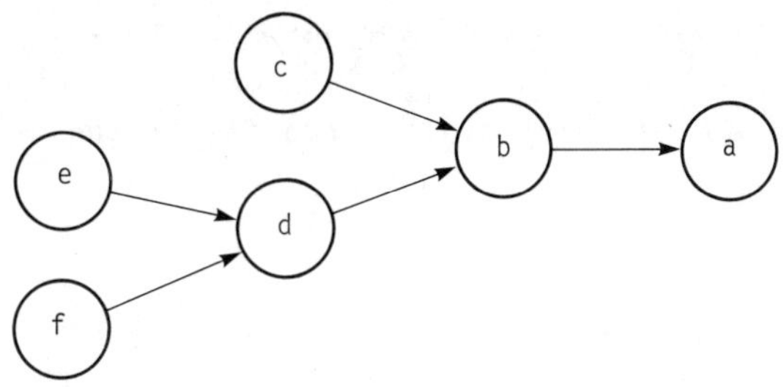

Figure 2: A small knowledge base

Suppose that the user has asked: 'How do you know that a is true?'. The answer can be generated by following the arrows in Figure 2 in the *backward* direction. From a the system sets to b and may answer:

'Because I know that
1 b is true.
2 a follows from b.'

The user can now further ask: 'How do you know that b is true?'. Using the same principle as above the system finds the justification for b in terms of c or d.

Now suppose the user has asked a 'why' type question: 'Why are you enquiring about c?'. The answer to this question can be generated by following the arrows in the *forward* direction, and the system can thus find the answer:

'Because I am investigating whether a is true, and I know that:

1 a follows from b.
2 b follows from c.'

If-then rules often define logical relations between concepts of the problem domain. Purely logical relations can be characterised as belonging to 'hard knowledge', 'hard' because they are always (absolutely) true. However, in some domains, such as medical diagnosis, 'soft knowledge' prevails; 'soft' in the sense that empirical regularities are usually valid only to a certain degree, ie often but not always. In such cases if-then rules are modified by adding a probabilistic qualification to their logical interpretation. For example:

'Conclusion A follows from condition B with certainty F.'

Figures 3, 4 and 5 show examples of if-then rules from three different knowledge-based systems: MYCIN for medical consultation (004), AL/X for diagnosing equipment failures (006), and AL3 for problem solving in chess (007).

PATTERN-DIRECTED SYSTEMS

Rule systems are closely related to a relatively new architecture of software systems called pattern-directed systems (008). This architecture is better suited for the implementation of expert systems than conventional system organisations. The main

<u>If</u> 1 the infection is primary-bacteremia, and
2 the site of the culture is one of the sterilesites, and
3 the suspected portal of entry of the organism is the gastrointestinal tract,

<u>then</u>
there is suggestive evidence (0·7) that the identity of the organism is bacteroides.

Figure 3: An if-then rule from the MYCIN system for medical consultation. The parameter 0·7 says to what degree the rule can be trusted.

<u>if</u> the pressure in V-01 reached relief valve lift pressure

<u>then</u>
the relief valve on V-01 has lifted [S=400, N=0·005]

<u>if</u> NOT the pressure in V-01 reached relief valve lift pressure
AND
the relief valve on V-01 has lifted

<u>then</u>
The V-01 relief valve opened early (the set pressure has drifted)
[S=2000, N=0.001]

Note:
AL/X treats uncertainty in the same way as Prospector. S and N above are 'sufficiency' and 'necessity' measures. S estimates to what degree the antecedent of the rule implies the consequent. N estimates to what degree the occurrence of the antecedent is necessary for the occurrence of the consequent.

Figure 4: Two rules from the AL/X system

<u>if</u>
1 there is a hypothesis, H, that a plan P succeeds, and
2 there are two hypotheses,
H1, that a plan R1 refutes plan P, and
H2, that a plan R2 refutes plan P, and
3 there are facts: H1 is false, and H2 is false

<u>then</u>
1 generate the hypothesis, R3, that the combined plan "R1 <u>or</u> R2" refutes plan P, and
2 generate the fact: H3 implies not(H)

Figure 5: A rule for plan refinement from the AL3 system

difference between conventional systems and pattern-directed systems is in the mechanisms of invocation of program modules. Figure 6 illustrates this difference. In conventional organisations of program systems, modules of the system call each other according to a fixed, predefined scheme. Each subprogram itself decides which subprogram will be executed next by explicitly calling other subprograms. The flow of execution is largely deterministic.

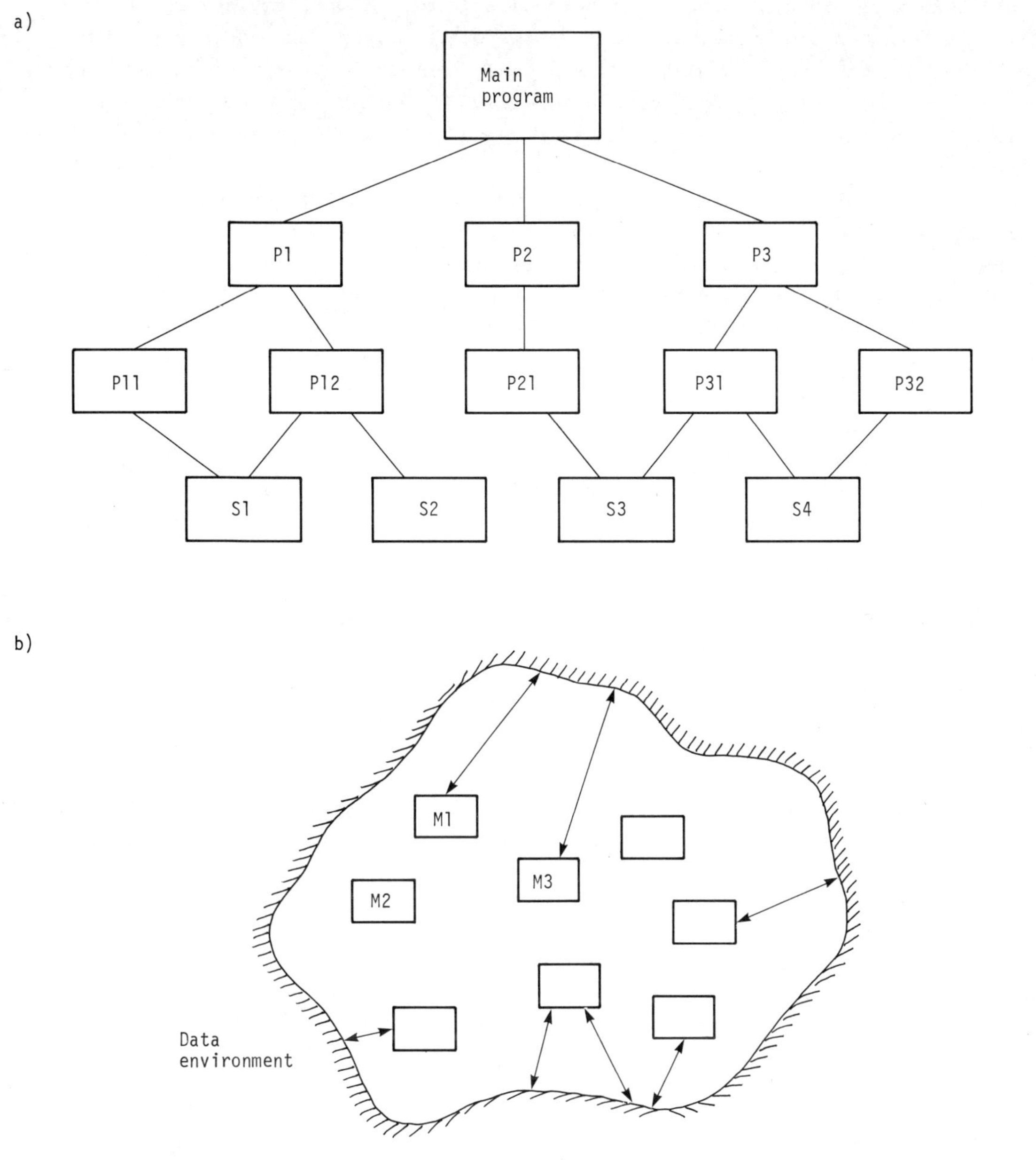

Figure 6a: *Example of conventional system organisation*
Figure 6b: *Example of pattern-directed system*
Figure 6: *Comparison of conventional and pattern-directed architecture*

In contrast to this, in pattern-directed organisation (Figure 6b) the modules of the system are not directly called by other modules. Pattern-directed modules are defined:

1 *A precondition pattern.*
2 *An action* to be executed if data matches the pattern.

Then the execution of program modules can be triggered by patterns that occur in the system's 'environment'. The data environment is usually also called the *database*.

Let us compare the structures in Figure 6 in more detail. The structure (a) certainly exhibits features that are generally considered good: it is neat, hierarchical, nicely ordered and enables good control and overview. The structure (b) is completely different. There is no hierarchy among modules. There is no explicit indication which module can invoke some other module. Modules communicate with the data environment rather than with other modules. The structure itself, in principle, permits execution of several modules simultaneously because the state of the database can be such as to simultaneously fire many modules. Consequently such an organisation can also serve as a natural model of parallel computation in which each module would be physically implemented by its own processor. This was studied by Nakamura (009).

From the viewpoint of the principles of structured program design, the structure (b) seems almost shocking. However, it also has certain advantages. One major advantage is that the design of the system does not require all the connections between modules to be carefully planned and defined in advance. Consequently, each module can be designed and implemented relatively autonomously, and is less dependent on other modules than in conventional systems. This renders a high degree of modularity. The level of modularity is manifested, for example, in that the removal of some module from the system is often not fatal. After the removal, the system would typically still be able to solve problems, only the way of solving problems might change. The same is true for the addition of new modules and for modifications of the existing modules. If similar modifications are carried out in systems with conventional organisation, at least the calls to other modules have to be properly modified.

This high degree of modularity is specially desirable in systems with complex knowledge bases because it is difficult to predict in advance all the interactions between individual pieces of knowledge in the base. The pattern-directed architecture offers a natural solution to this: each piece of knowledge, represented by an if-then rule, can be regarded as a pattern-directed module as illustrated in Figure 7.

Let us further elaborate the basic scheme of pattern-directed systems with implementational details. The scheme in Figure 6b suggests that the parallel implementation would be

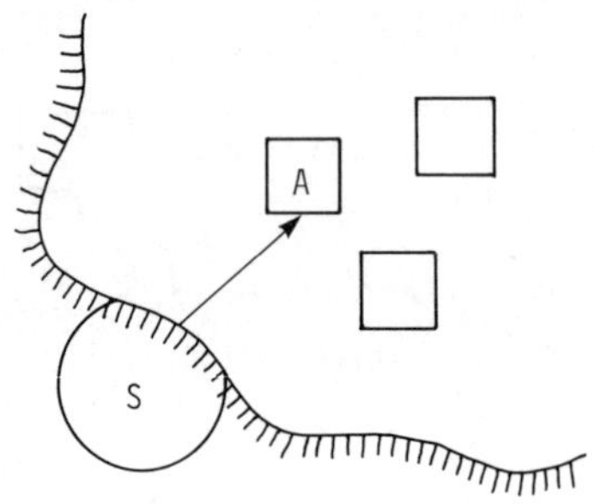

Figure 7: This situation corresponds to the rule: if situation S then action A

most natural. However, if the whole system is to be implemented on a traditional sequential processor, then in the case that the triggering patterns of several modules simultaneously occur in the database and there is a conflict, which of all these potentially active modules will be actually executed? The set of potentially active modules is called *conflict set*. In actual implementations of the scheme of Figure 6b on sequential processors there is an additional program module, called the *control module*. The control module resolves the conflict by choosing and activating one of the modules in the conflict set. One simple rule for resolving conflicts can be based on a predefined, fixed ordering of modules.

The basic life-cycle of pattern-directed systems is then composed of three steps:

1 *Pattern-matching*: find in the database all the occurrences of the condition-patterns of the program modules. This results in a conflict set.

2 *Conflict resolution*: choose one of the modules in the conflict set.

3 *Execution*: trigger the execution of the module that was chosen in step 2.

This implementational scheme is illustrated in Figure 8. For example, consider the set of if-then rules represented graphically in Figure 2. How can this set be operationalised into a pattern-directed system? One way is:

1 The database is composed of two lists which will be designated by F (for facts) and G (for goals). Elements of F and G can be a, b, c etc.

2 Each rule of Figure 2 corresponds to a pattern-directed module defined as:
- *Precondition*: the right-hand side of the rule appears in the list G
- *Action*: add the left-hand side of the rule to the list G.

3 There is an additional module defined as:
- *Precondition*: lists F and G have a common element
- *Action*: write ('Initial hypotheses have been proved') and stop the execution of the system.

4 The initial database is: the list F contains those things that are known to be true; the list G contains the hypothesis to be investigated. For example if the user knows that e is true, and is interested whether a is true, then the initial database would be:

    F = [e],   G = [a]

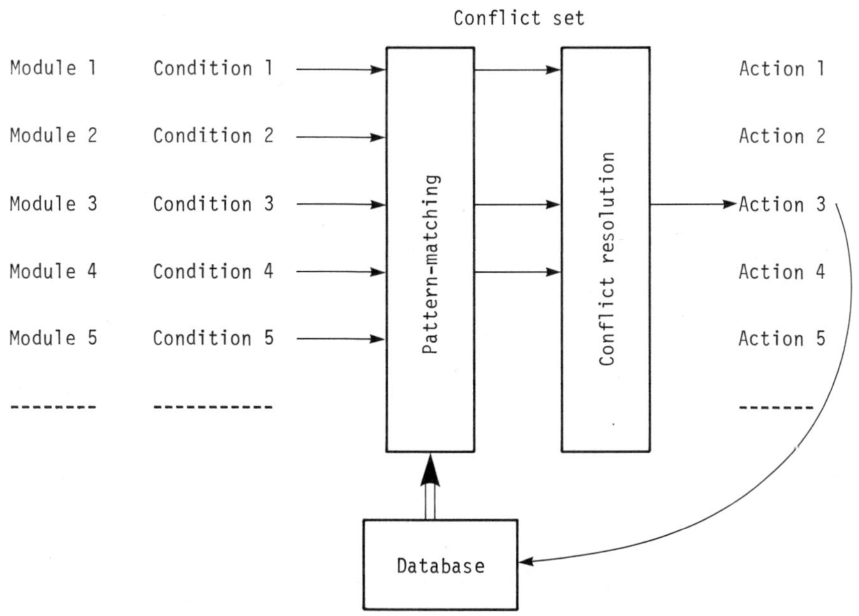

Note: In this example the database satisfies the condition pattern of modules 1, 3 and 4; module 3 is chosen for execution

Figure 8: Basic life-cycle of pattern-directed systems

5 The control schema: never execute any module that has already been executed; in case of conflict, first choose the module (3) above, and then other rules in the same order as they appear in Figure 2.

A trace of execution of this system is shown in Figure 9. This example gives an idea of using pattern-directed systems. Of course, some elaboration of the basic schema would be needed for dealing with larger knowledge bases and more complicated rules, such as those in Figures 3, 4 and 5. However, the mechanisms would be essentially the same.

F	G	Rule executed
[e]	[a]	b ---> a
[e]	[a,b]	c ---> b
[e]	[a,b,c]	d ---> b
[e]	[a,b,c,d]	e ---> d
[e]	[a,b,c,d,e]	stopping rule

Figure 9: Trace of example system when answering the question: Is a true if e is known to be true?

Our next example will show how pattern-directed programs can also be used to solve 'ordinary' programming exercises. We will implement the Euclid algorithm for finding the greatest common divisor of two natural numbers A and B. This algorithm can be written in procedural languages, like PASCAL, for example, as follows:

```
begin
   while  A ≠ B do
      if  A > B then  A := A-B
                else  B := B-A;
   write(A)
end
```

An equivalent rule-based program is:

```
RULE1:
[m(C1,A), m(C2,B), A > B] ---> [replace(m(C1,A), m(C1,A-B))]

RULE2:
[m(C,X)]  --->  [write(X), stop]
```

The names A, B, C1, C2 and X should be understood as universally quantified variables. Rule 1 can be read:

```
If
    there is a memory cell C1 whose content is number A
    and
    there is a memory cell C2 holding number B
    and
    A > B
then
    replace the content of C1 by A-B.
```

Conflict resolution schema is: first rule 1, then rule 2. Initially the database contains the numbers whose greatest common divisor is to be computed. If these numbers are 25 and 15 then the database would contain:

```
m(1,25),   m(2,15)
```

The final state of the database would be in this example:

```
m(1,5),   m(2,5)
```

The comparison between the PASCAL program and the rule-based program reveals that they in fact both implement the same algorithm. One (in this case small) advantage of the rule-based program is that it is not necessary to define an extra action for each of two cases: A > B and B > A. The matching for the precondition pattern of rule 1 always assigns the names C1 and C2 to the memory cells so that A > B.

It may appear now somewhat surprising that our rule-based program is also able to find the greatest common divisor of more than two numbers. If we initially store, for example, three numbers (30, 10 and 15) into the database then the program outputs the greatest common divisor of all three. The trace of the changes in the database is shown in Figure 10. This generality of the rule-based program is due to the condition pattern of rule 1 which only requires the existence of two unequal numbers in the database, regardless of other data. An extension of our PASCAL program so as to be able to deal with many numbers would require major modifications.

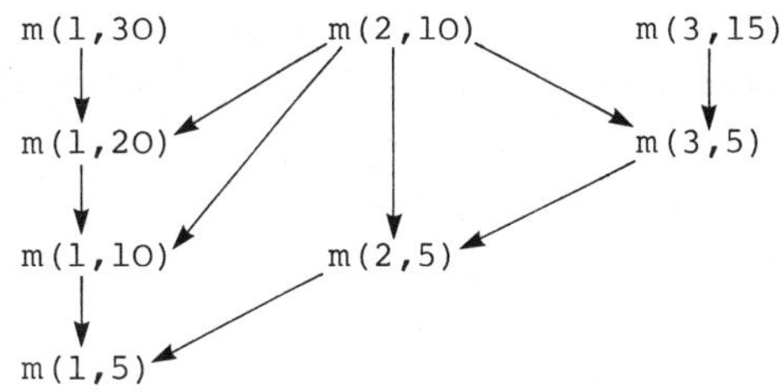

Figure 10: Modifications in the database during the computation of the greatest common divisor of 30, 10 and 15

PROLOG: INTRODUCTORY EXAMPLES

PROLOG is a programming language that is specially well suited for solving problems that involve objects and relations between objects. PROLOG programs themselves can be viewed as pattern-directed systems.

PROLOG is based on formal logic. Its syntax is basically the syntax of first order predicate calculus restricted to Horn clauses only. The idea of using logic for programming is developed in detail in Kowalski (010). PROLOG is usually introduced through formal logic; however, such a formal introduction is not necessary for practical programming in PROLOG. The beginner can easily obtain intuitive understanding of PROLOG syntax and meaning without formal treatment.

In this paper we will present PROLOG informally, mainly through examples to give some flavour of PROLOG programming. This is quite different from programming in 'ordinary', procedural languages.

PROLOG programs can be thought of as pattern-directed systems. Our example set of rules in Figure 2 can be straightforwardly translated into PROLOG. A corresponding PROLOG program can be:

```
a :- b.
b :- c.
b :- d.
d :- e.
d :- f.
e.
```

Throughout the paper we use the notational conventions of the Edinburgh implementation of PROLOG (011). The clause

```
a :- b.
```

can be read: 'a is true if b is true', or 'b implies a'. The last clause, 'e.', says that e is a fact (ie e is certainly true). The PROLOG program can now be asked whether a is true:

```
?- a.
```

The answer by the PROLOG system would be 'yes' because the system can logically derive a from the fact e, and from other statements in the program.

Our next example will illustrate how naturally one can solve problems in PROLOG involving objects and relations between objects. A small database in Figure 11 defines the parent relation. In PROLOG this relation can be defined by the following piece of program:

```
parent(tom,bob).
parent(tom,liz).
parent(bob,ann).
parent(bob,pat).
```

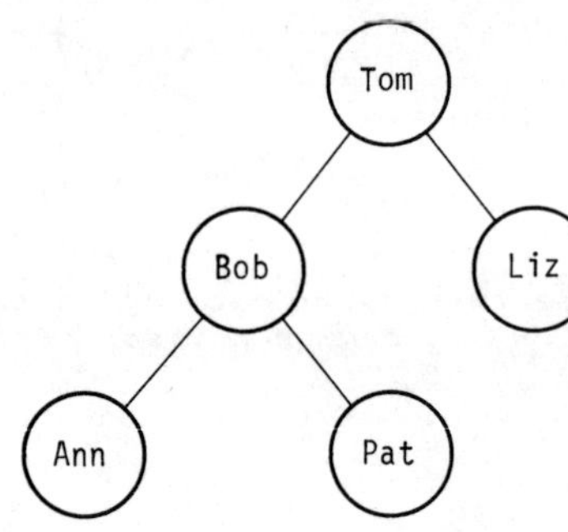

Figure 11: A family tree

The successor relation can be derived from the parent relation. The general rule defining the successor relation can be stated in PROLOG by two statements:

```
succ(X,Y) :- parent(Y,X).
succ(X,Y) :- parent(Y,Z), succ(X,Z).
```

The first statement above says: 'For all X and Y, X is a successor of Y if Y is a parent of X.'

The second statement recursively defines indirect successors and can be read: 'For all X and Y, X is a successor of Y if there exists a Z such that Y is a parent of Z and X is a successor of Z.'

Now the PROLOG system can be asked: Who are the children of Bob? This question to PROLOG is:

```
?- parent(bob,X).
```

PROLOG's answer is:

```
X = ann;
X = pat
```

We can also ask: Who are the predecessors of Pat? That is; we are looking for all the people whose successor is Pat.

```
?- succ(pat,Y).
```

Answer:

```
Y = bob;
Y = tom
```

We can also ask for all the pairs successor-predecessor:

```
?- succ(S,P).
```

PROLOG will answer with all instantiations of the variables P and S so that they satisfy the successor relationship:

```
P = tom, S = bob;
P = tom, S = liz;
P = tom, S = ann;
etc.
```

A SUMMARY OF THE SYNTAX AND MEANING OF PROLOG PROGRAMS

PROLOG is a non-procedural language. The execution of PROLOG programs can be viewed as the evaluation of relations. In this sense the nature of programming in PROLOG is much different from programming in algorithmic or procedural languages. This difference will be clarified by an example.

A basic computational operation in procedural languages is the assignment operation. An example is:

```
Y := f(X)
```

This can be read: compute the value of the function f(X) and assign the result to the variable Y. So this statement can be represented by the following diagram:

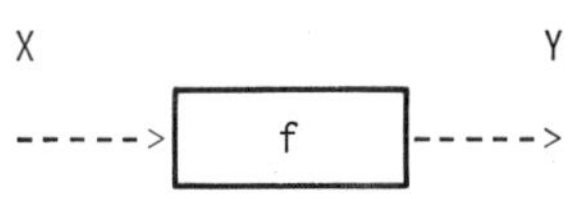

In PROLOG, a corresponding effect can be achieved by the statement

```
f(X,Y)
```

which says that the values of X and Y are such that they satisfy the relation f. If now the value of X is known then the evaluation of the relation f will instantiate the variable Y so that the relation f will be satisfied. If more than one value for Y satisfies f then the effect is non-deterministic. Depending on the context, all the corresponding values for Y may be generated.

The situation is here similar to that in the assignment statement:

> 'X is known, Y is unknown: Y is assigned a value, which corresponds to the same input/output view as in the above diagram.'

However, since here f is a *relation* rather than a function, there is no explicit demand on which of the arguments X and Y should be known or unknown. This makes possible other ways of using the statement f(X,Y). They are:

1 Y is known, X is unknown: the request f(X,Y) now works in the reverse direction: instantiate X so that f is satisfied.

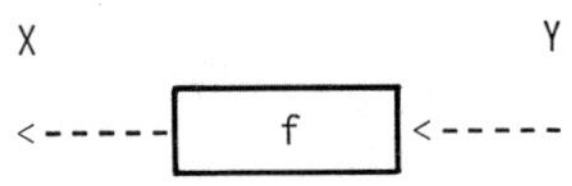

2 X and Y are both known: f(X,Y) behaves as a test whether the values of X and Y satisfy the relation f.

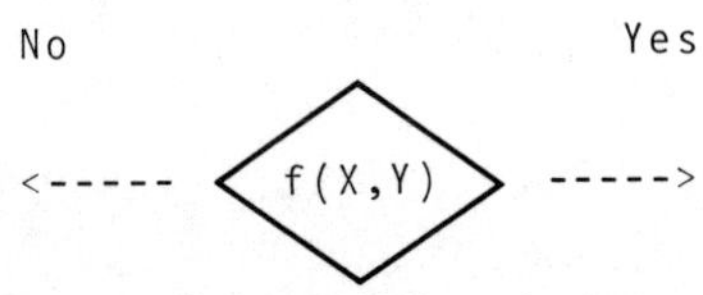

3 X and Y are both unknown: the request f(X,Y) will behave as a generator of all the pairs of values for X and Y such that they satisfy the relation f.

4 X and Y are partially known: for example, it may be only known that X is a family with two children, but their names and the names of parents, etc are not known. The effect of f(X,Y) would possibly be to further determine the values of X and Y.

The following is a brief, informal and incomplete review of the PROLOG syntax and semantics. Full description can be found eg in (012) and (013).

PROLOG programs consist of *clauses* of the form:

```
P :- Q1, ..., Qn.
```

Syntactically, P, Q1, ..., Qn are *terms* (defined later). P is the *head* of the clause, and the list Q1, ..., Qn is the *body*. PROLOG programs have both declarative and procedural meaning. For example, the clause

```
P :- Q, R.
```

can be read declaratively:

> 'P is true if Q and R are true', or

> 'Q and R imply P'

The procedural meaning defines how the program is actually executed by the PROLOG system. The procedural interpretation of the above example clause is:

'To solve P, first solve Q and *then*, if Q is true, solve R.'

Clauses that have empty body are used to represent facts. Queries to the system are stated in the form:

```
?- Q1, Q2, ..., Qn.
```

with the declarative meaning:

'Are Q1 *and* Q2 *and ... and* Qn true?'

The procedural reading is:

'Prove first that Q1 is true, and if Q1 is true then prove Q2, etc.'

Terms consist of predicate symbols and arguments, eg:

```
son(X,peter)
```

Arguments are data objects. The data objects are either:

1 Elementary objects.
2 Structured objects.

Elementary objects are:

1 *Atoms* eg: david, x, z23.
2 *Integers* eg: 5, 0, -19.
3 *Variables* which are syntactically recognised by that their names start with capital letters, eg: X, List, David, Y1B.

The syntax of structured objects is that of terms. All structured objects in PROLOG are trees. For example, a point in the three-dimensional space can be defined by three coordinates: X, Y, Z. So a point can be represented by a structured object which has three components, and the components are held together by a 'functor' (chosen by the user). Let us choose 'point' as the functor name. Then the structured object, representing a point, can be written:

```
point(X,Y,Z)
```

This can be graphically illustrated as a tree:

```
  point
  / | \
 /  |  \
X   Y   Z
```

For lists there is a convention that they are constructed by using the functor "." (dot). Arguments are the head and the tail of the list. The empty list is denoted by 'nil'. Then the list of atoms [a, b, c] can be written as:

```
.(a, .(b, .(c, nil)))
```

This corresponds to the tree

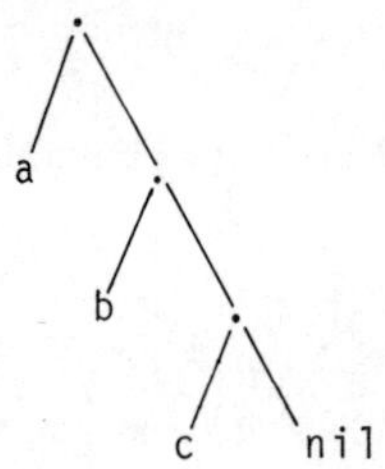

There is a 'syntactic sugar' for lists to provide a nicer (external) appearance of lists. The syntactic sugar also supplies a special notation for the separation of the prefix of the list and the rest of it. Our example list can be equivalently written in the following forms:

```
[a,b,c]  or  [a|[b,c]]  or  [a,b|[c]]
```

An important computational mechanism of PROLOG is *unification*. The unification process takes as input two terms and establishes whether they match. If they do then they are unified; that is the (yet uninstantiated) variables in both terms are instantiated so that both terms become identical. For example, the unification of the terms point (X1,Y1,5) and point(1,Y2,Z2) can be in PROLOG required by:

```
point(X1,Y1,5)  =  point(1,Y2,Z2)
```

The result is the following instantiation:

```
X1 = 1,  Y1 = Y2,  Z2 = 5
```

Such an instantiation of variables is also called the *most general unifier*. It is most general in the sense that the values of the variables set committed as little as possible. Another unifier would be in our example:

```
X1 = 1,  Y1 = 1,  Y2 = 1,  Z2 = 5
```

This unifier is less general than the one above because it unnecessarily strongly restricts the values of Y1 and Y2. Unification in PROLOG always produces the most general unifier.

The whole PROLOG program is a set of clauses. Declaratively, this set is interpreted as a set of statements that are all true. When the PROLOG system is answering a user query then the program clauses are used as axioms from which the answer is to be logically derived. Declaratively, the order in which the clauses appear in the program is not important. On the other hand, the procedural meaning of the program does depend on the order of clauses. The user query can be considered as a goal to be proved. The goal attempts to be unified with the heads of the clauses in the program. The clauses are tried in the same order as they appear in the program. If the unification succeeds then the terms in the body of the clause become additional goals to be proved, recursively using the program clauses as axioms. If there is no clause whose head can be unified with the current goal then the system *automatically backtracks* and tries to find another clause at some previous point that could be used.

PROGRAMMING EXAMPLES

Concatenation of lists can be expressed as a relation with three arguments, L1, L2 and L3, such that L3 is the concatenation of L1 and L2. For example:

```
conc([a,b],[c,d],[a,b,c,d])
```

The piece of program below that defines this relation is based on two observations:

1 If the first list is empty then the second and the third list must be equal.

2 If the first list is not empty then it can be decomposed into its head and tail. Then the head of the first list and the head of the third list must be equal (see Figure 12).

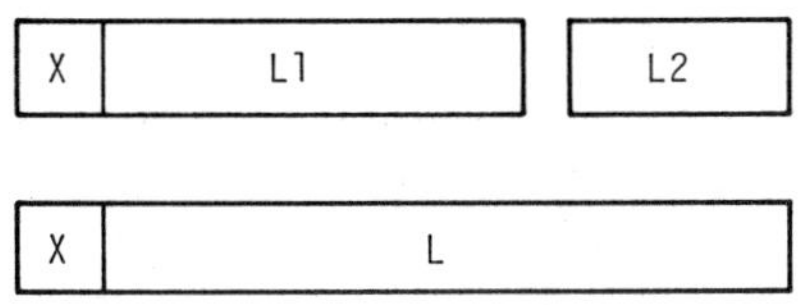

Figure 12: List concatenation

The same is said by the following two PROLOG clauses:

```
conc([],L,L).
conc([X|L1],L2,[X|L3])  :  conc(L1,L2,L3).
```

This program can now be used for concatenating given lists, and also for decomposing a given list into two lists, eg:

```
?- conc(L1,L2,[a,b,c]).
```

The PROLOG answer is:

```
L1 = [],  L2 = [a,b,c];
L1 = [a],  L2 = [b,c];
L1 = [a,b]  L2 = [c];
L1 = [a,b,c],  L2 = []
```

Let us now consider the list membership relation member(X,L) (X is a member of list L), eg:

```
member(b,[a,b,c,d])
```

Using the conc relation, the membership can be elegantly programmed by the clause:

```
member(X,L) :- conc(L1,[X|L2],L).
```

This can be read: X is a member of list L if L can be decomposed into two lists so that the second one of them begins with X.

The same idea, illustrated in Figure 13, can be used to define the sublist relation, eg:

```
sublist([c,d],[a,b,c,d,e])
```

The corresponding PROLOG clause is:

```
sublist(Sub,List) :- conc(S,S2,List), conc(S1,Sub,S).
```

Our final example is a simulator of a non-deterministic automaton. The simplicity of the solution will be enabled by automatic backtracking in PROLOG. The automaton itself is represented as a set of facts. For example, the automaton in Figure 14 is specified by the following part of PROLOG program which defines:

1 The final state of the automation.

2 The state transitions relation by the relation d with three arguments (state before transition, input symbol, state after transition):

```
final(s3).
d(s1,a,s1).
d(s1,a,s2).
d(s1,b,s1).
d(s2,b,s3).
d(s2,eps,s4).
d(s3,b,s4).
d(s3,eps,s1).
```

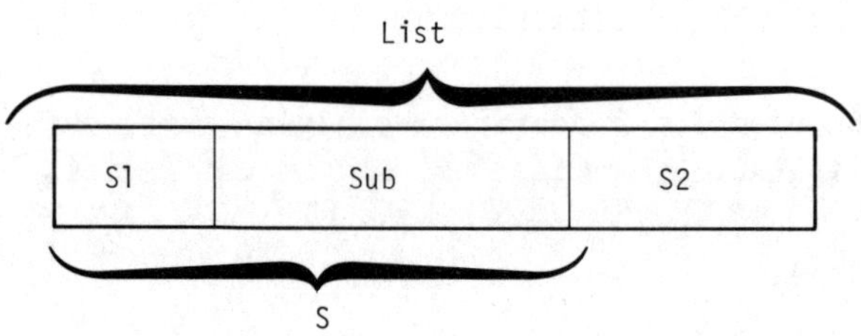

Figure 13: The sublist relation

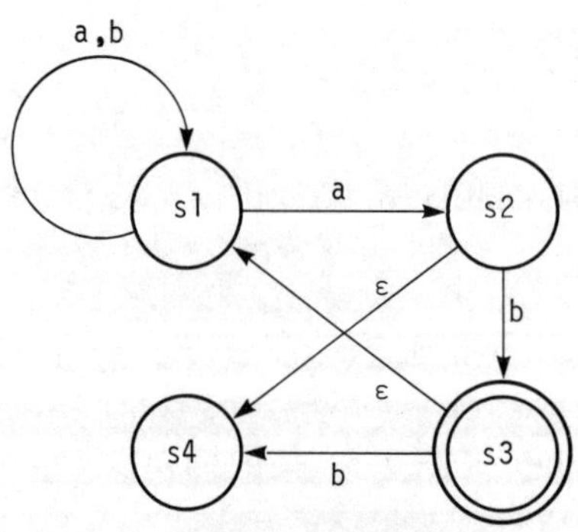

Figure 14: A non-deterministic automaton s3 is a final state, ε denotes the empty symbol

Input strings will be represented by lists; so the string 'aab' would be represented by [a,a,b] By definition, the non-deterministic automaton accepts a given input string if and only if (starting from the initial state), after having read the whole input string the automaton can (possibly) be in its final state.

The following simulator is programmed as a relation which defines the acceptance of a string from a given initial state. So:

```
accepts(S,String)
```

is true if the automaton would, starting from the state S as an initial state, accept the string String. The whole simulator is:

```
accepts(S,[]) :- final(S).
accepts(S,[A|Rest]) :- d(S,A,S1), accepts(S1,Rest).
accepts(S,String) :- d(S,eps,S1), accepts(S1,String).
```

The above clauses say:

1 The empty string is accepted from state S if S is a final state.

2 A non-empty string is accepted from state S if reading the first symbol can bring the automaton into a state S1, and the rest of the string is accepted from S1.

3 A string is accepted from state S if the automaton can make a 'silent' move ('reading' the empty symbol) from S to S1, and then it accepts the string from S1.

The program can be asked, for example, about the acceptance of the string 'aaab' by:

```
?- accepts(s1,[a,a,a,b]).
  yes.
```

PROLOG programs are often able to solve more general problems than problems for which they were originally developed. In our case we can also ask the simulator which state our automaton can initially be in so that it will accept the string 'ab'?

```
?- accepts(S,[a,b]).
```

The answer is:

```
S = s1;
S = s3
```

Amusingly, we can also ask: What are all the strings of length 3 that are accepted from the state s1?

```
?- accepts(s1,[X1,X2,X3]).

   X1 = a, X2 = a, X3 = b;
   X1 = b, X2 = a, X3 = b
```

SOME IMPLEMENTATIONS AND APPLICATIONS OF PROLOG

The following is a list of some PROLOG systems:

1 Interpreter in FORTRAN, University of Marseille (first implementation of PROLOG).

2 Interpreter (in Assembler) and compiler (in PROLOG) for DEC-10, University of Edinburgh.

3 Interpreter in Assembler for PDP-11 with the UNIX or RT-11 operating systems, University of Edinburgh.

4 Interpreter in LISP, embedded into LISP environment (University of Linkoeping).

5 A portable interpreter in Compiler Description Language (CDL), developed in Hungary and installed on a number of different machines (Siemens 7·755, IBM 370/145, IBM 3031, ODRA 1305 etc).

6 Interpreter for the Z-80 microprocessor, Imperial College, London.

The most known implementation is that of the Edinburgh University (012) which provides a friendly interactive environment with many built-in procedures and debugging facilities in the interpreter, and a compiler for (relatively) efficient execution of already developed programs. The compiler speeds up the execution by a factor of about 20 with respect to the interpreter. The above list of implementations shows that PROLOG can be run on very modest hardware although the way that data is typically represented and manipulated in PROLOG really indicates the use of more powerful resources, specially larger memories.

PROLOG is an efficient tool for non-numerical problems which involve objects and relations. It is, on the other hand, in its present form completely unsuitable for more traditional, numeric-type computations.

It is rather obvious that PROLOG is extremely well suited for the development of expert systems. It facilitates experimenting with alternative ways of representing and using knowledge in the system. Two examples of expert systems that are currently being developed and implemented in PROLOG are a system for regional planning (University of Lisbon (011), and a system for medical diagnosis and treatment advice in intensive care (J Stefan Institute, Ljubljana).

PROLOG has been successfully used in several other domains. Examples are as follows:

1 Systems for natural language communication, eg (014).

2 Compiler writing (015): the PROLOG compiler itself is written in PROLOG and generates efficient code; it takes typically a few seconds to compile programs of a few hundred clauses.

3 Knowledge-based problem solving systems: eg mechanics problems (014), and chess problems (007).

4 Drug design and chemical information handling (016).

5 Architectural design (017).

PROLOG can be naturally used as a query language for relational databases; this is investigated in (018). In (019) Bojadzijev *et al* report on using PROLOG as a specification language for information system design. A complex design documentation of a warehouse information system was directly translated into PROLOG. The result was an executable system specification which enabled the designers to test by simulation the proposed design specifications.

CONCLUDING REMARKS

Some tools and techniques of artificial intelligence for the design and implementation of knowledge-based systems have been reviewed: if-then rules for representing knowledge, pattern-directed architecture which is related to rule-based representations, and PROLOG as a programming vehicle. Throughout this paper, the advantageous features of these techniques have been mostly emphasised. If-then rules have proved to be a useful representation for complex knowledge. PROLOG programs tend to be compact, transparent and easily modifiable. It should be admitted, however, that systems based on these techniques, in one or another form have to do a lot of pattern matching or condition testing. This is often highly time consuming and typically causes problems of computational inefficiency. Practical applications show that in most cases this inefficiency can be tolerated. On the other hand, it is evident that much of the pattern-matching could be done in parallel. With special-purpose hardware tailored to the nature of these techniques, dramatic improvements in executional efficiency could be achieved. The Japanese study on the fifth generation computers (020) proposes a scheme for computer systems with a specialised processor for logic programming.

REFERENCES

001 FAHLMAN S E
NETL: a system for representing and using real-world knowledge
The MIT Press Cambridge Massachusetts (1979)

002 GOLDSTEIN I P and ROBERTS B
Using frames in scheduling
In *Artificial intelligence: an MIT perspective* P Winston and R H Brown (eds) vol 1 MIT Press (1979)

003 BRATKO I and MITCHIE D
A representation for pattern-knowledge in chess end-games
Advances in Computer Chess vol 2 M R B Clark (ed) Edinburgh Univ Press (1980)

004 SHORTCLIFFE E
Computer-based medical consultations
American Elsevier (1976)

005 DUDA R, GASCHNIG J and HART P
Model design in the Prospector consultant system for mineral exploration
In *Expert systems in the microelectronic age* D Mitchie (ed) Edinburgh Univ Press (1979)

006 REITER J
AL/X: an expert system using plausible inference
Univ of Edinburgh Machine Intelligence Research Unit (1980)

007 BRATKO I
Knowledge-based problem solving in AL3
Machine Intelligence vol 10
D Michie and Y H Pao (eds)
Ellis Horwood and Wiley (in press)

008 WATERMAN D A and HAYES-ROTH F (editors)
Pattern-directed inference systems
Academic Press (1978)

009 NAKAMURA K
Parallel production systems
J of the ACM (to appear)

010 KOWALSKI R
Logic for problem solving
North-Holland Publishing Co (1979)

011 PEREIRA L M, OLIVEIRA E and SABATIER P
An introspective expert system for biophysical resource evaluation
NATO symposium on *Artificial and human intelligence* Lyon (1981)

012 PEREIRA L M, PEREIRA F and WARREN D H D
User's guide to DEC system-10 PROLOG
Department of Artificial Intelligence
Univ of Edinburgh (1978)

013 CLOCKSIN W F and MELLISH C S
Programming in PROLOG
Springer-Verlag (1981)

014 BUNDY A, BYRD L, LUGER G, MELLISH C and PALMER M
Solving mechanics problems using meta-level inference
In *Expert systems in the microelectronic age* D Michie (ed) Edinburgh Univ Press (1979)

015 WARREN D H D
PROLOG and compiler writing
Department of Artificial Intelligence (DAI Rep) Univ of Edinburgh (1977)

016 DARVAS F
Logic programming in chemical information handling and drug design
Preprints of Logic Programming Workshop Debrecen Hungary (1980)

017 MARKUSZ Z
An application of PROLOG in designing many-storied dwelling houses
Preprints of Logic Programming Workshop Debrecen Hungary (1980)

018 GALLAIRE H and MINKER J
Logic and databases
Plenum Press (1978)

019 BOJADZIJEV D, LAVRAC N and MOZETIC I
Experience with PROLOG as a system specification language
J Slovene Society for Info Proc
Informatica (to appear 1982)

020 *Preliminary rep on study and research on 5th generation computers*
Japan Information Processing Development Center (1981)

DISTRIBUTED COMPUTING WITH LINKED MICROCOMPUTERS

C Crook

Zynar Ltd
Uxbridge
Middlesex

C CROOK began his early studies in microelectronics while working on tropospheric scatter systems for BMEWS rearward data link. He subsequently worked for the Plessey Company on computer design before joining Motorola, Geneva in 1969 and becoming involved in the development of Motorola's CMOS product line. In 1973 Mr Crook moved to the United States where he held various senior appointments with Motorola, his greatest technical achievement being the conception and development of the M68000 range of advanced microcomputers. In 1978 Mr Crook returned to the UK as Managing Director of Rank Precision Industries and in 1980 launched Zynar Ltd, a subsidiary of the Rank Organisation concerned with developing new opportunities in silicon systems technology. Mr Crook is a Chartered Engineer and in 1981 was appointed to the Fellowship of Engineers in recognition of his contribution to the development of the microcomputer.

DISTRIBUTED COMPUTING WITH LINKED MICROCOMPUTERS

A distributed computing system is not a fixed systems concept but involves a spectrum of options and capabilities involving control, processing and database. The specific user attributes of these systems are discussed in the context of a distributed systems approach using linked microcomputers. Particular attention is given to the newly evolving systems design using multiple microcomputers linked together over a local area network. The user's perception of the network and the distribution of its resources are discussed and an example of a current network of microcomputers is given. Key considerations for the use of network architectures are also discussed.

INTRODUCTION

Distributed computing has been discussed for some time with various interpretations applied to its definition. In fact, the liberal use of the term has resulted in a loss of definition. It is interesting to consider exactly what can be distributed within the definition of a computer/information system. The elements of the system are:

- Control
- Processing
- Database.

Distribution does not exclusively involve the physical aspect of hardware etc, but also involves the distribution of the way the system operates. In general the degree of distribution can be considered under the following points:

1 *Processing*: the spectrum runs from a single computer with exclusively local access, to separate specialised processors grouped together, to a single computer with remote access, to the final mode of multiple computers often physically apart.

2 *Control:* this capability can operate from centralised control, to full autonomous, to hierarchical, to the ultimate of decentralised, cooperating nodes.

3 *Database*: the database can be centralised, decentralised with central control, duplicated or finally physically distributed and partitioned.

In examining these key features which have been distributed according to the previous remarks, several observations can be made. The concept of a distributed system involves the 'degree' to which the system exhibits these characteristics.

We do have a spectrum of distribution. In terms of processing the use of multiple processors and multiple computers are the key interests. In the control area it is the multiple nodes cooperating on subtasks through to fully cooperating capability that is the interesting and relevant point. The database becomes interesting with distributed files using a single central directory. The ultimate node is a fully partitioned database with no master file or directory.

The resulting distributed system, therefore, is not a fixed systems concept, but involves a spectrum of options and capabilities involving control, processing and database.

The specific user attributes of these systems cover such things as:

- Reliability
- Availability
- Modular growth (cost/flexibility)
- Resource sharing
- Adaptability
- Graceful degradation
- Flexible growth path.

In discussing the distributed systems approach using linked microcomputers, the above attributes will be reviewed. This paper will not review the design of computer mainframes achieved by multiple microcomputer but will concentrate on the newly evolving systems design using multiple microcomputers linked together over a local area network. It is believed this approach will be the most relevant one over the next 10 years.

FUNDAMENTAL CHANGES REQUIRING CONSIDERATION

The developments in VLSI are now well known and the capability schedule is explicitly declared. (See Figure 1.)

Date	Chip density transistors	
1970	1K	
1975	10K	6800 type μprocessor
1980	100K	68 000 type μprocessor
1985	1M	? (fifth generation)
1990	10M	? (fifth generation)

Figure 1: Growth of chip density transistors

Once the semiconductor manufacturer is able to produce in massive volume, the mass consumer market becomes highly relevant. Current estimates for the personal computer market are staggering in their growth projections:

1980	1M machines
1990	200-500M machines!!

In addition to the phenomenal volume of machines, each one is going to have processing and general system attributes of current mini or mainframes, for example:

- Processing speeds - 1-3 MIPS
- Local memory - several Mbytes
- Local disk - 50 Mbytes
- Interface - high resolution and tuned to consumer/user acceptance.

The whole area of communications/information technology is expanding and presenting systems designers with the need to address both local and wide-area communications. Consequently, isolated stand-alone computer systems are unlikely to be very acceptable to the user. The ability to communicate with other systems over short or long distances or to access databases etc will be critical. This very fact will enhance the need for a distributed systems style of thinking.

Other relevant developments are those involving memory technology. Mass storage devices are becoming both cheaper and available in volume. Current Winchester disk and related technology looks like it will provide capacities of 1 gigabyte. Also optical memory technology will further enhance the cost/performance developments. The use of mass consumer software and such developments as 'expert systems' promises a revolution in the software industry. This is not yet perceived though some evidence is already beginning to appear.

In summary, we can see several fundamental forcing functions at play in the general market-place and technology. These are going to have a massive impact on all computer and information systems developments. The question of their relevance to distributed systems needs rapid evaluation.

Local, powerful, and distributed processing nodes (personal computer workstations) are the most obvious trend. Each node will also have a low cost and a plentiful front-end storage system. Mass back-end storage systems, involving again low-cost technology, will be accessed by many users as a common database. Multiple systems will be feasible due to the excellent price structure. The rapid developments in communications technology will facilitate high-capacity local-area (1 km) interconnects between nodes; access to a world-wide network will also be required by the user and the implementation will be feasible. Finally two levels of software will become very relevant; highly-tuned local user software with great appeal and capabilities and sophisticated system software. These two combined will create a very attractive total systems offering. It will be remembered that VisiCalc resulted from the personal computer market. Overall the trends favour a systems concept involving the distribution of processing, control and database. In essence the evidence suggests that we may finally see practical moves towards a 'true' distributed systems approach. Any concerns must surely lie in the systems-level software involving high-level operating systems. The classical design of operating systems consumes the availability of a large amount of systems information. This is not the case for a distributed system, with resulting complications.

MULTIPLE MICROCOMPUTER NODES

The classical user access to computing has been via a 'dumb' terminal into a mini/mainframe under a timesharing operating system. Recent developments have created the personal workstation. Here the user has dedicated processing power, control and memory. The computer is their own, with excellent personal appeal. Response is excellent and the user usually relates directly to the system. No longer is the 'computer' something at the end of a telephone line or a batch/line printer printout scheme. It has immediate and direct appeal.

The current product offering available in the market is typically:

- CPU - 8-bit microprocessor - 6502 type
- Speed - 0.3 million machine instr/sec
- 64K bytes of memory
- 140K bytes of 5¼-inch mini floppy.

New developments taking place are resulting in products which offer:

- CPU - 16/32 bits microprocessor - 68 000 type
- Speed - 3 million machine instr/sec
- + 512K bytes of memory
- Bit-mapped displays
- 5/10 Mbytes of mini Winchester disk storage.

Consequently, a 'typical' local network or community of linked microcomputers or personal workstations (10 - 30 nodes) constitutes a significant processing capability, albeit distributed and not usually cooperating under a central operating system.

In addition to the user or processing node, the community of linked microcomputers can have attached resources or 'servers'. These provide a range of special capabilities or services to which the user can gain access. A typical multinetwork system in use at Zynar in the UK has a total of 40 user nodes and 10 server nodes providing system-wide services.

Typical usage of the node at the beginning is strictly stand-alone with software running exclusively on that node. Any initial cooperation would usually be to use common resources. A compatible set of communications protocols must therefore be a prerequisite. In summary a large number of personal workstations with the power of current minicomputers, connected through a local area network and cooperating under a set of internetwork protocols, supported by a range of specialised servers, constitutes a basis for a distributed system. Considerable practical experience has already been gained on such low-cost but powerful distributed systems. This has tended to indicate that individual users work alone for significant portions of their time. They do, however, demand access to other users and to systems-wide resources which have a multiplying effect.

HOMOGENEOUS/HETEROGENEOUS MIX OF PROCESSING NODES

Various models of distributed systems involving local networks specify the ideal of a range of dissimilar processors all being able to communicate and perform tasks together. The practical attainment of such systems is very hard to identify. The advent of the low-cost personal computer has elevated this issue to one of immediate practical concern. It must be intuitively evident that a homogeneous mix of nodes greatly facilitates the cooperation of such nodes in a system, but even this coherent mix of nodes still presents non-trivial problems, involving a mix of languages and operating systems. A simple example is the ubiquitous Apple II personal computer:

- DOS 3.3
- UCSD PASCAL
- CP/M
- CIS-COBOL
- FORTRAN
- PILOT.

All of these languages/operating systems must operate transparently in the system with the user 'unaware' of the network. In this case two or more nodes can contemplate cooperating together.

However, consider the elementary problem of two different machines attempting to exchange a simple graphics display format. This is impossible between two different personal computers (say Apple and Tandy machines) without some effort at translating formats.

A mix of homogeneous machine nodes does facilitate the construction of practical distributed network systems capable of undertaking meaningful commercial tasks. Again, evidence has accumulated which supports the concept of local autonomy. Here the user simply wants the best of both worlds. The ability to operate in isolation and to select the optimum language, operating system or applications program for the issue at hand while at the same time accessing other nodes in the system and also utilising system resources and capabilities as transparently as possible.

AWARENESS OF NETWORK RESOURCES - DISTRIBUTION

A significant issue is that concerning the degree to which the user perceives the network and the distribution of its resources. The individual user ideally must see no network or systems software. Some consider this to be the 'art' of distributed or local network architecture. The ISO model attempts to layer the various levels of the system so that changes can take place at each level and yet not disturb the others. The layers of the ISO model are as follows:

1 Physical.
2 Link.
3 Network.
4 Transport.
5 Session.
6 Presentation.
7 Application.

It is not intended to discuss the details of the ISO model. An example can be made of the issues of transparency. The most elementary level is the actual physical interconnect for transmitting packets of information between nodes. The user really does not care about the physical method of connecting nodes. It could be broadband, baseband, fibre optics, token-passing, CSMA/CD etc etc. The only issue is the perception of the system the user arrives at, using the various interconnect techniques.

Having established a defined interconnect substrate, the technological improvements such as speed etc do not affect the higher levels of system software applications programs. Perhaps the only detectable impact would be the responsiveness of the system.

The issue becomes more complex with regard to more sophisticated system features. Issues of symbolic addressing such as 'print server' etc are examples. In general the most appropriate direction appears to be towards a rational compromise between total transparency and the need for a user to be aware of certain system features, either through the network operating system or at the applications level. In many ways the focus on local (ie node) autonomy will place emphasis on systems features being placed upon the applications software. It is this 'tuning' of the transparency which will require considerable effort.

CURRENT NETWORKS - AN EXAMPLE

The overall concept of microcomputers linked through a local area network represents the crucial thrust in future systems developments. It is evident however that considerable progress is needed. The Japanese Fifth Generation project, described below, involves a major development effort in this area. It is very instructive in the meantime to review current products available today and the likely progress expected.

When discussing distributed computing, the use of personal workstations places considerable emphasis on local autonomy. This reflects the actual way in which such computers are going to be used. The great appeal of the personal computer is exactly that! The computer is personal. Therefore many of these new distributed systems place great emphasis on local autonomy and responsiveness. Essentially the user perceives his/her own workstation with its dedicated processing power available exclusively. Local autonomous facilities are available such as printer, other input/output devices, and local bulk storage. In the case of the Zynar/Nestar system, this comprises an Apple II or III workstation with the full range of normal product attachments if required. Full local autonomy is achieved and access to a local area network covering 0.5km is available. Attached to this system is a community of other user nodes. The other nodes can choose to operate independently or to cooperate on system-wide tasks. The network makes available a wide range of attached special 'servers' or resources. These span the following:

1 Multiple file servers with a comprehensive range of software for multiuser use.

2 Print servers covering the ability to handle multiple networks, languages and operating systems, printer types etc.

3 Network gateways to both wide area networks and other networks/computers, eg:
   - File transfer server via dialled up lines via the PTT
   - Dial-in remote station server
   - Viewdata server
   - Telex server
   - 3780 server.

Consequently the user node has access to a very 'rich' set of capabilities previously not considered practical with small personal computers. The system therefore provides for three types of system components: the computing nodes, special servers, and a communications substrate.

Many of the tasks required by a user of the system are stand-alone but with access to system capabilities such as mass storage, communications etc. This is in contrast to many supposed distributed systems involving the execution of a total systems task over a complete set of fully cooperating nodes.

The claims made for distributed systems can be reviewed in the context of the local area network of microcomputers. Reliability is a major benefit. The absence of a central processing unit and the total distribution of the processing power among many nodes naturally reduces the risks. If an individual node fails then the fault is isolated in that node.

The costs of the workstation are such that a 'swap-out' is the likely maintenance procedure. Of more concern is the failure of a major server node such as a database. In this case dual servers with dramatically enhanced reliability can be employed. Availability is another key issue - the ability to move from one workstation to another and still perform the assigned task, together with the wide distribution of system assets, enhances the availability of the system as experienced by the user.

Modular growth, in terms of cost and flexibility, is a key feature. Above a specified minimum entry level, increases in capability can usually be achieved with a specific number of user nodes. The ability to increase in small increments provides for total efficiency. The alternatives of a large central processor resource always tend to imply under-utilised overheads. The purchaser does not wish to buy a system and then find out that the system is already operating at close to maximum capacity.

Resource sharing is another key feature. Expensive and high-grade professional server attachments can be added to a network. The costs are shared amongst the total user community.

Questions of adaptability, flexible growth, etc are also in the optimum solution framework for local networks of microcomputers. With the distribution of tasks to local nodes, the ability to respond to change is enhanced. Cooperation and coordination with other users is not a critical issue. In general, evidence suggests that the fairly global claims for distributed systems are justified for local networks.

KEY CONSIDERATIONS FOR NETWORK ARCHITECTURE

In evaluating network architectures, a series of considerations needs to be reviewed. The composition of a node defines the nature of a workstation or server. In general the personal computer type will define many features, going beyond performance and reflecting the type and availability of software and services available to the user. The number of nodes tends to indicate the overall capability of the system.

The system's total performance tends to be linearly related to the number of nodes. Attachable devices provide some evidence of the 'richness' of facilities that can be expected from the system. Network control is a key feature and reflects the distribution scale for the system as well as the sophistication potential for applications programs. Database is intrinsic to a network, whether in the form of a single multiuser file system or a distributed database. It also defines the degree of control to be expected. Considerable care is needed in evaluating this area. Access rules and program-to-program communications provide for applications capabilities as well. Again, these rules are critical in defining the type of network implied. Finally, communications (external) protocols and links are highly relevant to integrating the network into a wider scheme of things.

OTHER CONSIDERATIONS

Recent ideas have reflected upon the issue of developing programs which exploit spare computational capacity in a network during periods of low activity (eg at night). These programs represent one of the most difficult forms for distributed computing implementation. Given a local network involving many distributed nodes, then it is possible to conceive of an approach involving a program which can enter spare computational capacity existing at a node and use it. During quiescent periods the program can expand and use the network's full distributed capacity. During busy periods the program would retreat and 'lie low' in a small set of unused nodes. In essence, the program would start on one machine, then it would locate 'spare' machine capacity at a node. It would then enter that spare node and seize its processing power. Operating under a concept of segmentation and replication, the program could expand and contract according to network usage. (001) gives an excellent description of this concept, concluding that local networks supporting relatively large numbers of nodes provide a rich environment for experimenting with the concepts described. Such networks, involving a homogeneous mix of personal computers are now rapidly increasing in number and scope.

THE JAPANESE FIFTH GENERATION PROJECT

The well known and publicised Japanese Fifth Generation project pays attention to distributed systems. In particular it explicitly addresses the combinations of personal computers, local networks and high-level language machine groups. This is in support of the goals of high efficiency, high reliability, simple use and construction, easy adaptability to future technological improvements and the different machine/system levels and sophisticated functions expected. Their program is worthy of more detailed analysis in view of its close affinity to multiple microcomputers, and local area networks, in a distributed function context.

Project summary details

The distributed function architecture involves the development of an architecture in order to combine VLSI architectures with the new advanced ones. They would provide the goals described previously, namely high efficiency etc. The details involve the development of a basic distributed function system covering various R and D subprojects, eg dynamic architectures. The network architecture will be meant to loosely couple computer systems which are spaced apart. This will require the development of the techniques to combine systems with a global network and to build up a distributed information system based on a high-speed local network. Additionally a database machine will be developed with an architecture suitable to process databases and capable of high-speed accessing of large capacity databases. Another attachment would be a high-speed numerical computational machine. The distributed user node would involve input/output involving characters, speed, picture and image, and intelligent interaction with the user.

It can be seen that distributed functions involving personal computer nodes, local area network interconnect, specialised and very capable attached servers/resources, and a distributed architecture/operating system are fundamental to the whole project. Perhaps this gives some indication of the relevance of distributed computing involving linked microcomputers.

REFERENCES

001 SHOCH J F and HUPP J A
The WORM program etc
Communications of the ACM vol 25 no 3 (March 1982)

002 FORSDICK H C, SCHAUTZ R E and THOMAS R H
Operating systems for computer networks
Computer (Jan 1978)

003 CLARK D D and SVOBODOVA L
Design of distributed systems supporting local autonomy
IEEE CH1491

004 ENSLOW P H (Jr)
What is a distributed system?
Computer (Jan 1982)

005 PEEBLES R and MANNING E
Systems architecture of distributed data management
Computer (Jan 1978)

006 PEEBLES R and DOPIRAK T
Adapt: a guest view
IEEE CH1491

007 *Preliminary report on study and research on Fifth Generation computers*
Japan Information Processing Development Centre (1978-80)

008 Internal Zynar/Nestar product information

IMAGE PROCESSING

E R Davies

Royal Holloway College (University of London)
Egham
Surrey
UK

Acknowledgement

The support of the UK Science and Engineering Research Council for research on which some of the views expressed here are based, is gratefully acknowledged.

E R DAVIES received his BA in natural science in 1963, and his DPhil in solid state physics in 1967, both at Oxford University. After a further three years' research at Oxford he took up a lectureship in electronics at the Royal Holloway College (University of London) where he is now Senior Lecturer. Since then he has been doing research in the areas of magnetic resonance, the teaching of electronics at university level, pattern recognition, and image processing. His academic interests include analysis of the processes underlying vision, systematic design of image processing algorithms, development of languages for image processing, and hardware/software tradeoffs. At present he is engaged in the development of algorithms and hardware for automatic visual inspection tasks. Dr Davies is a member of the British Pattern Recognition Association, the British Robot Association, the IEEE Computer Society and the Institute of Physics.

IMAGE PROCESSING

This paper demarcates various sub-areas of image processing such as image analysis and image coding, and contrasts major techniques such as neighbourhood operations and global transform methods. The well known topics of noise filtering, image enhancement, image restoration, image segmentation and binary shape analysis are considered. It is shown that image analysis carried out purely in the image plane representation can in simple cases lead to object recognition and location. The number of fundamental operations needed to achieve this is estimated and the inherent need for hardware parallelism in image analysis is demonstrated. Finally, image understanding methods, pyramidal and quadtree approaches, and an interesting dichotomy between arithmetic and logical operations on images are discussed.

INTRODUCTION AND REVIEW

After more than two decades of development, the field of Image Processing (IP) is still expanding rapidly and now has a large range of industrial, commercial, medical, forensic, space, remote sensing, military and scientific applications. At the same time, the techniques of IP have crystallised into a number of rather separate areas of study including, in particular, image enhancement and restoration, image coding, image analysis for recognition, image reconstruction, and image database management.

Image database management is a special discipline in which satellite and aerial images are normalised in orientation and size, and corrected for geometric and projective distortions; and their borders, intensities, and colours are matched to help constitute a database which is then available (at least in principle) for a variety of geographic, cartographic, military, national and other needs (001,002).

Image reconstruction is a highly sophisticated technique which aims to reconstruct detailed images of the interiors of objects from sets of projections, using, for example, transmitted X-ray beams. The method has recently become important, under the name 'computed tomography', for providing remarkable brain and body scan pictures. Because of its mathematical complexity, details of this topic are outside the scope of this paper (see for example (003)).

Image coding is another specialised area of IP, where the aim is to compress image data for ease of storage or transmission, or for related purposes. Image analysis is related to image coding but has a different purpose - that of measuring and characterising images so as to aid subsequent recognition. Though similar techniques are employed in these two areas, space will not permit image coding to be considered further here (see for example (004)).

Image enhancement and restoration aim respectively to make images more easily interpretable by eye and to restore blurred images (degraded by atmospheric disturbances, motion smearing, etc) to a form as close to their original as practicable. Thus these types of IP are concerned with obtaining improved versions of images, and specifically transforming one image into another. This contrasts with image analysis, where images are transformed into data sets whose outputs may include coordinates of objects, size, and shape information, and so on.

This paper will emphasise analysis aspects of IP. Here descriptions of images, instead of whole images, will normally be passed on. The information will be received by some form of pattern recogniser whose purpose will be, for example, to instruct a robot manipulator to insert a bolt into an electric motor casing, or place it in a reject bin. The complete IP and recognition system can be refined considerably by a feedback loop wherein the recogniser is able to pass instructions on specific tasks to be performed back to the image processor. For the purpose of the present discussion, a pattern recogniser may be considered as a device which accepts abstract input data and classifies it into one of a number of categories, according to the data set it was trained on.

In not too complex situations, the complete pattern recognition (PR) and analysis problem can be solved by an image analyser whose output space may indeed *be* an image, on which a coded value indicates, eg, the centre of a nut, or the position of a chocolate to be rejected. The conditions when such a tradeoff can be achieved are studied in a later section of this paper.

Major IP techniques that will be discussed in this paper are image improvement (including image enhancement and restoration), image segmentation (including the thresholding of grey-scale images), binary image analysis, image understanding, and use of pyramidal data structures. In addition, problems of processing speed and hardware will be discussed towards the end of the paper. These topics are preceded by an examination of the fundamental methods of processing that are available for transforming one image into another.

Before proceeding further, it will be useful to mention recent texts covering IP. These include (001,003,004,005) and a new edition of the classic by Rosenfeld and Kak (006). Pattern recognition and a simple treatment of IP are covered in the elegant volume by Duda and Hart (007).

NEIGHBOURHOOD OPERATORS AND GLOBAL TRANSFORM METHODS

Perhaps the most basic function of IP is to generate one image from another. Clearly, the simplest way to do this is by a pixel-by-pixel copying operation. Convolution is an immediate generalisation of copying, which permits the output image to be closely related to the input image, while retaining a high degree of latitude in the form of the output picture. It is certainly not completely general in that (a) it is a linear operation and (b) its action is spatially invariant. While the latter property is normally useful in IP, restriction to linear processes may not be so relevant. On the contrary, linear processing precludes decision making and is therefore inappropriate for some image analysis and recognition tasks. Nonetheless, the simplicity of linear operations, coupled with the fact that theoretical analysis of their properties is mathematically tractable, results in their wide application in IP (004).

It is well known that the effects of convolution operations can be computed in the spatial frequency domain if their Fourier transforms are first obtained. In two-dimensional IP applications an initial conversion of an image to the spatial frequency domain is followed by multiplicative application of the transformed convolving functions, which is then followed by conversion back to the image domain. This means that three operations have been substituted for the original (single) direct operation implying an increase in computational complexity. Indeed, it will be clear that this 'global transform' approach results in making every new image pixel depend on every pixel of the original image, rather than (as is the case for a great number of IP tasks) depending on a limited number of pixels in the neighbourhood of the output pixel. (This comment is also valid for the other well known global transform methods, including Cosine, Hadamard, Karhunen-Loeve, etc, although these will not be considered further in this paper.) Thus there is likely to be a considerable processing overhead associated with the global transform approach (but see (008) for a more complete study of the tradeoff). This, coupled with the afore-mentioned fact that linear operators are not decision oriented, leads to global transform methods being, on the whole, unsuitable for image analysis applications - especially those where real-time processing is vital. The areas where global transform methods do come into their own is in image preprocessing, image enhancement and (particularly) image restoration. This will be examined next.

IMAGE IMPROVEMENT

The term 'image improvement' covers two broad areas:

- The area commonly called 'image preprocessing', which is the conditioning of images for subsequent automatic image analysis
- The other area including topics such as image enhancement wherein images are made more easily interpretable by human operators.

Noise suppression is a particularly important topic and appears in each of the above broad categories.

Noise suppression

One obvious technique for noise removal is multiple image averaging; another is spatial frequency filtering. In the latter case a low-pass spatial frequency filter may be beneficial for removing random noise, but for structured noise such as that due to the presence of TV scan lines, a band-reject spatial frequency filter may be more appropriate.

Often, processing by global transform methods is unnecessary and indeed too computationally expensive for the task in hand. All that may be needed is the application of a simple neighbourhood operator which replaces the centre pixel of

$$\begin{matrix} 1 & 1 & 1 \\ 1 & 0 & 1 \\ 1 & 1 & 1 \end{matrix}$$

by 1, and the centre pixel of

$$\begin{matrix} 0 & 0 & 0 \\ 0 & 1 & 0 \\ 0 & 0 & 0 \end{matrix}$$

by 0, throughout the image.

Impulse noise of these two types (often termed 'salt and pepper' noise) can thus be eliminated conveniently by a simple recognition and decision process applied to every part of a digital image. There are numerous variants on such noise removal processes: one modifies the centre pixel to the value expressed by all but one (rather than all) of the surrounding pixels; another (which is a generalisation to cover the case of grey-scale images) prevents the centre pixel being greater than the maximum of the surrounding values, or less than the minimum. A very commonly used variant is the median filter which essentially orders the values within the 3 × 3 window and returns the median value, this being better than the mean value in that it has a less deleterious effect on image detail. In fact, the median filter tends to produce a more pleasing effect than normal averaging (see below), and also copes well with impulse noise. All these filters can be applied several times to give greater smoothing effect, though it will often be more effective to apply a larger (5 × 5) implementation of the same general process (eg for the median filter one finds the median value of 25 instead of nine pixel values (004)).

Low-pass spatial frequency filtering by global transform methods can be mimicked by neighbourhood operators using local expand-then-shrink and shrink-then-expand operations (for binary images) or local max-then-min and min-then-max operations (for grey-scale images) (009). (See *Size analysis* below for detail of expand and shrink operations.) While such operators are non-linear, linearised versions can be constructed by employing averaging convolutions, of the following form:

$$\begin{matrix} 1 & 1 & 1 \\ 1 & 1 & 1 \\ 1 & 1 & 1 \end{matrix} \quad \text{or} \quad \begin{matrix} 1 & 2 & 1 \\ 2 & 4 & 2 \\ 1 & 2 & 1 \end{matrix} \quad \text{etc}$$

However, it is usual for the total weight to be normalised to unity, so that the average brightness of the image is unaffected by noise-filtering operations.

It should be noted that noise-removal operations can easily be taken too far, since there is a danger that edges and, particularly, texture will be smoothed out, thereby ruining later processing capabilities.

The topic of noise suppression has now reached an advanced stage, there being a choice of a considerable number of techniques, both linear and non-linear, with which to tackle noise problems (009); in addition, the simpler methods mentioned above are complemented by the more rigorous approach employed in image restoration (see below).

Contrast enhancement

In many circumstances the range of grey-scale values in an image will be inappropriate for reliable interpretation, either by human or by machine. It will then be necessary to normalise the range of permitted grey-scale values to a particular set, or even to adjust the shape of the histogram to a required profile. It will be evident that neither of these processes can increase the amount of information available for subsequent use and indeed the opposite must in general be true. What has to be achieved, however, is a suitable mapping of input to output grey-scale values which achieves the required normalisation while destroying as little information as possible. In order to avoid compressing the ends of the histogram into narrow spikes, a non-linear or piecewise-linear mapping may be employed. An interesting recent advance in this area is the interactive adjustment of the shape of the histogram (005).

Edge enhancement

Broadly, edge enhancement means improving the appearance of images that have become degraded by some possibly unknown blurring operation. This can be achieved in the spatial frequency domain by suitable high-frequency emphasis filtering. However, a simpler approach is often permissible using the technique of 'sharp/unsharp' masking. Here the new image is formed by subtracting a deliberately blurred version of the received image from a multiple of the received image and renormalising, in an attempt to cancel the blur (see Figure 1). Figure 2 shows the effect achieved by sharp/unsharp masking, using the following averaging convolution as the deliberate blurring function:

$$\frac{1}{16}\begin{pmatrix}1 & 2 & 1\\ 2 & 4 & 2\\ 1 & 2 & 1\end{pmatrix}$$

This crude method of emphasising high frequencies tends to produce such problems as 'ringing' (which takes the form of thin dark or light bands surrounding objects). However, applied carefully, it is efficient, effective, and useful.

Any technique of edge enhancement must, in principle, involve high-frequency emphasis filtering, and will therefore tend to emphasise noise: for this reason careful optimisation is called for. In this respect it is apt to quote from E L Hall (003):

> 'Much of the art of enhancement is knowing when to stop.'

This consideration leads to the topic of image restoration.

Image restoration

The range of techniques known as image restoration aims to make reliable estimates of the ideal form of any degraded image. For this purpose, accurate mathematical modelling of the blurring or other degradation process is necessary. For degradation processes which are spatially invariant over the image area, and linear, the mathematical analysis is tractable and leads to such well known transforms as Wiener filtering.

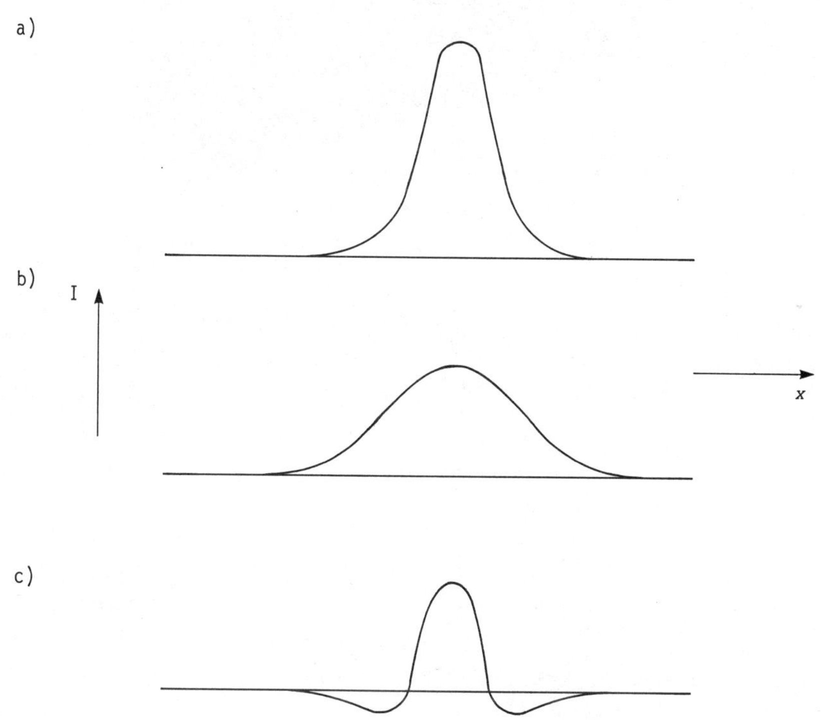

Figure 1a: Intensity variation of a light spot in a blurred image
Figure 1b:. Deliberately blurred version of the image
Figure 1c: The restoring effect of subtracting b from a
Figure 1: The principle of sharp/unsharp masking

a)

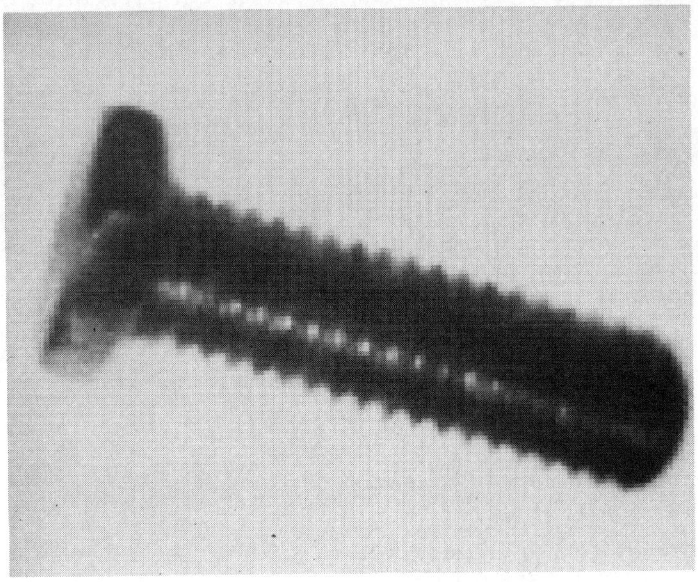

b)

Figure 2a: *Slightly out of focus image*
Figure 2b: *The effect of sharp/unsharp masking on the image shown in* a
Figure 2: *Effect of sharp/unsharp masking*

This is fortunate as many physical degradations approximate to linearity and spatial invariance. Even if they do not, the mathematics tends to rely on reducing the problem to a similar linear, spatially invariant one.

The main problems with the analysis include how to cope with non-unique solutions (if the underlying restoration problem turns out to be ill-conditioned), and how to model the noise present in a blurred image. To date, image restoration has been applied successfully to images degraded by the following (004):

- Motion smearing (caused by camera or object movement)
- Atmospheric turbulence
- Random noise
- Diffraction effects and other deficiencies of physical image systems
- Non-linearity of photographic film or emulsion
- Colour compensation problems.

IMAGE SEGMENTATION

The immediate purpose of image segmentation is to start the process of analysing images, by demarcating the edges of objects and other boundaries. For example, the facets of a nut might be outlined, or in an outdoor scene, a horizon line obtained.

In simple scenes composed, for example, of back-lit objects or dark components on a light conveyor belt, segmentation may consist only of thresholding the image at a convenient level. The latter may readily be obtained by automatic examination of the intensity histogram (see Figure 3). However, because of variations in background lighting it is likely that such a simple process will lead to serious error in at least part of the image (see Figure 4); it then becomes necessary for the thresholding level to be adjusted locally.

Often noise is also a devisive problem, and with low-contrast edges, techniques more powerful than simple thresholding need to be adopted. Existing methods fall under two main rather opposing headings - edge location and region growing.

Edge location procedures

While high-pass spatial frequency filters and Laplacian estimators have been used to locate edges in digital images, these methods tend to accentuate noise, and the usual approach is to estimate the grey-scale gradient. There are a number of suitable estimators, perhaps the most well known and widely used being the Roberts and Sobel operators, which employ 2 × 2 and 3 × 3 neighbourhoods respectively (007). The two

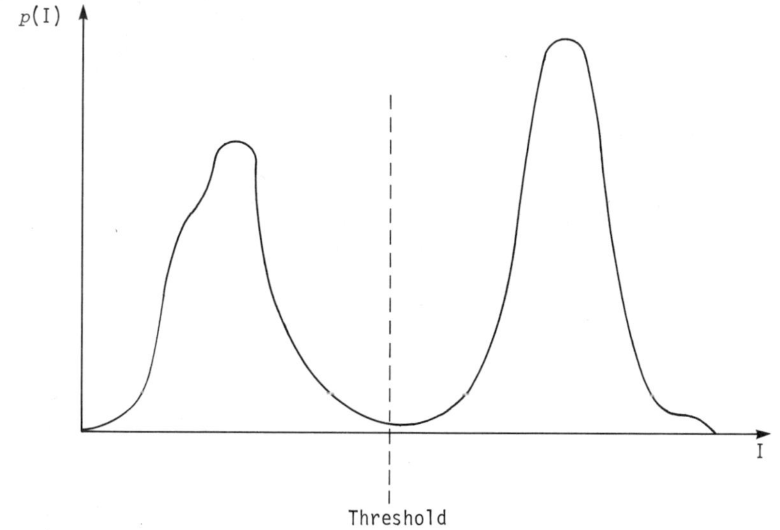

Figure 3: How a grey-level threshold may be selected from the intensity histogram. (The process is only straightforward for a bimodal distribution)

a)

b)

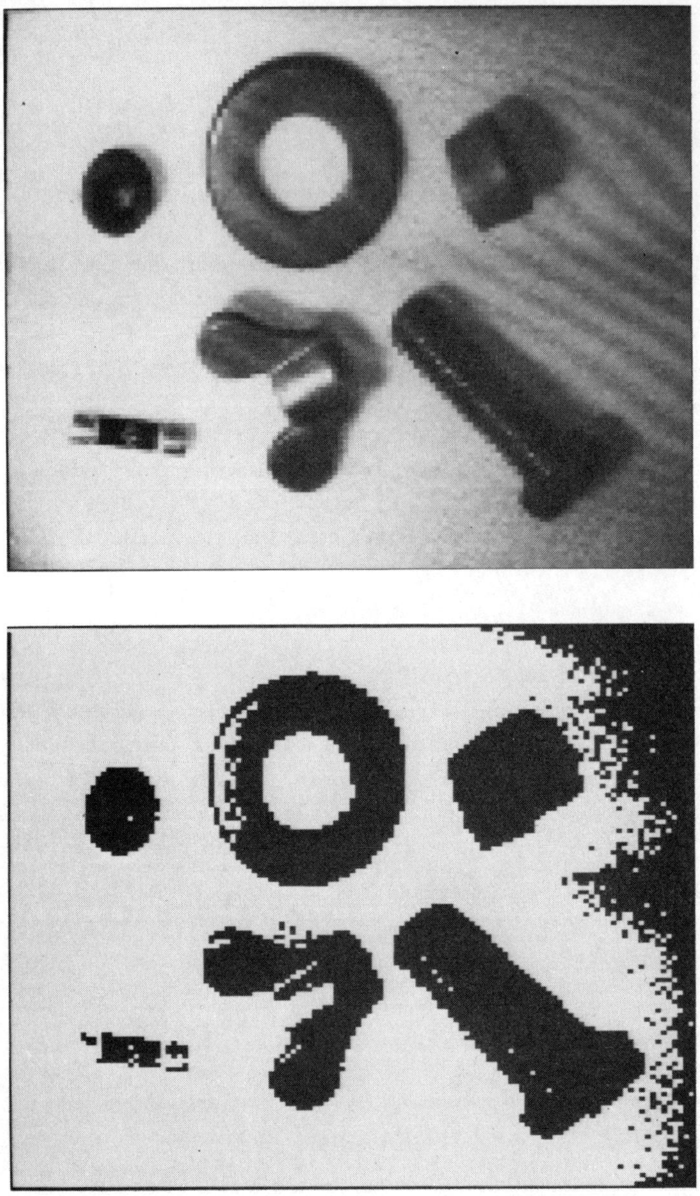

Figure 4a: *Image with non-uniform background lighting*
Figure 4b: *The effect of selecting a single (global) grey-level threshold (shadows and highlights add to the complexity of the problem)*
Figure 4: *Effect of employing a single grey-level threshold*

operators first compute components of the gradient using the following convolutions:

$$g_{R1} = \begin{pmatrix} -1 & 0 \\ 0 & 1 \end{pmatrix} \qquad g_{R2} = \begin{pmatrix} 0 & 1 \\ -1 & 0 \end{pmatrix}$$

$$g_{Sx} = \begin{pmatrix} -1 & 0 & 1 \\ -2 & 0 & 2 \\ -1 & 0 & 1 \end{pmatrix} \qquad g_{Sy} \begin{pmatrix} -1 & -2 & -1 \\ 0 & 0 & 0 \\ 1 & 2 & 1 \end{pmatrix}$$

They then estimate the gradient using the formulae:

$$g_R = (g_{R1}^2 + g_{R2}^2)^{\frac{1}{2}}$$

$$g_S = (g_{Sx}^2 + g_{Sy}^2)^{\frac{1}{2}}$$

However, for computational efficiency (but with little degradation in performance) it is usual to approximate these expressions as:

$$\tilde{g}_R = |g_{R1}| + |g_{R2}|$$

$$\tilde{g}_S = |g_{Sx}| + |g_{Sy}|$$

Many mask correlation schemes have been developed, but the recent Frei-Chen (010) method includes a number of the earlier ones as special cases. It involves the application of a set of nine masks, of which four correlate with edges and four correlate with lines (the ninth acting as a 'control', and completing the set of nine orthogonal basis functions). This set of masks is capable of providing an estimate of the precise direction of an edge or line, and indeed of differentiating between a line, an edge, and a plain point.

In the cases described so far, an enhanced edge image results: this must be thresholded to obtain a suitable set of (binary) outlines. The latter will often be thick and may even be broken. In such cases thinning and joining techniques will need to be applied before a useful binary edge image is produced. Curve-fitting methods may also be beneficial for producing meaningful sets of edges. In addition, prior to thresholding, some means of averaging edge information may be valuable for eliminating noise, and ensuring that a more globally significant set of edges is produced (009). Relaxation labelling is an iterative procedure that has recently been developed for this purpose (011).

Region growing techniques

The principle of this technique is to permit homogeneous regions of an image to 'grow', starting with contiguous pixels of roughly similar properties. Clearly, for this process to work, suitable pixel properties have to be chosen and similarity merging thresholds defined.

To generalise this approach, formal clustering techniques can be employed. These differ from normal PR clustering techniques (007) in that points within a cluster must be contiguous as well as having similar properties. After initially partitioning the image into regions, the latter are successfully merged or split as necessary, until a final solution is obtained (012).

Though this technique is basically complementary to the edge location procedures outlined earlier, it can more effectively take account of global characteristics of the image and may therefore be more stable and resistant to local noise (003). On the other hand, it may produce false regions (ie ones that, to the eye, appear as irrelevant subregions). Such effects are due more to pixel classification and PR than to IP as such, and will not be discussed further in this paper. Suffice it to say that pixel classification is an important aspect of image segmentation, both in the grey-scale case and for colour images (002).

An interesting recent development in this area is the global/local edge coincidence method (013) which combines the two major approaches to the subject. The procedure here is to merge regions until the boundaries match the local edges. This prevents local noise from adversely affecting the segmentation, and helps to ensure that the global edges that are found are locally significant.

Finally, it should be noted that the result of segmentation is not only to eliminate a large proportion of the noise of the original image, but also to reduce the input information to a small fraction of its original level. If outlines of objects and of their main facets are obtained, in binary format, then the processing problem is reduced enormously in scale at all subsequent stages. Since gross redundancy in the input data is the central problem facing any PR system, the importance of this type of preprocessing should not be underestimated.

BINARY IMAGE ANALYSIS

Here it will be assumed that images have already been segmented reliably and appear as a set of object outlines or as a set of regions. Discussion will be simplified by considering only images of separated objects such as chromosomes, block characters, nuts and bolts, flat metal pressings, or aircraft, viewed in profile. In these cases, a region image can unambiguously be presented in binary form, with foreground and background taking the values 1 and 0, respectively.

Under these circumstances, the problem of image analysis essentially becomes one of shape analysis. There are a number of approaches to shape analysis, some of which are relevant to a region representation of the image and some to an edge representation. Before these approaches can be examined in detail, it will be profitable to discuss problems concerned with connectedness and metrics in digital images.

Connectedness in digital images

When images are represented digitally in rectangular tessellation, a well known difficulty arises with the definition of connectedness. Consider the pattern:

$$\begin{matrix} 0 & 1 \\ 1 & 0 \end{matrix}$$

If identical diagonal elements are to be regarded as connected, then a background line crosses the foreground line: this is clearly unacceptable. If, on the other hand, identical diagonal elements are not to be regarded as connected, then the two foreground objects are separated from each other by a disconnected background line, which is again unacceptable. This paradox can be resolved by allowing foreground and background to assume different definitions of connectedness, foreground being '8-connected' and background being '4-connected' - ie diagonal neighbours are regarded as connected only if they are part of the foreground (014). This convention will be assumed in what follows.

Metric properties in digital images

Measurement of distance in a digital image is complicated by what is and what is not easy to calculate, given the types of neighbourhood operation that are common in IP. Distance can, of course, be estimated accurately in a digital image using the Euclidean metric:

$$d_E = \{ (x_1 - x_2)^2 + (y_1 - y_2)^2 \}^{\frac{1}{2}}$$

However, the 8-connected and 4-connected definitions of connectedness given above imply the following respective metrics:

$$d_8 = \max\ \{|x_1 - x_2|\ ,\ |y_1 - y_2|\}$$

and

$$d_4 = |x_1 - x_2| + |y_1 - y_2|$$

Thus constant distance loci appear under the d_E , d_8 and d_4 metrics as a circle, a square, and a diamond, centred at the reference point (007).

This gives rise to some difficulty in the rapid computation of, for example, the perimeter of an object. A simple way of estimating a perimeter is to treat horizontal or vertical edges normally, but to treat diagonal edges as $\sqrt{2}$ times the step length. Perimeter P is an important parameter since, in conjunction with area A, it can be used to give a useful initial indication of the shape of an object - via a calculation of the dimensionless quantity P^2/A. This quantity (often called 'complexity') is smallest for a circle and largest for an elongated object, but is independent of the size of the object. Other simple dimensionless measures include rectangularity and aspect ratio (001).

Size analysis

Accurate estimation of size can be undertaken using a Euclidean metric. However, it is frequently necessary in image analysis to perform unsophisticated but rapid size filtering operations. For example, it might be useful to eliminate very small or very thin objects as being due to 'noise', while rather large objects might be regarded as 'artefacts' which should also be filtered out. (The latter situation is not uncommon in the examination of biological material, where overlapping cells or debris might need to be ignored (015).)

A suitable operation can be provided by the shrink and expand functions mentioned above. The shrink function replaces any pixel in the (3 × 3) neighbourhood of a 0 by a 0, while the expand function replaces any pixel in the neighbourhood of a 1 by a 1. It will be clear that n successive shrink operations will eliminate objects of (maximum) diameter $2n$ or less, while a further n expand operations will restore the larger objects to their original size - though their shapes may be somewhat modified (see Figure 5). Propagation operations (016) may, if necessary, be used to restore the larger objects to their original shapes.

Large objects may be filtered out by first removing lesser-sized objects, and then performing a logical masking operation with the original image.

In other contexts, expand operations followed by shrink operations may be useful for joining nearby objects, filling in holes, and so on. Numerous refinements of, and additions to, these simple techniques exist (006).

Convex hull

The convex hull is a basic analogue descriptor of shape - being defined (in two dimensions) as the shape enclosed by an elastic band around the object in question.

a)

b)

Figure 5a: *Original image*
Figure 5b: *The effect of applying two shrink then two expand operations to the image shown in a. Small objects and fine detail are eliminated*
Figure 5: *Effect of applying shrink and expand operations*

The convex deficiency is defined as the combined shape that has to be added to a given shape to create the convex hull (see Figure 6).

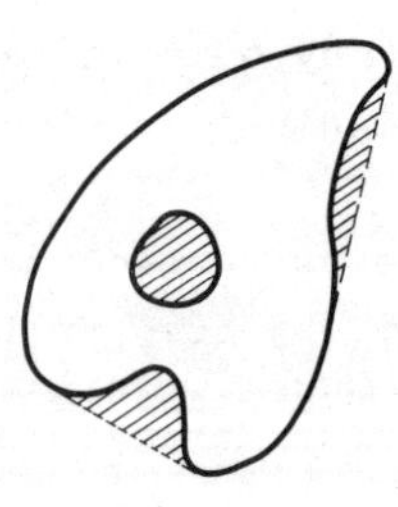

Note: The convex deficiency is the portion (shaded) that has to be added to the figure to make it convex

Figure 6: Convex hull and convex deficiency

The convex hull may be used for simplifying complex shapes, and for providing a rapid indication of the extent of an object. A particular application might be in locating the hole in a washer or nut, since the hole is that part of the convex deficiency that is not adjacent to the background. Finally, the convexity or otherwise of a figure is determined by finding whether the convex is (to the required precision) an empty set (007).

Obtaining a convex hull from an original shape is not trivial, as tests must be incorporated to ensure that separate limbs of the figure are in all cases connected. A simple means of achieving this (but not an accurate Euclidean one) is to repeatedly fill in the centre pixel of all neighbourhoods which exhibit a concavity; for example:

```
1 1 1          0 1 1
1 0 0   and    1 0 0
0 0 0          0 0 0
```

Skeletonisation

A powerful way of describing and analysing the shapes of binary objects is in terms of their skeletons. A skeleton may be defined as a connected medial line along the limbs of a figure, which in the case of thick hand-drawn characters is intended to be the path actually travelled by the pen. The simplest approach to skeletonisation is thinning. Thinning is a process whereby the outermost layers of a figure are stripped away until only the skeleton remains. A number of algorithms are available to carry this process out, more or less accurately, but a recent technique (017) allows a specified level of accuracy to be achieved and (if necessary) to be tested for. (The accuracy is of course limited ultimately by the d_8 metric implied by connectedness.)

Shape analysis may simply and conveniently be carried out by analysis of skeleton shapes and dimensions. Clearly, study of the nodes of a skeleton (points for which there are other than two skeletal neighbours) can lead to the classification of simple shapes, but not, for example, discrimination of all block capitals from each other (Figure 7). Many classification schemes exist which can complete the analysis, in terms of limb lengths and positions, but it is not fruitful to explore this further here (018).

A similar situation exists for analysis of the shapes of chromosomes, which take the form of a cross or a 'V' (001). For small industrial components, more detailed shape analysis is called for; this can still be approached with the skeleton technique, by examination of distance function values (object half-thickness values - see Figure 7) along the length of the skeleton. In general, shape analysis using the skeleton will proceed by examination in turn of nodes, limb lengths and orientations, and distance function values, until the required level of characterisation is obtained.

The particular importance of the skeleton as an aid in the analysis of connected shapes is not only that it is invariant under translations and rotations, but also that it embodies a highly convenient representation of the figure which (with the distance function values) essentially carries all the original information.

Other region description methods

Notable region description methods that have not so far been covered include topological analysis, moment descriptors and matching techniques. The polygonal approximation method of Pavlidis and Ali (019) should also be mentioned, since it forms an interesting alternative to skeletonisation. Topology is the study of properties of a figure that are unaffected by stretching or projective transformations (007). Space does not permit this topic to be dealt with here (though it has been touched on informally by skeletal node analysis above).

Moment approximations constitute a rather useful set of descriptors of region shapes (003). They involve approximating shape by a series of moments of the type.

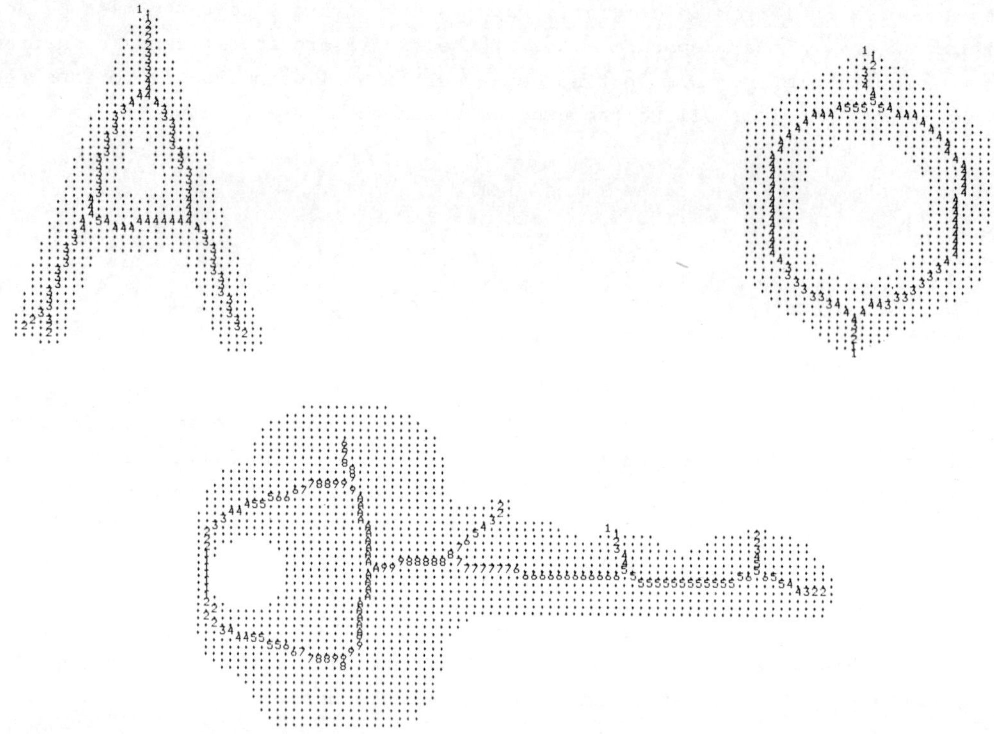

Note: The skeletons of the shapes shown were obtained by the Davies and Plummer method (017). *General topology of each shape is clear from the mode structure; distance function values give additional detailed shape information*

Figure 7: Skeletons of simple shapes

$$m_{pq} = \sum_x \sum_y x^p y^q f(x,y), \text{ for a picture function } f(x,y).$$

Moments that are invariant under translation, rotation, and scale change can be obtained by referring the original set to the centre of gravity of the shape and re-normalising (020). The value of using moment descriptors is that the number of moments employed in a particular application can often be made small without significant loss of precision, although the number required may not be evident without considerable experimentation (001).

Finally, matching techniques constitute a somewhat difficult and specialised topic. For example, direct matching of any but the smallest shapes tends to require the storage and comparison of impractically large numbers of masks of varying sizes, shapes, and orientations (021), although considerable advances have recently been made in this area (022,023). It should also be noted that the problem is eased if objects are of a fairly standard size and are oriented before inspection - as is permissible in some industrial environments.

Edge description methods

Edge descriptors fall into the following main categories:

- Curve fitting methods
- Fourier descriptors
- Angular sampling methods
- Chain coding.

Curve fitting methods can be regarded as the application of classical mathematical techniques (007) and will be omitted from detailed discussion here for reasons of space.

Fourier descriptors involve an analysis of how the curvature function $k(s)$ varies with distance s along the boundary of an object. Since $k(s)$ is periodic in s it is convenient to expand it as the Fourier series

$$k(s) = \sum_{n=-\infty}^{\infty} c_n \exp(2\pi ins/P).$$

Discontinuities in curvature caused by sharp corners in a boundary have to be dealt with specially (024). Other problems include the disrupting effects of small amounts of noise, and the differing spatial separations of sampling points at different orientations of the boundary. An excellent introductory discussion of this technique appears in (003).

An interesting method has recently been developed (025) which aims to reduce the computational effort involved in analysing shapes. The region boundary is first approximated by sampling at some constant incremental angle; shapes are then analysed in terms of the lengths of vectors from the controid to the sampling points, after the latter have been placed in their natural order along the boundary. Linear interpolations to shapes are found to be reasonably accurate, even for a 15° incremental angle.

Finally, the well known technique known as chain coding should be mentioned (026). This method recodes the boundary of a region into a sequence of octal digits, each one representing a boundary step in one of the eight basic directions relative to the current pixel position (denoted by *):

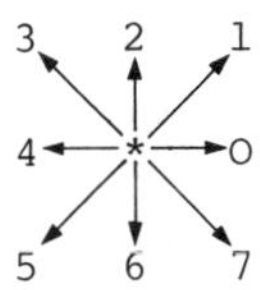

This code is important for presenting the shape information in such a way that it can be manipulated conveniently by computer, eg for shape-matching purposes.

IMAGE UNDERSTANDING

The purpose here is to outline the limitations of the approach to image analysis described above, and to indicate the relevance of the field of image understanding. Details will, however, be beyond the scope of this paper.

The last part of the paper dealt with images composed of separate small objects viewed in profile. It was found that some objects (such as bolts) can be recognised merely from topological properties of their skeletons. In such cases it is even possible for objects to be identified, and their positions marked in an output image, by analysis carried out entirely in the image plane. A slightly more complex situation arises when different types of chromosome are to be recognised: for this purpose limb length measurements may be taken from the skeleton and used to construct features for a statistical pattern recognition system (001).

Where more complex objects giving rise to several image regions are being examined, the more advanced techniques of image understanding are required. One such technique is the composition of an adjacency matrix (025) which holds information on the relative positions of various regions, and can be used to help analyse the image into several distinct objects. The general aim of image understanding is to describe natural scenes systematically in terms of hierarchical structures, starting with regions, and proceeding through surfaces, objects, groups of objects and thence to whole scenes. The two main approaches to this are the so called relational and syntactic representations, the former seeking to describe scenes through graphs showing the relationships of regions and objects to each other, and the latter describing them linguistically in terms of grammars of allowed structures. For detailed descriptions of these approaches the reader is referred to (001,003-007).

The reasons for employing these approaches are twofold:

1 So that *a priori* knowledge can be brought to bear on the interpretation of a scene.

2 So that the output information (which will necessarily be completely abstract in form by the time the image has been fully interpreted) can take full account of the abstract information that is already available after the preliminary stages of image analysis, and indeed so as to be able to provide some systematic base for this abstract information.

It will also be apparent that the image plane representation with its considerable implied redundancy is bound to be an impediment rather than an advantage after a certain stage of analysis is reached (except in the very simple cases mentioned earlier), and should then be phased out of consideration.

The situation is made considerably more poignant by the difficulty of interpreting fairly simple scenes where shadows interfere with normal outlines, highlights appear within the outlines of shiny objects (see Figure 4), objects are in contact with each other and hence are difficult to discern, and one object is partly occluded by another. These considerations confirm that the scope of (pure) IP is limited, and make it perhaps surprising that image analysis is able to achieve as much in the way of recognition as it does.

PYRAMIDAL DATA STRUCTURES IN IP

As an example of recent developments in IP it is worth mentioning pyramidal data structures. These are striking in terms of what has been said above because they bow to the need for incorporating hierarchical data structures in IP, though they retain a representation that is essentially imaged based. The much-used quadtree representation operates by successively averaging a $2^n \times 2^n$ image, in non-overlapping 2×2 neighbourhoods, to yield a pyramid of n images of resolutions ranging from $2^n \times 2^n$ down to 1×1. Images are then analysed using a tree structure to relate the information in this set of images. If each stage of the analysis proceeds at the highest possible level within the tree (ie at the lowest possible resolution) then the processing operations can be carried out efficiently and quickly. Recent work has shown this approach to be sound for a considerable number of processes (027). It remains to be seen how universal the quadtree method itself is. For example, an alternative pyramidal method has been found highly suited to the rapid registration and matching of two rather different views of the same scene obtained from optical and radar images (023).

ARCHITECTURES FOR IMAGE PROCESSING

Now it will be relevant to consider how the IP operations described earlier might be implemented in practice. To make the discussion more concrete, it will be instructive to consider the number of whole image operations needed to achieve various possible effects. It will be assumed that the image being processed has dimensions $N \times N$ and contains objects of maximum diameter $2n$ pixels or less.

Simple operations such as the removal of salt and pepper noise would require a single pass over the image, whereas more complicated operations such as skeletonisation would require about $4n$ passes (see (017)). Obtaining an intensity histogram for a grey-scale image would require one pass, and subsequent thresholding would require a further pass. Finding a convex hull and convex deficiency would require $n + 1$ passes, with a further n pass being needed to isolate a hole (eg in the centre of a nut). Shrink and expand operations for smoothing object profiles or for size filtering would necessitate (say) $n/2$ passes. Once a skeleton has been obtained, locating the 'T' node for a bolt would require one more pass, with up to n further passes being needed to confirm that the 'T' node was unique (apart from nodes corresponding to 'noise spurs'). Overall, for a 256×256 image containing objects of diameter 16 pixels or less, this leads to a figure of something like 50 passes over the image before bolts can be distinguished reliably from other small objects and their presence indicated by a coded pixel at the 'T' node.

This problem is probably not atypical of image analysis situations. The situation is much worse than it at first appears, since each pass over the image implies a total of 256^2 neighbourhood operations, each of which involves nine input pixels and one output pixel. Furthermore, even for the rather trivial expand and shrink operations described previously, computation of the output pixel value would involve nine basic machine computations per neighbourhood, plus (ideally) 10 memory accesses; although for a more typical task closer to 100 basic machine operations would be required. Thus the total number of machine operations for the complete bolt location problem would be close to $100 \times 256^2 \times 50 \simeq 300$ million. This implies that the recognition process would take of the order of three minutes on machines such as a PDP-11.

Clearly, this situation is unrealistic for real-time applications, and some form of hardware parallelism is required (028). One approach is to employ a parallel processor of the DAP (029) or CLIP IV (016) variety, which will handle whole image operations in one machine cycle. The other approach is to make use of the fact that many different IP operations are being implemented in sequence on a given image, so that a pipelined processor would operate efficiently (030). The parallel processor implementation would be able to handle the bolt problem in about 2 msec, while an optimised video-rate pipelined processor would carry it out in about 100 msec.

Pipelined processors are considerably cheaper than highly parallel processors, and lend themselves to the building of dedicated hardware for particular applications (031). In addition, different stages in the pipeline can readily be designed to cope efficiently with floating-point numbers, whereas parallel processors of the DAP variety are designed primarily for simple operations on logical and integer values.

Finally, it should be pointed out that the discussion in this paper has, for simplicity, been restricted to the use of parallel processes, which take input data from one image space and output it to a separate image space. Sequential processes are those in which a new pixel value is immediately written over the old pixel value in the same image space. For serial and pipelined processors this technique can result in more efficient processing (032) if suitable algorithms can be developed.

CONCLUDING REMARKS

This review has sought to indicate both the wide scope of the field of IP at its present stage of development, and the recent shift of emphasis towards hierarchical methodologies. The latter are significant as they herald the systematic integration of the subject with the formerly rather separate field of PR.

The paper has also commented on the nature of the basic processing techniques that are employed in this field. In this respect it is relevant to highlight an interesting dichotomy that exists in current IP methodology - that of traditional applied mathematical methods versus simple logical and integer operations on images. The former are typified by linear processing using Fourier transform techniques, curve-fitting by least squares calculations, shape description by moments, and so on. The latter are typified by shrink and expand operations, median filters etc: they broadly consist of the 3×3 neighbourhood operations discussed throughout this paper. As noted in the part on neighbourhood operations and global transform methods, the dichotomy sometimes holds implications about decision making and recognition processes. More often, however, it merely represents an alternative strategy for performing IP operations that has grown up largely by chance. Although it was implied that global transform methods are likely to be less efficient for image analysis applications, it is by no means obvious that traditional mathematical methods, which normally require inherently slow floating-point computations, will always be less efficient overall than processing requiring simple logical and integer operations. Until the dichotomy is fully understood the problem of optimising IP architectures will not finally be solved.

In the interests of brevity, much has had to be omitted from this review, and it has been considered better to concentrate on some topics such as image analysis at the expense of others. In particular, it should be noted that it has not been possible to cover colour, multispectral and textured images or to pay due attention to sequential processing methods.

REFERENCES

001 CASTLEMAN K R
Digital image processing
Prentice-Hall Inc Englewood Cliffs NJ (1979)

002 ROSENFELD A
Recent developments in image and scene analysis
Proc IoP Conf on *Machine-aided image analysis* pp 42-49 Institute of Physics London (1979)

003 HALL E L
Computer image processing and recognition
Academic Press New York (1979)

004 PRATT W K
Digital image processing
John Wiley & Sons Inc New York (1978)

005 GONZALEZ R C and WINTZ P
Digital image processing
Addison-Wesley Reading MA (1977)

006 ROSENFELD A and KAK A C
Digital picture processing
Academic Press New York
2nd ed (1981)

007 DUDA R O and HART P E
Pattern classification and scene analysis
John Wiley & Sons Inc New York
(1973)

008 HALL E L
A comparison of computations for spatial frequency filtering
Proc IEEE vol 60 no 7 pp 887-891
(1972)

009 ROSENFELD A
Image pattern recognition
Proc IEEE vol 69 no 5 pp 596-605
(1981)

010 FREI W and CHEN C C
Fast boundary detection: a generalisation and a new algorithm
IEEE transactions on Computing
vol 26 pp 988-998 (1977)

011 ZUCKER S, HUMMEL R and ROSENFELD A
An application of relaxation labelling to line and curve enhancement
IEEE transactions on Computing
C-26 pp 394-403 (1977)

012 BRICE C R and FENNEMA C L
Scene analysis using regions
Artificial Intelligence vol 1
pp 205-226 (1970)

013 HWANG J J, LEE C C and HALL E L
Segmentation of solid objects using global and local edge coincidence
Proc IEEE Conf on *Pattern recognition and image processing* pp 114-121
Chicago (1979)

014 ROSENFELD A
Connectivity in digital pictures
J ACM vol 17 pp 146-160 (1970)

015 SHIPPEY G A, BAYLEY R J H, FARROW A S J, RUTOVITZ D R and TUCKER J H
A fast interval processor
Pattern Recognition Special Issue
1980 Conf on *Pattern recognition*
pp 345-456 (1981)

016 FOUNTAIN T J and GOETCHERIAN V
CLIP4 parallel processing system
Proc IEE vol 127 part E no 5
pp 219-224 (1980)

017 DAVIES E R and PLUMMER A P N
Thinning algorithms: a critique and a new methodology
Pattern Recognition vol 14 nos 1-6
Special Issue 1980 Conf on *Pattern recognition* pp 53-63 (1981)

018 BEUN M
A flexible method for automatic reading of handwritten numerals
Philips Technical Review vol 33
pp 89-101 and vol 33 pp 130-137 (1973)

019 PAVLIDIS T and ALI F
Computer recognition of handwritten numerals by polygonal approximation
IEEE transactions on Syst Man Cybern SMC-6 pp 610-614 (1975)

020 HU M K
Visual pattern recognition by moment invariants
IRE transactions on Information Theory IT-8 pp 179-187 (1962)

021 ULLMANN J R and ROSENFELD A
Picture recognition and analysis
The Radio and Electronic Engineer vol 47 nos 1/2 pp 33-48 (1977)

022 ROSENFELD A and VANDERBRUG G J
Coarse-fine template matching
IEEE transactions on Syst Man Cybern SMC-7 pp 104-107 (1977)

023 WONG R Y and HALL E L
Performance comparison of scene-matching techniques
IEEE transactions on Pattern Analysis and Machine Intelligence PAMI-1 no 3 pp 325-330 (1979)

024 ZAHN C T and ROSKIES R Z
Fourier descriptors of plane closed curves
IEEE transactions on Computing vol 21 pp 269-281 (1972)

025 HWANG J J and HALL E L
Scene representation using adjacency matrices and sampled shapes of regions
Proc IEEE Conf on *Pattern recognition and image processing* pp 250-261 Chicago (1978)

026 FREEMAN H
On the encoding of arbitrary geometric configurations
IRE transactions on Electronic Computing EC-10 pp 260-268 (1961)

027 ROSENFELD A
Quadtrees and pyramids for pattern recognition and image processing
Proc 5th Intl Conf on *Pattern recognition* pp 802-807 (1980)

028 DANIELSSON P-E and LEVIALDI S
Computer architectures for pictorial information systems
Computer pp 53-67 (Nov 1981)

029 REDDAWAY S F
The DAP approach
State of the Art Rep *Supercomputers* vol 2 pp 309-329 Pergamon Infotech Maidenhead Berks (1979)

030 GERRITSEN F A and AARDEMA L G
Design and use of DIP-1: a fast, flexible and dynamically micro-programmable pipelined image processor
Pattern Recognition Special Issue 1980 Conf on *Pattern recognition* pp 319-330 (1981)

031 ULLMANN J R
Video-rate digital image analysis equipment
Pattern Recognition Special Issue 1980 Conf on *Pattern recognition* pp 305-318 (1981)

032 ROSENFELD A and PFALTZ J L
Sequential operations in digital picture processing
J ACM vol 13 pp 471-494 (1966)

DATAFLOW ARCHITECTURES

J Gurd

University of Manchester
Manchester
UK

J GURD obtained his PhD in Cybernetics at the University of Reading in 1976. He lectured in the Department of Cybernetics there for three years before moving to his present post of Lecturer in Computer Science at the University of Manchester in 1975. Since 1976, Dr Gurd has been involved with the Dataflow Research Project at Manchester. This group is currently constructing a prototype parallel dataflow computer, the first of its kind in the world. Research interests in the project include parallel system architecture, parallel language implementation, and parallel algorithm design.

DATAFLOW ARCHITECTURES

Dataflow architectures are considered in detail. Software parallelism is discussed and the need to use an effective notation to express potential parallelism in programs is illustrated. Generalised dataflow graphs are examined with particular reference to solutions for implementation problems, the use of structured data, and languages for the compilation of graph code. Parallelism in hardware is discussed and requirements for a dataflow system are examined. Static dataflow multiprocessors, an MSI dynamic-tagged dataflow processor, and a VLSI dynamic-tagged dataflow processor are assessed. Finally, a summary of dataflow hardware is given.

INTRODUCTION

In the recent search for improvements in computing speed, system reliability, software manageability and cost effectiveness, there have been several attempts to establish a viable alternative computer architecture to replace the traditional 'von Neumann' organisation on which our present computing practices are based. Dataflow is one possible alternative which shows promise of allowing very high-speed computing by efficient exploitation of vast software parallelism in a highly parallel system of processing hardware. The name 'dataflow' is derived from the graphical model of computation which is used to describe how programs are executed. In this model, as we shall see later, data is active and flows asynchronously through the two-dimensional program activating each instruction when all required input data has arrived. This is in direct contrast to the 'von Neumann' model in which data passively resides in store whilst instructions are executed one-at-a-time according to a defined sequence controlled by a 'program counter'.

Dataflow architectures, as described below, are only one alternative to traditional computers. Several other models with similar characteristics are emerging, and these are sometimes confused with dataflow systems, usually because they too are driven by their data. In particular, string reduction and graph reduction systems are important developments which will not be discussed in this paper. The set of systems described below are sometimes called *pure dataflow* architectures to distinguish them from these related schemes.

The paper is divided into two major sections; one covering software, the other describing hardware. In the software section we first consider the nature of software parallelism, possible ways of representing it, and implications for parallel machine-code. This will provide an introduction to pure dataflow notation and also demonstrate the important distinction between static and dynamic dataflow systems. To conclude the software discussion, we discuss techniques for compiling from various high-level programming languages into dataflow programs.

In the hardware section we consider the requirements for systems which can execute dataflow code and exploit the software parallelism which can be exposed. We then study three different system designs which have been or are being constructed as experimental research vehicles for further work on refining and applying dataflow techniques.

PARALLELISM IN SOFTWARE

Software parallelism can be found in two situations. Firstly when a common operation, or set of operations, is to be applied to many separate sets of data, eg when adding together several arrays element-wise, as in the FORTRAN program:

```
      DO  10  I = 1, 1, 100
          F[I] = A[I] + B[I] +C[I] + D[I]
   10 CONTINUE
```

Secondly, when different operations, or sets of operations, are to be applied to separate or common sets of data, eg when executing the following FORTRAN assignments:

```
A = E - G
B = H * J
C = E * H + F
D = E + G
```

These situations have been known for a long time now, and in 1966, M J Flynn, recognising the importance of instruction and data 'streams' to hardware parallelism, classified parallel hardware systems as SIMD (single instruction stream, multiple data stream) if they exploited the first type of software parallelism, and MIMD (multiple instruction stream, multiple data stream) if they exploited the second type of software parallelism (001).

Nowadays this classification is considered too simple, although no generally accepted taxonomy is emerging. The difficulty is that the hardware parallelism may be implemented at a different level of 'granularity' to the obvious software parallelism; eg in an instruction pipeline, where small parts of the execution of successive instructions are processed concurrently in an overlapped fashion, regardless of program parallelism. It would be helpful if a level-independent taxonomy existed, but in its absence we have found it useful to compare dataflow machines with conventionally-based parallel systems by distinguishing between 'regular' and irregular' parallelism.

Regular parallelism exists wherever the same task is to be performed many times over, usually on disjoint data. With connected data it may be necessary to exploit regular parallelism via a pipeline, as in the instruction pipeline cited above. Otherwise, eg for the first, or SIMD, kind of software parallelism, a lock-step parallel array of hardware, as in the DAP (002) or ILLIAC IV (003), can be used. In either case, the actions being performed concurrently are highly regular, and the performance of systems depends on the executing programs providing enough work with the required form of regularity.

Most of the parallel computers so far constructed exploit regular parallelism of one form or another, and in practice, it has proved extraordinarily difficult to arrange for programs to continually provide sufficient parallelism of the required regular nature. Consequently, the applications run at variable speed, the regular parts executing rapidly whilst other parts necessarily go more slowly. In many cases the slow segments dominate overall performance and reduce the total speed-up of programs to a fraction of the theoretical maximum.

Irregular parallelism exists wherever different tasks are potentially executable concurrently, sometimes on common data. This corresponds to the second, or MIMD, kind of software parallelism. An independent array of parallel hardware such as in the 6600 (004) (on a small scale) or the experimental multiprocessors C.mmp (005) and Cm * (006) (on a large scale), is necessary for implementation. Where common data is involved, complex interlocking mechanisms are needed to prevent unintended accesses from being made (eg reading before data has been defined, or writing before all prior reads have completed). Note that mechanisms to handle irregular parallelism are general enough to handle regular parallelism, although the reverse is not true.

Few parallel computers exist to exploit irregular parallelism on a large scale, and it is in this area that most of the interesting experiments in computer architecture are now being conducted. The best known examples use parallelism at the 'process' level in languages such as CONCURRENT PASCAL (007), MODULA (008), DISTRIBUTED PROCESSES (009) and COMMUNICATING SEQUENTIAL PROCESSES (010), implemented on shared-memory or message-passing multiprocessors. Dataflow systems attempt to exploit irregular parallelism at a lower level, approximating to the conventional machine-code 'instruction' level.

Whether parallelism is regular or irregular, the key issue in developing a system to exploit it is to use an effective notation for expressing potential parallelism in programs. We next develop a notation for instruction-level irregular parallelism by examining the nature of exposable parallelism in a small segment of conventional FORTRAN code.

PROGRAMS AS GRAPHS

Consider the following set of FORTRAN assignments which multiply together the variables A, B, C, D, E and F and put the result in variable K:

```
G = A * B
H = C * D
I = E * F
K = G * H * I
```

To discover the potential software parallelism we must discard the traditional view of a program as being a list of instructions which manipulate data in fixed storage locations in a defined sequence. Instead we need to concentrate on the role the individual storage locations play as they temporarily hold data values while these values pass between operations in the program. Indeed, the pattern of store accesses brought about by the sequence of activation of instructions is normally contrived by the programmer to achieve the combinations of data with operators required for the particular problem solved. The fact that this is specified as a one-at-a-time process owes more to the history of development of computers than to inherent constraints in the problems that computers are used to solve.

An alternative view of the combination of data with operators is obtained by constructing a data-dependence graph for the program. An algorithm for translation was first suggested in 1966, and since then versions for different forms of optimising compiler have been developed. In the simple example below, we simply draw a number of arcs over the program, one arc for each variable. The tail of an arc shows where the variable is assigned, and the head shows where it is consumed (by appearing on the right-hand side of an assignment statement). In more complicated examples more than one arc may be used for a variable because it appears in more than one right-hand side. Multiple assignments, by which a variable name is assigned more than once in a program, can be handled by transforming into a form without multiple assignments, using a well-known algorithm which we shall not study here. Where variables only appear on the right-hand side (ie they are not assigned) they are assumed to be input data to the program segment. The resultant code for our example is shown below:

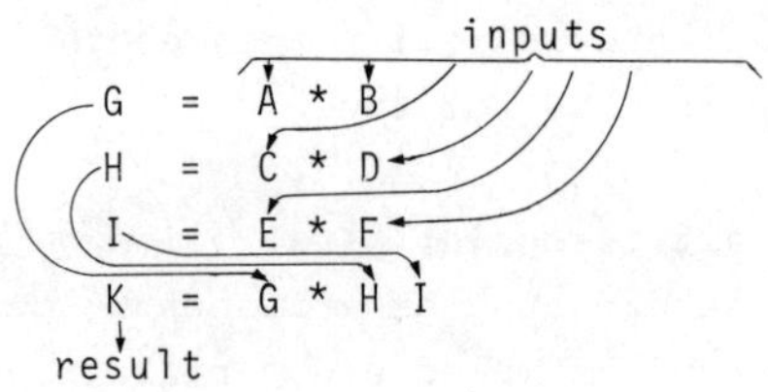

This diagram is more visually appealing if it is rearranged to show enforced sequence down the page, with potentially concurrent operations across the page, as follows:

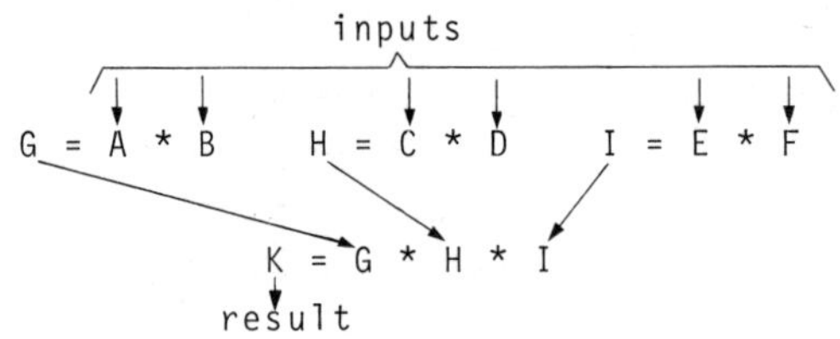

In this graphical form it is possible to omit all the variable names, since these are now superfluous, being constrained to be the same at head and tail of each arc. If names are required (as an aid to understanding, or for writing a textual version of the graphical program) they can be written just once, alongside the appropriate arc. Each assignment statement can be simplified to a description of the expression to be computed: in many cases this will be a simple arithmetic operation, eg multiply in our example:

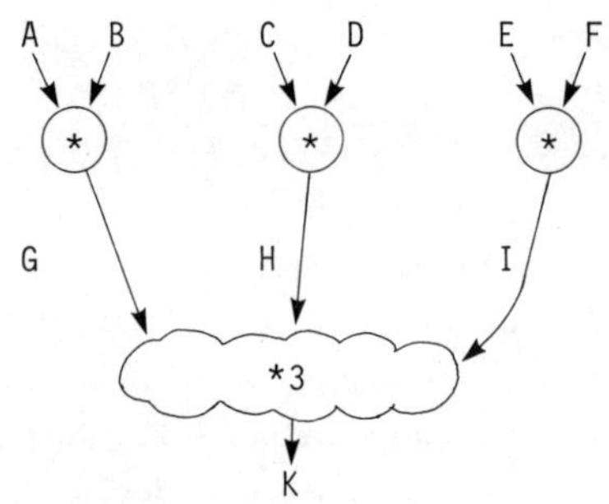

This sort of graph is called a simple *data dependence* or *dataflow* graph. Note that it still retains the semantics (or meaning) of the original program, but it now shows potential parallelism and enforced sequence in a two-dimensional format. In order to illustrate *all* the program parallelism that could be potentially exploited by hardware it is necessary to decompose the program completely to the machine-level. Of course, this level is completely arbitrary: we could build a machine that was capable of multiplying three numbers in one instruction, or we could go to the extreme of implementing only Boolean operators (AND, OR, NOT, etc) in hardware and building up the more complex operations using the appropriate, and well-known techniques. To retain familiarity, and permit easier comparison with present-day systems, we shall imagine a machine that executes instructions of the same complexity as a 16-bit minicomputer with extended arithmetic capabilities. Hence the straightforward monadic and dyadic arithmetic operators (negate, +, -, multiply and divide) are available for integer and floating-point numbers. Operators generating and manipulating Booleans will also be used where required.

In our example program, it will be noted that the top three expressions, which correspond to machine-level 'multiply' instructions, are different from the lower expression, which must be achieved by a combination of machine-level instructions. For example:

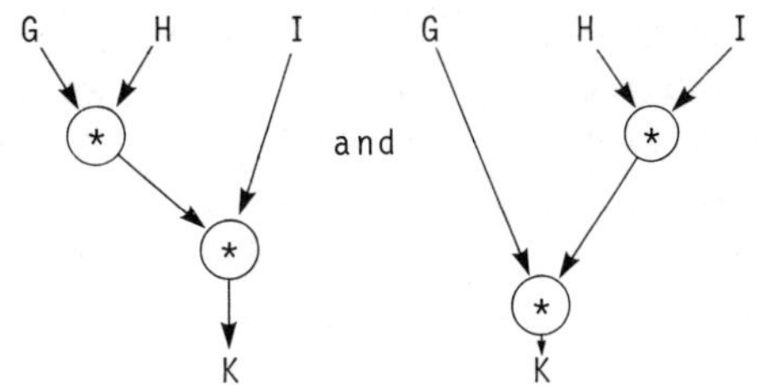

would compute the required expression. In this particular example it is immaterial which of these alternatives is used, and a compiler could choose arbitrarily from them. In other cases there will be 'good' and 'bad' alternatives for implementing expressions, and sensible compilers will attempt to choose the best one for the particular environment. To see how alternatives can differ, we need to consider the execution of machine-level graphical programs on parallel hardware. At this point it is simpler to define an abstract parallel implementation model, rather than describe a physical system. Since a formal definition is lengthy and somewhat obscure, we shall rely on an intuitive model in which we can see the progress of program execution on the program graph.

To see how this model works, consider a complete machine-level program graph for our example in which each multiply instruction is given an identification number.

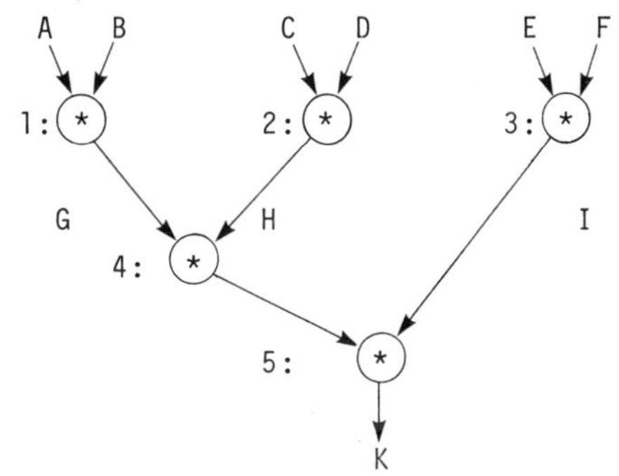

Remember that the idea of this notation is to allow all potentially concurrent instructions to execute simultaneously. In the original sequential program we would expect the multiplications to be performed in the order {1}, {2}, {3}, {4}, {5}, producing the answer in five multiplication times. On the graph we can see that either of the parallel execution orderings {1, 2, 3} ,{4} ,{5} or {1, 2} {3, 4} {5} will produce the answer in three multiplication times (given at least 3 and 2 multipliers, respectively). The problem for the parallel execution model is to cause one of these parallel execution orderings to occur: how can this be achieved?

In conventional systems there is a program counter which activates instructions one-by-one: could we use more than one such program counter (with processor) and arrange for multiple streams of instructions to be activated in sequence? In fact this is possible, but it is an awkward way of organising things. For one, exploitation of variable amounts of parallelism might require large numbers of processors which are sometimes idle. For another, the idea of a program counter is inextricably linked to the concept of a linear store with fixed locations for each variable: large numbers of active instructions would imply large numbers of active store locations with attendant problems of multiplexing accesses. In addition to this, each horizontal 'band' of instructions would have to be synchronised so that the next lower band could not start until all instructions had completed. This means that a program would proceed at the speed of the slowest operation in each band. In any case, organising the allocation of instructions to processors would be a very difficult task.

The above points have been laboured because together they form a compelling reason for abandoning program counters in instruction-level parallel computers. Dataflow researchers often feel persecuted because conventional computer scientists think they are studying obscure architectures for the sake of doing something different. In the context of the development of parallel computing, they are actually studying an *improvement* over conventional techniques. The key to this improvement is to notice that a data dependence graph shows how *instructions are dependent on data*. It makes no sense to execute an instruction before the data it requires is all available: conversely, once an instruction has finished executing, all other instructions that are waiting for its output data to be produced can safely be activated. The simplest way to execute a graph program is to send the data from instruction to instruction according to the data dependence arcs, and to allow each instruction to execute when and only when it has all the required input data available. In this way the graph program becomes *data driven*.

We can illustrate data-driven execution of graph programs by introducing data-carriers (usually called *tokens*, after Petri Net terminology) onto the data dependence graph. Each token carries one data value and is constrained to move (at any speed it can) from tail to head of one dependence arc. Tokens wait at the head of dependence arcs until all other arcs (if any) pointing to the subsequent instruction have tokens at their heads and then the subsequent instruction is executed, taking an arbitrary amount of time before producing (a) result token(s) at its output arc(s). The tokens causing the execution are no longer required, and they can be safely removed from the input arcs.

The sequence of 'snapshots' in Figure 1 shows how our example program can be used to evaluate 6! by sending tokens with values 1 to 6 inclusive to the inputs A to F, respectively. Tokens are shown on the dependence arcs as black disks with the associated value written alongside. The way in which the data appears to flow through the program graph during execution is the reason for the name 'dataflow'.

GENERALISED DATAFLOW GRAPHS

The original multiplication program we considered is not a very general example of conventional computing practice. The only arithmetic operation required is multiplication and there are no complex control structures, such as conditionals or loops, involved. In this section we consider enhancements to the dataflow graphical notation which help to accommodate more general programs.

The first point to be made is that *any* form of machine instruction can be represented by a node in a dataflow graph, and can hence be potentially executable in parallel with other instructions. This property makes the graph notation useful for exploiting the irregular software parallelism we discussed earlier. The simplest case in which this is advantageous is in the evaluation of arithmetic expressions, where all kinds of arithmetic instruction may be used. Arithmetic expressions can be represented as graphs quite readily; in fact most conventional compilers generate graphical 'expression evaluation trees' when parsing high-level programs, before generating appropriate linear machine code. The dataflow execution model demonstrates how such trees can be evaluated in time proportional to their height, using parallel instruction execution. At a higher level, the model also allows expressions themselves to be evaluated concurrently. Additional parallelism can be found when the control structures discussed below are invoked.

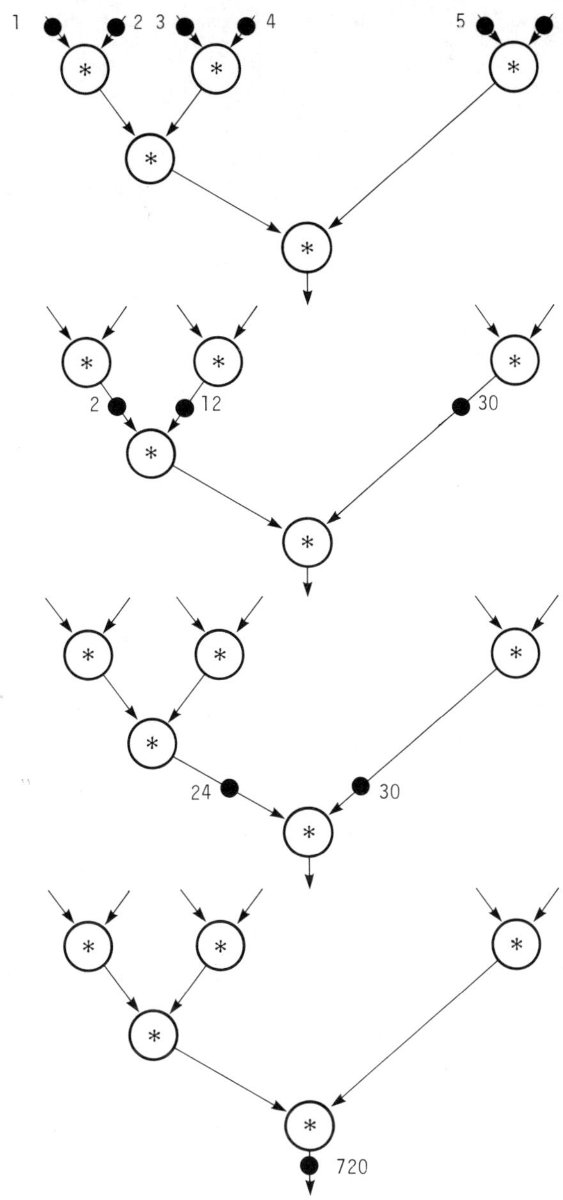

Figure 1: Example execution of dataflow program

The simplest control structure used to control a computation is the conditional, or if ... then ... else ... fi structure. We can handle this form when we construct a data dependence graph for a program by using special *conditional dependence arcs* which are controlled by the runtime evaluation of a Boolean condition. Such arcs can be implemented using two simple 'switching' machine-instructions known as *branch* and *merge*. These are best visualised as two-way switches inserted into the arcs of a graph: each switch selects one of two possible routes for a data token through the graph, the other route not being activated. The switch is controlled by a Boolean control token. The data and control tokens wait for each other exactly as they would at a dyadic arithmetic instruction.

Branch

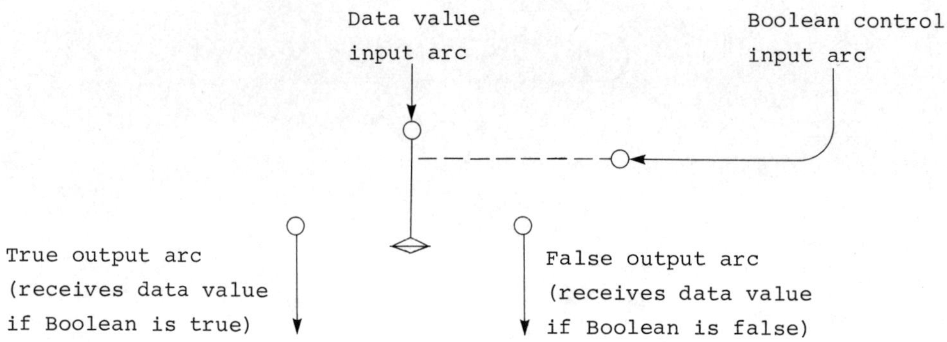

Merge

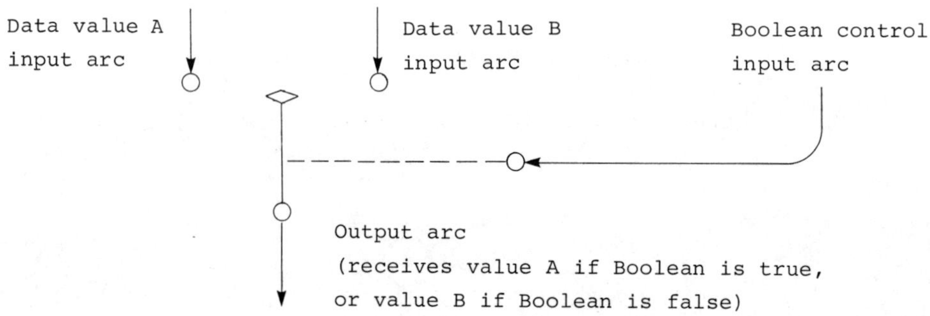

Where it is certain that only one of the data inputs to a merge switch will be generated, and in proper correspondence to the associated Boolean (eg from a previous branch using the same control value), the merge instruction can be omitted from the machine code and the two data arcs can simply be merged:

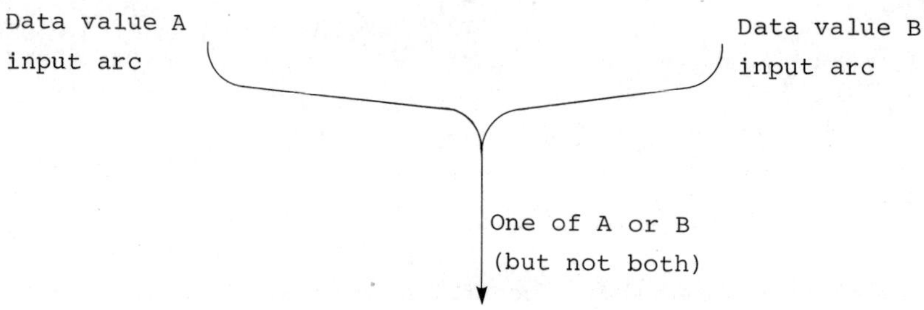

Using these instructions we can implement a FORTRAN conditional assignment such as:

```
C = A
IF (B.EQ.D)   C = F
```

as the following graph:

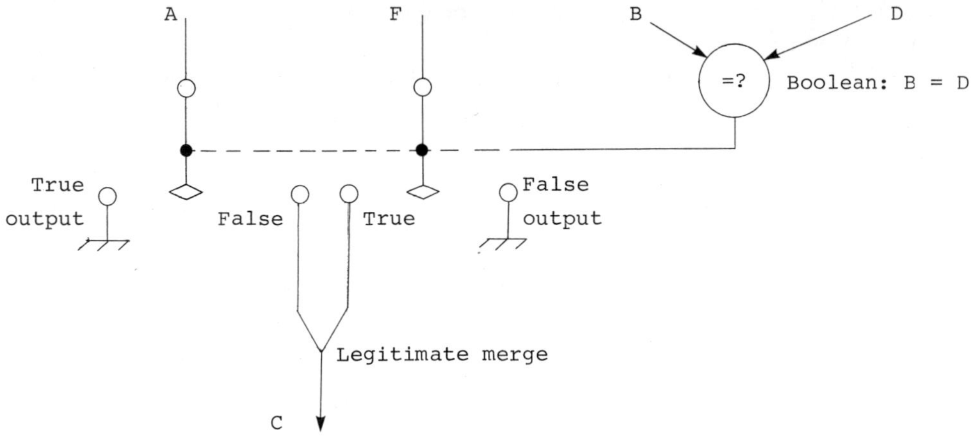

where ⊥ indicates that any token on this arc is destroyed, and the =? instruction generates a Boolean value indicating whether its data inputs are equal.

Switch instructions are most powerful when they are used to implement graphical loops and other re-entrant functions. These are important because they allow complex computations to be defined using relatively small programs, just as in conventional loops, subroutines and procedures. However, such re-entrant constructs pose substantial implementation problems in a parallel computational model because of the likelihood of simultaneous activation of the re-entrant code.

Dataflow researchers have determined three main methods for dealing with these implementation problems. The first method is the easiest to implement, but is not a general solution to re-entrancy problems since it prohibits concurrent re-entrancy by allowing only cycles and reactivating them in strict sequence. Although a limited amount of parallelism can be obtained for some applications by pipelining inside cycles within such a regime, the more general solutions of the other two implementation schemes allow more parallel execution to occur. Systems which allow only cyclic (sequential) re-entrancy are known as *static* dataflow systems, as opposed to the *dynamic* dataflow systems introduced below.

The second scheme permits concurrent re-entrancy by implementing a special *apply* instruction which creates a new copy of the re-entrant part of the graph it controls every time it is activated. All the required input tokens to this copy are gathered together at the apply instruction and they are then transferred to the unique new copy of the re-entrant code. A special *exit* instruction at the end of the re-entrant code copy gathers together all the output tokens for the activation and transfers them back to the output arcs of the appropriate apply instruction. The copy of the re-entrant code is then destroyed. This scheme is sometimes called the dynamic *code-copying* scheme, and its operation is analogous to macro-expansion in that extra code *and* data space is allocated whenever it is called for in order to avoid data having to share code concurrently.

The third scheme allows code to be shared in concurrently re-entrant graphs by 'tagging' data tokens as they enter into and exit from the re-entrant areas. This system is similar to the use of stacks for implementing conventional procedures and functions, except that the concurrent activation of shared graph code requires that each data value be *individually* tagged with the appropriate 'name-base', instead of using global stack registers to identify the currently active name-space. In visual terms, this can be thought of as colouring data tokens and modifying the execution rules so that only tokens of the same colour (ie carrying the same tag) can be grouped together to execute an instruction. Special instructions are needed to create new colours and to restore old colours at entry to and exit from the re-entrant code: tokens must carry round extra bits to denote the colour. This scheme is known as the dynamic *tagged*, or *code-sharing*, scheme.

Structured data

Compact conventional programs are also achieved by using data structures whereby one variable name can apply to a large collection of simple data items. Two implementation schemes have been developed to give them the same facilities in graph programs.

The first scheme uses separate storage to hold the structures, and represents each structure in the program graph as a *pointer* token. The special *structure store* is responsible for issuing the appropriate pointers. Other instructions operate on scalar data, or control the flow of pointer tokens through the program.

The alternative scheme uses the tagging system described above. Each element of a data structure carries a unique tag defining that element's position in the structure. Tag-sensitive instructions can be used to manipulate the structure in the required way. This scheme is particularly useful for implementing regular structures, such as arrays, whose elements are all being operated on (as, for example, in signal processing applications, etc).

Compilation of graph code

As has been demonstrated in the earlier examples, it is quite possible to generate dataflow graphs from conventional high-level programming languages such as FORTRAN. However, the analysis algorithm that forms the data dependency graphs for such programs is highly complex and takes a long time to execute. Other languages are known which are much more readily translated into graph code, and these are receiving most attention in dataflow research projects.

The Single-Assignment Languages (SALs) are one important group of high-level languages in this context. They have no concept of sequential execution and no direct control statements such as the GOTO. To combat the ambiguities that might arise from reassigning values to variables, the languages normally allow each variable to be assigned to only once in a program. Constructs are provided to permit controlled reassignment in special cases, such as loops. SALs also tend to use the kinds of data structure that can be readily implemented in dataflow graphs, such as arrays and streams. There are usually strict typing and scope rules in such languages: in particular, it is common to prohibit all forms of side-effect in re-entrant constructs. The net results are languages that look like attempts to provide a textual syntax for describing dataflow graphs. However, many were actually developed without reference to such an execution regime, and it is now becoming clear that the SALs are very similar to some languages which were developed without reference to any means of execution at all, namely the *functional* or *applicative* languages.

Functional languages are based on the mathematics of functional algebra and have no concepts of storage state and assignment. In fact, they are sometimes called Zero-Assignment Languages (ZALs). One interesting point that has recently emerged is that if assignment is restricted to occur only once for each variable in a program, the effect is the same as if there were no assignment at all, and 'assignment' statements were treated as *definitions* of variables. In this way SALs and functional languages are identical, and it is not surprising that absence of GOTOs and side-effects are common to them both. However, functional algebra allows higher level programming than most SALs permit by means of higher order functions and more comprehensive data structuring facilities. Consequently there is not a direct equivalence of the two. Nevertheless, they have enough in common to make it highly probable that functional languages will be amenable to efficient implementation on dataflow systems. Research is in progress to demonstrate operational compilers in this area.

Summary of dataflow graphs

Dataflow graphs are a convenient notation for representing parallel computation. They permit conditional computation, loops, functions (including recursion), and data structuring. Translation to dataflow graphs is feasible from a wide range of high-level programming languages.

There is a natural classification for dataflow schemes according to the way they handle re-entrant code. The three classes are: *static* schemes, *dynamic code-copying* schemes and *dynamic tagged* schemes.

PARALLELISM IN HARDWARE

Before considering possible hardware implementations for a dataflow computer, it is worth identifying the two fundamental parallel hardware configurations, and summarising their characteristics. The two configurations are known as the *pipeline* and the *parallel array*.

Pipelines are used where each hardware task (say an instruction) can be subdivided into several, or perhaps many, much shorter jobs that can be executed in sequence and, to a large extent, in isolation. Parallelism is exploited by overlapping the operation of the successive pipeline stages on successive program instructions. This situation is illustrated for a 6 stage pipeline in Figure 2. The stages of the pipeline are shown across the top of the diagram, and the optimum distribution of instructions through the hardware over a period of time are shown underneath. After an initial delay of $6\Delta t$, results are produced at the output every Δt period, even though each takes $6\Delta t$ to complete. The key assumptions made are:

1 Each subtask takes an identical, small, amount of time to perform.

2 There are no data dependencies between the modules other than the main path through.

3 There are no external constraints to providing input to the pipeline, or to disposing of the output, at the required regular rate.

If any of these assumptions is invalid, the distribution of instructions through the pipeline becomes uneven, and the average rate of processing is impaired.

Parallel arrays are used where each hardware task cannot be easily subdivided; where there are many tasks independently available for execution they may be distributed and executed concurrently. There are two ways of activating a parallel array, either serially or in parallel.

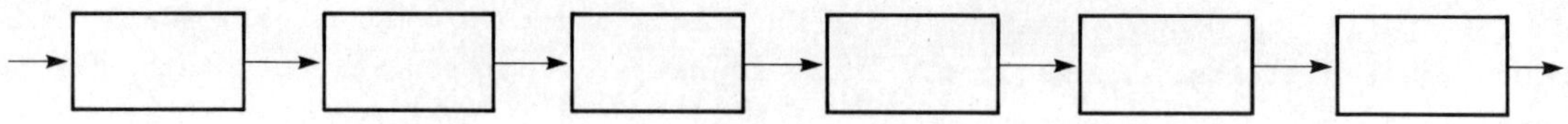

Time	Stage 1	2	3	4	5	6
0	task 1	-	-	-	-	-
Δt	task 2	task 1	-	-	-	-
2Δt	task 3	task 2	task 1	-	-	-
3Δt	task 4	task 3	task 2	task 1	-	-
4Δt	task 5	task 4	task 3	task 2	task 1	-
5Δt	task 6	task 5	task 4	task 3	task 2	task 1
6Δt	task 7	task 6	task 5	task 4	task 3	task 2
7Δt	task 8	task 7	task 6	task 5	task 4	task 3
8Δt	task 9	task 8	task 7	task 6	task 5	task 4
9Δt	task 10	task 9	task 8	task 7	task 6	task 5
10Δt	task 11	task 10	task 9	task 8	task 7	task 6
11Δt	task 12	task 11	task 10	task 9	task 8	task 7
12Δt	task 13	task 12	task 11	task 10	task 9	task 8
13Δt	|	|	|	|	|	|

Figure 2: Six-stage pipeline : delay per stage = Δt

In a serially activated system, the parallel array sits in a pipeline and is fed with tasks at a relatively high rate, each task going to a different module until all modules are active. The number of modules used is roughly the time per task divided by the time per input from the pipeline, so that the first module to be filled is emptied to the output pipe just as the last module is filled with its first task. This situation is illustrated for a 6 module array in Figure 3 in a similar fashion to the pipeline that was described earlier. In this case a finished task is output from the array at the same rate as for the pipeline. The key assumptions made are:

1 Each task takes an identical, relatively long time to perform.
2 There are no data dependencies between the modules apart from input/output.
3 Input and output occur at an appropriately fast rate.

Again, validity of any of these assumptions causes performance to deteriorate.

In a parallel-activated array, each module can be imagined to be executing a task independently, and output from each module usually enters a routing network which sends data to the input of the next required module. Perhaps the easiest way of visualising this is to imagine all the modules locked in step with one another executing many instructions literally in parallel. The distribution of tasks in a 6 module version of a system is illustrated in Figure 4. Now, however, 6 tasks start and finish at the end of each period of 6Δt time units, giving the same average throughput as for the cases studied above. Similar assumptions to those above have been made.

In the following sections we shall see how these structures can be configured to implement dataflow schemata in hardware. In practice it is difficult to ensure that the required assumptions are valid, to ensure maximum throughput, and so discussion will concentrate on the likely performance of the different configurations.

REQUIREMENTS FOR A DATAFLOW SYSTEM

From our earlier consideration of dataflow notation, it is apparent that any dataflow computer, static or dynamic, will have to perform at least three major jobs:

1 The program graph must be stored somewhere.

2 Data tokens which flow through the graph and match together with appropriate partners must be implemented.

3 Suitable data processing facilities must be provided.

Static and dynamic code-copying systems can implement tokens by providing additional data storage in the program graph store. Dynamic tagged systems require separate code and data stores. Instruction sets for the different schemes will reflect the needs described earlier, such as *apply* for code-copying and *change colour* for tagged systems.

In terms of system architecture, any of the schemes introduced in the previous section could be used. However, we would expect the obvious vehicle for implementing an instruction-level parallel execution schema to be a parallel-activated parallel array of instruction executors, especially if we intended to use conventional microprocessors as the basic processing facility. Consequently, we shall study two systems of this nature first. Two different refinements of this type of system will then be considered. Each system is either already in operation or currently under construction, so together they constitute a representative set of practical system designs.

STATIC DATAFLOW MULTI-MICROPROCESSORS

Two systems based on conventional microprocessor units connected in a parallel-activated parallel array identical to Figure 4 have been proposed. They mainly differ in microprocessor architecture, and in the nature of the communication switch. A research system built by a team led by Don Oxley at Texas Instruments in 1978 used four microprocessors connected together via a time-multiplexed packet-switching communication ring (011). A more powerful system is being implemented by Jack Dennis and his group at MIT using specialised bit-sliced microprocessors connected via a general-purpose unidirectional parallel routing network (012). In both systems the three major dataflow jobs are implemented by software in the microprocessors. The TI system can use the slow communication ring

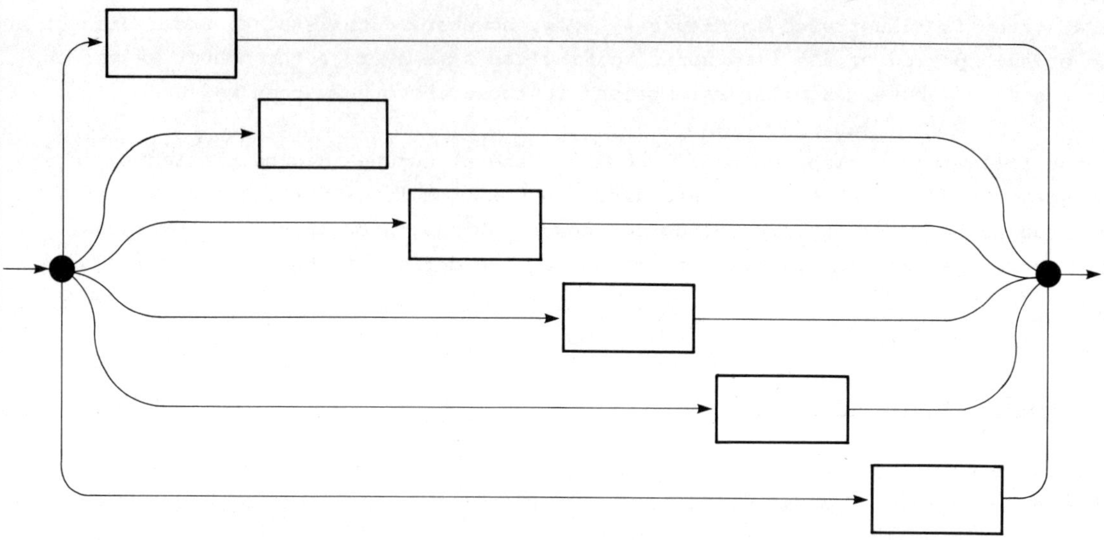

Time ↓ \ Module	1	2	3	4	5	6
0	task 1	-	-	-	-	-
Δt	task 1	task 2	-	-	-	-
$2\Delta t$	task 1	task 2	task 3	-	-	-
$3\Delta t$	task 1	task 2	task 3	task 4	-	-
$4\Delta t$	task 1	task 2	task 3	task 4	task 5	-
$5\Delta t$	task 1	task 2	task 3	task 4	task 5	task 6
$6\Delta t$	task 7	task 2	task 3	task 4	task 5	task 6
$7\Delta t$	task 7	task 8	task 3	task 4	task 5	task 6
$8\Delta t$	task 7	task 8	task 9	task 4	task 5	task 6
$9\Delta t$	task 7	task 8	task 9	task 10	task 5	task 6
$10\Delta t$	task 7	task 8	task 9	task 10	task 11	task 6
$11\Delta t$	task 7	task 8	task 9	task 10	task 11	task 12
$12\Delta t$	task 13	task 8	task 9	task 10	task 11	task 12
$13\Delta t$	|	|	|	|	|	|

Figure 3: Six-module pipeline-activated parallel array : delay per stage = $6\Delta t$

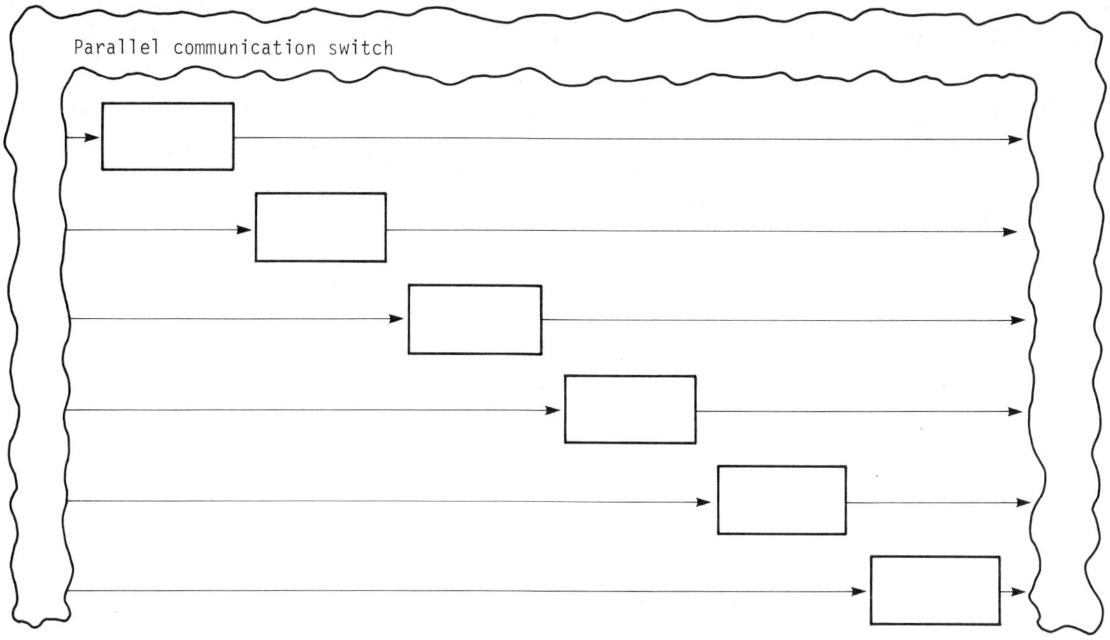

Module Time ↓	1	2	3	4	5	6
0	task 1	task 2	task 3	task 4	task 5	task 6
Δt	task 1	task 2	task 3	task 4	task 5	task 6
2Δt	task 1	task 2	task 3	task 4	task 5	task 6
3Δt	task 1	task 2	task 3	task 4	task 5	task 6
4Δt	task 1	task 2	task 3	task 4	task 5	task 6
5Δt	task 1	task 2	task 3	task 4	task 5	task 6
6Δt	task 7	task 8	task 9	task 10	task 11	task 12
7Δt	task 7	task 8	task 9	task 10	task 11	task 12
8Δt	task 7	task 8	task 9	task 10	task 11	task 12
9Δt	task 7	task 8	task 9	task 10	task 11	task 12
10Δt	task 7	task 8	task 9	task 10	task 11	task 12
11Δt	task 7	task 8	task 9	task 10	task 11	task 12
12Δt	task 13	task 14	task 15	task 16	task 17	task 18
13Δt	|	|	|	|	|	|

Figure 4: Six-module parallel-activated parallel array : delay per stage = 6Δt

because of the relatively slow processing time of its microprocessors, and the small number of them that have to be supported. In the MIT system the processors are faster and there are more of them, so the switch needs to handle much higher throughput. Both systems implement a static dataflow schema, with possible extension to a dynamic code-copying scheme.

Code for the TI system is mainly produced from standard FORTRAN programs, whereas a single-assignment language, VAL, has been defined and implemented to act as the high-level interface to the MIT machine (013). Arrays are provided in both languages, but streams are also anticipated in VAL.

A key point in the design of the MIT system is the ability to expand its computing power by adding extra processors via an extended communications switch. The switch itself is a network of simple 2 × 2 routers connected in such a way that any input port may reach any output port in a time proportional to the logarithm of the number of processors attached. The structure of this switch for 4, 8 and 16 processors is shown in Figure 5. Each 2 × 2 element operates a byte at a time.

The desire to expand computer power by adding hardware is common to all dataflow projects, and each of the architectural proposals outlined here uses a switch that is similar to that of Figure 4. There is keen debate as to how large a switch it is possible to construct (or will be possible in the foreseeable future). Obviously there is a relationship between the power of an individual processor, the overall required power, and the size of switch. Because the systems described in this section use conventional microprocessors to emulate the dataflow model by software, they run rather slowly, and large switches will be required for applications such as weather forecasting. It is implicit in this MIT proposal that switches of up to 500 × 500 can be implemented using byte-serial, bit-parallel 2 × 2 routers.

Other researchers are less confident that such switches will be practicable, and so their efforts have concentrated on improving the execution rates of individual processors by making them more directly dataflow oriented. The two projects discussed in the next sections follow this approach, and also implement dynamic tagged dataflow schemata.

THE MSI DYNAMIC-TAGGED DATAFLOW PROCESSOR

A research group at Manchester University (under the leadership of Ian Watson and myself) has constructed a specialised 'ring-structured' dataflow processor with funding from the Distributed Computing Systems Programme of the Science and Engineering Research Council of Great Britain (014).

In the basic ring-structured system the three dataflow tasks, namely matching tokens together, relating matched tokens onto the program graph, and performing the data processing, are implemented in three separate hardware modules. The individual actions in each of these modules are dependent only on the current input data, so that successive actions may be overlapped by connecting the modules in a pipeline. One additional pipeline module is provided to queue excess jobs when highly parallel programs are running. Hence the overall structure of the ring-structured processor is a four-stage pipeline as shown in Figure 6.

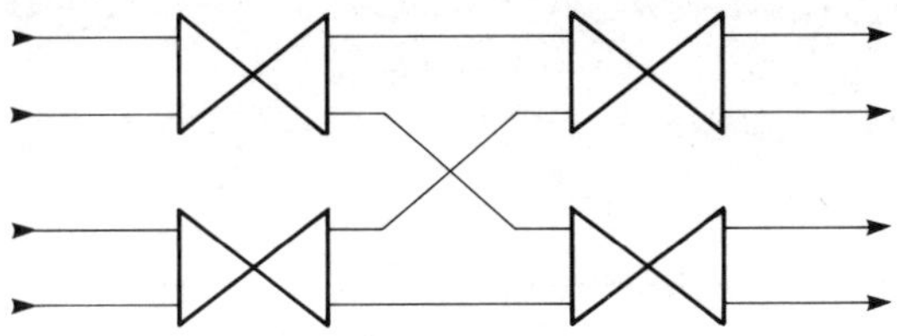

4 processors

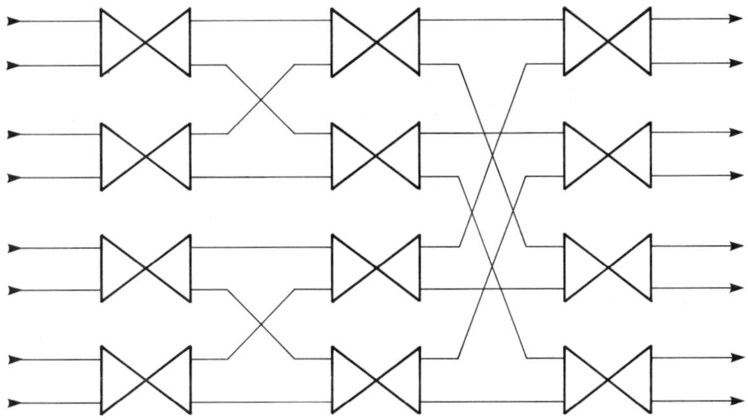

8 processors

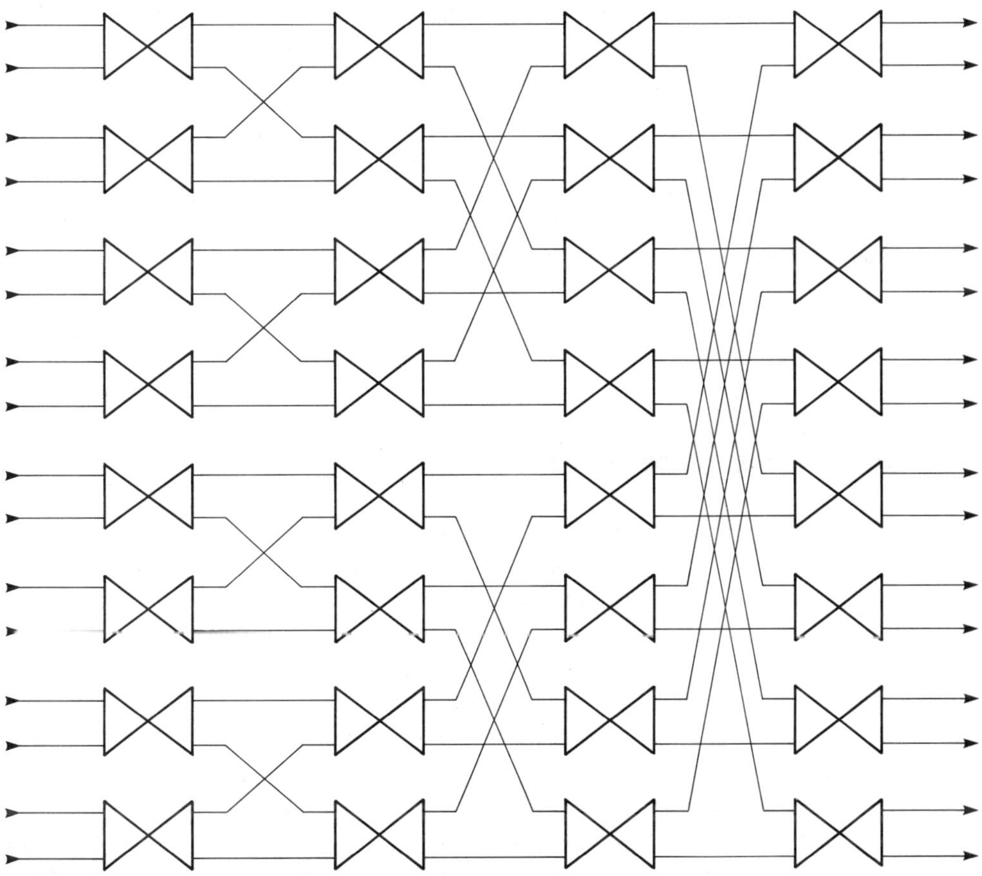

16 processors

Figure 5: Communication switch structure

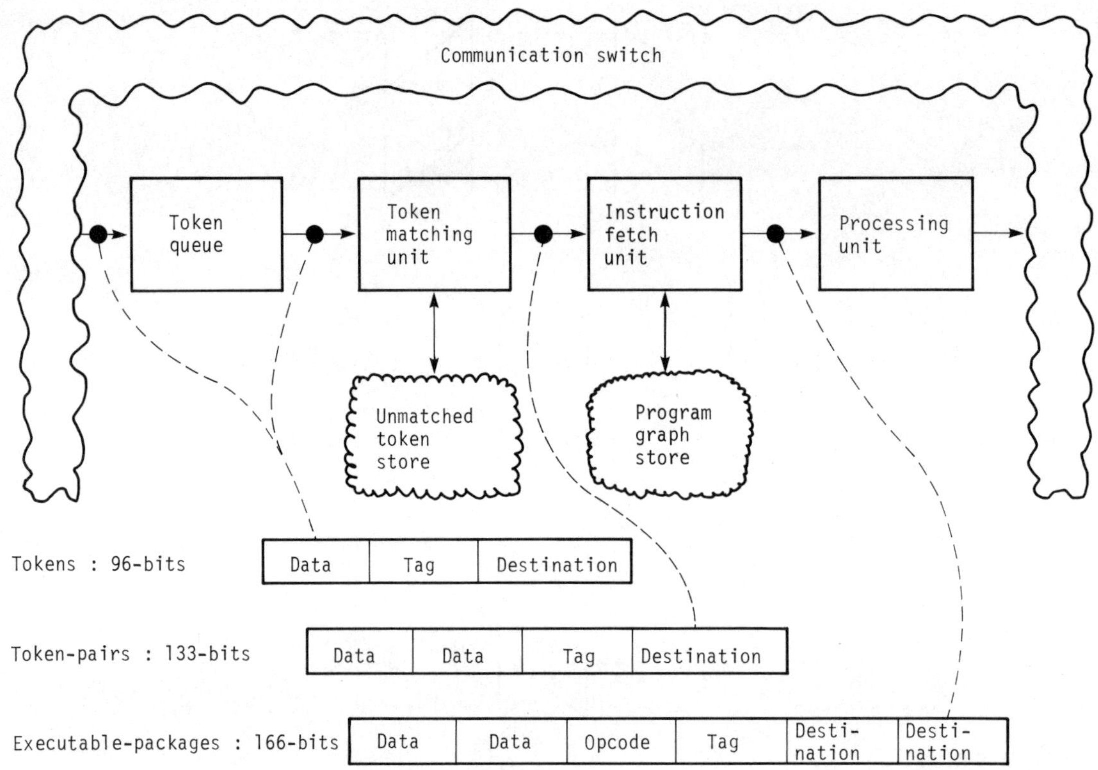

Figure 6: Ring-structured dataflow processor

The fundamental unit of information in the switch is a token-package, representing a notational tagged token on an arc of the graph. The token has a data value and tag, and the arc is represented by the address in the program graph store of the instruction at its head (the 'destination'). This token is the smallest data package, and so the queue module is inserted at this point. Queued tokens are presented one-at-a-time to the matching unit, which is responsible for grouping together tokens which have the same tag and are heading for the same destination. In the Manchester system tokens may only be grouped in ones and twos. Unmatched tokens, ie those that arrive at the matching unit before their partner (if they have one), are kept in the unmatched token store attached to the matching unit. After matching has successfully occurred, matched token-pairs are sent to the instruction fetch unit. The tag and destination fields for the pair are of necessity identical. The program graph is stored as an array of instructions, each one representing a node and its associated output arcs. The incoming destination is used to address the next instruction, which defines an opcode to perform at this point and up to two destinations to which the result should be sent. The now complete executable package is sent to the processing unit, which executes the required opcode on the input data, and sends the results back into the communication switch.

The critical point in this system is the matching unit. The task of pairing together matching tokens is essentially an act of association, and the unmatched tokens have to be saved in a pseudo-associative memory. Details of the operation of this unit are beyond the scope of this paper, but, in the technology chosen for implementation, the average match-time is 300 nsec (015). This limits the instruction execution rate of the processor to 3.3 million instr/sec. In fact, the data processing elements used to execute instructions are some 20 times slower than this in the prototype version, so a serially-activated parallel array of them is used to build the processing unit. The communications switch will be used in an extended system now under construction. This switch is to be constructed from 96-bit 2 × 2 routers and will control four ring-structured processors in the first instance.

This scale of implementation is made feasible by using simple existing MSI/TTL technology. Higher speed could be obtained by using faster switching components (eg ECL). Comparable speeds might be achievable if a similar system were manufactured in VLSI technology, and a practical study of such an approach is discussed next.

A VLSI DYNAMIC-TAGGED DATAFLOW PROCESSOR

A second research group at MIT, under the leadership of Arvind, is constructing a VLSI-based dynamic-tagged dataflow processor (016). An outline system design is shown in Figure 7. Its structure is quite complex but in essence it is similar to the ring-structured system. The two main differences are *firstly* that data structure accesses are handled differently from ordinary data token activities, and *secondly* that there is a two-tiered communication system.

Data structure operations are treated separately so that they can be performed quickly, and so that the related tokens do not fill up the unmatched token store. The two-tiered communication structure relieves the general communication switch of a lot of traffic as long as programs exhibit strong locality (ie local processing activity is likely to remain in the same area of the graph, and hence the same processor, rather than communicating randomly with all other processors). In fact, locality also benefits the size of unmatched token store, and current plans at MIT are to implement a 64-word store only, as opposed to the 16K-word store being used at Manchester.

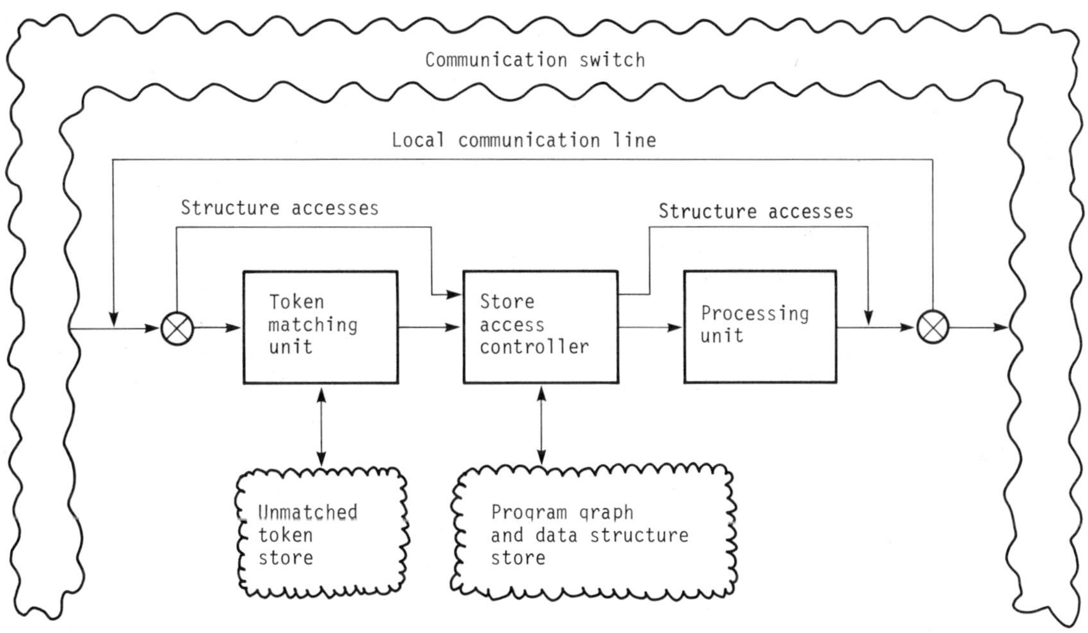

Figure 7: A VLSI-based dataflow processor

The reduced traffic in the communications switch allows bit-serial data paths to be used and so the proposed basic switch building block is an 8 × 8 unit, instead of the 2 × 2 byte and word units introduced above. Bigger switches can be constructed from such units, and, using locality again, can be made rather less complex than the networks shown in Figure 5.

This design relies heavily on there being locality in programs. The language ID has appropriate properties and the system is built around this language, which was also developed by Arvind's team (017).

SUMMARY OF DATAFLOW HARDWARE

The great advantage of dataflow notation is that individual actions in executing a graph program only interact with one another by token flow along the arcs. All necessary synchronisation of data and instructions can be achieved by the act of 'matching' tokens together. Hence, whether pipelines or parallel arrays are used for implementation, the parallel hardware can be kept occupied by simple distribution techniques without having to worry about inconvenient interlinking of constituent modules.

The systems presented above all have similar overall structure, but there are considerable differences in the detail. These are by no means the only designs for such systems, and at least three others are worth mentioning at this point, especially since they have been in operation for several years now. They were designed by the LAU project, led by Jean-Claude Syre at CERT Toulouse (018), the DDM1 project, led by Al Davis at the University of Utah (019) and a project at NTT in Japan led by Makoto Amamiya (020). Additional information on dataflow systems and languages has recently been published in a special issue of IEEE Computer (021).

Little has yet been published about the performance of dataflow systems in practical applications, but the existence of so much operational hardware should lead to a great expansion of assessment work and subsequent results in the near future.

REFERENCES

001 FLYNN M J
Some computer organisations and their effectiveness
IEEE Transactions on Computers
vol C-21 no 9 (Sep 1972)

002 REDDAWAY S F
DAP - a distributed array processor
Proc 1st Annual ACM Symposium on Computer Architecture (Dec 1973)

003 BARNES G H, BROWN R M, KATO M, KUCK D J, SLOTNICK D L and STOKES R A
The ILLIAC IV computer
IEEE Transactions on Computers
vol C-17 no 8 (Aug 1968)

004 THORNTON J E
Design of a computer: the CD6600
Scott Foresman & Co (1970)

005 WULF W A and BELL C G
C.mmp - a multiminiprocessor
Proc AFIPS FJCC vol 41 (Sep 1972)

006 SWAN R J, FULLER S H and SIEWIOREK D P
Cm - a modular multimicroprocessor*
Proc AFIPS NCC vol 46 (June 1977)

007 BRINCH HANSEN P
The programming language CONCURRENT PASCAL
IEEE Transactions on Software Engineering vol SE-1 no 2 (June 1975)

008 WIRTH N
MODULA: a language for modular multiprogramming
Software - Practice & Experience vol 7 no 1 (Jan 1977)

009 BRINCH HANSEN P
Distributed processes: a concurrent programming concept
Communications of the ACM vol 21 no 11 (Nov 1978)

010 HOARE C A R
Communicating sequential processes
Communications of the ACM vol 21 no 8 (Aug 1978)

011 JOHNSON D
Automatic partitioning of programs in multiprocessor systems
Proc IEEE Spring COMPCON (Apr 1980)

012 DENNIS J B, BOUGHTON G A and LEUNG C K C
Building blocks for dataflow prototypes
Proc 7th Annual ACM Symposium on Computer Architecture (May 1980)

013 ACKERMAN W B and DENNIS J B
VAL - a value-oriented algorithmic language: preliminary reference manual
Technical Rep TR-218 MIT Laboratory for Computer Science (June 1979)

014 GURD J R and WATSON I
Dataflow system for high-speed parallel computing
Computer Design vol 19 nos 6 and 7 (June 1980 and July 1980)

015 WATSON I and GURD J R
A practical dataflow computer
IEEE Computer vol 15 no 2 (Feb 1982)

016 ARVIND and KATHAIL V
A multiple processor dataflow machine that supports generalised procedures
Proc 8th Annual AMC Symposium on Computer Architecture (May 1981)

017 ARVIND, GOSTELOW K P and PLOUFFE W
An asynchronous programming language and computing machine
Dept of Information and Computer Science Technical Rep TR114a Univ of California at Irvine (Dec 1978)

018 COMTE D, HIFDI N and SYRE J C
The data-driven LAU multiprocessor system: results and perspectives
Proc IFIP '80 Congress (Oct 1980)

019 DAVIS A L
The architecture and system methodology of DDM1: a recursively structured data-driven machine
Proc 5th Annual ACM Symposium on Computer Architecture (Apr 1978)

020 AMAMIYA M, TAKAHASHI N, NARUSE T and YOSHIDA M
A dataflow processor array system for solving partial differential equations
Proc Intl Symposium on Applied Mathematics and Information Science
Kyoto Univ Japan (Mar 1982)

021 IEEE COMPUTER
Special issue on Dataflow Systems
vol 15 no 2 (Feb 1982)

AUXILIARY DATA STORAGE

A S Hoagland

IBM Research Laboratory
San Jose
CA

A S HOAGLAND is manager of Exploratory Magnetic Recording at the IBM San Jose Research Laboratory and immediate past president of the American Federation of Information Processing Societies. He joined IBM in San Jose in 1956, where he played a key role in the development of magnetic disk files. In 1962 he transferred to Europe as a consultant to IBM World Trade, and in 1964 joined the IBM Research Center in New York, where he was appointed director of technical planning for the research division in 1968. In 1971 he was assigned to the IBM Boulder, Colorado Laboratory to lead an inter-divisional program in mass storage, and in 1976 joined the San Jose Laboratory. A Fellow and past director of the IEEE and a past president of the IEEE Computer Society, Hoagland has held many positions in the IEEE, the Computer Society, and AFIPS. He is author of the book Digital magnetic recording *as well as some 30 technical publications. Mr Hoagland holds the BSEE, MSEE, and PhD degrees from the University of California at Berkeley.*

AUXILIARY DATA STORAGE

Electronic storage is discussed, with particular reference to Charge-Coupled Devices (CCDs) and Magnetic Bubble Memories (MBMs). Magnetic disks are assessed and floppy disks, the least expensive form of disk storage per unit, are also discussed. Tape storage devices and mass storage systems are examined, and the two 'mass storage' technologies currently under development (magnetic and optical) are also assessed. Finally, video disk technology and future growth directions are examined.

INTRODUCTION

Computerised information processing has grown over the past 25 years from incidental significance to become a pervasive influence in our society. A continuing concern, as the range of applications has grown, has been the cost and access time of data storage. A wide range of technologies has been investigated on a continuing basis to address this challenge. As rapid as progress in storage technology has been, the need for more capacity with improved access has increased even faster.

The use of storage technologies depends on three principal factors: cost per bit, access time, and unit device cost. Reduced cost per bit in all technologies derives primarily from an increase in density on the material being used for storage. Lower cost per bit is also associated with an increase in the physical size of the basic storage module. In low-end systems unit product cost is crucial.

The relative performance levels and corresponding costs for storage technologies are shown in Figure 1. This diagram reflects the relative cost per bit/access time tradeoff.

Since one must trade off improved access time against cost per bit, a memory/storage system generally consists of a hierarchy - a mix of device performance capabilities. The classical storage pyramid is shown in Figure 2, indicating the technology hierarchy and associated relative allocation of capacity.

A discussion of auxiliary storage will proceed by considering the different levels in the pyramid, starting downward from main memory.

ELECTRONIC STORAGE (CCD AND MBM)

Electronic storage involves data access with no physical motion. For auxiliary storage, where minimising cost per bit is paramount, techniques to reduce bit cell size and complexity, even at a price in access time, are explored - since there is ample design room for tradeoffs while still achieving considerably faster access times than those of mechanical devices. Two technologies appear as candidates in this category, Charge Coupled Devices (CCD) and Magnetic Bubble Memories (MBM).

The CCD is a memory design based on well established silicon technology. MOS RAM technology has been advancing at a rate such that chip capacity has quadrupled every two to three years over the last decade. The introduction of the N-channel single transistor cell greatly increased speed and bit density. 64-Kbit dynamic RAM is now

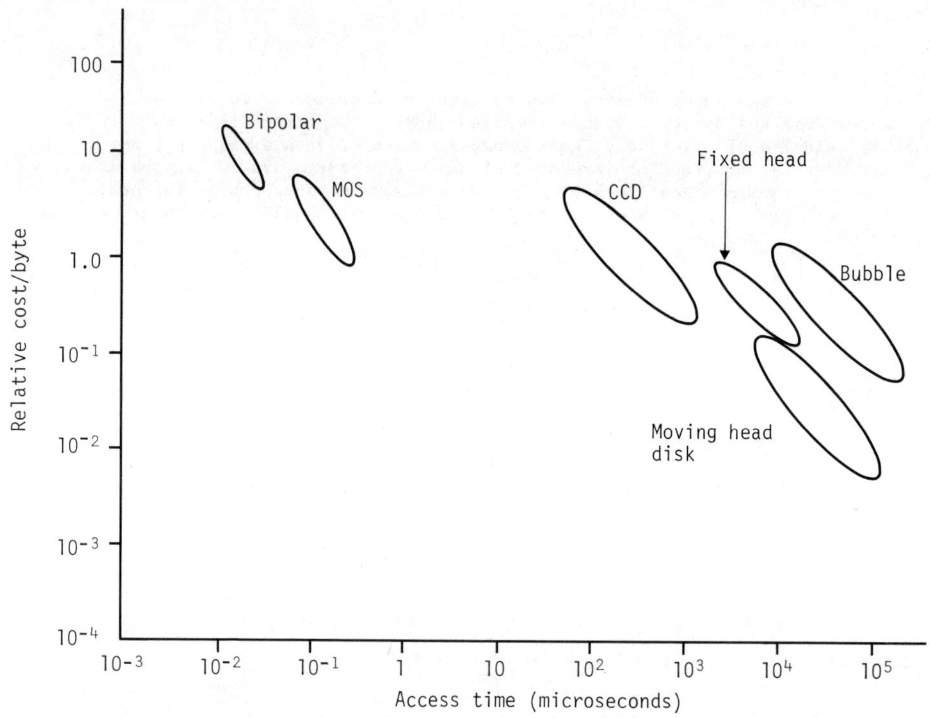

Figure 1: Performance levels and costs for storage technologies

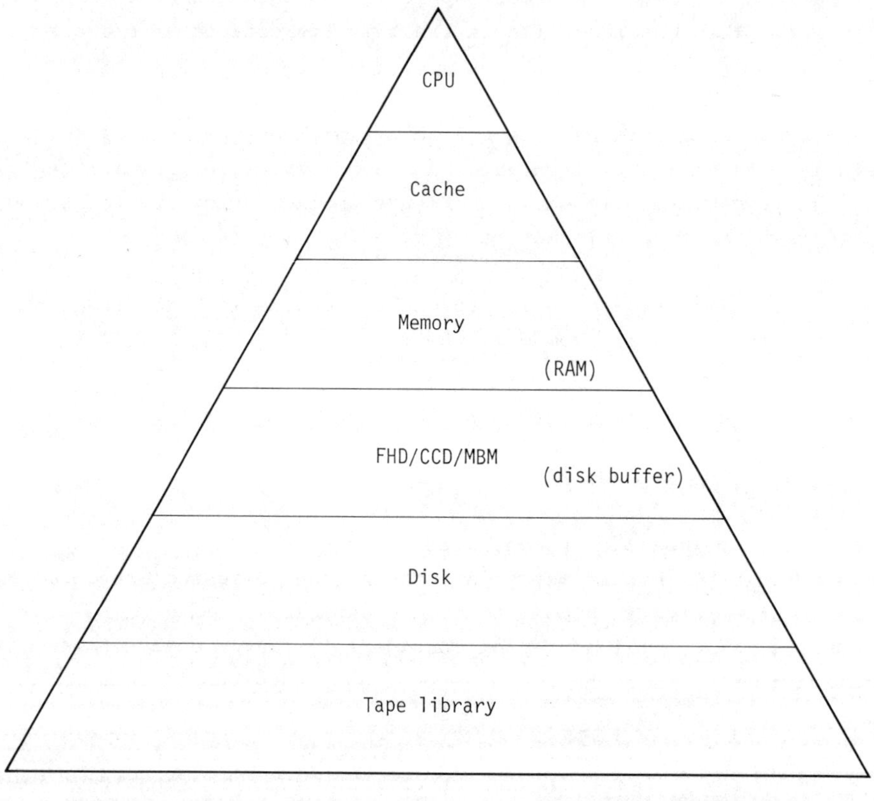

Figure 2: The classical storage pyramid

available and the introduction of electron and X-ray lithography will extend the miniaturisation underway. With a 1-μ channel length and a full wafer memory (based on defect-tolerant designs) 100 Mbits on a five-inch wafer has been projected as ultimately feasible (002).

CCD obtains a cost advantage over RAM by storing information in packets of charge rather than by means of bistable circuitry in a serial-parallel type organisation. The technological similarity, while a great asset, may in fact retard the wide acceptance of CCDs for storage because, compared to RAMs, the obtainable cost reduction may not be enough to offset the associated great decrease in access time, except in very specific applications.

The MBM also uses a shift-register type organisation. Magnetic bubbles are small cylindrical magnetic domains formed in certain thin magnetic films when an external magnetic bias field is applied normal to the plane of the film. These 'bubble' domains are magnetised in the reverse sense to that of the film itself. Information is coded in terms of the presence or absence of bubbles. MBM is non-volatile and non-mechanical. 1-Mbit chips are now being offered (2 to 3-μ bubbles). The factor curtailing the wider use of bubbles is cost, with the interface circuitry and power being significant factors. It is not clear that their cost will ever get lower than the rapidly moving semiconductor technology, much less disk.

Applications which can effectively exploit the unique attributes of bubbles need to be identified for the technology to find a niche. From the standpoint of cost per bit, neither CCDs nor MBMs are a threat to moving-head disks for the function of auxiliary storage.

MAGNETIC DISKS

These are available in both rigid and flexible form. Disks come in a wide range of access time capabilities, with the fixed-head systems at one extreme and floppies at the other. The primary characteristic of disks is direct access to all data in relatively short times.

Magnetic recording is a surface area technology and storage device capacity is a direct function of the storage medium surface area provided, the efficiency of its utilisation, and the areal density of recording.

As a recording type of storage, magnetic disks have the advantages of non-volatility, low cost, direct access, allocation flexibility, a simple, reliable recording process, and update in place. Their major disadvantage is that they involve mechanical motion with corresponding access time limitations.

One can consider the conventional rigid disk, in terms of solid-state terminology, as a wafer 14 inches in diameter (equivalent to 10 000 chips) that is processed and used as an entity (therefore, perfect 'wafers' are the rule). Bit cell length is currently about 1μ, with a head-medium 'dimension' of 0.2μ.

Higher storage densities have required improvement in magnetic recording resolution, which has been achieved through reductions in head gap, head-disk spacing, and medium thickness. Improved track densities have followed from the advent of the voice coil actuator and closed-loop track-following systems.

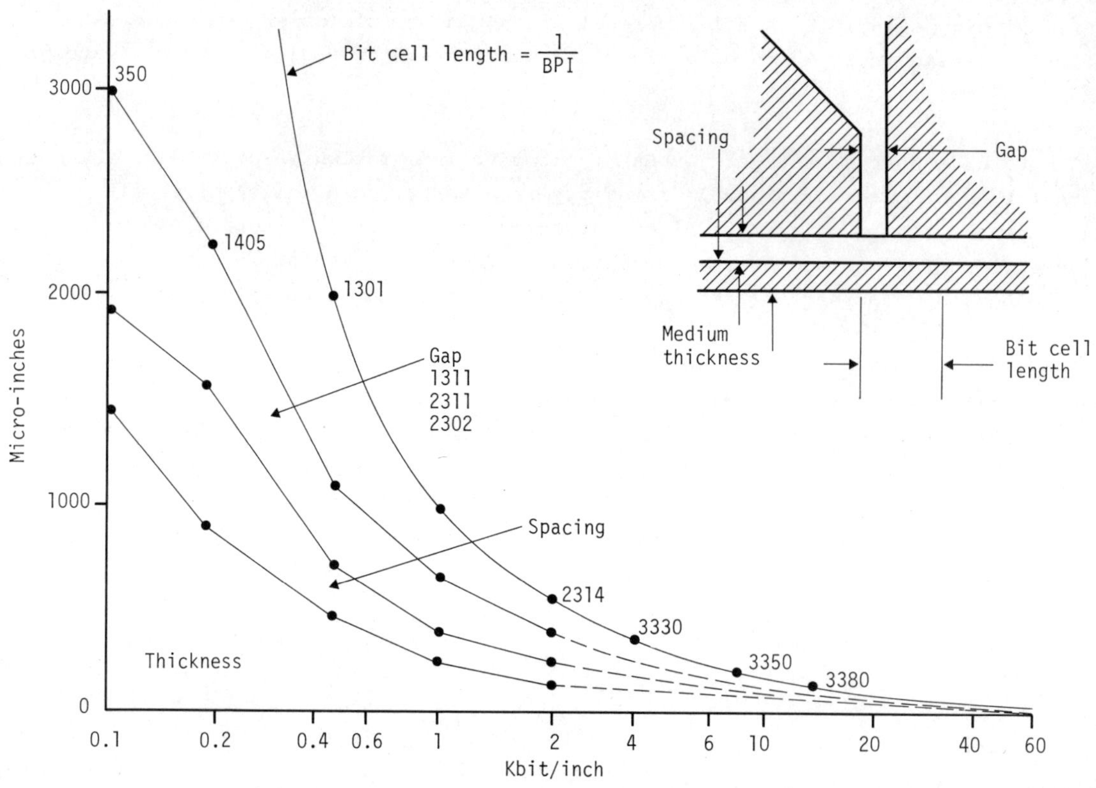

Figure 3: Bit cell length is related to physical recording parameters

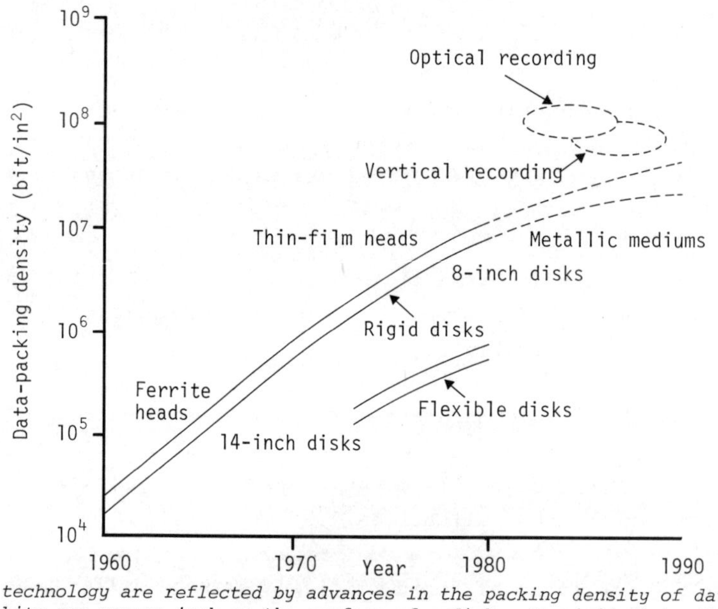

Note:
Advances in disk technology are reflected by advances in the packing density of data, expressed in this chart as bits per square inch on the surface of a disk. In rigid disks the magnetic medium is coated on an aluminium substrate; in floppy disks it is coated on Mylar plastic. Two improvements are foreseen for the magnetic technology: the use of metal film instead of iron oxide as the medium on rigid disks and the recording of data in regions of magnetisation oriented vertically, or perpendicular to the plane of the disk, instead of horizontally - the current practice. Optical disk technology might attain the greatest storage density.

Figure 4: Increase in areal density with time

Figure 3 shows how recording geometry has scaled down with increasing linear density, while Figure 4 shows the associated increase in areal density with time.

Non-removable packs are appearing in many of the new drives as they provide reduced tolerances and better environmental control, making it easier to increase density. Fortuitously, achievable capacities have reached a magnitude that minimises the utility of disk pack replaceability as long as a save/restore capability is available. As seen in Figure 5, disk storage density has increased from 2000 bit/in^2 to 1.55 Mbit/in^2 (2.4 × 104 bit/mm^2, with 550 bit/mm and 43 track/mm) - almost 10^4 increase in 25 years. Density increases should continue at this rate during the 1980s. Thus we have reached a capacity of almost 1 Gbyte/spindle. Access time has decreased from 1 sec to 16 msec in this same period.

Year	Device	Capacity	Bit/in^2	Bit/in	Track/in
1956	IBM 350	5	2K	100	20
1964	IBM 2311	7.3	110K	1100	100
1965	IBM 2314	29.1	220K	2200	100
1970	IBM 3330-1	100	775K	4040	192
1973	IBM 3330-11	200	1495K	4040	370
1973	IBM 3340	70	1650K	5600	300
1975	IBM 3350	317	3058K	6425	476
1978	STC 8650	635	6100K	6425	952
1979	IBM 3370	571	7800K	12 134	635
1980	IBM 3380	2500	12 000K	15 000	801
1981	NTT	3200	15 300K	13 970	1092

Figure 5: Disk development history

Progress in reducing the head-to-surface spacing has been the key factor in increasing the linear density of disk storage. A boundary layer of air is used to provide an air bearing, which in turn determines the spacing. Progress in air bearing technology has reduced head-to-disk spacing from 900 micro-inches to 10 micro-inches.

The molecular mean free path of air is approximately 3 micro-inches and is considered a lower limit for a true air bearing. However, disk manufacturing processes and attainable medium smoothness and durability have been the pacing factor in determining spacing.

Read/write head materials have been improved from laminated mu-metal, to ferrite, to batch fabricated thin film. The thin film approach offers higher frequency capability and much better control for the fabrication of narrow track widths. Fabrication technology has reduced the gap length a factor of 40, from 1000 to 25 micro-inches. Improved spin-coating processes have reduced particulate iron oxide coating thickness by a factor of 150, from 1200 to 20 micro-inches. To date, advances in disk media have been made by going to thinner and smoother particulate coatings to improve spatial resolution and reduce medium demagnetisation effects. With newer head materials that can provide higher write fields, higher coercive force media (which also reduce demagnetisation effects) and thin sputtered or chemically deposited metal films with high saturation magnetisation are being pursued. With these films it is easily possible to produce medium layers of less than 10 micro-inches.

Track density of moving-head magnetic disks is determined by the accuracy and tolerance of the head positioning mechanism and the transverse resolution of the read-write head: as long as an adequate signal/noise ratio is available track width is reduced. Over the same time period track density has increased from 20 to almost 1100 track/in. Placing servo information with the data and better head-disk assembly packaging will lead to further advances.

A large fraction of the cost of a disk drive is related to basic hardware: electronics, power, frames, motors etc required to support, drive, and provide environmental protection for the storage medium. The remaining fraction of the cost is associated with the heads, actuators, disks and recording channel electronics which determine the capacity or performance of the device. Because of this high fixed cost most designs have focused on increasing areal density and thus for slightly increased cost providing substantial improvements in cost/bit and data rate. Bit cost is almost inversely proportional to recording density.

Most of the improvements during this decade will continue to come from increased areal density. Increased linear densities will be achieved through continuing improvements in recording resolution, as a result of decreased medium thickness, head-gap and head-disk spacing, and through the increased use of sophisticated signal processing and error correction codes. Integration of pre-amplifiers with the heads will significantly improve the signal/noise ratio supporting this trend. A most important challenge is the development of manufacturing processes to meet the demanding requirements for further density increases.

With increasing density (and hence capacity) rigid disk technology is now being packaged in 8- and 51/4-inch drives for small systems applications and its introduction in new configurations will continue to grow. Power consumption is greatly reduced and mechanical design simplified.

In addition, for a given drive, as density increases throughput decreases as it tends to be inversely proportional to storage capacity per head positioner. Also a head-disk interface failure risks a much greater amount of data being lost. These aspects suggest more trading of density increases for smaller disks.

FLOPPY DISKS

Floppy disks and minifloppies provide the least expensive form of disk storage (per unit). They consist of a flexible disk of magnetically coated mylar. They have moving heads which record 'in contact'. The primary advantage of the floppy disk is low overall cost (though not in cost per bit). The medium is interchangeable and easily mailed.

The in-contact nature of the recording lends itself to very high linear recording densities but with some wear. Further, the inferior dimensional stability of the substrate (compared to rigid disks) diminishes its track density potential (today 96 track/in is becoming typical).

Recently, two new products have been announced that will further expand the growth of flexible disk devices. Sony has announced a 3.5-inch disk drive with a replaceable disk small enough to fit in a pocket and yet holding almost 500 Kbytes of data.

A drive has been announced that uses a thin flexible disk that conforms to the head and thus provides a small non-contact head-medium interface. This design allows higher surface speeds and performance closer to a rigid disk with potentially a low-cost replaceable storage medium.

TAPE STORAGE

Tape storage devices utilise a magnetically coated strip of mylar tape to record one or more tracks of sequential data. Half-inch, reel-to-reel 'start/stop' tape drives are the major medium used throughout the world for storage and exchange of digital data. Tape cassettes and cartridges are used where low cost is paramount and the storage requirements and access time are not critical. Tapes are used whenever large amounts of data can be stored off-line. Evolutionary improvements in coding, media, and head designs provide the capability for at least a factor of 10 improvement in storage density in the 1980s. Even so, the user areal storage density for ½-inch tape would be only one tenth that realised on hard disk. It has been the compatibility requirements associated with a replaceable medium often used for archival purposes that have constrained the implementation of technological advances on ½-inch tape.

MASS STORAGE SYSTEMS

The requirements for on-line databases have grown more rapidly than the disk device capacity. Two 'mass storage' technologies are being pursued for the 1980s: magnetic and optical.

The IBM 3850 is the only widely used, very large, mass storage device. These systems use a tape strip 2000 cm long wound on a spool and held in a cartridge. The cartridges are housed in a honeycomb cellular arrangement and when accessed, are mechanically extracted and moved to a read/write station where they are helically scanned. Present cartridges hold 50 Mbytes each and have an access time of several seconds. The total storage available is about 1000 Gbytes with a transfer rate of approximately 1 Mbyte/sec.

The consumer demand for video recorders capable of many hours of recording, a rapidly growing market, has led to rapid technical advances in the magnetic recording of images on flexible media. While consumer applications provide opportunities for rapid product innovations, in computer storage this has not been true in the past due to overall systems considerations involved with the integration of new devices. Magnetic video technology is ready for exploitation in mass data storage applications and will develop in this decade.

VIDEO (OPTICAL) DISK TECHNOLOGY

Optical video disk storage, while not a read/write type of device (ie data cannot be updated in place) is attractive because it provides a higher recording density than magnetic recording and because, for read-only applications, the stored information lends itself to replication. Both laser and stylus sensing are employed. The ablation of thin metallic films has been the most extensively investigated technique for postable (write once) optical recording.

With laser technology, a beam of modulated laser light is focused onto a spinning disk (either to produce a master from which copies are later reproduced or for directly recording upon an on-line storage medium). The recorded information can be retrieved by illuminating the disk with a somewhat less intense beam and then detecting the modulation of light either reflected back or transmitted by the disk. A track pitch of less than 2μ is used in video disks, giving approximately 15 000 track/in, and a minimum spot size of approximately 1μ is utilised.

The presumed attractive feature of the optical disk is its ability to store large amounts of information with archival permanence at very low media cost, currently estimated to be less than one tenth the cost of magnetic tape. The disadvantage is that information can be written only once or is read only; however, with low media cost, this disadvantage becomes much less severe. However, archivability presents a significant materials problem which is not yet solved.

With regard to track density, optical recording offers the advantage of a very low mass servo system and a focused circular beam so that high track density comes as easily as linear density. Also, the sensing energy is independent of the storage material. Optical storage may provide about a factor of 10 higher areal density than magnetic recording, primarily arising from the greater simplicity of tracking.

TECHNOLOGY DIRECTIONS - SUMMARY

It is frequently said that there are mature technologies and new technologies, with the inference that the rate of progress will be much greater in a new alternative. This can be misleading. For any technology to succeed it must offer something superior to a current technology at the time of its actual introduction. Existing technologies are moving targets. Thus one cannot begin at a rudimentary state with a new approach, but must develop the technology at least far enough to gain initial market acceptance. While no technology can be economically improved indefinitely, technological potential is not so much a function of newness as it is of intrinsic physical and engineering limits.

New directions in magnetic recording include higher coercive force film media, array (multi-element) heads and vertical recording. Vertical recording utilises a medium that can be magnetised normal to the plane of the medium (Figure 6). At high densities demagnetisation considerations favour this mode for the writing of narrow stable transitions. This approach calls for a departure from current media but could lead to a significant further gain in linear density.

In optical storage the wavelength of light places a limit on density due to diffraction, approximately a 1-μ spot size. The most fundamental limiting factor in magnetic recording is domain or particle size which is at least two orders of magnitude beyond the engineering limits being addressed today. Rather, it is the scaling or geometrical

Recording modes

	Vertical	Horizontal
	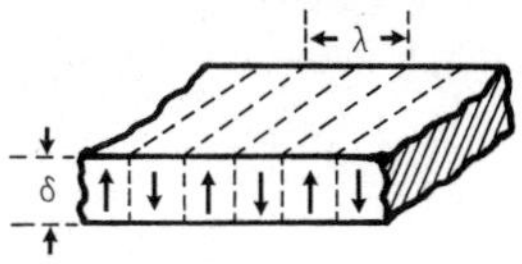	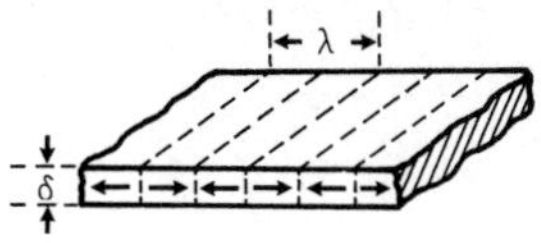
	$\lambda \to 0$	$\lambda \to 0$
	$H_d \to 0$	$H_d \to 4\pi M$
Head:	Single pole type or ring type	Ring type
Medium:	Thick δ High Ms, middle Hc Vertical anisotropy	Thin δ Low Ms, high Hc Horizontal anisotropy
Signal:	Digital (Sat.)	Analogue (non-Sat.) digital

H_d is demagnetising field

Figure 6: Features of vertical and horizontal recording

parameters which set the resolution of a bit cell and hence density. It is of interest to note that head-to-medium spacing is now in the range of 0.2μ, which is significantly less than the wavelength of light.

The continuing obsolescence of magnetic recording products has arisen not from alternatives but from advances in the technology itself. 100 Mbit/in^2 (1.6 × 105 bit/mm^2) should be achieved in the magnetic recording of digital data during the decade of the 1980s. Since the areal density on flexible disks is far less than on rigid disks, the relative rate of increase in flexible disk capacity will be greater. Magnetic recording will continue to be the dominating factor in storage as it moves to higher and higher densities. Optical storage will emerge in specific archival-like applications. The advent of consumer video recording has given magnetic recording a major new applications opportunity in high capacity mass storage and given optical data storage a new lease on life.

REFERENCES

001 HOAGLAND A S
'Magnetic Recording Storage'
IEEE Transactions on Computers vol C-25
no 12 pp 1283-1288 (Dec 1976)

002 TERAJIMA M
Proc IFIP 80 Congress
North-Holland Publishing Co
pp 127-135

STORE MANAGEMENT PROBLEMS IN VECTOR PROCESSORS

R N Ibbett

University of Manchester
Manchester
UK

R N IBBETT graduated in Physics at the University of Manchester in 1962 and went on to pursue research into the application of computer techniques in astronomical spectrometry. He obtained an MSc for this work in 1964 and a PhD from Hull University in 1967. Since that time he has been a member of the academic staff of the Department of Computer Science at Manchester. He became Senior Lecturer in 1975 and Reader in 1982. Until recently his major interest was the design implementation and evaluation of MU5, about which he has written and lectured extensively. His current research interests are local area networks and the architecture of vector processors.

STORE MANAGEMENT PROBLEMS IN VECTOR PROCESSORS

Vector processing is used in high-performance computer systems as a means of obtaining high arithmetic throughput. This throughput can only be sustained, however, if operands can be transferred to and from memory at high enough rates. In considering the problems of store management this is an important factor to be taken into account. Also important, however, are the effects of virtual addressing and the hardware-software interface of the system. In this paper these aspects of vector processing are considered with reference to the designs of the CDC STAR-100 and CYBER 205 systems, the CRAY-1 and CRAY X-MP, MU5, and the TI-ASC, and an indication is given of possible future architectural directions in this area.

INTRODUCTION

The design of a vector processing system involves a variety of considerations relating to main storage. Since vector processing is generally used as a means of obtaining high performance on scientific processing, the rate at which operands can be transferred between main storage and the floating-point execution unit is of prime importance. This is a 'real store' problem; in systems which use virtual addressing there are also 'virtual store' problems associated with the address translation mechanism. Also important is the nature of the hardware/software interface of the system (defined by the instruction set and the addressing structure) since this determines the amount of support which the hardware can provide for software running on the system. In seeking to obtain higher levels of machine performance these facets of design must all be taken into account, and an analysis of existing systems gives considerable insight into the problems involved. A useful starting point is the CDC STAR-100 (001), a machine developed in the mid to late 1960s in response to a requirement of the Lawrence Livermore Laboratories for a vector processor capable of executing 100 MFLOPS (millions of floating-point operations per second). A great deal of controversy raged about this machine in its early years, and many of the essential design issues and performance goals have been obscured. Despite the many difficulties which arose in the course of the STAR-100 programme, CDC remained convinced that the underlying architectural concepts of the STAR-100 were sound, and went on to produce a second version, the STAR-100A (which appeared commercially as the CYBER 203) followed by a completely re-engineered version, the STAR-100C, which is now produced commercially as the CYBER 205.

THE STAR-100

The fundamental premise on which the STAR-100 project was based was the provision of as much immediate access storage as was possible within engineering constraints. In the mid-1960s this meant using ferrite core technology, as semiconductor storage technology, while holding out a great deal of promise, was not sufficiently mature for its use in large quantities to be a realistic venture. The limitations on the amount of storage which could be provided using cores were physical space requirements, the physical interconnection problem, and overall reliability. These limitations led to a maximum memory size of one million 64-bit words using the 2D core memory developed for use as extended core storage in the CDC 6600. These stores had a 280 nsec access time and a 1280 nsec cycle time.

Coupled with the provision of large amounts of storage in the STAR-100 was a high bandwidth for the transfer of data between the store and the central processing unit. Because the access time to an individual store word was relatively long, however, it was clear from the outset that it would only be possible to use this bandwidth effectively if operand prefetching could be used in the same way as instruction prefetching is used in conventional machines. Instruction prefetching relies on the sequential nature of instruction execution; operand prefetching is similarly only effective if the processor can generate long sequences of contiguous addresses, a situation which arises quite naturally in vector processing. Thus the STAR-100 project was naturally geared to the provision of computing power for highly vectorisable problems, and vectors with up to 65 536 elements may be processed by a single vector instruction.

Memory bandwidth is obtained in the STAR-100 by a combination of eight-way interleaving of memory banks with wide store words (512 bits accessed per store cycle) and the pipelined transmission of each of these 'superwords' to the processor in four sequential groups of 128 bits. In order to handle this data rate in the processor, the STAR-100 uses two pipelined arithmetic units as shown in Figure 1, each of which can act as a

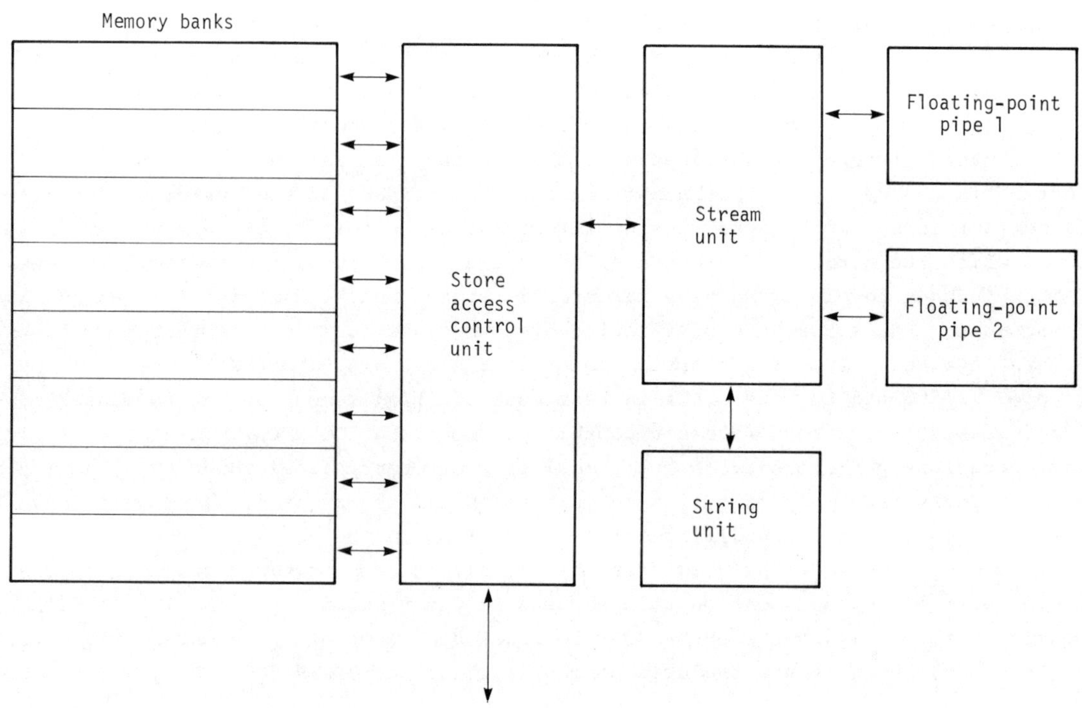

Figure 1: The STAR-100 processor

single 64-bit or a twin 32-bit unit. Floating-point pipe 1 performs floating-point operations such as add, subtract, multiply and compare, and also fixed-point address operations. Floating-point pipe 2 is similar, except that it includes a divide unit and a multipurpose unit which is used for special operations such as square root. For operations such as floating-point addition the two pipes act in parallel and can therefore accept the full 128 bits available from store in each clock period. For 32-bit operations this leads to an execution rate of four operations per 40 nsec clock period, equivalent to 100 MFLOPS.

The store is made up of eight sections, each containing four banks of 16K 64-bit words. 512 bits are read out from a bank in one store cycle, and the outputs of the four banks in any one section are multiplexed at 40 nsec intervals on to a 128-bit data trunk. The data trunks from each section are then multiplexed together in the store access control unit which provides a stream of operand store words to the processor. The outputs from the store access control unit cannot be fed directly into the arithmetic units, however, since in practice vectors cannot necessarily be expected to start on 512-bit word boundaries and the two operands making up a pair of source operands are normally taken from separate superwords. Thus the stream unit contains input shift networks which align the input operands correctly and a 'front-end precount' mechanism which discards any unwanted elements from the first superword received at the start of a vector order.

The stream unit must also align the result vector correctly, using an output shift network, and at the start and end of a result vector must ensure that only the appropriate parts of the store word are overwritten. Selective updating of the 512-bit superword in a given memory bank is carried out, on a 32-bit word basis, at the store interface. Thus the stream unit sends a four-bit 'write enable' control field with each 128-bit result, as illustrated in Figure 2, which shows the effect for eight 32-bit results positioned arbitrarily within a 512-bit superword.

Any read or write operation on a core store involves a read-write cycle and in the STAR-100 a word readout from a complete memory bank is held in a 512-bit holding register before being written back. The 'write enables' control the updating of the contents of this register by the results sent from the processor, giving the effect of a read-modify-write operation on the selected superword in the memory bank. Once the use of these write enables had been established as part of the design of the STAR-100, the concept of a control vector was an obvious extension. Control vectors became an important feature of the STAR-100 design and are used extensively, not only to define write enables, but also to control vector restructuring operations such as MASK, COMPRESS, and MERGE, which derive directly from the programming language APL.

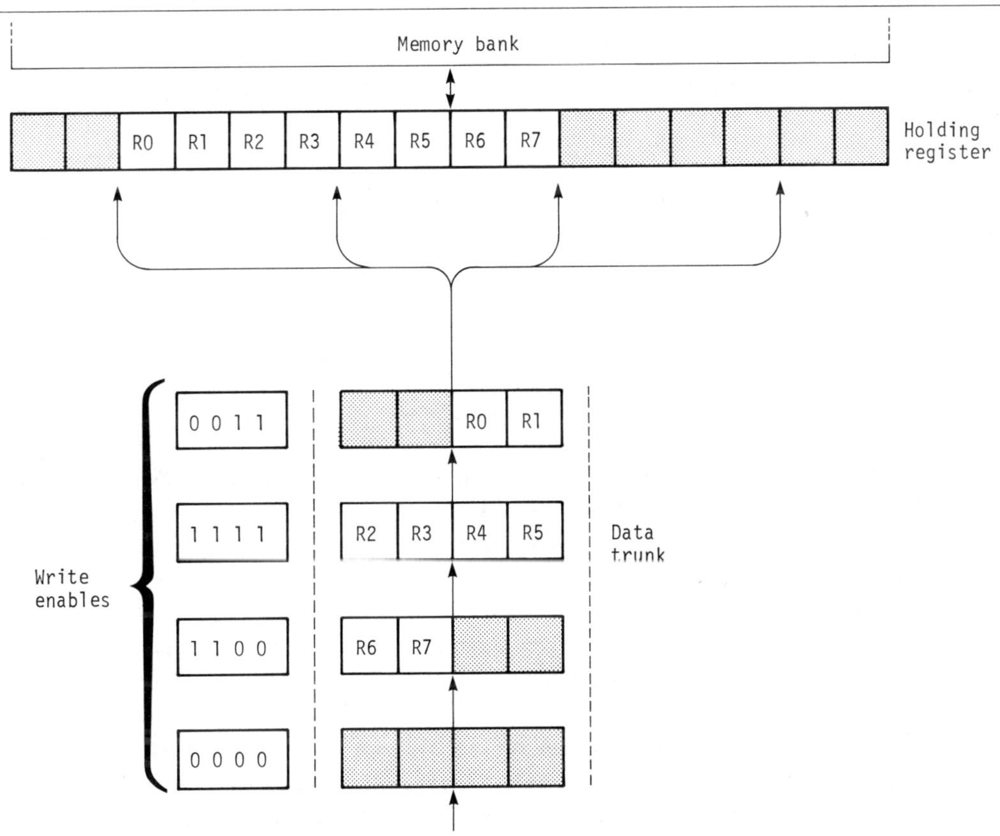

Figure 2: Result operand alignment in a STAR-100 superword

THE CDC CYBER 205

The STAR-100 was criticised on a number of grounds by users who wished to apply it to more general computing problems than those for which it was designed. The grounds for criticism were mainly the long vector start-up time and poor performance on scalar arithmetic, both of which were inevitable consequences of the design. These problems are largely overcome in the CYBER 205 (002) by the use of a very much faster (80 nsec access time) semiconductor memory and by the inclusion of a high-performance scalar unit. The overall performance of the CYBER 205 is further enhanced by its implementation in specially developed ECL LSI uncommitted logic array technology, allowing a reduction of the clock period from the 40 nsec used in the STAR-100 to 20 nsec.

Figure 3 shows the overall design of the CYBER 205 computer system, the major components

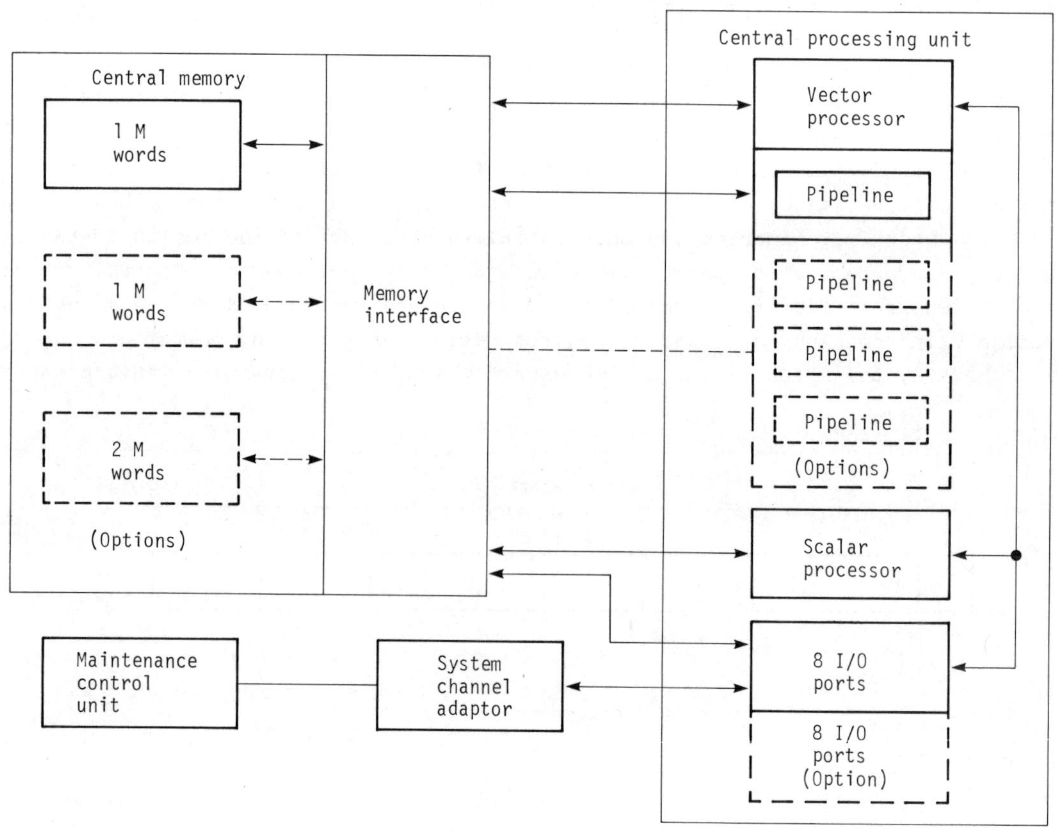

Figure 3: The CYBER 205 computer system

of which are the central processing unit (containing the vector processor, scalar processor and eight or 16 I/O ports), the central memory, and the maintenance control unit (linked to a standard I/O port via a system channel adaptor). Within the vector processor there can be one, two or four floating-point pipelines. The central memory of a basic system contains one million words, expandable to two or four million words (and with a capability to expand to eight million words as memory technology progresses) with each million words being connected to the memory interface via a 512-bit data highway.

Internally the memory is organised such that within each unit of one million words there are 16 interleaved 32-bit stacks allowing eight sequentially addressed 64-bit words (512 bits) to be accessed in parallel. Each stack is divided into eight independent banks, each holding 16K words. A new bank read access can be initiated in every clock period, provided it is to a bank which is not already busy, and the banks can share a single stack data path since this path is only required during the last clock period of the four clock period bank cycle.

Most vector instructions process data using two data input streams, one control vector input stream and one data output stream. These streams are specified by the origin addresses, field lengths and off-sets or indices selected from locations in a register file by the instruction before it leaves the scalar processor, and sent to the vector control unit (Figure 4) when the instruction is issued. During the setting up of a vector instruction within the vector processor, off-set values are added to the corresponding origin addresses and subtracted from the field lengths before being sent to the stream addressing unit. For each data stream the stream addressing unit generates sequential store addresses (normally to 512-bit words) by incrementing the origin address until the field length, which is decremented correspondingly, reaches zero.

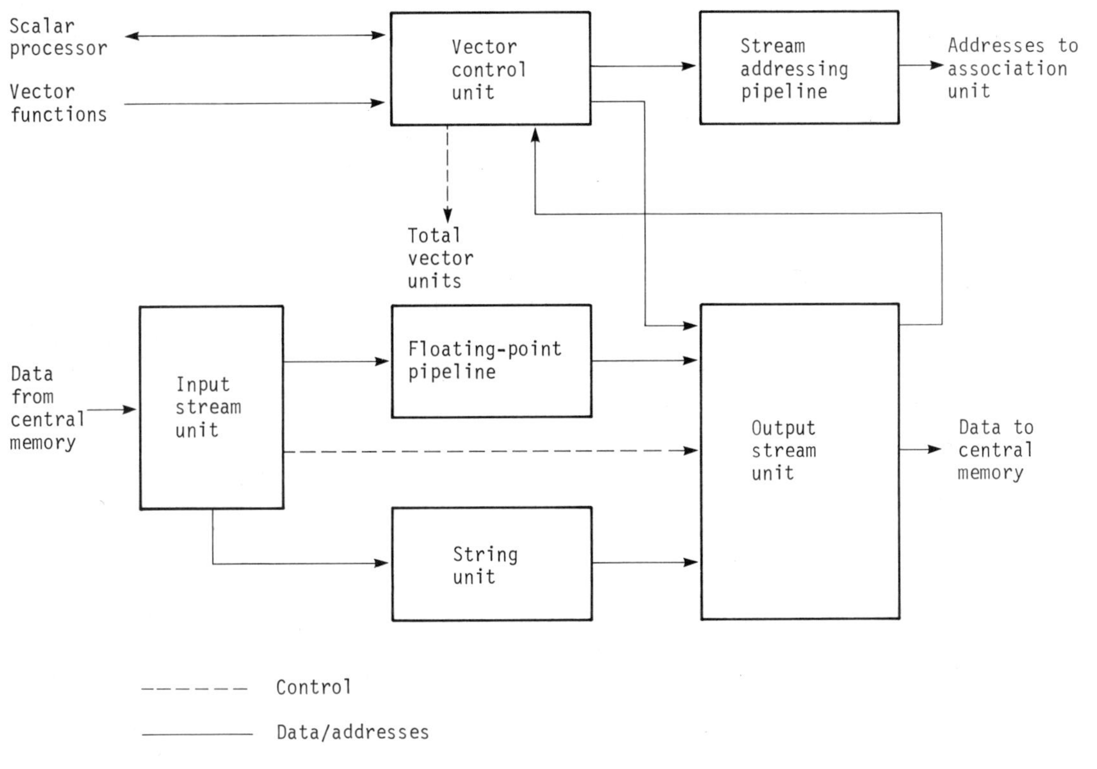

Figure 4: The CYBER 205 vector processor

The generation of addresses for each input and output stream is treated as an independent operation within the stream addressing unit. This allows each operation to be stopped and started independently, and allows the stream addressing unit to avoid bank busy conflicts in central memory. Since the banks have an 80 nsec cycle time, a request to any one bank causes a four-clock period busy condition, and a subsequent request to the same bank is not allowed to proceed until a further three clock periods have elapsed. In addition the priority of requests must be taken into account; within the vector processor input operand requests have highest priority, vector write requests have second priority, string write requests third, and control vector read requests fourth. A request of low priority must therefore be checked against higher priority requests to the same bank up to three clock periods ahead and up to three clock periods behind the clock period in which it will itself access central memory.

The stream addressing unit also controls the flow of data through the input and output stream units. The input stream unit contains a buffer for each input stream large enough to hold all data requested but not used. Associated with each buffer is a counter in the stream addressing unit which is incremented each time a 128-bit word is requested from central memory, and decremented each time a 128-bit word is removed from the buffer for use. If a counter indicates that the corresponding buffer is full, then further requests for that input stream are held up. For the output stream unit a counter in the stream addressing unit is incremented each time a result is entered into the output buffer, and decremented each time a write request is sent to central memory.

One of the criticisms levelled at the CYBER 205 is that, as in the STAR-100, vectors may only be accessed on the basis of a unit increment between successive elements, so that matrices stored by row, for example, cannot easily be accessed by column. However, the high memory bandwidth of the CYBER 205 is only obtainable because many adjacent elements can be read out in parallel in each memory cycle, and to allow different accessing patterns in standard vector orders would severely degrade performance. Provision of increments different from unity would also require changes to the instruction format, and alternative general mechanisms for the re-ordering of operands are provided instead. These mechanisms are invoked in indexed list operations which allow for the gathering or scattering of periodic or random data within a data structure.

During execution of a scatter operation (Transmit List -> Indexed C), for example, two source vectors (A and B) are normally read from memory and a result vector (C) is written to memory. Source vector A is a list of indices referring to positions in the result vector, while source vector B is the sequential list of 32-bit or 64-bit operands to be written. During each cycle of operation, the index taken from vector A is shifted appropriately and added to the result vector origin to form a memory address. This address is then sent to memory, accompanied by appropriate write control bits and by the corresponding operand taken from vector B. The index list may be formed either by geometrical considerations or by data-dependent considerations. Sparse vectors with a population density of the order of 0.1%, for example, can be dealt with more efficiently by this mechanism than by the alternative Boolean control vector technique which is also available in the CYBER-205, and which is suitable for population densities in the range 1 - 10%.

In a gather operation (Transmit indexed list -> C), source vector A is again a list of indices, but these indices refer to positions in source vector B rather than the result vector. Addresses formed by adding each index from vector A in turn to the origin of vector B are used to access operands from vector B, and these operands are then written to sequential result vector locations.

A number of variations on the general form of the gather and scatter operations may be invoked by appropriate settings of bits in the instruction. In particular, one option allows source vector A to be replaced by a fixed increment (a) taken from the register file location specified by A. In this case source vector addresses in a gather operation are of the form b, b+a, b+2a, b+3a, etc. (where b is the origin address of B), allowing access by column to a matrix stored by row, for example. An alternative variation allows groups of sequential B operands to be selected for each element of vector A.

As with ordinary vector operations, the stream units must avoid bank busy conflicts in memory during the execution of gather and scatter operations. A request to any one bank causes a four-clock busy condition, and a subsequent request to the same bank is not allowed to proceed until a further three clock periods have elapsed. In scatter operations these conflicts can occur on the write accesses, while in gather operations they can occur on read accesses to source vector B. These conflicts might be expected to affect performance quite severely in the case of non-sequential accesses. In practice, however, the number of memory banks provided is so large that, except when a specific sequence is presented in which each address has the same value modulo 64, few are found to be busy.

In the typical two-pipeline CYBER 205 system, two 64-bit operands can be transferred into the floating-point pipeline on each of its two input highways, and two 64-bit results transferred out, in one 20 nsec clock-period. This corresponds to an execution rate for 64-bit floating-point numbers of 100 MFLOPS, or 200 MFLOPS for 32-bit numbers. For linked triadic operations, or during the execution of the scalar product operation, this rate is doubled to 200 MFLOPS for 64-bit numbers or 400 MFLOPS for 32-bit numbers. The memory bandwidth required to support this execution rate is six 64-bit words per 20 nsec interval, or 300 Mwords/sec. Since the data highway between each one million words of central memory and the memory interface is 512 bits wide, and since a read or write transfer can occur every 20 nsec, memory bandwidth is actually 400 Mwords/sec. A one million word memory configuration can therefore support a two-pipeline system without difficulty. For the four-pipeline system at least two million words of central memory are required, with each one million words being connected to the memory interface via its own data highway. In this case the maximum execution rate is 800 MFLOPS for 32-bit linked triadic or scalar product operations.

Where accessing patterns involving non-unary increments are required, performance is reduced because the vector arithmetic instruction must be preceded by a gather instruction or succeeded by a scatter instruction. These instructions themselves run at less than the full arithmetic rate and have been measured to proceed at an average rate of 40 million operations per second. This performance is an average of many operations running at a rate of 50 million per second with occasional periods of 12.5 million per second.

Perhaps a more serious criticism of the CYBER 205 from the point of view of performance on general problems is the long vector start-up time. Whereas an execution rate of 100 MFLOPS for 64-bit numbers can in principle be obtained with a two-pipeline configuration, this rate can only be achieved in practice when very long vectors are used. As the length of the vectors being used becomes shorter, the start-up time has a progressively more serious effect, and Hockney (003) has used the vector length at which performance is halved as a measure of vector efficiency. For the CYBER 205 the nominal start-up time is 1 microsecond, and for a nominal result rate of 100 MFLOPS this length is clearly 100. Thus the CYBER 205 is best suited to problems in which long vector operations predominate. For more general problems, involving a higher proportion of scalar and short vector operations, the CRAY-1 usually offers higher performance.

THE CRAY-1

The CRAY-1 (004) can be seen as a logical development of the CDC 7600 processor, itself a development of the CDC 6600. All these machines use parallel functional units, as a means of obtaining high performance, and in the case of the 7600, the pipelining of these units makes possible a floating-point addition rate of one operation per clock period (1 FLOP/clock) and a floating-point multiplication rate of one operation in every two clock periods (0.5 FLOPS/clock). However the maximum possible total floating-point execution rate is limited to one operation per clock period, because only one instruction can be issued and only one result returned to the X registers in each clock period (005).

The problem of executing floating-point operations at a rate in excess of 1 per clock is overcome in the CRAY-1 processor (Figure 5) by the use of vector orders, which cause streams of up to 64 data elements to be processed as a result of one instruction issue. Vectors are contained in a set of eight V registers, each capable of holding 64 elements (each of 64 bits), and a typical vector instruction causes sets of operands to be taken from two V registers and the results to be returned to a third. In the following instruction sequence:

```
V0 <- V1 + V2
V3 <- V4 * V5
```

the second instruction uses different registers and a different functional unit from the first and can be issued one clock period after the first instruction. Subsequent

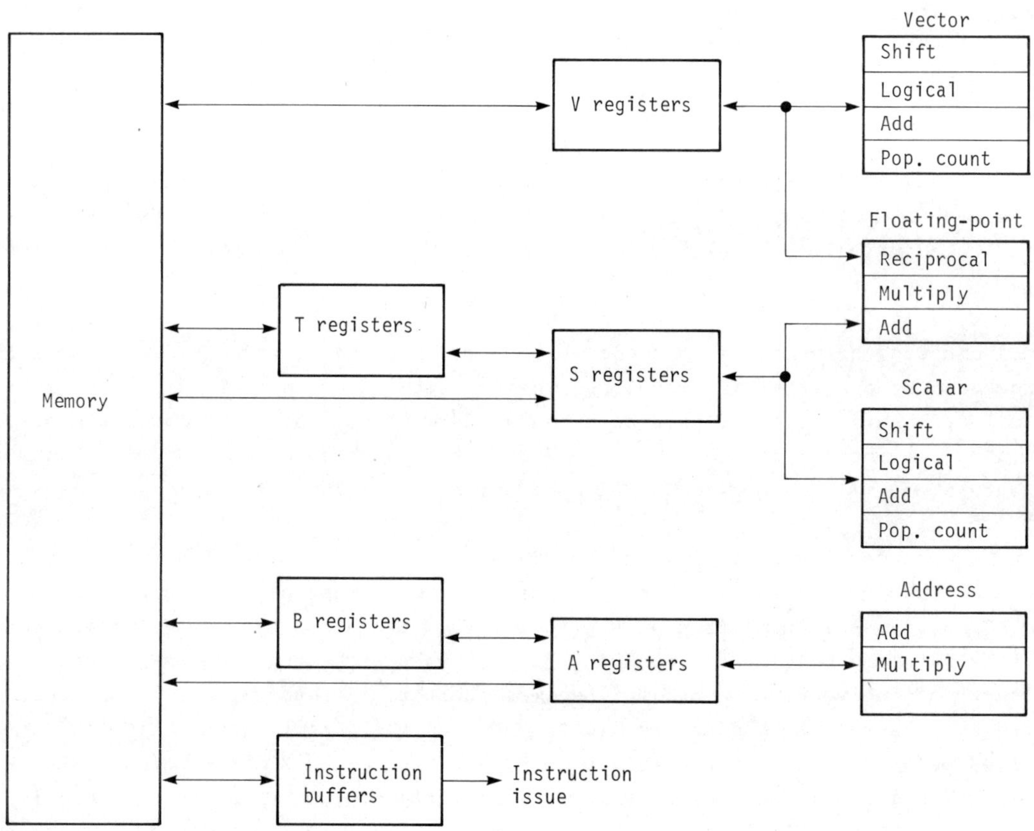

Figure 5: The CRAY-1 processor

to the pipeline start-up delays in the functional units (each of which can carry out operations at a rate of one per clock period), a floating-point result will appear from both the adder and the multiplier in each successive clock period. Thus if performance is estimated in terms only of floating-point addition and multiplication, the maximum floating-point execution rate is 2 FLOPS/clock. Furthermore, around 60 other instructions can be issued before these units require further instructions to keep them busy. Given that the clock period is 12.5 nsec, 2 FLOPS/clock corresponds to 160 MFLOPS.

The other serious bottleneck in the CDC 7600 architecture, namely the entry of results into the X registers at a maximum rate of one per clock period, is overcome in the CRAY-1 by the provision at the input to each vector register of multiplexor circuitry capable of selecting results from any of the six functional units which can produce vector results. Correspondingly, each vector functional unit has its own input multiplexors for selecting vector register operands. Without these circuits the CRAY-1 would also be limited to 1 FLOP/clock.

In addition to the eight 64-element V registers, there are eight 64-bit S (scalar) registers and eight 24-bit A (address) registers (corresponding to the X and A registers in the CDC 6600 and 7600) together with 64 B registers (each of 24 bits) and 64 T registers (each of 64 bits). The B and T registers are used in a different way from any of the registers in the 6600 and 7600, however, in that they act as buffer stores for A and S register values, respectively. The functional units take their input operands from the A, S and V registers only, and only return results to these registers.

The A registers are used primarily as address and index registers for scalar and vector memory references, but are also used for loop control, input-output operations, and to provide values for shift counts. An A register can be loaded either from a B register or direct from memory, while the B register contents can be transferred to or from memory in block copy operations. The S registers contain scalar operands, which may be used in scalar operations in the same way that X register values are used in the 6600 and 7600, but an S register in the CRAY-1 may also supply a scalar value required for a vector operation. S register values may be transferred to or from memory or the T registers, the latter allowing intermediate results of complex computations to be held in fast buffers rather than main memory. T register values can be transferred to or from memory in the same way as B register values.

Block copy operations between memory and the B or T registers, or between memory and a V register, normally proceed at a rate of one per clock period. The semiconductor memory has a cycle time of 50 nsec (four clock periods), and for contiguous addresses (such as those used in B or T block copy operations), must be at least 4-way interleaved to allow this rate to be achieved. In practice the memory in a CRAY-1 is 8-way or 16-way interleaved and contains 0.5M, 1M, 2M, or 4M words according to the configuration. When non-contiguous addresses are used, however, store clashes occur and the maximum rate cannot be maintained. When a vector is accessed from store into a V register a starting address and increment are supplied by the program. This allows for complete flexibility in accessing arrays by row, by column, or by diagonal, but can lead to store clashing if, for example, an increment of 16 is used in a 16-way interleaved store.

There is an additional problem related to chaining. Chaining occurs in the CRAY-1 when one of the V register inputs required by an instruction is also the output register of a previously issued instruction. Consider the sequence:

```
V2 <- V0 * V1
V4 <- V2 + V3
```

Provided the second instruction can be issued to the floating-point add unit when the first result element of the multiplication arrives back at V2, then elements destined for V2 can be sent, together with corresponding elements of V3, directly to the add unit at the same time as being written into V2. Chaining can also occur between the two operations in the following sequence:

```
V0 <- Memory
V2 <- V0 * V1
```

as vector elements destined for V0 arrive from memory. However, in the sequence:

```
V1 <- Memory
V0 <- Memory
V2 <- V0 * V1
```

the second instruction cannot issue until all the elements of V1 have been accessed from memory. There is thus an effective start-up delay in this sequence equal to the time required to load V1. The separation of store accessing and arithmetic operations within the instruction set of the CRAY-1 (made possible by the presence of the various processor registers) allows these activities to be overlapped to a large extent, but the start-up delay can nevertheless occur quite frequently and can reduce overall performance. The recently announced CRAY X-MP overcomes this problem by use of a multiport memory organisation instead of the single port used in the CRAY-1. The CRAY X-MP mainframe (Figure 6) contains the equivalent of two CRAY-1 processors, re-engineered to allow a clock-period of 9.5 nsec, and to allow both processors to occupy roughly the same physical space as a single CRAY-1 processor. These two processors share a common central memory, into which each has four independent access ports. The memory itself consists of 2M or 4M 64-bit words interleaved 32 or 64 ways according to the configuration. With this arrangement two vectors can be accessed in parallel from memory by either of the processors, provided there are no store clashes at the individual memory banks. If the two vectors reside in exactly the same set of memory banks, for example, then the accesses will become synchronised such that elements of one of the vectors are accessed one memory cycle behind the other. This gives an effective start-up time of one memory access time for one of the vectors, and a start-up time one memory cycle longer than this for the other vector, a considerable improvement over the CRAY-1 where the effective start-up time for this sequence could be of the order of 64 memory access times.

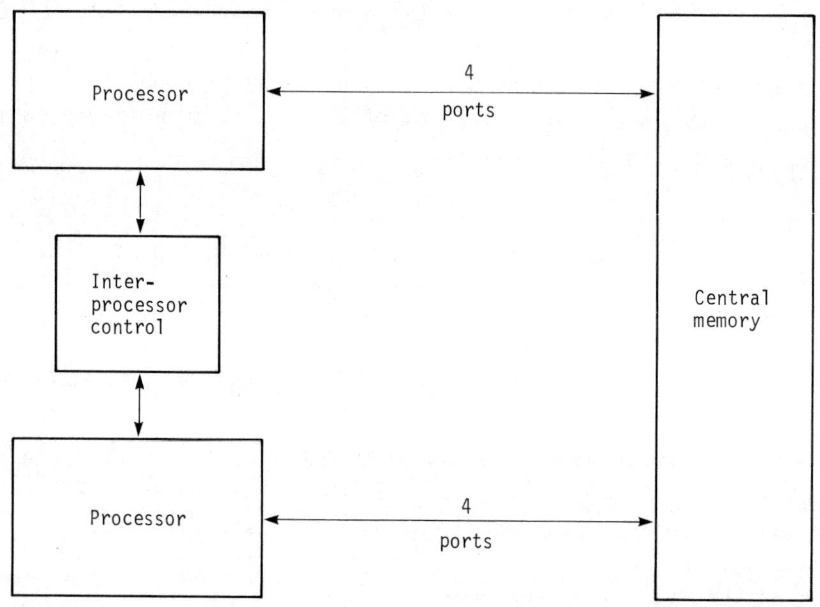

Figure 6: CRAY X-MP system organisation

Although the accessing mechanisms in the CRAY machines offer complete flexibility in areas such as the handling of vectors which are actually sub-arrays, the entire management of all forms of data structure is left to the software. Vectors with more than 64 elements, for example, must be broken up into sets of 64 elements or less and processed separately. This problem does not arise in the CYBER 205 unless vectors of more than 64K elements are used, and here each vector is essentially identified by a descriptor (containing an origin address and a length) held in the register file and accessed from there when required by an instruction. The use of descriptors to identify vectors can have a number of other benefits from a software point of view, as has been shown in the MU5 computer and its commercial derivatives at the top of the ICL 2900 Series.

VECTOR FACILITIES IN MU5

One of the design objectives of the MU5 computer system (006) was an instruction set through which information on the nature of operands could be transmitted to the hardware to allow optimal operand buffering. It was felt to be particularly important that scalar variables, of which only a small number are in frequent use at any one time, should be buffered separately from array elements, which are generally selected sequentially from a large group. It was also felt that hardware assistance should be provided for accessing elements of arrays and other data structures, particularly with regard to bound checking.

Both scalars and arrays appear as named objects in high-level languages. In MU5 an access to a scalar name produces its value directly; an access to a data structure element involves a primary access to the data structure name (the result of which is the descriptor of that data structure), followed by a secondary access involving the descriptor and possibly a modifier. Descriptors are of two main types:

Vector descriptor	Tv	BOUND	ORIGIN
	8	24	32
String descriptor	Ts	LENGTH	ORIGIN
	8	24	32

Vectors are normally used with computational instructions, and strings with a set of string processing orders which provide facilities for the manipulation of data records in languages such as COBOL, PL/1 and ALGOL 68. There are in addition some special descriptor types serving a variety of purposes.

Vector elements may be of size 1, 4, 8, 16, 32, or 64 as defined by bits within the type field (Tv), and are close-packed in store. A typical access to a vector element would involve the following instructions:

```
B = i
ACC = X[B]
```

The first of these instructions loads the variable i into the B register for use by the second instruction as a modifier. This instruction loads the named variable X into a descriptor register (DR) for interpretation. The hardware associated with this register first forms the address of the element by scaling the modifier according to the element size and adding the result to the origin address contained within the descriptor. It also checks that the modifier is greater than or equal to zero, and less than the bound; if not an interrupt is generated. This check incurs virtually no time penalty and removes the need for the costly software bound check which is often required on more conventional machines, particularly during program development. The address is then used to access the store, and the required vector element is selected from within the corresponding store word, right justified, and zero-filled for presentation to the accumulator (ACC). This mechanism is equally applicable to dynamic arrays whose starting address and bounds are known only at runtime, as in ALGOL-like languages, or to arrays where this information is available at load time, as in FORTRAN.

Operations on whole vectors are organised by program loops such as the following, which forms the scalar product of two vectors X and Y each of length LIMIT.

```
       B = 0
     ACC = 0
L1:  ACC* = X[B]   :: Stack ACC content and load with element of X
     ACC*   Y[B]   :: Multiply by element of Y
     B CINC LIMIT  :: Compare B against LIMIT and increment B
     ACC + STACK   :: Add Stack content to ACC
     IF /=, -> L1  :: Continue round loop until B = LIMIT
```

The arguments for processing vectors in this way, rather than by specific vector orders, are that the hardware can distinguish control and address calculation instructions from those operating on the vector elements, and can execute the former at the peak rate of the primary operand unit (PROP) pipeline, while the latter are queued in the secondary operand unit (SEOP) pipeline awaiting operand fetches (Figure 7). Furthermore, the

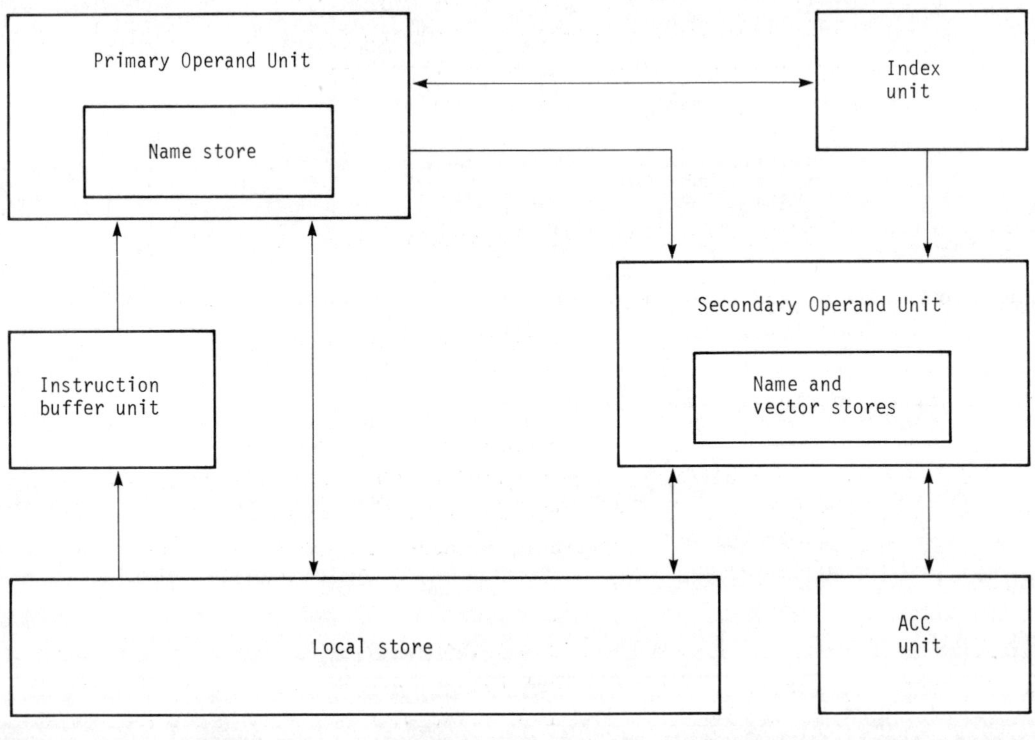

Figure 7: The MU5 processor

compilers generate conventional code in a straightforward way without intricate algorithms to decompile back to vector operations.

More complex descriptor mechanisms are also provided in MU5. Thus one of the special descriptor types (indirect) may be used to describe a structure containing other descriptors. Hence:

```
  B = i
 DR = X[B]
  B = j
ACC = D[B]  :: Use the current descriptor in DR
```

could be used to access an element X[i,j] of a two dimensional array using an addressing vector technique. This mechanism has the disadvantage in MU5 of requiring a descriptor to be accessed through the SEOP and returned to the front of it before the element access can begin. This destroys the overlap in the secondary pipeline and for simple languages an alternative multiplication technique in B has the advantage that the subscript calculations take place independently of operations queued in the secondary pipeline and can be substantially overlapped with them. The previous sequence becomes:

```
  B = i
  B * n
  B + j
ACC = X[B]
```

with a bound check on the overall limits of the array, rather than on each dimension. For languages where the lower bound of arrays is 1, a load and decrement B order is provided. A further, more elaborate, dope vector mechanism is convenient for arrays with dynamic lower bounds or for slices of arrays. The dope vector contains three 32-bit elements for each dimension, namely, a lower bound which is subtracted from the subscript, an upper bound against which the subscript is checked, and the stride by which it is multiplied. The special instructions SUB1 and SUB2 implement this facility, so X[i,j] becomes:

```
B = i
SUB1 X1    :: process first subscript, where X1 is the dope vector
B = j
SUB2       :: process next subscript
B = DO     :: move composite subscript to B (DO = Origin of DR)
ACC = X[B]
```

From a performance point of view these orders are worse than the indirect descriptor mechanism, since several of the actions implied by SUB1 and SUB2 require accesses to quantities which are to be returned to the front of the secondary pipeline. Some quite different structure from that of MU5 would be needed to obtain good performance using these orders.

All user addresses in both MU5 and the CYBER 205 are virtual addresses, in contrast with CRAY machines where all addresses are real. Real address-based systems have several attractions. Foremost from the performance point of view is the fact that an address generated by the CPU can be presented directly to the store, thus avoiding the time delay inherent in paging systems. Also the units of information delimited by address words, which are the units the system might automatically move from one level of store to another, can be complete logical entities (procedures or arrays, for example). This can be more efficient than moving fixed-size pages which represent arbitrary fragments of a program and its workspace. On the other hand, the problems of allocating and retrieving store in variable sized areas can lead to some store not being utilised, for example, because the empty areas may be too small. This has to be offset against the paging problem in which, even when all pages are in use, some will be partially occupied by unwanted information.

There are, however, other arguments in favour of virtual addressing. One of the most significant tasks of the operating system is store management, the dominant part of which is concerned with the automatic movement of information between levels of store. Such movement requires that the real addresses of the information moved be changed. If these real addresses are allowed to scatter through each program's private store, this task becomes complex. For example, the address words that require changing because of movement of information between levels of store are themselves subject to movement. The same address can also appear in several places. A much cleaner solution is to hold all information relating to the way a program maps into real store in a separate data structure outside the program and entirely under operating system control.

Virtual addressing also allows for better resource sharing in a multi-user environment. During the development of a major program, for example, only those parts of the program and its data required for a particular test run are brought into main memory. In a real address system the entire job must be swapped in and out of memory unless the programmer is prepared to run the risk of significantly altering the runtime job parameters. Not only does this swapping represent a significant loss of machine time in itself, but all other users are denied access to machine resources throughout the test run.

A further advantage of virtual addressing is the ease with which segmentation can be implemented. In MU5 the virtual address is subdivided into a segment number and a displacement within the segment. A typical process running on MU5 might use a segment for code, a segment for scalar variables, one or more segments for data structures, and so on. Information is thus sparsely distributed through the virtual store, and is mapped on to the (smaller) real store by the paging mechanism. From a store management point of view segmentation offers a number of advantages. Not only can individual segments be protected (eg read only, execute only) by hardware in the paging mechanism, but segments (containing arrays, for example) can be shared between users by the simple expedient of allowing different virtual address entries in the page table to access the same real address in store.

VIRTUAL ADDRESS TRANSLATION

The MU5 virtual addressing scheme and that used in the CYBER 205 both derive from the system used in Atlas. In the Atlas paging system (005) each associative page address register bore a one-to-one correspondence with a real page in the core store. In both MU5 and the CYBER 205, however, the number of associative registers is considerably smaller than the number of pages in real store, and the associative registers are therefore current page registers containing the most recently used virtual pages. In MU5 the absence of a match in the associative registers immediately causes an interrupt, whereas in the CYBER 205 the remainder of the page address translation table (the 'space table') is held in fixed locations in central memory, and if a particular page address is not found in one of the associative registers (the 'page table'), the space table is searched sequentially under microprogram control.

Entries in the page table registers (AR00 - 15) are held as an ordered list of most recent use. Whenever a virtual address is presented for association and a match occurs, the content of the register containing the matching address is moved to the top of the list (register AR00) and the contents of all those above the matching register move down one position. If no match is found, the content of AR15 is copied into a buffer register and the contents of registers AR00 - 14 move down one position leaving a null entry in AR00. The contents of all the associative registers are then copied into central memory and the contents of the space table are examined in sequence using the associative facilities of the page table registers. Thus the first entry in the space table is read and its location in central memory replaced by the previous content of AR15, held in the buffer register. After this first word has been examined it is itself copied into the buffer register. If no match occurs this cycle of events is repeated, with the second space table entry being read and replaced in central memory by the first word (now held in the buffer register), and so on. When a match occurs the page table registers are reloaded from central memory and the content of the matching address, held in the buffer register, is copied into AR00. Thus the ordering of entries in the page table also extends into the space table.

Since different programs running on the CYBER 205 require differing numbers of pages, a mechanism is required to prevent the hardware searching invalid page or space table entries. An 'end-of-table' marker is used for this purpose. If this marker is found in a page table register when there is a page fault, an interrupt is generated immediately and the space table is not searched. If the end-of-table marker is in the space table, however, then it will only be read and an interrupt generated after all valid entries in the space table have been examined. Such interrupts can, of course, occur during the execution of a vector order because the vector lengths associated with these orders are such that it is inevitable that the operand fetches will eventually cross a page boundary into a page for which no page or space table entry has been set up. While it might be possible to ignore some types of interrupt for the duration of one of these orders, a page fault must be dealt with immediately since the order itself cannot continue until the appropriate action has been taken. This requires a clean shut down of the order, the preservation of essential state information, and the transfer of control to the interrupt code. The use of a long arithmetic pipeline in the CYBER 205 and the presence of significant amounts of buffering in the stream units mean that in order to achieve the full vector rate, while still responding to these page fault interrupts, a one-page look-ahead is required on the output stream to ensure that operands progressing through the processor can be returned to store before shut down. Once the interrupt has been processed, the state information is restored and the order restarted from where it left off.

The choice of page size to be used is complicated in vector processing systems by the existence of long vectors. For general-purpose processing it has usually been found that a page size of 256 or 512 words gives the best overall performance in terms of internal and external fragmentation and operating system overheads in manipulating page tables. Such small page sizes are inappropriate for long vectors, however, and the CYBER 205 therefore allows large pages and small pages to co-exist. Large pages contain 65K words, the size of the largest directly addressable vector, while small pages may be chosen, for a particular job, to be 512 words, 2K words or 4K words long.

PARALLELISM IN VECTOR PROCESSORS

Many computer designers have been attracted to parallel processing as a means of obtaining high performance. One of the most successful examples of the use of parallelism is to be found in the CDC 6600 and its successor machines, the 7600 and the CRAY-1, where the parallelism is at the functional unit level. The CRAY X-MP also exhibits parallelism at the processor level, having two high-performance vector processors which share a common store, while the projected CRAY-2 will have four processors sharing a common store. Much higher degrees of processor parallelism are to be found in machines such as ILLIAC IV, C.mmp and Cm*, but none of the systems in this class have proved to be successful in a commercial sense. Most of the difficulties lie in the coordination of the activities of the parallel units.

The CYBER 205 exhibits parallelism within its vector processor by having one, two or four vector pipelines. This parallelism is not visible to the programmer, however, since only one vector order can be executed at a time and the pipelines are used to process, in parallel, groups of sequential elements taken from within the vectors being processed by that order. This is not the case in the Texas Instruments Advanced Scientific Computer (TI-ASC), which can also have up to four arithmetic pipelines, each of which can be executing a different vector order at any one time.

The basic structure of the central processor of the TI-ASC (007) is shown in Figure 8. The Memory Control Unit (MCU) allows two-way traffic between eight 256-bit wide processor ports and eight interleaved memory modules (plus an optional memory extension), with each processor port having full access to the 24-bit address space. The central processor design is such that one, two, three or four pipelined arithmetic units (AU) can be provided. Each AU is linked to the MCU through its own Memory Buffer Unit (MBU), the primary function of the latter being to supply, from memory, a continuous stream of operands to the arithmetic unit, and to return to memory a continuous stream of arithmetic results. Addresses for sustaining this continuity are computed in the MBU using parameters supplied through a vector parameter file at the start of a vector instruction, and double

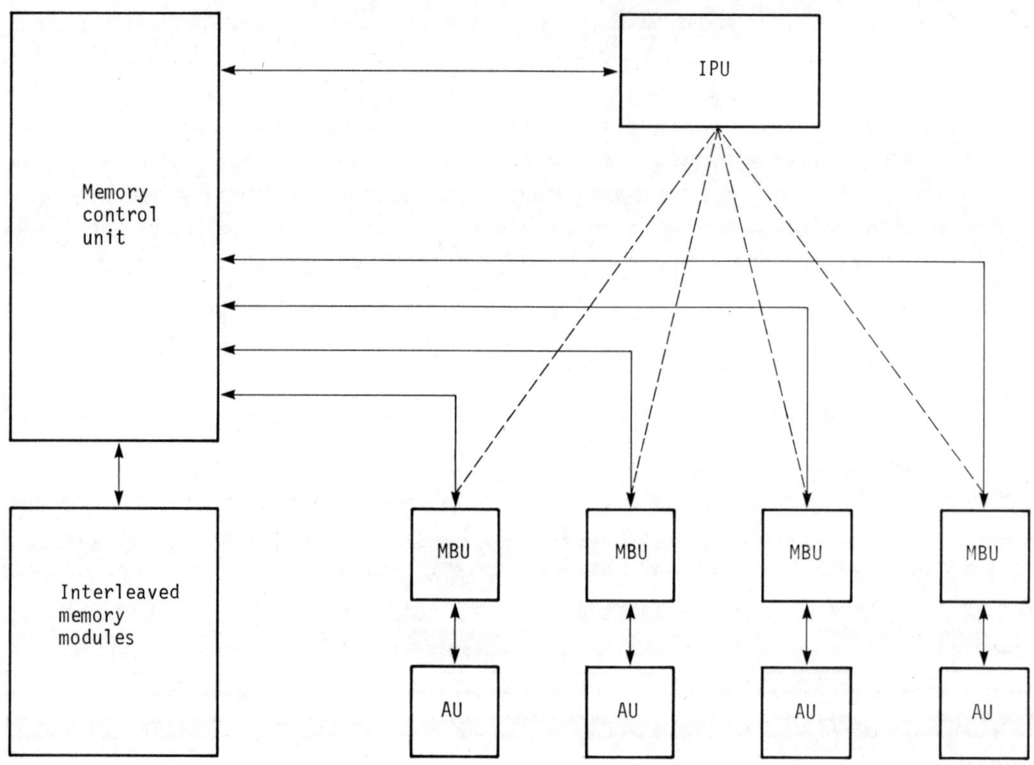

Figure 8: The Texas Instruments ASC

buffering (in units of eight 32-bit words) is provided for each of the operand streams. The vector parameter file contains a starting address field for each of the three vectors involved in a typical vector instruction, a vector length, inner and outer loop acounts, and increments to be added to each of the three starting addresses at the completion of each inner and outer loop. Information is supplied to the vector parameter file by the Instruction Processing Unit (IPU) which is mainly concerned with initiating operations in the MBU-AU vector processing pipelines, but also acts as a conventional scalar processor dealing with instruction fetching and decoding, address generation, control transfers, etc.

In general the number of vector units which can be operated in parallel successfully in a system of this type depends on two factors, one almost entirely hardware dependent, and the other program dependent (008). In considering the first factor, it is assumed that all vector units access a common main store. This store will have a maximum data rate which it can sustain (the store data rate) determined by its cycle time and degree of interleaving, and the vector units will have some data rate requirement which may vary according to the number of vectors involved in a given vector operation, and possibly the arithmetic involved. There will be some maximum possible requirement - the unit data rate - so that:

$$\text{Number of units} \leq \frac{\text{store data rate}}{\text{unit data rate}} \qquad (1)$$

In considering the second factor it is assumed that once initiated, a vector unit proceeds autonomously until the end of its operation, so that the IPU would be free to initiate operations in other vector units. The time taken to complete a vector operation depends on the vector lengths involved, and may vary for successive operations. The time taken to initiate an operation may also vary depending on the nature of the instruction set, but to a much lesser extent, and it can be assumed never to exceed some fixed maximum time, the unit set-up time. For successful operation, the IPU must be able to initiate all available vector units in a time less than or equal to the time taken by any one vector unit to complete its vector operation. Thus the number of vector units which can be successfully driven in parallel is determined by:

$$\text{Number of units} \leq \frac{\text{average vector operation time}}{\text{unit set-up time}} \qquad (2)$$

Ideally these two conditions should match, but since the first is essentially hardware dependent and the second largely program dependent, it is more instructive to view the second condition in an alternative form which gives the minimum vector length for which a system with a given number of vector units will operate efficiently. Thus if the vector length is L and successive results are produced at time intervals equal to the element operation time, then for efficient parallel operation:

$$L \geq \frac{\text{Number of units} \times \text{unit set-up time}}{\text{element operation time}} \qquad (3)$$

Equations (2) and (3) give a measure of the ability of the IPU to keep a number of vector processing units busy. In a system with four vector processing units each producing results at a rate of one every 20 nsec, for example, and a unit set-up time of 100 nsec, L must exceed 20 if the vector units are not to be left idle at some stage. If a TI-ASC operated at these speeds this would present no problem, since each of its vector processing units can be set up to execute a triple nested FORTRAN DO loop as a single operation. Loops of this type occur frequently in the seismic processing work for which the TI-ASC was designed. These long operations also minimise the effects of vector start-up times, but even where much shorter vectors are involved, a system with independent vector processing units would have some advantage over a system such as the CYBER 205 where the units act in concert. In a system with independent units the start-up time of one unit can be overlapped with full bore processing in others, and by having more units than can be supported by the store according to equation (1), which takes no account of start-up times, the full capability of the store data rate can be realised.

For very long vectors the performance offered by a given (small) number of parallel arithmetic units is obviously unaffected by whether they are operating on elements of different vectors (ie acting independently) or on a sequential set of elements from the same vector (ie acting in concert), but as the number of units increases, the end effects become more important, particularly for short vectors. Not only do the start-up and run-down times affect performance, but so also does the alignment problem discussed above under *The STAR-100* which led to the use of control vectors in the STAR-100 and CYBER 205 systems. As the number of bits being processed in one cycle increases, so does the amount of alignment buffering required, and so too does the number of store stacks cycled unnecessarily at the start and end of a vector operation. Independent pipelines would suffer less in this respect, and coupled with the use of a multiport memory such as that used in the CRAY X-MP, could offer greater performance.

Such a system would also require a different virtual-to-real address translation mechanism from that used in the CYBER 205. This mechanism would itself become a bottleneck if only one set of associative registers was used to translate all virtual addresses generated by the independent units. Thus multiple sets of associative registers would be required, and the coordination of these sets of registers into an integrated store management system represents a new challenge to designers of high-performance processors.

REFERENCES

001 HINTZ R G and TATE D P
Control data STAR-100 processor design
COMPCON 72 Digest pp 1-4 (1972)

002 LINCOLN N R
Technology and design tradeoffs in the creation of a modern supercomputer
IEEE Transactions on Computers vol C-31 pp 349-362 (1982)

003 HOCKNEY R W and JESSHOPE C R
Parallel computers
Adam Hilger (1981)

004 RUSSELL R M
The CRAY-1 computer system
Communications of the ACM vol 21 pp 63-72 (1978)

005 IBBETT R N
The architecture of high-performance computers
The Macmillan Press (1982)

006 MORRIS D and IBBETT R N
The MU5 computer system
The Macmillan Press (1979)

007 WATSON W J
The TI-ASC - a highly modular and flexible supercomputer architecture
Proc FJCC AFIPS pp 221-228 (1972)

008 IBBETT R N
Vector processing
ACM 6th European Regional Conference
pp 337-347 (1981)

SUPERCOMPUTERS: NEW DIRECTIONS IN APPLICATIONS - LOOKING FORWARD

E C Joseph

Anticipatory Sciences Inc
Minneapolis
MN

E C JOSEPH is President of Anticipatory Sciences Inc where he works as a futurist, researching the many aspects of future technology and providing a consultancy service on these topics. Mr Joseph is also adjunct professor at the University of Minnesota where he designs and teaches courses at graduate level. He has over 30 years' experience in computing, holds three computer patents, and is the system architect of five major computer systems. Mr Joseph has lectured and written widely on all aspects of computing and future technology.

SUPERCOMPUTERS: NEW DIRECTIONS IN APPLICATIONS - LOOKING FORWARD

Possible future developments in the computer field in general and supercomputer applications in particular are mapped, and multiple sets of future breakthrough expectations are depicted. Included are expectations for inference engines, three-dimensional and biogenetic chips, billion-gate wafer components, self-programming systems, new artificial intelligence directions and knowledge information utilities. Each subject is put into evolutionary context, delineating the possible path to a breakthrough, and a possible trend for the future. Forecasts are charted as 'future history maps' outlining events before and after milestones are reached.

INTRODUCTION

When reviewing the history of technology there is little doubt that one of the most versatile tools ever devised by humans, and one which has had the greatest amount of impact, has been the sophisticated modern computer. With its continued use and evolution, the indications are that it will become even more important in the future.

The digital computer has now been around for nearly 40 years, with newer and broader applications appearing annually. Over this time the computer has rapidly evolved new features and capabilities. The waves of technological advances come ever faster with each new generation. In this paper, forecasts of highly-likely future computer breakthroughs and the ensuing evolution are mapped as a future history for the next 40 years. Throughout their history (both past and expected future) supercomputer applications have played a key role in forcing many computer developments.

Interest in new breakthroughs in computer development for supercomputers is again growing. This new wave of interest stems, in part, from recent advances leading to such breakthroughs as the microprocessor, very high-speed integrated circuit (VHSIC) developments, and practical Artificial Intelligence (AI), as well as the Japanese thrust to excel beyond the USA and expectations for very high-speed circuits.

BREAKTHROUGH EXPECTATIONS

In spite of rapid and accelerated growth in past computer developments, there is no expectation that future breakthroughs will slow down at all. In fact, as this paper emphasises, there is considerable evidence to support even more rapid advances, and a growth in breakthroughs is to be expected both in the coming decades, and for the year 2000 and beyond.

Recently, computers have become small enough, cheap enough, and capable enough to be embedded with other hardware to make the resulting machines 'smart'. That is to say, these 'smart' machines are becoming the 'engines' of the Eighties, for raising productivity through the application of chip microcomputers. Shortly, 'inference engines' using the heuristics of AI and knowledge bases will be embedded to create 'intelligent' machines. These Knowledge Inference Processing (KIP) systems will also be applied as 'people amplifier tools/appliances', and will contain expert knowledge for amplifying the knowledge of professionals (eg doctors, pilots, managers, scientists etc). These special-purpose expert professional machines will later give way to a new generation of machines incorporating general intelligence. So far embedded device computer 'smarts' have been relatively slow, on the agenda for the future are very high-speed circuit components with circuits densities spanning the range from hundreds of thousands to billions per component depending on the timeframe considered and ranging from chip to wafer components.

Such developments usher in an era of 'component supercomputers' which turn open the door for the future to totally new supercomputer applications. As each new (future) computer generation breakthrough occurs, multiple embodiments of 'people amplifiers', 'robotic smarts' and intelligence will evolve and their usage will increase. Concurrently and/or following these breakthroughs, biochip technology, using recombinant DNA genetic material and 3-D chips, will emerge and vastly increase computer capabilities. Somewhat sooner, million gate/circuit chips will be used, followed by billion gate/circuit wafers. These developments will allow for 'component machines/computers', 'component systems/institutions', and 'component programs' to be cast in hardware as building-blocks for supercomputer machines. They, in turn, will be used to force other breakthroughs, such as sensor-based computers, smart and intelligent robots, artificial brain computers, biogenetic image processors, knowledge/intelligence computer utilities, ultra-high capacity biomemory, self-programmed systems, robot programmers, knowledge/inference processing networks, self-repairable systems, and much more.

How possible are such breakthroughs? Telescoping in on such futures reveals that the science required is largely at hand. Therefore, what is needed is the difficult and costly task of applied and advanced research and development. As we focus more closely on such futures, the natural evolutionary paths to their fruition become discernible. That is, the future breakthroughs as outlined herein, are no longer in the realm of speculation, but can now be mapped and developed.

To date, most supercomputer development has been in the realm of computational intensive computing (ie number crunching) as were early 1940-1950 general-purpose computers. An analogy could be drawn between the transition of supercomputers and their applications, and the path taken by general-purpose computers in the late 1950s, ie first towards data processing, then information processing and thirdly the possibility of moving towards inference processing.

Many trends characterise computer developments. One way to forecast the future is the extrapolation of such trends. For example, hardware complexity incorporated per component has been doubling annually for certain classes of computers since the early 1960s, but this trend has not moved as fast for supercomputers. As the current new US hardware development program leading to VHSIC wends its way deeper into this and the next decade, very high-speed and very dense circuit components for at least one class of future supercomputers can now be forecast to become reality.

Another trend that our known science would allow to advance at its past rate for at least a few more decades, is the doubling each year of computation speed - this rate of change in advancing the speed of supercomputers has been going on since 1951. However, since new supercomputers are not likely to be introduced each year, this speed curve should look more like a set of steps into the future - with each step taking a little longer to occur than the previous ones.

Supercomputer speed in the 1950s was measured in KOPS (1000s of operations performed per second). By the mid-1960 decade the measure became MIPS (millions of instructions per second) and typical supercomputer speed in the late Sixties and early Seventies ranged from 1 to 10 MIPS. Now the measure has become megaflops (millions of floating-point operations processed per second) - with a typical range of 1 to 100 megaflops (and with an average of 20 megaflops today). In the future, candidates for measures of the speed of supercomputers are:

- Megalips (millions of logic inference processing steps)
- BIPS (billions of instructions per second)
- B-Flops (billions of floating point instructions per second)
- APS (applications processed per second).

To meet and achieve the speed challenge required of supercomputers the trend from their beginning has been to do more processes in parallel. In the early days the trend was toward multiple bit multipliers, multiple and parallel executable arithmetic sections, instruction overlapping, pipelining of operations, multiprocessing, SIMD and MISD systems and vector computers. Today the trend is toward cellular multiprocessors, more sophisticated vector computer architectures, front-end and back-end processors, multiple I/O processors, multiple memory banks, MIMD-type computers and special-purpose attachable processors as speed-up accelerator units. In the future newer and more parallel MIMD types must be expected to be forthcoming and new types of AI logic inference processing engines. Further, the trend toward special-purpose accelerator/attachable processors will continue to evolve. As single chip/wafer VHSIC-type component application process engines emerge then very high speed special-purpose functions, for supercomputer building blocks, will force new types of architectures.

Throughout the history of supercomputers, when hardware and/or architectural advances were made a new list of supercomputer application capabilities also emerged - usually allowing scientists to get ever closer to simulating reality. This trend will continue. However, supercomputers are also approaching a new turning point whereby it will be possible to handle totally new types of application. One such area, as mentioned previously, is in the area of artificial intelligence type supercomputers for expert systems and knowledge inference processing systems - soon to be followed by the information utility, and later, knowledge utilities.

Further, the trend started early in the supercomputer era, for reorganising and reformatting large-scale application algorithms for optimising supercomputer performance, allowed faster computations and the trend will continue. Thus, the need to solve large-scale problems promotes supercomputer architectural developments, as do advances in hardware, and the rate at which our knowledge in algorithm development advances. The problem of course continues to be the structuring of new supercomputer architectures to maximise the number of operations which can be performed concurrently. However, in the past the operations maximised were primarily for number crunching. In the coming era, this trend will certainly continue, but with the additional trends for maximising the number of the following:

- I/O operations and system memory accesses
- Logic inference processing steps
- Knowledge processing steps
- Parallel application processing steps.

Needs and trends for supercomputers and their applications thus map as follows:

- Faster computations
- Faster numeric and non-numeric operations
- Faster and more parallel I/O
- Faster and more multiaccess memory
- More MIMD-type architectural alternatives
- Newer and better algorithms
- Lower cost systems
- More systems programs and standards
- More general-purpose applications programs
- More special-purpose accelerator/attachable processors.

FUTURE HISTORY MAPS

The following are numerous 'future history maps', delineating past, present, and possible future breakthroughs for the computer field - together with some evolutionary maps to and beyond these breakthroughs showing what to expect for the future. Included are lists of expected supercomputer trends and applications.

Past

- Analogue
- Digital
- Special purpose
- General purpose
- Computer systems
- Macro scale
  - small/medium/large/super
- Data processor
- Multiprocessor/multicomputer
- Associative processor
- Mini
  - 4-bit/8-bit/16-bit/32-bit/super
- DDP processor/computer/system
- Micro
  - 4-bit/8-bit/16-bit/32-bit/super
- Smart machines
- Attached special-purpose processor

Future

- Component
  - processor/computer/memory/ sensor/system
- Database
- Convivial machines
- Current awareness
- Knowledge processor
- Inference engines
- Knowledge based
- Ethnotronic
- Smart robot
- Non-von Neumann
- Sensor based
- Component institution
- Synergy amplifiers
- Code-spliced architecture
- Intelligent robot
- Artificial brain

Figure 1: Computers

Past

- Machine code
- Subroutines and SR libraries
- Monitors/supervisors
- Assemblers
- Microcode
- Macroprocessors
- Compilers and HOL languages - how type
- Program generators
- Program modules
- CAD/CAM/HDL
- Executive control
- Operating systems
- Portable/transportable
- HLL languages - how type
- User languages
- Structured programming
- Database management systems

Future

- HOL/HLL - what type
- VHD^2 L (very high-level design/ development language)
- Integrated
  - HLL/OS/CAD/CAM/CAE/MIS/DSS/DBMS
- Component SW - SW → HW
- Knowledge-based systems
- Provable correct programs
- Self-programmed systems
- Rule-based programmed systems
- General-purpose program structures
- SW automation systems - CAP
  - SW AI libraries
  - Problem-oriented descriptive systems
  - Problem-tailoring systems
  - Self-testing systems
- Robot programmers

Figure 2: Software and programming

Past	Future
Sequential machine	SP logic inference processing
Business/scientific	Image processing
Real-time	General inference processing
Data processor	Institutional functions
File management	Societal/cultural functions
Interactive	Universal intelligence
Concurrent tasks	
MIS	
Array processors	
DBMS	
DSS	
AI/expert/knowledge processing	

Figure 3: Computer processes

Past

Discretes
- Relays - tubes - transistors

Integrated circuit - microchips
- SSI (gate and micromemory)
- MIS (stage)
- LSI (function)
  - microprocessor
  - microcontroller
- VLSI (machine
  - component computer
  - component memory

Future

  - component system
  - component sensor
  - component SW
- Optical chips - 10^5 times faster
- Million gate chip

3-D components

Wafer components
- Component systems
- Component institution
- Billion-gate wafer

Biochips - 10^6 - 10^9 times denser
- Image processors
- Neurons and synapses
- Artificial brain
- Inference processors
- Hybrid - bio/HW/optical

Nuclear

Figure 4: Computer hardware

Past	Future
SW primitives → HW	Application primitives → HW
Instructions	Application parts → HW
Long/sequenceable instructions	Special-purpose programs → VHSIC/ VLSI/ULSI
Algorithms	Processes - sensor
Maths functions	AI rule-based/inference system
Language	Profession functions/ethnotronics
Executive control	Institutional
Processes - control/processor	General intelligence

Figure 5: Programs → hardware

Past	Future
C^2	Distributed smart machines
Real-time control	Distributed intelligent machines
Attached terminals	Computer/information utility
Computer systems	Knowledge inference networks
C^3	C^3I^2
Store and forward	Cooperative group amplifier networks
Multiple computers	
Message switching	
Timesharing	
Distributed/DDP	
C^3I	
Networks	
LAN	

Figure 6: Computer networks

Past	Future
Paper/cards	Database
Flipflops	Multiple data stream
Registers	Relational
Rotating/strip memory	Knowledge base
High-speed memory	Biomemory
Delay lines	
CRT	
Magnetic	
Semiconductor	
Optical	
Archival	
Buffers	
Associative	
Cache	
Boram	

Figure 7: Data structures/memory

Past	Future
Highly reliable components	**Secure systems**
Redundancy and back-up systems	**Self-repairable systems**
Error detection	**Maintenance-free systems**
Error detection and correction	
SW/executive error control	
Failsafe/failsoft systems	
Highly-integrated circuits	
Reconfigurable systems	
Bit/byte	

Figure 8: Systems availability

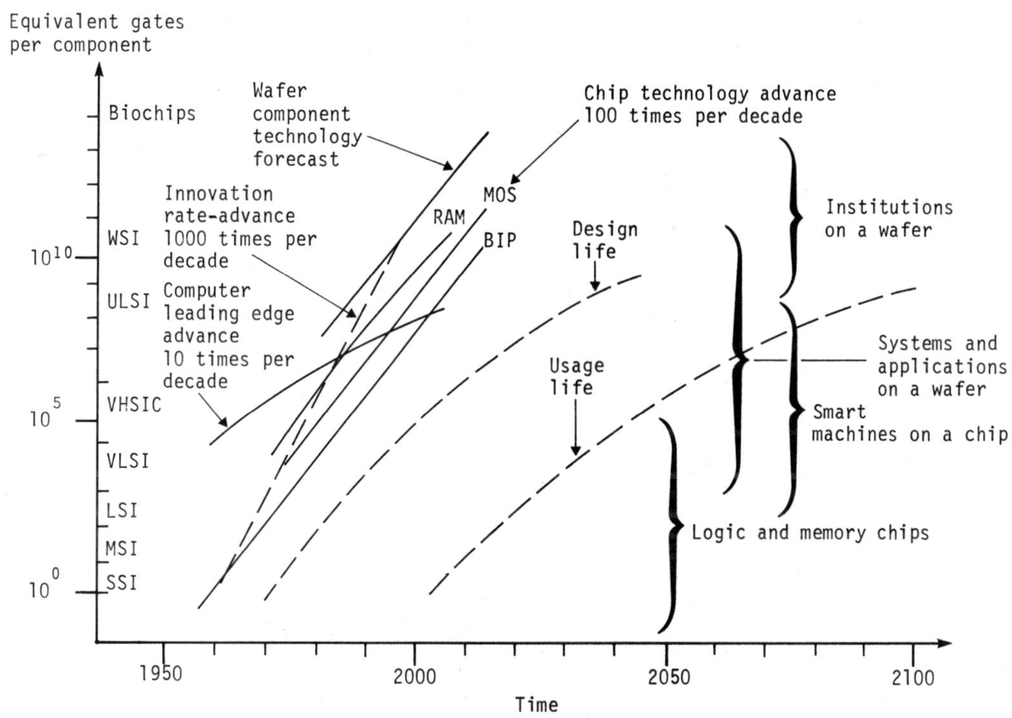

Figure 9: Forecasted harware future

1950s	-	Number processing
1960s	-	Data processing
1970s	-	Information processing
1980s	-	Smart processing
1990s	-	Knowledge processing
2000+	-	General-intelligence processing

Figure 10: Computer eras

1950s - Computer operations management
- Managing (computer) tool

1960s - Data processing management
- Managing computer, data, programs

1970s - MIS management
- Managing information and system

1980s - Information resource management
- Managing total information environment

1990s - Knowledge resource management
- Managing knowledge application

2000+ - Intelligence resource management
- Automated management of leadership

Figure 11: Computer management trends

1950s Computers
- Digital computers
- Data processors

1960s Information systems
- Computer families
- Minicomputers
- Multiprocessors
- Supercomputers

1970s Decision support systems
- Computer networks
- Microcomputers
- Distributed data processing
- Vectorcomputers
- Array computers
- Personal computers
- Factory robotic devices
- Superminicomputer
- MIMD machines

1980s Smart machines/systems
- Information utilities
- People amplifier appliances
- Information appliances
- Component computers
- Knowledge-based systems
- Smart robots
- Ethnotronic machines
- AI expert systems
- Supermicrocomputer
- Inference engine

1990s Smart ethnotronic systems
- Intelligent robots
- Knowledge utilities
- Intelligence amplifiers
- Smart cooperating machines

2000s Microinstitutions
- Component institutions
- Intelligence utilities
- Superbiocomputer
- General-intelligence amplifiers

Figure 12: A future history map

Past	Future
Calculation engine	Inference engine
Numerical arithmetics	Knowledge processing
Data manipulation engine	Ethnotronic people amplifier
Information processing	AI expert primitives
Smart machines	Robots
Embedded logics	

Figure 13: Computer types

1950s (Early)

- Instruction/computation primitives

  Multiply - divide ...

1950s (Late) and 1960s

- Algorithm primitives

  Indexing - floating point - trig functions ...

1960s and 1970s

- Language/control primitives

  Executive control - I/O - HLL ...

1970s

- Process/function primitives

  Controllers/processors

1980s (Early)

- Application primitives

  MIS - DBMS - courseware - profession ...

- System smarts

  Sensors/computer/machines

1980s (Late)

- Inference and system primitives

  Intelligence - systems - networks ...

1990s

- Institutional primitives

  Office - factory - society ...

2000+

- General intelligence

Figure 14: Programs into hardware eras

1980 Transitions

Boxes

Component computers/machines

Component systems/institutions

Figure 15: Computer trends

1 Word processing.
2 Smart word processing.
3 Communications-oriented word processing
4 Word processing and data processing marriage.
5 Office automation software.
6 Computer mail.
7 Computer conferencing.
8 Database computer.
9 Smart office machines.
10 People amplifier appliances.
11 Smart/automated offices.
12 Information appliances.
13 Knowledge-based machines.
14 AI expert systems.
15 Intelligent offices
16 Component/embedded offices
17 Bionic office systems
18 Human-office integration

Figure 16: Office-of-the-future generations

Present	Future
Chip based	Wafer based
	Biotechnology
	3D components

Figure 17: Trends in components and systems

Past/present	Future
Numerical calculation	Human intelligence Amplification networks
Business - bookkeeping	Knowledge utilities
Scientific	Future-office-of-the-future
Control/communications - C^2 - C^3 - C^3I	Real-time education
Real-time process control	Real-time professional amplifiers
Data processing	Expert/knowledge-base libraries
Systems support	Future-office/school-of-the-future
Language	(Remote office/school systems)
Information retrieval	Public MIS/DSS/expert systems/utilities
Business - financial/planning/forecasting	Corporative expert systems
Large systems of equations	Government/congressional law-making expert systems
Interactive	Total field taxonomy expert systems
Office/factory/professional	Automated factory
CAD/CAM/CAI/MIS/DSS	Real-world modelling and simulation
Humanities/arts	World models
Information processing	Electronic knowledge-based libraries
Laboratory analysis	World simulation assisted decision making
AI	
Personal computing	
Smart/intelligent machines	
Information utilities	
Robotics	
Expert systems - rule based	
Knowledge processing	

Figure 18: General-purpose and SC computer applications

Past	Future
SC Computation intensive number crunching	SC Computation/IO/memory/logic inference intensive operations
Physics	Information/knowledge utilities
• Atomic/thermonuclear/plasma	Knowledge information processors
• 3-D physical fields	Artificial humans
Aerodynamics	Global real-time cooperative networks
Seismology	Global/space ATC positioning
Meteorology	Space industrialisation
Weatherforecasting	Macroengineering projects
Business	Corporate management
• Large linear programs	Multinational cooperation
• Financial models	Global economic models
Government	
• World models	
• Multicriteria decision making	
Defence	

Figure 19: Supercomputer applications

COMPONENT TECHNOLOGY - THE NEXT 10 YEARS

D J Kinniment

University of Newcastle upon Tyne
Newcastle upon Tyne
Tyne and Wear
UK

D J KINNIMENT graduated from the Electrical Engineering Department of Manchester University in 1962, and after a period of postgraduate research in that department joined the Department of Computing Science at Manchester in 1964. Research at Manchester was concerned with the components and technology of computer systems; mainly new techniques for memory implementation. This work led to a PhD degree in 1968. Dr Kinniment contributed to the later stages of the ATLAS project as well as being largely responsible for development of an integrated circuit associative memory for the MU5 computer system. He now holds the Chair of Electronics at Newcastle upon Tyne University where his research interests are in the development of computer-aided design techniques for VLSI circuits.

COMPONENT TECHNOLOGY - THE NEXT 10 YEARS

A definition of VLSI is given and the contrasting approaches of the traditional semiconductor component engineer and the system designer to VLSI is discussed. Device dimensions are also considered and new developments in the design of systems on the chip are examined. Technological trends for the next 10 years are assessed, particularly possible limits to the reduction of dimensions in MOS devices. The problem of producing a correct design within an acceptable timescale is considered, with particular reference to design methodology and VLSI. Finally, uncommitted logic arrays are examined and gate array technology and design techniques are discussed.

INTRODUCTION

Undoubtedly one of the most significant influences on computer design over the next 10 years will be developments in an existing technology, one which has been around for at least 20 years and which shows no startling new device types or applications, but nonetheless has steadily developed to the point where the whole CPU of a computer of significant performance can now be fitted into a 7.5mm-square chip.

It is of course silicon technology, which is now the only fabrication technology capable of Very Large-Scale Integration (VLSI) in a cost-effective form. The implications of the probable reductions in system cost, and size, as well as the improvements in performance are such that in my opinion silicon VLSI will be the natural implementation medium for most computer systems, and its characteristics will be one of the main influences on the architecture of the machines themselves.

The importance of the technology has been realised by many of the advanced industrial nations who are currently investing considerable funds in the development, by 1990, of a VLSI capability able to take a significant share of the projected 40 billion-dollar market in VLSI semiconductors. Indeed it has been said by Carver Mead of Caltech, who foresaw many of the features of the present scene as early as 1971 that, 'the outcome of the VLSI struggle may well determine the future configuration of the world's power structure'.

VLSI

Because VLSI is a development of existing techniques it is important to define at what point LSI merges into VLSI, and why increases in component density are likely to be so far reaching in their consequences. There are at least two points of view on what represents VLSI, and perhaps these can be contrasted to indicate the difference between the traditional semiconductor component engineer's approach and that of the system designer who is likely to be most affected by developments.

Semiconductor companies have been involved since 1960 in a slow development of processing and photolithographic techniques which have brought about a gradual increase in the possible number of transistors per chip from 10-20 in 1960 to approximately 100 000 in 1980.

This is shown in Figure 1 which tabulates the increases in chip size and the simultaneous reduction in line width year by year. Since a silicon gate NMOS transistor can be represented by the intersection between a polysilicon gate of minimum width and an active area at right angles to the polysilicon it is possible to calculate the number of transistors that could be made on a single chip year by year.

WHAT IS VLSI?

'<2μ line widths'
'The point at which the problem of complexity overwhelms all other problems'

DATE	a) CHIP SIZE	b) MINIMUM LINE WIDTH	$(a/b)^2 \div 50$ TRANSISTORS/CHIP
1960	1mm × 1mm	30μ	18
1970	2.5mm × 2.5mm	10μ	1250
1980	6mm × 6mm	3μ	80 000
1990	10mm × 10mm	0.5μ	8 000 000

1M gates/chip by 1990?

Figure 1: Trends in integration

The possible levels of integration represented by the number of transistors per chip have in fact been closely followed by actual products and the curve of devices per chip against time (Figure 2) has become known as 'Moore's Law' after Gordon Moore of Intel who first produced the graph. To the fabrication line engineer conventional optical photolithography techniques are capable of defining line widths down to 2μ, beyond this electron beam or X-ray lithography may have to be used to define the patterns which produce 10^6 transistors or above. This is a view based purely on technological difficulty in fabrication and disregards the system problems. Those engineers who have designed chips of up to 1000 transistors know that while it is a demanding job, the difficulties are not severe and it is possible to produce a working chip in three months or less. A design of one million transistors on the other hand is a task which requires a team of engineers, each working on one part of a computer system, and is very unlikely to be correct the first time through. The balance of effort has now changed in that the system design aspects are very much more difficult, per chip, than the fabrication process which is common to a large number of designs.

Another definition of VLSI is therefore 'the point at which the problem of complexity overwhelms all other problems'.

Device dimensions

The current standard technology for the production of microprocessors and memory chips is silicon gate NMOS. There are good reasons for this in terms of the number of processes required and the yield of high-density high-performance devices, so that it is natural to look at advances in photolithography and processing techniques in terms of the NMOS process in order to predict the likely form of the 1990 device parameters.

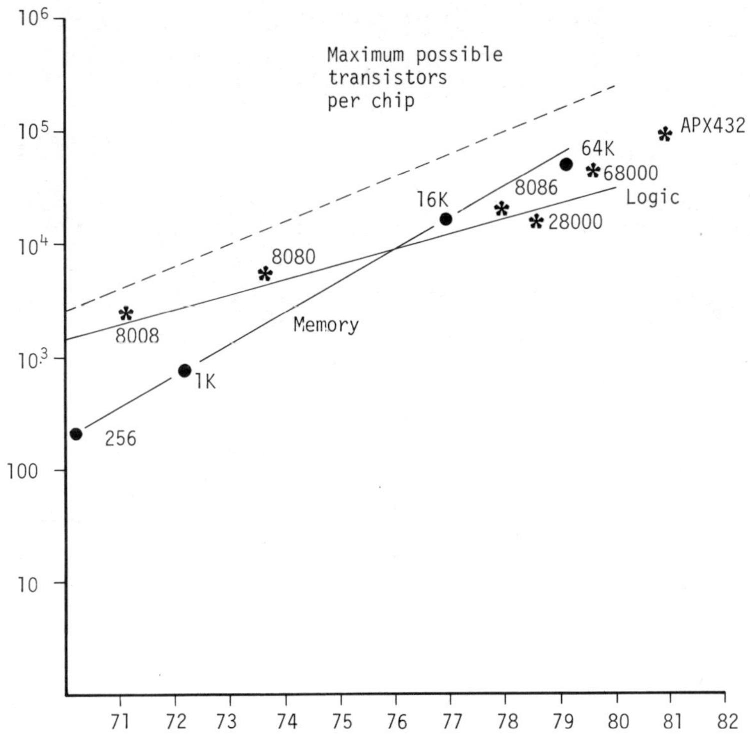

Figure 2: Trends in chip design (Moore's first law)

It is fortunate that, to the first order, models of NMOS transistors are relatively simple and the effects of reduced dimensions can be readily estimated. Figure 3 shows a cross-section through a typical transistor indicating the important dimensions.

The equations which govern the electrical performance of the transistor contain its gate length, width and depth as parameters and can be simplified as follows:

$$\text{Transistor current} \sim \frac{\text{gate width} \times (\text{voltage})^2}{\text{gate length} \times \text{gate oxide thickness}}$$

$$\text{Capacitance of a node (such as the gate)} \sim \frac{\text{gate width} \times \text{gate length}}{\text{gate oxide thickness}}$$

These relationships only hold if the fields within the device remain the same, so that if we reduce the lateral dimensions of the transistor we must also reduce the supply and other voltages to keep the field strength the same.

Since there are fields in both vertical and lateral directions, and because etching processes will only succeed in producing fine lines if the material thickness is reduced, the vertical dimensions of the transistor must be reduced in step with the lateral dimensions. A 'scaled' device may thus be produced which performs in the same qualitative way that the original transistor performed. Present standard technology produced line widths of 5μ in 1980 with corresponding gate delays of 5-10 nsec. By using techniques now available and likely to be in production by 1990, line widths as low as 0.25μ are possible, and the potential of this is a 400-fold increase in the level of integration. At the same time the supply voltage will be reduced by an order of magnitude, as will the transistor current. It is thus possible to see that the power per chip has not

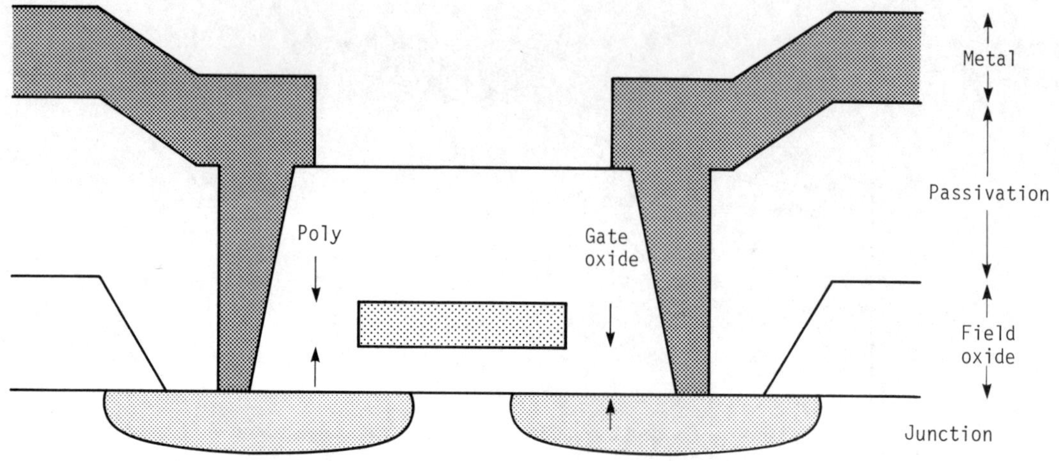

Figure 3: NMOS transistor

changed, but since the capacitance of all the nodes is reduced the gate delay has actually improved.

A considerable performance gain is the result of the scaling as well as the cost and reliability benefits of incorporating the whole CPU on a single chip.

There are, of course, several difficulties which may get in the way of this development and these are shown in Figure 4 which tabulates the dimensions and their effects in terms of λ, the minimum feature side on the chip (usually half the line width).

If all the dimensions on a chip were scaled by a factor of 10, the results predicted are those listed under the 'scaled' column in Figure 4. This is, however, not what most designers wish to do. The intention in reducing the device size is not to manufacture the same design smaller, but to produce a much bigger design on the same size chip, or to 'stuff' the chip with transistors. The effects of this are shown in the second column which takes into account the resistance of the power supply leads and interconnections.

Whilst the current per transistor has gone down, the current for the whole of the chip has gone up. This would be of little consequence except that the resistance of a given connection has also gone up, and connections will be longer in a large design leading to a further increase. The results of this are to magnify the relative effects of interconnections both from the point of view of supplying power to the chip, since the series resistance of the metal will present problems not previously encountered, and from the point of view of system performance, since although the individual gates have improved in performance the interconnect has become worse both in absolute and relative terms. As an example, a 10mm-long metal interconnect 5μ wide would have a delay of approximately 0.2 nsec. In a technology where 0.1μ-wide connection were possible the same 10mm length would have a 5 nsec delay, and a polysilicon connection might require 5 μsec.

Scaling	Now	Scale by 10
λ	2.5μ	0.25μ
Gate width	5μ	0.5μ
Gate oxide	0.1μ	100 Å
Poly	0.5μ	0.05μ
Metal	1.0μ	0.1μ
	Scaled	'Stuffed'
Device current	1/10	10
Capacitance	1/10	1
Gate delay	1/10	
Power	1/100	1
Resistance	10	100
RC connect	1	100
Wire current density	10	1000 (supply)

Limit λ = 0.12
Tunnelling
& Statistical variations
& Curvature

Figure 4: Scaling

The silicon foundry

The design of systems on the chip has, up to now, been the prerogative of relatively few people in semiconductor houses or large computer manufacturers such as IBM. The reasons for this are the very high capital costs of the fabrication equipment required and the reluctance of companies to share the details of their processes with competitors. This scene has recently undergone a dramatic change, partly aided by the emergence of relatively standard processes, partly by excess silicon capacity in the industry, but mainly by the need to tap design expertise wherever it exists.

This trend is best exemplified by the MultiProject Chip activity initiated at Caltech by Carver Mead and brought to maturity by Lynn Conway at Xerox PARC in 1979 (001). The emergence of Electron Beam Lithography has allowed several chip designs to be easily incorporated on the same mask, and hence manufactured on the same wafer. The costs of a mask set and the processing of a batch of wafers can thus be shared between the designs, reducing the cost per design to levels comparable to other implementation methods even on a one-off basis.

Costs quoted for the MPC79 exercise where 82 integrated circuit designs were implemented on two different wafer types were as follows:

Mask making $7500 per set	$15 000
Fabrication of two boat loads of wafers per mask sets	$10 000
Costs of data communications computing to merge designs, packaging and management	$15 000
	$40 000

This works out at less than $500 per design where designs were roughly equivalent to a printed circuit board's worth of MSI and SSI packages.

Other impressive aspects of MPC79 were the turn-around time of 29 days from design cut off to packaged chips, and the inclusion of a LISP microprocessor design 6mm × 7.5mm which functioned correctly first time. This was essentially a US university exercise but has since been repeated in other countries including the UK in 1981 (Figure 5 shows a Newcastle University project fabricated by SERC facilities). It is obvious that if this kind of design is economic from the system designer's point of view as well as the semiconductor house, then there will be an explosion of activity bringing together fabrication capacity with design expertise, and indeed this can already be seen to be happening with the formation of 'silicon brokerage' companies whose function is to act as the catalyst and to provide the bridge between design and implementation.

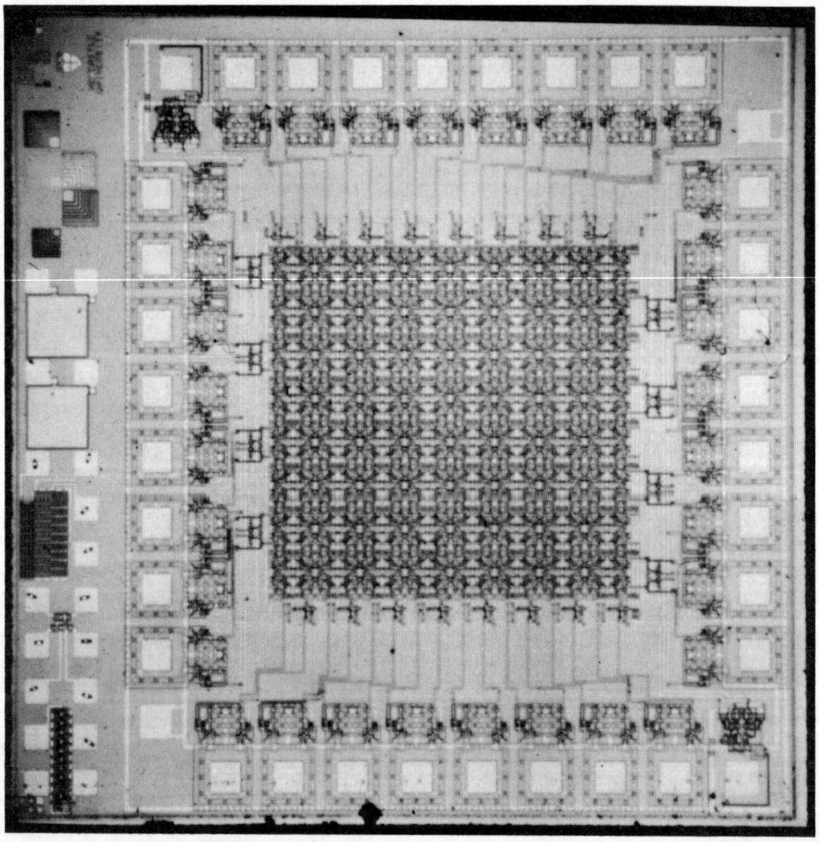

Figure 5: Chip design project

Trends in technology

As the improvements in photolithography and processing techniques are brought from the laboratory to the production line, smaller and faster NMOS transistors will result with continuous improvements up to 1990. The questions that arise from this statement are as follows:

1 What are the likely limits (if any) to this improvement?

2 How will similar improvements affect competitive technologies such as bipolar integrated circuits?

3 What are the chances of radically different technologies such as Josephson junction switches replacing silicon as the mainstream computer implementation medium?

There are a number of possible and established limits to reduction of dimensions in MOS devices: they include such effects as the probability of current carriers tunnelling through an extremely narrow transistor from source to drain, and the effects of discreteness of charge causing variations in the threshold level of the transistor. Both of these effects become important where the gate length is in the region of 0.25μ preventing the projection of simple theory much further (002). Another effect also limits the operation of a transistor as a digital switching element at about the same point. This is the effect of the curvature of the drain current/gate voltage characteristic at low currents. The curve is usually assumed to have a sharp threshold voltage below which no current flows, but in practice it is an exponential curve with an exponent of $\frac{qV}{kT}$. Thus as scaling requires that the voltages defining the logic levels are reduced, the curvature remains constant and eventually the device approximates more closely to a linear resistor over the range in question than a digital switch. Despite these limitations a factor of at least 10 in dimensions and 100 in packing density is likely before 1990.

Applying similar arguments to existing bipolar technology does not yield the same improvement factors. The main reason for this is that one of the important determinants of the speed of a bipolar transistor is the base transit time, and this is dependent on the base width of the transistor. Bipolar transistors are made in a different way from MOS devices, the base width being defined by the vertical difference between two diffusions rather than a surface dimension produced by photolithography. As a result it has been possible to produce transistors with base widths of less than 1μ for some years and ECL gates can currently be produced with propagation delays of 0.5 nsec or less. There is very little room for reduction in vertical dimensions of the transistor before quantum limits are reached, and also little room for reductions in gate output voltage swings which are already dangerously close to the curvature of the Vbe characteristic with voltage changes of 0.45V in ECL.

The only remaining possibility is a scaling of surface dimensions which would reduce collector currents at a similar rate to the corresponding capacitances. Gate speed thus remains fairly constant, and power per chip also remains constant in a 'stuffed' technology. Figure 6 summarises the present comparison in speed and shows that MOS is likely to catch up with the best bipolar technology over the next 10 years without the same penalty in process complexity.

Performance determined mainly by device transit times (may be worse with bipolar)

MOS $\tau = \frac{L^2}{\mu VDS}$ Bipolar $\tau = \frac{d^2}{4\mu\ KT/q}$

L = Source-drain d = Base width

	MOS		Bipolar
Dimensions now	5μ - 10μ		<1μ
VDS	5V/2	4KT/q	100mV
μ	800		1300
M τ	0.1 nsec - 0.4 nsec	τ 8	0.05 - 0.1 nsec
Gate delay	0.5-3 nsec 5τ upwards		0.25 - 1 nsec
1990	50 - 500 psec		100 - 500 psec

Figure 6: Bipolar versus MOS

Within MOS technology an important contender for the mainstream both as a general workhorse and for specialised computer systems is CMOS. Despite being more complex from the point of view of processing, it is possible to apply broadly the same scaling considerations so that similar increases in gate speed are likely. The great advantage of CMOS is that while conductor current densities will increase in the same way as NMOS, leading to the eventual dominance of power supply problems and interconnection performance limitations, the power requirements of a CMOS circuit start from a much lower base, typically 20 times less than the equivalent static NMOS device. It has much more mileage as a VLSI process, and also has the possibility of somewhat faster circuits. The greater silicon area required by CMOS is less of a difficulty in an environment where the circuit area is mainly occupied by interconnections in any case, and the need for many interconnection layers is likely to increase the process complexity required for NMOS.

Josephson junction logic

If it were possible to build MOS FET devices which would operate satisfactorily with only a few electrons on the gate, there would be no benefit in terms of device-switching energy in scaling the dimensions down. This is because the energy on the gate $E = \frac{1}{2}CV^2$ and $V = q/C$ where q is the charge on an electron. As C goes down, the switching energy and the time to switch then goes up.

Most Josephson junction devices such as SQUIDS operate with a value of flux trapped in a superconducting loop that is near the quantum limit of $\phi = 2 \times 10^{-15}$ webers. At a feature size of around 1μ, which is currently achievable in the laboratory, such devices have switching times of the order of 20 psec, which can be compared with a transition time of around 50 psec for an FET of the same size.

Because the power dissipation (at the device level) of a superconducting system is already very low, it is possible to increase the device currents and switching energy to make a circuit switching in less than 1psec. This fact, coupled with the improvement in interconnection path propagation delays likely to result from superconducting transmission lines, would result in a technology unsurpassed for raw speed, but the same disparity between the gate delay and the interconnection delay may exist as shown below.

	Gate delay	10mm interconnection delay	Ratio
Silicon at 0.5μ	100 psec	5 nsec	50:1
Josephson junctions	1 psec	50 psec	50:1

This comparison with FET gates says nothing of the power dissipation of the technology, which, while dissipation is very low in the actual Josephson device, is comparable for the same speed devices when the need to pump any heat produced up to room temperature using a Carnot cycle is taken into account, and much greater for high-speed devices.

An alternative might be to operate existing MOS devices at much lower temperatures allowing lower voltages and faster operation. In either case the penalty of the refrigeration is a cost that must be offset against the possibility of using concurrency to gain the same factor in speed improvement as can be obtained with low temperature operation.

THE DESIGN PROBLEM

As more and more complex chips become possible the difficulties of producing a correct design within an acceptable timescale are painfully apparent. Traditionally chip designers have achieved a constant rate of about 5-10 transistors committed to file per man-day over the brief history of semiconductor design. With the chips of 1000 transistors current in the early '70s three man-months was adequate to produce the design; now an effort of around 100 man-years is needed for a 32-bit microprocessor chip. This relationship has also been attributed to Gordon Moore (Figure 7), and Ian Barron recently pointed out that for a company with only 10 designers to attempt the next generation of chips with 10^6 transistors means a starting date of around 1930.

Clearly this law will have to be broken in the next few years, if progress is to be made, by the application of CAD and other methods.

Design methodology

CAD systems have been developed to a high level of sophistication over the past few years and have been applied very successfully to printed circuit board (PCB) design. The application of such systems to VLSI layout may not be as successful in the long term for a number of reasons. PCB layout is an exercise in manipulating between 20 and 100 objects (usually dual in line packages) and interconnecting them within the board. Here, runtimes of the software are related to the number of objects to be laid out, usually raised to the power of two. The area available for the interconnections is also relatively large since routing can be done under the packages as well as in the wide spaces between. If such techniques are applied directly to VLSI circuits, the computing task will be excessive for complex circuits and since routing is usually

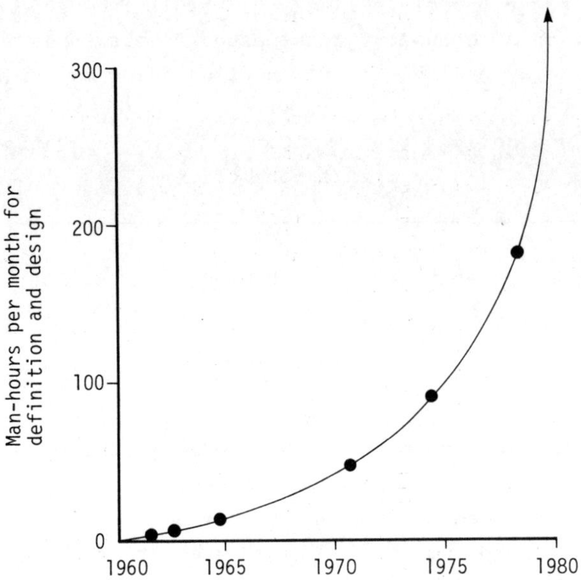

The man-hours per month required for ic product definition, design, and layout grow exponentially

Moore's 2nd law 5-10 transistors/day

(Barron's corollary: 1m transistors, 30 men = 10 years)

Figure 7: VLSI design effort

done between fixed connection points on the circuit modules, long and tortuous interconnections will result.

It has already been pointed out that the interconnections are likely to be the main performance limitation in VLSI systems, it is also likely that they will require an ever greater proportion of the silicon area, and methods which aggravate these tendencies will produce systems with low performance and high cost.

Many of the ideas already used to create large software systems may also be helpful in the design of VLSI hardware. In dealing with a complex problem, splitting the design up into a number of simple modules, each communicating with the others in a defined and predictable way, prevents the spread of design problems and allows the design of each part to proceed relatively independently. In addition to the existing software problems of complexity VLSI introduces a whole series of further difficulties:

- Each module must fit into a two-dimensional space
- Communication between non-adjacent modules is difficult
- Timing problems exist as well as those of sequencing
- The fabrication process is subject to faults as well as the possibility of designer error
- Turn-around time from design to chip is long, therefore testing difficulties are encountered.

These are problems which will have to be overcome before the idea of a 'silicon compiler' analogous to compilers of high-level languages can become a reality, and a specification can be compiled directly into a chip layout.

Despite this there are aspects of software management which can appropriately be used, particularly the notion of hierarchies of modules and simple testable interfaces which may ease the task.

The use of regular structures in design which are capable of topological modification without affecting their function, or functional modification without altering their shape also allows a top-down design approach in which a late change in the design of one module does not significantly affect its neighbours. The obvious example of this type of structure is the PLA (Figure 8) in which the mask specification can be automatically generated from a specification of the behaviour in terms of Boolean equations, and the position and interconnections required within the chip.

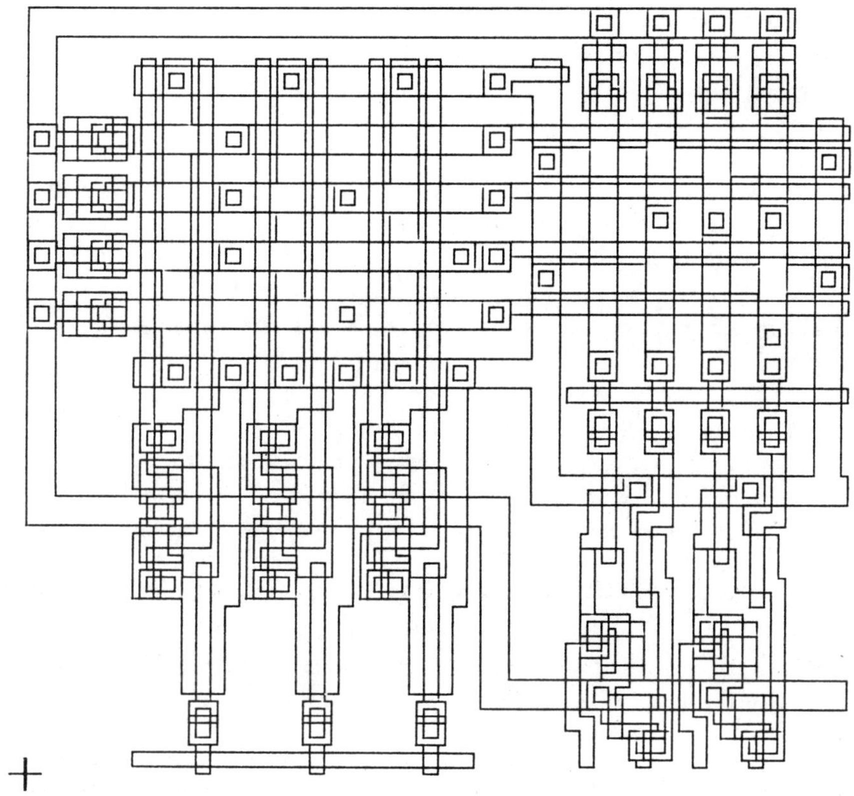

Figure 8: Programmable logic array

Methodologies are now being investigated where procedures to produce such regular structures are callable from a high-level language. The parameters of the procedures can thus be calculated as part of the main program and larger objects can be defined as an assembly of subprograms in a hierarchical way. The advantage of such methods is that the subsequent generation of a particular variant to suit the layout or function required is relatively easy.

VLSI and concurrency

Given the basic cost and performance advantages of VLSI, its adoption will probably lead to the use of computer architectures particularly suited to the characteristics of the medium.

In existing architectures a separation between the CPU and the memory has been traditional, partly because of the different implementation technology of magnetic memories and partly because of the batch processing advantage of producing many identical memory chips.

Transfer of information between the CPU and memory, however, requires a very high bandwidth, and is often the limit to system performance. Since the bandwidth limitation arises mainly because of the high cost of providing connections off the CPU chip and back onto the memory chips, and the transmission of the signals themselves is slowed by the process of amplification to high levels followed by translation back down onto chip levels, it makes sense to combine both the memory and the processing power on the chip.

This is just one illustration of the general principle that within VLSI computation is relatively cheap and communication relatively expensive. The interconnections even within a chip are costly in terms of silicon area and costly in terms of performance, so that if it is possible to avoid moving data long distances either on or off a chip it pays to do so.

A very large proportion of the activity involved in the execution of a program is concerned with movement of data from one place to another. Often, after the movement, very little in the way of calculation or modification is performed, thus by increasing the number of processing elements and placing them in positions near to the data to be processed considerable improvements could be gained in performance at little cost in silicon area.

Further improvements would be possible if the nature of the algorithm was such that similar actions could be performed by each processor on its own local data in parallel, but even if the algorithm was not naturally parallel the technology favours the use of multiple processing elements with local data.

The search for improved performance together with the advantages of reliability to be gained from multiprocessor or redundant systems is thus likely to combine with the natural characteristics of VLSI in advancing the cause of hardware concurrency despite the inherent difficulties in the design of concurrent systems.

UNCOMMITTED LOGIC ARRAYS

Full custom design of VLSI circuits requires a degree of sophistication and understanding of both the electrical characteristics of the process and the topological constraints involved in layout. Without some minimal level of understanding of these points it is impossible to produce a sensible design and the elegance and economy of the design is likely to improve with increasing skill and effort on the part of the designer. With the expansion of the market for LSI and VLSI devices into the system area, there are many applications for circuits in places where the economies and performance improvements which would be possible if existing SSI and MSI chip assemblies were replaced by a single chip could make a dramatic change to the viability of the product as a whole - the added value being orders of magnitude greater than the chip itself. In this case the emphasis is on production of a correct chip design in the minimum time regardless of elegance or cost effectiveness.

It is in this area of the market-place that uncommitted logic arrays are now making a significant impact, sales being expected to more than triple from $60 million per year in 1981 to $200 million by 1984. The cost per circuit (and the performance) of a ULA function implementation is likely to lie somewhere between full custom design and the same function implemented in standard off-the-shelf integrated circuits as shown in Figure 9.

The advantage in speed and ease of design comes from the fact that the chip is designed with an array of prediffused components allowing a range of standard gates or functions to be produced simply by interconnecting the components in a predefined way. This allows:

- The designer to think in terms of familiar objects such as gates or MSI components
- Easy conversion of Design Automation Software intended for PCBs
- The majority of masking stages to be done on a large scale before final commitment of the circuit to a particular design.

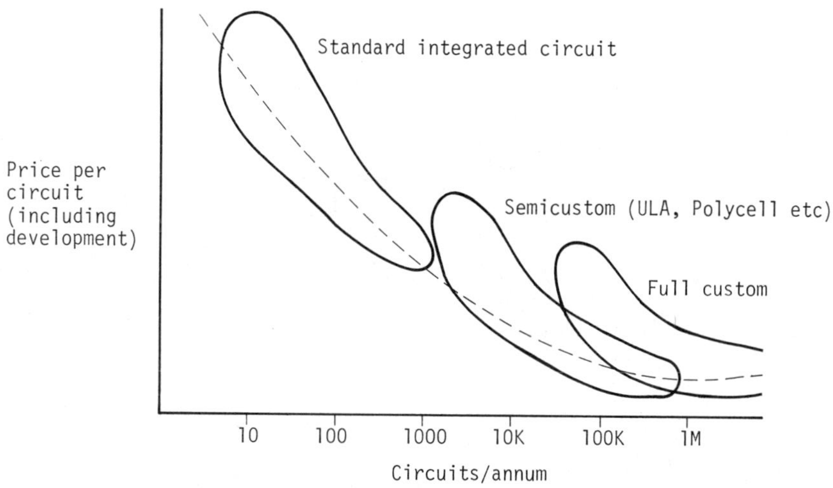

Examples: Ferranti CDI 200, 400, 900 gates

Plessey, ICL ECL 300, 600, 1000 gates

Many manufacturers CMOS 2000, 5000 gates

Figure 9: Uncommitted logic arrays

All of these factors make for a quick and easy design process though not necessarily an efficient one, again a turn-around time of three months from system specification to prototype chip in a commercial environment is typical. Computer manufacturers from IBM to Sinclair by way of DEC have all recently taken advantage of gate array technology.

Gate array technology

Both bipolar and CMOS gate array designs are now available commercially with capabilities of up to 1000 gates in bipolar and 5000 gates in CMOS. While bipolar arrays can offer sub-nsec gate delays, the power dissipation per chip required to achieve this performance is such that further increases in speed or density will be difficult.

No such limitation exists for CMOS arrays and in consequence they will dominate the market in the near future.

Figure 10 shows the cell structure of a typical three-input gate CMOS array showing how the cell can be connected to make either a NOR or a NAND gate by using two layers of interconnect metal. Other metallisation patterns can be used to make elements such as multiplexers and flipflops, but the very ease of design provided by familiar gate elements can be a trap which guides the designer to an inappropriate or inefficient chip.

An example of this is shown in Figure 11 which shows the gate level definition of a four-bit ALU which appears in many MSI data manuals as a description of the 74181 part.

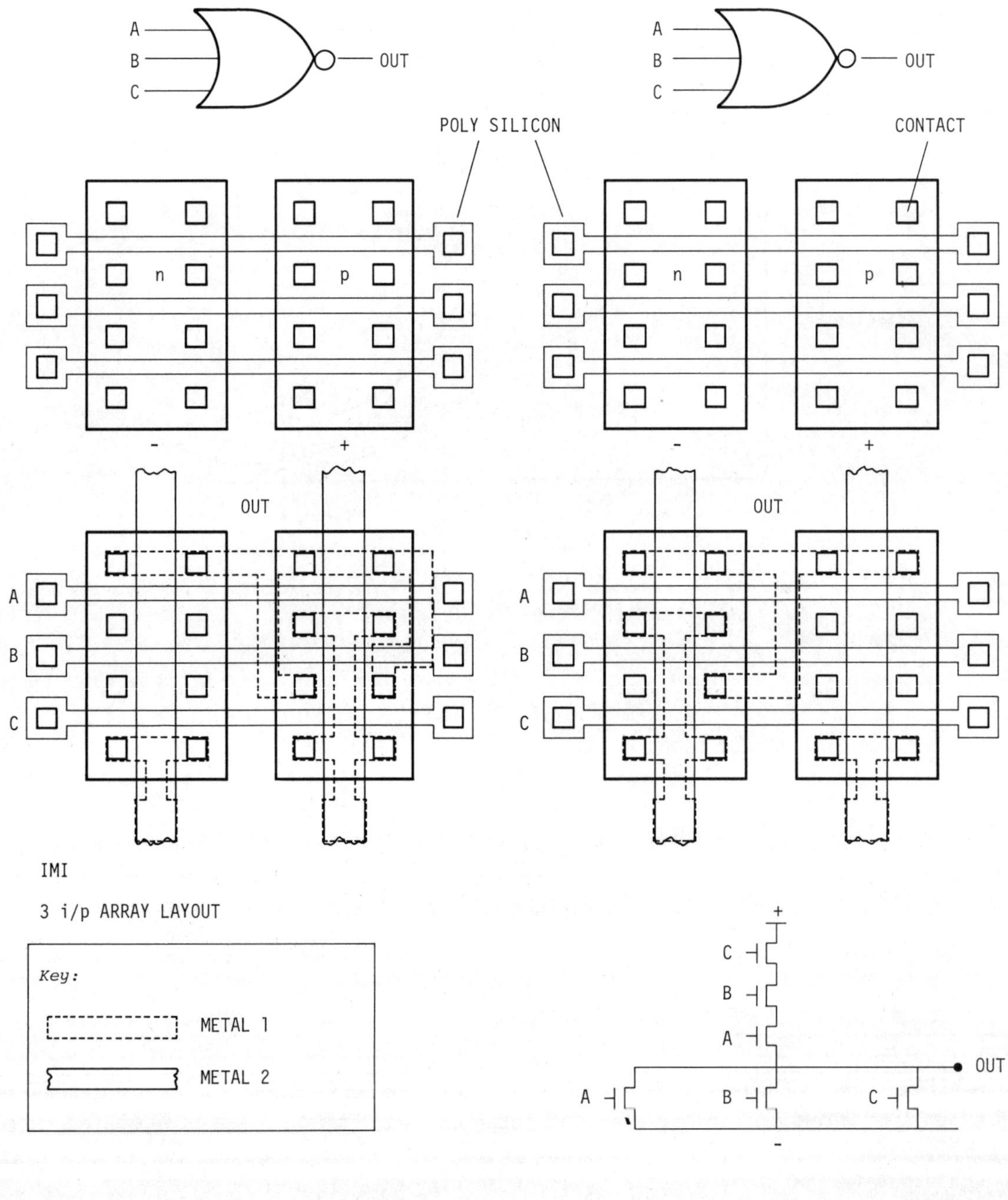

Figure 10: CMOS ULA cell structure

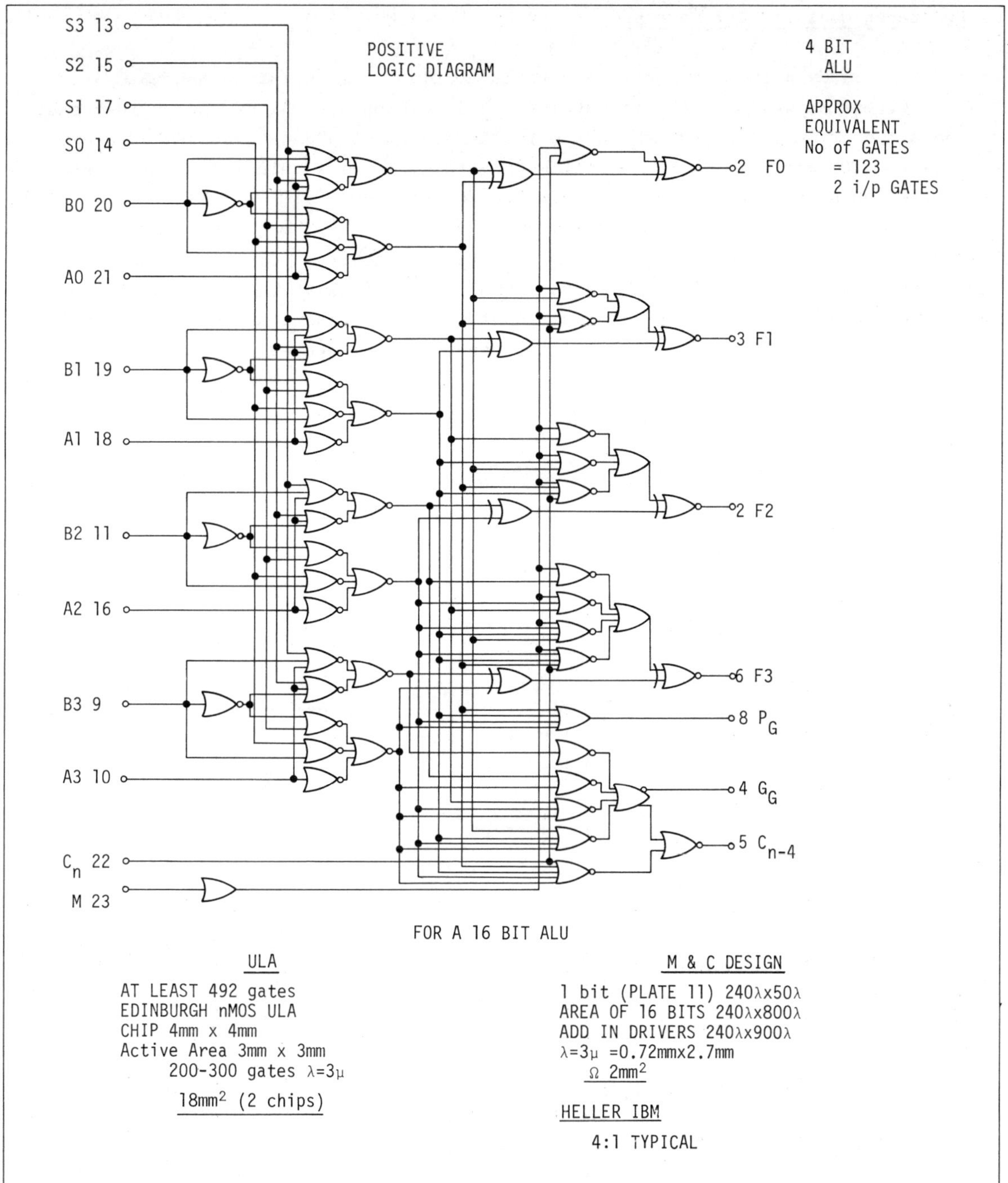

Figure 11: ALU logic gates

If this were to be mapped naively into an array of two input NAND gate cells approximately 123 cells would be required. Thus to produce a 16-bit ALU at least 412 cells or over 20% of a 6mm-square 2400 gate CMOS ULA would be required.

It is difficult to be sure that like is being compared with like when different designs are put alongside one another but using the same minimum feature size of $\lambda=2.5\mu$ it is certainly possible to produce a 16-bit ALU in CMOS technology in an area smaller than $2mm^2$ by using the regular structures described earlier and illustrated in the excellent book by Mead and Conway (003).

An area improvement of at least three to one is usually seen when translating gate array designs into fully custom designs and accompanying performance improvements are also likely.

Design techniques for gate arrays

There are already a number of software tools available to assist in the gate array design process as well as many in development. Perhaps typical of the current state of the art is Figure 12 which shows the block diagram of a design system development for Plessey ECL gate arrays at Newcastle University (004). This illustrates some of the differences between gate array design and PCB design.

The network is first specified in terms of gates and their interconnections, in a form which can provide the input to a digital simulator as well as the input to the auto layout software. The task of the layout software is to position the gates on cell locations as well as to find the paths for the interconnections. However, it is common for the area in between cells to be insufficient for the connections required, and in any case

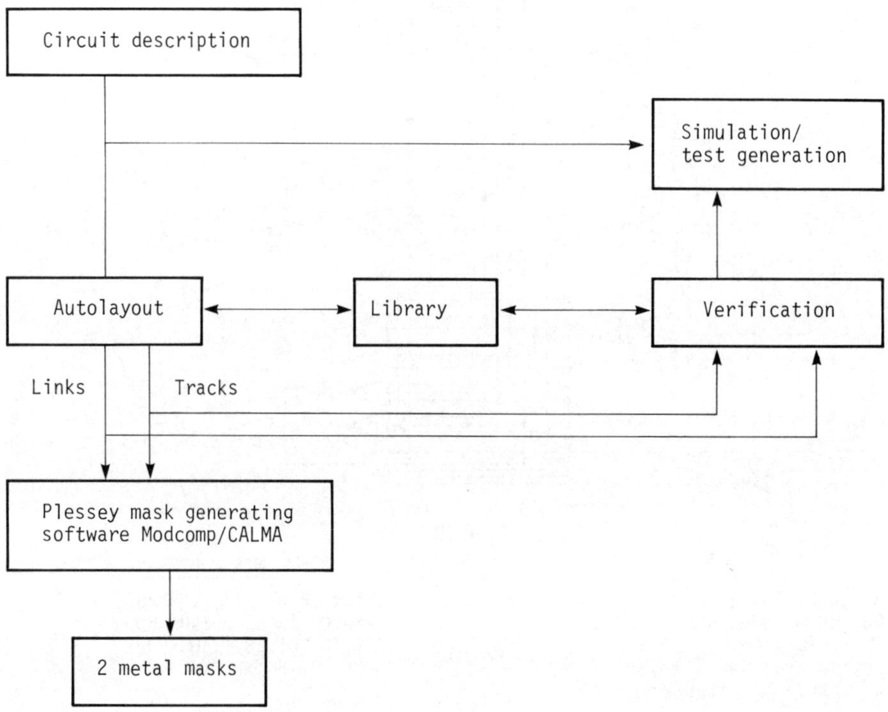

Figure 12: ULA design and verification system structure

layout programs are poor at recognising how placement of cells and routing of tracks can be optimised. As a result paths cannot be found for some tracks and manual intervention using computer graphics is required.

Any manual intervention to optimise a design which has already been verified by simulation can introduce errors and destroy the correspondence between the source text and the final product. At least two methods exist to solve this problem, either the graphical intervention may be constrained to operate in a way which maintains the correspondence by forcing the designer to connect only the points specified, or the resulting changes must be verified by reconstructing the network produced and comparing its behaviour with the original. It is the second method which is shown here, and which allows more flexibility in design at the expense of less certainty in the verification.

Whilst gate array design and structured design have been presented as different techniques, it is likely that difficulties in extending the software tools already in existence and the natural developments in the arrays themselves will force a convergence between methods.

Assemblies of cells are already being designed for large gate arrays which have many of the 'lego like' characteristics of the regular structures described earlier, and also allow the sort of butting connections that existing software cannot easily optimise. These developments and the increasing size of the arrays themselves are likely to make the two methodologies approach more closely in future.

CONCLUSION

It is clear that as far as developments in the technology are concerned and their possible influence on the computer architecture there will be at least as much change over the next 10 years as there was in the last 10 years, with major cost reductions and performance improvements. This in itself will project computer systems into an extremely wide market-place even in comparison with their position in society today.

REFERENCES

001 CONWAY L
The MPC adventures: experiences with the generation of VLSI design and implementation methodologies
Xerox PARC (1981)

002 KEYES R W
Physical limits in digital electronics
Proc IEEE vol 63 No 5 pp 740-767
(May 1975)

003 MEAD C and CONWAY L
Introduction to VLSI systems
Addison Wesley (1980)

004 MOLE G F, ALSHAHIB I A and KINNIMENT D J
A CAD verification system for ULA designs
IEE Conf on *Electronic design automation*
Brighton (1981)

THE FIFTH GENERATION: THE UK RESPONSE

R Malik

Freelance journalist
London
UK

R MALIK has been a freelance journalist for 25 years during which time he has written widely on computer technology, its development and applications, and its social, economic and political consequences. He is a frequent contributor to Computing *and* Computerworld USA *and is the London Correspondent of* 01 Informatique, *France. Mr Malik is the author of* And tomorrow the world? Inside IBM *and was an advisor to the BBC's* The Computer Programme.

THE FIFTH GENERATION: THE UK RESPONSE

The effect of Japan's plans for the Fifth Generation computer project are assessed with particular reference to the implications for UK research and development policy. Japan's additional research support programmes in software, CAD, supercomputers and other areas are also examined. One particular Fifth Generation target, machine assisted translation, is assessed. Possible UK responses are considered and the work of the Alvey Committee is discussed. The Committee's recommendations regarding current problems in the educational, financial and personnel areas are also considered.

INTRODUCTION

Current thinking about computing and long-term R & D policy in the West has been thrown into a state of confusion. The announcement of Japan's plans - the challenge of the Fifth Generation - has indeed put 'the cat among the pigeons'. Without this challenge, the West's R & D policy might well have gone on for years in roughly the same direction. What the Japanese have done is to introduce a discontinuity which has made everybody think.

The bundle of evolving documents in which the Japanese spell out their plans for the next ten to fifteen years has had a number of effects. This paper, however, will be restricted largely to their effect on the UK.

Firstly, the Japanese have mapped out the essential computing R & D agenda for the next ten to fifteen years. Other agendas would previously have been possible, but are now not likely. The Japanese challenge has to be met in some way, however, particularly as they have made it quite clear that this is the direction in which they are moving irrespective of any other country's R & D policies.

Anyone setting out an agenda with high ambitions and a short timescale, would probably come up with something similar to the Japanese proposals. What the Japanese have recognised is that the computing world is facing a situation in which the technology is dominated by one country, and that this technology has been developed in the light of the perceived needs and possible markets of that one country, ie the US. The way to end that dominance is not necessarily to challenge the US head on, but to change the basis of the technology, to introduce a major discontinuity. This is precisely what the Japanese are proposing. The best advice one can obtain outside Japan suggests that the basic programme they are proposing is probably achievable, perhaps even within the timescale planned. As far as anyone outside Japan is concerned then, it would be prudent to recognise what the Japanese are setting out to do and to adapt to it in some way, since the products of Japan's Fifth Generation will eventually arrive in the market-place whether jointly produced or as competitors.

Secondly, the Japanese proposals have exposed the short-term *ad hoc* nature of much of the long-term computing R & D policy elsewhere, particularly in the US and the UK. Japan apart, the only other country to have recognised that computing could introduce major social discontinuities, and to be prepared to create policies which recognise this, is France. In fact, what the Japanese are proposing is to tailor technology to people rather than expecting people to adapt themselves to technology, as has been the case for the last 30 years. In doing so they have exposed other countries' policies as lacking long-term social focus.

Next, the group of R & D support policies of which the Fifth Generation is the spearhead are closely related. It would be a mistake to think that the Fifth Generation is Japan's sole R & D policy. Also in progress are large-scale R & D support programmes in software, software tools development, Computer-Aided Design (CAD), supercomputers, opto-electronics, basic component technology, and, now up for approval, a R & D programme on intelligent robots, which can be thought of as the Fifth Generation with actuators, intelligent sensors and mobility. This R & D effort is so organised that the policies all support and buttress each other. Were the Japanese to fail with the Fifth Generation they would still become formidable competitors in conventional computing, but were they to have even minor success, which is more likely, they would radically affect the developing of computing and its markets. Indeed, they will transform computing as we have hitherto understood it. What is now conventional computing will become a subset of something much wider and more pervasive. For example, in the budget battles that have accompanied the beginning of the Fifth Generation programme (and it would be wise to remember that the Japanese too have such battles) the initial R & D aims have had to be narrowed. The Fifth Generation team have had to decide where their priorities lie, to cut the programme down to key and critical systems. Two of the targets that have been retained are shown in Figure 1, taken from the updated May 1982 proposals. A discussion of one of these targets, that of machine assisted translation, follows. It should be noted, though, that natural language comprehension, which in Figure 1 is found under the heading *Consultation systems*, is of direct relevance to such translation systems.

Any translation system of the kind the Japanese are proposing must be able to handle continuous speech. A device capable of handling this, which also has the ability to distinguish one voice from another (for that also is implicit) and to respond in what, to the user, appears to be real-time, will be truly revolutionary. In the future, this will lead to automatic translation telephone exchanges. With such systems, the PTTs could make most of the world's international telephone exchanges obsolete. True, there might still be a market for traffic where the countries concerned speak the same language, but it would be relatively small.

The Japanese target is for only 90 per cent accuracy. This creates more problems in print than in voice. In the latter case, given the redundancy of human speech, a system which allowed us to call, say, Japan in English, the receiver hearing what we say in Japanese (even if not perfect Japanese) and replying in Japanese while we hear the response in English, would be welcomed enthusiastically. In this field, we may in future see automatic translation machines which accept spoken input and then output printed copy. The world's literature could be stored and automatically translated on demand. It is worth pointing out, however, that the way in which conventional technology is developing, some forms of machine translation are likely to appear anyway well within ten years, even without any radical changes.

UK RESPONSE TO THE JAPANESE CHALLENGE

What response, if any, should the UK make to the Japanese challenge and their offer of collaboration? A response has to be made, for the Japanese government have made formal proposals which must sooner or later be replied to. The details of their proposals have not been made public at the time of writing, but after some weeks spent in Japan in the summer of 1982 and many discussions with the Japanese, the author can state that the proposals are probably as follows:

Machine translation system:

- Translations among multiple languages
- Vocabulary size: 100 000 words
- Machine to guarantee 90% accuracy, with the remaining 10% to be processed through intervention by man
- System to be an integrated system where computers participate in the individual stages ranging from text editing to printing of translations
- Total costs involved to remain at 30% or lower than those of translation by man.

Consultation systems:

- Specimen applications:
    - medical diagnosis
    - natural language comprehension
    - mechanical equipment Computer-Aided Design (CAD)
    - computer user consultation
    - computer systems diagnosis
- Number of objects: 5000 or more
- Inference rules: 10 000 or more
- Semi-automated knowledge acquisition
- Interfaces with system: natural languages and speech
- Vocabulary size: 5000 words or more.

Figure 1: Subjects and targets for basic applications systems

1 The countries taking part to agree on a detailed agenda of the areas in which they will each work.

2 All R & D results to be pooled.

3 Commercial exploitation to be left to the commercial judgement of those countries and companies involved.

This is the standard way in which the Japanese work within their own country. Unfortunately, there is no experience of this method of working at the international level, at least not in an area which mixes basic research with a technology so commercially charged. It may well be that this is the way it will work out in practice, but the weight of informed opinion in the UK in the summer of 1982 is against it.

It is not simply that there is a distrust of the Japanese, although this does exist; cultural and linguistic differences make it almost inevitable. It is rather that few people can see this methodology working in any more than one or two specialist areas. A joint programme of limited scope in, say, two or three areas might work. Nobody, however, can see how a broad attack on fundamental problems, in which research is spread across a number of countries could be successful. This is because it is difficult to see how such an attack may be mounted. To begin with, such a programme has to be headquartered somewhere and, however good the formal communications arrangements, the country in which it is headquartered has an advantage over the others. This would not matter too much in a slow moving technology, but in this case, where weeks can make a difference, it could be very important.

Another considerable problem is that the Japanese tradition of technical cooperation between major firms at the basic R & D level is an alien one to the UK at least. This is not just a matter of cultural ethos, although this is a major cause. More important are the practical consequences. The mechanics to make such cooperation possible do not even exist within the UK. They could be created, indeed as we shall see may well be created in the future, but it is asking much of British industry, given the pace at which institutional change takes place, to expect it to be able to cope on an international basis as well when the cooperation may well have to be more than just specifically item-related and not simply bilateral, but between a number of countries.

The Alvey Committee

Whether or not Her Majesty's Government eventually decides to cooperate with Japan, a study of what policies Britain might follow has been mounted by the Alvey Committee, chaired by John Alvey, a technical director of British Telecom. Members of the Committee include Iann Barron, Technical Director of INMOS, Phillip Hughes, Chairman of software house Logica, and Charles Read, Director of the Inter Bank Research Organisation, IBRO. The Committee is due to report to Kenneth Baker MP, Minister of State for Information Technology at the Department of Industry, shortly before the publication of this paper. Whether or not he will then choose to make it public is not currently known, and it is doubtful that it can be ascertained until the report has been finalised and studied.

Much of what the Committee has been considering, however, *is* known and some of its broad recommendations have become well known to the experts, largely because the Committee has made little secret of what it is doing (it could not do otherwise, since it has had to consult a wide range of experts and has commissioned a number of studies).

The Committee makes many breaks with past practice. To begin with, it is probably the first committee established by a government to look quite as deeply and as broadly into the development of a technology within a timescale of only a few months. Usually such an exercise would march in stately measure for a year or two at least. Because the Committee has to report within so short a space of time, it has had to concentrate on essential points - irrevelancies have been left aside.

The Committee is not charged with deciding whether or not the UK should join Japan, but rather with considering an internal British reaction to the Japanese challenge. What should Britain do first in order to 'put its house in order' and what should the next move be? What technologies should Britain as a country pursue where it might have some edge or expertise and where it would make long-term sense to do so? The one point on which everybody seems to be agreed is that the Japanese challenge is not just an R & D challenge, but a commercial challenge which, whether the UK cooperates or not, will have to be met in the market-place. Whether or not the UK decides to join the Japanese programme, the country's position will be greatly enhanced if the UK can first organise its own internal R & D policies.

The Committee, it appears, will recommend that British efforts should be concentrated (at least in the publicly funded R & D sector) in the following four areas:

- Software, particularly software tools
- VLSI, especially Britain's ability to tailor new circuits rapidly - known as *silicon brokerage*
- Man/machine interface development work (they are expected to accentuate this, probably taking the line that since much of the world's work is carried out in an English-speaking environment, we have some natural advantages we can build on)
- Intelligent Knowledge-Based Systems (IKBS).

This last belongs to the same class as the Expert System. One does not, for instance, have to look further than the medical diagnostic system in order to discover ways in which databases could be made considerably more intelligent than today's. What is more, it might be easier to build on what already exists without the upset of radical departures and the costs that would be involved, say, in a total re-ordering of data according to new schemata.

The Committee has found that the problem which faces the UK cannot be solved simply by addressing the problem of industrial R & D, which can then be said to be the responsibility of one ministry.

The Committee has discovered a number of institutional 'bottlenecks', and has made recommendations to help overcome them. The first of these involves intellectual resources and is a multifaceted problem. Due to the lack of resources committed to the IKBS field at the university level so far (partly due to current government policies, partly due to the lack of support policy generally over the last few years for work in this field) skilled personnel are leaving the country at an alarming rate. In one particular area, there were probably only 30 specialists in the country, yet *five* have left the country since the end of March 1982. Another absurdity is that, in the computing field, the University Grants Committee provides the buildings, but the separately funded and managed Science and Engineering Research Council provides the equipment. In addition, there is little concept of engineering in the British secondary school system. To solve the problem of intellectual bottlenecks, the country needs a larger pool of trained people (even at a basic level). This takes time, in some cases a great deal of time. Some effort must therefore be put into a number of educational areas if there is any progress to be made.

The problem, however, is not just a long-term one, but also a short-term one. The Committee, for instance, have had some discussions on the IKBS field. The initial recommendation was for a smaller R & D programme than has finally been recommended. This was because, whatever the amount of resources to be put in, it was not initially seen how the existing university system could absorb any more funds. The people to absorb these funds have to come from somewhere, and some of the Committee thought that the people resource or lack of it was a critical constraint. The existing system at the university level cannot absorb people without institutional change, university commitment and encouragement. The universities, however, are suffering from government cut-backs, and without extra funding many would be loth to engage in expansion, however economically desirable the country thought it to be.

The Committee recognises that education also needs to be carried within the broad spectrum of the computer industry. It is generally agreed that too many software support tools already in existence are not as widely and intensively used as they should be. This is so in universities and in R & D generally (including commercial R & D).

These are not the only problems. No R & D programme will provide the sole answer - there must also be commercial investment, but who is to invest and in what?

It is generally agreed that the growth point for the UK economy when faced with this challenge lies with the software houses. The high added value comes from assembly. Software houses assemble ideas into forms, where good returns can be obtained. It is doubtful, however, that if faced with the Japanese challenge the major earning software houses of the future will remain at all similar to the majority of those that exist today. In the sort of environment the Japanese envisage, the software house of the future will really be a software factory, dealing in tradeoffs between software and hardware. This means that the software house must be deeply immersed in simulation, which in turn means that it must become much more deeply immersed in the mastery of chip design technology. The successful software house 10 to 15 years from now will be quite capital intensive.

The Committee is believed to have recommended a £50 million per annum programme for the UK for at least five years. Not including other recommendations of a more general nature which involve ministries and departments across the country, we are left with what will probably be around 1000 specialists funded by public funds. Where will these specialists be located? Due to the length of time it would take to set up, the Committee is believed to have recommended that instead of copying the Japanese methodology (they have set up an Institute of New Generation Computer Technology) Britain should organise its research effort into consortia. These consortia would involve a mixture of researchers from industry, universities, and government laboratories. All would be owned by the government, but the government would in turn let out the results to industry, thus giving some return to the public purse. (This is a method much used in Japan where it is quite common for companies to involve their research staff in common R & D projects, paying a royalty to government on the eventual payoff.)

Naturally enough, the Committee hope for synergy, and one of the ways to achieve this even with a dispersed research effort, is to insist that all share common development tools. This of course means that investment for those tools must be available to all. For instance, in the IKBS area, the Committee is believed to have recommended a low-level start, because there is a need to acquire people with the right skills. Growth by at least a factor of ten within the scope of the programme is being talked of. In other areas, they are thought to be recommending that the number of skilled people be at least doubled. If these things can be done, then a pool of talent will be developed, a pool of a size large enough to permit movement of people as opportunities offer.

Opportunities will offer themselves. It is alright, for example, to talk of a bright future with VLSI, which everybody agrees exists. This is a statement of unexceptional generality, but the *truth* is different. As yet nobody really knows how to use the complexity of VLSI. Chip technology is almost reinvented with every complex chip. IBM is currently making much of the fact that its Essones plant in France is making 15 000 different kinds of chip. Given that the same plant makes no more than 20 million chips a year, this is absurd. This is proof, if it was ever needed, that the industry is still in its infancy.

Finally, the Committee recommends that the British programme should have a genuine R & D director. It will be interesting to see if this recommendation is accepted, because with it goes their only management suggestion. The suggestion is that the government should put up the funds, but place the management of the project in-house. The director should have real powers, and the usual British practice of project oversight (with ministerial and civil servant reviews, endless enquiries, the panoply of committees of review, enquiry and the rest of it - a structure which has always ensured that whatever is done is done at a slower pace in the UK than anywhere else) should be discarded. The director should have his terms of reference, his budgets, and the mechanics of cooperation set up, but then he and his team should be left to manage the programme alone.

What they are proposing, in effect, is an end to 'muddling through', that almost traditional British way of working. The evolution of this approach should be watched with great care. If it is accepted, then the Japanese challenge is being taken seriously, as is the Japanese timescale.

Will the British response be enough? An honest answer is that, as yet, nobody knows. What will determine this is whether or not the UK decides to cooperate with the Japanese, and that is not a decision likely to be taken for quite some time.

It may be possible, six months from now, say at the beginning of 1983, to provide some sort of sensible answer. Although today the policy options are all still open, they cannot remain so forever.

THE FIFTH GENERATION - PROGRESS IN JAPAN

T Moto-Oka

H Tanaka

University of Tokyo
Tokyo
Japan

T MOTO-OKA received the Bachelor of Engineering in electrical engineering in 1952 and the Doctor of Engineering in electrical engineering in 1958, both from the University of Tokyo. Since joining the Faculty of Engineering at the University of Tokyo in 1957, he has conducted various researches in the field of digital computers, that is, logic circuits, logic design automation, and memory systems. He was a Visiting Research Assistant Professor in the University of Illinois, and a Visiting Professor in Washington University in St. Louis. He is currently a Professor in the Electrical Engineering Department, University of Tokyo. His research interests include computer architectures, distributed computer systems and artificial intelligence.

H TANAKA received the degrees of Bachelor of Electrical Engineering, Master of Electrical Engineering and Doctor of Electrical Engineering from the University of Tokyo in 1965, 1967 and 1970, respectively. In 1970, he joined the faculty of Engineering, University of Tokyo, where he is now an associate professor. From 1978 to 1979, he was a Visiting Professor at City College of New York, NY. His current research interests are in computer architecture, operating systems for distributed processing, and distributed database systems. He is a member of Information Processing Society of Japan, IECE of Japan and IEEE.

THE FIFTH GENERATION - PROGRESS IN JAPAN

A project called Fifth Generation Computer Systems (FGCSs) is currently underway in Japan. The objective of this project is to develop the basic technology that is required to realise the FGCSs which will be used in the 1990s. These systems are oriented towards knowledge information processing systems, the basic elements of which are the problem-solving and inference system and the knowledge-base system. A 10-year research period has been set up, and this commenced on June 1, 1982. This paper presents the objectives, the configuration image, and the research and development schedule of this project.

INTRODUCTION

It has been 40 years since the first electronic computer was developed and hardware technology has progressed rapidly in this time. We now have single-chip computers whose processing power far exceeds that of the First Generation computers. Software technology has also progressed, and there are now various kinds of high-level languages, operating systems, and database systems. As a result, we can make programs for almost any kind of application, if its algorithms can be described explicitly. This means that computers can take the place of people in many areas because of their high-speed processing ability and their large memory capability. However, there are still some application fields in which computers have not been able to demonstrate their power satisfactorily; these are pattern recognition, natural language translation, summarising capability of sentences, learning capability of past experiences, global decision making through various kinds of information, and so on.

We are also facing a serious problem, namely the 'software crisis'. This arises because of the gap between the logic level required by applications and the one offered by high-level languages. As the application field expands more, the gap becomes broader and broader. This means that computers should support a higher logic level which is at the same time friendly and familiar for humans. We call such computer systems Fifth Generation Computer Systems (FGCSs). In other words, the FGCSs are Knowledge Information Processing Systems (KIPSs); they have knowledge bases and are able to infer from the knowledge and solve problems as humans do. Only when computers gain such capability, can they be truly useful and tide us over the software crisis. To realise such high-level computers, various kinds of technology are required such as knowledge representation, inference operation, knowledge acquisition, very efficient parallel execution mechanism, VLSI technology and so on. These technologies are not completed yet, but we think that the time is now ripe to start a project to develop Fifth Generation computers which are based on artificial intelligence.

In Japan, a few study groups were formed in 1979 made up of university professors, and researchers of national laboratories and industries. In the course of three years they fixed the image of Fifth Generation computers, and drew up a 10-year research plan divided into three terms of three, four and three years. A laboratory to lead this research and development was founded in June 1982 in Tokyo and funded by the Ministry of International Trade and Industry.

The following is a summary of this research and development plan.

BACKGROUND OF THE FIFTH GENERATION PROJECT

Changes of the era

Computers are not only used very widely for business applications and control of various kinds of systems, but are also related very closely to our daily life; they now constitute the nerve centre of society. On the other hand, the social circumstances surrounding computer systems are going to change very drastically because of many factors, not least the new computer technology. That is to say, we are going to face up to a great revolution in our society, characterised by a proliferation of technology on a scale unprecedented since the first Industrial Revolution. The symptoms of this revolution can already be seen in the changes already taking place: the many kinds of product now available, the various kinds of energy sources, and the advances taking place in the variety of information media.

Computers form a very strong means of realising this future society as harmoniously as possible. As we already have the fundamental technology, we expect rapid development of computer systems that will be able to adapt to the new era, through the Fifth Generation Computer Project.

Social requirements

The objective of this project is to realise new computer systems which will be needed in the 1990s. The roles expected of the Fifth Generation computers are:

1 To improve the productivity of low productivity fields such as non-fixed form business of tertiary industries.

2 To improve the utilisation efficiency of energy by minimising the energy consumption, optimally controlling the energy conversion, and so on.

3 To play an important role in medical treatment, to give educational assistance, and to solve numerous social problems.

4 To contribute to international society through international cooperation and automatic translation, and to help to internationalise Japanese society.

As stated above, the application field of computers will become many-sided in the 1990s, and the usage will spread from the world-wide gigantic information networks to the composed small elements of systems until everybody will use computers unconsciously in their daily lives. To realise such a society, we need to construct some friendly environment in which men and computers can communicate easily through information in various forms such as voice, sentences, figures and tables, which are a natural means for people to exchange information.

Technological background

The present generation of computers has been defined in terms of the basic circuit elements such as tubes, transistors, integrated circuits, and large-scale integrations. This means that there have been no substantial changes in the fundamental design philosophy and the application objectives of computers.

On the other hand, the Fifth Generation computers are expected to change their design philosophy and application fields as well as their circuit elements (the change to Very Large-Scale Integration (VLSI)). This change will be more drastic than the ones of previous computer generations. Up until now the design philosophy of computers has been based on the evaluation criteria that the hardware of computers should be as simple as possible, and almost all of the complicated logic should rely on the software, as the hardware elements have been very expensive, very large, short lived, and consumed a large amount of electric power. This philosophy has brought about the present giant computers, through the pursuit of high speed and large capacity, with the architecture of sequential control of the stored program. The major factors that require some novel design philosophy of computers at present are as follows:

1 The speed of circuit device is going to reach the limit of electric propagation speed.

2 In a few years, we will be able to use as much hardware as we need, as the hardware cost will decrease dramatically through VLSI technology.

3 Some parallel processing systems are required in order to make the best use of the mass production effect of VLSI.

4 Present conventional computers lack many of such basic functions as non-numerical data (such as voice, sentences, figures and images) processing, inference, association and learning that are required by the processing of artificial intelligence.

Computers were first designed as numerical calculation machines. Their application field expanded rapidly to such areas as control, information media processing, and artificial intelligence, without substantial change of their design philosophy. However, computers are required to get rid of the numerical calculation-oriented machines and to shift to such machines that can process artificial intelligence problems with the semantics of information taken into account. To achieve this objective, we should solve the problems listed below.

1 To realise such basic functions as inference, association and learning, as the nucleus functions of the Fifth Generation computers, which are going to be implemented by hardware.

2 To equip perfectly various kinds of basic software for artificial intelligence, thus mastering the basic functions.

3 To realise friendly man/machine interfaces which are natural for human beings, through utilising the research results of pattern recognition technology and artificial intelligence.

4 To realise some excellent developing support systems to resolve the so-called software crisis and to make the productivity of software high.

In the process of solving these problems, we should take the various research results into account, such as VLSI technology, software engineering and artificial intelligence.

CONCEPTUAL IMAGE OF FIFTH GENERATION COMPUTER SYSTEMS

Basic concept

The FGCSs are oriented to knowledge information processing that is based on the innovative theories and technologies offering the intelligent dialogue functions and the inference mechanism for knowledge bases that will be required in the 1990s. The functions of FGCSs can be divided into three kinds as follows:

1 Problem-solving and inference function.
2 Knowledge base management function.
3 Intelligent inferface function.

The problem-solving and inference function corresponds to the basic four arithmetic operations (plus, minus, multiply, divide) and the control functions needed to perform arithmetic calculations. The system which realises this function will be organised by the hardware inference mechanism, the control mechanism of parallel processing, the logic programs made up on these mechanisms, and the software system for higher-order predicate calculus. A language which includes the language PROLOG will be used as the interface between software and hardware. The knowledge-base management function is an innovative database management function which is enhanced by the processing function of semantic information. The relational data model is selected as the basic data model, which matches to PROLOG very well. The software of knowledge-base management will be implemented over the hardware function which processes the relational algebra in parallel.

Intelligent interface function, which corresponds to the input/output function of conventional computers at present, will consist of a collection of systems which process, recognise or synthesise many kinds of input/output media such as characters, voice, figures, and images. We think that it is very important to offer some friendly interfaces for humans to exchange information with FGCSs. These functions are realised through corresponding software and hardware systems. The conceptual image of FGCSs is shown in Figure 1, in which the modelling (software) system represents the final image of the software development, and the machine (hardware) system the hardware development, respectively. The upper half of the modelling system corresponds to the problem-solving and inference function, and the lower half to the knowledge-base management function. The left duplicated area with the circle of human systems corresponds to the intelligent interface function, which depends heavily on the previous two functions as shown in the Figure. This Figure shows that computers will closely approach the human system through a remarkable improvement of the logical level of the hardware system and by placing the modelling system between the hardware system and the human system.

In the knowledge-base system, three kinds of knowledge are stored: knowledge about problem domain; knowledge regarding languages, images etc which are used by the intelligent interface function; and knowledge about the machine system and knowledge representation.

When some problem is presented by the human system through some end-user language that uses voice, figures and images this problem is analysed and recognised by using knowledge about the language and the images, and is transformed into intermediate specifications which are given to the intelligent programming system. The problem is understood here using the knowledge about the problem domain, and the processing

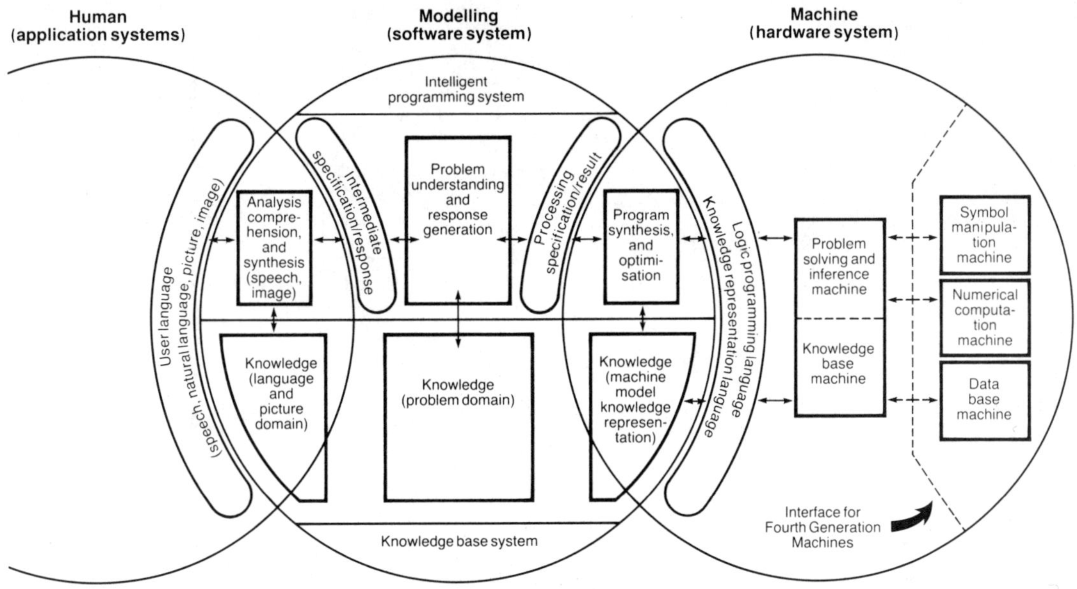

Figure 1: Conceptual diagram of the Fifth Generation Computer Systems

specification is made up as the result. This specification is transformed into a program and optimised through referencing the knowledge about the machine system and knowledge representation. The program, written in a logic programming language, is processed by the problem-solving and inference machine and the knowledge-base machine, both of which are in the hardware system of the FGCS. (The processing at the intelligent programming system is done using the machine system, of course.) We think that such hardware as the symbol manipulation machine, scientific calculation machine and database machine can be regarded as machines which undertake to subcontract from the problem-solving and inference machine and the knowledge-base machine. As all of the computer hardware up to the Fourth Generation play only the role of the subcontractor, we can say that the functions of hardware and software of FGCSs make the semantic gap between human and machine very small.

The processing results flow in the opposite direction, and are transformed into a response to the human system which is synthesised by the intelligent programming system into a form such as figures and voice which humans can understand easily.

Configuration image of FGCSs

The software and hardware systems which realise the three functions stated above are combined to make up a general-purpose machine, of which the configuration image is shown in Figure 2.

While the basic software system of FGCSs corresponds to the operating system of the present computers, it is made of three systems: the problem-solving and inference system, the knowledge management system and the intelligent interface system. These

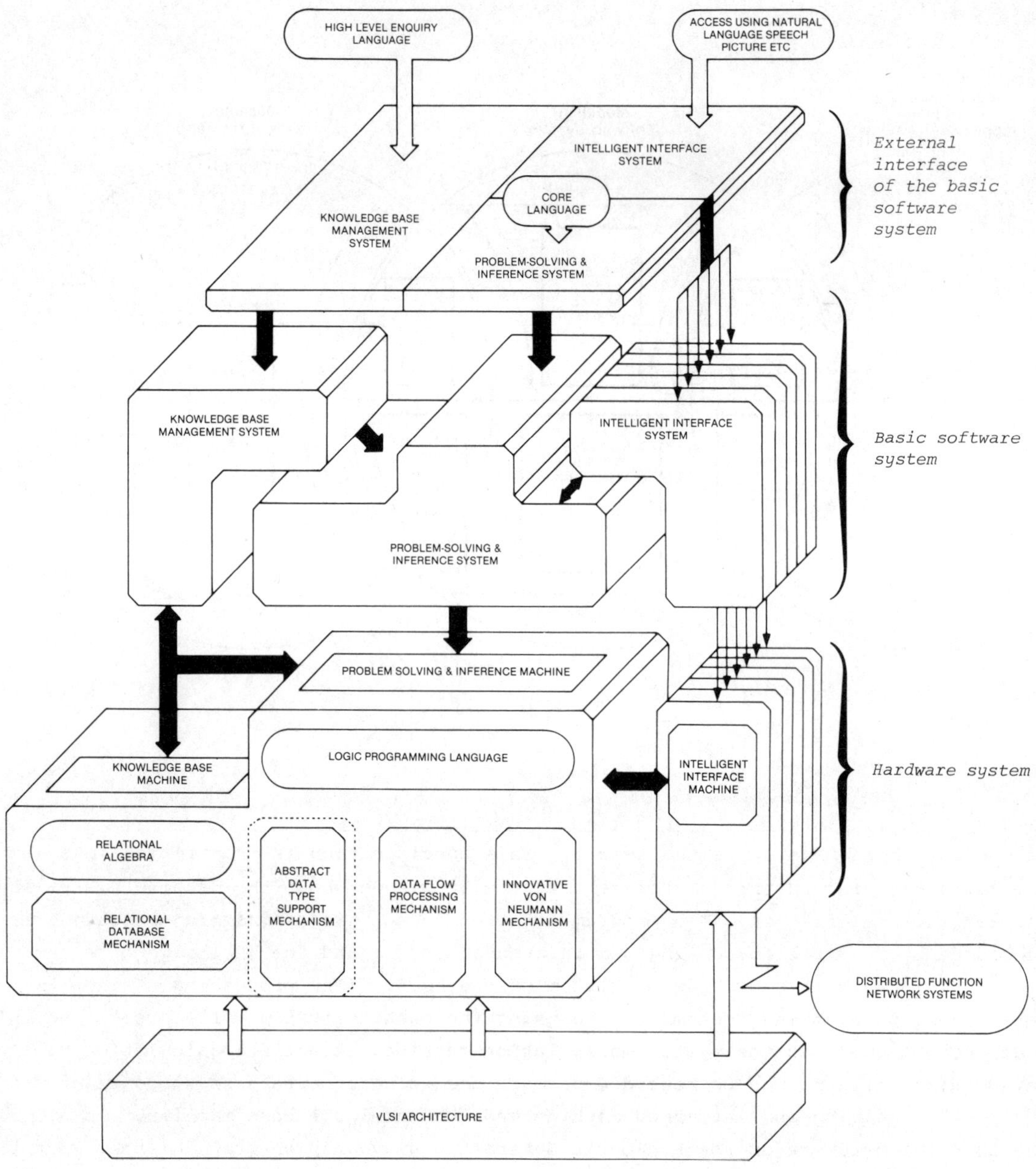

Figure 2: Basic configuration image of the Fifth Generation Computer Systems

three systems are supported by the problem-solving and inference machine, the knowledge-base machine and the intelligent interface machine, respectively. The problem-solving and inference machine which processes logic programming languages such as PROLOG is equipped with a high-power inference mechanism of hardware and a data-flow control mechanism for parallel processing. The innovative von Neumann mechanism will be provided to accept the conventional programs effectively. The abstract data type support mechanism is required from the viewpoint of data security, module programming, and many other reasons as well.

The knowledge-base machine will be realised by the combination of the relational database mechanism and the parallel processing machine of relational algebra operations, and be integrated with the problem-solving and inference machine through the supporting mechanism of abstract data types.

The intelligent interface machine will be organised as a set of many special machines dedicated to each medium such as voice-understanding/synthesising machine and image-understanding machine.

As the performance level required by each function will vary in practice depending on the needs, the system organisation is required to adapt to the various types of performance needs of the many application fields. Therefore, it will be necessary to build some special machines which are dedicated to any of the three functions.

These machines, of which machine language is a common kernel language for FGCSs, can be connected to each other to organise a distributed processing system. This kernel language interfaces the software system with the hardware system. All software systems are represented by this kernel language which the hardware system executes directly. For the implementation of this hardware, VLSI technology is indispensable as the number of gates required will be very large.

CONFIGURATION IMAGE OF SOFTWARE SYSTEMS

New computer software

The FGCSs need a lot of innovative software technology. The interface between hardware and software is the kernel language; defined by introducing the concept of a modal logic and higher order logic into the basic subset of first order predicate calculus. Though the level of this language is higher than the other conventional high-level languages at present, this is not one of the user-oriented languages. They will be developed as higher-level languages based on the kernel language. One of the highest-level languages can be thought to be a subset of a natural language.

Knowledge representation languages are required to store and adjust knowledge data. A knowledge management function is needed to add new knowledge data and change the stored knowledge. In order to realise such a capability for solving problems by utilising knowledge, it is necessary to develop a higher level of inference functions than the basic inference function realised by the kernel language. The functions of normal predicate calculus or other logic systems are realised by combining the functions of the kernel language. To execute inference operations very efficiently through combining adroitly the enormous amount of knowledge, some meta-inference functions, that is the inference about inference, are needed, which can be thought to be the control functions of inference. Knowledge acquisition, which is harder than the problems stated before, needs an induction function (ie hypothesising) which is organised by combining the meta-inference and the high-order inference.

We cannot expect to have some theoretically complete (algorithmic) methods, but will be using the less precise heuristic methods. These heuristic methods, which can be seen as meta-knowledge that represents knowledge about inference or knowledge about knowledge, should be developed with the establishment of their theoretical basis, which can be a methodology to select some proper subsystems, though they do tend to be seen as *ad hoc* methods.

The function of knowledge processing (problem-solving-oriented inference in other words), which is realised through the combination of the basic functions of kernel language, can be seen as an innovative programming for the Fifth Generation computers. We will be able to apply various methods which have been developed at the software engineering field, though we still have the problem of program productivity. These methods such as correctness verification of programs, transformation and synthesis of programs from specifications, algorithms bank, etc will be regarded as more natural ones and be simplified in the new environment so that they will be able to be applied to larger problems. We should seek to improve these methods.

On the other hand, the management and utilisation of knowledge needs higher-level functions for database handling. The relational database functions will be included into the kernel language, as its theory is based on the first order predicate calculus. Up to this time, programming languages and database languages have been developed as separate systems. However, these will be unified and fused into one at the kernel language development. It is also the premise of knowledge information processing.

The conversational functions of FGCSs should be natural for humans. We need natural language, and figures and so on from the information point of view, and voice and images from the media point of view. For example, to realise the conversational capability through natural languages, it will be necessary to have such capabilities as grammar and semantics processing, which the kernel language should be able to realise naturally and effectively. For voice utilisation, the recognition process needs some inference processing and is related to the natural language processing very closely, though the analysis and synthesis of voice waveforms belongs to signal processing technology.

The Fifth Generation computer software system

Global configuration

Besides the basic software system which offers the three basic functions stated above, the Fifth Generation computer software system includes the intelligent programming system which aims at the development of new software technology, and the basic application systems. Figure 3 shows the total configuration image of the Fifth Generation computer software system.

The software system offers various kinds of language which match very well to each level of FGCS users. System programmers make up programs utilising the kernel language itself. The engineers who develop some professional systems make up programs using the knowledge representation languages. Many kinds of consultation systems interact to users through somewhat limited natural languages, voice, figures, images etc. For each level of languages, the supporting system will be developed to help the users to use them easily.

Basic software system

The basic software system is composed of three systems: the problem-solving and inference system, the knowledge-base management system and the intelligent interface system. The final target of the program-solving and inference system is a cooperation program-solving system which solves a problem through the cooperation of more than two problem-solving systems.

For example, we can imagine a system that is a program-solving system on a knowledge

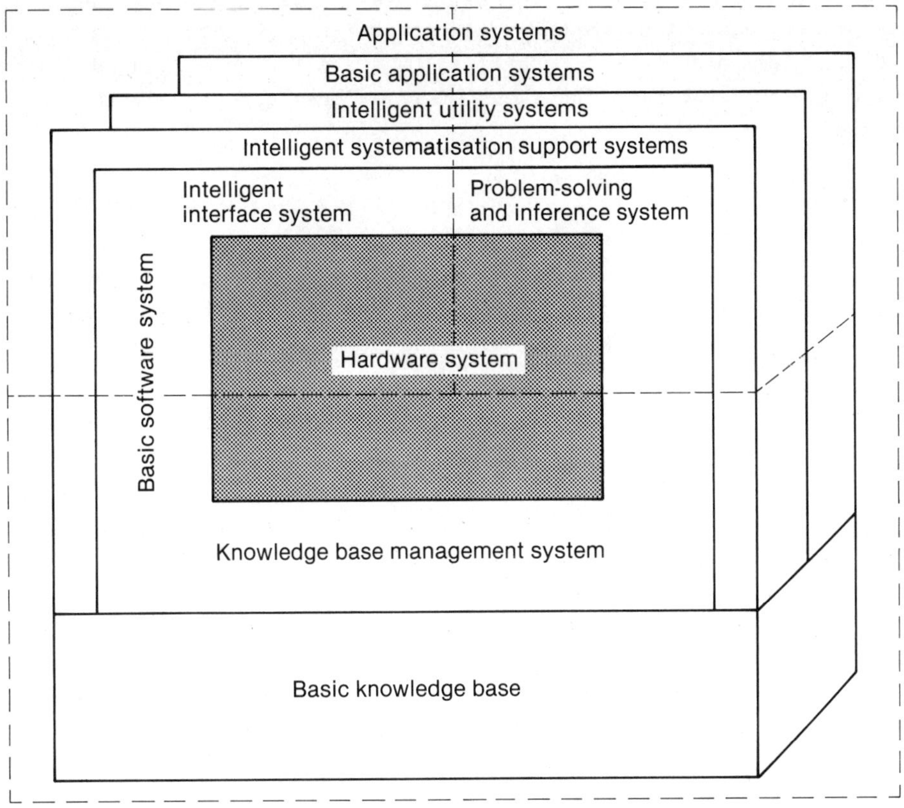

Figure 3: Configuration of the Fifth Generation computer software system

base which utilises an external large-scale database just as humans would use a library as a knowledge source. This system solves each problem through the cooperated work between the knowledge-base system corresponding to the library user and the large-scale database corresponding to the library, both of which are problem-solving systems equipped with inference capability. Another example is the case of cooperated diagnosis for medical treatment between a surgeon and a physician. For this cooperation, we need a meta-inference system that performs the inference about the inference process of each program-solving system, or the inference about the knowledge of the other party. This meta-inference system requires such functions as daily inference (implicit inference), inductive inference, and analogy, all of which are higher-level inference functions. These functions are going to be implemented by software using the kernel language of which the basic operation is the syllogism - the basic operation of deduction.

Functions implemented by the kernel language itself are as follows:

1 The control function for trial-and-error programs in which the threads of computation cannot be defined uniquely.

2 The deductive inference function.

3 A part of the meta-inference function (meta-inference basic function).

The kernel language can be seen as the specification of the hardware inference machine.

The software of the knowledge-base management function consists of the knowledge representation system, the knowledge-base design and maintenance support system, the large-scale knowledge-base system, the experimental knowledge acquisition system and the distributed knowledge-base management system. These systems will be integrated with the cooperative program-solving system. Especially, the knowledge acquisition is expected to be semi-automatic, that is, equipped with some learning capability. Functions that should be implemented by the kernel language are the relational database interface (the defining and the searching functions of relations) and part of the consistency check operations.

At the intelligent interface function, we can provide functions to enable human interaction with the computer very naturally through natural language, voice, figures and images. As natural language processing gives the basis of translation, the foreign languages (such as English) as well as Japanese can be set as the object languages. The final target is a system which can handle more than ten thousand basic words, with the exception of professional words, with less than two thousand grammatical rules, and can also analyse syntactically 99% of input sentences correctly.

The target of voice processing is a system which can handle multispeaker and continuous spoken Japanese with a vocabulary of more than 50 thousand words, and whose word-recognition rate is more than 95% at a rate three times faster than the real-time speech.

Regarding figure and image processing, we are going to develop a system which stores hundreds of thousands of pieces of figure and image information together with their structure information, and which can be used for the knowledge information processing system.

Intelligent programming system

The intelligent programming system is based on the kernel language developed on a new concept and the module programming derived from abstract data type technology, it aims at an automatic program synthesis and supports a consultation system for program development through software engineering technology. As a concrete target, it intends to realise the program synthesis at module level through the development of basic modules and the management of their data bank. The object software, which forms the basis of the basic modules, is used for such fields as office processing and robot control. The intelligent programming system is going to support users especially strongly at the design stage, and at the modification and improvement stage of programs, this is a particularly expensive procedure and takes up almost all of the software development cost. As a result, the total productivity of software is expected to be more than ten times higher than at present.

Basic application systems

The basic applications systems, which we imagine will be the basic and common systems for a wide variety of applications in the 1990s, are the machine translation system and the many kinds of consultation system. The machine translation system is expected to have the capability of translating several languages, and being able to handle hundreds of thousands of words with 90% precision, the rest of the translation is human aided. This system will be developed as a total system used by computers at each stage between the text editing and the final printing of translated results. The total translation cost is expected to be less than 30% of the cost of human translators.

Examples of consultation systems are found in medical diagnosis, natural language understanding, computer-aided design of machines, computer users' consultation, computer system diagnosis and so on. Each system will be made of more than five thousand objects and more than ten thousand inference rules, and use more than five thousand words. It is expected to have semi-automatic knowledge acquisition capability with the system interface of natural language and speech.

CONFIGURATION IMAGE OF HARDWARE SYSTEMS

New computer architecture

The Fifth Generation computer, which is oriented towards the knowledge information processing systems, should be supported by the basic functions of the computer architecture to realise such processing efficiently. Accordingly, the architecture of the Fifth Generation must satisfy the needs from knowledge information processing systems, with many new technologies to be taken into account. The technologies that will be closely related to the architecture are as follows:

1 VLSI technology which includes new high-speed devices.

2 Technology to realise parallel processing at a high level.

3 Distributed processing technology which integrates high-performance personal computers, distributed databases and computer networks.

4 Software technology, such as new programming languages, programming environment and automatic programming, to improve the productivity of software development.

5 Technology to process the many kinds of pattern information efficiently.

6 Artificial intelligence technology to realise knowledge bases, inference mechanisms and natural language processing.

7 Systematising technology to realise user systems.

The kernel functions of FGCSs are the following three functions as stated previously:

1 *Problem-solving and inference function*: means that it is necessary to establish a high-level architecture based on the computation models of a functional or predicate calculus type, which are higher in the logic level than the conventional von Neumann architecture.

2 *Knowledge-base management function*: aims at the realisation of large-scale databases which are needed to make up the many application systems of knowledge information processing, and at the perfect provision of high-speed inference and retrieval processing capability.

3 *Intelligent interface function*: the objective is to offer some friendly means which facilitates natural information processing for humans through dialogue with computers using voice, images, or natural languages.

The requirement of this high-level architecture is to shorten the semantic gap which is said to be one of the causes of low productivity and low reliability of software on conventional computers, and to utilise effectively new software technology such as modular programming based on the abstract data type concept, and program verification and synthesis. As the software of the Fifth Generation is going to build a very high level of functions, the program scale is expected to be very large, and such high-level architecture as stated above will be indispensable.

The processing performance and storage capacity of the inference and knowledge base will have to be 100~1000 times higher than the ones of conventional computers when the implementation of intelligent dialogue function is considered. Accordingly, it is necessary to use high-speed devices and a parallel processing architecture of a very high level, and to implement through VLSI. Moreover, as the inference and knowledge-base processing require very efficient processing capability for non-numerical information and symbols that cannot be handled efficiently on the conventional computers, it is necessary to develop some excellent architecture that will match processing.

Hardware elements of FGCSs

The basic hardware elements of an FGCS can be thought to be the following machines:

1 Problem-solving and inference machine which realises the high-level architecture and the high-speed of processing.

2 Knowledge-base machine, which supports large-scale data and has a high-speed retrieval capability for the knowledge-base system.

At the development process of these machines, we need to develop an experimental machine and other technology, as follows.

3 Inference machine of sequential type (a pilot model for the software development) which supports the kernel language of the Fifth Generation computers, and helps to improve the efficiency of software development.

4 VLSI technology and system architecture, which is essential to make up VLSI chips needed to build machine hardware and user-oriented systems.

Problem-solving and inference machines

There are two necessary conditions for the inference machines. Firstly, the architecture should be high enough to support the Fifth Generation computer kernel language and its computation model that defines the interface between software and hardware of the Fifth Generation computer. Secondly, it should have enough processing performance and storage capacity to implement the basic applications of knowledge information processing such as natural language processing and many kinds of consultation system. Regarding the high storage capacity architecture, the technology will be developed by the research of knowledge-base machines. Accordingly, the inference machine aims specially at high-speed processing.

We think that the data-flow architecture will fit the basic hardware mechanism of the inference machine very well. The data-flow architecture can not only pull out as many parallelisms contained in the program as possible, but also matches very well to functional languages which can be good interfaces to the inference processing.

The inference machine will provide the abstract data type mechanism which supports modular programming based on the abstract data type contained in the kernel language specification of Fifth Generation computers, and the description technology of parallel processing and distributed processing. Moreover, it will be supported by a parallel inference mechanism that enables the parallel execution of unification and resolution operations which are the principal ones for mechanical inference and are extracted directly from the predicate calculus and the computation model.

Knowledge-base machine

The hardware of the knowledge-base machine supports the large storage capability of the knowledge base and the high-speed processing of store, retrieve and modification operations. As the problem-solving and inference, and the knowledge-base management are closely related to each other, it will be impossible to divide both hardware units into perfect separate units of the Fifth Generation computer as with the controller and memory units of conventional computers. Accordingly, both functions will be fused into one unit for the prototype architecture of the Fifth Generation computers. However, at the first stage of development, both functions will be separated, and the research and development will be done in parallel for the problem-solving and inference machine, and the knowledge-base machine.

We regard the relational database machine as the basic mechanism of knowledge-base machine. The relational operations will be supported by high level of parallel and pipeline processing mechanism based on the concept of data flow and stream processing. On the mechanism which implements relational operation, some expansion and improvement will be done to support the knowledge operations. At the final stage of development, the basic processing mechanism of the knowledge base will be extracted from the fused mechanism of the inference function and the knowledge base management function rather than be based on the relational database machine.

Sequential inference machine

The pilot model for the development of software will be developed primarily to support the zero version of the Fifth Generation kernel language and to be used as the tool for the research of the kernel language specification, and additionally for the trial production of a processing system, and for the research and development of higher order inference and knowledge-base system software. This machine will be used not only as a workbench for the test of architecture, but also as the high-level function terminal for VLSI-CAD system. As this machine should be developed as soon as possible, it will be developed as a firmware-based machine which utilises high-speed microprocessors. It will be provided by a high-density display, input and output functions through voice and the Japanese language, a local network facility, and a relational algebra interface which enables connection to the experimental relational database machine. Furthermore, it will be equipped with the interpreter and the compiler of the zero version kernel language, debugging tools such as debugger and stepper, and word-processing software that includes an editor and Japanese facility.

VLSI technology and system architecture

It seems to us very natural that the computers in the 1990s will use VLSI including more than one million transistors per chip. The research of VLSI requires such a VLSI algorithm as to help specify the functions to be included in the chip, and the design support system (VLSI-CAD) which is needed to produce VLSIs. This VLSI-CAD system is going to be developed on a development support system, which will be used as the environment for software development, as well. The development support system, implemented using a high-speed local network, will be expected to grow to a knowledge information network including the Fifth Generation computer prototypes and a lot of personal inference machines. The members are connected through a very high-level interface and will be able to communicate with each other freely as if they are totally one system.

RESEARCH AND DEVELOPMENT SCHEDULE

Global research and development planning

The research and development of the FGCS aims at a very high level of objectives far beyond conventional computers. As this kind of research and development is evolutional and we have no such experiences, we have to build the object system by producing a lot of original ideas and repeating many trial and error procedures. However, the accumulation of fundamental researches which are expected to be the basis of such ambitious technology, such as knowledge information processing, is limited in its results and human resources at present. This is particularly evident in the software and fundamental theory fields. As the major objective of this project is to establish the basic computer technology which will be required in the 1990s, a very wide range of fundamental technology should be included and examined on the process of research.

Considering these conditions, we allowed 10 years for the period of research and development; divided into the initial stage of three years, the interim stage of four years and the final stage of three years. At the initial stage, research and development emphasis is placed on the evaluation and reorganisation of current technology in the field of knowledge information processing, and the development of a fundamental technology for the interim stage by selecting a few candidates in each theme.

At the interim stage, we are going to produce experimental subsystems of small or medium scale through setting up the basic computation model, the implementation algorithm, and the basic architecture, based on the evaluation results of the initial stage for elementary technology. At the final stage, we will be able to design the interface between software and hardware which balances their functions, matches their characteristics, and fixes the organisation of the total system.

So far as the concrete work procedures are concerned, many kinds of element modules of software and hardware will be built, and some experimental systems will be developed by combining the modules at the initial stage. These will include hardware simulators, software simulators, trial systems of language processors and experimental systems of natural language processing. At the interim stage, the improvement and expansion of the results of initial stage will be done, and two subsystems, the inference subsystem and the knowledge-base subsystem, will be developed by combining the results. These two subsystems, which necessarily must be developed independently will have many hardware and software problems to be solved before their completion. At the beginning of the final stage, we should evaluate the organisation of those software and hardware systems which were developed at the interim stage, and build up a detailed description of the final target. This description is expected to clarify the concrete image of the total system in which the two subsystems are fused.

Research and development themes

Following are the research and development themes to be executed:

1 Problem-solving and inference system:
- Problem-solving and inference mechanism
- Problem-solving and inference machine.

2 Knowledge-base system:
- Knowledge-base mechanism
- Knowledge-base machine.

3 Intelligent interface system.

4 Development support system:
- Pilot model for software development
- VLSI technology and system architecture.

5 Basic application systems:
- Machine translation system
- Consultation system
- Intelligent programming system.

Research and development schedule

The theme of the problem-solving and inference system is to develop a hardware inference machine and the software product of a cooperative problem-solving system. Three versions of kernel language will be developed, of which the zero and first versions will be developed within the initial stage, with the second version being developed at the interim stage. The development of the cooperative problem-solving system will be done at the interim stage on a full scale. Regarding inference machines, sequential inference machines will be developed as one of the development support systems using the zero version kernel language. At the interim stage, an inference machine subsystem will be developed using the first version of kernel language. To support this subsystem, elemental technology such as data-flow machine and hardware support for parallel inference operation will be developed at the initial stage. At the final stage, a total system will be developed integrating the inference machine and the knowledge-base machine. This system uses the second version of the kernel language.

The brief for the knowledge-base system, which handles the storage and management functions of data and rules, is to develop a very wide range of technology from the utilisation technology to the hardware technology. Regarding the utilisation technology, a knowledge representation system will be developed. A knowledge representation language and a development support system for knowledge-base design will be made up at the initial stage. At the interim stage or after, the emphasis of research will be placed on the knowledge acquisition. As for the research and development of hardware systems, a relational database machine and a database system of very large scale will be developed at the initial stage. Elemental technology which will be developed at the initial stage and be used at the interim stage includes the relational operation mechanism of highly parallel type, the implementation method of knowledge operations, and the organisation method of memory hierarchy systems. At the interim stage, we are going to develop a knowledge-base machine subsystem of parallel type and a distributed knowledge-base management system. The integration towards a total system will be done at the final stage.

The theme of the intelligent interface system will be focused on the research and development of natural language processing, and will be combined with voice processing. The initial stage will be oriented toward basic research, the interim stage toward an experimental system of small scale, and the final stage toward an experimental system of practical scale. The research of figure and image processing centres around the development of an image database from the knowledge representation point of view.

As for the development support system, a pilot model for software development will be developed within the initial stage. This pilot model will be used as the model of a super personal computer for logic programming, which will be used as the research and development tools for the interim stage or later. Moreover, it can be regarded as a system which leads to the inference subsystem and the knowledge-base subsystem.

The theme of VLSI technology and system architecture aims at the research and development of a knowledge information processing network which is evolved from the intelligent VLSI-CAD system and the distributed processing system. This network should be useful enough to be used as a research and development tool.

Among basic application systems, the research and development of an intelligent programming system will be started from the beginning. At the initial stage, a modular programming system will be developed, which will be used on the pilot model for software development. The automatic programming system will be investigated on a full scale at the interim stage. The research and development of machine translation systems and consultation systems will start from the interim stage. Their fundamental technology will be developed at the initial stage through the theme of knowledge representation system for the intelligent interface system. The fields of which consultation systems are going to be developed will be decided by the end of the initial stage. They should cover the wide application areas of knowledge information processing.

CONCLUSION

The Fifth Generation computer project intends to develop the knowledge information processing systems which are based on the problem solving and inference mechanism and the knowledge base. This means that the fundamental computer functions will be improved drastically and computer capability will be expanded largely beyond the one of present computers. When this objective is achieved, we can truly enjoy the computer power for the prosperity of human beings. However, we must solve a lot of difficult problems to attain the objective, as it is of a very high level compared to the functional level of conventional computers. Though Japan started this project, international cooperation is indispensable for the success of the project. We cannot expect to attain the objective within so short a period as 10 years without close international cooperation. We hope that the international cooperation will grow rapidly among many countries toward the common benefit of the world.

APPLICATIONS ON THE DAP

D Parkinson

Queen Mary College
London
UK

D PARKINSON became interested in computing whilst studying in Belfast for a PhD in Theoretical Physics, and was an early user of the Deuce computer. After completing his PhD Professor Parkinson worked for a number of years for the Atomic Energy Authority using large-scale computers for the solution of problems in science and technology. On leaving the Atomic Energy Authority Professor Parkinson worked in Italy for the European Space Organisation where he was responsible for a computer installation giving services to a technical laboratory. About seven years ago he joined ICL as a consultant in the use of computers for large-scale technical calculations and subsequently specialised in parallel processing systems. Professor Parkinson was responsible for the applicability of the ICL DAP. Since Spring 1979 he has been a Visiting Professor in the Department of Computer Science and Statistics of Queen Mary College and is Technical Head of the Specialist Unit (DAP Support Unit) which took delivery of the first production DAP in May 1980. He aids the user community in the use of this very new kind of facility.

APPLICATIONS ON THE DAP

Many problems do not appear to be parallel when examined from the point of view of serial implementation. This paper discusses the implementation of a number of problems on the highly parallel DAP system and shows how to discover hidden parallelism. A description of how to deal with problems larger than the size of a parallel computer is given and it is shown that often the adaptation of well known serial algorithms is appropriate. The bit-oriented nature of the DAP means that logical adaptations are extremely efficient. The paper concludes with a brief outline of a number of application areas studied by users of the Queen Mary College DAP.

INTRODUCTION

The DAP is a 64 × 64 array of identical bit-organised processing elements operated in Single Instruction Multiple Datastream (SIMD) environments. A very important question is 'What applications are well suited to the DAP architecture?'. Although the question is often posed in this form it is really a substitute for a more meaningful question, 'In an environment equipped with a classical serial computer and a DAP, what applications should be run on the DAP and what applications should continue to run on the serial machine?'.

The important difference between this question and the original question is the introduction of a comparison between a DAP approach and an alternative approach, rather than an attempt to evaluate the DAP in some absolute fashion. The reason for this change is that there may be applications which appear to use the DAP inefficiently but which use the alternative systems even more inefficiently. If we did not introduce this comparison then one might very easily reject good DAP applications just because they failed to meet some arbitrary efficiency measure.

In this paper we shall give a description of some of the considerations taken into account when examining applications for implementation on the DAP and describe some of the application areas that have so far been investigated using the DAP at Queen Mary College.

Before starting it is important to understand the environment in which the application studies are carried out. The DAP user has available a number of hardware/software tools, briefly these are:

1 A classical host computer with standard peripherals and software.

2 A 64 × 64 DAP attached to the host as a 2Mb memory enhancement.

3 A very low-level programming language (APAL) essentially for microprogramming the DAP.

4 A FORTRAN-like language (DAP-FORTRAN) which can be considered similar in efficiency to an assembly-level language.

The first and only golden rule for selecting suitable DAP applications is to choose only those applications whose performance is limited by processing power. The rule is obvious as applications limited by input/output capacity cannot show much benefit from increased CPU capacity. Provided that one has an application limited by CPU power and which requires large CPU resources then there appears to be every prospect that the DAP will be effective for the application, although some effort may be needed to develop an appropriate parallel algorithm. The greatest hurdle that a new programmer has to overcome is to learn to consider applications rather than algorithms. The last 30 years of application development have been concerned with exploiting the essentially serial nature of computer processing and finding methods which maximise the benefits to be gained by choosing a correct ordering. The advent of parallel computing means that many of the basic assumptions behind the algorithms are incorrect and that alternative ways of solving tasks are more efficient. The challenge for the application programmer is to discover the inherent parellelism in a task - a parallelism which has often been obscured by serial computer programming methodology.

HIDDEN PARALLELISM

There are many tasks which are obviously parallel in nature and which most programmers would see immediately are ideally suitable for parallel computation. Such obvious tasks are many of the so called 'vector operations' for operations such as matrix addition or subtraction. There are many other tasks which do not appear at all suitable for parallel computing and which the uneducated will therefore reject, even though the tasks are indeed highly parallel. A very instructive example occurs in the study of methods for the iterative solution of sets of linear equations. A typical problem arises from the need to solve sets of equations of the type:

$$a_{ij}\, x_{i-1,j} + b_{ij}\, x_{i,j-1} + c_{ij}\, x_{i,j} + d_{ij}\, x_{i+1,j} + e_{ij}\, x_{i,j+1} = f_{ij}$$

$$i = 1....: N; \quad j = 1....M$$

Such equations often occur in the solution of partial differential equations in two dimensions. The coefficients a, b, c, d and e often vary with (ij) but with no great loss of generality, we can study the equations in the form:

$$x_{i,j} = \alpha\left[x_{i-1,j} + x_{i+1,j} + x_{i,j+1} + x_{i,j-1}\right] + B_{ij}$$

These equations are often solved by iterative methods where $x^n_{i,j}$ is the n-th approximation to $x_{i,j}$.

There are many iterative schemes in the literature and it is not appropriate to discuss them all here, but we consider two typical schemes: Jacobi iteration which is an 'obviously parallel' algorithm and Gauss-Seidel iteration - an 'obviously sequential' algorithm.

The Jacobi scheme computes the n+1 iteration from the n-th iteration using the formulae:

$$x^{n+1}_{ij} = \alpha\left[x^n_{i-1,j} + x^n_{i+1,j} + x^n_{i,j} + x^n_{i,j-1}\right] + B_{ij} \quad \text{all } i \text{ and } j$$

If we assume that we have an estimate for $x^n_{i,j}$ for all i and j then it is evident that we can compute all the x^{n+1}_{ij} quantities in any order as the values are not dependent on each other, hence the Jacobi iteration scheme is easily implemented on a parallel computer and can readily use as many processors as there are unknowns $(N*M)$. Typical large problems may have 10^4 unknowns (or even 10^6 unknowns for the three-dimensional analogue) and it is easy to see that Jacobi-type algorithms will map onto highly parallel DAP-like systems.

Jacobi methods are not often used on serial computers for two reasons:

1 The convergence is usually slow.

2 They require excessive intermediate storage as all values of x^n and x^{n+1} must be available simultaneously.

If one attempts to program the Jacobi algorithm on a serial computer it is necessary to pick an order in which to compute the $n+1$ iteration. This order is usually implemented by pair of nested loops of the type:

```
for i:= 1 to N
     for j:= 1 to M
     compute x^{n+1}_{i,j}
```

The moment it is acknowledged that an ordering is used then the idea of always using the most recently updated values is attractive. This idea allows the programmer to overwrite old values and save store and has also been shown to speed convergence. The scheme is the well known Gauss-Seidel algorithm and is expressed by the iteration scheme:

$$x^{n+1}_{i,j} = \alpha(x^{n+1}_{i-1,j} + x^{n+1}_{i,j-1} + x^{n}_{i,j+1} + x^{n}_{i+1,j}) + B_{ij}$$

This scheme has no obvious parallelism and is just one example of an algorithm developed to maximise the benefits of serial computation. The uneducated programmer will dismiss this algorithm as unsuitable for parallel computation as 'obviously we cannot compute x^{n+1}_{ij} until $x^{n+1}_{i-1,j}$ and $x^{n+1}_{i,j-1}$ are known and so only one value may be computed at a time'. This view is incorrect! Let us examine the operations more carefully.

Suppose we have an estimate for $x^{n}_{i,j}$ for all i,j then the iteration scheme only allows us to compute a new value for $x^{n+1}_{1,1}$ as indeed our beginner would deduce. Once $x^{n+1}_{1,1}$ is known then we have all the information needed to compute $x^{n+1}_{1,2}$ and $x^{n+1}_{2,1}$ so two points may be computed in parallel. Once these two points have been computed it is possible to compute $x^{n+1}_{1,3}$; $x^{n+1}_{2,2}$; $x^{n+1}_{3,1}$ simultaneously. In general it turns out that one can compute simultaneously all values $x^{n+1}_{i,j}$; $i+j = k$ if $x^{n+1}_{i,j}$ for $i+j = k-1$ are known. The 'one degree' of parallelism has immediately turned into up to N degrees of parallelism ie a point at a time has turned into a diagonal at a time.

The analysis does not stop at this point, it is of the essence of the algorithm that many iterations are going to be done and therefore it is *not* essential to wait until one iteration is completed before the next is started. If we carefully examine the known data when we are about to compute:

$$x^{n+1}_{1,3} \; ; \; x^{n+1}_{2,2} \; ; \; x^{n+1}_{3,1}$$

we have computed:

$$x^{n+1}_{1,2} \; ; \; x^{n+1}_{2,1}$$

which are the two values needed to compute $x^{n+2}_{1,1}$! We therefore may start the next iteration. Further study shows that when the diagonal $x^{n+1}_{i,j}$ $\{i+j = K\}$ is being computed then we can:

compute the diagonal $K-2$ for iteration $n+2$
compute the diagonal $K-4$ for iteration $n+3$

compute the diagonal $K-6$ for iteration $n+4$
etc
etc.

The end result of this investigation is that by overlapping iterations we can compute every other diagonal simultaneously and hence update half the equations. This simple study has taken us from one degree of parallelism to N degrees of parallelism to $N^2/2$ degrees of parallelism without altering the fundamental mathematical processes. If the cells in the set $\{i,j\}$ were coloured red or black as in a chess board it will be seen that the Gauss-Seidel algorithm with overlapped iterations updates all cells of the same colour simultaneously and indeed the algorithm is identical to the RED-BLACK iteration scheme which is usually presented as if it were a separate parallel algorithm.

We have presented this algorithm at length as it shows a number of common aspects in the study of parallel application design. The two major lessons that the reader should learn are:

1 Be careful not to make hasty judgements about algorithms because they appear serial in nature.

2 Be careful not to put artificial unnecessary constraint on subproblems.

This second point is most important; if the programmer insisted on trying to replicate the subproblem of computing x^{n+1} given x^n then the maximum degree of parallelism is N. The task is not just to repeat the subproblem a large number of times, it is to solve the equations and artificially constraining the real task can lose the parallelism.

Another way of expressing this lesson is to realise that although loops in serial programs are indicative of potential parallelism it is often the case that the innermost loop is not the best one to exploit and a reordering of the loops is often beneficial.

This section has considered only the essential parallelism with a given task. The DAP, like any parallel computer, has only a fixed degree of parallelism, an important part of any application study is the matching of the parallelism of the system with the parallelism of the algorithm, we consider this task below.

MATCHING THE PROBLEM TO THE MACHINE

Many observers realise that the DAP type of architectures are well suited to matrix manipulation. In the case of the 64 × 64 DAP itself, it is evident that the system will be well adapted to manipulation of 64 × 64 data arrays, it is therefore natural to ask how one manipulates objects of different dimensionality. The question arises in a number of different contexts and has different answers depending on the context. Before considering some specific examples it is interesting to consider the major differences between parallel and sequential computing engines. Suppose we have a sequential computer which performs a certain operation in time t_s and we wish to perform that operation N times. The total time to complete the task will be:

$$T_s = Nt_s$$

For this discussion it is irrelevant what the operation being considered is - it could be a single multiplication or a payroll calculation, it is only relevant for this discussion that the operations are assumed to be independent of each other. Suppose we have a parallel computer made up from p processors each of which can perform the operation in time t_p. The total time to complete the task will be:

$$T_p = [N/p]\ t_p$$

where $[x]$ signifies the next integer above x when x is not an integer. The DAP user is interested in large degrees of parallelism so we have in Figure 1 plotted $\log_2 [T_s/t_s]$ and $\log_2 [T_p/t_p]$ versus $\log_2 N$.

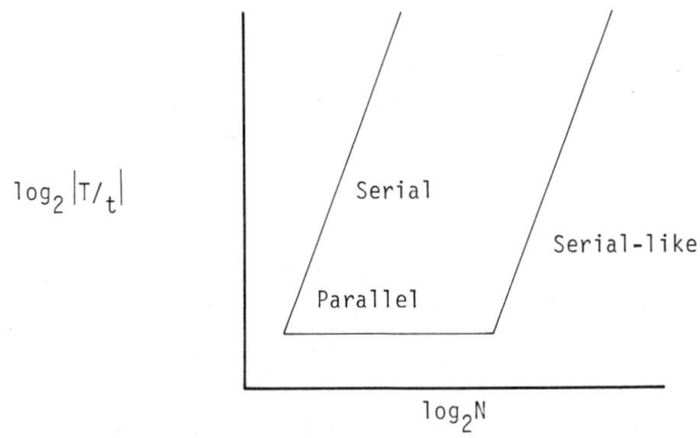

Figure 1: Plot of $\log_2[T_s/t_s]$ and $\log_2[T_p/t_p]$ versus $\log_2 N$

The performance curve for a serial computer is a simple straight line whilst that for the parallel computer has two components: a horizontal (the 'parallel') branch and a diagonal (the 'serial-like') branch. The 'serial-like' branch is parallel to the normal serial curve suggesting that the methods for solving large problems are similar to serial methods whilst small problems fall into the parallel branch and may exploit different algorithms.

The easiest example of the two types of algorithm occurs in the problem of matrix multiplication. The usual expression for defining the product of two matrices A and B to produce the product C is:

$$C_{ij} = \sum_k A_{ik} * B_{kj}$$

This expression will be interpreted by most readers as an expression involving scalar objects C_{ij}, A_{ik} and B_{kj}, but is equally valid if these objects were themselves matrices and represents, therefore, the well-known block or partition matrix multiplication. DAP programmers wishing to perform large matrix multiplication partition their large matrix into suitably sized partitions and then compute the sums of products of those partitions. Serial programmers do exactly the same thing except that they always choose partition of size 1×1. The problem when implementing matrix multiplication in a parallel environment is to decide a partition size for which it is convenient to use a special algorithm. The user of a serial machine chooses 1×1 partition because there is usually a special algorithm (the hardware multiplier) which facilitates 1×1 multiplications.

The DAP user chooses partitions of size 64×64 as this partitioning fits well onto the hardware facilities of the DAP and the outer product algorithm is efficiently implemented.

The DAP algorithm for the normal matrix product is the equivalent of the FORTRAN:

```
      DO 1 K = 1,N
      DO 2 I = 1,N
      DO 2 J = 1,N
 2    C(I,J) = C(I,J) + A(I,K)*B(K,J)
 1    CONTINUE.
```

The innermost two DO loops are executed in parallel so the execution time is only proportional to the number of times the outer loop is transversed and so the time for matrix multiplication varies linearly with partition size. On a serial computer the multiplication time for matrices varies as the cube of the matrix size and hence for matrices less than the DAP size the performance characteristics are qualitatively different from those of a serial computer.

If the matrices which arise in a particular application are very small compared with the DAP eg 4 × 4 then the application programmer is encouraged to examine the loop within which these multiplications occur and look for ways to perform many multiplications simultaneously.

A favourite non-problem which causes unnecessary worry to beginners is the question, 'How do you multiply 65 × 65 matrices on a 64 × 64 DAP?'. This problem is described as a 'non-problem' as in practice it has never occurred. DAP users find that they can either usually operate on 64 × 64 matrices or on multiples of that unit. The question of 65 × 65 matrices is a somewhat artificial problem of a similar nature to asking the user of a standard 32-bit serial computer about 33-bit arithmetic!

ALTERNATIVE ALGORITHMS

The matrix multiplication algorithm shown above is an example of a case where the parallel algorithm is different from the usual serial algorithm. The parallel algorithm is in this case a totally valid serial algorithm and indeed is a better algorithm on some pipelined systems. In some cases the parallel algorithm is not a good serial algorithm, by 'good' we mean has lowest operation count. A simple but very instructive example occurs when we examine algorithms for solving dense sets of linear equations.

The problem of solving $A\underset{\sim}{x} = \underset{\sim}{b}$ where A is a given dense N by N matrix and $\underset{\sim}{b}$ is a given N vector is a well-studied problem in numerical analysis. The most generally used algorithms are variants of the Gauss-elimination back-substitution algorithm or the LU decomposition algorithm.

The LU decomposition algorithm is typical of these 'triangularisation' methods; briefly A is decomposed into the product of two matrices $A = LU$ where L is a lower triangular matrix with unit entries along the main diagonal and U is an upper triangular matrix. Then to complete the solution of $Ax=b$ the following steps are performed:

y is evaluated from $L\underset{\sim}{y} = b$

x is evaluated from $U\underset{\sim}{x} = y$

The number of operations needed to perform the steps is well known (001).

The decomposition of A into L and U requires:

$\frac{n^3}{3} - \frac{n}{3}$ multiplications

$\frac{n^3}{3} - \frac{n^2}{2} + \frac{n}{6}$ additions

and n reciprocals.

The back substitution phase requires:

n^2 multiplications

and n^2-n additions.

Hence LU decomposition requires $\frac{n^3}{3} + O(n^2)$ multiplications and back-substitution requires $O(n^2)$ multiplications.

If different right-hand sides are needed with the same matrix A then the LU decomposition need only be performed once and each new set of equations requires only $O(n^2)$ operations for its full solution. The result is so powerful and widely known that it appears natural to ask, 'How does one perform LU decomposition in a parallel computer and how does one solve triangular systems on a parallel computer?'. These are the wrong questions - the correct questions are: 'How does one solve sets of equations on a parallel computer?', and 'How does one solve multiple sets of similar equations on a parallel computer?'.

The above suggests that there are two regimes to study:

1 Systems of equations very much larger than the degree of parallelism available.
2 Systems comparable or smaller than the available parallelism.

In the case of the DAP these two regimes become:

1 Systems with N equation where N>>64.
2 Systems with 64 or less equations.

The first regime is dealt with by a serial-like algorithm but based on 64 × 64 partition analogous in manner to the LU decomposition but the second regime is more interesting. When we try to solve N equations on a $N \times N$ parallel processor we find that the LU algorithm is inferior to the direct diagonalisation algorithm (the Gauss-Jordan algorithm) and that there is no benefit involved in obtaining the triangular forms even for the case of multiple right-hand sides. A very detailed exposition of this theory can be found in (002) but briefly the reasons are as follows.

The LU decomposition algorithm steps through the rows of the original matrix sequentially and subtracts a multiple of that row (the pivot row) from all rows so far unused. To implement this on a parallel computer with N rows and N columns requires fewer and fewer processors to be active at each step. The Gauss-Jordan algorithm subtracts multiples of the pivot row from all other rows and so exercises more processors in each step. As a result after N steps (each with one parallel add, multiplication, and division) the LU algorithm produces the decomposed form LU but the Gauss-Jordan algorithm has produced the full solution. Hence the Gauss-Jordan algorithm is faster than the LU algorithm for the solution of a single set of equations.

There is no known parallel algorithm for solving a triangular system of N equations in N unknowns (using N^2 processors) in less than N steps (one multiplication and addition per step) and hence the solution of the equations $LU\underset{\sim}{x} = b$ takes twice the time than the solution of the equations $A\underset{\sim}{x} = \underset{\sim}{b}$ (by Gauss-Jordan) hence the LU factorisation is inappropriate. The situation is even stranger - not only is the LU factorisation not appropriate for a parallel environment but, if the problem 'solve, using N^2 processors, the set of N equations $LU\ \underset{\sim}{x} = \underset{\sim}{b}$ for a set of different right-hand sides' was posed, then a good strategy would be to compute $A = LU$ and then solve $A\underset{\sim}{x} = b$, which is the very inverse of serial computing practice.

BIT-ORGANISED PROCESSORS

The results we have so far considered are valid on any SIMD computer with a large number of processors. The DAP is currently unique because of the bit-organised nature of its processors. The bit-organised nature means that relative costs of various operations on the DAP and on serial computers are very different. This becomes obvious to programmers in the following three ways:

1 Some common mathematical operations such as square root, exponential, and logarithm have essentially been microcoded and, therefore, are relatively not much more expensive than multiplication (indeed square root is faster than multiplication).

2 As all arithmetic is software-based, the system programmers have been able to provide a range of arithmetic precisions rather than the usual 'single' and 'double' precisions.

3 Logical operations are very efficient - especially in comparison with floating-point arithmetic.

The most important of these is the last point - the DAP is primarily a 'decision engine' and is therefore well suited to applications which require many data-dependent decisions. The realisation of this fact has been one of the most stimulating facets of our experience with the DAP. Initially it was felt that an ideal DAP problem would be one in which all processors would be kept fully occupied (ie problems such as matrix addition) and that performance degradation would take place if decisions required processors to be disabled. Comparison with other computers, however, shows that the relative performance improvement shown by DAP is greatest for problems with many data-dependent decisions. As decisions are implemented by 'switching-off' processors this leads to an apparently paradoxical result:

- Relative to classical serial machines the performance of the DAP rises as one switches off processors!

The paradox is resolved by realising that the measurement is relative and that what is really happening is that the performance of the serial machine is degraded by decisions and that degradation is greater than the degradation experienced by the DAP.

Applications which turn out to be suitable for the DAP have the following three main characteristics:

1 When implemented on serial computers they are strongly CPU limited.

2 When implemented on serial computers they consume large amounts of time.

3 It is possible to structure the problem so that the majority of the processor capacity is used by the repetition of a small number of routines or procedures which require several thousand operations for their execution.

The first two of these rules are obvious and require little further comment. Rule 1 eliminates I/O-dominated tasks and Rule 2 eliminates small tasks where programming ease is probably the dominating factor in the choice of computer solution. Rule 3 is vague and difficult to quantify but attempts to guard against analysis of applications at too low a level. The DAP is a tool for doing large numbers of operations simultaneously and application studies must take this into account. The correct unit of study for the DAP appears to be units of calculation with a minimum of 10 000 - 100 000 operations.

Rule 3 is very easy to break, on a number of occasions attempts have been made to implement too-trivial tasks with unsuccessful results. Typical of these failures was a study of a problem where it was discovered that 90% of the CPU time on a serial computer arose from calling a subroutine which performed 3 × 3 matrix multiplications. The thought was to replace the multiply routine with a DAP version. If the project had gone ahead it would have been unsuccessful. Experience will show what turns out to be the minimum computational packet for implementation on a parallel computer but early DAP experience suggests that if a system has N processors that computational packets with $N\sqrt{N}$ operations at least are appropriate. As $N = 4096$ for a DAP this means that the computational packets are non-trivial but represent an amount of work comparable with 64 × 64 matrix multiplication.

There are many application areas where large computational packets arise and therefore are well suited to the DAP. Some simple examples include any problem area which handles dense matrix algebra on matrices size 50 × 50 or larger. Such problems arise in crystallography, linear regression analysis, econometric modelling, panel or boundary integral methods in fluid dynamics, etc.

Partial differential equations are a fruitful source of problems suitable for the DAP. Complicated geometries can be efficiently handled using the logical masking facilities. There are some problems in retraining 'expert' programmers who feel that they have failed intellectually if they do not keep all processors active all the time. The cost of organising the work to avoid switching off processors can be excessive and the simple approaches are usually best.

The Boolean nature of the DAP processing elements means that character or low-precision variable manipulations seem to be rapid compared with floating-point operations. Text manipulation or image processing applications can exploit this characteristic and a number of workers are finding the DAP well suited for these tasks. Compilation, parsing of natural languages, algebraic processing, and image compression are areas where good results have been produced.

The main area for future research is probably going to be the area generally called 'sparse matrix methods'. These methods are important for such problems as network analysis or linear programming. The challenge for the designer of parallel algorithms arises from the extreme sophistication of serial techniques which tend to concentrate on very tight inner-loop computations. These 'inner loops' violate our Rule 3 and so do not form a suitable starting point for developing a DAP algorithm. Some progress is being made in network analysis but more work needs to be done. It is probable that the parallel algorithms will need to exploit problem structure. It is indeed a characteristic of parallel computers that they are more sensitive to data structure than are serial computers.

Experience with DAP has shown that parallel computing is different from serial computing but is applicable to nearly all computational tasks. The next few years in computational development will be based around various forms of parallel computation. The challenge will be to find methods of specifying problems in ways which do not destroy the inherent problem parallelism, as most existing programming languages do.

REFERENCES

001 KRONSJO L I
Algorithms, their complexity and efficiency
J Wiley and Sons Ltd (1979)

002 PARKINSON D
Parallel matrix multiplication, the ICL distributed array processor, linear equations and partial differential equations and bit-organised algorithms
Proc Conf on *Design of numerical algorithms for parallel processing*
Bergamo Italy (15-16 June 1981)
(not yet published)

INFORMATION SYSTEMS IN THE 1980s

B Soucek

University of Zagreb
Zagreb
Yugoslavia

B SOUCEK is a professor at the Institute Ruder Bosković and the University of Zagreb. His interests are cybernetics, digital instrumentation, and minicomputers- and microcomputer-based systems. For the last decade he has divided his time between teaching and research in Zagreb, Brookhaven National Laboratory, Upton, NJ and the State University of New York, Stony Brook, NJ. Professor Soucek is the author of Microprocessors and Minicomputers *and* Minicomputers in Data processing and simulation. *He is also coauthor with A D Carlson of* Computers in Neurobiology and behaviour.

INFORMATION SYSTEMS IN THE 1980s

The information industry is assessed and future investment areas are examined. Forecasting techniques are divided into two groups - exploratory or opportunity-oriented and normative or mission-oriented, and these are discussed. The influence of new technologies and microcomputer trends are examined and mainframe and system software trends are assessed. The trend of micros emulating minis is discussed and mass optical memories are examined. The movement towards user-oriented computer communication is examined.

INTRODUCTION

The paper covers the developments and prospects in the microprocessor, minicomputer, mainframe and supercomputer range and addresses the architecture and technology involved. The following topics are examined:

- The information industry and information society
- Small computer trends: from single chip microcomputers to minis and micros emulating the present day mainframes
- Mainframe trends: new ways of modular functional processors; future mass memories including video disks
- Hardware replacing software functions
- Computer communication trends: matching the expectations, needs and satisfactions of the user.

THE INFORMATION INDUSTRY

There is no single definition of 'information' that embraces all aspects of the primary information sector. Describing the operation of banking, J Martin says:

> 'Money is information. Payments of all sorts, called transactions require two forms of information: a record of transaction and certification, that the payer has the requisite wealth to make the transaction. Since it is information, money should be firmly in the province of the computer and be telephoned between machines like all other information.'

This is why banking is the largest sector in the application of computers and in communication integration.

Banking is only one example from the information industry. The end product of any information industry is knowledge. According to Porat (001):

> 'An information market enables the consumer to know something that was not known beforehand: to exchange a symbolic experience; to learn or relearn something; to change perception or cognition; to reduce uncertainty; to expand one's range of options; to exercise rational choice; to evaluate decisions; to control a process; to communicate an idea, a fact, or an opinion. An information market may sell topical knowledge with a very short useful life; it may exchange long-lasting knowledge. It may involve a completely specialised or unique configuration of knowledge, useful only to one person in one situation, or it may be public know-

ledge available to all simultaneously and generally useful in many contexts. It could be extremely costly to produce, or it may involve only very simple processing and transmission approaching zero marginal cost. Information could be a lengthy process spanning a whole lifetime (such as invention), or it could be a burst of data occurring in a millionth of a second (such as pulses in an experiment).'

Figure 1 shows eight major classes of industries that in some way produce, process, disseminate or transmit knowledge or messages. The information industry employs *information workers*. Information workers are therefore primarily engaged in the production, processing or distribution of information, and their jobs include a broad range of professions – from scientific and technical workers to the machine operators and telecommunication workers (see Figure 2).

Knowledge production and inventive industries

- R&D and inventive industries (private)
- Private information services

Information distribution and communication industries

- Education
- Public information services
- Regulated communication media
- Unregulated communication media

Risk management

- Insurance industries (components)
- Finance industries (components)
- Speculative brokers

Search and coordination industries

- Search and non-speculative brokerage industries
- Advertising industries
- Non-market coordinating institutions

Information processing and transmission services

- Non-electronic-based processing
- Electronic-based processing
- Telecommunication infrastructure

Information goods industries

- Non-electronic consumption or intermediate goods
- Non-electronic investment goods
- Electronic consumption or intermediate goods
- Electronic investment goods

Selected government activities

- Primary information services in the Federal Government
- Postal service
- State and local education

Support facilities

- Information structure construction and rental
- Office furnishings

Figure 1: Typology of primary information sector industries, US (001)

Figure 3 shows a four-sector aggregation of the US workforce for the period 1860 to 1980. Agriculture was predominant in Stage I (1860 to 1906) and industry was predominant in Stage II (1906 to 1954). In the current period, Stage III, information occupations are predominant.

<u>Markets for information</u>

Knowledge producers

- Scientific and technical workers
- Private information services

Knowledge distributors

- Educators
- Public information disseminators
- Communication workers

<u>Information in markets</u>

Market search and coordination specialists

- Information gatherers
- Search and coordination specialists
- Planning and control workers

Information processors

- Non-electronic based
- Electronic based

<u>Information infrastructure</u>

Information machine workers

- Non-electronic machine operators
- Electronic machine operators
- Telecommunication workers

Figure 2: Typology of information workers, US (001)

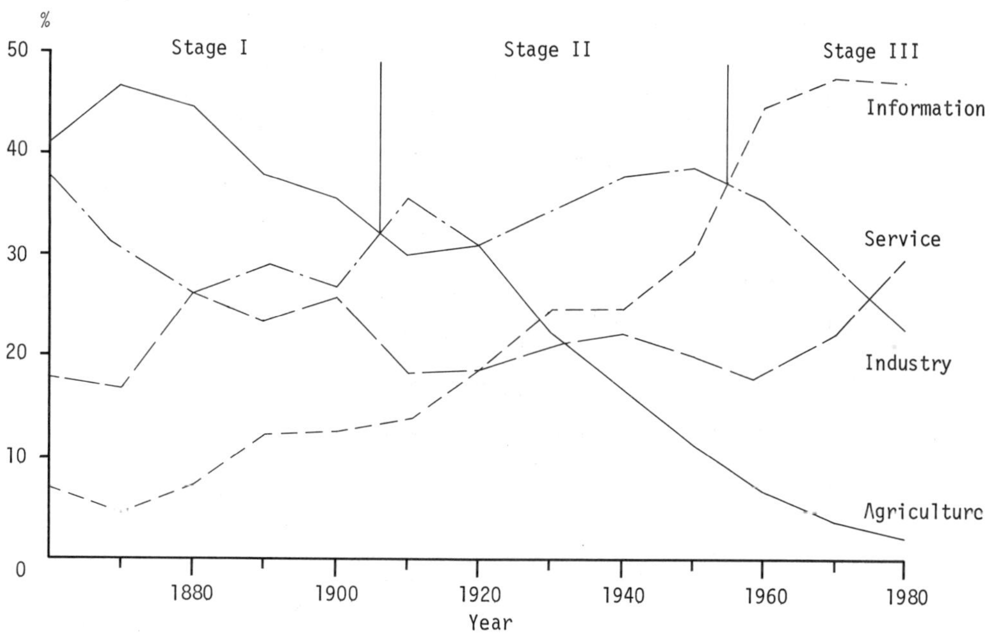

Figure 3: Four-sector aggregation of the US workforce by percentage, 1860 1980, using median estimates of information workers (001)

Hence we could call Stage III the *information society*, the *knowledge economy* (Fritz Machlup), the *technetronic age* (Zbigniew Brzezinski); the *post-capitalist society* (Rudolf Dahrendorff), the *post-modern society* (Amitai Etzioni) or the *post-industrial society* (Herman Kahn). The major activity of the information society involves the handling and processing of information, and not just the production of 'objects' as was the case in the agricultural and industrial societies. The side effects of the information society are 'information shock', 'information pollution', and 'information illiteracy'.

'The entire knowledge system in society is undergoing violent upheaval. We are increasing the rate at which we must form and forget our images of reality', says Alvin Toffler in *Future Shock*.

What society needs is the synthesis, repackaging and consolidation of information. Dispersed information is of low value, condensed and preprocessed information is of high value (see Figure 4).

INVESTMENTS

Microcomputers are very inexpensive. As a result they are being used as building material for very elaborate information systems. Most important information systems are distributed-network-oriented systems. Such systems are needed in industrial production, business, administration, health care, banking, national security, education

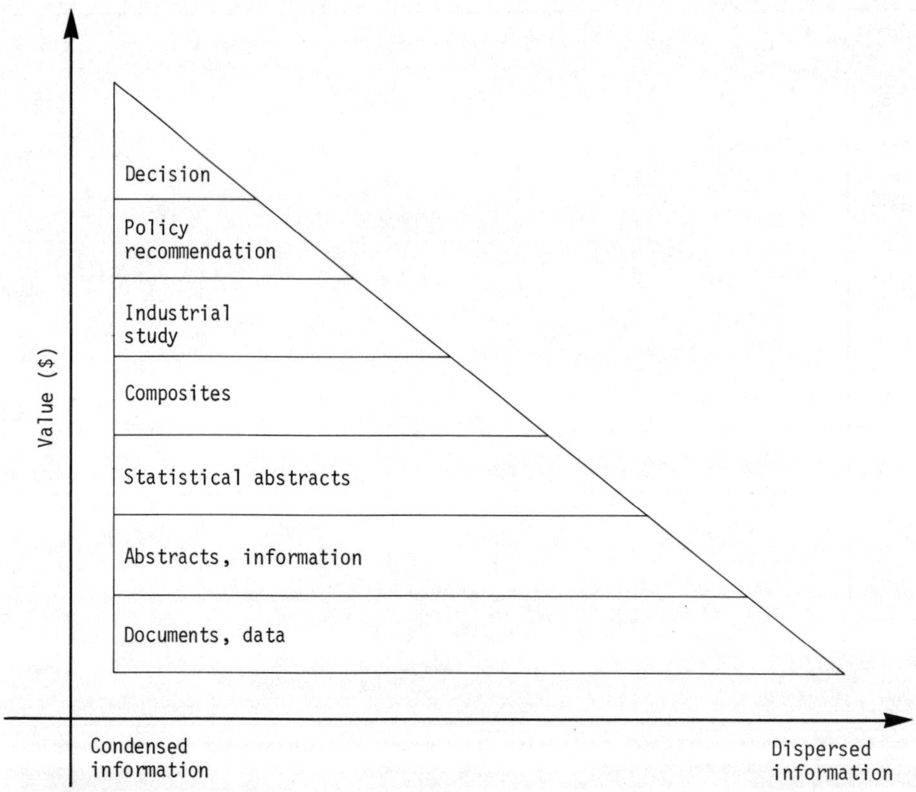

Figure 4: Dispersed information is of low value, condensed information is of high value

etc. A moderate number of these systems were built in the 1970s, based on mainframes and fixed wired terminals. A new wave of systems is expected in the 1980s. In parallel to the new mainframes, the basic elements in these systems will be microcomputer-based minicomputers, as well as microcomputer-based distributed units/terminals.

At the end of the '70s, the total value of installed computing equipment approached $100 billion. It has been estimated that another $100 billion has been invested in software. IBM alone operates with an annual budget of over $1 billion for research and development. The total investment in operating software for one family of computers has reached $100 million.

Computer networks and data transmission networks are spreading over cities and countries, and frequently over whole regions of the world. One of the leading corporations in this field, AT&T, operates with revenues of $33 billion. By the end of 1980 the number of installed computers will reach $300 000 (not including microcomputers and portable computers). The investment per capita at this moment is about $200 in the USA, or about $50 in Spain, or in Yugoslavia.

Mini and microcomputers are expected to be the basic building material for gigantic information systems in the 1980s. Although minis and micros are inexpensive, the information systems will mean substantial investments. One typical information system could run to $1 million – $20 million or more. Information systems can be grouped in the following way:

- Small information systems: 10 to 20 minis and micros; typical application - process control, data acquisition
- Medium size information systems: 20 to 100 minis and micros; typical application - corporation management systems
- Gigantic information systems: 100 to 1000 or more minis and micros; typical application - on-line banking, data retrieval, national/international networks.

The distribution of computers in industry is shown in Figure 5 and the distribution in other fields is shown in Figure 6. Figures 5 and 6 use Japan as an example (approximately 40 000 installations, total value $10 billion in 1976). One could speculate that a substantial percentage of these applications will be taken over by the new wave of powerful minis and micros of the '80s.

FORECASTING

Forecasting techniques can be divided into two large groups as follows:

- Exploratory or opportunity oriented
- Normative or mission oriented.

Exploratory- or opportunity-oriented forecasting starts from the present state of the art and explores future trends. This could be done using a trend extrapolation technique, an analytical model, by analogy, or simply in the intuitive way, gathering and comparing the opinions of knowledgeable individuals or groups. The last approach has been known for centuries; the Delphic oracle, whose prophecies, vague and ambiguous as they were, were famous throughout the Mediterranean area.

Industry	No of units	Value (million $)
Agriculture	23	1·6
Forestry	15	0·6
Fisheries	99	6·3
Mining	65	13·9
Construction	670	121·5
Foods	1251	146·0
Textile	918	96·9
Paper and pulp	315	32·0
Publishing/printing	300	60·3
Chemical/petroleum	1412	374·5
Glass/cement	285	59·3
Steel	587	368·9
Non-ferrous metals	623	105·5
Machineries	860	186·1
Electric equipment	1882	1064·0
Shipping	721	438·2
Precision equipment	329	64·4
Other manufacturing	1343	128·8

Figure 5: Computer distribution in industry (Japan 1976)

Application	No of units	Value (million $)
Retail/wholesale	12 252	1112·3
Banking	4314	1941·3
Insurance	202	340·9
Securities	189	142·3
Real estate	99	11·1
Communication/transportation/mass media	1233	277·3
Utilities	162	173·5
Service	2759	714·5
(Information services)	(1361)	(168·8)
(General services)	(1398)	(545·7)
Hospitals	122	26·4
Universities	633	210·3
High schools	246	22·1
Other schools	86	17·7
Local government	670	212·7
National government	388	382·7
Government corporations	607	810·1
Foundations/farmers' cooperation	2104	256·6
Religious institutions	10	1·0
Unclassified	106	28·5

Figure 6: Computer distribution outside industry (Japan 1976)

The trend extrapolation and analytical models search for the expected saturation limits of current technologies. They can produce reasonably good predictions if technology progresses in a continuous manner.

Normative- or mission-oriented forecasting starts with future goals and then goes back and investigates the technologies that might possibly achieve these goals. One of the most critical steps in this kind of forecasting is the definition of the future goal. The goal should be described in terms of its components. Each component and the interaction between components must be described in quantitative terms.

Mini-microcomputer technology forecasting is exploratory- or opportunity-oriented. It is mostly based on a single component technology: semiconductor-integrated circuits. It is also based on a single technological approach: the electron beam method of producing extremely narrow conducting and insulating areas. Also some elements of normative forecasting may be used, searching for the technology that could produce faster circuits, lower power consumption, greater packing densities, new kinds of mass memories, and new kinds of input/output devices and man/machine communications. A special problem involves the forecasting of software development.

One should always separate careful forecast from the creation of buzz words. Says W L Frank (002):

> 'New ideas are often christened with catchy names in order to promote research and developmental support. A great name or a new acronym can do wonders for sales literature and trade journal articles and can possibly influence buyers to join the bandwagon. Now, on the threshold of the 80s, we have decided to review the buzz words of the past, and categorise them by levels of realisation.' (See Figure 7 and Figure 8.)

	CATEGORY		
CLASSIFICATION	A. 'Insignificant impact, unproven, has practically disappeared'	B. 'Low profile, not yet significant may still make it'	C. 'Prospects look good, not yet fully accepted or respectable'
Software development	Higher-order language Automatic programming Universal computer-oriented language Implicit programming International algebraic language Software transportability	Problem-oriented language Decision tables Flowchart Program generator	Modular programming On-line programming Non-procedural languages Software products
Systems/organisations	Automated display systems Associative memory Content-addressable memory Hierarchical storage Polymorphic systems Self-organising systems Graceful degradation Integrated database PERT/CPM	Multicomputers Automated resource allocation Self-diagnostic systems Parallel computing Firmware Facility management	Value-added network Packet switching
Application	Management information systems Language translation	Automatic abstracting Computer assisted instruction Pattern recognition Automated factory Artificial intelligence Medical diagnosis	Source data entry Word processing

Figure 7: Current status of old buzz words (002)

CLASSIFICATION	CATEGORY A 'Insignificant impact, unproven, has practically disappeared'	B. 'Low profile, not yet significant, may still make it'	C. 'Prospects look good, not yet fully accepted or respectable'
Software development	Advanced languages Structured programming	Design technology User development systems Application generator	Data dictionary Implementation systems Transaction development system Programmer's workbench
Systems/organisation	Robustness, forgiving User-oriented, friendly Data-as-a-resource Database administrator Personal computer Compatible systems	Software engineering System security Home computer Voice recognition Distributed database	Distributed processing Relational databases User workstation Transaction processing
Applications	Electronic files Paperless office Office of the future Teleconferencing Total information systems	Automated office Electronic funds transfer Videotex systems Robotics	Electronic mail Query systems

Figure 8: Future status of new buzz words (002)

One could draw many conclusions from Figures 7 and 8. Proposals and buzz words promising 'universal', 'total', 'international' or 'integrated' solutions, usually have insignificant impact (ie, universal computer language, international language, total information system, integrated database etc). The organisation of Figures 7 and 8 is based on statistics. This means that, although some of the techniques have not been accepted by the majority, the minority that use them claim good results (personal computers, structured programming).

THE INFLUENCE OF NEW TECHNOLOGIES

When an improved or new technology becomes available to a computer designer, there are four paths the designer can take to incorporate the technology:

1 Use the newer technology to build a *cheaper* system with the same performance.

2 Hold the price constant and use the technological improvement to get an *increase in performance*.

3 Push the design to the limits of the new technology, thereby increasing *both performance and price*.

4 Find a *drastically new structure* using the computer as a basic archetype such that the design can be considered off the evolutionary path.

Applying the above design strategies over several generations produced the plot given in Figure 9 (003). The computer classes can be distinguished by price and named as follows: submicro, micro, mini, midi, maxi and super. The classes midi and maxi are sometimes referred to as mainframe.

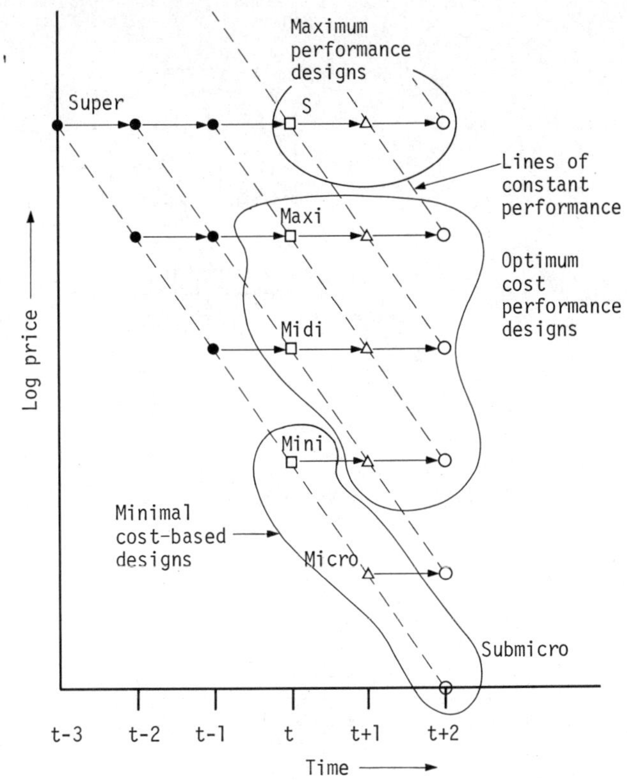

Figure 9: Price versus time for each machine class (003)

MICROCOMPUTER TRENDS

In the last few years we have witnessed tremendous advances in semiconductor technology. The number of bits per chip for a Metal Oxide Semiconductor (MOS) memory doubles every two years (Moore's Law (004)). Currently, complete processors are available on single chips. In the future even large processors and complete computers will be placed on single chips (see Figure 10 (005)).

During 1977 total sale of microchips exceeded $4 billion. In 1978 and 1979 the sales continued to grow. The cost of unit hardware is decreasing all the time: a micro-computer on the board costs $300; a personal computer with keyboard and screen costs $2000; a professional portable computer is less than $10 000. One could get a powerful microprocessor for less than $50. As a result, microprocessors are everywhere — in cars, typewriters, programmable instruments etc.

The increase in software development requirements has led to an increased percentage of software costs in relation to total cost. Low microcomputer hardware costs versus high software development cost leads towards two solutions as follows:

- Modular and automated software production
- Microcomputer — receiver of standardised solutions (software products).

Figure 11 outlines the basic trends in the development and application of microcomputers (006,007).

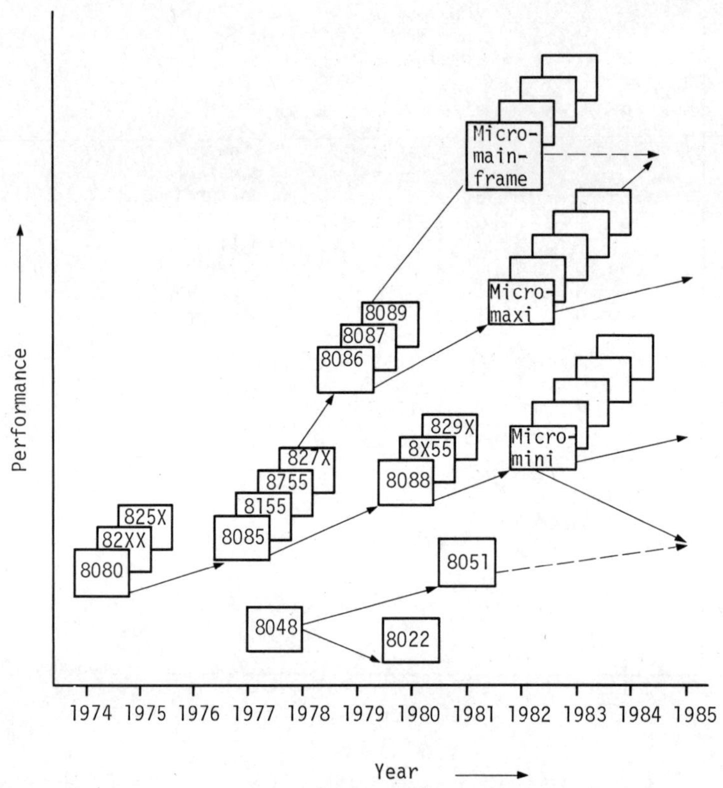

Figure 10: Intel's plans for the 1980s (005)

MAINFRAME TRENDS

The dominant share of the mainframe market is in the hands of the IBM corporation. For this reason it is important to analyse IBM's technological and marketing strategies. Figure 12 is a forecast of IBM strategies in the 1980s. It is believed that the major steps in this strategy will involve three groups of machines: E, H and S/80 series.

It is very difficult to predict anything about IBM. Still, it seems that the E and H series will represent the evolution of the System 370. The E series should replace the low end of the 370 family, with a two-to-three times improved performance/price ratio. The H series should replace the upper end of the 370 family. The prices and timing in Figure 12 should be considered only as approximations.

As regards price and size, the E series could be considered as 'minicomputers' (less than 1 m^3, less than \$200 000). At the same time the E series emulates the 370 family with all its power, and with a tremendous software from the past. One could also expect major changes in computer peripheral units. Magnetic bubble memories will soon reach the market as a part of mass memory systems. It is expected that such systems will replace fixed-head disks by 1980.

The E and H series from IBM and similar systems from other vendors could be the major new wave in the first half of the 1980s. In the second half, we can expect more revolutionary changes. Within the IBM range, we shall call these revolutionary machines System 80, (008).

TREND 1:	Improvements of established families of microcomputers (example: 8008, 8080, 8080A, 8085 ...)
TREND 2:	New powerful single chip microcomputers with 16-bit and 32-bit word length (example: MC2=16 bits, 350 mW, 875 nsec)
TREND 3:	Microcomputer emulation of established minicomputers (example: IM6100 versus PDP-8 or LSI-11 versus PDP-11)
TREND 4:	Microchip-based emulation of established mainframes, using already existing software (example: IBM 4341 versus IBM 370)
TREND 5:	Standardisation and diversity (example: microcomputers based on international standard IEEE 488; custom-made computers)
TREND 6:	Hardware replacing software (example: firmware operating systems; ROM compilers; fast computational sequences)
TREND 7:	Expansion of personal and home computers (example: viewdata service using home television; one microcomputer per capita in 1980s in USA)
TREND 8:	Information networks (example: European Information network)
TREND 9:	Modular application software development; software products (example: application generators similar to RPG II)
TREND 10:	More direct man/computer communication (example: voice communication; non-procedural languages)

Figure 11: Microcomputer trends

System 80 from IBM, and similar systems from other vendors, should present the second wave of computers later in the 1980s. These machines should take advantage of technological advances in hardware, software and architecture. Perhaps one could describe these new mainframes in one sentence:

Mainframe = composition of functional microcomputers.

One should expect the following characteristics from these machines (see Figure 13):

- Multiprocessing: distribution of functions between several 'functional' microprocessors
- Memory hierarchy
- High-speed, universal internal buses
- Intelligent, microcomputer driven input/output channels
- Non-procedural languages
- Increased use of firmware
- Operation system = microcode in firmware
- Relational database (maybe based on CODASYL standards) etc.

Basic mainframe trends are outlined in Figure 14.

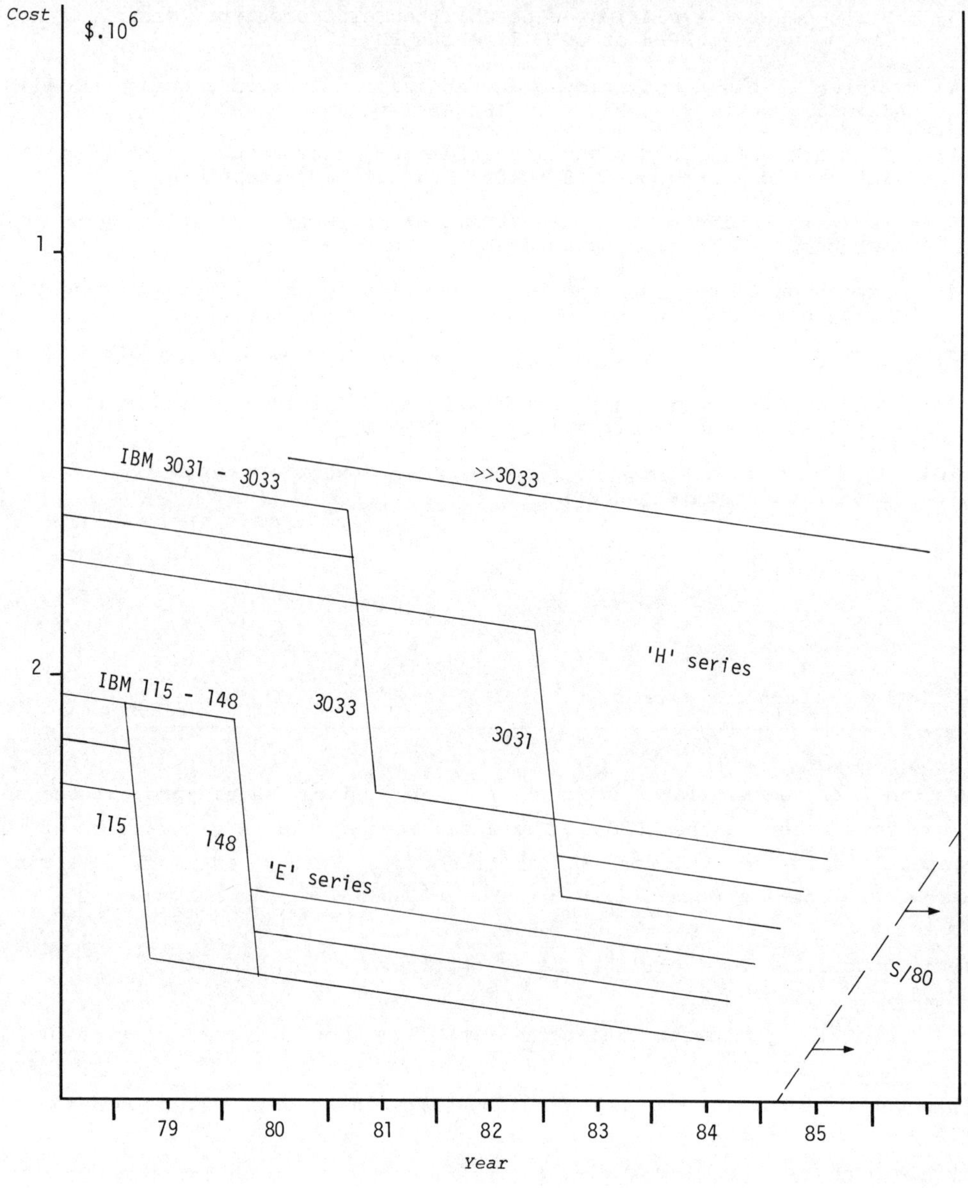

Figure 12: Mainframes of the 1970s being replaced by software compatible minicomputers of the 1980s.

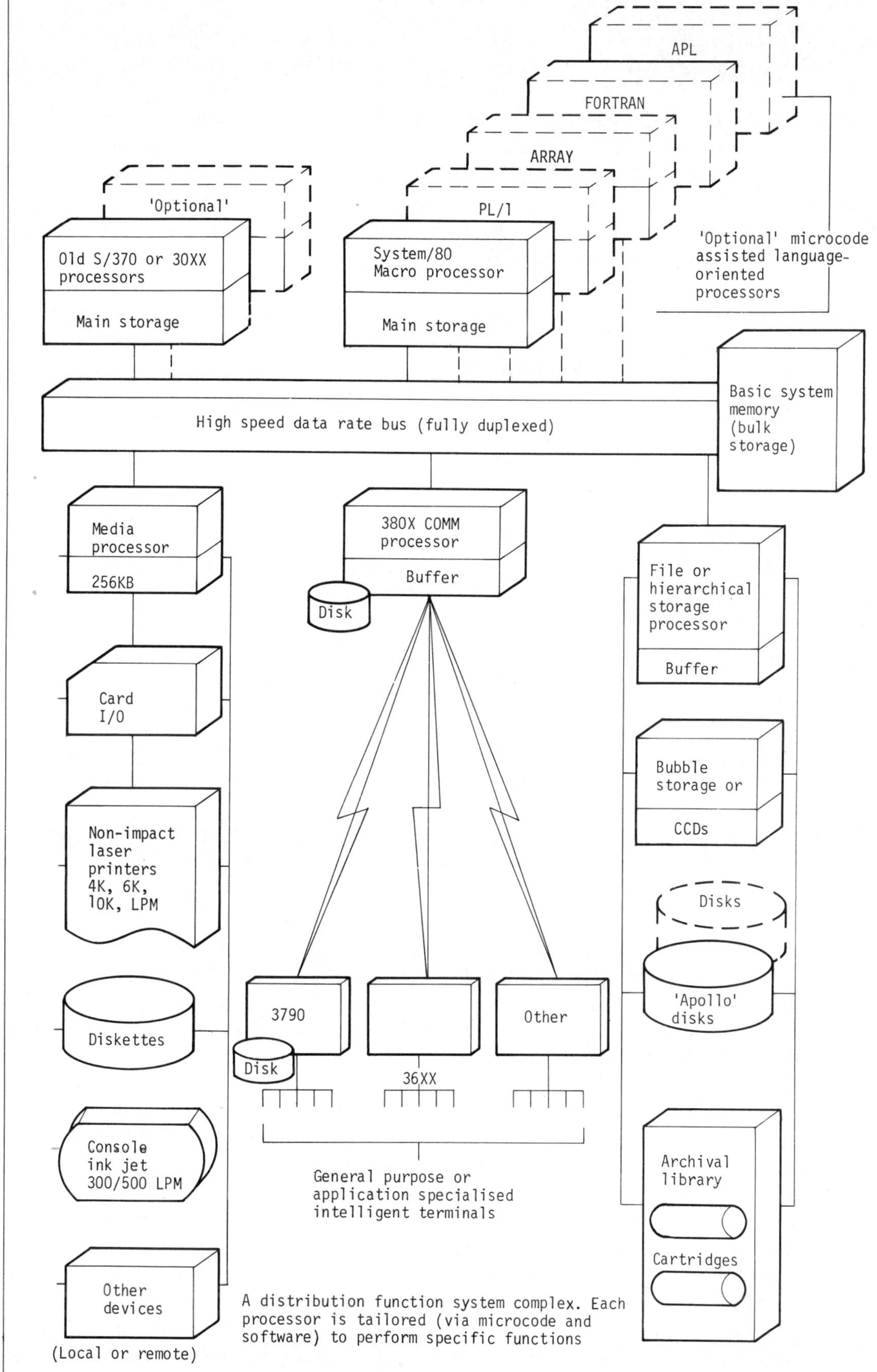

Figure 13: Mainframe architecture based on functional processors (008)

TREND 1: Mainframes of the '70s becoming minicomputers in the beginning of '80s running the old software (example: low end IBM 370 versus IBM E series)

TREND 2: More powerful mainframes in the '80s, but software compatible with largest machines of the '70s (example: upper end of IBM 370 versus IBM H series)

TREND 3: Minicomputers of the '70s becoming portable microcomputers in the early '80s running the old software

TREND 4: New mainframes, middle of the '80s. New architecture: mainframe = composition of functional microcomputers; non-procedural languages; relational database (example: series 80)

TREND 5: New technologies (example: magnetic bubble memories replacing fixed-head disks; video disk; Josephson effect logic etc)

Figure 14: Mainframe trends

SYSTEM SOFTWARE TRENDS

In system software one can detect an important new trend which could be described as 'switching from software to hardware'. The trend is obvious in two areas:

1 Control operations presently performed by system software (scheduling, I/O control, compilers, interrupts etc) will be implemented in hardware in the 1980s.

2 Special-purpose microsystems with almost everything burned into ROMs, including the application software (word processing systems; accounting systems; inventory control systems; process control systems etc).

A summary of system software trends is shown in Figure 15, and hardware/software innovations are outlined in Figure 16.

An example of a hardware compiler system is the new PASCAL Microengine from the Western Digital Corporation. A 16-bit computer chip set, directly executes PASCAL object programs at least five times faster than is possible with conventional system software, and eliminates the host operating system and interpreter previously required. The chip set standardises a version of PASCAL on that offered by the University of California. The chip set comprises four LSI components as follows:

- An arithmetic chip that contains micro-instruction decode, an Application Logic Unit (ALU), and the register file
- A microsequencer chip that contains macro-instruction decode portions of the control circuitry, a micro-instruction counter, and I/O control logic
- *Two* MICROM chips (each 22 bits × 512) that contain the micro instruction ROMs and microdiagnostics

Control operations performed presently by software, that might be implemented in hardware in the 1980s

1 Timesharing and multiprogramming
- Memory
- Processor and task scheduling
- Priorities
- Swapping
- Protection

2 File and list management
- Searching
- Sorting
- Comparisons
- Swapping
- Copying
- Indexing

3 Direct higher-order language execution, reducing the need for compilers, assemblers, editors and debugging programs

4 Fault protection and detection
- Memory protection
- Diagnosis
- Some self repair

5 Fast computational sequences based on large read-only memories and on large sets of micro-instructions

Figure 15: System software trends: hardware replacing software functions

Programming transparency	*High-level language processors*	*Executive and operating system transparency*
The programmer does not have to know details of the system structure	Computer instructions are equivalent to the high-level language statements	Scheduling, interrupts, I/O control – made available as higher-order language instructions

Natural man/computer interaction

- Intelligent terminals
- Interpreters
- Speech recognition and voice generation interfaces

Figure 16: Switching from software to hardware

EMULATION TRENDS

It is obvious that software development is now playing a dominant role in the computer world. This is why so many micros are emulating the established minicomputers. With steadily improving technology and with microprogramming, we are now at the stage when medium-scale computers are being emulated with microchip sets. As a result, the mainframes of the 1970s will be replaced by software-compatible minicomputers in the 1980s, and the minicomputers of the 1970s will be replaced by microcomputers in the 1980s (see Figure 12).

Micros emulating minis present an already established trend. Here are a few examples:

- PDP-11 – LSI-11
- Nova – Micronova
- PDP-8 – IM 6100
- TI 990 – TMS 9900.

As semiconductor technology produces more powerful chips, we can expect a growing number of such emulations in the future. Perhaps we are approaching the level of being able to emulate today's mainframes with the microchip set.

An obvious reason for the emulation of leading classical computers is the tremendous amount of software developed for these machines in the last few years, as well as the practical experience gained on them. Unlike today's microcomputers, the micros that emulate established minis support all major high-level languages (FORTRAN, BASIC, FOCAL, COBOL, ALGOL) and are fully software supported by an advanced operating system, including file-handling text editors, symbolic assemblers, loaders, debugging techniques, batch processors and system utilities.

Four basic emulation approaches can be described as follows:

1 *Hardware emulation.* A special family of microchips is developed with an architecture that is similar to the architecture of the mini. Some simplifications in the architecture result through the usage of Programmed Logic Arrays (PLA). (Example: IM6100 versus PDP-8.)

2 *Emulation through microprogramming.* The minicomputer is organised around an inner computer with its own internal control store. Such an inner computer operates at a clock rate about 10 times faster than the rest of the mini. The microprograms are stored in the control read-only memory and are used to implement the mini's assembly-level instruction set. (Example: LSI-11 versus PDP-11.)

3 *Systems based on slice-oriented micros.* Two- and four-bit wide slices through the data processing section of a digital computer have been developed. Combining the slices in a parallel network one can build a 16- or 32-bit computer. The instruction set is defined by microprograms stored in control read-only memory. (Example: Intel 3000.)

4 *Systems that extend through both the micro and mini range.* The microchip is designed to be compatible with the established mini. The family extends from the chip set (component level), through the computer-on-a-board, all the way to the well equipped mini (system level). (Example: Micronova versus Nova.)

In some systems one can detect a mixture of these four approaches. Concrete examples of minis emulated by micros are presented. Mass production of such systems, with the basic price tag below $1000, has a significant impact in many application areas.

MASS OPTICAL MEMORIES

The new video disk technology presents the 'write only once' memory or read-only memory. This will not matter much, for with essentially infinite storage, one can store each new version of a program at a new physical location until the disk is full.

Two main types of disk are in competition. RCA uses variations in capacitance to record information with an arm and head which track the grooves and pick up the signal. Such disks can only be accessed serially; like a magnetic tape or audio cassette. To access a record, one must pass over all the records between the initial position and the desired record. Philips and MCA Division have developed optical players which use a laser to scan the disk. Information is stored in micropits less than a micron in diameter and these produce changes in the beam which are detected by photodiodes. These optical systems are direct access. The recently advertised Philips 'Diode Laser Memory' stores 500 000 typewritten pages on a 12-inch disk. Any address of the giant read-only memory can be accessed in 250 nsec.

The status of development of video disk is outlined in Figure 17. It provides an essentially infinite storage at negligible cost.

Information formats in video disk are shown in Figure 18 and potential uses of such inexpensive mass memories are shown in Figure 19. Very large application software and mathematical libraries are possible with very small investment, leading towards possible new trends: microcomputer + video disk = receiver of a standardised problem solution.

- For less than $1000
- Directly accessible in 10-50 milliseconds
- Data transmission rate 15 000 000 bits per second
- On-line capacity of 4000 000 000 bytes
- Storage unit costing $2 each
- 'Write-once' memory
- Philips, MCA Discovision
- Optical players which use a laser to scan the disk
- Micropits less than a micron in diameter
- Changes in the beam detected by photodiodes
- Direct access capability

Figure 17: The characteristics of video disk

- Colour video (36 000 colour video frames on one plastic disk)
- Black and white video
- Digital storage (2^{32} bytes)
- Voice or music
- High resolution frames to replace microfilm and fiche in libraries and homes

Figure 18: Information formats in video disk

- Electro-optical professional libraries
- School libraries
- Education at home via disk
- Database
- Application software and mathematics library*
- Data communication over 10^6 gigaHertz bandwidth laser networks of the future

  * Application programmer of tomorrow?

Figure 19: Usage of inexpensive mass memories (video disk)

COMPUTER COMMUNICATION TRENDS

In computer communication, the industry is changing from technology-oriented criteria to criteria based upon concepts of matching the expectations, needs and satisfactions of the user.

There is a general asymmetry in communication flow: man to computer communication is weak, slow in data rate, inaccurate and unnatural; computer to man communication is strong, fast, precise and well-matched to human data - input system.

Human input is multichannel and very flexible although it is slow it has a wide dynamic range. Human output is multichannel and multi-axis, it is slow but very flexible.

Computer input is usually manual at present; limited hearing mode and visual modes are being developed. Computer input can be very fast. Computer output is usually visual at present but limited speech mode is developed, again this can be fast.

Figure 20 shows an acoustic mode of communication. Figure 21 shows a concrete example of the usage of acoustic communication: the pay by phone principle. Figure 22 presents the video input-output and Figure 23 presents a concrete example of the usage of video input-output: the cheque-image banking system.

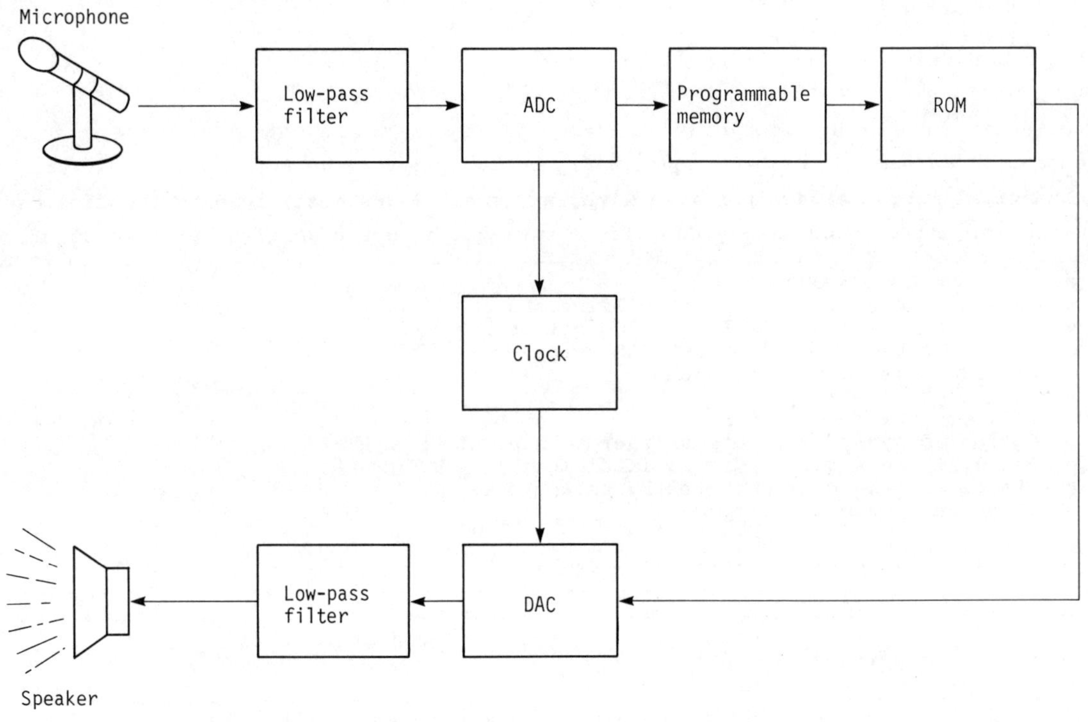

Figure 20: Computer controlled vocal input/output

- Phone a bank
- Enter account number
- Enter ID code of merchant
- Enter amount of payment
  - all entries are confirmed with voice response of the system

  (Union Commerce Bank, touch-tone)

Figure 21: Pay-by-phone

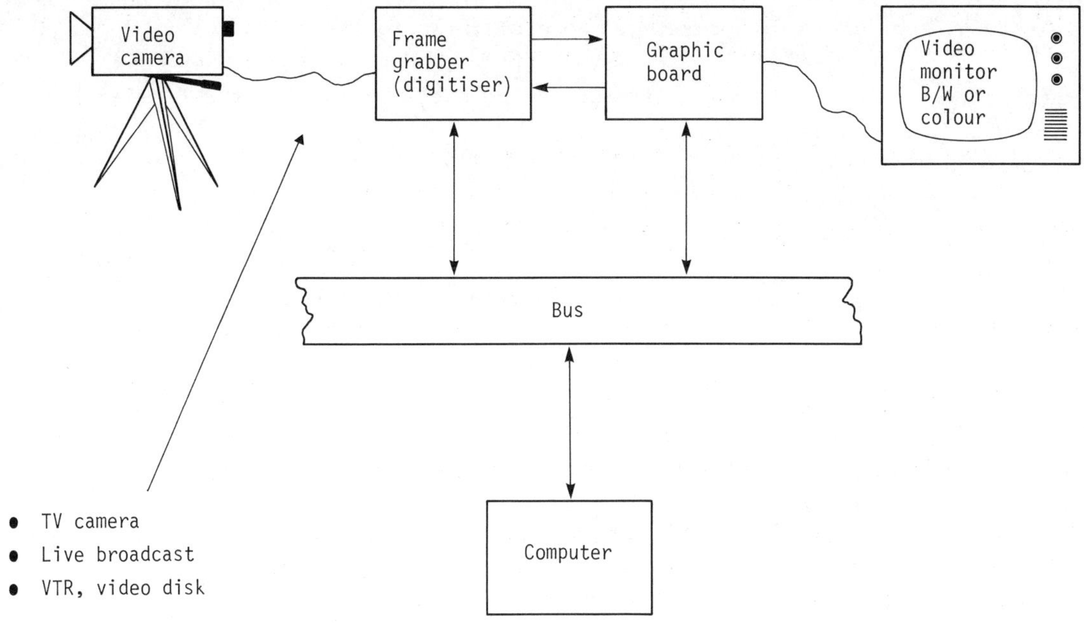

Figure 22: Video input-output

- Input through CCD or other sensitive cameras (image ports)
- Turn cheque into digital replica
- Store, transmit, display, reproduce, truncate the cheque (Projects:
  - Bank of America with NCR
  - Midland Bank with Burroughs)

Figure 23: Cheque-image banking system

CONCLUSION

The increase in software development requirements has led to an increased percentage of software costs in relation to total cost. Low microcomputer hardware costs versus high application software development costs leads towards two solutions as follows:

- Automated software production, where possible
- Computer = receiver of standardised solutions, (software products).

W L Frank (002) says:

> 'While there is no doubt the production of software requires a disciplined foundation if we are to succeed in adequately predicting and fulfilling software project forecasts, there is no engineering discipline that can be imposed, so that programming can move from its current art form to a more scientific basis; I do not see much promise for software engineering.'

Optimistic opinions of software engineering also exist (009). By applying top-down design and stepwise refinement and using suitable tools and strategies one could improve the efficiency of application programming. Some of these tools include:

- Interactive programming aids (editors; debug facilities; interpreters etc)
- Application generators
- Software project database
- String preprocessors
- Block-diagram languages etc.

Application software production will benefit from advances in other areas as well:

1 Application software depends on hardware trends:

  - CPU improvements
  - Word length steadily increasing
  - Multiple specialised execution units
  - RAM, ROM and mass memories; cycle time will drop to a few nanoseconds, capacity will reach 10^{10} bits by the 1980s
  - New microchips.

2 Application software depends on system software trends:

  - Control operations performed presently by software that might be implemented in hardware in the 1980s
    - timesharing
    - scheduling
    - priorities
    - swapping
    - protection
    - searching
    - sorting
  - Direct higher-order language execution
  - Fast computational sequences based on large ROMs, and special-purpose microchips.

3 Application software depends on emulation trends:

  - Microcomputers emulating established minis (example PDP-11 versus LSI-11);
    - microchip-based minicomputers emulating established mainframes (example IBM 370 versus IBM E series)
  - Computers of the 1980s but software of the 1970s.

4 Application software depends on mass optical memories:

  - Video disk
    - storage capacity of one Gbyte on a storage unit costing $20
  - Electro-optical professional libraries
  - Database for a small business
  - Application software and mathematical libraries
  - Microcomputer + video disk = receiver of a problem solution (software products).

REFERENCES

001 PORAT M U
The information economy: definition and measurement
Rep no 77-12(1) Office of Telecommunication US Department of Commerce

002 FRANK W L
Buzz words revisited
Datamation p 159 (Jan 1980)

003 BELL C G, MUDGE J C and McNAMARA I E
Computer engineering
Digital Press (1978)

004 MOORE G
VLSI: some fundamental challenges
IEEE Spectrum pp 30-37 (Apr 1979)

005 POSA J G
Intel takes aim at the '80s
Electronics pp 89-95 (28 Feb 1980)

006 SOUCEK B and LERCH Z
Advanced microcomputer application programming
In *Microcomputer software* pp 231-256 Infotech State of the Art Rep Infotech Limited Maidenhead UK (1979)

007 LERCH Z and SOUCEK B
Machine-oriented high-level languages, preprocessors and structured techniques on microcomputers
In *Microcomputer software* pp 121-137 Infotech State of the Art Rep Infotech Limited Maidenhead UK (1979)

008 LECHT C P
The waves of change
ACT New York (1977)

009 BOEHM B W
Software engineering
IEEE Transactions on Computers (1976)

010 SOUCEK B
Microprocessors and microcomputers
J Wiley & Sons New York (1976)

PASCAL ON THE CRAY-1

I R Wilson
N H Madhavji
F C de Moura

University of Manchester
UK

ACKNOWLEDGEMENTS

Our thanks are due to CRAY RESEARCH, INC as a company, to Dick Hendrickson and his CFT team for intellectual and technical support, and to CRAY-UK for their financial assistance. An earlier draft of this paper was presented at the SIGPLAN symposium on Compiler Construction 1982 at Boston, Massachusetts.

I R WILSON has been a lecturer in Computer Science at Manchester University since 1969. His early work developed the concepts of the Compiler Compiler into various system programming languages on Atlas and the MU5 computers. Work on software tools led to automated techniques for code production including diagrammatic representations. In recent years his interest in the PASCAL language has resulted in a standard textbook and compilers on machines at all levels, from the hobby-sized to the CRAY-1 supercomputer.

N H MADHAVJI produced his thesis work at Manchester on software design and was a major contributor to the CRAY PASCAL project as a research assistant financially supported by CRAY RESEARCH. He is now a lecturer at the University of Illinois at Urbana-Champaign where he has an interest in expert systems and formal specifications.

F C de MOURA is studying system programming at Manchester, on leave from the Minho University in Portugal. His investigations into vectorisation have contributed to the CRAY PASCAL project.

PASCAL ON THE CRAY-1

A PASCAL compiler has been added to the software repertoire of the CRAY-1 computer. Here the structured nature of PASCAL statements and data structures is contrasted with the 'powerful computing engine' nature of the CRAY-1 hardware. The accepted views of PASCAL as a simple one-pass language and the CRAY-1 as a purely vector processor are laid aside in favour of a multipass approach, taking account of the machine's scalar capabilities. The compiler is aimed at the production of highly efficient runtime code for applications likely to be programmed in PASCAL. Some statistics are given to indicate the nature of such applications. Though the statistics are not encouraging, the approach taken to vectorisation is discussed.

INTRODUCTION

CRAY PASCAL - a multipass language on a scalar machine! This expletive is not intended to deny the simplicity of the design of PASCAL or the vector processing capabilities of the CRAY-1. The power of this computer is often related to its performance improvement over earlier powerful scalar machines such as the CDC 7600, for example Baskett and Keller (001) give a brief description of the machine and quote a ratio of a factor of two to three for scalar processes and two to ten for vector processes. Indeed, the CRAY X-MP is expected to add a further factor of two to five in performance. However, as Baskett and Keller state, viewing this machine purely as a vector processor does not do justice to its general-purpose capabilities. Further, the extension of the use of vector processors into more general-purpose environments, such as universities, shows benchmark results which resist improvement due to a base load of non-vectorisable work (002). This becomes relatively more significant as the vectorisable component is more efficiently processed.

PASCAL compilers are commonly based on one of the three compilers (003, 004, 005) originally implemented at Zurich, each for a different level of language provision. These compilers are single pass, with a recursive-descent recognition directly producing code for an interpretive or real machine. This reflects the simple LL(1) nature of the syntax and semantics of the language. However, a high degree of code optimisation necessitates knowledge of the complete program being compiled, which in turn implies a multipass compilation technique, see Wulf *et al* (006). This is also recognised by Faiman and Kortesoja (007) who describe a PASCAL compiler for the DFC 10, which is among the notable exceptions to the simple PASCAL compilers described above.

A statistical investigation of the nature of PASCAL programs was carried out at an early stage of the CRAY PASCAL project. This highlights the scalar nature of some PASCAL programs, see Brookes (008). Traditionally, most use of PASCAL has been for non-numeric applications such as system programming. Thus, gathering a significant representative sample of non-numeric programs involved little effort - whereas a corresponding sample of numeric applications was more difficult to obtain. A discussion of the results appears later, but it is interesting to note that there is statistical support for an intuitive feeling that the two application areas are different. This suggests that the vectorisable content of PASCAL programs may be smaller than typical CRAY FORTRAN programs and that an examination of the relevance of other CRAY-1 features may be productive in this context.

CRAY-1 FEATURES CONCERNING PASCAL

A description of the CRAY-1 hardware may be found in CRAY RESEARCH manuals, but some specific features concerning PASCAL are of interest here. With high memory-to-register and register-to-register transfer rates, a PASCAL program on the CRAY-1 is expected to achieve high execution speeds. However, the ratio of memory-to-register to register-to-register transfer speeds is 1:11. Therefore, it is important to minimise the number of store/loads in a procedure by devising a suitable register allocation scheme and by interleaving instructions so as to minimise 'hold' conditions arising from store accesses. This interleaving carried out by the compiler is called 'scheduling'.

With reference to the scalar capabilities of the CRAY-1, there are 64 intermediate B/T registers each. Hence, there is a possibility of utilising these registers as cache memory. Surprisingly, it will be shown that this number is more than the average number of variables declared in a procedure and comparable to the total number of variables declared in a program. Consequently, use of B/T registers to hold variable values is a major factor in reducing the number of store/loads required in a program.

With reference to the vector capabilities, there are eight vector registers, each of which has sixty-four 64-bit elements. While these are obviously utilised for vector processing, it is conceivable to utilise them as an 8:64 scalar cache memory. A closer investigation suggests that the benefits thus gained, compared to store/loads, may not be significant, especially when the selection of a particular vector register is difficult and an A-register load is required. Also, a store/load may not result in a significant delay if data transfer overlaps with concurrent processing. This is a scheduling problem.

In computers with small memory size there generally has to be a tradeoff between runtime efficiency and compiler size/speed. Runtime efficiency generally induces complexity, which in turn increases compiler size and representation data size. In contrast, the 8 Mbyte typical memory size of the CRAY-1 enables an optimising multipass PASCAL compiler to be feasible. In general, this should assist in runtime efficiency of PASCAL programs on the CRAY-1.

In addition to the parallelism implied in vector operations and autonomous store accesses, the CRAY-1 has independent pipelined functional units which may carry out several arithmetic and logical operations concurrently. The pipelining also permits each unit individually to accept functional requests at 12.5 nsec clock intervals even if the functional operation occupies several clocks. To take advantage of this, the compiler must further interleave the instructions by choosing registers and scheduling appropriately.

The high proportion of control transfers inherent in PASCAL programs (discussed below) suggests careful examination of the instruction buffering mechanism on the hardware. This is significant in size, the 256 instruction units being approximately five times that on a CDC 7600. It also has a minimal structure consisting of four separately loaded buffers, but has no intelligence regarding choice of release, look-ahead filling, or heuristics and each buffer must be treated as a contiguous unit. Clearly, loops which fit totally into these buffers and cover no more than four disjoint address spaces, will benefit from a lack of hold conditions arising from instruction store fetches. However, any deviation from these rules incurs the penalty of apparently increased time to process a control transfer, from a minimum of 2 clocks in the case of no-transfer conditional to a worst case buffer 'thrashing' of 25 clocks.

PASCAL FEATURES CONCERNING THE CRAY-1

Procedure abstraction

With the provision of the procedural abstraction facility in PASCAL and a wide acceptance of structured programming principles, a large usage of procedures is expected in PASCAL programs to be run on the CRAY-1, and this will be demonstrated later. Hence, it is important to have an efficient procedure calling sequence. Also, in some cases it may be possible to perform macro-substitution. This could be a textual substitution at an early stage, or code substitution at a later stage.

The principal advantages of the substitution would be a continuity in the usage of the scratch B/T registers and the elimination of the procedure entry/exit code sequence. On the other hand, a main disadvantage could be that there is no localisation of variables on which B/T cache register allocation is dependent. Thus, some registers could be artificially locked out. Further, an increased size of the compiled code due to multiple substitution may cause a frequently obeyed sequence to overflow the instruction buffers.

In the CRAY-1 PASCAL Compiler (CP) the substitution of suitable procedures is neither performed by a preprocessor nor by the code generator. Instead, it is performed at the internal representation level, where there is a knowledge of the properties of the procedure concerned, and the cache register allocation scheme has already been applied.

Strongly typed

PASCAL is a strongly typed language. This enables compile-time selection of a suitable type of register for an operand, since conversion, subrange information, etc is known at compile-time. Consider the following declarations as an example:

```
var I : 1..10; (*index variable*)
    B : boolean
```

A 24-bit A-register is more suitable than a 64-bit S-register, given the bounds of variable I; whereas, an S-register is more suitable for variable B, since logical operations on the CRAY-1 are performed in these registers. This contrasts with the lack of such information in FORTRAN.

Recursion

While recursive procedures entail a stack mechanism, it will be shown in later discussion that recursive procedures are a small percentage of all procedures. For recursion, a structured machine (see 009) with a hardware stack is more suitable. However, the B/T register allocation scheme designed for the compiler emulates a structured machine. This scheme is based on processing a table of information on each procedure. After reserving some registers to reduce recursive call overheads and scratch registers to prolong the life of loaded operands, an appropriate number of B/Ts are allocated to the main program and noted in the procedure/function table entry. The subprocedure call tree is analysed to allocate registers at each mode, with the last allocated to its parent node as a base. As a recursive procedure may call a static one, all the non-static procedures are examined for the calls of static ones, and a list of calls formed. Each element in the list is now processed as an independent tree.

Structured objects

The ability to manipulate complete structures by comparisons and assignments suggests the possibility of vector operations, though not vectorisation in the sense of parallel calculations.

THE NATURE OF PASCAL PROGRAMS

The analysis of the static nature of PASCAL programs mentioned in the introduction was carried out by modifying the Belfast ICL 1900 PASCAL compiler described by Welsh and Quinn (010). By replacing the code generation with frequency counting statements, a file of statistics on various programs could be built up. Brookes (008) describes this process in detail, but Figure 1 shows some relevant measures.

	PASCAL non-numeric	PASCAL numeric
% assignment	36.9	39.3
% call	30.1	24.3
% if	12.6	10.9
% loops	3.8	10.0
% global variables	38.0	26.0
Average leading spaces	14.2	11.3
Count of arrays	13.1	39.3
For : while and repeat	0.9	10.1
Minimum % assignments	22.5	31.8
Maximum % calls	55.4	32.3
INTEGERS : REALs	42.5	1.1
Maximum average leading spaces	29.9	12.8

Figure 1: Summary of static analysis results

With reference to Figure 1, it may be argued that the sample was not representative and that anything may be proved from an analysis of such measures. However, it may be reasonable to conclude that the more common non-numeric applications have fewer declared REALs, use fewer arrays, are more heavily procedured, use testing rather than counting loops and, by virtue of a greater level of indentation, would appear to be more logically complex. Such tentative conclusions would only be fully confirmed by a dynamic analysis of running applications on a CRAY-1, which the authors may not yet perform, though a similar analysis on compilers only, by Shimasaki *et al* (011), gives some support.

Taking the suggested nature of applications as a starting point, it is worth noting that the total number of scalars, for all procedures and the main program, but excluding parameters, was 87:83 per program. The number of single word object parameters per procedure was approximately four and there were less than two declared scalars per procedure. Further, only approximately 12% of procedures appeared to be recursive and the ratio of all structured accesses to variable accesses was approximately 0:8.

It is suggested that the application profile emerging from this discussion is one with a heavy use of procedures which are largely non-recursive and with a significant proportion of control constructs and of structure accessing. Further, the number of variables is significantly fewer than one might expect in a language which is not block-structured and whose declarations are not mandatory, for example FORTRAN.

There is a need for careful optimisation of procedures. The control construct nature of programs (gotos were non-existent) is beneficial in demonstrating control-flow, but emphasises the need for optimisation of jumps at coincident construct boundaries. This is particularly true, in view of the control transfer times already mentioned.

The significant use of structure accesses suggests close attention be paid to common sub-expression analysis, as avoiding re-evaluation of recurring address calculations and indirections would be as or more critical than avoiding explicit arithmetic re-evaluations, particularly as store access times for indirection are significantly greater than functional arithmetic times. This type of optimisation is sometimes ignored on machines with sophisticated operand buffer mechanisms and hardware controlled cache stores, for example the local Manchester machine MU5 (009).

One other feature of PASCAL programs which is of interest, is the distribution of literal sizes. The scalar enumeration types and subranges of PASCAL encourage the implicit and explicit use of small positive constants, and a separate investigation by Wilson (012) suggests a distribution as shown in Figure 2. This distribution corresponds to the provision in the CRAY-1 hardware of a load six-bit literal instruction.

COMPILATION PROCESSES

It has been suggested by Fischer (013) that compilation itself is a vectorisable task, as a vector of text is matched with internal vectors (syntax, property lists, code skeletons etc) to produce a vector of instructions. However, the complexities involved in optimisation and the limited nature of the vector operations available on current machines do not appear to make practical use of this technique directly viable. This does not mean that the vector hardware is eschewed - three categories of use are apparent, namely search operations, as an additional cache, and for structured comparisons and assignments.

These techniques make it desirable to use operand manipulation in preference to control flow logic where possible, particularly in view of the jump times given above and the expected benefits of scheduling store/load waits. The recursive-descent technique, employed by most PASCAL compilers, might appear to be critical in this respect. However, an analysis of the time spent in the recognition phase of the simplest of PASCAL compilers given by Oliviera (014) (see Figure 3), shows this to be much less important than name look-up, for example. It should be noted that the measures in this table are, in fact, distorted by inefficient symbol table manipulation and the simplistic code generation required by the interpretive system which was analysed.

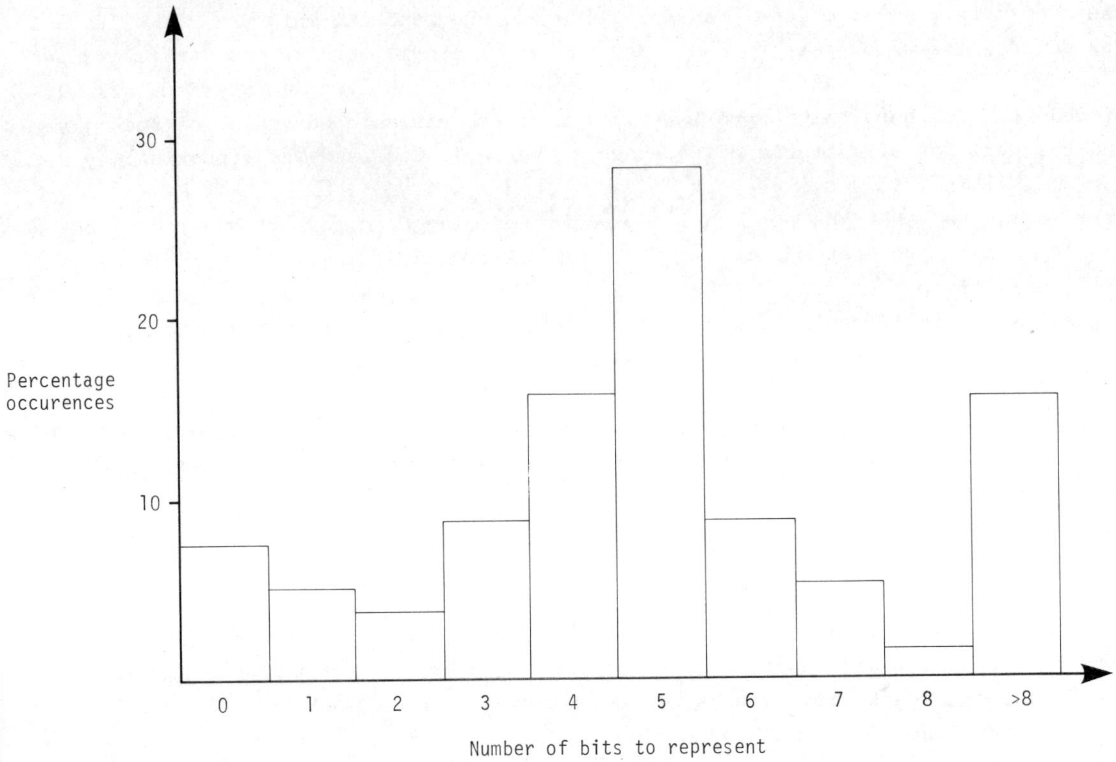

Figure 2: Distribution of literal sizes

	Percentage of compilation time
Scanning	26
Itemisation	9
Symbol table	51
Syntax recognition	2
Error recovery	3
Code generation	9

Figure 3: Performance of a simple compiler

Because of the necessity to open and close the scope of identifiers frequently (as record fields are selected and with statements applied), most PASCAL compilers use a tree-structured symbol-table. This has the benefit of a logarithmic look-up time, but may involve significant control flow logic and typically five levels of tree-node (ie five store accesses and indirections). An analysis of hash table techniques given in Figure 4, shows that the use of vector registers as hash tables, with any reasonable hash formula, would reduce the store accesses by a factor of four (to approximately one), while simplifying the control logic in the look-up process. Note the importance of this improvement due to the 1:11 ratio of register speed to memory speed mentioned earlier. In practice, record-file identifiers do not take advantage of this hashing to reduce the overhead of scope open/close operations. In Figure 4 the name is abcd..z, length n and the hash value is taken as modulo 64.

Hash formula	Average number of store accesses
a + b + c . . .	1.26 - 1.50
((a"2 + b)"2 + z)"2 + n	1.11 - 1.61
(. . . ((a"2 + b)"2) . . .+z)"2	1.73 - 2.16

Figure 4: Store accesses per symbol table search

THE INTERNAL REPRESENTATION

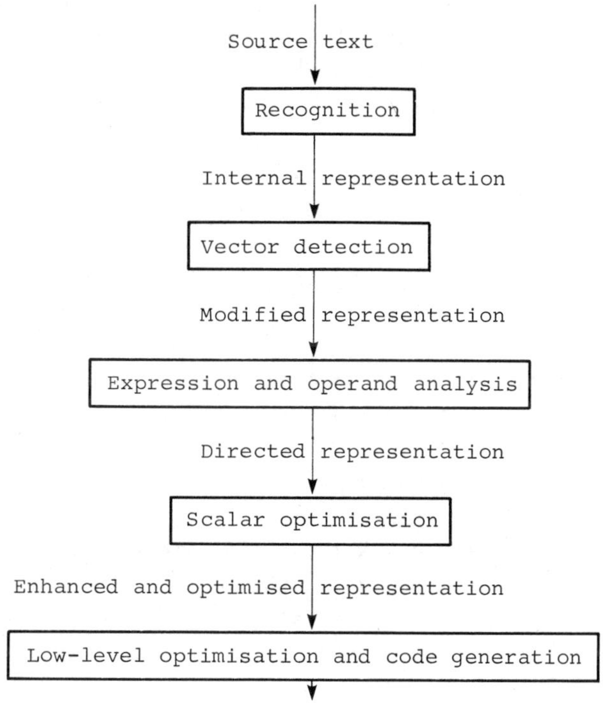

Figure 5: Overall operation of the compiler

The internal representation referred to in Figure 5 is produced during recognition and is in five parts:

1 Procedure table.
2 Constant pool.
3 Property lists.
4 Statement tree.
5 Triple vector.

The procedure table indicates whether a procedure is recursive, performs I/O or accesses non-locals (side effects), and shows how many local variables of different types are present, etc. The recursive nature is determined by a set of rules which guarantee that a recursive procedure is so marked. At the end of recognition, the register allocation algorithm described earlier is applied to associate the intermediate B/T registers with variables of the procedures.

Some usage count information is retained in the procedure table. However, the structured nature of PASCAL programs is used to avoid necessity of GOTO analysis and determining areas of usage of variables as required in FORTRAN subprograms, which are textually larger.

It is hoped that the discrimination of different kinds of procedure (eg recursive, non-local accessing, etc) will permit overheads comparable with machine coding standards. This may not obviate the need for macro-substitution, where possible.

The control construct of a program is represented in a bracketted form within the expression triples to assist low-level optimisations. However, the separate existence of the statement tree mitigates the disadvantages of the often quoted fixed nature of triples (Aho and Ullman (015)) while maintaining the advantages of compactness. The level of operand representation is chosen such that two references to the same object (eg two matching variant fields or two named constants with the same value) are identical. This implies the use of actual offsets rather than property list addresses - though these are retained where a global analysis is required (eg vectorisation). This approach also contrasts with the register rather than operand representation used in CRAY-1 FORTRAN (CFT).

OPTIMISATION OF STRUCTURED/DYNAMIC OBJECTS

Scalar optimisations are performed on the internal representation of a program (discussed above). In general a program is optimised one procedure at a time. Within a given procedure, the flow of control information is appropriately represented in the triple vector. This drives the optimiser according to the properties of a control construct, and according to nested and sequential constructs.

On recognition of a control construct, a local table is initiated. This table holds the information about the operands in the construct while the construct is being processed. Hence the table is referred to as the <operand,reference> (or <opd,ref>) table. Clearly, the <opd,ref> table behaves like a stack, as constructs are opened and closed.

An <opd,ref> table entry generally consists of an operand and its properties. The properties include the class of the operand; the class of register use; the reference of the operand in the triple vector; the availability, category, dependency, state and the usage order of the operand, and its dynamic linkages. This information, which is gathered while processing a construct, is also useful during the later phases of the compilation process (eg register allocation).

Associated with each triple is a row of entries in the usage-chain column for the left operand, the right operand, and the complete triple. As each operand position can be distinguished within a row, the operand entries in the <opd,ref> table enable different operand-value usage-chains to be constructed. These chains connect the appearances of operands all known to have the same value. The operands themselves are connected to a direction to the first appearance of the value. This is invaluable for detecting common subexpressions, but is also useful during code generation.

While a wide range of scalar optimisations are performed with these internal mechanisms, those which performed as a result of the idiosyncrasies of PASCAL are of particular interest: structured objects, dynamic objects, record variants, pointers, etc.

Unlike simple operands, complex operands (such as array elements, fields of records, complete structured objects, etc) form separate triples. In order to detect common subexpressions using such complex variables, the variables themselves participate in the detection process. For this purpose, structured objects maintain additional information in the <opd,ref> table.

Records and dynamic data structures

For dynamic data structures, not only the references of individual elements, but also the structural relationships have to be considered. Particularly in view of the possibility of aliasing where an object may be accessed via two different routes, for example A in the example below. The propagation and common subexpression detection for these objects involves accessing the appropriate structures via static pointers. Consider the following dynamic variable accesses:

```
        P^.K^.A and Q^.A
   where Q := P^.K;
```

The internal representation of the relationships, emanating from the <opd,ref> table is as shown in Figure 6.

```
                                   :<opd,ref> table:
                                   :               :
                            g<-----:----<P,ref>    :
                            :      :               :
                 <k,ref><-----0<P^> :              :
                 :                 :               :
                 g<----------------:----<Q,ref>    :
                 :                 :               :
       <A,ref><------0<P^>K^>      :               :
                                   :               :
```

Figure 6: <opd,ref> table dynamic linkages

In the dynamic representation in Figure 6, <P,ref> is the entry for the static pointer P; g designates a GATE, to enable aliasing pointers to refer to a same dynamic object; 0 designates a dynamic record and <A,ref> is the field representation of object P^.K^.

Knowledge of a static record, unlike the dynamic case, is held directly in the <opd,ref> table. However, the representations for fields of a static record are held as dynamic linkages. Moreover, as there is no aliasing involved in this case, GATES are not necessary.

Availability of objects

On an assignment to a field, an object obtains a right-hand-side reference. Further, the complete reference of the containing record is disabled, so that a next use of the record object is not detected as common to its previous definition. In essence, the record enters a new state. Consider the following example:

```
DOPRINT (P^);  (*value parameter *)
P^.NAME := NEWNAME;
TEST := P^ = Q^;
```

As there is an intervening assignment to P^.NAME, the detection of the second occurence of object P^ is inhibited. Instead, object P^ obtains a new reference which can be propagated further. For an assigned field which is multiple levels within a structure, all the higher level containing structured objects is disabled. This higher level inhibition process is terminated on encountering a pointer. On the other hand, an assignment to a complete record object implies copying of the knowledge of assigned-object fields. This technique enables the detection of the assigned-to object fields as common.

For pointer assignments, not only the right-hand-side reference is allocated, but structural changes also take place. For instance, new linkages are formed such that a common dynamic object is accessible via a common GATE. The implication of this is that the usages of the same object referenced by aliasing pointers are detected as common.

Upon recognition of a triple for dynamic data structure, an appropriate structure is created, and if the structure is used (as opposed to assigned-to) then its reference is enabled. Subsequent use of this structure is detected as common to its first occurrence. The linkages of the structure exist in the local table for the duration of the current control construct. In theory, knowledge of suitable structures could be propagated into the outer loops, but this may introduce excessive compiler complexity.

Where side effects are present, the precise nature of the affected pointers must be determined. For instance, assigning to a field could cause aliasing problems if another, apparently unrelated, pointer also has access to the field (eg non-local pointers). This is the case in the following example:

```
if <boolean-expression> then
  begin
    write(P^.A);
    Q^.A := maxint;
    Q := Q^.NEXT;
    write(P^.A)
 end (*if*);
```

Here, it may not be safe to detect the second occurrence of P^.A as common, unless it is known that P and Q are not aliasing pointers. The dynamic linkages are of some assistance here.

In general, there are pointers whose access-right information is available, and these are termed 'GREEN pointers'; others are termed 'RED pointers'. The colour of a pointer can be deduced from the pointer entry in the local table. A GREEN pointer is allocated the highest dependency number (infinity); whereas a RED pointer is allocated a dependency number equivalent to its creation point in the triple vector.

Separate uses of RED pointers to an unknown alias structure, have no side effects, but they may not be identified as common. As a result of an assignment to an object requiring an indirection through a RED pointer, all other RED objects are deleted. Thus, no affected RED object is wrongly detected as common. This is achieved by using the dependency values to limit the search region to the offending assignment point forward.

Record variants

An assignment to, or creation of a variant field may overwrite one or more existing variant fields, whose space ranges overlap the former field. Given the field displacements and sizes, overlapping fields can be detected and knowledge of their values erased. Since, at a given time, only unique fields exist in the field representations, different variant fields of the same size and displacement are not distinguished internally. The effect of this technique may be compared to that of the optimising DEC 10 PASCAL compiler (007) by considering the following example text:

```
 type R = record
            A : integer;
            case B : boolean of
              true : (C1 : integer);
              false: (C2 : integer)
          end;
var P, Q : ^R;
      .
      .
      P^.C1 := 10;
      Q^.C2 := 20;
      if P^.C1 = 10 then ...
```

Whereas in the DEC 10 compiler, at the last statement, P^.C1 is equal to 10; in CP, P^.C1 is equal to 20. Thus, CP enables the optimisation of record structures even in the presence of 'free unions'. This is particularly useful in some machine-dependent applications, where it may be necessary to map a value onto another one of a different type.

As the dynamic linkages (see Figure 6) simulate the runtime behaviour of dynamic data structures, it is possible to detect some runtime faults at compile time, in a similar manner to assignments of variables with disjoint defined ranges. An example of the kind of dynamic data-structure fault detected, is accessing through a DISPOSEd structure.

VECTORISATION

The figures given in Figure 1 appear discouraging when full use of the CRAY vector capabilities is envisaged. The common non-numeric applications have few REALs and few arrays, whereas the vector hardware is most effective when processing arrays of real numbers. Vector operations are more likely to be present in scalar operations within a FOR loop, but these are infrequent in the non-numeric class. Indeed, the balance of statement types as a whole is discouraging, with loops infrequent and IF/call statements (which give vectorisation difficulties) more frequent. However, it is a matter of observable experience that programmers and applications on a CRAY-1 are self selecting, with much emphasis put on the class of problems for which the machine was purchased. The samples for Figure 1 were taken before CP implementation and therefore were not, of course, specifically CRAY applications.

Vector facilities can be provided by language extension as in CFD on the ILLIAC IV, by provision of subroutines which may be called by the user as in the STAR FORTRAN on the CDC STAR-100 and CFT on the CRAY-1 or by use of an entirely new language which reflects the vector parallelism as does the ACTUS language of Perrot (016). These approaches have obvious benefits in guaranteeing the maximum extraction of vector parallelism at a minimum compilation cost. However, they do put a varying degree of burden on the user and remove all possibility of porting the application to or from other (possibly scalar) processors. PASCAL enthusiasts would see this latter point as particularly important in a context where a CRAY-1 is necessarily part of a multimachine configuration. Thus CRAY-1 CFT and CRAY PASCAL have been aimed at automatic vectorisation of standard scalar written programs.

In an attempt to isolate the nature of loops and those features which were preventing vectorisation, the static analysis presented earlier was extended. The static analyser program was modified to detect the occurrence of constructs within FOR loops which were known to enforce scalar operation. Where no such difficulty was detected, a data dependency analysis of the statements within the loop was undertaken. This was capable of determining whether the loop was a vector one or could be manipulated to be so. The results in Figure 7 for a program known to be highly numerical in content, show relatively few vectorisable loops (16 out of 191). Of course, it is possible that the knowledge in CP of the form of side effects in each user procedure would permit the elimination of a procedure call as a definitive block to vectorisation.

The detection of vector operations during compilation may be achieved at one of several points. The source text may be preprocessed into a vector form, as may be achieved in the PARAFRASE system described by Kuck *et al* (017). Alternatively, vectorisation may be achieved within the compiler by operating on the internal representation of the program, either before or after scalar optimisations. In the case of CP, scalar optimisations require the modifiable tree-structure representation to be changed to a directed graph form. In contrast, vectorisation may involve changing the structure of the program by loop splitting, for example. Thus in CP, vector operations are detected prior to scalar optimisations and a modified form of the triples is produced.

CODE GENERATION

The enhanced and optimised representations mentioned under *The internal representation* above are used in the final stages of compilation to perform code generation. This contains several areas with conflicting requirements, as in Figure 8.

Summary of vector failures

Inner loop found	18	10.98
Procedure/function found	63	38.41
Nested if found	4	2.44
Index expression failed	2	1.22
Goto/label found	5	3.05
Case statement found	2	1.22
LHS is constant	61	37.20
Const inc expression expected	8	4.88
Non-index use of control variable	1	0.61

Total failures = 164

Data dependence analysis of 27 loops

Led to:

3 scalar , 15.79

16 vector , 84.21

Figure 7: Vectorisation static analysis

In particular, the optimal allocation of registers, interleaving of instruction sequences (to minimise waiting on the arrival of operands), and peephole optimisation of juxtaposed instructions, all conflict. Optimisation of register usage may clearly only be performed with real functional registers, and the ordering of instructions is one factor in the choice of operand for register release. Contrarily, the allocation of real registers is an inhibiting factor on the scheduling process. Note the example of Figure 9 with operands from store, where <u>fewer</u> registers is a slower schema, but the cost of the use of an additional register is dependent on the surrounding code.

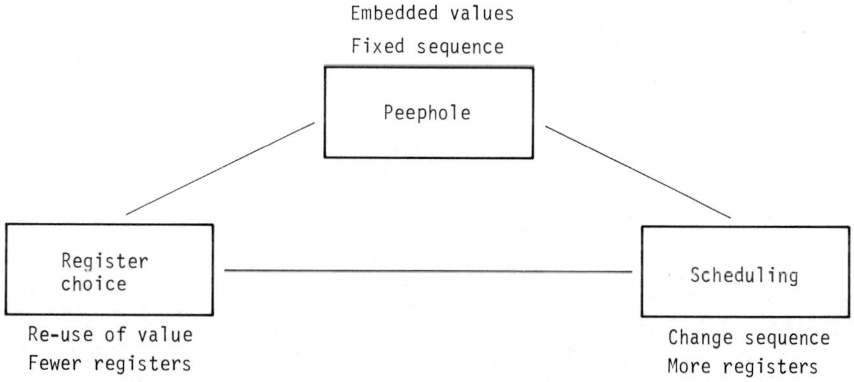

Figure 8: Conflicting optimisations

Two register	Start time	Finish time
S1 = a	0	11
S2 = b	2	13
S1 = S1*S2	13 - wait for b	20
S2 = c	14	25
S1 = S1+S2	25 - wait for c	31

Three register	Start time	Finish time
S1 = a	0	11
S2 = b	2	13
S3 = c	4	15
S1 = S1*S2	13 - wait for b	20
S1 = S1+S3	20 - wait for *	26

*Figure 9: 2/3 register coding of a*b + c*

CFT gives priority to scheduling by performing this with virtual registers, whereas CP allocates registers on the basis of a tree walk of the expression, leaving maximum freedom for later scheduling. Which technique is more beneficial is not immediately apparent and, no doubt, an experimental analysis will lead to more interaction of the two requirements. The IBM PL.8 compiler (018), for example, schedules twice - before and after register choice.

CONCLUSIONS

Traditionally PASCAL compilers based on the Zurich recursive descent one-pass compiler have comprised 3000 to 12 000 lines of PASCAL source. Not surprisingly the CRAY PASCAL source is longer - approximately 25 000 lines - and will no doubt suffer from compute-time penalties. Arguments advanced by Faiman and Kortesoja (007) suggest that a degradation factor of two to four may be expected in comparison with the most simplistic compilers. For systems programming or production of frequently used applications this is thought to be acceptable in order to gain the benefit of optimal runtimes.

This PASCAL project was begun fresh from a subset implementation for total CRAY-1 register size and also a P-code implementation. Thus, we see that the only interesting numbers are 0, 1 and ∞.

REFERENCES

001 BASKETT F and KELLER T
An evaluation of the CRAY-1 computer
In *High speed computer and algorithm organisation* D J Kuck *et al* (eds)
Academic Press (1977)

002 Personal Communication with CDC and CRAY technical sales staff (1981)

003 WIRTH N
PASCAL - S A subset and its implementation
ETH Zurich Report 12

004 NORI K *et al*
The PASCAL <P> implementation notes
ETH Zurich (1975)

005 WIRTH N
The design of a PASCAL compiler
Software - Practice and Experience vol 1 p309 (1971)

006 WULF W *et al*
The design of an optimising compiler
Elsevier (1975)

007 FAIMAN R and KORTESOJA A
An optimising PASCAL compiler
IEEE Transactions on Software Engineering vol SE-6 no 6 (1980)

008 BROOKES G
Compilation analysis techniques for vector processing methods
MSc Thesis University of Manchester (1981)

009 MORRIS D and IBBETT R
The MU5 computer system
Macmillan Press (1979)

010 WELSH J and QUINN C
A PASCAL compiler for the 1900 series computers
Software-Practice and Experience vol 2 p73 (1972)

011 SHIMASAKI M *et al*
An analysis of PASCAL programs in compiler writing
Software-Practice and Experience vol 10 p149 (1980)

012 WILSON I R
PASCAL for school and hobby use
Software-Practice and Experience Vol 10 p659 (1980)

013 FISCHER C
On parsing and compiling arithmetic expressions on vector computers
ACM Transactions on Programming Languages vol 2 p203 (1980)

014 OLIVIERA J
PASCAL on small microcomputers
MSc Thesis University of Manchester (1981)

015 AHO A and ULLMAN J
Principles of compiler design
Addison Wesley (1977)

016 PERROT
A language for array and vector processors
ACM Transactions of Programming Languages and Systems vols 1 and 2 (1979)

017 KUCK D J, KUHN P H, LEASURE B, and WOLFE M
Structure of an advanced vectoriser for pipelined processors
IEEE 4th International CPM computer software and applications (Oct 1980)

018 AUSLANDER M and HOPKINS M
An overview of the PL.8 compiler
Sigplan Symposium on Compiler Construction Boston, Mass (June 1982)

BIBLIOGRAPHY
AND
ANALYSIS REFERENCES

AN ANNOTATED BIBLIOGRAPHY OF SUPERCOMPUTER SYSTEMS TECHNOLOGY

F Sumner

Manchester University
Manchester
UK

AN ANNOTATED BIBLIOGRAPHY OF SUPERCOMPUTER SYSTEMS TECHNOLOGY

INTRODUCTION

In Section 1 of the Analysis it was argued that the title Supercomputers should be extended to cover not only the highly parallel floating-point engines typified by the CRAY and CYBER 205, but also other specialised computers for all forms of pattern recognition, database management, and the new architectures which should be more suitable for the support of languages designed for the implementation of knowledge-based systems.

It was also argued that the key to advances in performance was in technology, particularly in the area of memories where it was felt that hierarchies ranging from sub-10 nsec buffers to Gbyte disks would continue to be the solution for efficient data storage and data access.

The contents of the Bibliography reflect these arguments and hopefully supply the user with a selection of papers supporting, and in some cases arguing against, these beliefs.

The contents of the Bibliography have been chosen to give a picture of the development of the technology, architecture, and application of supercomputers. In a subject with such a very high rate of change and development the vast majority of the papers selected have been published within the last three years. Earlier ones either provide background or are included because they were attempts to look into the future and it is interesting to compare their extrapolations with actual developments.

The Bibliography is arranged in alphabetical order of the first named author. In order to try to provide a structured index a set of headings is given below together with the reference numbers of the papers which come under that heading; naturally several papers appear under more than one heading.

A few books are included as they give excellent surveys of their field and references to earlier publications which will permit the user to trace developments in the different areas. The same is true of various review articles generally taken from the ACM Computing Surveys. The majority of other references are to papers published in the proceedings of specialist conferences in, for example computer architecture and in parallel processing. The general practice in computing seems to be for workers at the leading edge of their subject to present papers at such conferences rather than submit them to more conventional journals. A final source of high quality papers are editions of *Computer* or special issues of the *IEEE Transactions on Computers* which are dedicated to specific areas. Included below is a list of the recent and forthcoming special issues which shows very clearly the degree of interest in the subjects covered in this Report.

IEEE Transactions on Computers special issues (July 1982 - May 1983)

- Reliable and fault-tolerant computing
- Computer architecture for pattern analysis and image database management
- Performance evaluation of multiple processor systems
- Parallel and distributed processing
- Computer arithmetic
- Recent developments in the design and implementation of families of computers.

CROSS-REFERENCE LISTING

Subject	*Reference*
Applications:	
Databases	113,127,140,161,167,182
Knowledge-based systems	122,171
Numerical and scientific	109,134,174,180
Picture processing	102,103,115,118,123,129,130,132,178,185,186, 187,188,195,197
Speech	124
Architecture:	
Array processors	114,147,148,155,169
Arrays of processing elements	156,158,187,196
Dataflow	120,121,135,136,137,152,191,193
Fault tolerance	101,106,166
General	117,148,172,177
Interconnection networks	101,126
Memory organisation	119,147,157,170,175
Multiprocessors	104,105,150,164,166,184
Parallel computing	108,111,128,134,138,139,141,145,163,168,190
Pipelines	114,146,147,148,149,159,160,181
Hardware and technology	110,116,125,133,144,153,160,161,162,176, 179,183,189
Languages:	
for dataflow	100,173
for other new architectures	107,165,192
for parallel systems	112,131,143,151,154
Microprocessors	142,194

ABSTRACTS

100 ACKERMAN W B
Dataflow languages
Computer vol 15 no 2 pp 15-25 (1982)

Ackerman argues that the language properties that a dataflow computer requires are beneficial in themselves and are very similar to some of the properties that are known to facilitate the understanding of maintainable software. The paper contains a nice description of dataflow languages with particular reference to VAL and ID. Ackerman makes the point that dataflow languages must avoid the use of a global memory manipulated by the sequential execution of commands.

101 ADAMS III G B and SIEGEL H J
The Extra Stage Cube: a fault-tolerant interconnection network for supersystems
IEEE Transactions on Computers vol C-31 no 5 (May 1982)

The Extra Stage Cube (ESC) interconnection network, a fault-tolerant structure, is proposed for use in large-scale parallel and distributed supercomputer systems. It has all of the interconnecting capabilities of the multistage cube-type networks that have been proposed for many supersystems. The ESC is derived from the generalised cube network by the addition of one stage of interchange boxes and a bypass capability for two stages. It is shown that the ESC provides fault tolerance for any single failure.

102 AGGARWAL J K, DUDA R O and ROSENFIELD A
Computer methods in image analysis
IEEE Press 466 pp NY (1977)

This book is a collection of papers on the general topic of image analysis by computer. The papers are divided into seven sections:

1 Correlation and matching.

2 Segmentation: regions.

3 Region representation and description.

4 Segmentation: boundaries.

5 Boundary representation and description.

6 Scene analysis: the blocks world.

7 Scene analysis: the natural world.

Each section is preceded by a short introduction.

103 AHUJA N and SCHACHTER B J
Image models
ACM Computing Surveys vol 13 no 4 p 373 (1981)

Models of spatial variation used in the computer processing of pictorial information are surveyed. Models of images depicting homogeneous textures are reviewed under the categories of pixel-based and region-based models. Pixel-based models are further divided into one-dimensional time series models, random field models, and syntactic models.

104 ARDEN B W and GINOSAR R
MP/C: a multiprocessor/computer architecture
IEEE Transactions on Computers vol C-31 no 5 455 pp (May 1982)

A computer architecture for concurrent computing is proposed which has the shared memory aspect of tightly-coupled multiprocessor systems and also the connection simplicity associated with message-connected, loosely-coupled multicomputer systems. A large address space is dynamically partitioned into contiguous segments that can be accessed by a single processor.

105 ARVIND V K and GOSTELOW K P
A computer capable of exchanging processors for time
Proc IFIP Congress pp 849-854 (1977)

The subject of this paper is the design of a computing system which can achieve parallel execution using arrays of processing elements. Arvind and Gostelow present an architecture which is based on dataflow languages. The design is presented as a description of an interpreter for a selected dataflow language. From this description, some of the properties and possible hardware realisations of parts of a total system are deduced.

106 AVIZIENIS A
Fault tolerance: the survival attribute of digital systems
Proc IEEE 66 pp 1109-1125 (Oct 1978)

This paper discusses the concept of fault tolerance, the reasons for its inclusion in digital system architecture, and the methods of its implementation. A chronological view of the evolution of fault-tolerance systems and an outline of some goals for its further development conclude the presentation.

107 BACKUS J
Function-level programs as mathematical objects
Proc ACM Conf on *Functional programming languages and computer architecture* (1981)

This paper discusses the 'functional level' approach to building programs. This approach applies program forming operations to the given programs to form a succession of programs culminating in the desired program.

108 BATCHER K E
Bit-serial parallel processing systems
IEEE Transaction on Computers vol C-31 no 5 p 377 (May 1982)

This paper describes a recent development of 2-bit serial parallel processing systems. One system is an airborne associative processor in a volume less than 0.5 cubic feet, with approximately the same processing power as STARAN, and a second system is described with approximately 100 times the power of STARAN, capable of 100 MFLOPS or up to 3000 million instr/sec for 16-bit integer arithmetic.

109 BURKE P G, DAVIES B W and EDWARDS D P
Some research applications on the CRAY-1 computer at the Daresbury laboratory 1979-1981
SERC Rep Daresbury Laboratory (1982)

This report is a collection of papers describing work done on the CRAY-1 during the first two years of its operation. It provides a good illustration of the range of fields which have benefited from the use of supercomputers. It contains 16 reports.

110 CHI C S
Advances in computer mass storage technology
Computer vol 15 no 5 pp 60-74 (1982)

The paper gives a nice review of the developments in magnetic recording with extrapolations to 1988. It discusses 'think-film recording' and the possible advantages of perpendicular mode recording and concludes with a discussion of optical disks.

111 CHIANG A M
A new CCD parallel processing architecture
Proc Conf on *VLSI systems and computations* pp 408-415 Carnegie Mellon Univ (1981)

This is a description of a CCD parallel processing architecture which will allow devices to be built that can perform many high-level mathematical operations such as vector-matrix products, matrix-matrix products, and triple matrix products.

112 CONERY J S and KIBLER D F
Parallel interpretation of logic programs
Proc ACM Conf on *Functional programming languages and computer architecture* p 163 (1981)

This paper presents an abstract model that exploits the parallelism due to non-deterministic choices in a logic program. A working interpreter is described together with various models.

113 CONNETT J
Database software or database machine?
IUCC Bulletin (GB) vol 3 no 3 pp 131-132 (1981)

This paper examines one existing and one suggested design for database machines, and describes how these machines might be used. Both database machines are designed to have low cost and good performance.

114 CONTROL DATA CORPORATION
Final report, preliminary study for a numerical aerodynamic simulation facility
NASA CR-152068-9 (1977)

CONTROL DATA CORPORATION
Numerical aerodynamic simulation facility preliminary study extension
NASA CR-152108 (1978)

BURROUGHS CORPORATION
Final report, numerical aerodynamic simulation facility preliminary study
NASA CR-152060-2 (1977)

BURROUGHS CORPORATION
Numerical aerodynamic simulation facility preliminary study extension
NASA CR-152107 (1978)

The above four papers provide detailed descriptions of proposals by Control Data and Burroughs of two designs of supercomputers with speeds of approximately 2 GFLOPS. The Burroughs design is based on an array of 512 processors and a sophisticated memory switch. The Control Data machine is a multipipe version of the CYBER 205.

115 DANIELSSON P E and LEVIALDI S
Computer architectures for pictorial information systems
Computer vol 14 no 11 pp 53-67 (1981)

The hardware and software for pictorial information systems are discussed. Several parallel processors are reviewed including GLOPR, Picap I and II, CLIP IV, MPP, and DAP, and there is also a short section on programming language considerations.

116 DANSKY A H
Bipolar circuit design for a 5000-circuit VLSI gate array
IBM J of Research and Development vol 25 pp 116-125 (May 1981)

This paper presents the design of a one-chip 370-compatible processor. It describes the technology selection and the chip design process.

117 DARLINGTON J and REEVE M
ALICE - a multiprocessor reduction machine for the parallel evaluation of applicative languages
Proc ACM Conf on *Functional programming languages and computer architecture* p 65 (1981)

In this paper a scheme is presented for the parallel evaluation of a wide variety of applicative languages together with an overview of the architecture of a machine on which it may be implemented. The approach is compared with other proposed schemes for the parallel evaluation of applicative languages and future developments are discussed.

118 DAVIS E W
Parallel systems for imagery data processing and storage
Proc IEEE Computer Society Workshop pp 57-61 (1981)

An architecture is described which has parallelism of processing components, and extends the parallelism to secondary storage via bubble memories. The result is a device capable of storing imagery data and processing parallel algorithms on the images.

119 DEB A
A regular non-periodic skewing scheme for optimal conflict-free memory access
Proc IFIP Congress p 193 (1980)

In parallel computation, the access to large arrays by rows, columns, main diagonal, etc presents considerable problems for a memory organised in a normal way. This paper describes the result of a skewing mechanism which increases memory utilisation and the speed of data transfer.

120 DENNIS J B
The varieties of dataflow computers
Proc IEEE 1st Intl Conf on *Distributed computing systems* pp 430-439 (Oct 1979)

Architectures of computer systems based on dataflow concepts are attracting increasing attention as an alternative to conventional sequential processors. The paper discusses and contrasts several approaches to dataflow computation representative of current work on experimental prototype machines.

121 DENNIS J B
Dataflow supercomputers
Computer (USA) vol 13 no 11 pp 48-56 (1980)

Dennis provides new strategies to attain programmability with increased performance, including two approaches to dataflow architecture, dataflow multiprocessors, and the cell block architecture.

122 DINCBAS M
*A knowledge-based Expert System for automatic analysis and synthesis in CAD**
Proc IFIP Congress p 705 (1980)

The introduction of artificial intelligence techniques in Computer-Aided Design (CAD) aims at increasing the aid brought to the designer by the machine. Some aspects of expert systems are discussed. An expert program for the analysis and synthesis of electronic circuits is discussed with emphasis on knowledge representation and resolution strategy. Examples which demonstrate problem solving are included.

123 DUFF M J B
Cellular processors
Proc IEE Colloquium on *New types of*

digital processing elements p 3/1-2 (1981)

Currently, only two cellular logic arrays are in operation, one of which, DAP, is in commercial production. The other, CLIP IV, is the sixth array to be constructed at University College London as part of a continuing design study on cellular logic image processing.

124 ERMAN L D, HAYES-ROTH F, LESSER V R and RAJ-REDDY D
The HEARSAY-II Speech-Understanding System integrating knowledge to resolve uncertainty
ACM Computing Surveys vol 12 no 2 pp 213-253 (1980)

This is an excellent survey of the problems of computer recognition of speech. The paper discusses the characteristics of the speech problem in particular, the special kinds of problem-solving uncertainty in that domain, the structure of the HEARSAY-II system developed to cope with that uncertainty, and the relationship between HEARSAY-II's structure and those of other speech-understanding systems.

125 FAIRBAIRN D G
VLSI: a new frontier for systems designers
Computer vol 15 no 1 pp 87-96 (1982)

Highly parallel systems require large amounts of hardware and there are also structural properties which make the application of VLSI very promising. This paper is written on the premise that parallel and other VLSI machines of the future must be designed by systems people to have a detailed understanding of VLSI. It contains a useful list of universities offering VLSI design courses, generally based on the Mead and Conway text.

126 FENG T
A survey of interconnection networks
Computer vol 14 no 12 pp 12-27 (1981)

Concurrent processing depends on interconnection networks for communication among processors and memory modules. The article considers various topologies and switching strategies.

127 FENG T Y
A very large database computer
Proc IEEE Computer Society Workshop pp 12-24 (1981)

Feng proposes a very large database computer following a discussion on the classification and characteristics of various database machines.

128 FLYNN M J and HENNESSY J L
Parallelism and representation problems in distributed systems
IEEE Transactions on Computers vol C-29 no 12 pp 1080-1086 (Dec 1980)

A hierarchical view of program representation is used to explain the problems of matching various representations to underlying distributed architectures. If a program is to use a distributed computer system effectively, it is necessary to represent and detect a high degree of parallelism. Methods for detecting such parallelism and their limitations are discussed.

129 FOUNTAIN T J
Towards CLIP 6 - an extra dimension
Proc IEEE Computer Society Workshop pp 25-30 (1981)

A new architecture is described, which offers greater resolution, performance/cost advantages, and a set of primitive operations better fitted to the multivalued nature of the data. Various possible implementations of this idea are proposed and the advantages and disadvantages of each are discussed.

130 FRALICK S *et al*
The IIP - an Interactive Image Processor
Proc IEEE Computer Society Workshop pp 149-153 (1981)

The Interactive Image Processor (IIP), as an add-on module to existing digital display systems, is designed to greatly increase the processing power and speed of response of image workstations.

131 GAJSKI D D, PADUA D A, KUCK D J and KUHN R H
A second opinion on dataflow machines and languages
Computer vol 15 no 2 pp 58-69 (1982)

This article summarises the principle and practice of dataflow computation and identifies a number of its short-comings as a method of high-speed computation. An alternative approach is postulated leading to higher speed computation from the higher level use of dependence graphics.

132 GOLDWASSER S M
A generalised segment display processor architecture
IEEE Computer Society Workshop (USA) pp 301-308 (Nov 1981)

The overall organisation and functional logical architecture for an image processing and display system based on the segment descriptor block concept are presented. This generalised approach provides key operational and developmental advantages when compared with existing systems.

133 GOSLING J B
Design of arithmetic units for digital computers
The Macmillan Press Ltd (1980)

This book gives a practical description of the algorithms for performing the various arithmetic operations and explains how they are implemented. It also deals with more advanced concepts and more powerful units.

134 GOTTLIEBB A and SCHWARZ J T
Networks and algorithms for very large-scale parallel computation
Computer vol 15 no 1 pp 27-35 (1982)

The approach to very large-scale parallel computation is described using standard high-performance microprocessor chips tightly coupled by a suitable network. The designs assume the availability in the near future of 20 Mcycle microprocessors and 1 Mbyte memory chips. The paper also discusses the possibility of using modifiers to existing programming languages for parallel processors.

135 GURD J R and WATSON I
Dataflow computers
Proc IEE Colloquium on *New types of digital processing elements* pp 2/1-4 London (1981)

Gurd and Watson discuss dataflow computer architectures and compare these to other parallel architectures. They then consider the graphical computation approach and look at iterative and recursive cycles. The Manchester prototype system is looked at briefly.

136 GURD J and WATSON I
Data-driven system for high-speed parallel computing (Part I)
Computer Design pp 91-100 (June 1980)

137 GURD J and WATSON I
Data-driven system for high-speed parallel computing (Part II)
Computer Design pp 97-106 (July 1980)

Very high-speed computer organisation has become an area for extensive research because of the continuing demand for such systems. Part I of this two-part article discusses the result of one such research effort, suggesting that the classical approach to computing be abandoned in favour of a data-driven model that allows the full potential for parallelism both in hardware and in software. Part II describes the architecture of a prototype system that implements the data-driven model of computing.

138 GUZMAN A
A parallel hierarchical machine for high-level language processing
Proc IEEE Intl Conf on *Parallel processing* pp 64-71 (1981)

A computer architecture is presented that processes in parallel programs written in high-level languages capable of being expressed in the Lambda notation (applicative languages). The architecture has been developed for the LISP language, although other applicative languages are also possible.

139 GUZMAN A
A hierarchical multimicroprocessor LISP machine
IEEE Computer Society Workshop (USA) pp 309-317 (Nov 1981)

This paper presents the architecture of a parallel, general-purpose computer that uses LISP as its main programming language. It is built from several dozens of microprocessors (Z-80s), each of them executing a part of the program.

140 HAWTHORN P
Is there an ideal database machine?
Proc COMPCON pp 104-7 (Spring 1981)

Four basic types of database machine are described. These are pseudo-associative search engines, multi-processor systems, functionally complete back-end systems, and integrated machines.

141 HAYNES L S, LAU R L, SIEWIOREK D P and MIZELL D W
A survey of highly parallel computing
Computer vol 15 no 1 pp 9-24 (1982)

This paper gives a very good survey of highly parallel structures which the authors define as being composed of a large number of computing elements used to solve one single problem at a time. There is a brief description of each of the different types of parallel system. The major part is devoted to MIMD systems, in particular the Carnegie-Mellon Cm*, and processor intercommunication. There is also a section on applications of highly parallel systems and an excellent list of some 94 references.

142 HEERING J
The Intel 8086, the Zilog Z8000 and the Motorola MC68000 microprocessors
Euromicro J vol 6 pp 135-143 (May 1980)

Heering compares three recent 16-bit systems with respect to several important aspects: software and hardware portability, high-level languages (compiler and interpreter support), multiprocessing, and distributed processing.

143 HEWITT C and BAKER H
Laws for communicating parallel processes
Proc IFIP Congress p 987 (1977)

Laws are postulated which must be specified by computations involving communicating parallel processes. The laws take the form of stating plausible restrictions on the histories of parallel computations to make them physically realisable. The laws are justified by appealing to physical intuition. The laws are used to analyse the mechanisms by which you will be able to process and communicate the work effectively together to solve difficult problems.

144 HOAGLAND A S
Storage technology: capabilities and limitations
Computer vol 12 no 5 pp 12-18 (1979)

Hoagland argues against the commonly held belief that CCDs, bubbles, and optical disks will begin to replace magnetic recording media as a form of mass storage. He argues that there are substantial improvements in cost and bit density in magnetic recording. He also argues that memory hierarchies will continue to be the solution to storage organisation.

145 HOCKNEY R W and JESSHOPE C R
Parallel computers
Adam Hilger Ltd Bristol (1981)

This is probably the best currently available book on parallel computer architecture. It discusses the design of pipeline computers and processor arrays. There is a section on parallel languages and another on parallel algorithms. All aspects are treated very thoroughly and there are extensive references.

146 HWANG K, SU S P and NI L M
Vector computer architecture and processing techniques
Advances in Computers vol 20 pp 115-197 (1981)

Two major classes of parallel machines are discussed: pipeline computers and SIMD processors. Recent research work on pipeline and SIMD processors is also summarised. The topics examined in the paper include language aspects and features of vectorising compilers.

147 IBBETT R N
The architecture of high-performance computers
The Macmillan Press Ltd (1982)

This book discusses the techniques which have been used to obtain high performance in computer systems, in particular storage hierarchies, pipelines, instruction buffering, parallel functional units, and vector processors.

148 ILIFFE J K
Advanced computer design
Prentice-Hall Inc (1982)

The following topics are covered: interpreters, microprogrammable machines, prepacked micromachines, direct execution of languages, micro-system design, high-speed data, active memory operations, parallel procedures, and image enhancement functions.

149 IRWIN M J
Reconfigurable pipeline systems
Proc ACM Annual Conf vol 1 pp 86-92 (1978)

This paper provides a useful tutorial on pipeline architectures. Examples are taken from four large computer systems: IBM 360/91, Texas Instruments ASC, CRAY-1, and CDC STAR-100. The paper ends with a proposal for a future reconfigurable pipeline system.

150 JONES A K and SCHWARZ P
Experience using multiprocessor systems - a status report
ACM Computing Surveys vol 12 no 2 p 121 (1980)

Only when the hardware, operating system, utility software, and application are considered can one determine whether the potential of a multiprocessor has been realised. There are a number of myths about the inherent complexity or simplicity and efficiency or inefficiency of multiprocessors, which are discussed.

151 KAHN G and MacQUEEN D B
Coroutine and networks of parallel processors
Proc IFIP Congress p 993 (1977)

The language is presented based on processing communication that facilitates well-structured programming with dynamically evolving networks of processes. Some sample program proofs are given.

152 KATHAIL A and KATHAIL V
A multiple processor dataflow machine that supports generalised procedures
Proc IEEE 8th Annual Symposium on *Computer architecture* pp 291-302 (May 1981)

Among the proposed dataflow machines, few support procedures in any generality. Kathails' machine, which is a hardware realisation of the U-interpreter for dataflow languages, provides support for a variety of procedure-calling conventions.

153 KETCHEN M B
AC-powered Josephson miniature system
Proc IEEE Intl Conf pp 874-7 New York (1980)

The design and operation of a Josephson miniature system is presented. Transfer of information between Josephson logic gates powered by a regulated bipolar power supply is demonstrated down to a cycle time of 1.25 nsec.

154 KOTOV V E
On basic parallel language
Proc IFIP Congress p 229 (1980)

The problem of a general-purpose programming language with well-developed capabilities for the description of various forms of computational parallelism is discussed. The language must be based on a model of highly parallel computation which can be implemented in programs and computers of the next decade.

After a brief analysis of the current situation in parallel computation, the main principles of Basic Parallel Language are described. In conclusion, the language is considered as a base for future computer architecture.

155 KUCK D J
The Burroughs Scientific Processor (BSP)
IEEE Transactions on Computers vol C-31 no 5 p 363 (May 1982)

This paper describes a high-performance scientific processor of roughly the same performance as the CRAY-1. It combines parallelism and pipelining and pays particular attention to providing conflict-free memory access for most indexed arrays. CMOS memory is used as a high bandwidth secondary memory.

156 KUNG H T
Why systolic architectures?
Computer vol 15 no 1 pp 37-46 (1982)

The basic principle of a systolic architecture replaces a single processor element with an array of PEs with one memory access serving all the PEs. The crux of this approach is to ensure that once a data item is brought from memory it can be used effectively in each cell. The wide variety of possible interconnections is discussed and the implication in VLSI is considered.

157 LAWRIE D H and VORA C R
The prime memory system for array access
IEEE Transactions on Computers vol C-31 no 5 p 435 (May 1982)

The design of a memory system for conflict-free array access is described. The design is based on the use of a prime number of memories and permits efficient parallel access to the required sections of an array, eg a row, a column, a diagonal, etc.

158 LEHMAN P L
A systolic (VLSI) array for processing simple relational queries
Proc Conf on *VLSI systems and computations* pp 285-295 Carnegie Mellon Univ (1981)

Lehman discusses the use of systolic arrays to produce VLSI capable of processing simple relational database queries, which are by far the most frequently executed queries in practical large database systems.

159 LINCOLN N R
A safari through the Control Data STAR-100 with gun and camera
Proc AFIPS National Computer Conf (June 1978)

This paper looks back to the STAR-100 project, which started in 1965. It discusses the problems of providing a sufficiently large memory with the then available technology of two-dimensional core and the problems of implementing virtual memory on a vector processor. It also describes the arithmetic unit pipelines. It is worth reading this paper in conjunction with Lincoln's later paper on the CYBER 205.

160 LINCOLN N R
Technology and design tradeoffs in the creation of a modern supercomputer
IEEE Transactions on Computers vol C-31 no 5 p 349 (May 1982)

The interaction of technology, architecture, manufacturing, and user demands gives rise to compromises and design decisions which challenge the supercomputer developer. The nature of some of these challenges and their resolution, in the case of the production of the Control Data CYBER 205, is discussed in this paper in an attempt to elevate supercomputer development from the mystique of being an art to the level of a science of synergistic combination of programming, technology, structure, and packaging.

161 LIU J W S and JINO M
Intelligent magnetic bubble memories and their applications in database management systems
IEEE Transactions on Computers vol C-28 no 12 pp 888-906 (Dec 1979)

Three bubble chip organisations - major-minor loop, on-chip decoder, and bubble lattice - are briefly described. The paper then discusses how the bits, words, and pages of a memory should be distributed over a set of bubble chips. File processing operations, relational data processing and the architecture of a relational database machine are also outlined.

162 LOGUE J C *et al*
Techniques for improving engineering productivity of VLSI designs
IBM J of Research and Development vol 25 pp 107-115 (May 1981)

At present, design capability lags far behind the ability to fabricate ever increasing numbers of chips on a wafer. Present practices to achieve reduced design times rely on a compromise that shortens design time at the expense of circuit density. Logue *et al* propose a design approach that tends to combine large circuit density and efficient design procedure.

163 LOVE H H
The highly-parallel supercomputers: definitions, applications, and predictions
Proc AFIPS Conf pp 181-190 Anaheim (1980)

Love describes some of the highly parallel computer organisations and the applications suitable for them. General criteria for applicability are also given. The implications of VLSI with respect to these supercomputers and to fault-tolerant capability are explained.

164 LUNDSTROM S F
A controllable MIMD architecture
Proc IEEE Intl Conf on *Parallel processing* pp 19-27 (1980)

These proceedings describe the strategies adopted for making a many-processor multiprocessor controllable and efficient.

165 MacLENNAN B J
Introduction to relational programming
Proc ACM Conf on *Functional programming languages and computer architecture* p 213 (1981)

This paper discusses a style of programming in which entire relations are manipulated rather than individual data.

166 MANNER R, SCHNEIDER W, DE LUIGI B and POSNER K
A general-purpose multimicrosystem with high fault-tolerance and unlimited system-capacity
Euromicro J vol 6 pp 388-390 (Nov 1980)

This paper describes the Heidelberg multiprocessor system which consists of up to 300 processing modules and up to 100 I/O modules accessing several global memories via multiple shares buses (fault tolerance being a major design consideration).

167 MARYANSKI F J
Back-end database systems
ACM Computing Surveys vol 12 no 1 p 3 (1980)

Back-end database systems have been proposed as a solution to the problems of overloaded data processing installations. This tutorial examines back-end database systems in terms of their basic structure, their potential benefits and drawbacks, and the problems facing developers of such systems. Several prototype systems are described, and research on extensions of the back-end concept is discussed. The structure of the hardware and software components of back-end database systems is presented in detail. The performance problems encountered in recent prototypes are pointed out and potential solutions indicated.

168 MEILANDER W C
History of parallel processing at Goodyear Aerospace
Proc IEEE Intl Conf on *Parallel processing* pp 5-15 (1981)

The techniques of associative memories and associative processors are described, followed by a description of a microcomputer array processor, and the massively parallel processor. The capabilities of these two machines in image processing and electronic warefare are also discussed.

169 MILLSTEIN R E and MUNTZ C A
The ILLIAC IV FORTRAN compiler
SIGPLAN Notice vol 10 no 3 pp 25-33 (Mar 1975)

This paper describes a system for the execution of ANSI standard FORTRAN on the ILLIAC IV. Standard code is first converted by a parallelism analyser and synthesiser to IVTRAN. Although the system was actually written it does not seem to be preferred by the ILLIAC user community. The languages most commonly user are GLYPNIR and CFD, which both exhibit the explicit parallelism of the ILLIAC IV.

170 MYERS G J and BUCKINGHAM B R S
A hardware implementation of capability-based addressing
Operating Systems Review (USA) vol 14 no 4 pp 13-25 (1980)

The SWARD architecture, an experimental higher level architecture, contains the naming and protection concept of capability-based addressing. After discussing the merits of capability-based addressing, its general representation in the SWARD architecture is discussed.

171 NISHIDA T and DOSHITA S
A knowledge-based literature guide system - a new approach to document retrieval
Proc IFIP Congress p 699 (1980)

This paper presents a new approach to document retrieval based on a semantic model for natural language. The content of a document is represented using the hierarchical model of knowledge representation. Sentences of a document are translated into logical representations, which are integrated into the knowledge base as an organised knowledge structure. Queries are also in natural language, from which retrieval commands are automatically generated. Answers are synthesised from the results of retrieval. A working system has been constructed that can answer questions based on integrated abstracts of scientific literature.

172 ORGANICK E I
New directions in computer systems architecture
Euromicro J vol 5 pp 190-202 (July 1979)

This expanded version of Organick's keynote address from the Euromicro '78 Conference highlights four forces for change and why they have had little effect on the computer system architecture. Architecture development has been remarkably stable despite demands made by applications and systems, reliability, language and programming, and technology. This paper takes a brief yet good look at these problems.

173 OSMON P E
Hierarchical language derived dataflow architectures
Proc 6th ACM European Regional Conf pp 445-453 (1981)

A strategy for deriving dataflow architectures is introduced. The strategy is to iterate around a loop comprising programming problems, language facilities, and models of computation. The model is then used as a basis for proposing real architectures which can be investigated, at the register transfer level, using a simulation package.

174 PETERSON V L
Computational aerodynamics and the numerical aerodynamic simulation facility
In *Future computer requirements for computational aerodynamics* NASA CP-2032 (1977)

Computational aerodynamics provides a rapid and inexpensive means of simulating aerodynamic flows, through the numerical solution of approximating sets of the fluid dynamics equations (Navier Stokes equations) using fast computers. This is an excellent description of the problem and the levels of approximation which are possible with different high-performance computer systems.

175 POHM A V and SMAY T A
Computer memory systems
Computer vol 14 no 10 pp 93-110 (1981)

While the paper starts with a brief survey of the performance of various memory technologies, the main theme is the discussion of storage hierarchies. Various designs of cache memory are discussed and also the design of virtual memory systems. The final conclusion is that memory hierarchies will continue to play a key role in cost-effective systems, although the speeds and sizes of the different levels in the hierarchies will continue to change as technology advances.

176 PRICE J E
LSI chip architecture for large high-performance computers
Proc IEEE Intl Conf pp 497-502 New York (1980)

The potential benefits of LSI are analysed with respect to the requirements of large computers. Evolutionary trends in integrated circuit chip architecture from 1960 to 1980 are described, and conclusions are drawn as to the best chip architecture for large high-performance computers.

177 RECOQUE A
Survey of main trends in computer hardware architecture
Proc IFIP Congress p 115 (1980)

A top-down approach is used to study the main trends in computer architecture. It starts with an identification of what makes a good system from the point of view of the user and is followed by the implementation of these features in hardware and software. The limits of von Neumann architecture are considered and alternative architectures are briefly described.

178 REEVES A P
Computer architectures for image processing in the USA
Signal Processing (Netherlands) vol 3 no 3 pp 217-230 (July 1981)

Innovative computer architectures have been developed to meet the high-speed computation needs of image processing applications. These architectures take advantage of the highly structured characteristics of image data and image processing algorithms. Several alternative architectures for image processing are discussed and some current hardware development projects in the USA are described.

179 ROBERTS D H and HIRST G E C
Silicon-based microelectronics - background and future prospects
Proc Microelectronics Symposium
p 3 (1979)

The dramatic improvements in cost and performance of silicon-integrated circuits over the past two decades, together with the emergence of the user-programmable microprocessor explain why 'microelectronics' is recognised as the key industrial technology for the next few decades. This paper considers the factors which are inherent within this technology and which may restrict its growth, and then goes on to suggest ways in which these inhibiting factors may themselves be overcome or bypassed.

180 RODRIGUE G, GIROUX E D and PRATT M
Perspectives on large-scale scientific computation
Computer vol 12 no 10 pp 65-80 (1979)

This article describes numerical modelling, hardware, and software used at the Lawrence Livermore National Laboratory. A very strong case is made for the value of computer simulations. There is a section on numerical modelling and a brief description of the vast amount of high-performance hardware available at the Laboratory. The article concludes with the statement that a key requirement for large scientific computation is for hardware and software which is optimised for solving partial differential equations and other equations describing physical systems.

181 RUSSEL R M
The CRAY-1 computer system
Communications of the ACM vol 21 no 1 pp 63-72 (Jan 1978)

One of the most powerful commercially available mainframes is described in this paper. The CRAY-1 is a pipelined vector processor with 12 independent clock-segmented functional units. It is not surprising that the architecture is somewhat similar to that of the CDC 7600. The paper gives a good description of the architecture of the CRAY-1 and outlines some of the major problems encountered in production.

182 SHAW D E
A relational database machine architecture
Proc ACM 5th Workshop on *Computer architecture* (USA) pp 84-95 (1980)

Algorithms are described and analysed for the efficient evaluation of the project. Shaw also discusses join operators of a relational algebra on a proposed non-von Neumann machine based on a hierarchy of associative storage devices.

183 SHEPHERD A A and PEARSON J D
Trends in microelectronic device manufacture and application
Proc Microelectronics Symposium
p 13 (1979)

Views on the types of integrated circuit that will be used during the next decade are presented and reasons given for these views. The forces that will determine the direction of the integrated circuit industry are not predominantly those of semiconductor technology but are determined by the commercial interests of the users, and particularly the size of the available market for each type of device.

184 SHYUE B and LIU M T
A cluster structure as an interconnection network for large multimicrocomputer systems

IEEE Transactions on Computers vol C-30 no 4 pp 254-264 (Apr 1981)

This paper deals with cluster structures as a means of interconnecting a large number of microcomputers for parallel and distributed processing. Such a structure is a conceptual interconnection scheme in which system components (processors, memories, processing elements, or microcomputers) are grouped into levels of subclusters forming a hierarchical organisation. Shared buses are used as the basic interconnection media and indirect communication is established among microcomputers by message passing.

185 SRIHARI S N
Representation of three-dimensional digital images
ACM Computing Surveys vol 13 no 4 p 399 (1981)

Three-dimensional digital images are encountered in a variety of problems, including computed tomogrophy, biological modelling, space planning, and computer vision. A wide spectrum of data structures is available for the computer representation of such images. This paper is a tutorial survey of three-dimensional spatial-data representation methods emphasising techniques that apply to cellular (or voxel-based) images.

186 STERNBERG S R
Parallel architectures for image processing
Proc COMPSAC for IEEE Conf pp 712-717 (1979)

Image processing operations are defined which permit image processing algorithms to be written as algebraic expressions whose variables are whole images. Highly parallel computing architectures for evaluating these expressions are presented.

187 TANIMOTO A L
Systolic cellular logic: inexpensive parallel image processors
Proc IEEE Computer Society Conf pp 306-309 (1981)

The tradeoffs of processing for time and flexibility are discussed. A new architecture is presented based on systolic arrays which offers several advantages over the total parallel and the pipelined architectures. Considerations for VLSI implementation of systolic cellular logic are discussed.

188 TANIMOTO S I and PFEIFFER Jr J J
An image processor based on an array of pipelines
IEEE Computer Society Workshop (USA) pp 201-208 (Nov 1981)

Parallel processors for image processing can be designed in a wide variety of configurations. One class of these is that of cellular-logic machines. A design approach is described that uses 'virtual processing elements' to increase the number of cells on each VLSI chip of a cellular-logic image processor.

189 TERAJIMA M
Recent progress in memory devices and their prospects
Proc IFIP Congress p 127 (1980)

The design and capacity of dynamic RAM chips is discussed with extrapolations for the future. This paper also reaches the conclusion that magnetic disk files have the potential to excel other technologies for at least the next 10 years. There is also some discussion of magnetic bubble memories.

190 TRELEAVEN P C
Exploiting program concurrency in

computing systems
Computer vol 12 no 1 pp 42-53 (1979)

This paper describes the limitations of doing concurrent computation with the usual sequential type of computer. The author then describes a design of the new type of architecture he developed. For special classes of computation he estimates that speed-up ratios in the neighbourhood of 40:1 could be achieved by the use of the new type of architecture. Some examples are given to illustrate the new type of concurrent execution.

191 TRELEAVEN P C and HOPKINS R P
Decentralised computation
Proc IEEE Annual Symposium on *Computer architecture* pp 279-290 (May 1981)

This paper examines dataflow, control flow, and reduction models and presents a classification for their underlying concepts. In addition, it describes a computational model called recursive control flow, which is a synthesis of these concepts and which directly supports dataflow, control flow, and reduction computation.

192 WADLER P
Applicative style programming, program transformation and list operators
Proc ACM Conf on *Functional programming languages and computer architecture* p 25 (1981)

This paper examines how list operators can be used to guide the transformation process. It describes a small set of list operators that possess a 'complete' set of transformation rules, allowing transformations to be performed very efficiently. Whereas most previous transformation methods resemble proofs, this transformation method resembles algebraic manipulation.

193 WATSON I and GURD J
A practical dataflow computer
Computer vol 15 no 2 pp 51-57 (1982)

A dataflow machine, which ran its first program in October 1981, is described. The architecture is greatly influenced by the labelled dataflow model and is built on TTL technology with a basic pipeline bit of 200 nsec. Extensions which should permit an execution rate of 3.3 million instr/sec are described.

194 WISE K D, CHEN K and YOKELY R E
Microcomputers: a technology forecast and assessment to the year 2000
John Wiley & Sons Inc (1980)

In this book, informed judgements are made about future microcomputer technology and its impacts on society for the period 1976 to 2000. The bases of the judgements are a synopsis of physical and engineering principles, pertinent literature review, and interviews with knowledgeable persons at the forefront of microcomputer development and applications.

195 YAMAGUCHI K and JUNII T L
Local framework of a picture database computer
IEEE Computer Society Workshop (USA) pp 284-292 (Nov 1981)

The logical framework of a picture database computer (PICCOLO) is presented. The logic has two major advantages; one is that the computer design based on this logic can handle varieties of picture structures universally and is suitable for the implementation by VLSI. Another advantage is that a set of data items that is generated by rules, such as texture data, is stored in the picture computer efficiently.

196 YEN D W L and KULKARNI A V
The ESL systolic processor for signal and image processing
IEEE Computer Society Workshop (USA) pp 265-272 (Nov 1981)

This paper describes the structure of the systolic 'cells' being implemented and the algorithms that can be executed using a linear array of such cells. A brief description of the hardware and software organisation is also presented, followed by some performance figures for a 20-cell system.

197 ZOBRIST A L and NAGY G
Pictorial information processing of Landsat data for geographic analysis
Computer vol 14 no 11 pp 34-41 (1981)

This paper gives a very clear indication of the problems of data storage associated with the processing of image data patterns from satellites

ANALYSIS REFERENCES

200 HOCKNEY R W and JESSHOPE C R
See (145)

201 LINCOLN N R
See (160)

202 IBBETT R N
See (147)

203 ROBERTS D H
See (179)

204 ANACKER
IBM J of Research and Development vol 24 no 2 (Mar 1980)

205 EDEN *et al*
The prospects for ultra high-speed VLSI GaAs digital logic
IEEE Transactions on Electronic Devices ED-26 pp 299-317 (1979)

206 TERAJIMA M
See (189)

207 FLYNN M S
Very high-speed computing systems
Proc IEEE vol 54 no 12 (Dec 1966)

208 SHAW J H
Second thoughts on parallel processing
Computing and Electrical Engineering vol 1 pp 95-109 (1973)

209 ANDERSON G A and JENSON E D
Computer interconnection structures: taxonomy characteristics and examples
ACM Computing Surveys vol 7 no 4 (Dec 1975)

210 KASCIC Jr M J
Vector processing on the CYBER 200
In *Supercomputers* D Morsley (ed) Pergamon Infotech State of the Art Rep vol 2 Pergamon Infotech (1979)

211 CONTROL DATA CORPORATION (CDC)
Technical document (1981)

212 MORSLEY D (editor)
Supercomputers
Pergamon Infotech State of the Art Rep vol 1 Pergamon Infotech (1979)

213 *CRAY X-MP*
Cray Research publicity release (1982)

214 *CRAY CHANNELS*
vol 4 no 1 (1982)

215 MAI TIN
PhD Thesis
Univ of Manchester (1981)

216 STEVENS Jr K G
Numerical aerodynamic simulation facility project
In *Supercomputers* D Morsley (ed)
Pergamon Infotech State of the Art Rep vol 2 Pergamon Infotech (1979)

217 LAWRIE D H
Access and alignment of data in an array processor
IEEE Transactions on Computers C-24 pp 1145-1155 (1975)

218 JONES A K and SCHWARZ P
See (150)

219 RODRIGUE G, GIROUX E D and PRATT M
See (180)

220 LINCOLN N R
See (159)

221 POHM A and SMAY T A
See (175)

222 CRAY RESEARCH LTD
Technical document (1981)

223 CONTROL DATA CORPORATION (CDC)
Technical document (1981)

224 COLE R
Computer communications
The Macmillan Press Ltd (1981)

225 STOKES A V (editor)
Networks
Pergamon Infotech State of the Art Rep Pergamon Infotech (1981)

226 WHITE C H (editor)
Distributed databases
Pergamon Infotech State of the Art Rep vol 1 Pergamon Infotech (1979)

227 AUSTIN J H
The Burroughs scientific processor
In *Supercomputers* D Morsley (ed)
Pergamon Infotech State of the Art Rep vol 2 Pergamon Infotech (1979)

228 HOCKNEY R W
Supercomputer architecture
State of the Art Rep Pergamon Infotech (1977)

229 JESSHOPE C R and CRAIGIE J A I
Small is OK too
DAP Newsletter vol 4 (1980)

230 *Some research applications of the CRAY-1*
See (109)

231 *CRAY CHANNELS*
vol 3 no 2 (1981)

232 SERC
Report on image processing
SERC Rutherford Appleton Laboratories

233 DANIELSSON P E and LEVIALDI S
See (115)

234 POTTER J L
The STARAN architecture
Proc AFIPS p 1041 (1978)

235 DUFF M J B
Review of the CLIP image processing system
Proc AFIPS p 1055 (1978)

236 MORI K I *et al*
Design of local parallel processors for image processing
Proc AFIPS p 1025 (1978)

237 NUDD G R
Image processing architectures
Proc AFIPS p 377 (1980)

238 MARYANSKI F J
See (167)

239 SU S Y W *et al*
Database machines and some issues on DBMS standards
Proc AFIPS p 191 (1980)

240 HSIAO D K
Future database machines
In *Future systems* Pergamon Infotech State of the Art Rep
Pergamon Infotech (1977)

241 DARLINGTON J and REEVE M
See (117)

242 REEVE M
The ALICE compiler target language
(To be published)

243 d'AGAPEYEFF A *et al*
BCS specialist group report on Expert Systems
British Computer Society (1982)

244 PERIERA L M, PEREIRA F and WARREN D H D
Users' guide to DEC-10 PROLOG
Artificial Intelligence Unit Univ of Edinburgh (1978)

245 CLOCKSON W F and MELLISH C S
Programming in PROLOG
Springer-Verlag (1981)

246 Datamation
(Jan 1982)

REFERENCE SOURCES

Some abbreviations of journal titles are used in the list of references. The full title is given below together with the address from which the journal is available. The second part gives the addresses of publishers of the books cited in the Bibliography.

Reference	*Full title and publisher's name*
ACM	Association for Computing Machinery Inc ACM Order Department 11 West 42nd Street New York NY 10036 USA
ACM Computing Surveys	ACM Computing Surveys (*See* ACM)
Advances in Computers	Advances in Computers (*See* ACM)
Artificial Intelligence Unit	Artificial Intelligence Unit Kings Buildings University of Edinburgh Mayfield Road Edinburgh EH9 3JZ UK
British Computer Society	British Computer Society 13 Mansfield Street London UK
Communications of the ACM	Communications of the ACM (*See* ACM)
Computer	Computer (*See* IEEE Computer Society)
Computing and Electrical Engineering	Computing and Electrical Engineering Pergamon Press Maxwell House Fairview Park Elmsford NY 10523 USA
Computer Design	Computer Design 11 Goldsmith Street Littleton Massachusetts 01460 USA

Control Data Corporation (CDC)	Control Data Corporation 8100 34th Avenue South Minneapolis Minnesota 55120 USA
Cray Channels	Cray Channels Cray Research Inc 1440 Northland Drive Mendota Heights Minnesota 55120 USA
Cray Research Ltd	Cray Research Ltd (*See* Cray Channels)
DAP Newsletter	DAPSU Queen Mary College Mile End Road London E1 4NS UK
Datamation	Datamation 35 Mason Street Greenwich CT 06830 USA *Outside US/Canada* J B Tratsart Ltd 154a Greenford Road Harrow Middlesex HA1 3QT UK
Euromicro	Euromicro (*See* North-Holland Publishing Co)
IBM J of Research and Development	IBM Journal of Research and Development International Business Machines Corp Armonk NY 10504 USA
IEEE	The Institute for Electrical and Electronic Engineers 345 East 47th Street New York NY 10017 USA

IEEE Computer Society	The Institute for Electrical and Electronic Engineers Computer Society 5855 Naples Plaza Suite 301 Long Beach CA 90803 USA
IEEE Transactions on Computers	IEEE Transactions on Computers (*See* IEEE)
IEEE Transactions on Electronic Devices	IEEE Transactions on Electronic Devices (*See* IEEE)
IUCC Bulletin	IUCC Bulletin Miss M J Day Computer Lab University of Cambridge Corn Exchange Street Cambridge CB2 3QC UK
NASA	Ames Research Center NASA Moffett Field CA USA
Operating System Review	Operating System Review (*See* ACM)
Proc ACM Annual Conf	Proceedings of the ACM Annual Conference (*See* ACM)
Proc ACM Conf on Functional Programming Languages and Computer Architecture	Proceedings of the ACM Conference on Functional Programming Languages and Computer Architecture (*See* ACM)
Proc ACM 5th Workshop on Computer Architecture	Proceedings of the ACM Fifth Workshop on Computer Architecture (*See* ACM)
Proc ACM Regional Conf	Proceedings of the ACM Regional Conference (*See* ACM)
Proc ACM 6th European Regional Conf	Proceedings of the ACM Sixth European Regional Conference (*See* ACM)
Proc AFIPS Conf	Proceedings of the AFIPS Conference AFIPS Press 210 Summit Avenue Montvale NJ 07645 USA

Proc AFIPS National Computer Conf	Proceedings of the AFIPS National Computer Conference (*See* Proc AFIPS Conf)
Proc COMPCON	Proceedings of COMPCON (*See* IEEE Computer Society)
Proc COMPSAC	Proceedings of COMPSAC (*See* IEEE Computer Society)
Proc IEE Colloquium	Proceedings of the IEE Colloquium Institute of Electrical Engineers Savoy Place London WC2 OBC UK
Proc IEEE Computer Society Conf	Proceedings of the IEEE Computer Society Conference (*See* IEEE Computer Society)
Proc IEEE Computer Society Workshop	Proceedings of the IEEE Computer Society Workshop (*See* IEEE Computer Society)
Proc IEEE 1st Intl Conf on Distributive Computing Systems	Proceedings of the IEEE First International Conference on Distributive Computing Systems (*See* IEEE Computer Society)
Proc IEEE 8th Annual Symposium on Computer Architecture	Proceedings of the IEEE Eighth Annual Symposium on Computer Architecture (*See* IEEE)
Proc IEEE Intl Conf New York	Proceedings of the IEEE International Conference New York (*See* IEEE)
Proc IEEE Intl Conf on Parallel Processing	Proceedings of the IEEE International Conference on Parallel Processing (*See* IEEE Computer Society)
Proc IFIP	Proceedings of the IFIP (*See* North-Holland Publishing Co)
Proc IFIP Congress	Proceedings of the IFIP Congress (*See* North-Holland Publishing Co)
Proc Microelectronics Symposium	Proceedings of the Microelectronics Symposium British Association for the Advancement of Science Fortress House 23 Saville Row London W1X 1AB UK

Proc VLSI Systems and Computation's Conf — Proceedings of the VLSI Systems and Computation's Conference
Carnegie Mellon University
Pittsburg
Pennsylvania
USA

SERC Daresbury Laboratories — SERC Daresbury Laboratories
Daresbury
Cheshire
UK

SERC Rutherford Appleton Laboratories — SERC Rutherford Appleton Laboratories
Didcot
Berkshire
UK

Signal Processing (Netherlands) — (*See* North-Holland Publishing Co)

SIGPLAN Notices — Newsletter of the Special Interest Group on Programming Languages
(*See* ACM)

<u>Book publishers</u>

Adam Hilger Ltd
Techno House
Redcliffe Way
Bristol BS1 6NX
UK

IEEE PRESS
(*See* IEEE)

The Macmillan Press Ltd
Houndmills
Basingstoke
Hampshire RG21 2XS
UK

North-Holland Publishing Co
Box 211
Amsterdam
The Netherlands

Prentice-Hall Inc
Englewood Cliffs
NJ 07632
USA

66 Wood Lane End
Hemel Hempstead
Herts
UK

Springer-Verlag New York Inc
175 Fifth Avenue
New York
NY 10010
USA

John Wiley and Sons Ltd
Baffins Lane
Chichester
Sussex
PO19 1UD
UK

John Wiley Inc
605 3rd Avenue
New York
NY 10016
USA

INDEX

INDEX